The **Rough Guide** to

Rajasthan, Delhi and Agra

written and researched by

Daniel Jacobs and Gavin Thomas

ROUGH
GUIDES

NEW YORK · LONDON · DELHI

www.roughguides.com

Contents

Forts and palaces of Rajasthan colour section following p.208

Rajasthani Crafts colour section following p.320

◄◄ Jaisalmer, Rajasthan ◄ The Taj Mahal, Agra

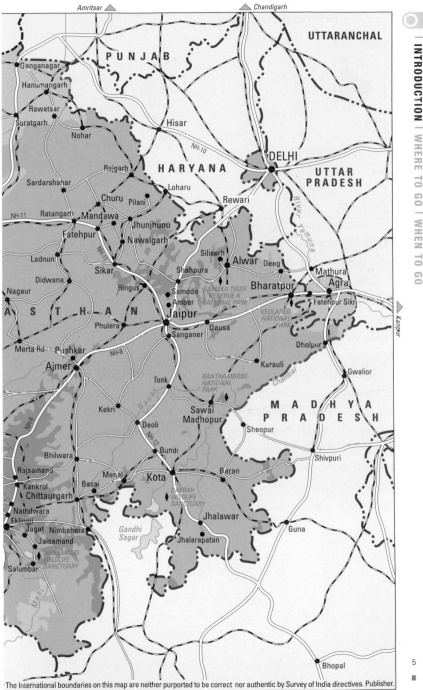

Amritsar △   △ Chandigarh

UTTARANCHAL

PUNJAB

Ganganagar

Hanumangarh

Rawatsar

Suratgarh

Nohar

Hisar

NH-10

DELHI

HARYANA

UTTAR
PRADESH

Rajgarh

Sardarshahar

Loharu

Churu   Pilani

Rewari

River Yamuna

NH-11   Ratangarh   Mandawa

Fatehpur

Jhunjhunu

Ladnun

Nawalgarh

Siliserh

Alwar   Deeg

Mathura

Agra

Sikar

Shahpura

NH-11

Didwana

Ringus

Nagaur

Samode

SARISKA TIGER
RESERVE &
NATIONAL PARK

Bharatpur

Fatehpur Sikri

Kanpur △

A   S   T   H   A   N

Amber

Jaipur

KEOLADEO
NATIONAL
PARK

Phulera

Sanganer

Dausa

Merta Rd

Pushkar

NH-8

Dholpur

Ajmer

Tonk

Karauli

Gwalior

Banas

RANTHAMBORE
NATIONAL
PARK

Chambal

Kekri

M A D H Y A
P R A D E S H

NH-8

Deoli

NH-12

Sawai
Madhopur

Sheopur

Bhilwara

Bundi

Baran

Shivpuri

Rajsamand

Menal

Kota

Kankrol

Bassi

Chittaurgarh

DARRAH
WILDLIFE
SANCTUARY

Nathdwara

Eklingji

Jagat   Nimbahera

Gandhi
Sagar

Jhalawar

Guna

Jaisamand

Jhalarapatan

JAISAMAND
WILDLIFE
SANCTUARY

Salumbar

Mahi

Bhopal

The International boundaries on this map are neither purported to be correct nor authentic by Survey of India directives. Publisher.

Introduction to

Rajasthan, Delhi and Agra

When most foreigners imagine India, they are probably thinking of somewhere in Rajasthan, Delhi or Agra. This is the Subcontinent at its most iconic, from the Taj Mahal and the great Mughal mosques and mausoleums of Delhi and Agra to the fairy-tale landscapes of Rajasthan, with its mighty hilltop forts, remote desert citadels and extravagant royal palaces. The region as a whole richly fulfils every romantic expectation one might have about Indian life and culture, with picturesque crowds of men in top-heavy turbans and women dressed in vibrantly coloured saris; crowded bazaars overflowing with sumptuous fabrics, embroidery and jewellery; or the vivid orange flash of a tiger or leopard seen padding quietly through the undergrowth of a national park. Taken as a whole, the area's myriad attractions offer a recipe for Subcontinental sensory overload, and explains why this is the place to which most first-time visitors to the country immediately head.

The irony is that the region thought of as representing all that is most quintessentially Indian is in fact the one which has been most profoundly shaped by external forces and foreign cultures. Northwest India has always been the meeting point between the Subcontinent's indigenous traditions and incoming marauders from Central Asia, from the earliest Aryan invaders through to the Mughals. This geographical location has made the region one of the most fascinatingly diverse in India and an absorbing study in contrasts, between Hindu and Islamic, militaristic and artistic, and progressive and

6

Fact file

• **Rajasthan**, with 56.5 million people (89 percent Hindu, 8.5 percent Muslim, 1.4 percent Sikh, 1.2 percent Jain), is India's largest and eighth most populous state. It came into existence following Independence in 1947, formed from a union of nineteen princely states, plus Ajmer, which had been under direct British rule. The main languages are Hindi and Rajasthani. Rajasthan is ruled by the Bharatiya Janata Party (BJP), India's main opposition. The economy is mainly agricultural, along with mines for copper and zinc, and quarries for sandstone and marble.

• **Delhi**, India's federal capital and second-largest city (after Mumbai) is home to 13 million people (82 percent Hindu, 12 percent Muslim, 4 percent Sikh, and around one percent each of Jains and Christians). Not part of any state, it has its own legislative assembly and Capital Territory status, and is ruled by the Congress Party. Most employees work in the public sector, but IT, telecommunications and the media are important industries.

• **Agra**, populated by 1.3 million people (predominantly Muslim), is the third-largest city in the state of Uttar Pradesh (UP). Its politics are dominated by the largely local, socialist Samajwadi Party, which promotes the rights of the lower castes and religious minorities.

traditional – from the cosmopolitan restaurants and malls of Delhi to the deeply conservative villages of Rajasthan; or from the crowded bazaars of Agra and Jaipur to the great expanses of uninhabited desert around Jaisalmer and Bikaner

For the visitor, the region's attractions are obvious. The Taj Mahal and the Islamic monuments of Agra and Delhi; the unforgettably romantic lakeside palaces of Udaipur and the remote desert fortress of Jaisalmer; the bazaars of Jaipur's Pink City or the mighty Mcherangarh Fort at Jodhpur – all rank amongst India's most spectacular and memorable sights, though there are also countless less heralded places to seek out, and even repeated visits to the region are unlikely to exhaust its extraordinarily rich array of attractions.

Where to go

Most visitors to the region arrive in **Delhi**, and pretty much everyone spends at least a few days exploring India's historic capital, although you could spend weeks wandering the city's countless

▼ Pink City, Jaipur

monuments, museums and bazaars, including the soaring Qutb Minar, erected by the city's first Muslim ruler, the Mughal-era Red Fort (Lal Qila) and Jama Masjid and the grandiose imperial creations of the British.

From Delhi it's a short train journey south to **Agra**, home to an astonishing collection of Mughal monuments, including the superlative Taj Mahal, and also conveniently close to the remarkable abandoned city of **Fatehpur Sikri**. West of Agra lies the bustling city of **Jaipur**, the third point of the famous "Golden Triangle", and the capital of the state of Rajasthan, home to an intriguing collection of monuments and bazaars.

> This is the Subcontinent at its most iconic, from the Taj Mahal and the great Mughal mosques and mausoleums of Delhi and Agra to the fairy-tale landscapes of Rajasthan

Jaipur is also the starting point for forays into eastern Rajasthan. Immediately north of Jaipur, the fabulous painted havelis of the **Shekhawati** region are attracting increasing numbers of foreign visitors, though the region is best known for **Keoladeo National Park** at Bharatpur, one of the world's finest bird-spotting destinations, and **Ranthambore National Park**, one of the easiest places on the planet to see tigers in the wild.

▲ Pushkar lake

Rajasthan's ethnic minorities

Like most Indian states, Rajasthan has a number of "tribal" peoples who live outside the social mainstream. Many are nomadic, and often called "Gypsies" – indeed the Romanies of Europe are thought to have originated among these Rajasthani Gypsy tribes. The most prominent are the **Kalbeliyas**, found largely in Pushkar. The Kalbeliyas discovered how to charm snakes, and they used to sing and dance for royalty, as they now do for tourists, but living in on the margins of society, they suffer much the same discrimination as their brethren in Europe.

Similarly, the **Bhopas** are a green-eyed tribe of nomads who used to work as entertainers to the maharajas, and to this day they exist as itinerant poets and storytellers. They are asked to perform particularly where someone is sick, as their songs are believed to aid recovery.

In the Jodhpur region, many tourists take an excursion into the countryside to visit the **Bishnoi** (see p.295), a religious rather than strictly ethnic group, whose tree-hugging beliefs chime with those of hippies in the West. Living in close proximity to them, though with a very different lifestyle, are the **Bhils**, great hunters who used to hire themselves out as soldiers in the armies of the Rajput kingdoms. They have their own language and religion, and their dances have become very popular, especially at Holi.

West of Jaipur, the pretty little town of **Pushkar** is famous for its astonishing annual camel fair, and has long been Rajasthan's principal backpacker hangout. By contrast, surprisingly few tourists venture out to the historic nearby city of **Ajmer**, Rajasthan's most important Muslim settlement. West of Ajmer, **Jodhpur** also remains relatively overlooked by travellers, despite boasting arguably Rajasthan's most spectacular fort.

Beyond Jodhpur, the Thar Desert begins in earnest, its rolling, scrub-covered sands enveloping Rajasthan's two remotest cities. The first, **Bikaner**, is renowned for its superb Junagarh fort and for the unique Karni Mata shrine, or "rat temple", at Deshnok. The second, **Jaisalmer**, is one of the archetypal Rajasthan destinations: a fairy-tale walled city marooned amidst the sands of the Thar, its narrow streets lined with fantastically carved havelis and ornate temples.

In stark contrast to the deserts of western Rajasthan, the southern part of the state is notably green and hilly. The main attraction here is the beautiful city of **Udaipur**, with its romantically tangled skyline of palaces and havelis

▼ Chandni Chowk, Delhi

▼ Bundi bazaar

strung out around the sylvan waters of Lake Pichola. North of Udaipur, the massive **Kumbalgarh** fort and the superb Jain temples at **Ranakpur** are both easily visited as a day-trip, while there are further spectacular Jain temples west of Udaipur at the engaging little hill station of **Mount Abu**.

Heading east from Udaipur, the superb fort at **Chittaurgarh** is amongst the most spectacular and historically important in the state, while further east the city of **Kota** is one of Rajasthan's most heavily industrialized, but compensates with some outstanding murals at its grand city palace. Even finer examples of Rajasthani painting can be seen nearby at the small town of **Bundi**, whose laid-back charms are attracting increasing numbers of western visitors.

When to go

Rajasthan's **climate** reaches the extremes common to desert regions; in general, the western half of the state is drier and hotter than the eastern and southern areas. The **best time to visit** is between October and March, when daytime temperatures hover around the 25°C mark, though night-time temperatures can fall to near freezing, and mornings can be chilly. However, hotels tend to get booked up during this period and room rates are at their highest. During the **summer**, from April to September, average daytime temperatures push up into the mid-30s, and can top 45°C in May and June. On the plus side, hotel rates fall significantly at many places from around April to September, and pretty much everywhere has vacancies. The **monsoon** arrives (and temperatures fall) in July and August (in theory, at least – rainfall in recent years has been sporadic and unpredictable, with widespread drought in parts of the state and

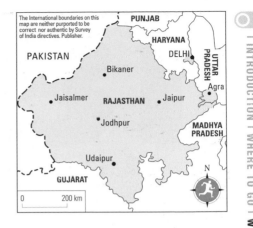

catastrophic flooding in others). **Delhi** and **Agra** enjoy a similar climate to Rajasthan, though without ever quite reaching the extremes of heat experienced in western Rajasthan.

Average temperatures (in °C) and rainfall (in mm)

	Jan	Feb	Mar	Apr	May	Jun	Jul	Aug	Sep	Oct	Nov	Dec
Agra												
Max/min	22/7	26/10	32/16	38/22	42/27	41/29	35/27	33/26	33/25	31/19	29/12	24/8
Rainfall	16	9	11	5	10	60	210	263	151	23	2	4
Bikaner												
Max/min	22/8	25/11	32/16	38/23	42/28	42/29	38/28	37/27	37/26	36/22	30/14	24/9
Rainfall	6	6	5	4	14	30	81	90	32	4	2	4
Delhi												
Max/min	21/7	24/10	30/15	36/21	41/27	40/29	35/27	34/26	34/25	35/19	29/12	23/8
Rainfall	25	22	17	7	8	65	211	173	150	31	1	5
Jaipur												
Max/min	22/8	25/11	31/15	37/21	41/26	39/27	34/26	32/24	33/23	33/18	29/12	24/9
Rainfall	14	1	8	9	4	10	54	193	239	90	19	4
Jaisalmer												
Max/min	24/8	28/11	33/17	38/21	42/25	41/27	38/27	36/25	36/25	36/20	31/13	26/9
Rainfall	2	1	3	1	5	7	89	86	14	1	5	2
Jodhpur												
Max/min	25/9	28/12	33/17	38/22	42/27	40/29	36/27	33/25	35/24	36/20	31/14	27/11
Rainfall	7	5	2	2	6	31	122	145	47	7	3	1
Udaipur												
Max/min	24/8	28/10	32/15	36/20	38/25	36/25	31/24	29/23	31/22	32/19	29/11	26/8
Rainfall	9	4	3	3	5	87	197	207	102	16	6	3

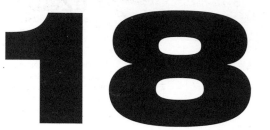

things not to miss

It's not possible to see everything that Rajasthan, Delhi and Agra have to offer in a single trip – and we don't suggest you try. What follows is a selective taste of the region's highlights: outstanding monuments, memorable wildlife and spectacular festivals. Attractions are arranged in five colour-coded categories with a page reference to take you straight into the guide, where you can find out more.

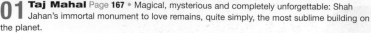

01 Taj Mahal Page **167** • Magical, mysterious and completely unforgettable: Shah Jahan's immortal monument to love remains, quite simply, the most sublime building on the planet.

11 Baha'i Temple, Delhi Page **136** • Delhi's answer to the Sydney Opera House – a remarkable modernist temple, modelled in the form of a giant unfolding lotus.

13 Keoladeo National Park, Bharatpur Page **253** • India's most famous ornithological hotspot, its wetlands attracting vast flocks of migrant birds from across Asia and beyond – drought permitting.

14 Pink City, Jaipur Page **207** • The original heart of old Jaipur, and still Rajasthan's most vibrant commercial district, with streets full of imposing pink mansions, crammed with colourful bazaars.

12 Fatehpur Sikri Page **186** • The enigmatic abandoned capital of the great emperor Akbar – a hauntingly deserted showcase of Mughal architecture.

15 Jaisalmer Page **298** • Honey-coloured city marooned amidst the sands of the Thar Desert, its streets crammed full of extravagantly carved temples and havelis.

16 Red Fort, Delhi Page 116 • The centrepiece of Mughal Delhi, the Red Fort (Lal Qila) offers an absorbing insight into the public pageantry and private life of its creator, Shah Jahan, and his imperial successors.

17 Udaipur Page **331** • The most romantic city in India, with a spectacular array of ornate palaces and havelis clustered around – or floating amidst – the peaceful waters of Lake Pichola.

18 Camel trekking in the Thar Page **306 & 317** • Climb aboard a camel and sally forth into the rolling sands of the Thar Desert, one of India's quintessential wilderness experiences.

Basics

Basics

Getting there

The most practicable way of getting to the region from abroad is by plane. You can fly direct to Delhi from London, New York, Los Angeles or Toronto, though you may find it cheaper to take an indirect flight, changing planes en route, and if you are starting from other airports in the British Isles or North America, or from Australia, New Zealand or South Africa, you will need to do this in any case. If you're already in India, internal flights are often the quickest way to Delhi and Rajasthan, but it's also worth considering the train, particularly the Rajdhani and Shatabdi express services which run to Delhi from major cities nationwide including Mumbai (Bombay), Chennai (Madras), Kolkata (Calcutta), Bangalore, Trivandrum and Guwahati.

International airfares vary slightly with the **season**, and in the northern hemisphere, you'll usually get the best fares in January and February, after the Christmas period, when fewer people are travelling, higher fares around July and August, and the highest around Christmas and Easter, and also over Diwali, which usually falls in November. From the southern hemisphere, cheapest fares are usually in July and August, with higher fares in the summer (November to March), and the highest over Christmas, Easter and Diwali. The prices we quote are inclusive of tax.

It's worth shopping around for the most convenient **arrival times**; nearly all of the cheaper flights land in the middle of night and it can be worth shelling out a little extra to arrive in the morning, particularly if this is your first trip to India.

Packages

A large number of operators run **package holidays** to the region. Specialist tours range from steam locomotives and textiles to religion and food. Even if you book a general sightseeing tour, most firms offer a tour of Rajasthan or the "Golden Triangle" of Delhi, Agra and Jaipur. Some also offer wildlife tours or the luxury *Palace on Wheels* train journey (see p.32). In addition, many companies will arrange **tailor-made tours**, and can help you plan your own itinerary.

Flights from the UK and Ireland

London's Heathrow is the only airport in the UK with **direct flights** to Delhi, operated by BA, Air India, Virgin Atlantic, and currently by a couple of independent Indian airlines, Air Sahara and Jet Airways. Flying time is around seven and a half hours, and longer coming back.

From elsewhere in the UK or Ireland, you will either have to make your way to London, or else take an **indirect flight**, changing planes at London, or in Europe or the Middle East. Royal Jordanian is a good choice, as you change planes at Amman, roughly halfway, and arrive in Delhi nice and early in the morning. KLM offer the advantage of flying from a number of British and Irish airports, with a change of planes at Amsterdam.

If you want to fly **to Jaipur**, you will probably have to change planes at Delhi or Mumbai (Bombay). One possible alternative, if you want to visit the UAE on route, is to fly to Dubai, then take an onward flight to Jaipur with Air Arabia (Ⓦwww.airarabia.com) out of Sharjah.

Expect to pay over £400 from London to Delhi in January, around £500 in summer and more than £650 over Christmas. Flying from Dublin, fares are typically around €700 in January, or €850 in summer and €1800 over Christmas.

Flights from the US and Canada

If you live on the East Coast it's quicker to go via Europe, while from the West Coast it takes less time to go via the Pacific, but either way it's a long haul: fourteen hours to fly direct to Delhi from New York or Toronto, and twenty hours from Los Angeles.

There are **direct flights** to Delhi from New York (with Air India or Continental), Toronto (with Air India or Air Canada), Los Angeles (with Air India) and currently also from Chicago (with American Airlines) and Houston (with Continental), but from any other airport in North America, you'll have to take an **indirect flight**, changing on your way at one of those five airports, or in Europe, the Middle East or East Asia. East Asian airlines usually offer the best standards of comfort, but are only convenient if flying from the West Coast.

Sample fares are US$1150 to fly from New York to Delhi in January, US$1250 in summer, and at least US$1500 over Christmas. From Los Angeles, it costs around US$1350 in January, US$1450 in summer, and US$2500 at Christmas.

Flying out of Toronto or Montreal, tickets start at Can$1400 in January, Can$1550 in July and August, and Can$2000 or more at Christmas. From Vancouver, expect to pay Can$1850 off-season, Can$1950 in summer, and upwards of Can$3000 at Christmas.

Flights from Australia, New Zealand and South Africa

There are no direct flights to Delhi from Australia or New Zealand or South Africa, so you will have to change planes en route. However, you can fly direct from South Africa to Mumbai.

Flying **from Australia**, you will have to make at least one change of plane in a Southeast Asian hub city (usually Hong Kong, Kuala Lumpur, Singapore or Bangkok). You can get to Delhi with just one change of plane from Sydney, Melbourne, Perth, Adelaide or Brisbane. Singapore, Thai, Malaysia Airlines and Cathay Pacific (who also serve Cairns) are among the airlines flying from these airports to Delhi via Southeast Asia. Qantas can offer through tickets in combination with an Indian airline. Expect to pay around AUS$1250 in July or August and AUS$1900 in January. Flying over Christmas, you'll be paying upward of AUS$2500. A flight from Sydney to Delhi with a change of plane at Bangkok will typically take around seventeen hours.

From New Zealand, it's a similar story, except that your choice of carriers will be more limited and you may need to change more than once. Your widest choice of flights will be out of Auckland, served by the same Southeast Asian carriers that fly from Australia, but you can also fly out of Wellington or Christchurch. Prices start at NZ$1120 for most of the year, rising to around NZ$2000 at Christmas.

From South Africa, there are no direct flights to Delhi, but the national carrier, SAA, does fly five times weekly from Johannesburg straight to Mumbai (Bombay), where you can make your way to Delhi or Rajasthan by train or by internal flight. Otherwise, your most direct route to Delhi is via East Africa, usually with Ethiopian Airlines, changing planes at Addis Ababa. It is also possible to fly via the Middle East or even – rather a long way round – via Europe. Expect to pay around R7300 for the cheapest ticket to Delhi in July or August, R13,500 in January and R18,650 over Christmas. A flight from Johannesburg to Delhi changing at Addis will take around fifteen hours. A direct flight from Johannesburg to Mumbai takes just over nine hours. From other South African airports, you'd need to get first to Johannesburg and continue from there.

RTW flights

If northern India is only one stop on a longer journey, you might want to consider buying a **Round the World** (RTW) ticket. Some travel agents can sell you an "off-the-shelf" RTW ticket that will have you touching down in about half a dozen cities; others will have to assemble one for you, which can be tailored to your needs but is likely to be more expensive. Figure on £1600/US$3000/ €2300 for an "off-the-shelf" ticket including Delhi. Some tickets allow for arrival at Delhi and departure out of Mumbai (Bombay) or Kolkata (Calcutta), travelling overland in between. If you plan to arrive in Delhi and travel southwards through Rajasthan, ending up at Mount Abu or Udaipur, then it may well suit you to continue down to Mumbai and fly on from there.

Flights from elsewhere in India

Delhi is easily reached by plane from almost

Fly less – stay longer! Travel and climate change

Climate change is the single biggest issue facing our planet. It is caused by a build-up in the atmosphere of carbon dioxide and other greenhouse gases, which are emitted by many sources – including planes. Already, flights account for around 3–4 percent of human-induced global warming: that figure may sound small, but it is rising year on year and threatens to counteract the progress made by reducing greenhouse emissions in other areas.

Rough Guides regard travel, overall, as a global benefit, and feel strongly that the advantages to developing economies are important, as are the opportunities for greater contact and awareness among peoples. But we all have a responsibility to limit our personal "carbon footprint". That means giving thought to how often we fly and what we can do to redress the harm that our trips create.

Flying and climate change

Pretty much every form of motorized travel generates CO_2, but planes are particularly bad offenders, releasing large volumes of greenhouse gases at altitudes where their impact is far more harmful. Flying also allows us to travel much further than we would contemplate doing by road or rail, so the emissions attributable to each passenger are greater. For example, one person taking a return flight between Europe and California produces the equivalent impact of 2.5 tonnes of CO_2 – similar to the yearly output of the average UK car.

Less harmful planes may evolve but it will be decades before they replace the current fleet – which could be too late for avoiding climate chaos. In the meantime, there are limited options for concerned travellers: to reduce the amount we travel by air (take fewer trips, stay longer!), to avoid night flights (when plane contrails trap heat from Earth but can't reflect sunlight back to space), and to make the trips we do take "climate neutral" via a carbon offset scheme.

Carbon-offset schemes

Offset schemes run by **climatecare.org, carbonneutral.com** and others allow you to "neutralize" the greenhouse gases that you are responsible for releasing. Their websites have simple calculators that let you work out the impact of any flight. Once that's done, you can pay to fund projects that will reduce future carbon emissions by an equivalent amount (such as the distribution of low-energy lightbulbs and cooking stoves in developing countries). Please take the time to visit our website and make your trip climate-neutral.

www.roughguides.com/climatechange

all main cities in India, and even from places as far afield as Leh and Imphal. There are currently around 45 flights a day from Mumbai (Bombay), 25 from Bengaluru (Bangalore), 18 from Chennai (Madras), 17 from Kolkata (Calcutta), 14 from Hyderabad and 9 from Guwahati. On all of these major routes, you have a choice of operators, including Indian Airlines, Air Deccan, Air Sahara, Jet Airways, Kingfisher, SpiceJet and IndiGo Air, though the national carrier, Air India, flies only on the Mumbai–Delhi route. For airline contact details, see pp.22–23.

If you prefer to fly in to **Jaipur**, you could take one of the direct flights from Kolkata,

Mumbai, Bengaluru and Hyderabad, there are also flights from Mumbai to **Jodhpur**.

Typical return **fares** are Rs7510 from Mumbai (1hr 55min), Rs7760 from Kolkata (2hr), Rs9410 from Chennai (2hr 30min), Rs9320 from Bengaluru (2hr 30min), or Rs8530 from Guwahati (2hr 15min).

Trains

Getting to **Delhi** by train is usually straightforward enough, though journeys from the south and east can take well over a day. There are fast Rajdhani Express services from Mumbai, Chennai, Kolkata and Guwahati, to Delhi, as well as direct express and mail services from major cities nationwide.

Agra and Rajasthan are less well connected than Delhi, but **Agra** and **Jaipur** can be reached fairly easily by daily train from Mumbai and Kolkata.

Full details of direct train services from any major stations in India to Delhi, Agra or Rajasthan, and fares, can be found on the Indian Railways website at ⓦwww.indianrail .gov.in.

The only **international train service** currently running into India is the twice-weekly Samjhauta Express from Lahore in the Pakistani part of the Punjab to Amritsar in the Indian part, though political tensions sometimes affect the running of this service, and there may be extended delays at the border. All being well, however, you depart from Lahore on a Tuesday or a Friday at 8am, arriving at 3pm in Amritsar, from where a Shatabdi Express leaves for New Delhi at 5pm, arriving around six hours later. In 2006, a service was introduced from Karachi to Jodhpur (the Thar Express, leaving Karachi 11pm Friday, arriving Jodhpur around 9.30pm Saturday). It was suspended when the line was damaged by floods, but should be reinstated soon. Foreign tourists have not so far been permitted to use this service, but that may change.

For further information on train reservations and rail passes, see pp.29–31.

Buses

The most useful **bus services** into Delhi are from the mountainous areas to the north, such as Kashmir, and most of Himachal Pradesh and Uttarakhand, which are not served by train. There is also a bus service from Lahore in Pakistan, run by the Pakistan Tourism Development Corporation (PTDC; ☎042/575 5940 or 587 5359) and the Delhi Transport Corporation (DTC), leaving from 66-D/1 Gulberg-III, near Liberty Market on Wednesday and Saturday at 6am, and taking thirteen hours.

Buses can also be handy if you are going directly to Rajasthan – and especially southern Rajasthan – from Mumbai (Bombay) or Gujarat. The daily bus from Mumbai to Udaipur takes around twelve hours, and there are regular buses from the Gujarati capital of Ahmedabad to Jaipur, Jodhpur and Udaipur, among other Rajasthani destinations.

Airlines, agents and operators

Online booking

ⓦwww.expedia.co.uk (in UK) ⓦwww.expedia .com (in US) ⓦwww.expedia.ca (in Canada)
ⓦwww.lastminute.com (in UK)
ⓦwww.opodo.co.uk (in UK)
ⓦwww.orbitz.com (in US)
ⓦwww.travelocity.co.uk (in UK) ⓦwww .travelocity.com (in US) ⓦwww.travelocity.ca (in Canada)
ⓦwww.zuji.com.au (in Australia) ⓦwww.zuji .co.nz (in NZ)

Airlines

Aer Lingus Republic of Ireland ☎0818/365 000, Northern Ireland ☎0870/876 5000, ⓦwww.aerlingus.com.

Aeroflot UK ☎020/7355 2233, US ☎1-888/340-6400, Canada ☎1-416/642-1653, Australia ☎02/9262 2233, ⓦwww.aeroflot.co.uk, ⓦwww.aeroflot.com.

Air Canada Canada ☎1-888/247-2262, ⓦwww.aircanada.com.

Air France UK ☎0870/142 4343, US ☎1-800/237-2747, Canada ☎1-800/667-2747, ⓦwww.airfrance.com.

Air India UK ☎020/8560 9996 or 8745 1000, US ☎1-800/223-7776, Canada ☎1-416/865-1033, Australia ☎02/9283 4020, NZ ☎09/631 5651, ⓦwww.airindia.com.

Air Sahara UK ☎0870/128 8026, ⓦwww.airsahara.net.

Alitalia UK ☎0870/544 8259, Ireland ☎01/677 5171, US ☎1-800/223-5730, Canada ☎1-800/361-8336, ⓦwww.alitalia.com.

American Airlines US ☎1-800/433-7300, ⓦwww.aa.com.

Asiana Airlines US ☎1-800/227-4262, ⓦwww.flyasiana.com.

British Airways UK ☎0870/850 9850, Ireland ☎1890/626 747, US and Canada ☎1-800/ AIRWAYS, ⓦwww.ba.com.

Cathay Pacific US & Canada ☎1-800/233-2742, Australia ☎13 17 47, NZ ☎09/379 0861, ⓦwww.cathaypacific.com.

China Airlines US & Canada ☎1-917/368-2003, Australia ☎02/9231 5588, NZ ☎09/308 3364, ⓦwww.china-airlines.com.

Continental Airlines US and Canada ℡1-800-523-3273, Ⓦwww.continental.com.

Delta US & Canada ℡1-800/221-1212, Ⓦwww.delta.com.

Emirates UK ℡0870/243 2222, US ℡1-800/777-3999, Ⓦwww.emirates.com.

Ethiopian Airlines South Africa ℡011/289 8077 or 8, Ⓦwww.ethiopianairlines.com.

Gulf Air UK ℡0870/777 1717, Ireland ℡0018/272 828, US and Canada ℡1-888/FLY-GULF, Ⓦwww.gulfairco.com.

Indian Airlines UK ℡0800/034 4000, US ℡1-866/435-9422, Canada ℡1-866/770-7799, Ⓦindian-airlines.nic.in.

Jet Airways UK ℡020/8970 1525, US ℡1-925/866 1205, Ⓦwww.jetairways.com.

Kenya Airways South Africa ℡011/881 9795, Ⓦwww.kenya-airways.com.

KLM (Royal Dutch Airlines UK ℡0870/507 4074, Ireland ℡1850/747 400, US ℡1-800/225-2525, Ⓦwww.klm.com.

Kuwait Airways UK ℡020/7412 0006, US & Canada ℡1-201/582-9200, Ⓦwww.kuwait-airways.com.

Lufthansa UK ℡0870/837 7747, Ireland ℡01/844 5544, US ℡1-800/645-3880, Canada ℡1-800/563-5954, Ⓦwww.lufthansa.com.

Malaysia Airlines Australia ℡13 26 27, NZ ℡0800/777 747, Ⓦwww.malaysia-airlines.com.

Qantas Australia ℡13 13 13, NZ ℡0800/808 767 or 09/357 8900, Ⓦwww.qantas.com.

Qatar Airways UK ℡020/7896 3636, US ℡1-877/777-2827, Canada ℡1-888/366-5666, Ⓦwww.qatarairways.com.

Royal Jordanian UK ℡020/7878 6300, US ℡1-800/223-0470, Canada ℡1-800/363-0711 or 514-288-1647, Ⓦwww.rja.com.jo.

SAA (South African Airways) South Africa ℡11/978 1111, Ⓦwww.flysaa.com.

Singapore Airlines Australia ℡13 10 11, NZ ℡0800/808 909, Ⓦwww.singaporeair.com.

Swiss UK ℡0845/601 0956, Ireland ℡1890/200 515, US ℡1-877/FLY-SWIS, Ⓦwww.swiss.com.

Syrian Airlines UK ℡020/7631 3511, Ⓦwww.syrianairlines.co.uk.

Thai Airways Australia ℡1300/651 960, NZ ℡09/377 3886, Ⓦwww.thaiair.com.

Virgin Atlantic UK ℡0870/380 2007, US & Canada ℡1-800/821-5438, Ⓦwww.virgin-atlantic.com.

Discount agents

ebookers UK ℡0800/082 3000, Ⓦwww.ebookers.com, Ireland ℡01/488 3507, Ⓦwww.ebookers.ie. Low fares on an extensive selection of scheduled flights and package deals.

North South Travel UK ℡01245/608 291, Ⓦwww.northsouthtravel.co.uk. Friendly, competitive travel agency, offering discounted fares worldwide. Profits are used to support projects in the developing world, especially the promotion of sustainable tourism.

Trailfinders UK ℡0845/058 5858, Ireland ℡01/677 7888, Australia ℡1300/780 212, Ⓦwww.trailfinders.com. One of the best-informed and most efficient agents for independent travellers.

Travel Cuts Canada ℡1-866/246-9762, US ℡1-800/592-2887, Ⓦwww.travelcuts.com. Canadian youth and student travel firm.

STA Travel US ℡1-800/781-4040, Ⓦwww.statravel.com, UK ℡0870/163 0026, Ⓦwww.statravel.co.uk, Australia ℡1300/733 035, Ⓦwww.statravel.com.au, NZ ℡0508/782 872, Ⓦwww.statravel.co.nz, South Africa ℡0861/781 781, Ⓦwww.statravel.co.za. Specialists in independent travel; also student IDs, travel insurance, and more. Good discounts for students and under-26s.

USIT Republic of Ireland ℡01/602 1904, Northern Ireland ℡028/9032 7111, Ⓦwww.usit.ie. Ireland's main student and youth travel specialists.

Tour operators

Adventure Center US & Canada ℡1-800/228-8747, Ⓦwww.adventurecenter.com. Trekking and cultural tours including Mughal Highlights (Delhi, Agra, Jaipur, Amber, Sariska National Park) also to the "Golden Triangle" of Delhi, Agra and Jaipur.

Audley Travel UK ℡01869/276218, Ⓦwww.audleytravel.com. Privately guided, tailor-made itineraries including several good Rajasthan options, and *Palace on Wheels* train tour (see p.32).

Bales UK ℡0845/057 1819, Ⓦwww.balesworldwide.com. Upmarket escorted tours including a sixteen-day "India of the Maharajas" Rajasthan tour, and a nine-day "Magic of India" tour featuring Delhi, Agra, Jaipur and Amber.

Butterfield & Robinson US & Canada ℡1-866/551-9090, Ⓦwww.butterfield.com. Bespoke tours, with an emphasis on cycling and walking, including a very varied ten-day Rajasthan tour.

Cox & Kings UK ℡020/7873 5000, Ⓦwww.coxandkings.co.uk, US ℡1-800/999-1758, Ⓦwww.coxandkings.com. Established in India in 1758, with upmarket tailor-made and off-the-shelf tours including the "Golden Triangle" and a couple of Rajasthan tours, and short breaks in Agra, Jaipur, Udaipur, Bharatpur, Ranthambore or Mount Abu.

Essential India UK ℡01225/868544, Ⓦwww.essential-india.co.uk. A 14-day "Colour and

Craft" tour of Rajasthan, Delhi and Agra, with an emphasis on crafts such as block printing, jewellery, stonecutting and miniature painting.

Exodus UK ☎0870/240 5550, Ireland c/o Abbey Travel T01/804 7153, US and Canada c/o G.A.P. ☎866/732-5885, Australia and New Zealand c/o Peregrine (see opposite), South Africa c/o Mask Expeditions ☎011/807 3333, ⓦwww.exodus .co.uk. Overland adventure including several options in Rajasthan alone or with Delhi and/or Agra, and a seventeen-day Rajasthan cycling tour.

Explore Worldwide UK ☎0870/333 4001, Ireland c/o Maxwells Tours ☎01/677 9479, US c/o Adventure Center ☎1-800/227-8747, Canada c/o Trek Holidays ☎1-888/456 3522, Australia c/o Adventure World ☎02/8913 0700, New Zealand c/o Adventure World ☎09/524 5118, South Africa c/o Shiralee Travel ☎028/313 0526, ⓦwww.explore .co.uk. Highly respected small-groups adventure tour operator with a sixteen-day Rajasthan tour or a ten-day "Mughal Highlights" tour in Rajasthan, Delhi and Agra.

Greaves India UK ☎020/7487 9111, US & Canada ☎1-800/318-7801, ⓦwww.greavesindia.com. Upmarket operator offering a two-week "Essence of Rajasthan" tour that includes a few off-beat sites as well as Delhi, Jaipur and Udaipur. Also offers a ten-day tour featuring Delhi, Agra, Jaipur and Udaipur.

High Places UK ☎0114/275 7500, ⓦwww .highplaces.co.uk. Sheffield-based specialists in

trekking and mountaineering, including a sixteen-day cycling, trekking and wildlife-viewing Rajasthan tour.

Imaginative Traveller UK ☎0800/316 2717 or 01473/667 337, ⓦwww.imaginative-traveller .com. Options include a deluxe 21-day "Amongst the Maharajahs" tour, or a 15-day "Rajasthan in Style" tour, both staying in heritage hotels, or a more adventurous 22-day Rajasthan safari.

Indus Tours UK ☎020/8901 7320, ⓦwww .industours.co.uk. Specialists in "tailor-made" tours, who also offer a number of excellent off-the-shelf Rajasthan options, some including Delhi and Agra too.

Mountain Travel/Sobek US & Canada ☎1-888/687-6235 or 510/594-6000, ⓦwww .mtsobek.com. Adventure travel firm offering an "easy to moderate" 15-day Rajasthan tour (including Delhi and Agra), with some hiking and/or camel riding, staying in hotels and deluxe tented camps.

Nature Expeditions International US & Canada ☎1-800/869-0639 or 954/693-8852, ⓦwww .naturexp.com. Offers quite a varied 18-day tour covering Rajasthan, Delhi, Agra and also Varanasi (Benares).

Peregrine UK ☎01635/872 300, Australia ☎1300/854 444 or 03/8601 4444, ⓦwww .peregrine.net.au. Trekking specialists with a wide range of tailored group and individual tours; tours offered by their budget section, Gecko's, include a 12-day Rajasthan tour which also takes in Delhi and Agra.

Pettitts India UK ☎01892/515966, ⓦwww .pettitts.co.uk. Tailor-made holidays off the beaten track, and off-the-shelf itineraries including an unusual 21-day rural Rajasthan tour as well as a 19-day tour of Rajasthan's forts and temples, and a more conventional 14-day tour of Delhi, Agra and Rajasthan's major sights.

San Michele Travel Australia ☎1800/222 244, ⓦwww.asiatravel.com.au. Budget and upmarket air and accommodation packages, tailor-made trips for groups or individual travellers, or a twelve-day Delhi, Agra and Rajasthan tour.

Trans Indus Travel UK ☎020/8566 2729, ⓦwww.transindus.co.uk. Excellent fixed and tailor-made tours from Delhi, Rajasthan and Agra; specialists in wildlife, fishing and trekking.

Voyages Jules Verne UK ☎020/7616 1000, ⓦwww.vjv.co.uk. Upmarket cultural tour operator with several Rajasthan options including the *Palace on Wheels* (see p.32).

Western & Oriental Travel UK ☎0870/499 1111, ⓦwww.westernoriental.com. Award-winning, upmarket agency with tailor-made itineraries and three excellent Rajasthan tours.

Wilderness Travel US & Canada ☎1-800/368-2794, ⓦwww.wildernesstravel.com. Three Rajasthan tours, staying in heritage hotels and, in two cases, travelling on the *Palace on Wheels* (see p.32).

Worldwide Quest Adventures US & Canada ☏ I-800/387-1483 or 416/633-5666, ⓦ www .worldwidequest.com. Sightseeing plus trekking, cycling, camel safaris and cultural tours.

Indian Railways sales agents abroad

Australia Adventure World, Level 20, 141 Walker St (PO Box 480), N Sydney, NSW 2059 ☏ 02/8913 0755, ⓦ www.adventureworld.com.au.

Canada Hari World Travel Inc, 1 Financial Place, 1 Adelaide St E, Concourse Level, Toronto, ON M5C 2V8 ☏ 1-416/366-2000, ⓦ www.hariworld.com.
South Africa M.K.Bobby Naidoo Travel Agency, PO Box 2878, Durban 44001 ☏ 021/309 3628, Ⓔ mkbobby@iafrica.com.
UK SD Enterprises Ltd, 103 Wembley Park Drive, Wembley, Middlesex HA9 8HG ☏ 020/8903 3411, ⓦ www.indiarail.co.uk.
USA Hari World Travel Inc, 30 Rockefeller Plaza, Shop 21, North Mezzanine, New York, NY 10112 ☏ 1-212/957-3000, ⓦ www.hariworld.com.

Entry requirements

Everyone except citizens of Nepal and Bhutan needs a visa to visit India. If you're going to Delhi, Rajasthan or Agra on business or to study or work, you'll need to apply for a special student or business visa; otherwise, a standard tourist visa will suffice. These are valid for six months from the date of issue (not of departure from your home country or entry into India), and usually cost £30/US$60/€50 (but are free for South Africans). You're asked to specify whether you need a single-entry or a multiple-entry visa, and as the same rates apply to both, it makes sense to ask for the latter (just in case you decide to go back within six months). For details of other kinds of visas, contact your nearest Indian embassy or high commission, or check their website.

The best place to get a visa is in your country of residence, from the embassies and high commissions listed on p.26; you can download an application form from the embassy and consulate websites, or from ⓦ www.india-visa.com. Bear in mind that Indian high commissions, embassies and consulates will observe Indian public holidays as well as local ones, so always check opening hours in advance. To apply for a visa in Britain and North America, you'll need a passport valid for at least six months, two passport photographs and an application form, obtainable in advance by post or on the day; address applications to the Postal Visa Section of the consulate in question. In Australia and New Zealand, one passport-sized photo and your flight/travel itinerary are required, together with the visa application form. As a rule, visas are issued in a matter

of hours, although embassies in India's neighbouring countries often drag their feet, demand letters of recommendation from your embassy, or make you wait and pay for them to send your application to Delhi. In the US, postal applications take a month as opposed to a same-day service if you do it in person – check with your nearest embassy, high commission or consulate. Make sure that your visa is signed by someone at the embassy, as you may be refused entry into the country otherwise.

In many countries it's possible to pay a **visa agency** (or "visa expediter" – see list on p.27) to process the visa on your behalf, which typically costs £40–50/$80–100, plus the price of the visa. This is an option worth considering if you're not able to get to your nearest Indian high commission, embassy or consulate yourself. Prices vary a little from company to company, as do turnaround times. Two weeks is about standard, but you can get a visa in as little as 24hrs if you're prepared to pay premium rates (typically £80/$150 on top of the cost of your visa). For a full rundown of services, check the company websites opposite, from where you can usually download visa application forms.

Visa extensions

It is no longer possible to **extend a tourist visa** in India, though exceptions may be made in special circumstances. If your tourist visa is about to expire and you need more time in the region, you could pop across the border to Pakistan, or even to Bangkok, Colombo or Kathmandu, and apply for a new one. However, in recent years this has been something of a hit-and-miss business, with some tourists having their requests turned down for no apparent reason. The Indian High Commission in Kathmandu is particularly notorious for this.

If you stay in India for more than 120 days, you are supposed to get a **tax clearance certificate** before you leave the country to show that you have no outstanding tax liabilities. The certificate is available at the foreigners' section of the income-tax department in Delhi. It is free, but you should take bank receipts to show you have changed your money legally. In practice, tax clearance certificates are rarely demanded, but you never know. For further information on visa extensions, visit the Bureau of Immigration website at ⓦwww .immigrationindia.nic.in.

Indian embassies, high commissions and consulates abroad

For a comprehensive and up-to-date list of India's diplomatic representation worldwide, go to ⓦmeaindia.nic.in.

Australia 3–5 Moonah Place, Yarralumla, Canberra, ACT 2600 ☎02/6273 3999, ⓦwww .hcindia-au.org; Level 27, 25 Bligh St, Sydney, NSW 2000 ☎02/9223 9500, ⓦwww .indianconsulatesydney.org; 15 Munro St, Coburg, Melbourne, Vic 3058 ☎03/9384 0141, ⓦwww .cgindiamel-au.org; Level 2, 4 Ventnor Ave, West Perth, WA 6005 ☎08/9486 9011, ⓔconsul @wa1.quik.com.au; 175a Swann Rd, Taringa, Qld

4068 ☎07/3871 3362, ⓔindcon@optusnet .com.au.
Canada 10 Springfield Rd, Ottawa, ON K1M 1C9 ☎1-613/744 3751, ⓦwww.hciottawa.ca; 365 Bloor St E, Suite 700, Toronto, ON M4W 3L4 ☎1-416/960-0751 or 2, ⓦwww.cgitoronto .ca (no walk-in visa service); 325 Howe St, 2nd floor, Vancouver, BC V6C 1Z7 ☎1-604/662 8811, ⓦwww.cgivancouver.com.
Ireland 6 Leeson Park, Dublin 6 ☎01/497 0843, ⓔindcons@eircom.net; also in Belfast (see below).
Nepal PO Box 292, 336 Kapurdhara Marg, Kathmandu ☎01/441 0900, ⓦwww.south-asia .com/Embassy-India.
New Zealand 180 Molesworth St, PO Box 4005, Wellington 6015 ☎04/473 6390, ⓦwww.hicomind .org.nz.
Pakistan G-5, Diplomatic enclave, Islamabad ☎051/220 6950 to 54, ⓔhicomind@isb.compol .com; India House, 3 Fatima Jinnah Rd, PO Box 8542, Karachi ☎021/522 275.
South Africa 852 Schoeman St (cnr of Eastwood St), PO Box 40216, Arcadia 0007, Pretoria ☎012/342 2593, ⓦindia.org.za; 1 Eton Road, Parktown, PO Box 6805, Johannesburg 2000 ☎011/482 8484 to 9, ⓦwww.indconjoburg.co.za; The Old Station Building (4th floor), 160 Pine Street, PO Box 3276, Durban 4001 ☎031/307-7020, ⓦwww.indcondurban.co.za.
Sri Lanka 36–38 Galle Road, PO Box 882, Colombo 3 ☎01/232 7587, ⓦwww .indiahcsl.org; 31 Rajapihilla Mawatha, PO Box 47, Kandy ☎08/234 545, ⓔahciknd@telenett.net.
UK India House, Aldwych, London WC2B 4NA ☎020/7836 8484, ⓦwww.hcilondon.net; 20 Augusta St, Jewellery Quarter, Hockley, Birmingham B18 6JL ☎0121/ 212 2782, ⓦwww .cgibirmingham.org; 17 Rutland Square, Edinburgh EH1 2BB ☎0131/229 2144, ⓦwww.cgiedinburgh .org; c/o Andras House Ltd, 60 Great Victoria St, Belfast BT2 7BB ☎028/9087 8787, ⓔdsrana @andrashouse.co.uk.

Duty free allowances

Anyone over 17 can bring in two litres of wine or spirits, plus 200 cigarettes, or 50 cigars, or 250g tobacco. You may be required to register anything valuable on a tourist baggage re-export form to make sure you can take it home with you, and to fill in a currency declaration form if carrying more than $10,000 or the equivalent.

USA 2536 Massachusetts Ave, Washington, DC
20008 ☎1-202/939-7000, ⊛www.indianembassy
.org; 3 E 64th St (between Madison and 5th Ave),
New York, NY 10021 ☎1-212/774-0600, ⊛www
.indiacgny.org; 540 Arguello Blvd, San Francisco,
CA 94118 ☎1-415/668-0662, ⊛www.cgisf.
org; 455 North City Front Plaza Drive, NBC Tower
Building, Suite 850, Chicago IL 60611 ☎1-
312/595 0405, ⊛chicago.indianconsulate.com;
1990 Post Oak Blvd, Suite 600, Three Post Oak
Central, Houston, TX 77056 ☎1-713-621-5576,
⊛www.cgihouston.org.

Visa agencies

CIBT US ☎1-800/929-2428, ⊛www.cibt.com.
Gold Arrow UK ☎0870/165 7412,
⊛www.goldarrow.info.
Travel Document Systems US ☎1-800-874-
5100 or 1-202/638 3800, ⊛www.traveldocs.com.
Visa Connection US ☎1-877/847-2362, Canada
☎1-866/566-8472, ⊛www.visaconnection.com.
Visa Service UK ☎0870/890 0185,
⊛www.visaservice.co.uk.
Visa Link Australia ☎1902/211 133,
⊛www.visalink.com.au.

Getting around

Local transport may not be the fastest or the most comfortable in the world, but
it's cheap, covers more or less all the routes between Delhi, Agra and the cities of
Rajasthan, and generally gives you the option of train or bus, occasionally even
plane. Transport around town comes in even more permutations, ranging from
bicycle rickshaws, auto-rickshaws and Ambassador taxis to – in Delhi – a
spanking new metro system.

By rail

Travelling by train is one of the great experiences of India. Trains are often late of course,
sometimes by hours rather than minutes, but
they're cheap and much more comfortable
than buses, and they connect Delhi, Agra
and almost every part of Rajasthan. The
main destinations not served directly by train
are Pushkar and Mount Abu, which are a
short bus ride away from rail stations at,
respectively, Ajmer and Abu Road.

On longer journeys (Udaipur or Jaisalmer
to Jaipur or Delhi, for example), an
overnight train can save you a day's travelling and a night's hotel bill. Between 9pm
and 6am anyone with a bunk reservation is
entitled to exclusive use of their bunk as a
bed, but before 9pm, the middle and lower
bunks may be used as seats: the upper
bunk has the advantage that you can stretch
out on it at any time. When travelling
overnight, it's a good idea to padlock your
bag to your bunk; an attached chain is

usually provided beneath the seat of the
lower bunk.

Indian Railways do have a relatively high
accident rate, with four to five hundred
crashes nationwide every year, and seven to
eight hundred fatalities, making it the most
dangerous rail network in the world. Train
passengers, however, can take solace in the
fact that travelling by rail is considerably safer
than using buses since, according to official
statistics, an average of 85,000 people die
on the country's roads every year.

Routes and types of train

Inter-city trains, called "express" or "mail",
vary a lot in the time taken to cover the same
route. Slow by Western standards, they're
still much faster than local **"passenger"
trains**, which you need only use to get off
the beaten track. Note that express and mail
trains cost a fair amount more than ordinary
passenger trains, so if travelling unreserved
make sure you buy the right ticket.

Distance chart (in km)

	Agra	Ajmer	Alwar	Bharat-pur	Bikaner	Chittaur-garh	Delhi
Agra	–	388	172	56	665	579	195
Ajmer	388	–	272	332	233	191	392
Alwar	172	272	–	116	462	463	163
Bharatpur	56	332	116	–	497	523	251
Bikaner	665	233	462	497	–	424	470
Chittaurgarh	579	191	463	523	424	–	583
Delhi	195	392	163	251	470	583	–
Jaipur	232	138	143	175	354	345	259
Jaisalmer	853	490	762	822	333	657	882
Jodhpur	568	205	477	537	243	372	597
Kota	453	200	383	418	432	158	504
Mount Abu	737	375	647	707	569	297	767
Nawalgarh	370	207	164	280	239	398	292
Sawai Madhopur	230	252	228	233	485	283	484
Udaipur	637	274	551	581	506	112	664

New Delhi station is connected by super-fast air-conditioned trains to Agra, Jaipur and also Ajmer and Abu Road. Of these, the **Rajdhani expresses** are overnight services travelling on to destinations at the far end of India, while the **Shatabdi expresses** are daytime trains which connect major cities (the only Shatabdi routes relevant to this book are between New Delhi, Jaipur and Ajmer, and New Delhi and Agra). Bottled water, snacks and good meals are included in the ticket price of these services.

Classes of train travel

Indian Railways (IR; ⓦ www.indianrail.gov .in) distinguishes between no fewer than seven **classes** of travel, but most travellers (not just those on low budgets) choose to travel second class, which keeps you in contact with the world outside, while first and air-conditioned classes involve being sealed away behind glass, often virtually opaque.

Second-class unreserved is crowded and noisy with no chance of a berth if travelling overnight, but it's incredibly cheap. Far more civilized and costing only around fifty percent more is **second-class sleeper**, which are usually reasonably comfy, and should be booked in advance even for daytime journeys (unreserved second-class tickets are not valid in sleeper carriages). If you have only been able to get an unreserved ticket and want a sleeper, go and see the Ticket Controller (TC) in the sleeper section as soon as you board the train. If there are any sleepers available, you should be able to get one by paying the extra fare, but of course there may be none, so it is far better to book your sleeper in advance if possible.

First class costs about five times as much as sleeper class. It insulates you to a certain extent from the hustle and bustle, but is not always available, and is gradually being phased out.

Air-conditioned travel falls into four categories. The best value is the **a/c chair car** (often denoted as CC), with comfortable reclining seats at roughly two and a half times the price of a second-class sleeper. Shatabdi expresses are exclusively chair car but come in two classes – ordinary a/c chair car and, for double the price, an executive a/c chair car. **Air-conditioned three-tier sleepers**

Jaipur	Jaisalmer	Jodhpur	Kota	Mt Abu	Nawal-garh	Sawai Mad	Udaipur
232	853	568	453	737	370	230	637
138	490	205	200	375	207	252	274
143	762	477	383	647	164	228	551
175	822	537	418	707	280	233	581
354	333	243	432	569	239	485	506
345	657	372	158	297	398	283	112
259	882	597	504	767	292	484	664
–	543	317	242	465	138	164	347
543	–	285	690	572	540	742	545
317	285	–	404	326	347	457	260
242	690	404	–	455	407	161	270
465	572	326	455	–	582	580	185
138	540	347	407	582	–	306	481
164	742	457	161	580	580	–	395
347	545	260	270	185	185	395	–

(3AC) cost slightly less than normal first class, and can feel a bit cramped. They are less common than **a/c two-tier sleepers** (2AC), which cost half as much again as ordinary first class. Top of the tree is **a/c first class** (1AC), with two- to four-person compartments, carpet and more presentable bathrooms. Bed linen is provided free on most a/c services while meals are also included on Rajdhani and Shatabdi trains.

For more detailed descriptions, along with photographs of seats and carriages in the different classes, plus good advice and information on train travel, visit the Man in Seat 61's India pages at Ⓦwww.seat61.com/India.htm.

Bed rolls (sheet, blanket and pillow) are available in first class and a/c second for that extra bit of comfort – book these with your ticket, or before you board the train.

Ladies' compartments exist on all overnight trains; they are usually small and can be full of noisy kids, but they exclude male nuisance-mongers, and can be a good place to meet Indian women, particularly if you like (or are with) children. Some stations also have ladies-only waiting rooms.

Timetables and tickets

Indian Railways publish a **timetable** of all mail and express trains – in effect, all the trains you are likely to use – called *Trains at a Glance* (Rs30), available from information counters and newsstands at all main stations, and from IR agents abroad. You can also consult rail timetables and fares, and check availability at Ⓦwww.indianrail.gov.in.

All rail fares are calculated according to the exact **distance** travelled. *Trains at a Glance* prints a chart of fares by kilometres, and also gives the distance in kilometres of stations along each route in the timetables, making it possible to calculate what the basic fare will be for any given journey.

Each individual train has its own **name and number,** prominently displayed in station booking halls.

Reserving tickets

To make a reservation, you fill in a form specifying the train you intend to catch, its number, your date of travel, and the stations you are travelling to and from, plus your age

Delhi–Jaipur: comparative fares

For comparison, here are the fares for different forms of transport between Delhi and Jaipur, a journey of just under 260km by road, or just over 300km by rail.

Train

2nd class unreserved	Rs80	2nd class sleeper	Rs177
1st class	Rs905	AC chair car	Rs465
AC three-tier	Rs441	AC two-tier	Rs610
AC first	Rs1045		

Bus

Ordinary state bus	Rs145	Semi-deluxe state bus	Rs172
Silver line (deluxe)	Rs270	Gold Line (AC deluxe)	Rs460
Deluxe private bus	Rs180	Private sleeper bus	Rs200

Plane

Economy discount	Rs2350	Economy full-fare	Rs4610
Business class	Rs6530		

and sex (this helps conductors to determine who you are). Most stations have **computerized booking counters** (these are listed in *Trains at a Glance*), and you will be told immediately whether or not seats are available. There's a small fee to book a seat or sleeper in second class; in other classes this is already included in the price of the ticket.

Reservation offices in the main stations are often in a separate building and generally open from Monday to Saturday from 8am to 8pm, and on Sunday to 2pm. In larger cities, the major stations have special **tourist sections** to cut the queues for foreigners and Indian citizens resident abroad, with helpful English-speaking staff. Bear in mind, if you don't pay in pounds sterling or dollars (traveller's cheques or cash), you may be asked to produce an encashment certificate (see p.74) to back up your rupees. Elsewhere, buying a ticket can often involve a long wait, though women get round this at ticket counters which have "**ladies' queues**"; travelling in a mixed group or couple, a woman will find it easier to get a ticket. Alternatively, many travel agents will secure tickets for a reasonable Rs25–50 fee. Failure to buy a ticket at the point of departure will result in a stiff **penalty** when the ticket controller (TC) finds you.

It's important to **plan your train journeys in advance**, as the demand often makes it impossible to buy a long-distance ticket on the same day that you want to travel (although the new **Tatkal** quota system – see opposite – has made life a little easier if you're happy to pay extra). Travellers following tight itineraries tend to buy their departure tickets the moment they arrive, to avoid having to trek out to the station again later. At most large stations, it's possible to reserve tickets for journeys starting elsewhere in the country. You can even book tickets for specific journeys before you leave home, with Indian Railways representatives abroad (see p.25). They accept bookings up to six months in advance, with a minimum of one month for first class, and three months for second.

Indian Railways online

Online ticket reservation is now available across the network via the Indian Railways' website, ⓦ www. indianrail.gov.in, though there's a lengthy sign-up and login process. Generally, foreign travellers are better off either purchasing tickets in person or paying a travel agent to do so on their behalf. That said, the website is extremely useful as a means of **checking fares, timetables and availability of berths** – information that you would normally have to travel to a station and queue for.

If there are no places available

If there are **no places available** on the train you want, you have a number of choices. First, some seats and berths are set aside as a **"tourist quota"** – ask at the tourist counter if you can get in on this, or else try the stationmaster. Alternatively, you can stump up the extra cash for a **Tatkal** ticket (see below), which guarantees you access to a special ten percent of unreserved tickets on most trains, though certain catches and conditions apply.

RAC – or "Reservation Against Cancellation" – tickets are another option, giving you priority if sleepers do become available – the ticket clerk should be able to tell you your chances. With an RAC ticket you are allowed onto the train and can sit until the conductor can find you a berth. The worst sort of ticket to have is a **wait-listed** one – identifiable by the letter "W" prefixing your passenger number – which will allow you onto the train but not in a reserved compartment; in this case go and see the ticket inspector as soon as possible to persuade him to find you a place if one is free: something usually is, but you'll be stuck in unreserved if it isn't. Wait-listed ticket holders are not allowed onto Shatabdi and Rajdhani trains. You could **travel unreserved**, but if the train is full (as it will be on major routes) travel in second class will be extremely uncomfortable. If you get on where the train starts its journey, **baksheesh** may persuade an official to "reserve" you an unreserved seat or, better still, a luggage rack where you can stretch out for the night (station porters may be able to act as middlemen in this regard, taking a cut themselves, of course). You could even fight your way on with everybody else and try to grab a seat or a luggage rack yourself, but your chances are slim. For short journeys, or on minor routes where trains are not so crowded – between the towns of Shekhawati for example – you won't need to reserve tickets in advance.

Indrail passes

Indrail passes, sold to foreigners and Indians resident abroad, cover all fares and reservation fees for periods ranging from half a day to ninety days, but are considerably more expensive than buying your tickets individually. The pass is designed for nation-wide travel, so if you are only using it between Delhi, Agra and the cities of Rajasthan, you will certainly not be getting your money's worth. The pass does, however, save you queuing for tickets, and it allows you to make and cancel reservations with impunity (and without charge), and generally smooths your way in, for example, if you need to find a seat or berth on a "full" train, passholders get priority for tourist quota places. Indrail passes are available in sterling or US dollars, at main station tourist counters in India, and outside the country at IR agents (see p.25), and sometimes at Air India and Indian Airlines offices. A seven-day pass costs US$80 in second class, US$135 in first, and US$370 in AC class; thirty days is US$125/248/495; ninety days is US$235/530/1060; a full schedule of prices is available at ⓦ www.indianrail.gov.in.

Tatkal tickets

Indian Railways has a late-availability reservation system for train travellers called **Tatkal**, which has been controversial in India, but looks set to be a great help for foreign tourists. A quota of ten percent of places on most trains is reserved under this scheme, bookable at any computerized office. Tickets are released from 8am, five days before the train departs, and there's an extra charge of Rs150 in Sleeper or Chair Car and Rs300 in First or a/c sleepers. There's a catch, however, as you will need to pay for the entire length of the journey from originating to terminating station, regardless of how much or little of the ride you do. Therefore, Tatkal is not such a good deal, for example, if you want to get from Jaipur to Bikaner on the Howrah Express from Kolkata. If you're covering most of the route, though, it's worthwhile, and you're pretty well guaranteed to find a place, especially if you get in early, as a lot of resident Indians have been put off by the price supplement.

Tourist trains

Inspired by the Orient Express, Indian Railways offers holiday packages aboard luxury **tourist trains** – with exorbitant prices in dollars to match. The flagship of the scheme is the **Palace on Wheels**, with sumptuous ex-maharajas' carriages updated into modern air-conditioned coaches, still decorated with the original designs. An all-inclusive, one-week whistle-stop tour (Sept–April weekly) starts from Delhi and travels through Jaipur and Jodhpur to the sands of Jaisalmer before turning south to Udaipur and returning via Agra; prices start at US$2205 per person for the full trip, with discounts off-season (Sept & April). The service has proved so popular that it is often booked up for months ahead, and a less expensive second service, *Heritage on Wheels*, has now been introduced to supplement it. This offers a three-day trip from Jaipur to Bikaner and Shekhawati starting at US$450 per person.

Both trains can be booked through the Rajasthan Tourism Development Corporation (RTDC), Bikaner House, Pandara Road, New Delhi 110011 (☎011/2338 1884, ⓦwww.rajasthantourism.gov.in) or *Hotel Swagatam*, Jaipur 302006 (☎0141/220 3620). Or you can call toll-free to book in North America (☎877/463-4299), the UK (☎0800/845 6201), Australia (☎1800/156671) or New Zealand (☎0800/442510), or on line at ⓦwww.palaceonwheels.net or ⓦwww.heritageonwheels.net.in.

Another option is the **Fairy Queen**, driven by the oldest working steam engine in the world, which takes a two-day trip through eastern Rajasthan to Alwar and the Sariska tiger reserve (Oct–Feb twice monthly; Rs7500/US$165).

The *Fairy Queen* can be booked through the same RTDC offices as the *Palace on Wheels*, and also at the Government of India Tourist Office, 88 Janpath, New Delhi (☎011/2332 0005 or 8), or the International Tourist Bureau at New Delhi station (☎011/2340 5156 or 2334 6804, ⓔitbnrind@nda.vsnl.net.in), or Delhi's National Rail Museum (☎011/2688 1816 or 0939, ⓔsmehranrm@hotmail.com). Alternatively, you can book all of these trains online at ⓦwww.indiarailtours.com.

Cloakrooms

Most stations in India have **cloakrooms** (sometimes called parcel offices) for passengers to leave their baggage. These can be extremely handy if you want to go sightseeing in a town and move on the same day. In theory, you need a train ticket or Indrail pass to deposit luggage, but staff don't always ask; they may, however, refuse to take your bag if you can't lock it. Losing your reclaim ticket causes problems; the clerk will be assumed to have stolen the bag if he can't produce it, so there'll be untold running around to obtain clearance before you can get your bag without it. Make sure, when checking baggage in, that the cloakroom will be open when you need to pick it up. The standard charge is currently Rs10 per 24 hours.

By bus

Although trains are the definitive form of transport in India, and generally more comfortable than **buses**, there are places (such as the desert towns around Jaisalmer) where trains don't go, where they are inconvenient, or where buses are simply faster. Buses go almost everywhere in Rajasthan, and are generally more frequent than trains, though they travel mostly in daylight hours.

Services vary somewhat in price and standards. The state transport companies – Delhi State Transport (DTC; ⓦdtc.nic.in) in Delhi, the Rajasthan State Road Transport Corporation (RSRTC; ⓦwww.rsrtc.org) in Rajasthan, the Uttar Pradesh State Road Transport Corporation (UPSRTC; ⓦwww.upsrtc.com) in Uttar Pradesh, which includes Agra – cover most routes. RSRTC have ordinary and express buses, bog-standard in terms of comfort, as well as deluxe "silver line" and air-conditioned "gold line" buses, which are a good deal more comfortable (and expensive). Popular trunk routes may also be covered by **private buses**, which tend to be more comfortable than the ordinary state services. Whichever you choose, try to avoid the back seats, which can be very bumpy indeed.

Luggage travels in the hatch of private buses. On state-run buses, you can usually squeeze it into an unobtrusive corner, or under your seat, though it may get dirty there, or you may sometimes be requested to put it in the hold or up on the roof; in the latter case, check that it's well secured (ideally, lock it there) and not liable to get squashed. Whether on the roof or in the hold, baksheesh is in order for whoever puts it thoro for you.

Buying a bus ticket is usually less of an ordeal than buying a train ticket, although at large city bus stations there may be several counters, assigned to different routes. You can always get on ordinary state buses without a ticket, and at bus stands outside major cities you can usually only pay on board, so you have to be sharp to secure a seat. Prior booking is usually available and preferable for express and private services, and it's a good idea to check with the agent exactly where the bus will depart from. You can often pay on board private buses too, though doing so reduces your chances of a seat.

By air

Given the cheap and plentiful train connections and the relatively short distances involved, you may not feel the need to use planes to get around between Delhi and the cities of Rajasthan, but it is possible. Jaipur, Jodhpur and Udaipur all have airports, and all of them have flights to Delhi should you want to use them. Indeed, you can also fly from Udaipur to Jodhpur or Jaipur. Most of these routes have only one to three flights a day, though the Delhi–Jaipur route has extra flights on Wednesdays and Sundays. In particular, a flight between Delhi and Udaipur or Jodhpur can save you a long train journey. Discounted seats are available but often sell out quickly, so it's a good idea to book early, or you may have to pay the full fare. Indian Airlines and the independent airline Jet Airways (considered slicker and more dynamic) both fly Delhi–Jaipur, Delhi–Udaipur, Delhi–Jodhpur. In addition, Indian Airlines flies Jodhpur–Udaipur, and Jet flies Jaipur–Udaipur. Flight times and frequencies are listed in the "Moving On" sections at the end of each Guide chapter.

Agra and Jaisalmer have airports, but they are not currently used for commercial passenger flights, though this may change in the future. Alliance Air, a subsidiary of Indian Airlines, operated passenger flights between Delhi and Agra as recently as 2005.

Domestic airlines

Air India ☎1800/227 722 or 0124/234 8888, ⓦwww.airindia.com.
Air Deccan ☎3900 8888 ʋɪ 080/4114 8190, ⓦwww.airdeccan.net.
Air Sahara ☎1800/223 020, ⓦwww.airsahara.net.
GoAir ☎1800/222 111 or 022/6741 0000, ⓦwww.goair.in.
Indian Airlines ☎1800/180 1407 or 011/2211-6869, ⓦindian-airlines.nic.in.
IndiGo Air ☎0/991 038 3838 or 011/4351 3186, ⓦbook.goindigo.in.
Indus Air ☎011/3254 8463, ⓦwww.indusair.biz.
Jet Airways ☎1800/225 522 or 011/3984 1111, ⓦwww.jetairways.com.
Kingfisher Airlines ☎1800/180 0101 or 0124/274 4700, ⓦwww.flykingfisher.com.
SpiceJet ☎1800/180 333, ⓦwww.spicejet.com.

By car

Driving in India is not for beginners. If you do drive yourself, expect the unexpected, and expect other drivers to take whatever liberties they can get away with. Traffic circulates on the left, but don't expect anybody to obey road regulations. Lane discipline is non-existent, and almost nobody bothers to indicate when turning. Overtaking is willy-nilly on either side. Generally the vehicle in front seems to have right of way, so at busy intersections or roundabouts (rotaries) drivers try and get out in front as soon as possible. Another unstated law of the road is that might is right.

Traffic in the **cities** is heavy and undisciplined; vehicles cut in and out without warning, and pedestrians, cyclists and cows wander nonchalantly down the middle of the road. In the **country** the roads are narrow, in terrible repair, and hogged by overloaded "Tata" trucks that move aside for nobody, while something slow-moving like a bullock cart or a herd of goats can take up the whole road. To **overtake**, sound your horn (an essential item on Indian roads) – the driver in front will signal if it is safe to do so; if not, he will wave his hand, palm downwards, up and down. A huge number of potholes don't make for a smooth ride either. Furthermore, during the monsoon roads can become flooded. Ask local people before you set off, and proceed with caution, sticking to main highways if possible.

You should have an **international driving licence** to drive in India, but this is often overlooked if you have your licence from home. **Insurance** is compulsory, but not expensive. Car **seat belts** are compulsory in Delhi and Rajasthan, and strongly recommended in any case. Accident rates are high, and you should be on your guard at all times. It is particularly dangerous to drive at night – not everyone uses lights, and bullock carts don't have any. If you have an **accident**, it might be an idea to leave the scene quickly and go straight to the police to report it; mobs can assemble fast, especially if pedestrians or cows are involved, and drivers involved in accidents with local people are frequently roughed up.

Fuel is reasonably cheap (around Rs45 a litre for leaded or unleaded petrol, Rs32 for diesel), but the state of the roads will take its toll on your car, and mechanics are not always very reliable, so some knowledge of vehicle maintenance is handy, as is a checkup every so often. Luckily, if you get a flat tyre, puncture-wallahs can be easily found almost everywhere.

The classic Indian automobile is the Hindustan Ambassador (basically a Morris Oxford), nowadays largely superseded by more modern vehicles such as the Maruti Suzuki. Renting a car, you'll probably have a choice of these two or others.

It is much more usual for tourists to be driven in India than it is for them to drive themselves; **car rental** firms operate on the basis of supplying **chauffeur-driven vehicles**, and taxis are available at cheap daily rates. Arranged through tourist offices or local car rental firms, a chauffeur-driven car will run to about £25/US$50 per day, rather more if you arrange it through one of the international car rental franchises.

Car rental agencies

Avis UK ☏ 0870/606 0100, Ireland ☏ 021/428 1111, US ☏ 1-800/230-4898, Canada ☏ 1-800/272-5871, Australia ☏ 13 63 33 or 02/9353 9000, NZ ☏ 09/526 2847 or 0800/655 111, South Africa ☏ 0861/113 748, ⓦ www.avis.com.
Budget UK ☏ 0870/156 5656, Ireland ☏ 090/662 7711, US ☏ 1-800/527-0700, Canada ☏ 1-800/268-8900, Australia ☏ 1300/362 848, New Zealand ☏ 0800/283 438, South Africa ☏ 011/398 0123 or 086/101 6622, ⓦ www.budget.com.
Europcar UK ☏ 0870/607 5000, Ireland ☏ 01/614 2800, US & Canada ☏ 1-877/940 6900, Australia ☏ 1300/131 390, ⓦ www.europcar.com.
Hertz UK ☏ 020/7026 0077, Ireland ☏ 01/870 5777, US & Canada ☏ 1-800/654-3131, NZ ☏ 0800/654 321, South Africa ☏ 021/935 4800, ⓦ www.hertz.com.

By motorbike

Riding a motorbike around India has long had a strong appeal, but is not without its hazards. Beside the appalling road conditions (see p.33) and the ensuing fatigue, **renting a motorbike**, unless you are well versed in maintenance, can be a bit of a nightmare, with breakdowns often in the most inconvenient places. Motorbike rental is available in some tourist towns and useful for local use, but the quality of the bikes is never assured. Helmets are best brought from home.

A few tourists buy themselves a motorbike in India, and aficionados of classic bikes love the Enfield Bullet (350 model), an Indian-made version of an old British model, the Royal Enfield. Motorcycles of various sorts can easily be bought new or secondhand. In Delhi, the Karol Bagh area is renowned for its motorcycle shops. For a short stay, buying a bike when you arrive and selling it again when you leave seems like a lot of trouble to go to, but given the right bargaining skills, it is possible to buy a used bike and sell it again later for a similar price, to a dealer or by advertising it in hotels and tourist hang-outs. A certain amount of bureaucracy is involved in transferring vehicle ownership, but a garage should be able to put you on to a broker ("auto consultant") who, for a modest commission (around Rs500), will help you find a seller or a buyer, and do the necessary paperwork.

It's worth noting that a motorbike can be taken in the luggage car of a **train** for the same price as a second-class passenger fare (get a form and pay a small fee at the station luggage office).

By bicycle

For getting around between cities, a bicycle is in many ways the ideal form of transport, offering total independence without loss of contact with local people. You can camp out, though there are cheap lodgings in almost every village – take the bike into your room with you – and, if you get tired of pedalling, you can put it on top of a bus as luggage, or transport it by train.

Bringing a bike from abroad requires no carnet or special paperwork, but spare parts and accessories may be of different sizes and standards in India, and you may have to improvise. Bring **basic spares** and **tools**, and a **pump**. Panniers are the obvious thing for carrying your gear, but fiendishly inconvenient when not attached to your bike, and you might consider sacrificing ideal load-bearing and streamlining technology for a backpack you can lash down on the rear carrier.

Buying a bike in India presents no great difficulty, and there are cycle shops in most big towns. The advantages of a local bike are that spare parts are easy to get, locally produced tools and parts will fit, and your bike will not draw a crowd every time you park it. Disadvantages are that Indian bikes tend to be heavier and less state-of-the-art than ones from abroad; mountain bikes are beginning to appear in cities and bigger towns, but with insufficient gears and a low level of equipment, they're not worth buying. Selling should be quite easy: you won't get a tremendously good deal at a cycle market, but you may well be able to sell privately, or even to a rental shop.

Bicycles can be **rented** in most towns, usually for local use only: this is a good way to find out if your legs and bum can survive the Indian bike before buying one. Rs25–50 per day is the going rate, occasionally more in tourist centres, and you may have to leave a deposit, or even your passport as security. One or two adventure tour operators, such as Exodus (see p.24), offer bicycle tours of Rajasthan with most customers expected to bring their own cycles.

City transport

Transport around towns takes various forms, with **buses** the most obvious, usually single-decker. City buses can get unbelievably crowded, so beware of pickpockets, razor-armed pocket-slitters, and "Eve teasers" (see p.63). Visitors to Delhi are often amazed by the clean efficiency of its **metro system**.

You can also take **taxis**, usually rather battered Ambassadors (painted black and yellow in the large cities) and Maruti omnivans. With luck, the driver will agree to use the **meter**; in theory you're within your rights to call the police if he doesn't, but the usual compromise is to agree a **fare** for the journey before you get in. Naturally, it helps to have an idea in advance what the fare should be, though any figures quoted in this or any other book should be treated as being the broadest of guidelines only. From places such as main stations, you may be able to find other passengers to share a taxi to the town centre; some stations, and most airports, operate prepaid taxi schemes with set fares that you pay before departure.

The **auto-rickshaw**, that most Indian of vehicles (though increasingly appearing elsewhere too), is the front half of a motor-scooter with a couple of seats mounted on the back. Cheaper than taxis (they're metered, but it's highly unlikely they will use it so agree a fare before setting off) and better at nipping in and out of traffic, auto-rickshaws are a little unstable and their drivers often rather reckless, but that's all part of the experience. In major tourist centres auto-wallahs may hustle people for business on the street, usually with the aim of overcharging them, or taking them to commission-paying shops before going to the destination they've asked for. Moreover, agreeing a price before the journey will not necessarily stop your auto-wallah reopening discussion when the trip is underway, or at its end (you can treat this as an invitation not to tip). It is invariably better to hail an auto yourself than to take one that hustles you for business, and it's also worth avoiding autos that hang around outside hotels. Delhi now has a number of pre-paid auto stations where you buy a ticket to your destination in advance from a kiosk rather than paying your auto-wallah on arrival.

Slower and cheaper still is the **cycle rickshaw** – basically a glorified tricycle.

Foreign visitors often feel uncomfortable about travelling this way, as rickshaw-wallahs are invariably emaciated pavement dwellers who earn only a pittance for their pains. In the end, though, to deny them your custom on those grounds is spurious logic; they will earn even less if you don't use them, and you are always free to be generous when tipping. Tourists in any case usually pay a bit more than locals. As with autos, it's best to hail a rickshaw yourself rather than take one which hails you. Note that cycle rickshaws are rather slow, so not worth taking if you're in any sort of hurry.

Here and there (most notably in Fatehpur Sikri and also around Taj Ganj in Agra), you'll also come across horse-drawn carriages, or **tongas**. Tugged by underfed and often lame horses, they cost about the same as cycle rickshaws.

If you want to see a variety of places around town, consider hiring a **taxi**, rickshaw or auto-rickshaw for the day. Find a driver who speaks English reasonably well, and agree a price beforehand. You will probably find it a lot cheaper than you imagine, and the driver will invariably act as a guide and source of local knowledge. Again, though the price may be low, you are free to be generous with the tip.

Health

You hear a lot of scare stories about the health risks of travelling in India, but coming down with a serious tropical illness is very much the exception rather than the rule. Risks do exist, and yes, travellers do sometimes come down with malaria, dysentery, hepatitis or even typhoid, but generally speaking, such diseases can be avoided by taking elementary precautions, and if you're careful, you should be able to get through with nothing worse than a mild dose of "Delhi belly". It is extremely important, however, to keep your resistance high and to be aware of the health risks of untreated water, mosquito bites and undressed open cuts.

What you **eat** and **drink** is crucial: a poor diet lowers your resistance. Meat and fish are obvious sources of protein for non-vegetarians in the West, but not necessarily in India: eggs, pulses (lentils, peas and beans), rice, paneer and curd are all protein sources, as are nuts. Overcooked vegetables lose a lot of their vitamin content, but eating plenty of peeled fresh fruit helps keep up your vitamin and mineral intake. It's also important to drink plenty of water. And make sure you eat enough – an unfamiliar diet may reduce the amount you eat – and **get enough sleep** and rest: it's easy to get run down if you're on the move a lot, especially in a hot climate.

If you do fall ill, and can't get to a doctor, it's worth knowing that almost any medicine can be bought over the counter without a prescription, though heavy-duty drugs such as antibiotics should not be taken without medical advice, except perhaps in case of dire emergency.

Precautions

The lack of sanitation in India can be exaggerated. It's not worth getting too worked up about it or you'll never enjoy anything, but a few **common-sense precautions** are in order, bearing in mind that things such as bacteria multiply far more quickly in a tropical climate, and your body will have little immunity to Indian germs.

For details on the **water**, see box opposite. When it comes to **food**, be particularly wary of prepared dishes that have to be reheated – they may have been on display in the heat and exposed to flies for some time. Anything that is boiled or fried (and thus sterilized) in your presence is usually all right, though meat can sometimes be dodgy if the electricity supply (and thus refrigerators) is unreliable. Anything that has been left out in the open for any length of time is definitely suspect. Raw, unpeeled fruit and vegetables should always be viewed with suspicion, and you should avoid salads unless you know they have been soaked in an iodine or potassium permanganate solution. Wiping down a plate before eating is sensible, and avoid straws as they are often dusty or secondhand. As a rule of thumb, stick to cafés and restaurants that are doing a brisk trade, and where the food is thus freshly cooked, and you should be fine.

Be vigilant about **personal hygiene**. Wash your hands often, especially before eating, keep all cuts clean, treat them with iodine or antiseptic, and cover them to prevent infection. Be fussier than usual about sharing things like drinks and cigarettes, and never share a razor or toothbrush. It is also inadvisable to go around barefoot – best to wear flip-flops even in the shower.

Advice on avoiding **mosquitoes** is offered under "Malaria". If you do get bites or itches try not to scratch them: it's hard, but infection and tropical ulcers can result if you do. Tiger balm and even dried soap may relieve the itching.

Finally, especially if you are going on a long trip, have a **dental check-up** before you leave home – you don't want to go down with unexpected tooth trouble in the middle of rural Rajasthan. If you do, and it feels serious, head for Delhi, and ask a foreign consulate to recommend a dentist, or try Delhi Dental Centre (see p.151).

Vaccinations

No **vaccinations** are legally required for entry into India, but meningitis, typhoid, and hepatitis A jabs are recommended, and it's

What about the water?

One of the chief concerns of many prospective visitors to India is whether the water is safe to drink. To put it simply, it's not, though your unfamiliarity with Indian micro-organisms is generally more of a problem rather than any great virulence in the water itself.

As a rule, it is not a good idea to drink **tap water**, although in big cities such as Delhi and Jaipur it is usually chlorinated. However, you'll find it almost impossible to avoid untreated tap water completely: it is used to make ice, which may appear in drinks without being asked for, to wash utensils and so on.

Bottled water, available in all but the most remote places these days, may seem like the simplest and most cost-effective solution, but it has some major drawbacks. The first is that the water itself might not always be as safe as it seems. Independent tests carried out in 2003 on major Indian brands revealed levels of **pesticide** concentration up to 104 times higher than EU norms. Top sellers Kinley, Bisleri and Aquaplus were named as the worst offenders.

The second downside of bottled water is the **plastic pollution** it causes. Visualize the size of the pile you'd leave behind you after getting through a couple of bottles per day, and imagine that multiplied by millions, which is the amount of non-biodegradable land-fill waste generated each year by tourists alone.

The best solution from the point of view of your health and the environment is to purify your own water. **Chemical sterilization** is the cheapest method. **Iodine** isn't recommended for long trips, but **chlorine** is completely effective, fast and inexpensive, and you can remove the taste using neutralizing tablets or lemon juice. Alternatively, invest in some kind of **purifying filter** which uses chemical sterilization to kill even the smallest viruses. An ever-increasing range of compact, lightweight products is available these days at outdoor shops and large pharmacies, but anyone who's pregnant or suffers from thyroid problems should check that iodine isn't used as the chemical sterilizer.

worth ensuring that you are up to date with tetanus, polio and other boosters. All vaccinations can be obtained in Delhi if necessary; just make sure the needle is new. If you're arriving in India from a country infected with Yellow Fever (which mainly means tropical Africa), you'll be asked for an inoculation certificate.

Hepatitis A is not the worst disease you can catch in India, but the frequency with which it strikes travellers makes a strong case for immunization. Transmitted through contaminated food and water, or through saliva, it can lay a victim low for several months with exhaustion, fever and diarrhoea, and may cause liver damage. The Havrix vaccine has been shown to be extremely effective; though expensive, it lasts for up to ten years. The protection given by gammaglobulin, the traditional serum of hepatitis antibodies (now rarely used), wears off quickly and the injection should therefore be given as late as possible before departure: the longer your stay, the larger the dose. Symptoms by which you can recognize hepatitis include a yellowing of the whites of the eyes, nausea, general flu-like malaise, orange urine (though dehydration could also cause that) and light-coloured stools. If you think you have it, avoid alcohol, and get lots of rest. More serious is **hepatitis B**, passed on like HIV through blood or sexual contact. There is a vaccine, but it is generally only given to those planning to work in a medical environment.

Typhoid, also spread through contaminated food or water, is endemic in India, but rare outside the monsoon. It produces a persistent high fever with malaise, headaches and abdominal pains, followed by diarrhoea. Vaccination can be by injection (two shots are required, or one for a booster), giving three years' cover, or orally – tablets are more expensive but easier on the arm.

Cholera, spread the same way as hepatitis A and typhoid, causes sudden attacks of watery diarrhoea with cramps and debilitation. It only appears during periodic epidemics. If you get it, take copious amounts of water with rehydration salts and seek medical treatment. There is currently no effective vaccination against cholera.

Most medical authorities now recommend vaccination against **meningitis** too. Spread by airborne bacteria (through coughs and sneezes for example), this illness attacks the lining of the brain and can be fatal. The symptoms appear at first to be similar to those of a cold, but they progress rapidly to include (not necessarily all at once) fever, a severe headache, vomiting, intolerance to light, stiffness in the neck and in some cases a rash, whose spots do not lighten when pressed against a glass; note that the rash may be hard to spot if you have dark skin. If you suspect that you have meningitis, it is vital to seek medical help quickly, as it can be fatal if left untreated.

You should have a **tetanus** booster every ten years whether you travel or not. Tetanus (or lockjaw) is picked up through contaminated open wounds and causes severe muscular spasms; if you cut yourself on something dirty and are not covered, get a booster as soon as you can.

Assuming that you were vaccinated against **polio** in childhood, only one (oral) booster is needed during your adult life. Immunizations against **mumps**, **measles**, **TB** and **rubella** are a good idea for anyone who wasn't vaccinated as a child and hasn't had the diseases.

Rabies is a problem in India. The best advice is to give dogs and monkeys a wide berth, and not to play with animals at all, no matter how cute they might look. A bite, a scratch or even a lick from an infected animal could spread the disease; wash any such wound immediately but gently with soap or detergent, and apply alcohol or iodine if possible. Find out what you can about the animal and swap addresses with the owner (if there is one) just in case. If the animal might be infected or the wound begins to tingle and fester, act immediately to get treatment – rabies is invariably fatal once symptoms appear. There is an (expensive) vaccine, which serves only to shorten the course of treatment you need, and is only effective for a maximum of three months.

Medical resources for travellers

For up-to-the-minute information, make an appointment at a **travel clinic**. These clinics

A travellers' first-aid kit

Below are items you might want to carry with you, especially if visiting remote areas of Rajasthan. All are available in India at a fraction of what you might pay at home:

• Antiseptic cream
• Insect repellent and cream such as Anthisan for soothing bites
• Plasters/band aids
• A course of Flagyl antibiotics
• Water sterilization tablets or water purifier
• Lint and sealed bandages
• Knee supports
• Imodium (Lomotil) for stop-gap diarrhoea treatment
• Paracetamol or aspirin
• Multi-vitamin and mineral tablets
• Rehydration sachets
• Hypodermic needles and sterilized skin wipes
• condoms
• iodine or potassium permanganate solution

also sell travel accessories, including mosquito nets and first-aid kits. Information about specific diseases and conditions, drugs and herbal remedies is provided by the websites on p.43. Highly recommended for travel to India and other tropical countries is the *Rough Guide to Travel Health* by Dr Nick Jones.

Malaria

Protection against **malaria** is absolutely essential. The disease, caused by a parasite carried in the saliva of female **Anopheles mosquitoes**, is endemic in Delhi and Agra, and throughout Rajasthan, and is regarded as one of the biggest killers in the Indian Subcontinent. It has a variable incubation period of a few days to several weeks, so you can become ill long after being bitten. Programmes to eradicate the disease by spraying mosquito-infested areas and distributing free preventative tablets have proved disastrous; within a short space of time, the Anopheles develop immunities to the insecticides, while the malaria parasite itself constantly mutates into drug-resistant strains, rendering the old cures ineffective.

It is vital for travellers to take **preventative tablets** according to a strict routine, and to cover the period before and after your trip. The drug used is **chloroquine** (trade names include Nivaquin, Avloclor and Resochin), usually two tablets weekly, but India has chloroquine-resistant strains, and you'll need

to supplement it with daily **proguanil** (**Paludrine**) or weekly **Maloprim**. In India chloroquine is easy to come by but proguanil isn't, so stock up before you arrive. An alternative is the highly effective weekly antimalarial **Larium (Mefloquine)**, which can be bought over the counter in India, but note that this can cause horrible side effects in some people (see below), and should not be used without medical advice unless you have used it before and are sure that you will not suffer an adverse reaction. Australian authorities are now prescribing the antibiotic **Doxycycline** instead of Mefloquine, and there is another drug called **Malarone** which can also be used as an alternative. As the malaria parasite can incubate in your system without showing symptoms for more than a month, it is essential to continue taking preventative tablets for at least four weeks after returning home. Most people who catch malaria as a result of foreign travel do so because they forget to keep taking the pills when they get home – don't join them. If you go down with a fever within three months of getting home, be aware that it could be malaria, and seek medical help quickly if you suspect that it may be.

Side-effects of anti-malaria drugs may include itching, rashes, hair loss and sight problems. In the case of Larium some people may experience disorientation, depression, sleep disturbance and even delusions; if you're intending to use Larium you should begin to take it two weeks before you depart to see whether it will agree with your metabolism, though normally you only need to begin taking anti-malaria medication a week before your departure date.

Malarial symptoms

The first **signs of malaria** are remarkably similar to a severe flu, and may take months to appear: if you suspect anything go to a hospital or clinic for a blood test immediately. The shivering, burning fever and headaches come in waves, usually in the early evening. Malaria is not infectious, but certain strains can be fatal if not treated promptly, in particular, **cerebral malaria**. This virulent and lethal strain of the disease, which affects the brain, is treatable, but has to be diagnosed early. Erratic body temperature, lack of energy and aches are the first key signs.

Preventing mosquito bites

The best way of combating malaria is of course to stop yourself getting bitten: malarial mosquitoes are active from dusk until dawn and during this time you should use **mosquito repellent** and take all necessary precautions. Sleep under a **mosquito net** if possible – one which can hang from a single point is best (you can usually find a way to tie a string across your room to hang it from), burn **mosquito coils** (widely available in India, but easy to break in transit) or electrically heated repellents such as All Out. An Indian brand of repellent called Odomos is widely available and very effective, though most travellers bring their own from home, usually one containing the noxious but effective compound **DEET**. DEET can cause rashes and a strength of more than thirty percent is not advised for people with sensitive skin, though they should still use DEET on clothes and nets. Mosquito "buzzers" – plug-in contraptions which make a noise that supposedly deters mosquitoes – are pretty useless but wrist and ankle bands are as effective as spray and a good alternative for sensitive skin. Though active from dusk till dawn, female Anopheles mosquitoes prefer to bite in the evening, so be especially careful at that time. Wear long sleeves, skirts and trousers, avoid dark colours, which attract mosquitoes, and put repellent on all exposed skin, especially ankles and feet.

Dengue fever

Another illness spread by mosquito bites is **dengue fever**, whose symptoms are similar to those of malaria, plus aching bones. However, unlike malaria, which is spread by the anopheles mosquito, dengue is spread by the aedes "tiger" mosquito (identifiable by its black and white body), which tends to bite in daylight hours, especially early morning and late afternoon. There is no vaccine available and the only treatment is complete rest, with drugs to assuage the fever.

Intestinal troubles

Diarrhoea is the most common bane of travellers. When mild and not accompanied by other major symptoms, it may just be your stomach reacting to unfamiliar food. Accompanied by cramps and vomiting, it could well be food poisoning. In either case, it will probably pass of its own accord in 24–48 hours without treatment. In the meantime, it is essential to replace the fluids and salts you're losing, so drink lots of water with oral **rehydration salts** (commonly referred to as ORS, or called Electrolyte in India). If you can't get ORS, use half a teaspoon of salt and eight of sugar in a litre of water, and if you are too ill to drink, seek medical help immediately. Travel clinics and pharmacies sell double-ended moulded plastic spoons which measure the exact ratio of sugar to salt.

While you are suffering, it's a good idea to avoid greasy food, heavy spices, caffeine and most fruit and dairy products. This can be surprisingly difficult in India – you quickly become aware of just how much food is fried in ghee with heavy spices. Bananas and pawpaws are good, as are plain rice or *kitchri* (a simple dhal and rice preparation) and rice soup and coconut water, while curd or a soup made from Marmite or Vegemite (if you happen to have some with you) are forms of protein that can be easily absorbed by your body when you have the runs. Drugs like Lomotil or Imodium simply plug you up – undermining the body's efforts to rid itself of infection – though they can be useful if you have to travel. If symptoms persist for more than a few days, a course of antibiotics may be necessary; this should be seen as a last resort, following medical advice.

Sordid though it may seem, it's a good idea to look at what comes out when you go to the toilet. If your diarrhoea contains blood or mucus and if you are suffering other symptoms including belches and rotten-egg farts, the cause may be **dysentery** or giardia. With a fever, it could well be caused by **bacillic dysentery**, and may clear up without treatment. If you're sure you need it, a course of antibiotics such as tetracycline should sort you out, but they also destroy "gut flora" in your intestines (which help protect you – curd can replenish them to some extent). If you start a course, be sure to finish it, even after the symptoms have gone. Similar symptoms, without fever, indicate **amoebic dysentery**, which is much more serious, and can damage your gut if untreated. The usual cure is a course of Metronidazole (Flagyl) or Fasigyn, both antibiotics which may themselves make you feel ill, and must not be taken with alcohol. Symptoms of **giardia** are similar – including frothy stools, nausea and constant fatigue – for which the treatment is again Metronidazole. If you suspect that you have either of these, seek medical help, and only start on the Metronidazole (750mg three times daily for a week for adults) if there is definitely blood in your diarrhoea and it is impossible to see a doctor.

Finally, bear in mind that oral drugs, such as malaria pills and the contraceptive pill, are likely to be largely ineffective if taken while suffering from diarrhoea.

Bites and creepy crawlies

Worms may enter your body through skin (especially the soles of your feet), or food. An itchy anus is a common symptom, and you may even see them in your stools. They are easy to treat: if you suspect you have them, get some worming tablets such as Mebendazole (Vermox) from any pharmacy.

Biting **insects** and similar animals other than mosquitoes may also aggravate you. The obvious suspects are bed bugs – look for signs of squashed ones around beds in cheap hotels. Head and body **lice** can also

be a nuisance, but medicated soap and shampoo (preferably brought with you from home) usually see them off. Avoid scratching bites, which can lead to infection. Bites from ticks and lice can spread typhus, characterized by fever, muscle aches, headaches, and, later, red eyes and a measles-like rash. If you think you have it, seek treatment (tetracycline is usually prescribed).

Snakes are unlikely to bite unless accidentally disturbed, and most are actually harmless in any case. If you do get bitten, remember what the snake looked like (kill it if you can), try not to move the affected part, and seek medical help immediately: antivenoms are available in most hospitals.

Scorpions can also be a problem in much of Rajasthan. They usually live under stones and in crevices, but they come out at night. Be particularly wary if camping (don't sleep directly on the ground, and shake your shoes out before putting them on in the morning. If you do get stung, follow the same procedure as for a snake bite; you can also put a cold compress on the area if you have one at hand.

Black widow **spiders** are also found in Rajasthan. Only the shiny black female is venomous. The bite itself is not painful and may pass unnoticed, but the reaction, including abdominal pain, cramps and nausea, can lay you out for some days, though it is not usually fatal in adults. First aid procedures are the same as for a scorpion sting.

The sun and the heat

The sun and the heat can cause a few unexpected problems. Many people suffer a bout of **prickly heat** rash before they've had time to acclimatize. A cool shower, zinc oxide powder (sold in India) and loose cotton clothes should help. **Dehydration** is another possible problem, so make sure you're drinking enough fluids; if you want to optimize water absorption by your body, add rehydration salts (see opposite). The main danger sign for dehydration is irregular urination (only once a day for instance); dark urine definitely means you should drink more, though it could also indicate hepatitis.

As well as the obvious dangers of sunburn, the **sun** can also cause sunstroke, and a high-factor sun block is vital on exposed skin, especially when you first arrive; pay attention to areas newly exposed by haircuts or changes of clothes. A light hat is also a very good idea, especially if you're doing a lot of walking around in the sun.

Finally, be aware that overheating can cause **heatstroke**, which is potentially fatal. Signs are a very high body temperature, without a feeling of fever but accompanied by headaches and disorientation. Lowering body temperature (taking a tepid shower for example) and resting in an air-conditioned room is the first step in treatment; also take in plenty of fluids, and seek medical advice if the condition doesn't improve after 24 hours.

HIV and AIDS

The rapidly increasing presence of **HIV/AIDS** has only recently been acknowledged by the Indian government as a national problem. The reluctance to address the issue is partly due to the disease's association with sex, a traditionally closed subject in India. As yet only NGOs and foreign agencies such as the World Health Organization have embarked on awareness and prevention campaigns. As elsewhere in the world, high-risk groups include prostitutes and intravenous drug users. It is extremely unwise to contemplate casual sex without a condom – carry some with you (preferably brought from home as Indian ones may be less reliable; also, be aware that heat affects the durability of condoms), and insist on using them if you do have sex with a new partner.

Should you need an injection or a transfusion, make sure that new, sterile equipment is used; any blood you receive should be from voluntary rather than commercial donor banks. If you have a shave from a barber, make sure he uses a clean blade, and don't undergo processes such as ear-piercing, acupuncture or tattooing unless you can be sure that the equipment is sterile.

Getting medical help

Pharmacies can usually advise on minor medical problems, and most doctors in India speak English. Also, many hotels keep a doctor on call; if you do get ill and need medical assistance, take advice as to the

---

Ayurvedic medicine

Ayurveda, a Sanskrit word meaning the "knowledge for prolonging life", is a five-thousand-year-old holistic medical system that is widely practised in India. Ayurvedic doctors and clinics in large towns deal with foreigners as well as their usual patients, and some **pharmacies** specialize in Ayurvedic preparations, including toiletries such as soaps, shampoos and toothpastes.

Ayurveda assumes the fundamental sameness of self and nature. Unlike the allopathic medicines of the West, which depend on finding out what's ailing you and then killing it, Ayurveda looks at the whole patient: disease is regarded as a symptom of **imbalance**, so it's the imbalance that's treated, not the disease. Ayurvedic theory holds that the body is controlled by three forces, which reflect the forces within the self: *pitta*, the force of the sun, is hot, and rules the digestive processes and metabolism; *kapha*, likened to the moon, the creator of tides and rhythms, has a cooling effect, and governs the body's organs; and *vata*, wind, relates to movement and the nervous system. The healthy body is one that has the three forces in balance. To diagnose an imbalance, the Ayurvedic **vaid** (doctor) responds not only to the physical complaint but also to family background, daily habits and emotional traits.

Imbalances are typically treated with herbal remedies designed to alter whichever of the three forces is out of whack. Made according to traditional formulae, using indigenous plants, Ayurvedic medicines are cheaper than branded or imported drugs. In addition, the doctor may prescribe various forms of yogic cleansing to rid the body of waste substances. To the uninitiated, these techniques will sound rather off-putting – for instance, swallowing a long strip of cloth, a short section at a time, and then pulling it back up again to remove mucus from the stomach.

best facilities around. Basic medicaments are made to Indian Pharmacopoea (IP) standards, and most medicines are available without prescription (always check the sell-by date). Hospitals vary in standard: **private clinics** and mission hospitals are often better than state-run ones, but may not have the same facilities. Hospitals in the big cities, including university or medical-school hospitals, are generally pretty good, and cities such as Delhi boast state-of-the-art medical facilities, but at a price. Many hospitals require patients (even emergency cases) to buy necessities such as medicines, plaster casts and vaccines, and to pay for X-rays, before procedures are carried out. Remember to keep receipts for insurance reimbursements.

However, **government hospitals** provide all surgical and after-care services free of charge and in most other state medical institutions, charges are usually so low that for minor treatment the expense may well be lower than the initial "excess" on your insurance. You will, however, need a companion to stay, or you'll have to come to an arrangement with one of the hospital cleaners, to help you out in hospital – relatives are expected to wash, feed and generally take care of the patient. Beware of scams by private clinics in tourist towns such as Agra where there have been reports of overcharging and misdiagnosis by doctors to claim insurance money. Addresses of foreign consulates in Delhi (who will advise in an emergency) can be found on p.151, and addresses of clinics and hospitals can be found in the Listings sections for major towns in this book.

Medical resources for travellers

CDC US ☎ 1-877/394-8747, ⊛ www.cdc.gov/ travel. Official US government travel health site.
Canadian Society for International Health ⊛ www.csih.org/en/travelhealth/index.asp. Extensive list of travel health centres in Canada.
International Society for Travel Medicine US ☎ 1-770/736-7060, ⊛ www.istm.org. Their website has a list of travel health clinics worldwide.
Travellers Abroad UK ☎ 0113/238 7575, ⊛ www .masta.org. Clinics throughout Britain; call or check online for the nearest one to you.
Travellers' medical and Vaccination Centre Australia ☎ 1300/658 844, ⊛ www.tmvc.com. au. Lists travel clinics in Australia, New Zealand and South Africa.
Tropical Medical Bureau Ireland ☎ 1850/487 674, ⊛ www.tmb.ie. Has a list of clinics in the Republic of Ireland.

Accommodation

On the whole, accommodation, like so many other things in India, provides good value for money, though in Delhi especially, luxury establishments with Western-style comforts and service also charge international prices.

Inexpensive hotels

While accommodation prices are generally on the up, there's still an abundance of **cheap hotels**, catering for backpacking tourists and less well-off Indians. Most charge Rs150–350 for a double room, and some in rural and small-town Rajasthan have rates below Rs150 (£1.75/$3.40/€2.60). The rock-bottom option may be in a dormitory of a hostel or budget hotel, where you'll be charged anything from Rs50 to 100 for a bed. Budget accommodation varies from filthy fleapits to homely guesthouses and, naturally, tends to be cheaper the further you get off the beaten track; it's most expensive in Delhi, where prices are at least double those for equivalent accommodation elsewhere. Many budget hotels, especially at the bottom of the scale,

Accommodation price codes

All **accommodation prices** in this book are **coded** using the symbols below. The prices given are for the cheapest double room in high season. Where hotels have a number of room options available this is shown by a spread of price codes; in the case of dorms, we give the price in rupees. Most mid-range and all expensive and luxury hotels charge a luxury tax of between 8–12.5 percent. All taxes are included in the prices we quote.

Delhi, Agra and Rajasthan don't really have a **tourist season** as such, though certain resorts and some spots on established tourist trails do experience some variation and will be more expensive, or less negotiable, when demand is at its peak, which tends to be in the winter months, and particularly around Christmas.

① under Rs200   ④ Rs700–Rs1000   ⑦ Rs2500–Rs4000
② Rs200–Rs400   ⑤ Rs1000–Rs1500   ⑧ Rs4000–Rs6000
③ Rs400–Rs700   ⑥ Rs1500–Rs2500   ⑨ Rs6000 and above

lack hot running water, though cold showers are not too much of a hardship in summer, and even the cheapest places will supply hot water in a bucket. Bathroom facilities may well be shared, and it's always wise to check out the state of the bathrooms and toilets before taking a room. A room with its own private bathroom is known as an **"attached"** room in India. Bed bugs and mosquitoes are other things to check for – blood spots on the sheets and on the walls where people have squashed them are tell-tale signs.

If a taxi driver or auto- or rickshaw-wallah tells you that the place you ask for is full, closed or has moved, it's more than likely because he wants to take you to a hotel that pays him commission, which will often be added to your bill. Hotel touts likewise work by getting commission from the hotels they take you to; they usually operate at New Delhi station, among other places (see p.69). Never let touts attach themselves to you and accompany you to a hotel, and don't accept alternative hotels offered by taxi, auto- or rickshaw-wallahs who are unwilling to take you to the place you've asked for; either insist that they take you there (and make sure it really is the same place), or ask to be dropped off nearby. Indeed, it's a wise policy not to allow a taxi driver or rickshaw-wallah to accompany you into a hotel in any case.

Mid-range hotels

These often have large clean rooms, with a freshly made bed, your own spotless (often sit-down) toilet, and hot and cold running water, all for around Rs500 ($11.30/£5.80/€8.70) or under. You'll pay more for a TV, a balcony, and, above all, **air-conditioning** (a/c). This is not necessarily the advantage you might expect – in some hotels you can find yourself paying double for a system that is so dust-choked, wheezy and noisy as to preclude any possibility of sleep – but providing it entitles a hotel to consider itself mid-range. Some also offer a halfway-house option known as **air-cooled** – noisy and not as effective as full-blown a/c, but better than nothing in severe heat.

Rajasthan's state government runs its own hotels, similar to private mid-range establishments, but often also offering pricier a/c rooms and cheaper dorms, though they tend to be rather run-down. We've indicated such places throughout this guide by including the state acronym RTDC (Rajasthan Tourist Development Corporation).

Upmarket hotels

Most **luxury hotels** in India fall into one of two categories: old-fashioned institutions brimming with class, and modern jet-set chain hotels, largely confined to large cities and tourist resorts.

The faded grandeur of the **Raj** lingers on in a few former imperial hangouts such as Delhi's *Oberoi Maidens* hotel (see p.101). In Rajasthan, however, where most of the Rajputs remained substantially independent of British rule, there are some magnificent old forts and **palaces** (*thikanas*) from feudal estates, and **havelis**, the former homes of aristocratic families, now designated **heritage hotels**.

Modern deluxe establishments – slicker, brighter, faster and far more businesslike – tend to belong to **chains**. Some of these, such as the Taj and Oberoi hotels, along with the India Tourist Development Corporation's Ashok chain, are Indian-owned. International firms include Hilton, Hyatt, Marriott and Sheraton. Most deluxe chain hotels quote tariffs in US dollars, starting at around $100, and up to around $500 for a double room, and some may require you to pay in foreign currency – for which you may even get a better deal. In Rajasthan's palaces and heritage hotels, however, you'll still get excellent value for money, with rates only just beginning to approach those of their counterparts in Europe.

Note that when it comes to five-star and other high-end hotels, it's worth shopping around online, as some websites provide access to rates that may be far lower than the standard rack rates you'll be quoted over the phone or if you walk in. Upmarket tour operators at home may also be able to organize a package including the hotel of your choice at a lower price than you would pay if you book the room yourself.

Other options

Many **railway stations** have **"retiring rooms"** where passengers can sleep. These rooms can be particularly handy if you're catching an early morning train, though tend to get booked up well in advance. They vary in price, but generally charge roughly the same as a budget hotel, and have large, clean, if somewhat institutional rooms; dormitories, where you can bank on being woken at the crack of dawn by a morning chorus of throat-clearing, are often available. Occasionally you may come across a main station with an air-conditioned room, in which case you will have found a real bargain. Retiring rooms cannot be booked in advance and are allocated on a first-come-first-serve basis; just turn up and ask if there's a vacancy, but note that you normally need to have a train ticket to use the station retiring rooms.

In one or two places, it's possible to rent rooms in people's **homes**. In Rajasthan, the tourist office runs a **"paying guest house" scheme** to place tourists with families offering lodging. Servas (ⓦwww.indiaservas .org), established in 1949 as a peace organization, is now devoted to providing homestays; you have to join before travelling by applying to your local Servas secretary (if you are not Indian, go via the international

---

Accommodation practicalities

Check-out time is often noon, but confirm this when you arrive: some expect you out by 9am, but many others operate a 24-hour system, under which you are simply obliged to leave by the same time as you arrived. Some places let you use their facilities after the official check-out time, sometimes for a small charge, others won't even let you leave your baggage after check-out unless you pay for another night.

Unfortunately, not all hotels offer **single rooms**, so it can often work out more expensive to travel alone; in hotels that don't, you may be able to negotiate a slight discount. However, it's not unusual to find rooms with three or four beds – great value for families and small groups.

In cheap hotels and hostels, you needn't expect any additions to your basic bill, but as you go up the scale, you'll find **taxes** and **service charges** creeping in. Service is generally ten percent; taxes are determined by state governments, but in Rajasthan this varies between eight and twelve and a half percent; in Delhi, it's always twelve and a half percent, and in Agra five percent.

Like most other things in India, the price of a room may well be open to **negotiation**, especially off-season. If you think the price is too high, or if all the hotels in town are empty, try haggling. You may get nowhere – but nothing ventured, nothing gained.

website (W)www.servas.org), and you will be interviewed to check you are suitable. You then get a list of hosts to contact in the place you are visiting. Some people provide free accommodation, others are just day hosts. There is no guarantee a bed will be provided – it's up to the individual.

Camping is possible too, though it's hard to see why you'd want to be cooped up in a tent overnight when you could be sleeping on a cool *charpoi* (a sort of basic bed) on a roof terrace for a handful of rupees – let alone why you'd choose to carry a tent around in the first place. It's not usual to simply pitch a tent in the countryside, though some hotels allow camping in their grounds.

There are HI **youth hostels** in Delhi, Jaipur, Jodhpur, Jaisalmer, Bikaner and Alwar, and also at Shahpura, 70km west of Bundi, but with accommodation so cheap anyway, there's probably no reason for staying in them. We've included the two most useful ones, in Delhi (p.101) and Bikaner (p.318). Some, such as Delhi, are open to HI members only, but most are open to all. Further information can be found on (W)www .yhaindia.org, or by calling the youth hostel in Delhi on (T)011/2611 0250 or 2687 1969.

Occasionally, and especially if you have a particular interest in religion, you may be able to stay in a Hindu, Sikh or Jain **temple**, for which a donation may be expected, and is certainly appreciated.

Food and drink

Rich, aromatic, and of course spicy, Indian food has a well-deserved reputation across the globe. If you're a vegetarian, you've come to the right place, as around half of India's restaurants are vegetarian ("veg"), and even non-veg restaurants offer plenty of vegetarian options. In northern India, and particularly in old Mughal centres like Delhi and Agra, there is a strong tradition of non-veg cuisine, while Rajasthan has two parallel traditions – meat dishes, particularly "mutton" (which in India means goat), eaten by the warrior Rajput class, and strictly vegetarian dishes eaten by Brahmins and Jains, and the merchant class.

Restaurants

The cheapest kind of restaurant in India is a **dhaba**, or roadside diner, or a **bhojanalaya** (sometimes called a "hotel", though it does not have accommodation); to a large extent the two terms are interchangeable, though *dhaba* suggests somewhere a little more basic than *bhojanalaya*. Food in *dhabas* and *bhojanalayas* is simple – usually just a veg curry with dhal and bread or perhaps rice – but it's often good and invariably cheap. Some *dhabas* and *bhojanalayas* are spotlessly clean; others can be quite grubby, so give them a once-over before you commit yourself to eating there. In general, they are not used to catering for foreigners, but they'll

often have a menu in English tucked away somewhere; if not, you'll have to ask what they've got, or just point to what you want.

Proper **restaurants** vary in price and quality, and can be veg or non-veg, offering a wide choice of dishes much like Indian restaurants anywhere else in the world. They'll always have a menu in English, and the best ones will usually specialize in a particular type of cuisine, be it Punjabi, Mughlai, tandoori or whatever, though some will be "multi-cuisine" with standard Indian dishes plus "Continental" (which tends to mean Western in general) and Chinese dishes, of a sort. In places with a large contingent of foreign tourists – Jaisalmer,

Pushkar, Delhi's Paharganj or Agra's Taj Ganj, for example, you'll find eating places catering specifically for that market, with pancakes, toast and fruit salad. They may well miss the mark by a long way, and they are not of course authentically Indian, but they can offer a break from fried and spicy food, especially if you've got tummy troubles. **Deluxe restaurants** such as those in five-star hotels can be very expensive by Indian standards, but they offer a chance to try classic Indian cooking of very high quality: rich, subtle, mouthwatering. Try to have a meal in one at least once.

Following Sikh tradition of offering hospitality to all and sundry, Sikh **gurudwaras** (temples) serve a simple meal of rice and dhal twice a day, and all visitors to the *gurudwara*, regardless of their religion, are welcome to partake.

Veg and non-veg

Because so many people in India are **vegetarian**, a large proportion of restaurants serve only vegetarian food, and all restaurants offer vegetarian options. Most religious Hindus don't eat meat, fish or eggs, while some orthodox Brahmins will not eat food cooked by anyone outside their household (or onions or garlic, as they are considered to inflame the baser instincts). Jains are even stricter, eschewing not only animal products (apart from dairy), but also all root and tuber vegetables such as onions, potatoes and carrots. **Veganism** is not common, however, and though vegetarian food in India usually excludes eggs, it does not exclude dairy products, and particularly ghee (clarified butter), in which most things are fried. In fact, one of the most common ingredients in Indian veg cooking is **paneer**, a mild cheese made without rennet.

All eating places in India specify whether they are **veg** or **non-veg**, though meat-eaters should exercise caution even when meat is available – its quality is not assured except in the best restaurants, and you won't get much in a dish anyway. Hindus, of course, do not eat beef and Muslims shun

pork, so you probably won't find those anywhere, except perhaps in the odd European or Chinese restaurant.

Indian food

What Westerners call a **curry** covers a variety of wet dishes (that is, dishes in a sauce, or "gravy"), each made with a different mix of spices, or masala. Curry powder is not used in India, the nearest equivalent being *garam masala* ("hot mix"), a combination of dried ground black pepper and other spices, in theory added to a dish at the last stage of cooking to spice it up, but often used as a substitute for other aromatics. Commonly used **spices** include chilli, turmeric, garlic, ginger, cinnamon, cardamom, cloves, coriander – both leaf and seed – cumin, and even saffron. These are not all added at the same time, and some are used whole, so beware of chewing on them. Fenugreek, the spice that gives ready-made curry powder its distinctive taste, is actually used much more sparingly in India.

It's the Indian penchant for **chilli** that alarms many Western visitors. The majority of foreigners develop a tolerance for it; if you don't, you'll just have to stick to mild dishes such as korma and biryani where meat or vegetables are cooked with rice, and eat plenty of chapati. Indians tend to assuage the effects of chilli with chutney, *dahi* (a type of yoghurt, commonly referred to as **curd**) or *raita* (curd with mint and cucumber, or other herbs and vegetables). Otherwise, **beer** is one of the best things for washing chilli out of your mouth; the essential oils that cause the burning sensation dissolve in alcohol, but not in water.

Vegetarian curries are usually identified (even on menus in English) by the Hindi names of their main ingredients (see p.433 for a food and drink glossary), such as *alu gobi* for potato and cauliflower. Terms like "curry" and "masala" don't really tell you what to expect; meat curries are more often given specific names such as korma or dopiaza, to indicate the kind of masala used or the method of cooking.

A main dish – which may be a curry, but could also be a dry dish such as a kebab, or a tandoori dish without a masala – is usually served with a dhal (lentils) and bread such as

For advice on **drinking water** in India, see p.37.

chapatis or nan. Rice is usually an optional extra in north India. Many restaurants offer a set meal or **thali**. This is a stainless steel tray with a number of little dishes in it, containing a selection of curries, a chutney and a sweet. In the middle you'll get bread and usually rice. In many places, waiters will keep coming round with refills until you've had enough.

Many people in India prefer to eat with their fingers (to feel the food as well as taste it) and in some cheap places you may have to ask for cutlery. Avoid getting food on the palm of your hand by eating with the tips of your fingers, and wash your hands both before and after eating. Wherever you eat, remember to use only your right hand.

In north India, food is usually served with bread, which comes in a number of varieties, all of them flatbreads rather than loaves. **Chapati** is a generic term for breads, but tends to refer to the simplest, unleavened type. It's usually made from wheat flour, but in Rajasthan you may come across chapatis made from millet. The term **roti** is likewise generic, and a roti can be exactly the same as a chapati, but the term tends to refer more to a thicker bread baked in a tandoor. In Rajasthan you get quite a variety of rotis, made with different flours and spices. **Naan** is a leavened bread, thick and chewy, and invariably baked in a tandoor; it's a favourite in non-veg restaurants as it best accompanies rich meaty dishes. You may also come across fried breads, of which **paratha** (or parantha) is rolled out, basted with ghee, folded over and rolled out again several times before cooking, and often stuffed with ingredients such as potato (*alu paratha*); it's popular for breakfast. Less common in the region, **puri** balloons out like a puffball when fried, and needs to be served immediately. **Poppadum** (papad) is a crisp wafer made from lentil flour and is typically served as an appetizer.

Mughlai and tandoori cuisine

The classic cuisine in Delhi and Agra is **Mughlai**, the food of the Mughals. Mostly non-veg, Mughlai cooking is extremely rich, using ingredients such as cream, almonds and saffron. A Mughlai meal is usually accompanied by **makhania dhal**, which is made with cream. **Korma** is a typical Mughlai dish, consisting of meat (or vegetables) cooked in curd, and usually quite mild in terms of spices. Also typical of Mughlai cooking is **biryani**, in which rice and meat are cooked together. A **pulao** is very similar, except that the meat and gravy are added to the rice at a later stage (and pulaos tend to be wetter than biryanis). **Kebabs** also feature strongly in Mughlai cuisine, particularly kebabs such as *seekh kebab* (minced lamb grilled on a skewer) and *shami kebab* (small minced lamb cutlets). Another classic Mughlai dish is **rogan josh**, a rich mutton curry with tomatoes and saffron. Although in principle Mughlai cusine is non-veg, vegetarian versions of most Mughlai dishes are available, often made with paneer. Mughlai food is typically eaten with naan. A *mughlai masala* normally indicates a mild, creamy one. *Mughlai paratha* is a paratha with egg.

The other big (and mainly non-veg) north Indian style of cooking is **tandoori**, which you'll find right across Rajasthan, Delhi and Agra, though the region with which it is most strongly associated is **Punjab**. The name refers to the deep clay oven (tandoor) in which the food is cooked. **Tandoori chicken** is marinated in yoghurt, herbs and spices before cooking. Boneless pieces of meat, marinated and cooked in the same way are known as **tikka**. Tandoori meats may be served in a medium-strength masala, one thickened with almonds (**pasanda**), or in a rich butter sauce – if chicken is involved, this is known as **murg makhani** or butter chicken. Breads such as naan and roti are also baked in the tandoor. Though tandoori food is most often chicken (wags have it that tandoori chicken is Punjab's national bird), it can also be made with mutton, paneer or even fish.

Rajasthani food

Rajasthan's ruling Rajput class, as warriors, have always eaten a largely non-veg cuisine, very similar to that of the Mughals. The merchant class as well as Brahmins and Jains, however, have traditionally eschewed meat in favour of strictly vegetarian cooking.

The most popular of all Rajasthani dishes is **dhal bati churma**, which consists of *bati* (bread) – a baked wheatflour ball with a tough crust; dhal, as ever, a soupy lentil stew; and *churma*, a sweet made of coarse-ground wheatflour cooked with ghee and sugar. The three are served as a thali, sometimes with other veg curries to accompany them.

Another vegetarian Rajasthani speciality is **gatta**, small dumplings of gram flour (made from ground chickpeas) cooked in a masala- or yoghurt-based sauce. *Gatta* recipes vary across the state, but the best known is *govind gatta*, in which the dumplings are round and quite large. *Gatta ki sabji* is gatta with vegetables. There is also a lentil-flour dumpling called **mangodi**, most typically served in a curry with potatoes (*alu mangodi*), though it can come with fenugreek leaves (*methi mangodi*) or onions (*mangodi piaza*).

A couple of delicious but unfamiliar **vegetables** that you may come across in Rajasthan are **sangri**, the long pods of the *khejri* tree, and **kair**, the caper-like fruit of a shrub that grows in the same region. The two are typically cooked and served together in villages of the Bishnoi people, to whom the *khejri* tree is sacred (see p.295).

Among meat dishes, Rajasthan's pride is **lal maas** or **laal maans** ("red meat"), a spicy dish of lamb marinated in chilli. A less fiery alternative is **safed maas** ("white meat"), which is mutton in a mild cashew, curd and cream curry. **Sula** (or *maas ka sula*) is a Rajasthani tandoori kebab, whose distinctive marinade includes kachri, a vegetable that tenderizes the meat.

Food from other regions of India

Along with Rajasthani, Mughlai and Punjabi food, you'll also come across restaurants specializing in cuisine from other parts of India. **Gujarati cuisine**, from the state adjoining Rajasthan, is generally spicy, often quite tangy, and mainly vegetarian. In Rajasthan, Delhi and Agra, it most commonly appears in the form of a Gujarati thali, which is generally a good way to sample it.

South Indian food is even more popular, and you'll find south Indian restaurants all over the place. South Indian curries are very

For a **glossary** of food items, see pp.432–436.

spicy and served with rice. More commonly, however, you'll come across light meals based on either *dosa*, *iddli*, uttapam or vada. **Dosa** is a crispy rice pancake which, when filled with a lightly spiced potato mix, is called a **masala dosa**, and served with a coconut chutney, and with **sambar**, a tangy vegetable soup containing tamarind and asafoetida. Sambar is also commonly served with **iddli**, a steamed rice cake. **Uttapam** is likewise made of rice, but thinner and flatter than iddli, more like a pancake, while **vada** is a doughnut-shaped fried lentil cake.

Snacks and street food

Snack food (**chhat**) is ubiquitous, and should be approached with caution when sold on the street. The guiding principle is that frying will sterilize anything, but leaving it out for any length of time allows germs to breed, so stick to freshly cooked food and steer clear of items that have been lying in the open for hours.

Favourite snack foods include **samosas**, pastry triangles filled with meat or potato. There's even a sweet version (*mawa samosa*) that's filled with a kind of milk fudge and drizzled with syrup. A speciality of Jodhpur is **mirchi bada**, a large chilli fried in a thick batter of wheatgerm and potato.

Puris may appear in the form of **chana puri**, served with a chickpea curry, or **bhel puri**, a speciality of Mumbai (Bombay) that you may nonetheless run across in Delhi, Agra or Rajasthan, consisting of small a mix of puffed rice, deep fried vermicelli, potato, crunchy puri with tamarind sauce. **Gol gappa** is a kind of stuffed puri. Similar but larger is **raj kachori**, a crisp shell usually filled with chickpeas and doused in curd and sauce, a mix of flavours that explodes inside your mouth.

Also popular, and more portable, are **namkeens**, the dry snacks that make up what is known in the West as "Bombay mix". In India these are available individually or in various combinations, with or without masala seasoning. Bikaner in particular is known for them, and especially for **Bikaneri bhujia** – thin, vermicelli-like sticks made from gram and lentil flour, which are supposed to be extra crisp in Bikaner because of the dry climate.

Paan

You may be glad to know that the red stuff people spit all over the streets isn't blood, but juice produced by chewing **paan** – a digestive, commonly taken after meals, and also a mild stimulant.

Paan consists of chopped or shredded nut (called betel nut, though in fact it comes from the areca palm), wrapped in a leaf (which does come from the betel vine) that is first prepared with ingredients such as *katha* (red paste), *chuna* (slaked lime), *mitha masala* (a mix of sweet spices, which can be ingested) and *zarda* (chewing tobacco, not to be swallowed on any account). The triangular package thus formed is wedged inside your cheek and chewed slowly, and in the case of *zarda* paans, spitting out the juice as you go.

Paan, and *paan masala* (a mix of betel nut, fennel seeds, sweets and flavourings), are sold by paan-wallahs, often from tiny stalls squeezed between shops. Paan is an acquired taste; novices should start off, and preferably stick to, the sweet *mitha* variety, which can safely be swallowed.

International food

Delhi has a wide choice of international cuisines, including Thai, Japanese, Italian and French, particularly in upmarket restaurants in South Delhi, and in five-star hotels. In Agra and Rajasthan, you'll find **Chinese food** on the menu in a surprising number of places, though it isn't what you'd call authentic. **Western** ("Continental") **food** is variable, but you can get some decent pasta dishes on occasion, and even fish and chips. In big cities, you'll also find the usual junk food franchise chains. Tourist centres such as Pushkar, Udaipur, Agra's Taj Ganj and Delhi's Paharganj offer a fair choice of Western and also Middle Eastern (Israeli) food, often including some quite passable hummus. The same places will also serve what has become the international fare of backpackers across Asia, such as porridge, toast, omelettes, banana pancakes, and fruit salad with yoghurt, which can be especially welcome at **breakfast** time. Indian breakfasts include *chana puri* or *alu paratha* with dhal, but these can be a little spicy for some. Alternatives include South Indian snacks such as masala dosa or *iddli sambar*.

Sweets

Many Indians have rather a sweet tooth and Indian **sweets**, usually made of milk, can be very sweet indeed. Of the more solid type, **barfi**, a kind of fudge made from milk which has been boiled down and condensed, varies from moist and delicious to dry and powdery.

It comes in various flavours from plain creamy white to *pista* (pistachio) in livid green and is often sold covered with silver leaf (which you eat). Round, smoother-textured **penda** and thin diamonds of cashew nut called **kaju katli** are among many other sweets made from *chhana* or boiled-down milk. Gelatinous **halwa** (not to be confused with the sesame sweet of the Middle East) originates in Sindh, now in Pakistan, but has become popular across the Subcontinent. **Ladoo** comes in balls made from wheat or gram flour with sugar, and often other ingredients such as raisins. A lot of sweets in Rajasthan are made with *mawa* (solidified condensed milk), and you can even get *mawa* samosas and *mawa* kachoris. Bikaner is best known for its sweets, but confectionery is generally good throughout Rajasthan.

Getting softer and stickier, **jalebis** are syrup-filled, deep-fried batter tubes, and are as sickly as they look. Other syrup-laden sweets tend to be Bengali in origin, but some towns in Rajasthan have made quite a name for their own versions. **Gulab jamuns** are deep-fried cream cheese sponge balls soaked in syrup, and **rasgullas** are rosewater-flavoured cream cheese balls floating in syrup. **Ras malai** is similar but soaked in cream instead of syrup.

Western-style ice cream is not great in India (and stay away from street ices unless you have a seasoned constitution), but do try **kulfi**, a pistachio- and cardamom-flavoured frozen sweet which is India's answer to ice cream and extremely delicious, even in its mass-produced versions. **Kheer**, a wonderfully aromatic rice pudding, is also a popular dessert.

Fruit

What **fruit** is available varies with region and season, but there's always a fine choice. Ideally, you should **peel** all fruit including apples, or soak them in strong iodine or potassium permanganate solution for half an hour. Roadside vendors sell fruit which they often cut up and serve sprinkled with salt and even masala – don't buy anything that looks like it's been hanging around for a while.

Mangoes of various kinds are usually on offer, but not all are sweet enough to eat fresh – some are used for pickles or curries. Indians are picky about their mangoes, which they feel and smell before buying; if you don't know the art of choosing the fruit, you could be sold the leftovers. Among the species appearing at different times in the season, which lasts from spring to summer, look out for alphonso and langra. Bananas of one sort or another are also on sale all year round, and oranges and tangerines are generally easy to come by, as are sweet melons and thirst-quenching watermelons.

Among less familiar fruit, the *chiku* (sapodilla) looks like a kiwi and tastes a little bit like a pear. It comes from the tree whose sap is used to make chewing gum. The watermelon-sized jackfruit, whose spiny green exterior encloses sweet, slightly rubbery yellow segments, each containing a seed, is sometimes sold in individual segments at roadside stalls.

Tea and coffee

India sometimes seems to run on **chai** (tea), which is sold by chai-wallahs on just about every street corner. Interestingly, although it was introduced from China by the East India Company in 1838, its consumption was only popularized by a government campaign in the 1950s.

Chai is usually made by putting tea dust, milk and water in a pan, boiling it all up, straining it into a cup or glass with lots of sugar and pouring back and forth from one cup to another to stir. Ginger and/or cardamoms are sometimes added. If you're quick off the mark, you can get them to hold the sugar. English tea it isn't, but most foreign visitors get used to chai. "Think of it as a drink in its own right rather than tea," advise some. From time to time, especially in tourist spots, you might get a pot of European-style "tray" tea, generally consisting of a tea bag in lukewarm water – you'd do better to stick to the pukka Indian variety.

Coffee is all too frequently instant, but sleek cafés selling espresso, cappuccino, frappés and the like have sprung up in Delhi and other large towns, and filter coffee is sometimes available.

Soft drinks

Sodas (known as cold drinks in India) are ubiquitous. Coca-Cola and Pepsi returned to India in the early 1990s after being banned from the country for seventeen years and have taken over most of the indigenous brands such as Thums Up and Limca.

Plain soda, served alone or with lime juice, is much more refreshing, than straight water (see also p.37), either treated, boiled or bottled; bear in mind though, the recent reports of high concentrations of pesticides in bottled water (see p.37). There are also cartons of Frooti, Jumpin, Réal and similar brands of fruit juice drinks, which come in mango, guava, apple and lemon varieties. If the carton looks at all mangled, it is best not to have it as it may have been "recycled". At larger stations, there will be a stall on the platform selling apple juice from the state of Himachal Pradesh. Street stalls often sell delicious freshly pressed sugar cane juice, but be choosy where you get it from, as not all of them are tremendously hygienic.

India's greatest cold drink, **lassi**, is made with beaten curd and drunk either sweetened with sugar, or salted, or mixed with fruit. It varies widely from smooth and delicious to insipid and watery, and is sold at virtually every café, restaurant and canteen in the country. Don't knock salted lassi until you've tried it: it's surprisingly good, and a lot more refreshing than the sweet variety. In some places, lassi may be spiced – sweet lassi with cardamom or saffron, salted lassi with cumin. In western Rajasthan, and particularly Jodhpur, you'll get deliciously rich makhania lassi, made with saffron and cream. Bhang lassi contains cannabis, and should be approached with caution (see p.59).

Freshly made milkshakes are commonly available at establishments with blenders. They'll also sell you what they call a fruit juice, but which is usually fruit, water and sugar (or salt) liquidized and strained. With all such drinks, however appetizing they may seem, you should exercise **caution** in deciding where to buy them: consider in particular where the water is likely to have come from.

Alcohol

Prohibition, once widespread in India, is no longer fully enforced in many places, but it does apply in Pushkar. Even in the rest of Rajasthan, bars, other than those in hotels, can be few and far between, but in practice, restaurants in most guesthouses do in fact serve alcohol, though strictly speaking it is illegal. There are also "dry" days when alcohol cannot be bought or served; in Rajasthan and Agra only three days are dry, namely Republic Day (26 Jan), Independence Day (15 Aug), and Gandhi Jayanti (2 Oct), but Delhi has no less than 21 dry days in its annual calendar. The minimum legal age for buying alcohol is eighteen in Rajasthan, but 25 in Delhi and Agra. Despite the lower drinking age, Rajasthani society remains conservative in its attitude to alcohol, which is seen as rather a low-life pursuit, but amongst the wealthier classes in Delhi, on the other hand, a pub culture not dissimilar to that of the west has taken root.

Alcohol is usually cheaper in Delhi than it is in Rajasthan or Agra.

Kingfisher is the leading brand of **beer**, but there are plenty of others. Prices vary from Rs70–150 for a 650ml bottle. All lagers tend to contain chemical additives including glycerine, but they are palatable enough if you can get them cold. In certain places or on "dry" days, beer may be sold in the form of "special tea" – a teapot of beer, which you pour into and drink from a teacup to disguise what it really is.

Spirits usually take the form of "Indian Made Foreign Liquor" (IMFL), although the recently legitimized foreign liquor industry is expanding rapidly. Some scotch, such as Seagram's Hundred Pipers, is now being bottled in India and sold at a premium, as is Smirnoff vodka amongst other known brands. Some of the brands of Indian whisky are not too bad and are affordable in comparison; gin and brandy can be pretty rough, while Indian rum is sweet and distinctive. Steer well clear of *arak*, which is distilled illegally and often contains methanol (wood alcohol) and other poisons. A look through the press, especially at festival times, will soon reveal numerous cases of blindness and death as a result of drinking bad hooch (or "spurious liquor" as it's called). Unfortunately, the Indian **wine** industry, though slowly improving with vineyards such as Grovers, is not up to scratch and the wines are pricey, while foreign wine available in upmarket restaurants and luxury hotels comes with an exorbitant price tag.

The media

BASICS | The media

Though few people in India speak English at home, most literate people can speak it, and a lot of the media, particularly print media, is in English, which makes it very easy to keep up with Indian and foreign news while you are in the country.

Newspapers and magazines

There are a large number of English-language daily newspapers; most prominent of the nationals are the *Times of India* (Ⓦ timesofindia.indiatimes.com), *The Hindu* (Ⓦ www.hinduonline.com), *The Statesman* (Ⓦ www.thestatesman.net), the *Hindustan Times* (Ⓦ www.hindustantimes.com), the *Economic Times* (Ⓦ economictimes .indiatimes.com) and the *Indian Express* (Ⓦ www.indianexpress.com; usually the most critical of the government). All are pretty dry and sober, and concentrate mainly on Indian news, often with Delhi or Rajasthan editions that have sections devoted to regional news too. Online, the *Times of India*, *The Hindu* and the *Hindustan Times* provide the most up-to-date and detailed news services.

India's press is the freest in Asia, and attacks on the government are often quite outspoken. However, as in the West, most papers can be seen as part of the political establishment, and are unlikely to print anything that might upset the "national consensus", particularly on topics such as Kashmir. If you want to look outside the box, try the independent media website Ⓦ india .indymedia.org.

In recent years, a number of *Time/ Newsweek*-style **news magazines** have hit the market, the best being *India Today* (Ⓦ www.india-today.com) and *Frontline* (Ⓦ www.frontline.in), published by *The Hindu*. Others include *Outlook* (Ⓦ www.outlookindia .com), plus there are magazines and periodicals in English covering all sorts of popular and minority interests, so it's worth checking newsstands to see what's available.

Foreign publications such as the *International Herald Tribune*, *Time*, *Newsweek*, *The Economist* and the international edition of the British *Guardian* can be found in the main cities. The *Guardian* has an excellent archive of articles on India on its website at Ⓦ www.guardian.co.uk/india.

For a read through the British or American press in Delhi, try the British Council or American Information Resource Center (see p.144 for addresses).

Radio

India's national **radio** service, All India Radio, runs the popular Vividh Bharati Seva station, with a mix of music (mainly *filmi*), comedy and news in several languages, including English, though most of its talk shows are in Hindi. It can be picked up on medium wave throughout the region, broadcasting on 819kHz, 666kHz and 1017kHz (280m, 366m and 450m) in Delhi, 1530kHz (196m) in Agra, 1476 (203m) in Jaipur, and several AM and FM frequencies in different parts of Rajasthan (see Ⓦ allindiaradio.org/schedule/freq_nr.html for full details). Recent years have seen a plethora of independent FM stations spring up following a relaxation of government restrictions on radio broadcasts. Delhi in particular is well blessed with music stations, some of them, like Radio One (94.3MHz), off-shoots from stations originally established in Mumbai. Others, such as Adlab Radio's Big FM (92.7MHz), are homegrown. The Entertainment Network of India's channel, Radio Mirchi (98.3MHz), broadcasts in Jaipur as well as Delhi. All play a mix of Indian and foreign pop hits. Others include Red FM (93.5MHz), Hit FM (95.0MHz) and Fever FM (104.0MHz).

If you want to hear **foreign news stations**, BBC World Service radio (Ⓦ www.bbc.co .uk/worldservice), with news on the hour, can be picked up on short wave at 15.31MHz (19.6m) roughly between 8.30am–10.30pm (Indian time). Alternative frequencies include 9.74MHz (30.1m),

11.92MHz (25.2m), 11.96MHz (25.1m) and 17.79MHz (16.9m). The Voice of America (Ⓦ www.voa.gov) can be found on 15.75MHz (19m), 71.25MHz (42m), 97.60MHz (30.7m) and 96.45MHz (31.1m), among other frequencies. Radio Canada (Ⓦ www.rcinet .ca) broadcasts in English on 93.65MHz (32m) from 6.30–7.30am and on 58.4MHz (51.3m) from 8.30–9.30pm.

Television

The government-run **TV** company, Doord-arshan, which broadcasts a sober diet of edifying programmes, now has to compete with the onslaught of **satellite TV**. The main broadcaster in English is Rupert Murdoch's Star TV network, which incorpo-rates BBC World Service TV and Zee TV (with Z News), a progressive blend of Hindi-oriented chat, film, news and music programmes. Star Sports and ESPN churn out a mind-boggling amount of cricket with an occasional sprinkling of other sports. Others include CNN, some sports channels, the Discovery Channel, the immensely popular Channel V, hosted by scantily clad Mumbai models and DJs, and a couple of American soap and chat stations. There are now several local-language channels too.

Festivals and holidays

Virtually every temple in every town or village has its own festival. The biggest and most spectacular in Rajasthan include the camel fair at Pushkar in November, and the Gangaur festival in March or early April. While many festivals are religious in nature, merrymaking rather than solemnity are generally the order of the day, and onlookers are usually welcome. Indeed, if you are lucky enough to coincide your visit with a local festival, it may well prove to be the highlight of your trip.

Hindu, Sikh, Buddhist and Jain festivals follow the Indian **lunar calendar** and their dates therefore vary from year to year against the plain old Gregorian calendar. Determining them more than a year in advance is a highly complicated business best left to astrologers. Each lunar cycle is divided into two *paksa* (halves): "bright" (waxing) and "dark" (waning), each consisting of fifteen *tithis* ("days" – but a *tithi* might begin at any time of the solar day). The *paksa* start respectively with the new moon (*ama* or *bahula* – the first day of the month) and the full moon (*purnima*). Lunar festivals, then, are observed on a given day in the "light" or "dark" side of the month. The lunar calendar adds a leap month every two or three years to keep it in line with the seasons. Muslim festivals follow the **Islamic calendar**, whose year of exactly twelve lunar months loses about eleven days per annum against the Gregorian. Islamic festival dates are only approximate as they depend on the actual sighting of the new moon at the start of each month.

You may, while in the region, have the privilege of being invited to a **wedding**. These are jubilant affairs with great feasting, always scheduled on auspicious days. A Hindu bride dresses in red for the ceremony, and marks the parting of her hair with red *sindhur* and her forehead with a *bindi*. She wears gold or bone bangles, which she keeps on for the rest of her married life. Although the practice is officially illegal, large dowries often change hands. These are usually paid by the bride's family to the groom, and can be contentious; poor families feel obliged to save for years to pay for their daughters to get married.

Festivals

The festivals are listed below under the Hindu calendar months (in brackets) in which they occur as most of the festivals listed are Hindu, and in any case, Sikhs, Buddhists and Jains use the same months.

Jan–Feb (Magha)

H Vasant Panchami (20 Magha; 11 Feb 2008, 31 Jan 2009, 20 Jan 2010, 8 Feb 2011): One-day spring festival in honour of Saraswati, the goddess of learning, celebrated with kite-flying, the wearing of yellow saris, and the blessing of schoolchildren's books and pens by the goddess.

N Nagaur Fair (22–25 Magha): One of Rajasthan's biggest cattle fairs, held at Nagaur, with sales of steers, horses and camels, plus camel racing, tug-of-war games and general celebrations.

H Baneshwar Fair (11–15 Magha): Held where the Mahi and Som rivers meet near Dungarpur, this is the main Bhil festival of the year, celebrated with acrobatics and magic shows, and a silver image of Mavji, one of Vishnu's incarnations, carried in procession on horseback.

N Jaisalmer Desert Festival (28–30 Magha): A three-day cultural display, with Gair tribal dancers, fire dancers, and even a turban-tying contest.

H Makar Sankranti/Uttarayan (14 Jan): The passing of the sun into Capricorn marks its move into the astrological northern hemisphere, and is celebrated with competitive kite flying.

N Republic Day (26 Jan): A military parade in Delhi typifies this state celebration of India's republic-hood, followed on Jan 29 by the "Beating the Retreat" ceremony outside the presidential palace in Delhi. (RDA)

M Ashura (10 Muharram; approximately 19 Jan 2008, 7 Jan & 27 Dec 2009, 16 Dec 2010): Festival to commemorate the martyrdom of the (Shi'ite) Imam, the Prophet's grandson and popular saint, Hussain. (RDA)

Feb–March (Phalguna)

N Bharatpur Braj Festival (2–4 Feb): Singing and dancing in the streets mark this festival in honour of Lord Krishna, in particular the Raslila dance depicting the story of Krishna and his consort Radha.

> **Key: B=Buddhist; C = Christian; H=Hindu; J=Jain; M=Muslim; N=non-religious; S=Sikh; R = public holiday in Rajasthan; D = public holiday in Delhi; A = public holiday in Agra.**

N Taj Mahotsav (18–27 Feb): A ten-day craft fair with music and dance held at the Shilpgram crafts village in Agra.

H Shivratri (14 Phalguna; 20 Mar 2008, 9 Mar 2009, 27 Feb 2010, 17 Mar 2011): Anniversary of Shiva's tandav (creation) dance, and his wedding anniversary. Popular family festival but also a sadhu festival of pilgrimage and fasting. (A)

H Holi (15 Phalguna): Hugely popular water festival held during Dol Purnima (full moon) to celebrate the beginning of spring. Expect to be bombarded with water, paint and coloured powder (which can permanently stain clothing, so don't go out in your Sunday best). (RDA)

N Jaipur Elephant Festival (15 Phalguna): Held on Holi, and featuring parades of elephants, naturally, plus elephant-back polo and even a people vs. elephants tug-of-war.

M Mawlid (approximately 20 Mar 2008, 9 Mar 2009, 26 Feb 2010, 15 Feb 2011): Birthday of the Prophet Mohammed, celebrated with feasting, processions and gatherings to discuss the life and deeds of the Prophet. (RDA)

March–April (Chaitra)

H Cheti Chand (1 Chaitra; 6 Apr 2008, 27 Mar 2009, 16 Mar 2010, 4 Apr 2011): Lunar New year, more popularly celebrated in the south of India. (A)

H Gangaur (3–4 Chaitra): Rajasthani festival in honour of the goddess Parvati, marked with singing, dancing and processions bearing an image of Parvati in her manifestation as Gauri, goddess of marital happiness. Jaipur, Jodhpur, Jaisalmer, Bikaner, Udaipur and Nathdwara have the biggest processions; around Bundi, Kota and Jhalawar the goddess is festooned with garlands of opium poppies.

H Kaila Devi Fair (12 Chaitra): Held at the village of Kaila, 24km south west of Karauli, in honour of the goddess Laxmi, as worshipped at the local temple.

H Ramanavami (9 Chaitra): Birthday of Rama, the hero of the **Ramayana**, celebrated with readings of the epic and discourses on Rama's life and teachings. (RDA)

N Tilwara Cattle Fair (11–26 Chaitra): One of the biggest cattle fairs in Rajasthan, and barely a tourist in sight. See p.297.

J Mahaveerji Fair (24 Chaitra): A festival in honour of the 24th Jain tirthankara, held at a temple dedicated to him in the village of Chandangaon, 29km north of Karauli, with a procession carrying his image in a golden chariot hauled by four bullocks to the river to be bathed.

C Good Friday (movable): Crucifixion of Jesus. (DA)

April–May (Vaisakha)

HS Baisakhi (13 or 14 April): To Hindus, it's the solar new year, celebrated with music and dancing; to Sikhs, it's the anniversary of the foundation of the Khalsa (Sikh brotherhood) by Guru Gobind Singh.

H Parshuram Jayanti (3 Vaisakha; 8 May 2008, 27 Apr 2009, 16 May 2010, 5 May 2011): Birthday of Parshuram, the sixth avatar of Vishnu. (A)

J Mahavir Jayanti (13 Vaisakha): Birthday of Mahavira, the founder of Jainism. The main Jain festival of the year, observed by visits to sacred Jain sites, and with present-giving.

N Mount Abu Summer Festival (13 Vaisakha; 18 May 2008, 7 May 2009, 26 May 2010, 15 May 2011): Folk and classical music recitals, plus tribal dancing for this three-day carnival celebrating the arrival of summer.

B Buddha Purnima (15 Vaisakha): The holiest day in the Buddhist calendar, as according to tradition Buddha was not only born on this day, but achieved enlightenment and also died on the same date. (DA)

June–July (Ashadha)

M Urs Ajmer Sharif (6 Rajab; approximately 9 July 2008, 29 June 2009, 18 June 2010): Muslim pilgrims from all over India come to pay homage at the tomb of Ajmer's Sufi saint. Poems are recited, Sufi chants are performed, and huge vats of *kheer* (a kind of milk pudding) are cooked up.

July–Aug (Shravana)

H Teej (3 Shravana; 4 Aug 2008, 24 July 2009, 12 Aug 2010, 2 Aug 2011): Festival in honour of Parvati, to welcome the monsoon. Celebrated particularly in Jaipur.

H Raksha Bandhan/Narial Purnima (15 Shravana): Festival to honour the sea god Varuna. Brothers and sisters exchange gifts, the sister tying a thread known as a *rakhi* to her brother's wrist. Brahmins, after a day's fasting, change the sacred thread they wear. (RA)

N Independence Day (15 Aug): India's biggest secular celebration, on the anniversary of independence from Britain. (RDA)

Aug–Sept (Bhadrapada)

H Kajli Teej (3 Bhadrapada; 18 Aug 2008, 8 Aug 2009, 26 Aug 2010, 15 Aug 2011): Bundi's celebration of Teej, a month later than everyone else's.

H Janmashtami (8 Bhadrapada; 4 Sept 2007, 28 Aug 2008, 14 Aug 2009, 2 Sept 2010): Krishna's birthday, an occasion for fasting and celebration, especially in Agra. (RDA)

M Ramadan or Ramzan (first day approximately 2 Sept 2008, 22 Aug 2009, 12 Aug 2010, 1 Aug 2011): The holy month during which Muslims may not eat, drink, smoke or have sex from sunrise to sunset.

Sept–Oct (Ashvina)

H Dussehra (9–10 Ashvina; 7 Oct 2008, 26 Sept 2009, 15 Oct 2010, 4 Oct 2011): Two days' public holiday (with an eight-day run-up) associated with vanquishing demons, in particular Rama's victory over Ravana in the **Ramayana**, and Durga's over the buffalo-headed Mahishasura. Dussehra celebrations include performances of the *Ram Lila* (life of Rama). Celebrated particularly in Kota and Alwar. (RDA)

H Marwar Festival (14–15 Ashvina): Music and dance festival celebrated in the region around Jodhpur.

N Mahatma Gandhi's Birthday (2 Oct): Solemn commemoration of Independent India's founding father.

M Id ul-Fitr (approximately 13 Oct 2007; 1 Oct 2008, 21 Sept 2009, 10 Sept 2010, 31 Aug 2011): Feast to celebrate the end of Ramadan, after 28 days of fasting. Fatehpur Sikri is one of the best places to celebrate this. (RDA)

Oct–Nov (Kartika)

N Pushkar Camel Fair (7–15 Kartika; 17 Nov 2007, 5 Nov 2008, 25 Oct 2009, 13 Nov 2010). Camel herders don their finest attire for this massive livestock market on the fringes on the Thar Desert.

H Chandrabhaga Fair (14 Kartika): Held by the Chandrabhaga River at Jhalawar, where pilgrims come to bathe while cattle are brought to be traded.

H Diwali or Deepavali (15 Kartika; 9 Nov 2007, 28 Oct 2008, 17 Oct 2009, 5 Nov 2010, 26 Oct 2011): Festival of lights, and India's biggest, to celebrate Rama and Sita's homecoming in the **Ramayana**. Festivities include the lighting of oil lamps and firecrackers, and the giving and receiving of sweets and gifts. Diwali coincides with Kali Puja, celebrated in temples dedicated to the wrathful goddess. (RD one day; A two days)

J Jain New Year (15 Kartika): Coincides with Diwali, so Jains celebrate alongside Hindus.

S Nanak Jayanti (16 Kartika): Guru Nanak's birthday marked by prayer readings and processions. (RDA)

Nov–Dec (Margashirsha, or Agrahayana)

M Id ul-Zuha or Bakr Id (10 Duhl-Hijja; approximately 20 Dec 2007, 8 Dec 2008, 28 Nov 2009, 17 Nov 2010, 7 Nov 2011): Pilgrimage festival to commemorate Abraham's preparedness to sacrifice his son Ismail. Celebrated with slaughtering and consumption of sheep. (RDA)

Dec–Jan (Pausa)

C Christmas Day (25 Dec): Birth of Jesus. (RDA)
N Bikaner Camel Festival (14 Pausa; 21 Jan 2008, 10 Jan 2009, 30 Dec 2009): Camels dressed up in colourful camel costumes, ridden by proud Rajasthanis in all their finery.
M Muslim New Year (1 Muharram; approximately 10 Jan & 29 Dec 2008, 18 Dec 2009, 7 Dec 2010).

Sports and outdoor activities

Camel trekking

The way to experience the desert in style is from the top of a camel. The one-humped Arabian camel, or dromedary, common in desert regions of Rajasthan, is well adapted to the terrain, with long double eyelashes to keep sand out of its eyes, nostrils that it can close, and broad, soft, padded feet that are ideal for walking on sand. Riding on a camel is smoother than riding on a horse because the camel moves its left and then right legs together, rather than front and then back legs like a horse, giving it a more rolling gait. They are usually docile, good-tempered animals, but the male goes into rut in spring, when it becomes rather grumpy and can kick and bite, and spit its regurgitated stomach contents in anger.

Camel treks can be arranged at Jaisalmer (see p.306), Bikaner (see p.317), Khuhri (see p.313) and also at Mandawa in Shekhawati (see p.237). In fact, arriving in Jaisalmer, you can barely move for touts trying to sell you a camel safari, but dodgy operators abound, so beware.

Some treks stick to the beaten track, and take you to the popular tourist sights. Others specialize in heading off deep into the desert for a feeling of isolation and remoteness. Typically, camel treks include two days in the saddle and a night spent camping in the desert, but you can opt for longer or shorter trips. For more on camel trekking, see box, p.306.

Horse riding

Udaipur is Rajasthan's main centre for horse riding, followed by Mount Abu, while several places in Shekhawati, Udaipur (see p.347) and around Bundi offer horse riding activities. Other places include Rohet Garh near Jodhpur (see p.286) and Roop Niwas in Nawalgarh (see p.230); the same company also offers horse safari packages (see Ⓦwww.royalridingholidays.com), as do Muir's tours in the UK (Ⓦwww.nkf-mt.org.uk) and Equitours in the US (Ⓦwww.ridingtours.com).

Spectator sports

Cricket is by far the most popular spectator sport in India, and a fine example of how something quintessentially British (well, English) has become something quintessentially Indian. Travellers to India will find it hard to get away from the game – it's everywhere. Expectations are high and disappointments acute; India versus Pakistan matches are especially emotive.

Test matches are a rare event so if you want to see a game live, interstate cricket is your best bet. States (plus some city and occupational teams) compete between October and March for the Ranji Trophy, the country's most prestigious award, equivalent to England's County Championship or Australia's Pura Cup.

Horse racing can be a good day out, especially if you enjoy a flutter. The course at Delhi has races every Tuesday (see p.145). Other spectator sports include **polo**, originally from upper Kashmir, but taken up by the British to become one of the symbols of the Raj. A number of Rajasthani cities, including Jodhpur and Mount Abu, still have polo grounds, as does Delhi, and the sport remains hugely popular among upper-class Rajasthanis. The Maharaja of Jodhpur's website (⬤www.maharajajodhpur.com) has a section devoted to polo.

Golf is extremely popular and relatively inexpensive in India, and Delhi has several golf courses and plenty of enthusiasts.

One indigenous sport you may see is **kabadi**, played on a small (badminton-sized) court, and informally on any suitable open area. The game, with seven players in each team, consists of a player from each team alternately attempting to "tag" as many members of the opposing team as possible in the space of a single breath (cheating is impossible; the player has to maintain a continuous chant of kabadikabadikabadikabadi etc), and getting back to his/her own side of the court

without being caught. The game can get quite rough, with slaps and kicks in tagging allowed, and the defending team must try to tackle and pin the attacker so as not to allow him or her to even touch the dividing line. Tagged victims are required to leave the court. Although still an amateur sport, kabadi is taken very seriously with state and national championships, and now features in the Asian Games.

Popular with devotees of the monkey god, Hanuman, Indian **wrestling**, or **kushti**, has a small but dedicated following. Wrestlers are known as *pahalwaans* or "strong men" and can sometimes be seen exercising early in the morning with clubs and weights along river *ghats*. In Delhi, matches are held every Sunday near the Jama Masjid (see p.120).

Crime and personal safety

In spite of the crushing poverty and the yawning gulf between rich and poor, India is, on the whole, a safe country to travel in, and that includes not only Rajasthan and Agra, but also Delhi, despite its size and metropolitan character. As a tourist, however, you are an obvious target for thieves (who may include some of your fellow travellers), and stand to face serious problems if you do lose your passport, money and ticket home. Common sense, therefore, suggests a few precautions.

If you can tolerate the encumbrance, carry valuables in a money belt or a pouch around your neck at all times. In the latter case, the cord should be hidden under your clothing and not be easy to cut through. Beware of **crowded locations**, such as packed buses or trains, in which it is easy for pickpockets to operate – slashing pockets or bags with razor blades is not unheard of, and even itching powder is sometimes used to distract the unwary. Thieves often work in teams, one member distracting your attention – for example by bumping into you – while another swipes your bag. In hotels, don't leave valuables lying around in your room. Upmarket establishments will have a room safe; budget

hotels will often have a safe at reception to keep them in.

Budget travellers would do well to carry a **padlock**, as these are usually used to secure the doors of cheap hotel rooms and it's reassuring to know you have the only key; strong combination locks are ideal. You can also use them to lock your bag to seats or racks in trains. Don't put valuables in your luggage for bus or plane journeys: keep them with you at all times. If your baggage is on the roof of a bus, make sure it is well secured. On trains and buses, the prime time for theft is just before you leave, so keep a particular eye on your gear then, beware of deliberate diversions, and don't put your belongings next to open windows.

Druggings leading to theft and worse are rare but not unheard of, and so you are best advised to politely **refuse food and drink** from fellow passengers or passing strangers, unless you are completely confident it's the family picnic you are sharing or have seen the food purchased from a vendor.

However, don't get paranoid; the best way to enjoy your visit is to stay relaxed but have your wits about you. Crime levels in India are

Drugs

Rajasthan, and particularly the region around Chittaurgarh and Kota, is a major centre for the legitimate production of **opium**, which is used to make medicines for the pharmaceutical industry. Traditional use of opium is ingrained in Rajasthani culture: Rajputs used to take a dose before battle to assuage fear, or in case of injury, pain; their wives took it before committing *sati*. Even today, in many Rajasthani villages, opium is commonly offered as a sign of hospitality. The drug makes you drowsy, and is pleasurable but addictive. If you are offered some on a village tour and don't want to fall under its effects, you could accept a very small token crumb of it just to be polite, though it is of course illegal and you are quite within your rights to refuse it outright. In Rajasthan, it is not smoked, but drunk in the form of a tea. It is also used medicinally. Some people do become addicts, and opium addiction can be a social problem, particularly if the family's main bread-winner spends all his income on the drug and all his time under its influence. Heroin ("brown sugar") is not widespread in rural communities, but it's an increasing problem among the urban poor. In central Delhi particularly, you may well see homeless people smoking it on the street.

Cannabis comes in three forms. **Bhang** (marijuana leaf, usually boiled and pounded) is used in religious celebrations and is legal. It is most commonly stirred into drinks, though it can also be made into sweets, and it is sold in licensed bhang shops at several places in Rajasthan. Cafés and restaurants in places like Pushkar and Udaipur may also serve bhang lassis. Because there is no legal restriction on it, you may be tempted to try bhang, but if you are not used to the effects of cannabis, beware: the drug does not agree with everybody, and when eaten (bhang is not usually smoked), the dosage is notoriously difficult to gauge, and the effects can last for some hours, sometimes causing intense, and protracted, psychological distress. Also be aware that potentially dangerous adulterants such as datura or even tranquillizer pills are sometimes added to bhang drinks to increase their effect.

The other two varieties of cannabis – **ganja** (marijuana bud) and **charas** (cannabis resin, hashish) – are generally mixed with tobacco and smoked in a pipe called a chillum, which was originally the bowl of a hookah. Both drugs are illegal, though sadhus (religious mendicants) are allowed to smoke ganja as part of their religious devotion to Shiva, who is himself apparently partial to a smoke.

Aside from such religious use, and the festive consumption of bhang, the use of cannabis is considered a low-life habit (if you see anyone in a movie smoking a chillum, you can be sure it's the baddie), and the **law** against it is harsh. Anyone arrested with less than five grams which they can prove is for their own use is liable to a maximum of six months in prison, but cases can take years to come to trial (two is normal, and eight not unheard of). For more than five grams, you can expect a hefty prison sentence. "Paying a fine now" may be possible on arrest (though it will probably mean all the money you have), but once you are booked in at the station, your chances are slim; most of the foreigners languishing in Indian jails are there on drugs charges. Police raids on budget hotels in Delhi's Paharganj area are not unknown (though we haven't heard of any in recent years), and in Pushkar, where hippy tourism is still the order of the day, the police also keep a sharp eye out. If you are arrested, expect no sympathy from your consulate. Best advice is to steer clear of all illegal drugs including *charas* and ganja.

a long way below those of Western countries, and violent crime against tourists in Rajasthan, Delhi and Agra is extremely rare. Virtually none of the people who approach you on the street intend any harm: most want to sell you something (though this is not always made apparent immediately), some want to practise their English, others (if you're a woman) to chat you up, while more than a few just want to add your address to their book or have a picture taken with you. Anyone offering wonderful-sounding moneymaking schemes, however, is almost certain to be a con artist.

If you do feel threatened, it's worth looking for help. Tourism police are found sitting in clearly marked booths in main railway stations, some bus stations and major tourist centres throughout Rajasthan, and in Delhi and Agra.

Be wary of **credit card fraud**; a credit card can be used to make duplicate forms to which your account is then billed for fictitious transactions, so don't let shops or restaurants take your card away to process – insist they do it in front of you or follow them to the point of transaction.

It's not a bad idea to keep US$100 or so separately from the rest of your money, along with your traveller's cheque receipts, insurance policy number and phone number for claims, and a photocopy of the pages in your passport containing personal data and your Indian visa. This will cover you in case you do lose all your valuables.

If the worst happens and you get robbed, the first thing to do is **report the theft** as soon as possible to the local police. They are very unlikely to recover your belongings, but you need a report from them in order to claim on your travel insurance. Dress smartly and expect an uphill battle – city cops in particular tend to be jaded from too many insurance and traveller's cheque scams.

Losing your passport is a real hassle, but does not necessarily mean the end of your trip. First, report the loss immediately to the police, who will issue you with the all-important "complaint form" that you need to be able to travel around and check into hotels, as well as claim back any expenses incurred in replacing your passport from your insurer. A complaint form, however, will not allow you to change money or traveller's cheques. If you've run out of cash, your best bet is to ask your hotel manager to help you out (staff will have seen your passport when you checked in, and the number will be in the register). The next thing to do is telephone your nearest embassy or consulate in the region. Normally, passports have to be applied for and collected in person, but if you are stranded, it is usually possible to arrange to receive the necessary forms in the post. However, you still have to go to the embassy or consulate to pick up your new passport. "Emergency passports" are the cheapest form of replacement, but are normally only valid for the few days of your return flight. If you're not sure when you're leaving the country, you'll have to obtain a more costly "full passport" from your country's embassy in Delhi.

Culture and etiquette

Western visitors will find that cultural differences in India extend to all sorts of things. While allowances will usually be made for foreigners, those unacquainted with Indian customs may need a little preparation to avoid causing offence or making fools of themselves. The list here is hardly exhaustive: when in doubt, watch what Indian people are doing and follow suit.

Eating and the right-hand rule

In Rajasthan, Delhi and Agra, cutlery is usually supplied in eating places, but sometimes you may have to eat the traditional way – with your fingers. In such cases, the rule is that you should **eat with your right hand only**. In India, as right across Asia, the left hand is for wiping your bottom, cleaning your feet and other unsavoury functions (you also put on and take off your shoes with your left hand), while the right hand is for eating, shaking hands, and so on.

People nowadays, especially in Delhi, don't tend to be too strict about this (washing hands before and after eating is more of an issue), but especially in rural areas, it is best to follow the rule. While you can certainly hold a cup or utensil in your left hand, and use both hands to tear your chapati, you should not pass food or put it into your mouth with your left hand. Best to keep it out of sight below the table.

In theory, this rule extends beyond food too. In general, it is best to avoid passing things to people with your left hand, or pointing at people with it, and the same applies to putting it in your mouth.

The other rule to beware of when eating or drinking is that your lips should not touch other people's food – *jhuta* or sullied food is strictly taboo. Don't, for example, take a bite out of a chapati and pass it on. When drinking out of a cup or bottle to be shared with others, don't let it touch your lips, but rather pour it directly into your mouth. It is customary to wash your hands before and after eating.

Temples and religion

Religion is taken very seriously in India; it's important always to show due respect to religious buildings, shrines, images, and people at prayer. When entering a temple or mosque, remove your shoes and leave them at the door (socks are acceptable). Some temples – Jain ones in particular – do not allow you to enter wearing or carrying leather articles, and forbid entry to menstruating women. Sikh temples do not allow you to enter with alcohol, tobacco or any other drug, and a couple of Hindu temples in Delhi that are popular with tourists require you to deposit cameras and mobile phones at the entrance. When entering a religious establishment, dress conservatively (see below), and try not to be obtrusive.

In a mosque, you won't normally be allowed in at prayer time and women are sometimes not allowed in at all. In a Hindu temple, non-Hindus may be asked not to enter the inner sanctum, and it is not usually permitted to take **photographs** of images of deities inside temples. Indeed, it's best not to wield your camera inside a temple at all without at least checking with someone beforehand. In some cases you will have to leave your camera at the door, so it may be best not to bring it with you. Never take photos of funerals or cremations.

Dress

Some Indian people can be quite conservative about **dress**. This is not so much true in cities, and particularly among the upper and middle classes, but in the countryside women usually dress modestly, with legs and shoulders covered. Trousers are acceptable, but wearing shorts and short skirts is rather risqué – no problem in a Delhi nightclub perhaps, but definitely not the done thing if visiting a village in rural Rajasthan, while men should not wander around in public without a shirt. These rules go double in temples and mosques. Cover your head with a cap or cloth when entering a *dargah* (Sufi shrine) or Sikh *gurudwara*; women in particular are also required to cover their limbs. Men are similarly expected to dress appropriately with their legs and head covered. Caps are usually available on loan, often free, for visitors, and sometimes cloth is available to cover up your arms and legs.

In general, Indians find it hard to understand why rich Westerners should wander round in ragged clothes or imitate the lowest ranks of Indian society, who would love to have something more decent to wear. Staying well groomed and dressing "respectably" vastly improves the impression you make on local people, and reduces sexual harassment too.

Drinking and smoking

While lots of Indian men smoke anything from bidis to chillums, it is not the done thing for women to smoke, especially in public, and doing so will give a very bad impression, and lead some to regard you as a loose woman, which means a potential target for harassment.

Drinking alcohol is also to some extent considered a low-life occupation, for members of both sexes, but especially for women. This is not so much the case at the upper end of the market – and in Delhi particularly, you will find plenty of upmarket bars where both men and women can quite happily drink without fear of opprobrium – but women in particular do not frequent low-class bars if they are respectable, and this is especially true in Rajasthan, where hotel bars are usually your best bet if you are female.

Other possible gaffes

Kissing and **embracing** are regarded in India as part of sex: do not do them in public. In more conservative areas (ie outside Westernized parts of big cities), it is not even a good idea for couples to hold hands,

though Indian men can sometimes be seen holding hands as a sign of "brotherliness".

Be aware of your **feet**. When entering a private home, you should normally remove your shoes (follow your host's example); when sitting, avoid pointing the soles of your feet at anyone. Accidental contact with one's foot is always followed by an apology.

Meeting people

Westerners have an ambiguous status in Indian eyes. In one way, they represent the rich sahib, whose culture dominates the world, and the old colonial mentality has not completely disappeared. On the other hand, as a non-Hindu, they are outcaste, their presence in theory polluting to an orthodox or high-caste Hindu, while to members of all religions, Western morals and standards of spiritual and physical cleanliness are suspect.

As a traveller, you will constantly come across people who want to strike up a **conversation**. English not being their first language, they may not be familiar with the conventional ways of doing this, and thus their opening line may seem abrupt if at the same time very formal. "Excuse me good gentleman, what is your mother country?" is a typical one. Many people will simply come up to you and demand to know your name or nationality, but while this may seem an odd way to begin, they are merely trying to start a conversation. Straight questions about your name, origin, family and occupation are considered polite conversation between strangers in India, and help people place one another in terms of social position. Indian English can be very formal and even ceremonious. Indian people may well call you "sir" or "madam", even "good lady" or "kind sir". At the same time, you should be aware that your English may seem rude to them. In particular, swearing is taken rather seriously in India, and casual use of the F-word is likely to shock.

Things that Indian people are likely to find strange about you are lack of religion (you could adopt one), travelling alone, leaving your family to come to India, being an unmarried couple (letting people think you are married can make life easier), and travelling second class or staying in cheap hotels when, as a foreign tourist, you are obviously relatively rich. You will probably end up having to explain the same things many times to many different people; on the other hand, you can ask questions too, so you could take it as an opportunity to ask things you want to know about India. English-speaking Indians, and members of the large and growing middle class in particular, are usually extremely well informed and well educated, and often far more *au fait* with world affairs than Westerners.

Sexism and women's issues

India is not a country that provides huge obstacles to women travellers. In the days of the Raj, upper-class eccentrics started a tradition of lone women travellers, taken up enthusiastically by the flower children of the hippy era. Plenty of women keep up the tradition today, but few get through their trip without any hassle, and it's good to prepare yourself to be a little bit thick-skinned.

Indian streets are almost without exception male-dominated – something that may take a bit of getting used to, particularly if you find yourself subjected to incessant staring, whistling and name calling. This can usually be stopped by ignoring the gaze and quickly moving on, or by firmly telling the offender to stop looking at you. Most of your fellow travellers on trains and buses will be men, who may start up most unwelcome conversations about sex, divorce and the freedom of relationships in the West. These cannot often be avoided, but demonstrating too much enthusiasm to discuss such topics can lure men into thinking that you are easy about sex, and the situation could become threatening. At its worst in larger cities, all this can become very tiring. You can get round it to a certain extent by joining women in public places, and you'll notice an immense difference if you join up with a male travelling companion. In this case, expect Indian men to approach him (assumed, of course, to be your husband – an assumption it is sometimes advantageous to go along with) and talk to him about you quite happily as if you were not there. Beware, however, if you are (or look) Indian with a non-Indian male companion: this may well cause you

harassment, as you might be seen to have brought shame on your family by adopting the loose morals of the West.

In addition to staring and suggestive comments and looks, **sexual harassment**, or "Eve teasing" as it is bizarrely known, is likely to be a nuisance, but not generally a threat. Expect to get groped in crowds, and to have men "accidentally" squeeze past you at any opportunity. It tends to be worse in cities than in small towns and villages, but anywhere being followed can be a real problem.

In time you'll learn to gauge a situation – sometimes wandering around on your own may attract so much unwanted attention that you may prefer to stay in one place until you've recharged your batteries or your male fan club has moved on. It's always best to dress modestly – a *salwar kameez* is perfect, as is any baggy clothing – and refrain from smoking and drinking in public, which only reinforces prejudices that Western women are "loose" and "easy".

Returning an unwanted touch with a punch or slap is perfectly in order (Indian women often become aggressive when offended), and does serve to vent a little frustration. It should also attract attention and urge someone to help you, or at least deal with the offending man – a man transgressing social norms is always out of line, and any passer-by will want to let him know it. If you feel someone getting too close in a crowd or on a bus, brandishing your left shoe in his face can be very effective.

To go and watch a Bollywood movie at the cinema is a fun and essential part of your trip to India but, at cheap cinemas especially, such an occasion is rarely without hassle. If you do go to the cinema, it's best to go to an upmarket theatre, or at least to go with a group of people and sit in the balcony area, where it's a bit more expensive but the crowd is much more sedate.

Violent sexual assaults on tourists are extremely rare, but the number of reported cases of rape is rising, and you should always take precautions: avoid quiet, dimly lit streets and alleys at night; if you find a trustworthy rickshaw/taxi driver in the day keep him for the night journey; and try to get someone to accompany you to your hotel whenever possible. While Indian women are still quite timid about reporting rape – it is considered as much a disgrace to the victim as to the perpetrator – Western victims should always report it to the police, and before leaving the area try to let other tourists, or locals, know, in the hope that pressure from the community may uncover the offender and see him brought to justice. In Delhi there's a police helpline for women in distress (☏1091), and a special police unit to deal with crimes against women (☏011/2573 7951 for central Delhi), and the women's organization JAGORI lists Delhi helpline numbers on their website at ⒲jagori.org /resources/helplines. Rajasthan does not have such resources, but if you prefer to contact a women's group rather than go straight to the police, you could try VIVIDHA on ☏0141/276 2932.

The **practicalities of travel** take on a new dimension for lone women travellers. Often you can turn your gender to your advantage. For example, on intercity buses the driver and conductor will often take you under their wing, and there will be countless other instances of kindness wherever you travel. You'll be more welcome in some private houses than a group of Western males, and may find yourself learning the finer points of Indian cooking round the family's clay stove. Women frequently get preference at bus and railway stations where they can join a separate "ladies' queue", and use ladies' waiting rooms. On overnight trains the enclosed ladies' compartments are peaceful havens (unless filled with noisy children); you could also try to share a berth section with a family where you are usually drawn into the security of the group and are less exposed to lusty gazes. In hotels watch out for "peep-holes" in your door (and in the common bathrooms), be sure to cover your window when changing and when sleeping.

Lastly, bring your own supply of **tampons**, which are not widely available outside main cities.

Toilets

A visit to the loo is not one of India's more pleasant experiences: toilets can be filthy and stink. They are also major potential breeding grounds for disease. And then there is the squatting position to get used to; the traditional Asian toilet has a hole in the ground and two small platforms for the feet, instead of a seat. Paper, if used, often goes in a bucket next to the loo rather than down it. Indians use instead a jug of water and their left hand, a method you may also come to prefer, but if you do use paper, keep some handy – it isn't usually supplied, and it might be an idea to stock up before going too far off the beaten track as it is not available everywhere. Travelling is especially difficult for women as facilities are limited or nonexistent, especially when travelling by road. However, toilets in the a/c carriages of trains are usually kept clean, as are those in mid-range restaurants. In tourist areas, most hotels offer Western-style loos, even in budget lodges.

Baksheesh

As a presumed-rich sahib or memsahib, you will, like wealthy Indians, be expected to be liberal with the **baksheesh**, which takes three main forms.

The most common is **tipping**: a small reward for a small service, which can encompass anyone from a waiter or porter to someone who lifts your bags onto the roof of a bus or keeps an eye on your vehicle for you. Large amounts are not expected – ten rupees should satisfy all the aforementioned. Taxi drivers and staff at cheaper hotels and restaurants do not necessarily expect tips, but always appreciate them, of course, and they can keep people sweet for the next time you call. Some may take liberties in demanding baksheesh, but it's often better just to acquiesce rather than spoil your mood and cause offence over trifling sums.

More expensive than plain tipping is paying people to **bend the rules**, many of which seem to have been invented for precisely that purpose. Examples might include letting you into a historical site after hours, finding you a seat or a sleeper on a train that is "full", or speeding up some bureaucratic process. This should not be confused with bribery, a more serious business with its own risks and etiquette, which is best not entered into.

The last kind of baksheesh is **alms giving**. In a country without a welfare system, this is an important social custom. People with disabilities and mutilations are the traditional recipients, and it seems right to join local people in giving out small change to them. Kids demanding money, pens, sweets or the like are a different case, pressing their demands only on tourists. In return for a service it is fair enough, but to yield to any request encourages them to go and pester others.

Shopping

So many beautiful and exotic souvenirs are on sale in Rajasthan, Delhi and Agra, at such low prices, that it's sometimes hard to know what to buy first. On top of that, all sorts of things (such as made-to-measure clothes) that would be vastly expensive at home are much more reasonably priced here. Even if you lose weight during your trip, your baggage might well put on quite a bit – unless of course you post some of it home.

Rajasthan in particular is well blessed with all kinds of wonderful crafts, while Delhi, as the nation's capital, has emporiums full of goods from all over India, and also from neighbouring countries such as Tibet. For more information on shopping in Rajasthan, see the *Rajasthani crafts* colour section.

Where to shop

Quite a few items sold in tourist areas are made elsewhere and, needless to say, it's more fun (and cheaper) to pick them up at source. Best buys are noted in the relevant sections of the Guide, along with a few specialities that can't be found outside their regions. India is awash with **street hawkers**, often very young kids. Although they can be annoying and should be dealt with firmly if you are not interested, do not write them off completely as they sometimes have decent souvenirs at lower than shop prices and are open to hard bargaining.

Virtually all the state governments in India run handicraft "**emporiums**", and most of them have branches in Delhi, where there is also a **Central Cottage Industries Emporium** (Ⓦwww.cottageemporiumindia .com), selling goods made by artisans from across India. Goods in these places are generally of a high quality, even if their fixed prices are a little expensive, and they are worth a visit to get an idea of what crafts are available and how much they should cost.

Rajasthan is particularly known for its textiles, but there's also the blue ceramic ware of Jaipur, as well as jewellery, miniature paintings and leatherware. In **Agra**, the top souvenir is marble inlay work in the same style as that in the Taj Mahal. The *Rajasthani crafts* colour section has more detail about what's available in the way of arts and crafts, but there are plenty of more everyday goods that are worth buying, including books (cheaper here than at home), DVDs (especially Hindi films with English subtitles), Bollywood film posters, stainless steel tiffin boxes, tea from Assam or Darjeeling, spices, essential oils and joss-sticks.

Buying metals and gemstones

Among precious metals, **silver** is generally a better buy than gold but is difficult to distinguish from cheap white metal often palmed off as silver in curio shops. **Gold** is usually 22 carat and very yellow, but relatively expensive due to taxes (smuggling from the Gulf to evade them is rife) and to its popularity as a form of investment – women traditionally keep their wealth in this form, and a bride's jewellery is an important part of her dowry. Silver varies in quality, but is usually reasonably priced, with silver jewellery generally heavier and rather more folksy than gold. Gold and silver are usually sold by weight, the workmanship costing very little.

Buying **gemstones** can be something of a minefield; scams abound, and you would be most unwise to even consider buying gems for resale or as an investment without a basic knowledge of the trade. That said, some precious and semiprecious stones can be a good buy in Rajasthan, particularly those which are indigenous to India, such as garnets, black stars and moonstones. Jaipur is a major centre for gems, but also for con tricks, so tread carefully.

Finally, things **not to bring home** include ivory and anything made from a rare or protected species, including snakeskin and turtle products. As for drugs, don't even think about it.

Bargaining

Whatever you buy (except food and cigarettes), you will almost always be expected to **haggle** over the price. Bargaining is very much a matter of personal style, but should always be lighthearted, never acrimonious. There are no hard and fast rules – it's really a question of how much something is worth to you. It's a good plan, therefore, to have an idea of how much you want to pay. Bid low and let the shopkeeper argue you up. If he'll settle for your price or less, you have a deal. If not, you don't, but you've had a pleasant conversation and no harm is done.

Don't worry too much about the first quoted prices. Some people suggest paying a third of the opening price, but it really depends on the shop, the goods and the shopkeeper's impression of you. You may not be able to get the seller much below the first quote; on the other hand, you may end up paying as little as a tenth of it. If you bid too low, you may be hustled out of the shop for offering an "insulting" price, but this is all part of the game, and you'll no doubt be welcomed as an old friend if you return the next day.

"Green" tourists are easily spotted, so try and look like you know what you are up to, even on your first day, or leave it till later; you could wait and see what the going rate is first.

Haggling is a little bit like bidding in an auction, and similar rules apply. Don't start haggling for something if you know you don't want it, and never let any figure pass your lips that you are not prepared to pay – having mentioned a price, you are obliged to pay it. If the seller asks you how much you would pay for something, and you don't want it, say so.

Sometimes rickshaw-wallahs and taxi drivers stop unasked at shops; they get a small commission simply for bringing customers. In places like Jaipur and Agra where this is common practice, tourists sometimes even strike a deal with their drivers – agreeing to stop at five shops and splitting the commission for the time wasted. If you're taken to a shop by a tout or driver and you buy something, you pay around fifty percent extra. Stand firm about not entering shops and getting to your destination if you have no appetite for such shenanigans. If you want a bargain, shop alone, and never let anybody on the street take you to a shop – if you do, they'll be getting a commission, and you'll be paying it.

Travelling with children

Indians are very tolerant of children so you can take them almost anywhere in India without restriction, and they always help break the ice with strangers, but the attention they receive can be relentless, and sometimes a problem in itself.

Foreign children in some parts of India can be a novelty, and lots of people will want to pick them up and have their picture taken with them. This is especially the case in places where foreigners are less common. Often, these approaches can be extremely intrusive; people may simply pick up your child without asking permission. If your child is comfortable with it, then you may as well go with the flow, but if not, then you will need to be firm, and preferably avoid crowds and perhaps less touristy places.

Extra protection is needed from the sun, unsafe drinking water, heat and unfamiliar food. Chilli in food also may be a problem, if they're not used to it. Remember too, that diarrhoea, perhaps just a nuisance to you, could be dangerous for a child: rehydration salts (see p.40) are vital if your child goes down with it. Make sure, if possible, that your child is aware of the dangers of rabies; keep them away from animals, and consider a rabies jab before you go. Children should also be made aware that monkeys can be dangerous if teased.

For babies, **nappies** (diapers) are available in most large towns at similar prices to the West, but it's worth taking an additional pack in case of emergencies, and bringing sachets of Baby Calpol, which aren't easily available in India. A changing mat is another necessity. And if your baby is on powdered milk, it might be an idea to bring some of that: you can certainly get it in India, but it may not taste the same. Dried baby food could also be worth taking – any café or chai-wallah should be able to supply you with boiled water.

For touring, hiking or walking, child-carrier backpacks are ideal; some even come with mozzie nets these days. When it comes to **luggage**, bring as little as possible. If your child is small enough, a fold-up buggy is also well worth packing, even if you no longer use a buggy at home, as kids tire so easily in the heat.

On Indian Railways, children under five **travel free**, and those aged between five and twelve pay half the adult fare. On a plane, children under twelve pay half fare, unless they are under two and sharing a seat with an adult, in which case they pay ten percent of the adult fare.

Travel essentials

Costs

For visitors to Rajasthan, Delhi and Agra, a little foreign currency can go a long way.

The costs we give below are only an approximation of what you can expect to spend on a daily basis. On a good day, you may spend very little, but it's always worth making room for unexpected expenses, such as the odd splurge, or buying souvenirs.

As a foreigner in the region, you are penalized by double-tier entry prices to museums and historic sites as well as in upmarket hotels, all of which are levied at a higher rate and in dollars. Even at the lower end of the market, you will generally be paying more for goods and services than Indian people would pay. Some tourists resent this, but to be fair, even a budget traveller is far better off than most Indians, and it's worth bearing this in mind and accepting the surcharge with good grace.

What you spend depends on where you are: Delhi is rather more expensive than most places for both accommodation and food. Pushkar, on the other hand, is cheaper, particularly for accommodation. On a budget of as little as Rs500 (US$11.50/£6/€9) per day, you'll manage if you eat in local *dhabas* and don't move about too much. On Rs1000 ($23/£12/€18) a day, you'll be able to afford mid-range hotels, as well as meals in smarter restaurants, regular rickshaw or taxi rides and entrance fees to monuments. If you're happy spending around Rs1500 (US$35/£17.50/€26) per day, however, you can really pamper yourself; to spend much more than that, you'd have to be doing a lot of air-conditioned travelling, flying instead of taking trains, consistently staying in swish hotels and eating in the top restaurants.

Generally speaking, you can usually find an inexpensive hotel for around Rs150 (US$3.50/£1.75/€2.60) per person per night, and a basic veg meal for half that or less, while a mid-range hotel will cost around Rs500 (US$11.50/£6/€9) per person and a good meal in a moderately-priced restaurant shouldn't set you back much more, even if you throw in a beer or two. Even in a classy restaurant, you'll be hard pushed to pay more than Rs1500 for a meal. Bear in mind that service is often added to the bill (usually ten percent), along with 12.5 percent VAT. For typical transport costs, see box, p.30.

If service isn't included, ten percent is an acceptable **tip** in a restaurant. You might also consider tipping taxi drivers and auto- or rickshaw-wallahs, though they don't necessarily expect it. In a hotel, you might tip the porter Rs10–20.

Disabled travellers

Disability is common in India; many conditions that would be curable in the West, such as cataracts, are permanent disabilities here because people can't afford the treatment. Disabled people are unlikely to get jobs (though there is a famous blind barber in Delhi), and the choice is usually between staying at home to be looked after by your family, and going out on the street to beg for alms.

For the **disabled traveller**, this has its advantages and disadvantages: disability doesn't get the same embarrassed reaction from Indian people that it does from some able-bodied Westerners. On the other hand, you'll be lucky to see a state-of-the-art wheelchair or a disabled loo, and the streets are full of all sorts of obstacles that would be hard for a blind or wheelchair-bound tourist to negotiate independently. Kerbs are often high, pavements uneven and littered, and ramps nonexistent. There are potholes all over the place and open sewers. Some of the more expensive hotels have ramps for the movement of luggage and equipment, but if that makes them accessible to wheelchairs, it is by accident rather than design. Nonetheless, the 1995 Persons with Disabilities Act specifies access for all to public buildings, and is sometimes enforced. A visit to Delhi by the wheelchair-bound astro-physicist Stephen Hawking resulted in the appearance of ramps at several Delhi tourist sights including the Red Fort, Qutub Minar and Jantar Mantar. Following a 1997 court case, Delhi airport has also been made a lot more accessible for chair users. Meanwhile, Delhi's new metro system has been deliberately designed for accessibility, and has step-free access from street to platform at every station.

If you walk with difficulty, you will find India's many street obstacles and steep stairs hard going. Another factor that can be a problem is the constant barrage of people proffering things (hard to wave aside if you are, for instance, on crutches), and all that queuing, not to mention heat, will take it out of you if you have a condition that makes you tire quickly. A light, folding camp-stool is one thing that could be invaluable if you have limited walking or standing power.

Then again, Indian people are likely to be very helpful if, for example, you need their help getting on and off buses or up stairs. Taxis and rickshaws are easily affordable and very adaptable; if you rent one for a day, the driver is certain to help you on and off, and perhaps even around the sites you visit. If you employ a guide, they may also be prepared to help you with steps and obstacles.

If complete independence is out of the question, going with an able-bodied companion might be on the cards. Contact a specialist organization for further advice on planning your trip. In Delhi, Timeless India (℡011/2617 4205 or 6, ⊛www.timelessexcursions.com) offers an "accessible tour" for wheelchair-bound visitors, covering Delhi, Agra and Jaipur as well as Mumbai and a Goa beach resort. Otherwise, some package tour operators try to cater for travellers with disabilities – Bales and Somak among them – but you should always contact any operator and discuss your exact needs with them before making a booking. You should also make sure you are covered by any insurance policy you take out.

For more information about disability issues in Rajasthan, Delhi or Agra, check the Disability India Network website at ⊛www.disabilityindia.org.

Electricity

India's electricity supply is 230V 50Hz AC. Most sockets are triple round-pin (accepting European-size double round-pin plugs). British, Irish and Australasian plugs will need an adaptor, preferably universal; American and Canadian appliances may need a transformer too, unless multi-voltage. Power cuts and voltage variations are very common; voltage stabilizers should be used to run sensitive appliances such as laptops.

Gay and lesbian travellers

Homosexuality is not generally open or accepted in India. Sexual intercourse between men is illegal and carries a ten-year sentence under article 377 of the penal code, while laws against "obscene behaviour" can be used to arrest gay men for cruising or liaising anywhere that could be considered a public place.

For **lesbians**, making contacts is rather difficult; even the Indian women's movement does not readily promote lesbianism as an issue that needs confronting. The only public faces of a hidden scene are the organizations in Delhi listed on p.70.

For **gay men**, homosexuality is no longer solely the preserve of the alternative scene of actors and artists, and is increasingly accepted by the upper classes, but Mumbai remains much more a centre for gay life than Delhi, let alone traditionalist Rajasthan.

One group of people you may come across are **hijras**, who look like transvestites and are accepted as a transitional "third sex" between male and female. Many, but far from all, hijras are eunuchs, who undergo castration or join the hijra community for various reasons related to the fact that it allows them to live with an ambiguous sexuality. Most hijras were born as boys, but a few were born as girls; not all originally-male hijras are gay, and some have female partners. They live in their own "families" and have a niche in Indian society, but not an easy one. At weddings, their presence is supposed to bring good luck, and they are usually given baksheesh for putting in a brief appearence. Generally, however, they have a low social status, face widespread discrimination, and make a living by begging or prostitution. Violence against them is quite common.

Gay and lesbian contacts and resources

You will need to contact the following places in advance for information as most addresses are PO boxes:

Campaign for Lesbian Rights (CALERI)/Shakhi PO Box 3526, Lajpat Nagar, New Delhi 110065 Ⓔ caleri@hotmail.com. Collective working for lesbian rights.

Humrahi PO Box-3910, Andrews Ganj, Delhi 110049 Ⓦ www.geocities.com/WestHollywood/ Heights/7258. Organization for gay men in New Delhi; meets Saturdays 7pm at D-45 Gulmohar Park, New Delhi.

Humsafar Trust Ⓦ www.humsafar.org. Set up to promote safe sex among gay men, but the website has lots of links and up-to-date information.

Indian Dost Ⓦ www.indiandost.com/delhigay.php. The Delhi page of a website for gay men in India.

International Gay and Lesbian Human Rights Commission Ⓦ www.iglhrc.org. Latest news on the human rights situation for gay people worldwide, including regular bulletins on India.

Purple Dragon Lobby of the Tarntawan Place Hotel, 119/5-10 Suriwong Road, Bangkok 10500, Thailand ☎ +662/634-0273, toll-free from US and Canada ☎ 1-866/414-1076, from UK ☎ 0800/471 5180, Ⓦ www.purpledrag.com. Thai-based gay-friendly tour operator covering India with tours of Delhi and the "Golden Triangle".

Queer India Ⓦ queerindia.blogspot.com. Interesting blog on gay issues in India.

Rainbow High Vacations 506 Church Street, Suite 200 Toronto, Ontario, Canada M4Y 2C8 ☎ 1-416/962-2422 or 1-800/387-1240, Ⓦ www.rainbowhighvacations.com. Offers a 15-day gay/lesbian tour of Rajasthan, Delhi and Agra plus Mumbai and Varanasi.

Sangini PO Box 7532, Vasant Kunj, New Delhi 110070. Lesbian information, support and contacts. Helpline Tuesday noon–3pm and Friday 6–8pm on ☎ 011/5567 6450.

Timeless India 340 Somdutt Chamber-II, 9 Bhikaji Cama Place, New Delhi 110066 ☎ 011/2617 4205 or 6, Ⓦ www.timelessexcursions.com. Tour operator offering a gay-oriented tour of Rajasthan, staying in gay-friendly heritage hotels.

Insurance

In the light of the potential health risks involved in a trip to Rajasthan, Delhi or Agra – see p.36 – travel insurance is too important to ignore.

In addition to covering medical expenses and emergency flights, travel insurance also insures your money and belongings against **loss** or **theft**. Before paying for a new policy, however, it's worth checking whether you are already covered: some all-risks home insurance policies may cover your possessions when overseas, and many private medical schemes include cover when abroad. In Canada, provincial health plans usually provide partial **medical cover** for mishaps overseas, while holders of official student/ teacher/youth cards in Canada and the US are entitled to meagre accident coverage and hospital in-patient benefits. Students will often find that their student health coverage extends during the vacations and for one term beyond the date of last enrolment.

Internet

You'll find plenty of **Internet** offices in Delhi, Agra, and all major towns in Rajasthan. Charges range from Rs20 to Rs50 per hour for checking mail and browsing, and extra for printing. ISDN broadband connections are increasingly common.

Laundry

In Rajasthan, Delhi and Agra, no one goes to the laundry: if they don't do their own, they

---

Rough Guides has teamed up with Columbus Direct to offer you travel insurance that can be tailored to suit your needs. Products include a low-cost **backpacker** option for long stays; a **short break** option for city getaways; a typical **holiday package** option; and others. There are also annual **multi-trip** policies for those who travel regularly. Different sports and activities can be usually be covered if required.

See Ⓦ www.roughguidesinsurance .com for eligibility and purchasing options. Alternatively, UK residents should call ☎ 0870/033 9988; US citizens should call ☎ 1-800/749-4922; Australians should call ☎ 1-300/669 999. All other nationalities should call ☎ +44 870/890 2843.

send it out to a dhobi. Wherever you are staying, there will either be an in-house person, or one very close by to call on. The dhobi will take your dirty washing to a *dhobi ghat*, a public clothes-washing area (the bank of a river for example), where it is shown some old-fashioned discipline: separated, soaped and given a damn good thrashing to beat the dirt out of it. Then it is hung out to dry in the sun and, once dried, taken to the ironing sheds where every garment is endowed with razor-sharp creases and then matched to its rightful owner by hidden cryptic markings. Your clothes will come back from the dhobi absolutely spotless, though this kind of violent treatment does take it out of them: buttons get lost and eventually the cloth starts to fray. If you'd rather not entrust your Savile Row made-to-measure to their tender mercies, there are dry-cleaners in most main towns.

Living in Delhi, Agra or Rajasthan

It is illegal for a foreign tourist to work in India, and there's no shortage of English teachers, but you may consider doing some voluntary charitable work. Several charities welcome volunteers on a medium-term commitment, say over two months. People visiting India on business or with employment arranged in advance may apply for a business visa, and non-resident Indians are entitled to stay for up to five years.

If you want to spend your time working as a volunteer for an **NGO (Non-Governmental Organization)**, you should make arrangements well before you arrive by contacting the body in question, rather than on spec. Special visas are generally not required unless you intend to work for longer than six months. For information about which NGOs are operating in Rajasthan, Delhi and Agra, log on to ⊛www.indianngos.com.

It is also possible to study in Delhi as part of an exchange programme.

Charities and NGOs

Animal Aid 4505 SW Massachusetts St, Seattle, WA 98116, USA ☎1-206/935-2670; 27C Neemach Mata Scheme, Dewali, Udaipur 313004, Rajasthan; ⊛www.animalaidsociety.org. Animal welfare group working to alleviate animal suffering in Udaipur (see p.397). No special skills are required, though volunteers with veterinary knowledge are especially welcome.

Concern India Foundation A-52, 1st Floor, Amar Colony, Lajpat Nagar-IV, New Delhi 110024 ☎011/2622 4482 or 3, ⊛www.concernindia.org. Charitable trust supporting grassroots NGOs working with disadvantaged people.

DISHA Foundation Disha Path, Near JDA Park, Nirman Nagar-C, Jaipur 302019, Rajasthan ☎0141/239 3319, ⊛www.dishafoundation.org. Resource centre for children with cerebral palsy. Needs donations, sponsors, and volunteers with time or specific skills.

Friends of Shekhawati c/o Apani Dhani, Nawalgarh 333042, Rajasthan ☎01594/222 239, ⊛www.apanidhani.com/friend. Conservation group aiming to save Shekhewati's art heritage; needs writers, photographers, architects and architecture students to volunteer their services.

Help in Suffering Maharani Farm, Durgapura, Jaipur 302018, Rajasthan ☎0141/276 0803, ℮hisjpr@datainfosys.net. Animal welfare group concentrating on eradicating rabies from Jaipur's feral dog population. Volunteers need to be vets or at least have veterinary experience.

Mandore Medical and Relief Society 1U-D Near Government Bus Stand, Paota, Jodhpur 342006, Rajasthan ☎0291/254 5210, ⊛www.mandore .com. Takes on volunteers for periods as short as a week to work in health awareness and education projects in rural areas around Jodhpur.

Salaam Baalak Trust A12/5, Vasant Vihar, New Delhi 110057 ☎011/2358 4164, ⊛www .salaambaalaktrust.com. Charity working to help street children in Delhi's Paharganj (see p.108). Their website has an application form for volunteers.

Seva Mandir Old Fatehpura, Udaipur 313004, Rajasthan ☎0294/245 1041 or 0960, UK ☎020/7235 7897, US ☎1-732/393 0034 ext 36, ⊛www.sevamandir.org. NGO working in "tribal" villages in the Udaipur district; takes interns to help with development projects.

SOS Children's Villages of India A-7 Nizamuddin (West), New Delhi 110013 ☎011/2435 9450, ⊛www.soscvindia.org. SOS has projects in different parts of India, including Delhi and Rajasthan, giving shelter to distressed children by providing a healthy environment and education including vocational training.

Mail

Mail can take anything from three days to four weeks to get to or from India, and will be faster from Delhi, Jaipur and Agra than from rural Rajasthan. Stamps are not expensive: sending a postcard to anywhere in the world costs Rs8; an aerogramme is Rs8.50. Ideally, you should have mail franked in front of you.

Poste restante (general delivery) services are pretty reliable, though exactly how long individual offices hang on to letters is more or less at their own discretion. Letters are filed alphabetically. To avoid misfiling, your name should be printed clearly, with the surname in large capitals and underlined, but it is still a good idea to check under your first name too, just in case. Have letters addressed to you c/o Poste Restante, GPO (if it's the main post office you want), and the name of the town and state. Don't forget to take ID with you to claim your mail. American Express in Delhi (see p.151) will keep mail for holders of their charge card or traveller's cheques.

Having **parcels** sent out to you in India is not such a good idea – chances are they'll go astray. If you do have a parcel sent, have it registered.

Sending a parcel abroad can be quite a performance. First you have to get it cleared by customs at the post office (they often don't bother, but check), then you take it to a tailor and have it wrapped in cloth, stitched up and sealed with wax. In big city GPOs, people offering this service will be at hand. Next, take it to the post office, fill in and attach the relevant customs forms (it's best to tick the box marked "gift" and give its value as less than Rs1000 or "no commercial value", to avoid bureaucratic entanglements), buy your stamps, see them franked, and dispatch it. Parcels should not be more than 1m long, nor weigh more than 20kg. Surface mail is incredibly cheap, and takes an average of six months to arrive – it may take half, or four times that however, and sometimes it goes astray, or may arrive damaged. It's a good way to dump excess baggage and souvenirs, but don't send anything fragile. Books and magazines can be sent more cheaply, unsealed or wrapped around the middle, as **printed papers** ("book post").

For further information about Indian mail services, visit ⓦwww.indipost.gov.in.

Alternatively, there are numerous **courier** services. These are not as reliable as they should be and there have been complaints of packages going astray; it's safest to stick to known international companies such as DHL, FedEx or UPS. Note that packages from India are likely to be suspect at home, and will often be searched or X-rayed.

Maps

The maps in this book should be sufficient for tourist needs, but you may well need a good road map if you're driving. Road maps of Rajasthan are easy to find at bookshops and newsstands in any town in the state, or in Delhi. The best is published by TTK, on a scale of 1:1,200,000. The same firm also produces reasonably detailed street maps of Jaipur and Agra. In Delhi, the best maps are published annually by Eicher (see p.91 for more on Delhi city maps).

You can find a few interesting maps, including some quite quirky ones (a mineral map of Rajasthan, for example, or a map of the shopping complexes of New Delhi) on the Maps of India website at ⓦwww.mapsofindia.com/maps/rajasthan for Rajasthan, ⓦwww.mapsofindia.com/maps/delhi for Delhi, or ⓦwww.mapsofindia.com/maps/agra for Agra.

Money

India's unit of currency is the **rupee**, usually abbreviated "Rs" and divided into a hundred **paise**. Almost all money is paper, with notes of 10, 20, 50, 100, 500 and 1000 rupees: a few notes of 1, 2 and 5 rupees are still in circulation. Coins come in denominations of 1, 2 and 5 rupees; 10, 20, 25 and 50 paise coins exist but are rarely used.

Banknotes, especially lower denominations, can get into a terrible state, but don't accept **torn banknotes**; no one else will be prepared to take them, so you will be left saddled with the things, though you can change them at the Reserve Bank of India and large branches of other big banks. Don't

Big Numbers

A hundred thousand is a lakh, written 1,00,000; ten million is a crore, written 1,00,00,000. Millions, billions and the like are not in common use.

pass them on to beggars; they can't use them either, so it amounts to an insult.

Outside of big cities, large denominations can also be a problem, as change is usually in short supply. Many Indian people cannot afford to keep much lying around, and you shouldn't necessarily expect shopkeepers or rickshaw-wallahs to have it (and they may – as may you – try to hold onto it if they do). Paying for your groceries with a Rs100 note will probably entail waiting for the grocer's errand boy to go off on a quest to try and change it. Larger notes – like the Rs500 note – are good for travelling with and can be changed for smaller denominations at hotels and other suitable establishments. A word of warning – the Rs500 note looks remarkably similar to the Rs100 note.

At the time of writing, the **exchange rate** was approximately Rs85 to £1 sterling, Rs46 to US$1, Rs58 to €1, Rs40 to Can$1, Rs35 to Aus$1, Rs30 to NZ$1.

Carrying your money

The easiest way to access your money is with **plastic**, though it's a good idea to also have some back-up in the form of cash or traveller's cheques. You will find ATMs to withdraw cash at main banks in all major towns and tourist resorts, though your card issuer may well add a foreign transaction fee, and the Indian bank will also charge a small fee, generally around Rs25. The daily limit on ATM cash withdrawals is usually Rs15,000.

Credit cards are accepted for payment at major hotels, top restaurants, some shops and airline offices, but virtually nowhere else. American Express, MasterCard and Visa are the likeliest to be accepted. Beware of people making extra copies of the receipt, to fraudulently bill you later; insist that the transaction is done before your eyes.

One big downside of relying on plastic as your main access to cash, of course, is that cards can easily get lost or stolen, so take along a couple of alternative ones if you can, keep an emergency stash of cash just in case, and make a note of your home bank's telephone number and website addresses for emergencies.

US dollars are the easiest **currency** to convert, with euros and pounds sterling not far behind. Major hard currencies can be changed easily in tourist areas and big cities, less so elsewhere. If you enter the country with more than US$10,000 or the equivalent, you are supposed to fill in a currency declaration form.

In addition to cash and plastic (or as a generally less convenient alternative to the latter), consider carrying some **traveller's cheques**. You pay a small commission (usually one percent) to buy these with cash in the same currency, a little more to convert from a different currency, but they have the advantage over cash that, if lost or stolen, they can be replaced. Not all banks, however, accept them. Well-known brands such as Thomas Cook and American Express are your best bet, but in some places even American Express is only accepted in US dollars and not as pounds sterling.

It is illegal to carry rupees into India, and you won't get them at a particularly good rate in the West anyhow (though you might in Thailand, Malaysia or Singapore). It is also illegal to take them out of the country.

Banks and forex bureaux

Changing money in regular **banks**, especially government-run banks such as the State Bank of India (SBI), can be a time-consuming business, involving lots of form-filling and queuing at different counters, so change substantial amounts at any one time. Banks in Delhi, Jaipur and Agra are likely to be most efficient, though not all change foreign currency, and some won't take **traveller's cheques** or currencies other than dollars or sterling.

Also in the main cities and the tourist centres, there are usually **forex bureaux**, which are a lot less hassle than banks, though their rates may not be as good. In small towns, the State Bank of India or the State Bank of Jaipur and Bikaner are your best bets but you may want to ask around for an alternative. Rates of commission vary – most banks charge a percentage, many forex bureaux charge none, and some charge a flat rate, so it's always worth asking before you change.

Outside **banking hours** (Mon–Fri 10am–2/4pm, Sat 10am–noon), large hotels may change money, usually at a lower rate, and exchange bureaux have longer opening hours. In Delhi, Thomas Cook at New Delhi station is open 24 hours.

Hold on to **exchange receipts** ("encashment certificates"); they will be required if you want to change back any excess rupees when you leave the country, and to buy air tickets and reserve train berths with rupees.

If you are having **money wired**, many larger post offices act as agencies for Western Union (ⓦwww.westernunion.com), while Moneygram (ⓦwww.moneygram.com) is represented by Trade Wings, Indusind Bank and Thomas Cook. **American Express** (ⓦwww.americanexpress.com/india) and **Thomas Cook** (ⓦwww.thomascook.co.in) both have offices in Delhi and agents in Agra and Jaipur.

Card issuers

Emergency numbers for lost or stolen credit cards.
American Express ☏1800/180 126 or 0124/280 1800
Diners Club ☏044/852 2484
MasterCard ☏000-800/100 1087
Visa ☏001-410/581 9994 or 001-410/581 3836

Opening hours and public holidays

Standard **shop opening hours** in India are Mon–Sat 9.30am–6pm: Most big stores, at any rate, keep those hours, while smaller shops vary from town to town, religion to religion, and one to another, but usually keep longer hours. **Post office** hours are surprisingly variable, and small branch offices may open longer than a town's head post office or GPO. Typically, expect the GPO to open Mon–Sat 10am–3.30pm for services like parcel dispatch or poste restante, with branch offices open 10am–5pm for sale of stamps. **Banks** are typically open Mon–Fri 10am–2/4pm, Sat 10am–noon.

India has only four national **public holidays** as such: Republic Day (26 Jan), Independence Day (15 Aug), Gandhi's birthday (2 Oct) and Christmas Day (25 Dec). In addition, each state sets its own calendar of official holidays, so those in Rajasthan may differ from those in Delhi or Agra. In fact, however, most major Hindu and Muslim holidays, plus the most important Sikh and Christian ones,

are public holidays in Rajasthan, Delhi and Uttar Pradesh (which includes Agra) alike, so you won't find shops or offices in any of those places open on Holi, Dussehra, Diwali, Ashura, Id ul-Fitr, Id ul-Zuha, Christmas Day or Guru Nanak's birthday. For a complete list of festivals, including all those which are public holidays in Rajasthan, Delhi and Agra, see pp.55–56.

Phones

Privately run **phone services** with international **direct dialling** facilities are very widespread. Advertising themselves with the acronyms **STD/ISD** (subscriber trunk dialling/international subscriber dialling), they are extremely quick and easy to use; some even stay open 24 hours. To call abroad, dial the international access code (00), followed by the code for the country you want – 44 for the UK, for example – the appropriate area code (leaving out any initial zero), and the number you want; then you speak, pay your bill, which is calculated in seconds, and leave. Prices vary from office to office, and are usually cheaper in Delhi than in Agra or Rajasthan. Calls to the UK or North America are usually around Rs7–14 per minute, a little more to Ireland, Australasia or Europe, and more again to South Africa. Calling from hotels will be much more expensive. "Call back" (or "back call", as it is often known) is possible at most phone booths and hotels, although check before you call and be aware that, in the case of booths, this facility rarely comes without a charge of Rs3–10 per minute.

Home country direct services are now available from any phone to the UK, the USA, Canada, Ireland, Australia, New Zealand, and a growing number of other countries. These allow you to make a collect or telephone credit card call to that country via an operator there. To use it, you normally dial 000, followed by the country code, and 17; the exception is Canada, for which you dial 000-127.

To **call India** from abroad, dial the international access code (00 in most countries, but generally 011 from North America, 0011 from Australia) followed by 91 for India, the local code minus the initial zero (11 for Delhi, for example), and then the number.

Mobile Phones

Call charges to and from **mobile phones** are far lower in India than western countries, and many foreign tourists sign up to a local network while in the country. To do this you'll need to buy an Indian SIM card from a mobile phone shop; these cost around Rs600, which includes some Rs350-worth of calls. Your retailer will help you get connected. They'll also advise you on which company to use. Airtel and Hutch should cover Rajasthan, Delhi and Agra. Cheaper options are available (from around Rs300), but the problem with these is that, to use your phone outside the company's coverage you'll need to shell out extra for a roaming facility – otherwise, you'll have to buy a new SIM card each time you change state, for example if travelling between Rajasthan and Delhi or Agra. When roaming, both you and your caller pay for incoming calls.

Indian mobile numbers are ten-digit, starting with a 9. However, if you are calling from outside the state where the mobile is based (but not from abroad), you will need to add a zero in front of that.

Photography

Camera **film**, sold at average Western prices, is widely available (but check the date on the box, and note that false boxes containing outdated film are often sold – some firms print holograms on their boxes to prevent this). It's fairly easy to get films developed, though the pictures don't always come out as well as they might at home; Konica and Kodak film laboratories are usually of a good standard. If you're after slide film, slow film or fast film, buy it in the big cities, and don't expect to find specialist

brands such as Velvia; it is rare to find a dealer who keeps film refrigerated. Getting **digital** shots burned onto CD is very easy – a lot of Internet cafés will do it.

When taking photographs, beware of pointing your camera at anything that might be considered "strategic", including airports and anything military, but even at bridges, railway stations and main roads. Remember too that some people prefer not to be photographed, so it is always wise (and only polite, after all) to ask before taking a snapshot of them. Quite often, you'll get people, especially kids, volunteering to pose. Also, remember to guard your equipment from dust – reliable repair is extremely hard to come by in India.

Time

India is on GMT+5hr 30min, which means it is 5hr 30min ahead of Britain and Ireland (4hr 30min when those places are on summer time), 10hr 30min ahead of the US east coast, Ontario and Quebec (9hr 30min when those places are on daylight saving time), 13hr 30min ahead of the US and Canadian Pacific coast (12hr 30min when those places are on daylight saving time), 2hr 30min behind Western Australia, 4hr 30min behind eastern Australia (5hr 30min when daylight saving time is in force there), 6hr 30min behind New Zealand (7hr 30min when daylight saving time is in force there), and 3hr 30min ahead of South Africa. Indian time is referred to as IST (Indian Standard Time, which cynics refer to as "Indian stretchable time").

Tobacco

Indian cigarettes, such as Wills, Gold Flake, Four Square and Charms, are rough but hardly break the bank (Rs10–30 per pack), Alternatively, stock up on imported brands, or rolling tobacco, which is available in the bigger towns and cities. One of the great smells of India is the *bidi*, the cheapest smoke, made of a single low-grade tobacco leaf. If you smoke roll-ups, avoid Indian Capstan cigarette papers which are thick and don't stick very well; Rizlas, where available, are pretty costly, and usually king-size.

Tourist information

The main tourist website for India is ⓦwww .incredibleindia.org.

Delhi and the states of Rajasthan and Uttar Pradesh (which includes Agra) have their own tourism departments, all of which publish an array of printed material, from city maps to glossy leaflets on specific destinations, and can generally answer any specific queries you might have about accommodation and visiting tourist sights.

The Indian government's tourist department has offices in Delhi, Agra and Jaipur, and in major cities and tourist destinations across India, including Mumbai (Bombay), Kolkata (Calcutta), Chennai (Madras) and Bengaluru (Bangalore), plus offices in several foreign countries (see opposite). Uttar Pradesh's tourist information department, UP Tourism, maintains an office in Delhi, and one in Agra, with others elsewhere in Uttar Pradesh, while Rajasthan's Tourism Development Corporation (RTDC) has offices in Delhi, Mumbai, Kolkata and Chennai, as well as throughout Rajasthan. Locations of tourist offices in each town are given in the text.

All of these state and federal tourism organizations, aside from giving out advice and information, sell a wide range of travel facilities, including guided tours, car rental and their own hotels. The federal tourism department's corporate wing, the Indian Tourism Development Corporation (ITDC), for example, runs the Ashok chain of hotels, and operates tour and travel services, frequently competing with its state counterparts.

Indian government tourist offices abroad

Australia Level 2, Piccadilly, 210 Pitt St, Sydney NSW 2000 ☎02/9264 4855, ⓔinfo@indiatourism .com.au.
Canada 60 Bloor St (West), Suite 1003, Toronto, ON M4W 3B8 ☎1-416/ 962-3787 or 8, ⓔindiatourism@bellnet.ca.
The Netherlands Rokin 9–15, 1022 KK, Amsterdam ☎020/620 8991, ⓦwww .indiatourismamsterdam.com.
Singapore 20 Karamat Lane, 01–01A United House, Singapore 228773 ☎6235 3800.
South Africa PO Box 412542, Craighall 2024, Hyde Lane, Lancaster Gate, Johannesburg 2000 ☎011/325 0880, ⓔgoito@global.co.za.
UK 7 Cork St, London W1S 3LH ☎020/7437 3677, ⓔinfo@indiatouristoffice.org.
USA 1270 Ave of Americas, Suite 1808 (18th floor), New York, NY 10020 ☎1-212/586-4901, ⓔrd@itony.com; 3550 Wilshire Blvd, Suite 204, Los Angeles, CA 90010-2485 ☎1-213/380-8855, ⓔindiatourismla@aol.com.

State tourist office websites

Delhi Tourism and Transport Development Corporation (DTTDC) ⓦdelhitourism.nic.in
Rajasthan Tourism Development Corporation (RTDC) ⓦwww.rajasthantourism.gov.in
Uttar Pradesh Tourism ⓦwww.up-tourism.com

Travel advice

Australian Department of Foreign Affairs ⓦwww.smartraveller.gov.au
British Foreign & Commonwealth Office ⓦwww.fco.gov.uk
Canadian Department of Foreign Affairs ⓦwww.voyage.gc.ca
US State Department ⓦwww.travel.state.gov

Guide

Guide

Delhi

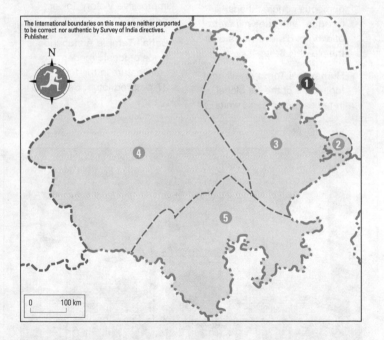

The International boundaries on this map are neither purported to be correct nor authentic by Survey of India directives. Publisher.

N

0   100 km

CHAPTER 1 # Highlights

* **Rajpath** The centrepiece of Lutyens's imperial New Delhi, this wide boulevard epitomizes the spirit of the British Raj. See p.104

* **Red Fort** Delhi's most famous monument, a huge palace-cum-fortress that formed the heart of the Mughal Empire under Shah Jahan. See p.116

* **Jama Masjid** Shah Jahan's pompous congregational mosque, with huge minarets offering bird's-eye views over the old city. See p.119

* **Humayun's Tomb** An elegant forerunner of the Taj Mahal in red sandstone and white

marble, whose lovely gardens offer an escape from the heat. See p.127

* **Safdarjang's Tomb** A decadent rococo successor to the Taj, built at the tail end of the Mughal era. See p.130

* **Qutb Minar Complex** The ruins of Delhi's first incarnation, a thirteenth-century city dominated by an impressive Victory Tower. See p.132

* **Baha'i Temple** A stupendous piece of iconic modern architecture in the form of a 27-petalled lotus. See p.136

△ Jama Masjid

Delhi

Delhi is the symbol of old India and new . . . even the stones here whisper to our ears of the ages of long ago and the air we breathe is full of the dust and fragrances of the past, as also of the fresh and piercing winds of the present.

Jawaharlal Nehru

Site of no fewer than eight successive cities, India's capital **DELHI** is the hub of the Indian Subcontinent, a buzzing international metropolis which draws people from across India and the globe, utterly dwarfing Agra, Jaipur and the cities of Rajasthan, not only in size and density, but also in culture and sophistication. Home to 1.3 crore (thirteen million) people, it's big and it's growing. The National Capital Territory, which marks the city's limits, encompasses 1,483 square kilometres, but burgeoning suburbs like Faridabad, Gurgaon and Noida are expanding beyond its perimeter into the neighbouring states of Haryana and Uttar Pradesh (UP). Yet tucked away inside Delhi's modern suburbs and developments are tombs, temples and ruins that date back centuries; in some areas, the remains of whole cities from the dim and distant past nestle among homes and highways built in just the last decade or two. You'll even find a touch of rural India, in the form of villages where life appears to carry on in its sleepy way, as if they were still out in the countryside rather than slap-bang in the middle of one of the most dynamic cities on earth. The result is a city full of fascinating nooks and crannies that you could happily spend weeks or even months exploring if you've a mind – or the time – to.

Although Rajasthan has three airports currently served by passenger flights, Delhi is where you'll probably land if flying into the region from abroad, and for someone new to India, it isn't a bad place to start. Of all the cities in the region, Delhi is the most cosmopolitan and is quite used to outsiders; you'll find a wide range of hotels at all levels that cater specifically for tourists, and an endless stream of fellow travellers who can give you tips and pointers on anything you're unsure of. Meanwhile, there's no shortage of things to see and do while you acclimatize to Indian ways.

Delhi is an increasingly self-confident city, with stylish shops and fine restaurants, though many Delhiites struggle hard to get by, and poverty is still very much in evidence on its streets. It's the opposite of most cities in having a spacious centre surrounded by older and more densely populated neighbourhoods, in whose narrow thoroughfares the street life is full-on and relentless. Shoppers, hawkers and chai-wallahs all vie frantically for space with stallholders, handcarts, rickshaws, and of course cows.

From a tourist's point of view Delhi is divided into two main parts. **Old Delhi** is the city of the Mughals, created by Shah Jahan and dating back to the

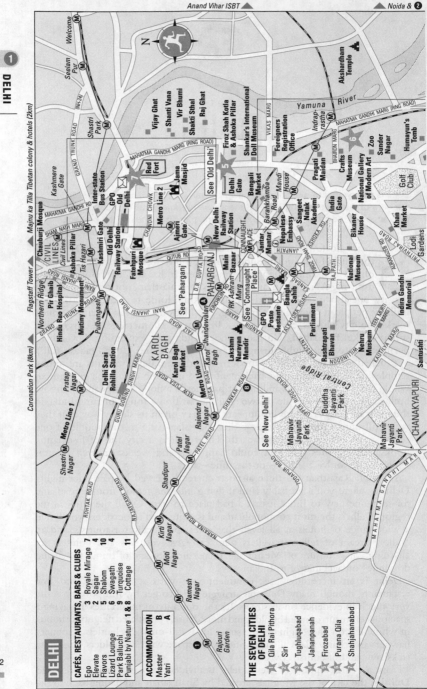

Anand Vihar ISBT ▲

▲ Noida & **2**

N

Yamuna River

Coronation Park (8km) ▲ Flagstaff Tower ▲ Majnu ka Tilla Tibetan colony & hotels (2km) ▲

Akshardham Temple

Seelam Pur Ⓜ

Welcome Ⓜ

NH-24

Shastri Park

Vijay Ghat
Shanti Vana
Vir Bhumi
Shakti Sthal
Raj Ghat

Firoz Shah Kotla & Ashoka Pillar
Shankar's International Doll Museum

VIKAS MARG

Indrap-rastha Ⓜ

MAHATMA GANDHI MARG (RING ROAD)

Foreigners Registration Office
Pragati Maidan Ⓜ
Crafts Museum
National Gallery of Modern Art
Zoo
Sunder Nagar
Humayun's Tomb

BHAIRON MARG

6

Golf Club

Kashmere Gate Ⓜ

GRAND TRUNK ROAD

MAHATMA GANDHI MARG (RING ROAD)

Chauburji Mosque

Civil Lines

CIVIL LINES

Inter-state Bus Station
Red Fort
Jama Masjid
Delhi Gate
Bengali Market
Mandi House
See 'Old Delhi'
5
7

Khan Market

Lodi Gardens

India Gate

Pir Ghaib
Hindu Rao Hospital
Mutiny Monument

Northern Ridge
Flagstaff Tower

GRAND TRUNK ROAD

RANI JHANSI ROAD

Old Delhi
GPO
Old Delhi Railway Station
Chandni Chowk Ⓜ
Metro Line 2
Ajmeri Gate Ⓜ

SHAM NATH MARG

Ashoka Pillar
Kashmiri Gate
Tis Hazari Ⓜ

Fatehpuri Mosque

QUTUB RD
QUTUB ROAD

New Delhi Railway Station Ⓜ
Main Bazaar

See 'Paharganj'

PAHARGANJ

R K Ashram Marg Ⓜ

Jhandewalan Ⓜ

Pulbangash Ⓜ

See 'Connaught Place'
CONNAUGHT PLACE

Jantar Mantar
Nepalese Embassy
Sangeet Natak Akademi
Bikaner House

JANPATH

National Museum
Indira Gandhi Memorial

TEEN MURTI MARG

Sangeet Akademi

Barakhamba Road

SIKANDRA RD

KAROL BAGH

Karol Bagh Market
Karol Bagh Ⓜ

FAIZ ROAD
NEW ROHTAK ROAD
DESH BANDHU GUPTA ROAD

RAJENDRA PLACE
Rajendra Nagar Ⓜ

PUSA ROAD
SHANKAR ROAD

Lakshmi Narayan Mandir

PANCHKUIAN ROAD

Bangla Sahib
GPO Poste Restante
Parliament
Rashtrapati Bhavan

SANSAD MARG

MANDIR MARG

ASHOKA ROAD

Nehru Museum

Santushti

CHANAKYAPURI

Central Ridge

See 'New Delhi'

Buddha Jayanti Park

Mahavir Jayanti Park

Mahavir Jayanti Park

UPPER RIDGE ROAD

CRESCENT ROAD

WILLINGDON

KAUTILYA MARG
SHANTI PATH

PRITHVIRAJ ROAD
AURANGZEB RD

Shastri Nagar Ⓜ

Metro Line 1

Pratap Nagar

Delhi Sarai Rohilla Station

GURU GOBIND SINGH MARG

Shadipur Ⓜ

Patel Nagar Ⓜ

PATEL ROAD

ROHTAK ROAD

Kirti Nagar Ⓜ

Moti Nagar Ⓜ

Ramesh Nagar Ⓜ

Rajouri Garden Ⓜ

1

NAJAFGARH ROAD

RANI JHANSI ROAD
NEW TUSA ROAD

MAHATMA GANDHI MARG

TODAPUR ROAD

▲ Sulabh Museum of Toilets (2km)

DELHI

CAFÉS, RESTAURANTS, BARS & CLUBS

Ego	3
Elevate	2
Flavors	5
Lizard Lounge	6
Park Balluchi	9
Punjabi by Nature	1 & 8
Royale Mirage	7
Sagar	4
Shalom	10
Swagath	4
Turquoise Cottage	11

ACCOMMODATION

Master	B
Yatri	A

THE SEVEN CITIES OF DELHI

☆☆ Qila Rai Pithora
☆☆ Siri
☆☆ Tughluqabad
☆☆ Jahanpanah
☆☆ Firozabad
☆☆ Purana Qila
☆☆ Shahjahanabad

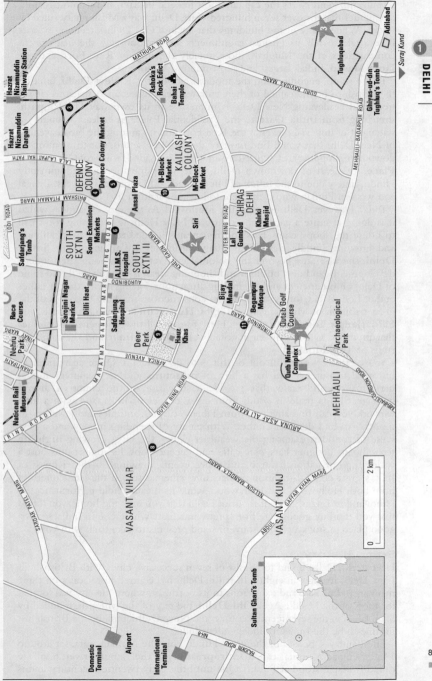

DELHI

Mathura Road

Hazrat Nizamuddin Railway Station

Hazrat Nizamuddin Dargah

Ashoka's Rock Edict

Bahai Temple

Guru Ravidas Marg

Tughluqabad

Adilabad

Ghiyas-ud-din Tughluq's Tomb

Suraj Kund

Mehrauli-Badarpur Road

La Lajpat Rai Path

Defence Colony Market

Defence Colony

N-Block Market

Kailash Colony

M-Block Market

Bhisham Pitamah Marg

Ansal Plaza

Siri

Lal Gumbad

Chirag Delhi

Khirki Masjid

Outer Ring Road

Khel Gaon Marg

Safdarjang's Tomb

Ring Road

South Extn I

South Extn II

South Extension Markets

A.I.I.M.S. Hospital

Aurobindo Marg

Bijay Mandal

Begampur Mosque

Qutb Golf Course

Race Course

Sarojini Nagar Market

Dilli Haat

Safdarjung Hospital

Mahatma Gandhi Marg

Deer Park

Hauz Khas

Africa Avenue

Qutab Minar Complex

Aurobindo Marg

Archaeological Park

National Rail Museum

Nehru Park

Shantipath

Vinay Marg

Ring Road

Sardar Patel Marg

Outer Ring Road

Aruna Asaf Ali Marg

Mehrauli

Mehrauli-Gurgaon Road

Vasant Vihar

Nelson Mandela Marg

Gaffar Khan Marg

Vasant Kunj

Abdul Ghaffar Khan Marg

Domestic Terminal

Airport

International Terminal

NH-8

Rajokri Road

Sultan Ghari's Tomb

0   2 km

Gurgaon Fun n Food Village

seventeenth century. It's the capital's most frenetic quarter, and its most Islamic, a reminder that for over seven hundred years, Delhi was a Muslim city, ruled by sultans. While many of the buildings that enclose Old Delhi's teeming bazaars have a tale to tell, its greatest monuments are undoubtedly the magnificent constructions of the Mughals, most notably the mighty **Red Fort**, and the **Jama Masjid**, India's largest and most impressive mosque.

To the south, encompassing the modern city centre, is **New Delhi**, built by the British to be the capital of their empire's key possession. A spacious city of tree-lined boulevards, New Delhi is impressive in its own way. The **Rajpath**, stretching from **India Gate** to the Presidential Palace, is at least as mighty a statement of imperial power as the Red Fort, and it's among the broad avenues of New Delhi that you'll find most of the city's museums, not to mention its downtown shopping area, centred around the colonnaded facades of **Connaught Place**, the heart of downtown Delhi. Here, the population is predominantly Hindu, largely due to the influx of Hindu (and Sikh) refugees from east Bengal and western Punjab who came here following Partition in 1947.

Today, however, Delhi is spreading southward. As the city expands – which it is doing at quite a pace – the centre of New Delhi is becoming too small to house the shops, clubs, bars and restaurants needed to cater to its affluent and growing middle class. Thus many businesses are moving into **South Delhi**, the vast area beyond the colonial city. Yet here, among the modern developments, and new business and shopping areas, is where you'll find some of Delhi's most ancient and fascinating attractions. Facing each other at either end of Lodi Road, for example, lie the constructions marking two ends of the great tradition of Mughal garden tombs: **Humayun's Tomb**, its genesis, and **Safdarjang's Tomb**, its last gasp. Here too, you'll find the remains of cities that preceded Old Delhi, most notably the **Qutb Minar** and the rambling ruins of **Tughluqabad**.

You certainly won't run out of things to do in Delhi. Quite apart from its historical treasures, Delhi has a host of **museums** and art treasures, cultural performances and crafts that provide a showcase of the country's diverse heritage. **Shops** trade in goods from every corner of India, and with a little legwork you can find anything from Tibetan carpets, antiques and jewellery to modern art and designer clothes. With plenty of spending money and a new sense of confidence among the wealthier classes, the city's growing **nightlife** scene boasts designer bars, chic cafés and decent clubs. Its auditoriums host a wide range of national music and dance events, drawing on the richness of India's great classical traditions. Smart new cinemas screen the latest offerings from both Hollywood and Bollywood, while its theatres hold performances in Hindi and in English. And if it's from Delhi that you're flying home, you'll find that you can buy goods here from pretty much anywhere else in India, so it's a good place to stock up with souvenirs and presents to take back with you.

Some history

Historically, Delhi is said to consist of seven successive cities, with British-built New Delhi making an eighth. In truth, Delhi has centred historically on three main areas: **Lal Kot** and extensions to its northeast, where the city was located for most of the Middle Ages; **Old Delhi**, the city of the Mughals, founded by Shah Jahan in the seventeenth century; and **New Delhi**, built by the British just in time to be the capital of independent India.

The Pandavas, heroes of the great Hindu epic the Mahabharata, set around 1450 BC, had a capital called **Indraprastha** on the Yamuna river; a village called Indrapat stood at Purana Qila until the early twentieth century, and is generally assumed to have been the same place. In 1060, a Rajput clan called the **Tomars** founded **Lal Kot**, considered the first city of Delhi. A hundred years later, a rival Rajput clan, the **Chauhans** from Ajmer, made themselves overlords of the Tomars and expanded Lal Kot, renaming it **Qila Rai Pithora**, but they only kept it till 1191, when the city fell to the armies of Muhammad of Ghor, a Turkic Muslim from Afghanistan, thus ushering in six centuries of Islamic rule.

Muhammed left Delhi in the charge of his general, **Qutb-ud-din Aibak**, and went back to Afghanistan, where he was assassinated. Qutb-ud-din then set himself up as an independent ruler, thus founding the state that was to become known as the **Delhi Sultanate**. Qutb-ud-din had originally held the status of a slave so his heirs were known as the **Slave Dynasty**. His son-in-law and successor **Iltutmish** (1211–36), greatest of the early Delhi sultans, expanded his territory both eastward and westward, making Delhi the capital of lands stretching all the way from Punjab to Bengal.

Another group of Central Asian Turks, the **Khaljis**, took over the Delhi Sultanate from the Slave Dynasty in 1290, and it was their most illustrious ruler, **Ala-ud-din** (1296–1316), who in 1303 founded **Siri**, known as the "second city of Delhi", though it was actually just a citadel to give the unpopular king a base outside the city. Ala-ud-din's son and successor was assassinated by a power-hungry subordinate, giving Ala-ud-din's lieutenant, **Ghiyas-ud-din Tughluq**, the excuse to step in and become sultan himself, and so instituting the **Tughluq dynasty**. It was Ghiyas-ud-din who had Delhi's third city built at **Tughluqabad**, 8km east of Lal Kot in 1321. His successor, **Muhammad Tughluq** – despite an abortive attempt to move the capital 1100km south to Daulatabad – was responsible for Delhi's "fourth city", **Jahanpanah**, really just a northeastward extension of Lal Kot, filling in the area between that and Siri. The energies of the next sultan, **Firoz Shah**, were mostly taken up with suppressing rebellion, but he left his mark by building a fortified palace at Firoz Shah Kotla in 1354. It was evidently meant to be the stronghold of a new city called **Firozabad**, considered Delhi's fifth incarnation, but he never actually built beyond the citadel.

In 1398, Delhi fell to the forces of Timur the Lame (Tamerlaine), a Central Asian warlord, who completely ransacked it. Many of its residents fled, including the sultan, leaving a deserted city and a power vacuum, which was eventually filled by **Khizr Khan**, a follower of Timur. He founded a new dynasty of sultans, the **Sayyids** (1414–44), but they ruled little more than Delhi and its hinterland; the days of a powerful Delhi sultanate were over, and the Sayyids' reign was fractious, frequently reduced to civil war by internal power struggles. Out of these emerged a new sultan, **Buhlul Lodi**, a Punjabi ruler originally called in to support one of the Sayyid factions. He enlarged Delhi's territory and established the **Lodi dynasty**, whose tombs grace Lodi Gardens (see p.129), but his son Sikandar moved his capital to Agra, thus ending the Delhi Sultanate once and for all. It was Sikandar's son, Ibrahim, however, who laid the foundations for the empire that would succeed it, by being such a tyrant that one of his nobles asked for help from the founder of the Mughals, **Babur**.

Babur's 1526 victory at Panipat (see p.382) made him master of Delhi and Agra, but his son **Humayun**, lost them, along with most of his father's conquests, to the Afghan king **Sher Shah Suri**. Sher Shah is credited with building the "sixth city of Delhi" at **Purana Qila**, again just a citadel, though, as with Firozabad, it's likely a new city was intended to be built around it. Humayun retook Delhi in 1555, but died the following year, and was succeeded by his son **Akbar**, who, like Sikandar Lodi, moved his court to Agra. Akbar's grandson, **Shah Jahan**, shifted it back, creating Delhi's "seventh city", Shahja-hanabad, now known as **Old Delhi**. Shah Jahan was eventually deposed and imprisoned by his ruthless son, **Aurangzeb**, who ruled from Delhi until 1681, and then transferred the capital to Aurangabad on the Deccan plateau, though his son and successor **Bahadur Shah I** moved it back in 1712.

After Aurangzeb's death in 1707, as the Mughal empire started to disinte-grate, Delhi fell victim to successive invasions by rebels and opportunistic outsiders. In 1739, in an echo of Timur's invasion, **Nadir Shah** of Persia sacked the city and slaughtered an estimated twenty thousand of its inhabit-ants. A decade later, with Nadir Shah's ally, Ahmad Shah Durrani, threatening Delhi, the Mughal governor of Avadh (eastern Uttar Pradesh), **Safdarjang**, took over as vizier and saved the day. When he was ousted for being a Shi'ite, his son led Avadh to independence, reducing Delhi's hinterland still further, so that the empire's tax base was not even sufficient to finance its army. In 1757, Ahmad Shah Durrani took Delhi just to plunder it, and of the next emperor, Shah Alam II (1761–1805), it was said, "The kingdom of Shah Alam/ Runs from Delhi to Palam", Palam being a village near Dwarka, just northwest of Delhi airport. Urdu poets even developed a new genre of verse called *shahr ashob* ("ruined city") to lament the city's decline. In 1784, the **Marathas** (see p.385) subdued Delhi and made the emperor their vassal. They bit off more than they could chew, however, when they took on the **British**, who in 1803 beat them in battle at Patparganj (near Akshardham Temple) and brought Delhi into the North-Western Provinces of the East India Company's Bengal-based empire. The Brits allowed the emperor to stay on under their control, but his position was now purely ceremonial.

The Mughals' final undoing was the **1857 uprising** against the British – the Mutiny or First War of Independence. It began at Meerut, 64km to the northeast, with a revolt by sepoy troops in the Company's army, who then made for Delhi to seek the blessing of emperor **Bahadur Shah II**. He had little choice but to give it, committing himself to a full-scale rebellion to restore Mughal rule and throw out the foreign occupiers. Sepoys and mobs of rioters killed any Christian Europeans and Indian converts they could find, as their comrades from other regiments poured into Delhi to support them, along with jihadist militants, and the British took up a position overlooking the city on the Northern Ridge, around the Flagstaff Tower and Hindu Rao's house (now part of the Hindu Rao Hospital; see p.126). Most Delhiwallahs, particularly the poor, supported the uprising, though the rich were more ambivalent, especially when mobs started looting the city's havelis while gangs of sepoys robbed and extorted its inhabitants. With little discipline, strategy or intelligence about the enemy, the insurgents failed to destroy the British position when they had the chance. Meanwhile, bandits took control of the surrounding countryside, and the British called in reinforcements from the Punjab. When they finally recaptured the city, they went on a rampage of destruction and murder, killing some three thousand people in bloody and indiscriminate **reprisals**. Bahadur Shah was packed off to exile in Burma, and almost Delhi's entire population was turfed out, its Muslims not allowed to return for two years.

After abolishing the East India Company, along with the Mughal empire, in the wake of the 1857 uprising, the British, in their new incarnation as the **Raj**, at first kept their administration in Calcutta, but in 1911 decided to make Delhi India's new capital. Fervent construction of bungalows, parliamentary buildings and public offices followed, and in 1931, **New Delhi** – the city's eighth incar-nation – was officially inaugurated as the capital, the same year the British agreed in principle to India's eventual independence.

The Seven Cities of Delhi (plus one)

1. **Lal Kot (Qila Rai Pithora)** The area around the Qutb Minar, at the heart of medieval Delhi, founded by the Tomars in 1060 (see p.134).

2. **Siri** Actually a fortress rather than a city, commissioned by Ala-ud-din in 1303 (see p.131).

3. **Tughluqabad** A fortified city built for Ghiyas-ud-din Tughluq in 1321 but deserted soon after (see p.136).

4. **Jahanpanah** Founded by Muhammad Tughluq in 1326 as an extension of Lal Kot, joining it to Siri (see p.131).

5. **Firozabad** A fortified palace, Firoz Shah Kotla, is the only part of this supposed city that we know of for sure, founded by Firoz Shah in 1354 (see p.124).

6. **Purana Qila** Built as a fortress for Sher Shah in 1533, possibly on the site of ancient Indraprastha (see p.111).

7. **Old Delhi (Shahjahanabad)** Founded by Shah Jahan in 1638 to be the capital of Mughal India (see p.113).

8. **New Delhi** Inaugurated by the British in 1931 as the capital of their prize colony, which gained independence just sixteen years later (see p.102).

When **Independence** finally came, in 1947, it was in Delhi that the British handed over power to India's first democratically elected government under **Jawaharlal Nehru**. In the wake of **Partition**, however, Hindu mobs turned on Delhi's Muslim population, nearly half of whom fled to Pakistan, ending centuries of Muslim dominance in the city. They were replaced by Hindu and Sikh refugees from the Pakistani sectors of Punjab and Bengal, so many, in fact, that whole new districts had to be created to house them (Chittaranjan Park in South Delhi, for example, was originally EBDPC – East Bengal Displaced Persons' Colony, and it remains predominantly Bengali to this day).

In 1957, in the wake of a huge rise in the capital's population, the **Delhi Development Authority (DDA)** was founded to plan the city's development, and has largely been responsible for the shape of its expansion. For many Delhiites, the DDA's most visible activity has been in housing, with something like half the city's population now living in DDA-built homes.

Indira Gandhi's **Emergency** in 1975–77 saw violent evictions of Old Delhi's predominantly Muslim slum-dwellers, who were sent to live in disease-ridden housing out of town, an event recalled by Salman Rushdie at the end of his novel *Midnight's Children*. Following Indira's 1984 assassination by her Sikh bodyguards, it was the turn of the city's Sikh population to fall victim to **sectarian riots** (Khushwant Singh's novel, *Delhi*, reviewed on p.424, records that evil episode in fiction).

In 1992, having previously been a Union Territory, administered directly by the federal government, Delhi gained a status similar to that of Washington DC or ACT's Canberra, with its own government, but lesser powers than those of a state. The Hindu sectarian BJP won power that year in the first **Capital Territory** election, but lost in 1998 to Congress, who have controlled the administration since then.

Delhi's most obvious demographic change in the last couple of decades has been the **rise of the middle class**, with increasing numbers of relatively prosperous professionals, particularly in South Delhi. The area around Delhi's "first city" at Lal Kot is among those that are becoming quite gentrified, and saw the opening of a plush multiplex cinema in 1997 and a golf course in 2000.

The explosion of telephone **call centres**, of which the first opened in 1998, has brought lucrative jobs to many English-speaking Delhiites; call centre workers typically earn Rs12,000–14,000 for a 50-hour week, which is around three times the wage of an unskilled industrial worker. The latest trend, however, is for more prosperous Delhiites to move out of town, to satellite suburbs such as Gurgaon and Noida, and often now even further afield. Meanwhile **forced relocation** of shantytown dwellers continues, in a more low-key manner than during the Emergency. Despite this, unemployed rural migrants in search of work continue to pour into Delhi's slums from India's poorer and less developed states, often facing outright hostility from some of Delhi's existing residents. Clearly, Delhi is on the up, but despite its evident prosperity, it still has a number of difficult issues to resolve.

Arrival

Delhi is India's main point of arrival for overseas visitors, and the major transport hub for foreigners heading to Rajasthan and Agra, as well as the rest of north India. The **airport**, 20km southwest of the centre, has two separate terminals – one handling international flights, the other domestic services; although adjacent, they're 6km apart by road. The capital is served by four long-distance **train stations**, but the vast majority of services used by tourists arrive and depart from either Old Delhi or New Delhi stations, although a few useful services use Hazrat Nizamuddin in the southeast and Sarai Rohilla in the northwest. State **buses** from all over the country pull into the Maharana Pratap ISBT in Old Delhi, while a few services from Uttar Pradesh and Uttarakhand use the Anand Vihar ISBT in the east of the city.

By air

International flights land at **Indira Gandhi International (IGI) Airport** Terminal 2, while domestic services land at Terminal 1. There are no ATMs at the airport (though this may change), but State Bank of India and Thomas Cook in the arrivals lounge offer 24hr money-changing facilities; be sure to get some small change for taxis and rickshaws. For those seeking accommodation, 24hr desks here, including Indian Tourism (ITDC) and Delhi Tourism (DTTDC), have a list of approved hotels and will secure reservations by phone. A free AAI **shuttle** bus runs hourly between the two terminals.

From the international airport the easiest way to get into Delhi is by **taxi**, particularly advisable if you arrive late at night. There are several official pre-paid taxi kiosks in the restricted area outside the arrival hall; the fare will be around Rs250 to the city centre, with a 25 percent surcharge between 11pm and 5am; prices vary from kiosk to kiosk, so you might check a few before plumping. It's worth noting, however, that even some of these pre-paid taxi drivers may try to take you to hotels not of your choice (see box opposite).

Alternatively there's the **bus** (Rs50; 40min). Tickets for the ex-servicemen's shuttle (EATS) and the Delhi Transport Corporation (DTC) are available from their respective counters in the arrival hall. Both services go via the domestic terminal and take around thirty minutes; EATS drops you off at Connaught Place F-block in the city centre, DTC much less conveniently at Maharana Pratap ISBT in Old Delhi, which is only really handy if you're staying in Majnu ka Tilla.

The **auto-rickshaws** that wait in line at the departure gate constitute the most precarious and least reliable form of transport from the airport, especially

Delhi scams

Delhi can prove a headache for the first-time visitor because of the numerous **scams** designed to entrap the unwary – one of the dirtier dodges is to dump dung onto visitors' shoes, then charge ridiculous amounts to clean it off. The most common scheme, though, is for taxi drivers or touts to convince you that the hotel you've chosen is full, closed or has just burned to the ground. More sophisticated scammers will pretend to phone your hotel to check for yourself, or will take you to a travel agent (often claiming to be a "tourist office") who will do it, dialling for you (a different number); the "receptionist" on the line will corroborate the story, or deny all knowledge of your reservation. The driver or tout will then take you to a "very good hotel" – usually in Karol Bagh market – where you'll be pressured into parting with a hefty sum of money for one night's accommodation – rates vary according to how gullible/stressed/tired/affluent you seem to be. To **reduce the risk of being caught out**, write down the registration number of your taxi (make sure the driver sees you doing it), and absolutely insist on going to your hotel, and without any stops en route. If you're heading for Paharganj, your driver may well attempt to take you to a hotel of his choice rather than yours. To avoid such conflict, you could ask to be dropped at New Delhi railway station and walk to your hotel from there. You may even encounter fake "doormen" outside hotels who'll tell you the place is full; check at reception first, and even if the claim turns out to be true, never follow the tout to anywhere he may recommend. Bear in mind, though, that most problems can be avoided by **reserving a room in advance**; many hotels will arrange for a car and driver to meet you at your point of arrival.

New Delhi railway station is the worst place of all for touts; assume that anyone who approaches you here – even in uniform – with offers of help, or to direct you to the foreigners' booking hall, is up to no good. Most are trying to lure travellers to the fake "official" tourist offices opposite the Paharganj entrance, where you'll end up paying way over the correct price, often for unconfirmed tickets. And don't believe tall tales that the foreigners' booking hall has closed. On **Connaught Place** and along **Janpath**, steer clear of phoney "tourist information offices" or travel agents that falsely claim to be "government authorized" – some are even decorated with GOI tourist posters. The official Government of India tourist office is at 88 Janpath and the DTTDC is in Block N, Middle Circle.

Finally, be aware that taxi, auto and rental-car drivers get a hefty commission for taking you to certain shops, and that commission will be added to your bill should you buy anything. You can assume that auto-wallahs who accost you on the street do so with the intention of overcharging you, or of taking you to shops which pay them commission rather than straight to where you want to go. Always hail a taxi or auto-rickshaw yourself, rather than taking one whose driver accosts you, and don't let them take you to places where you haven't asked to go.

at night, though they're cheaper than a taxi; fares are around Rs100–150. Many hotels, including some of the Paharganj budget options, now offer **pick-up services** from the airport, where you will be met with a driver bearing your name on a placard. This presents the smoothest and most reliable method of getting to your hotel from the airport, though prices vary considerably, starting from as little as Rs200 to more than the cost of a prepaid taxi.

By train

Delhi has two major **railway stations**. **New Delhi Station** is at the eastern end of Paharganj Main Bazaar, within easy walking distance of many of the area's budget hotels. The station has two exits: take the Paharganj exit for

Connaught Place and most points south, and the Ajmeri Gate exit for Old Delhi. Cycle rickshaws ply the congested main bazaar toward Connaught Place – which is just 800m down the road – but cannot enter Connaught Place itself. Auto-rickshaws start at Rs20 for Connaught Place, or Rs35 to Old Delhi – agree a price before getting in. **Old Delhi Station**, west of the Red Fort, is also well connected to the city by taxis, auto-rickshaws and cycle-rickshaws; for autos there's a booth selling fixed-price pre-paid tickets – Connaught Place is Rs40, plus Rs5 per piece of baggage. Both rail stations are notorious for **theft**: don't take your eyes off your luggage for a moment. These stations are also on the metro, but travelling on it with heavy baggage is prohibited. The other long-distance stations are **Hazrat Nizamuddin**, southeast of the centre, for trains from Agra (except the Shatabdi Express); and **Sarai Rohilla**, west of Old Delhi station, for some services from Rajasthan. Hazrat Nizamuddin has a pre-paid auto booth; Connaught Place is Rs50, and around the same from Sarai Rohilla. If you're lucky you may connect with a local train into New Delhi, but these tend to be sardine-can packed, and buying a ticket can be a real scrum.

By bus

Buses run by Rajasthan Roadways, as well as state-run buses from other north Indian states, pull in at the **Maharana Pratap Inter-state Bus Terminal (ISBT)**, north of Old Delhi railway station. Auto-rickshaws to New Delhi or Paharganj take around fifteen minutes (and cost approximately Rs50), cycle rickshaws take twice that (around Rs30). There's a pre-paid auto-rickshaw booth at the terminal (on the west side, and also just southeast of the terminal on Dr HP Hedgewar Marg, under the elevated metro line). The metro station is by the terminal (Kashmere Gate). RTDC buses from Jaipur, Ajmer, Jodhpur and Udaipur drop you at **Bikaner House** near India Gate (Connaught Place is Rs30 by auto). **Private buses** from Agra and some from Rajasthan may deposit you at **Sarai Kale Khan ISBT** by Hazrat Nizamuddin train station (cross over by the footbridge for pre-paid autos; Rs50 to Connaught Place). Private buses may also pull up in the street outside New Delhi railway station; some even drop passengers in Connaught Place. A few services, mainly from Uttarakhand, leave you at **Anand Vihar ISBT**, across the Yamuna towards Ghaziabad in east Delhi, which also has a pre-paid auto-rickshaw booth (an auto into town should cost around Rs60), and is served by bus #85 to Connaught Place.

Information

There are reasonably helpful tourist offices at the international and domestic airports, railway stations and bus terminals, and the **Government of India (GOI) tourist office** at 88 Janpath, just south of Connaught Place (Mon–Fri 9am–6pm, Sat 9am–2pm; ☎011/2332 0005 or 8, ⓦwww.incredibleindia.org), is a good place to pick up information on historical sites, city tours, shopping and cultural events, as well as free city maps. You can change money and reserve accommodation at the extremely useful **DTTDC** (Delhi Tourism and Transport Development Corporation) office, N-36, Bombay Life Building, Middle Circle, Connaught Place (Mon–Sat 9am–6pm, ☎011/5152 3073, ⓦdelhitourism.nic .in). For travel information as such, DTTDC have another office with longer hours (daily 7am–9pm; ☎011/6539 0009) in *Coffee House*, 1 Annexe, Emporium Complex, Baba Kharak Singh Marg, opposite Hanuman Mandir, which does not have money-changing facilities. They also have a kiosk a little further along the same street, and others in New Delhi rail station (☎011/2374 2374), Hazrat Nizamuddin station (☎011/6547 0605), and at the airport. Beware of any other firms that look like or claim to be tourist offices (see box, p.89).

Exhibitions and cultural events are listed in local **magazines** such as the weekly *Delhi Diary* and fortnightly *Delhi City*; both with comprehensive directories and a basic city map. The monthly *First City* is more like a proper listings magazine, with features and editorial content. All three are available from bookshops and street stalls; *Delhi Diary* can sometimes be found for free at big hotels or at the GOI tourist office. **Online**, apart from the DTTDC's website, it's worth checking the Delhi pages of India for You at ⓦ www.indfy.com/delhi .html for sightseeing information, the Delhi city government's tourism pages at ⓦ dclhigovt.nic.in/page.asp for general information, and for current listings the My CityPedia site at ⓦ www.delhi-india.net or the DelhiLive site at ⓦ www .delhilive.com. There's also an excellent Delhi blog with news and views about the city at ⓦ thedelhiwalla.blogspot.com.

Should you need a more detailed **map**, Eicher's *Delhi Road Map* (Rs75 from bookshops or newsstands) is one of the best; the same firm produces a even more comprehensive *Delhi City Map* in book form, with street index, for Rs290. If you're going to spend some time in Delhi and want an in-depth **guide** to its ancient monuments, *Delhi: a Thousand Years of Building* by Lucy Peck (INTACH/Roli, 2005) covers just about every building or ruin of historical or architectural interest in the city, with exhaustive descriptions of each, and detailed maps showing their locations.

City transport

Despite a spanking new metro system, **public transport** in Delhi is still inadequate for the city's population and size, and increased car ownership is adding to the general chaos. **Cows** have been banned from much of central Delhi, but in the city's more traditional districts they still amble along, or sit down for a rest in the middle of the street, leaving traffic to career round them. In an effort to reduce pollution, the city's buses, taxis and auto-rickshaws have all now been converted from petrol and diesel to run on **compressed natural gas** (CNG), but most inner-city thoroughfares are still choked with exhaust fumes and congested.

The metro

New Delhi's brand new **metro system** opened in December 2002, with the capacity to carry two hundred thousand passengers daily. It's being built in several phases, with work projected to continue until at least 2021. There are three lines, two traversing the city from east to west, and a shorter one running north to south. The **red line** (line 1) runs from Barwala in the northwest to Shahdara across the Yamuna river in the northeast. The **yellow line** (line 2) runs from Vishwa Vidyalaya in the north to the Central Secretariat, interchanging with the red line at Kashmere Gate (by Maharana Pratap ISBT), and continuing to Old Delhi (Chandni Chowk) and New Delhi rail stations and Connaught Place (Rajiv Chowk). The **blue line** (line 3) starts at Dwarka in the southwest and terminates at Indrapastha near Purana Qila, interchanging with the yellow line at Rajiv Chowk. All three lines are due to be extended at both ends in the near future, most notably the yellow line, which will continue southward to

DELHI METRO

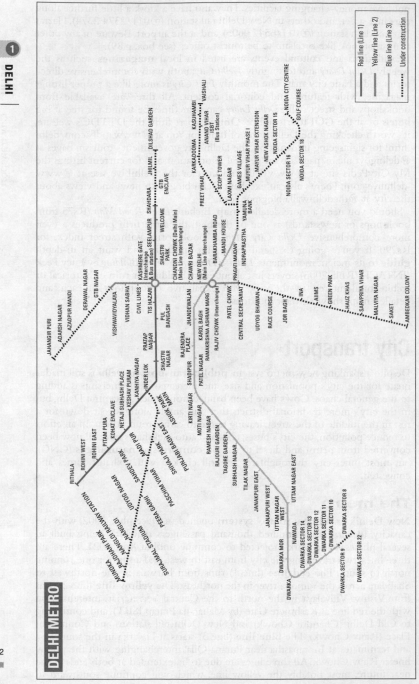

Red line (Line 1)

Yellow line (Line 2)

Blue line (Line 3)

Under construction

City and regional tours

The DTTDC tourist office (see p.90) organizes a/c bus **tours** of New Delhi (9am–2pm; Rs105), and Old Delhi (2.15–5.15pm; Rs105), plus a full-day tour which covers both (9am–5.15pm; Rs205). All start outside the DTTDC office opposite the Hanuman Mandir on Baba Kharak Singh Marg. From the same place, they run a "Delhi by Evening" tour (Tues–Sun; Rs150), which includes sound and light at the Red Fort, and an Agra day-trip (depart 7am, return 10pm; Rs950). Delhi Transport Corporation (☎011/2884 4192) run one-day tours for Rs100, starting from New Delhi rail station at 9.15am, Scindia House in Connaught Place (corner of Janpath) at 9.30am, or the Red Fort at 9.45am. All the five-star hotels offer their own, door-to-door packages, and many hotels in and around Paharganj, such as *Namaskar* and *Metropolis*, can arrange city tours by taxi for Rs500–600, which is good value when shared between three or four people.

Hauz Khas and beyond, while the blue line will be extended to Anand Vihar ISBT and Noida. For progress updates, ask at the tourist offices (see p.90) or visit ⓦ www.delhimetrorail.com.

The minimum fare on the metro is currently Rs6, and tokens to open the electronic gates can only be purchased at metro stations. It is also possible to get tourist cards which allow unlimited travel for a day (Rs70) or three days (Rs150), but since the highest fare from the centre is currently Rs15, you are unlikely to profit by buying one. Long-term stayers in Delhi may want to consider a stored-value card, which can be charged up with Rs100, Rs200 or Rs500 at a time, valid for a year from the last charge-up. The metro is wheelchair accessible, and each station should have an ATM. Children under 90cm (3ft) tall travel free if accompanied by an adult. Note that photography is strictly prohibited on the metro.

Especially in the centre of town, metro trains can become very crowded at certain times of day (mid-mornings and early evenings). Delhiites are still developing metro etiquette which natives of other cities may take for granted; people stand on both sides of the escalators, for example, and sometimes don't let passengers off the train before barging on, so you may have to fight your way off at busy stations such as Rajiv Chowk, though the authorities are addressing the problem, and things should change in the near future.

Buses

With auto- and cycle rickshaws so cheap and plentiful, only hardened shoestring travellers will want to use Delhi's confusing and overcrowded **buses**. The first digit of the three-digit route number shows the direction of each bus – thus routes starting with "5" head south from the centre towards Mehrauli, and those starting with "4" travel southeast towards Kalkaji through Nizamuddin, while those starting with "1" go north through Old Delhi. **Useful bus routes** include the #505 from Ajmeri Gate and Connaught Place (Super Bazaar and the corner of Kasturba Gandhi Marg) to the National Museum, Safdarjang's Tomb, Hauz Khas and the Qutb Minar. Connecting Old and New Delhi, bus #246 runs from Shivaji Terminal, off Connaught Place behind Block P, to the Red Fort. Bus #101 goes from Shivaji Terminal to Maharana Pratap ISBT, and bus #85 runs from Connaught Place (Outer Circle, opposite the Plaza Cinema) to Anand Vihar ISBT. The #181, #893 and #966 connect Connaught Place (Outer Circle, opposite the Plaza Cinema) with Humayun's Tomb and Nizamuddin. It is possible to check bus routes **on** line at ⓦ delhigovt.nic.in/dtcbusroute/dtc/Find_Route/getroute.asp, but the website still needs a little honing, and the lists of bus stops currently given do not always use names that will be familiar to tourists – for buses from Connaught Place, for example, you would need to check Jantar Mantar, Regal Cinema, Scindia House (the stop in Kasturba Gandhi Marg), Shivaji Stadium (the terminal behind Block P) and Super Bazar.

Auto-rickshaws and cycle rickshaws

Auto-rickshaws ("autos") – India's three-wheeler taxis – are the most effective form of transport around Delhi, although their drivers are notoriously anarchic. Some auto-wallahs will offer to use the meter, but in general you'll need to negotiate a price before getting in, and try to have the exact change ready; prices for foreigners vary considerably according to your haggling skills and the mood of the driver, but as a sample fare, it should cost about Rs40 from Connaught Place to Old Delhi. Auto stands, which dot the city, are the best places to pick up auto-rickshaws, though they can also be hailed in the street. In Connaught Place itself, there's a pre-paid auto-rickshaw kiosk, charging certified official fares, on the innermost circle between the two halves of Palika Bazaar, and another on Janpath outside the Government of India tourist office.

Cycle rickshaws are not allowed in Connaught Place and parts of New Delhi, but are handy for short journeys to outlying areas and around Paharganj. They're also nippier than motorized traffic in Old Delhi. Rates should be roughly half that demanded by autos.

While auto- and rickshaw-wallahs may well try to take advantage of you by overcharging, do bear in mind that cycle rickshaw-wallahs in particular are among the city's poorest residents, and it really isn't worth haggling them down to the absolute minimum fare or arguing with them over what will amount in the end to a trifling sum. Most tourists accept that they are going to pay a bit more than local residents, and when you see how hard your rickshaw-wallah has to work, you may well feel he deserves a hefty tip on top of that.

Taxis

Delhi's **taxis** (white, or black and yellow) cost around fifty percent more than auto-rickshaws and are generally safe and reliable. Drivers belong to local taxi stands, where you can make bookings and fix prices; if you flag a taxi down on the street you're letting yourself in for some hectic haggling. A surcharge of around 25 percent operates between 11pm and 5am. Alternatively, Dial-a-Cab (☏1920) and Mega Cabs (☏1929) offer a 24-hour call-a-cab service with air-conditioned cars (in summer at least), and tamper-proof digital meters, though expect to pay a bit more than usual.

From New Delhi (Connaught Place) to Old Delhi (eastern end of Chandni Chowk, opposite the Red Fort), there's a **shared jeep taxi** service costing Rs6 and leaving when full.

Car and cycle rental

For local sightseeing and journeys beyond the city confines, **chauffeur-driven cars** are very good value, especially for groups of three to four. Many budget hotels offer cars and drivers, as does the DTTCC tourist office (see p.90), and the booths at the southern end of the Tibetan Market on Janpath. DTTDC rates are Rs630 for an eight-hour day within Delhi, which includes 80km mileage;

if you want an a/c vehicle, the rate is Rs870. Alternatively, there's Kumar Tourist Taxi Service, K-14 Connaught Place (☎011/2341 5930, ⓦkumar.tt.free.fr). Driving yourself in Delhi can be dangerous, and we don't really advise it, but if you are confident of your ability to negotiate the city's traffic, car rental agency addresses can be found on p.151.

Cycling in the large avenues of New Delhi takes some getting used to and can be hazardous for those not used to chaotic traffic. **Bicycle rental** is surprisingly difficult to come by; try Mehta Cycles (☎011/2358 9239) at 5109–10 Main Bazaar, Paharganj, almost opposite *Hotel Vishal*, who rent pushbikes for Rs50 a day.

Accommodation

Delhi has a vast range of **accommodation**, from dirt-cheap lodges to extravagant international hotels. Its deluxe hotels are as good as you'll get anywhere in the world, and in terms of service in particular, often far superior to their counterparts in the west, while the mid-range hotels offer unbeatable value for money, though you do have to pick and choose. Bookings for upmarket hotels can be made at airport and railway station tourist desks, but even budget hotels can be booked by phone or e-mail, though it's often touch and go whether such bookings will be honoured if you turn up late in the day. Most hotels in Delhi have a noon checkout time.

The hotels in **Connaught Place** are handy for banks, restaurants and shops, and transport connections to the main sights, but you do pay more to stay there. North of Connaught Place, the busy market area of **Paharganj** and the adjacent **Ram Nagar**, close to New Delhi railway station, feature the best of the budget accommodation. Many of Delhi's luxury hotels are located in the **south**, where you'll also find the city's **youth hostel**. North of Old Delhi, the Tibetan colony of **Majnu Ka Tilla** has a few good places to stay, but is a little bit out of the way.

Connaught Place and around

You pay a premium to stay on **Connaught Place** itelf, so if you want value for money, stay elsewhere. To its south, grander hotels on and around **Janpath** and along **Sansad Marg** cater mainly for business travellers and tourist groups, but there are some very good ones among them. Most upmarket hotels have plush restaurants and swimming pools, and some require non-Indian residents to pay in foreign currency. Of the budget travellers' lodges that used to dot the lanes off the northern end of Janpath, only a couple survive, and they're often full, so book ahead.

Unless otherwise stated, the hotels listed below are marked on the Connaught Place **map** (p.96).

Alka 16/90 P-Block, Connaught Place ☎011/2334 4328, ⓦwww.hotelalka.com. "The best alternative to luxury," they reckon, but the rooms, though a/c and carpeted, are pretty poky – the cheaper ones don't even have a window, though they do try to make up for it with mirrors to create an illusion of more space. The staff, on the other hand, don't give out any smiles to create an illusion of friendliness. On the plus side, there's a reasonable veg restaurant, and an annex on M-block for when the main hotel is full. ⑦

Bright M-85, Connaught Place ☎011/4151 7766, ⓔhotelbright@hotmail.com. A mixed bag of rooms, some attached, at this slightly ramshackle but decent enough city-centre hotel. The best room is no.11, spacious with big windows, but others are a bit on the dingy side, so try before you buy. Upstairs, *Blue* (☎011/2341 6666,

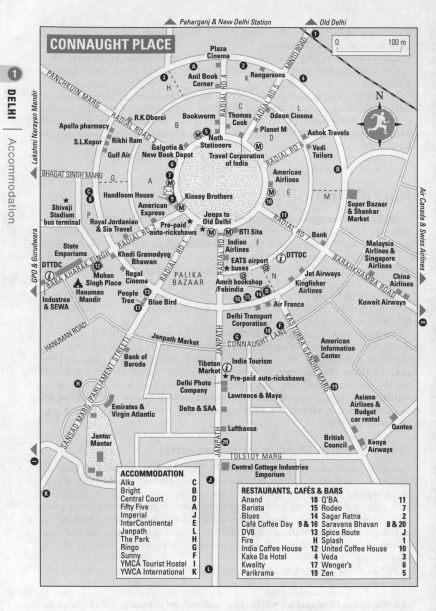

ⓔhotelbluedelhi@hotmail.com) has the benefit of a terrace and is a decent fallback option. ❹–❺
Central Court N-Block, Connaught Place ☎011/2331 5015 to 7. A rooftop establishment with a nice terrace overlooking Connaught Place. The rooms are rather drab, though each has a fridge and a/c. Upstairs rooms are huge (quadruple

in fact) and attached, off a large terrace overlooking Connaught Place, whereas those downstairs are smaller, with their own bathroom, but not attached to the room. ❺–❻
Fifty Five H-55, Connaught Place ☎011/2332 1244, ⓦwww.hotel55.com. Rooms here are small but they're quiet, clean and well kept, with a/c and

a TV (though management ask you not to watch certain channels which apparently charge extortionate rates for the privilege). There's a small terrace upstairs to take tea or snacks, and the staff are generally sweet and obliging. ❼

Imperial Janpath, Connaught Place end ☎011/2334 1234, ⓦwww.theimperialindia .com. See also New Delhi map, p.103. Delhi's classiest hotel, in a beautiful 1933 Art Deco building set amid large, palm-shaded gardens. The rooms are stylish, as is the cool lobby done out in cream and gold, while corridors double up as galleries depicting rather fascinating eighteenth- and nineteenth-century prints of India. Staff maintain just the right degree of courteousness, and there are a number of excellent restaurants including the renowned *Spice Route* (see p.140). Doubles from US$478. ❾

InterContinental off Barakhamba Rd and Tolstoy Marg, southeast of Connaught Place ☎011/4444 7777 or 1800/111 000, ⓦwww.intercontinental .com. See also New Delhi map, p.103. Brash and monolithic upmarket hotel frequented by business travellers, that's all opulence and mod cons, conference meetings and general comings and goings. Has a choice of restaurants, bars and a disco, and lots of shops. When the hotel's at its busiest, doubles start from US$422, but prices are lower when business is slack. ❾

Janpath Janpath ☎011/2334 0070, ⓔjanpath @ndf.vsnl.net.in. See also New Delhi map, p.103. Like an upmarket hotel in a provincial Indian town, and catering for reasonably well-heeled Indian out-of-towners rather than for foreigners, this place is just on the wrong side of deluxe, though the services are all there. Its rooms are large, and comfortable enough, if slightly scuffed around the edges, and the long lobby has some good restaurants, foreign exchange facilities, shops and a travel counter. Doubles from US$149. ❾

Le Meridien Windsor Place, Raisna Rd ☎011/2371 0101, ⓦwww.lemeridien-newdelhi .com. See New Delhi map, p.103. Busy five-star with glass-walled elevators that take you up to bedrooms set around a massive atrium. The whole ensemble looks like a housing scheme in a sci-fi movie, though the rooms are spacious and comfortable within, and service is excellent. Facilities include a swimming pool, health club and a choice of restaurants and bars. Prices start from US$484 per double. ❾

Master R-500 New Rajendra Nagar ☎011/2874 1089, ⓦwww.master -guesthouse.com. See Delhi map, pp.82–83. A lovely little *pension*-style guesthouse, comfortable,

secure and family-run, with only four a/c double rooms of different sizes (a bathroom between each pair), and a secluded roof terrace. Located on the edge of the green belt only 10min by auto-rickshaw from Connaught Place (or bus #910 from Shivaji Terminal behind Block P) and not far from Karol Bagh metro. Veg meals are available. Book ahead. ❻

The Park 15 Sansad Marg ☎011/2374 3000, ⓦwww.theparkhotels.com. See also New Delhi map, p.103. They don't come much snazzier than this place, from the super-cool lobby to the ultra-modern rooms, the decor is state-of-the-art, down to the LCD TV in each room and the frosted glass walls that screen off the en-suite bathrooms. Service is snappy, the atmosphere is relaxed, and all the facilities you'd expect are here, including a bar, a good restaurant and a pool. A cut above your run-of-the-mill five-star. Doubles from US$396. ❾

Ringo 17 Scindia House, Connaught Lane ☎011/2331 0605, ⓔringo_guest_house@yahoo .co.in. An old backpacker favourite that's traded in its dorms for single and double rooms, which are plain but decent, some attached, and arranged around a central terrace that makes a pretty congenial little hangout. ❷–❸

Sunny 152 Scindia House, Connaught Lane ☎011/2331 2909, ⓔsunnyguesthouse123 @hotmail.com. Open 24hr with friendly staff and a sociable rooftop restaurant, this is the last remaining backpacker dorm hotel from a gaggle that once flourished in the vicinity. As well as the dorms (Rs90), there are some rather box-like single and double rooms, some attached, with hot water at 20 minutes' notice. ❷–❸

YMCA Tourist Hostel Jai Singh Marg, southwest of Connaught Place ☎011/2336 1915, ⓦwww .newdelhiymca.org. See also New Delhi map, p.103. A rather staid establishment popular with American budgeteers (though it isn't all that cheap), the institutional corridors belie the spacious if simple rooms, and there are good restaurants, a large swimming pool (open Apr–Oct only) and attractive gardens. Rates include breakfast and supper. ❻–❼

YWCA Blue Triangle Ashok Rd, southwest of Connaught Place ☎011/2336 0133, ⓦwww .ywcaindia.org. See New Delhi map, p.103. Open to men and women, rooms here are nice and big, with large attached bathrooms. The whole place is clean, quiet and respectable, with lawns outside to relax on. Rooms bookable in advance, dorms (Rs410) day-by-day depending on availability, with groups given preference. Rates include breakfast. ❻

YWCA International 10 Sansad Marg, southwest of Connaught Place ℡ 011/2336 1561, ⓦ www.ywcaindia.org. See also New Delhi map, p.103. Clean and airy a/c rooms with private bathrooms, though not quite as nice as at the *Blue Triangle*; set meals are available in the restaurant. Women are given priority but men can also stay. Rates include breakfast, and you even get a free copy of *The Times of India* every morning. ⑥

Paharganj

Running west from New Delhi railway station, the **Paharganj** area is prime backpacker territory, with innumerable lodges offering inexpensive and mid-range accommodation. Some are homely and extremely good value, while others offer very little for very little. Several hotels, particularly those with all-night restaurants, can suffer from slamming-door syndrome and people shouting till dawn, so choose carefully if you value a quiet night; this is especially true in the many hotels whose rooms only have windows facing inwards onto the communal

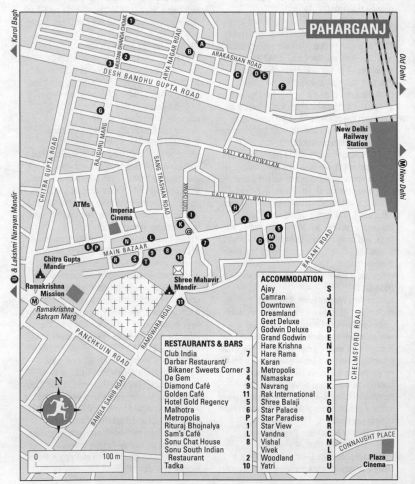

PAHARGANJ

New Delhi Railway Station

Old Delhi

Ⓜ New Delhi

Karol Bagh

ⓤ & Lakshmi Narayan Mandir

MULTANI DHANDA CHOWK

ARYA NAGAR ROAD

ARAKASHAN ROAD

DESH BANDHU GUPTA ROAD

RAJGURU MARG

CHITRA GUPTA ROAD

SANG TRASHAN ROAD

QUTUB ROAD

GALI KASERUWALAN

GALI HALWAI WALI

BASANT ROAD

ATMs

Imperial Cinema

MAIN BAZAAR

Chitra Gupta Mandir

Ramakrishna Mission

Ⓜ Ramakrishna Ashram Marg

PANCHKUIN ROAD

RAMDWARA ROAD

BANGLA SAHIB ROAD

Shree Mahavir Mandir

CHELMSFORD ROAD

CONNAUGHT PLACE

Plaza Cinema

N

0   100 m

RESTAURANTS & BARS

Club India	7
Darbar Restaurant/ Bikaner Sweets Corner	3
De Gem	4
Diamond Café	9
Golden Café	11
Hotel Gold Regency	5
Malhotra	6
Metropolis	P
Rituraj Bhojnalya	1
Sam's Café	L
Sonu Chat House	8
Sonu South Indian Restaurant	2
Tadka	10

ACCOMMODATION

Ajay	S
Camran	J
Downtown	Q
Dreamland	A
Geet Deluxe	F
Godwin Deluxe	D
Grand Godwin	E
Hare Krishna	N
Hare Rama	T
Karan	C
Metropolis	P
Namaskar	H
Navrang	K
Rak International	I
Shree Balaji	G
Star Palace	O
Star Paradise	M
Star View	R
Vandna	C
Vishal	N
Vivek	L
Woodland	B
Yatri	U

stairwell. Some hotels here run a 24-hour checkout system, which means you check-out at the same time you checked in – good if you arrived late, but bad if you arrived early. The area is easily accessible by Metro, with Ramakrishna Ashram Marg the most convenient station. One major irritation for visitors to Paharganj are the notorious hotel **touts**; see box, p.89 for ways to avoid them.

Unless otherwise stated, the hotels listed below are marked on the Paharganj **map** (opposite).

Ajay 5084-A Main Bazaar ☎011/2358 3125, ⓦwww.anupamhoteliersltd.com/html/ajay.htm. Tucked away down an alley off the Main Bazaar, this well-run place with marble decor has clean rooms, some a/c, most with baths and TV, but not all with windows. There's a pool table, Internet access, and a 24hr bakery downstairs, next to a big café area for breakfast or snacks. 24hr checkout. ❷

Camran 1116 Main Bazaar ☎011/3297 4474, ⓔsubhashthakur@yahoo.com. A small, somewhat run-down lodge in part of a late-Mughal period mosque, with some character and a panoramic rooftop terrace. The cheapest rooms are box-like cubicles (though they *are* cheap), or you can pay more for a better room with its own bathroom. Dorm beds also available (Rs80). ❶–❷

Downtown 4583 Main Bazaar ☎011/4154 1529, ⓔltctravel@rediffmail.com. This friendly lodging, just off the Main Bazaar, is not bad value, but it's worth paying Rs50 more to get a spacious room with an outside window. Minus points include an 11am checkout. ❷

Hare Krishna 1572–3 Main Bazaar ☎011/4154 1341, ⓦwww.anupamhoteliersltd.com/html/hare .htm. A friendly and reasonably cosy place. The rooms vary, but the best are spacious, most are attached, and they're all clean. There's hot running water and a pleasant rooftop café-restaurant, but the lower floors can be pretty noisy. 24hr checkout. ❷

Hare Rama T-298 off Main Bazaar ☎011/3536 1301 or 2, ⓔharerama_2000@hotmail.com. Decent, clean attached rooms at this busy, good-value hotel down an alley off the Main Bazaar. 24hr checkout. ❷

Metropolis 1634 Main Bazaar ☎011/2358 5766, ⓦwww.metropolistravels.com. Main Bazaar's most upmarket and comfortable hotel, though somewhat overpriced for what you get. A few double rooms have large windows and bathtubs, though others don't have a window. All are a/c with a TV, fridge and balcony, and there's a good restaurant and bar, with seating downstairs or on the roof terrace. ❺–❻

Namaskar 917 Chandiwalan, Main Bazaar ☎011/2358 2233, ⓔnamaskarhotel@yahoo.com. Popular family-run budget hotel off the Main Bazaar with a variety of attached a/c rooms, but

not all with hot showers, and not all with outside windows. Many people rave about this place, though not everybody comes away happy. The staff are very attentive, but they also run tours which they're rather pushy about selling, and are less than happy with guests who admit to buying tours elsewhere. Airport pick-up service, though it's pricey at Rs400. ❷–❸

Navrang Tooti Chowk, 820 Main Bazaar ☎011/2352 1965. More like a down-at-heel lodge in a remote small town than a city hotel in the middle of Delhi, but it's very friendly, if somewhat basic. On the other hand, you get what you pay for, and at these rates it isn't bad value. The rooms are attached but without hot running water (they'll bring you a bucket for Rs10). ❶

Rak International Tooti Chowk, 820 Main Bazaar ☎011/2358 6508, ⓔhotelrakint@yahoo.com. One of the most consistently popular Paharganj choices, in a small square off the main bazaar; good value with large, cool rooms, a/c, TV, fridge and hot water, and a nice rooftop too, but it could definitely do with a lick of paint. ❸

Shree Balaji 2204 Rajguru Marg, Chuna Mandi ☎011/2353 2212. Between the Main Bazaar and Ram Nagar, this is one of the better hotels along this street in terms of comfort and cleanliness. All rooms have en-suite bathrooms with hot water on tap, but most have no shower. ❷

Star Palace 4590 Main Bazaar ☎011/2358 4849, ⓦwww.stargroupofhotels.com. Rooms here are well equipped for the price (en-suite bathroom, phone, a/c, satellite TV), but they're also a bit cell-like, with no outside windows. If the hotel is full, the staff will direct you to one of their slightly pricier sister establishments, the *Star Paradise* opposite, or the *Star View* at the other end of Paharganj. ❷–❸

Vishal 1575–80 Main Bazaar ☎011/2356 2123, ⓔvishalhotel@hotmail.com. There's a choice here between rather bare, cheap rooms with outside bathroom, and much nicer large attached ones, and there's a good restaurant too, but check the sheets before you take a room. ❸

Vivek 1534–50 Main Bazaar ☎011/5154 1435 or 6, ⓔreservation@vivekhotel.com. A longstanding travellers' favourite, with a 24hr rooftop restaurant, and decent if unremarkable rooms, most with attached baths and hot water, some a/c; the best have windows facing the street. There's even room service. **②**

Yatri 3/4 Jhansi Rd, off Punchkuin Rd, by Delhi Heart and Lung Institute ☎011/2362 5563, ⓦwww.yatrihouse.com. See also Delhi map pp.82–83. This guesthouse, tucked away up a small residential street ten minutes' walk from Paharganj, is like staying in a private home, with clean and quiet attached rooms, hot water, TV and a small enclosed garden for breakfast or just for relaxing. Book well in advance if you want to stay here. **⑥**

Ram Nagar

Directly north of Paharganj, five minutes' walk from New Delhi railway station and just beyond the flyover section of D.B. Gupta Road, **Ram Nagar** is lined with hotels and a few restaurants. It's within easy reach of the Main Bazaar, but you're spared the incessant noise and commercial atmosphere. The area's accommodation tends to be a little more expensive than in Paharganj, but the rooms are generally bigger, brighter and cleaner.

The hotels listed below are marked on the Paharganj **map** (p.98).

Geet Deluxe 8570 Arakashan Rd ☎011/2361 6140 to 43. A cut above the other mid-range options in this area, well-kept with nice touches and a certain charm, and clean, decent-sized rooms, all with TV, and either a/c or air-cooled. **③–④**

Godwin Deluxe 8501/15 Arakashan Rd ☎011/2351 3795 to 8, ⓦwww.godwinhotels.com. Well-run hotel with bright, clean a/c rooms, 24hr room service, TV, and excellent staff. If an ordinary "deluxe" room isn't good enough, you can opt for a bigger "super deluxe" version. **④–⑤**

🏃 **Grand Godwin** 8502/41 Arakashan Rd ☎011/2354 6891 to 8, ⓦwww .godwinhotels.com. As its name suggests, a slightly grander sister hotel to the *Godwin Deluxe*. Rooms start at merely "semi-deluxe" (which means they're on the ground floor), but they're all well appointed and well kept, and there are even suites, as well as a multi-cuisine restaurant. Rates include a buffet breakfast. **⑤–⑥**

Vandna and **Karan** 47 Arakashan Rd ☎011/2362 8821 to 3. Two hotels next to each other and jointly run. The *Karan* has smaller and simpler rooms, while the *Vandna* – with mosaics of Krishna and the Qutb Minar flanking the doorway – has slightly larger rooms and costs a bit more, but all the rooms in both hotels are attached with hot water and TVs, though mattresses are rather hard. **②–③**

Woodland 8235/6 Multani Danda, Arakashan Rd ☎011/4154 1304 to 6, ⓦwww.hotelwoodland .com. Popular hotel with a choice of big a/c, or less expensive smaller, non-a/c rooms. If you want a cheaper room still, they'll send you to their sister establishment, the *Dreamland*, just across the street. **②–③**

Old Delhi

Few tourists stay in **Old Delhi**: it's less central than Connaught Place and Paharganj, and it's dirtier, noisier and more crowded, with hotels geared mostly to Indian visitors rather than foreigners. The hotels around Old Delhi station in particular are bad value. On the other hand, there are a couple of good upmarket options on the area's fringes, and some reasonable budget hotels around the Jama Masjid, and of all the areas in town to stay in, this is the most colourful and it has lots of character.

Unless otherwise stated, the hotels listed below are marked on the Old Delhi **map** (p.113).

Ambar 6477 Katra Bariyan ☎011/2396 5081. This relatively new, tourist-friendly hotel behind Fatehpuri Mosque is one of the area's better offerings, although hot water comes in buckets rather than out of the shower, and the windows all face inward. **②**

Broadway 4/15A Asaf Ali Rd ☎011/2327 3821 to 5, ⓔbroadway@vsnl.net. On the southern edge of Old Delhi, close to Delhi Gate, this mid-range hotel has a lot of old-fashioned charm, and an excellent restaurant specializing in Kashmiri feasts (see p.141), plus two bars, and tours through Old Delhi are available. Rooms are a little bit sombre, but they're clean and well equipped, and some look out over the Jama Masjid. Prices include breakfast. **⑦**

Diamond Palace 3696 Netaji Subhash Marg
℡011/2324 3786 or 7, ℻011/2314 3789.
Comfortable carpeted a/c rooms above the hubbub
of Netaji Subhash Marg on the east side of Old
Delhi. 24hr checkout. ⑤
New City Palace 725 Jama Masjid Motor Market
℡011/2327 9548, ℻011/2328 9923. Though it
doesn't quite live up to its billing of "a home for
palatial comfort", this budget hotel is clean and
well situated, directly behind the Jama Masjid
(reserve ahead if you want a room with a view).
Showers are hot and the best rooms have a/c,

though not all the cheaper ones have outside
windows. 24hr checkout. ②–③
Oberoi Maidens 7 Sham Nath Marg, Civil
Lines; metro Civil Lines ℡011/2397 5464,
Ⓦwww.oberoihotels.com. See main Delhi map
pp.82–83. A nice bit of understated luxury in a
lovely old colonial mansion dating back to
Company days; quiet and relaxing with comfortable
period rooms, big bathrooms and leafy gardens as
well as a swimming pool and a good restaurant.
Doubles from $197. ⑨

South Delhi

Most of the accommodation **south of Connaught Place** lies firmly in the
luxury category, although there are a few guesthouses in Sundernagar, the odd
mid-range hotel tucked away in a residential area and a modern youth hostel
near the diplomatic enclave of Chanakyapuri.

The hotels listed below appear on the New Delhi **map** (p.103).

Ambassador Sujan Singh Park, off Subramaniam
Bharti Marg ℡011/2463 2600, Ⓦwww.tajhotels
.com. Low-key but smart, well-run and classy, this
is a friendly place with comfortable-sized rooms
and huge bathrooms, plus a couple of good
restaurants and free use of the pool and health
club at the other Taj Group hotel, Taj Mahal.
Doubles start from US$253. ⑨
The Claridges 12 Aurangzeb Rd ℡011/4133
5133, Ⓦwww.claridges.com. One of Delhi's oldest
and finest establishments, oozing elegant 1930s
style from its façade to its rooms and even its
bathrooms. Facilities include tennis courts,
restaurants and a swimming pool. Doubles start at
US$332. ⑨
La Sagrita 14 Sundernagar ℡011/2435 1249,
Ⓦwww.lasagrita.com. Tucked away down a quiet
side street in an exclusive colony, opposite a small
park and next-door to the Grenadian high commission, this small guesthouse might just suit if you want
to escape the din of central Delhi. The rooms are
cosy, carpeted, attached and tastefully done out, and
there's a little garden out front to relax in. ⑦–⑧

Maurya Sheraton Sardar Patel Marg,
Chanakyapuri ℡011/2611 2233, Ⓦwww
.itcwelcomgroup.in. An extremely plush hotel on
the edge of Chanakyapuri, opposite the Ridge
forest, with an imposing range of individually
designed luxury rooms, and some of the best
dining in Delhi (see p.142). It regularly hosts
visiting heads of state, with Bill Clinton and
Jacques Chirac among those who have
stayed here. Full-price room rates start at
US$500, but promotional rates are often
available. ⑨
Youth Hostel 5 Nyaya Marg, off Kautilya Marg,
Chanakyapuri ℡011/2611 6285, Ⓦwww
.yhaindia.com. Away from the bustling city
centre, this ultra-modern and eco-friendly grey
concrete building, with dorms (a/c Rs270; non-
a/c Rs90) and a/c or non-a/c singles and
doubles, is the showpiece-cum-administration
centre of the Indian YHA. You need to be an HI
member to stay here (maximum stay seven days)
but you can join on the spot (Rs250). Rates
include breakfast. ②

Majnu ka Tilla

If you want to avoid Delhi's hustle and bustle, or to have a change from Indian
culture and cuisine, the Tibetan colony at **Majnu ka Tilla** offers excellent-
value budget hotels with immaculately kept rooms, much nicer than what you'd
get for the same price in Paharganj, in a relatively quiet district with Tibetan
food, Internet facilities and money changers close at hand, but it isn't very
convenient for central Delhi (Connaught Place is Rs80 away by auto, Vidhan
Sabha metro Rs15 by rickshaw). Book ahead if you intend to stay here as hotels
are often full up. There's only one main drag in Majnu ka Tila, so everything's
pretty easy to find.

Lhasa House 16 New Camp, just east of the main street ☎ 011/2393 9777 or 9888, ✉ lhasahouse@ rediffmail.com. The rooms are a little bit smaller and simpler than at *Wongdhen House* next door, but all are attached, with TV and fan. Cheapest rooms are on the top floor. ❷–❸

White House 44 New Camp ☎ 011/2381 3544 or 3644 or 3944, ✉ whitehouse02@rediffmail .com. On the Tibetan colony's main street (such as it is), 100m north of the other two hotels mentioned here; the rooms are quite large,

attached, with TV, and certainly well kept, but the mattresses are a bit on the hard side. ❷–❸

Wongdhen House 15-A New Camp, just east of the main drag, next to *Lhasa House* ☎ 011/6415 5330, ✉ wongdhenhouse@hotmail .com. Friendly guesthouse with a choice of rooms, some attached and some overlooking the River Yamuna. There's also a good restaurant (Tibetan food, or breakfast items) and a terrace with a great river view. ❷–❹

The City

Delhi is both daunting and alluring, a sprawling metropolis with a stunning backdrop of ancient architecture. Once you've found your feet and got over the initial impact of the commotion, noise, pollution and sheer scale of the place, the city's geography slowly slips into focus. Monuments in marble and sandstone, which stand in assorted states of repair, are dotted around the city, concentrated mainly in **Old Delhi** and in southern enclaves such as Hauz Khas. The modern city, built by the British, centres on Connaught Place, the heart of **New Delhi** (though actually on its northern edge), from which it's easy – by taxi, bus, auto-rickshaw or metro – to visit pretty much anywhere else in town.

New Delhi

At the 1911 durbar (ceremonial gathering), Britain's King George V, in his role as emperor of India, announced that Delhi would replace Calcutta as India's capital. The real reason for this was that opposition to British rule in Bengal had grown so strong that the colonialists wanted to move their admin-istration to somewhere less militant. Architect **Edwin Lutyens**, thus far known mainly for building country houses in England, was commissioned to design the administrative centre, and decided to place this **New Delhi** on a rise between Old Delhi and the city's more ancient incarnations at Lal Kot and Firozabad. Tombs, temples and buildings of historical importance were incorporated into the new area, but homes and a handful of villages were simply knocked down to make way for it. The new city was spacious, with wide tree-lined avenues, fine residential bungalows and solid colonial archi-tecture. Its low density in such a populated city is rather peculiar, but Delhiites (or, more correctly, Delhiwallahs) are justifiably proud of its grand scale, and it does make for a splendid centre of government.

The axis of Lutyens' city is the arrow-straight royal mall, **Rajpath**, running from the presidential palace, **Rashtrapati Bhavan**, in the west, to **India Gate** in the east. In the spacious avenues to the south, the residences of Jawaharlal Nehru and Indira Gandhi have been preserved as memorials, as has **Gandhi Smriti**, where the Father of the Nation, Mahatma Gandhi, met his death. At the north edge of the new capital lies the thriving business centre, **Connaught Place** ("CP"), where neon advertisements for restaurants, bars and banks adorn the roofs and verandas of the buildings that circle its central park. On the fringes of New Delhi lie older areas: **Purana Qila**, Delhi's sixth incarnation, with its nearby **Crafts Museum**; and **Paharganj**, once a village, now the city's favourite backpacker hangout.

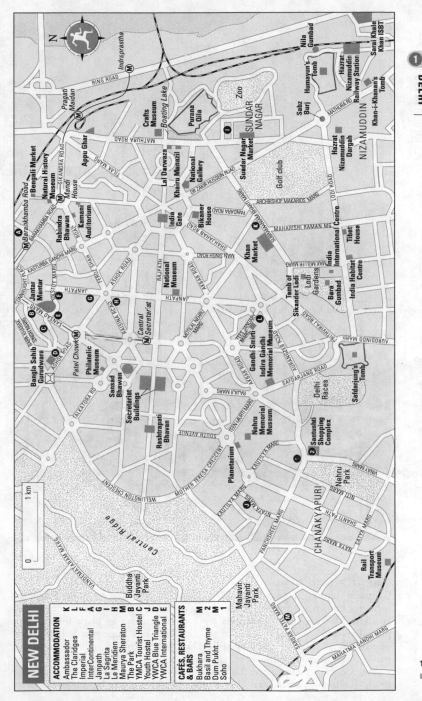

NEW DELHI

ACCOMMODATION
Ambassador	K
The Claridges	L
Imperial	F
InterContinental	A
Janpath	G
La Sagrita	I
Le Meridien	H
Maurya Sheraton	M
The Park	B
YMCA Tourist Hostel	C
Youth Hostel	J
YWCA Blue Triangle	D
YWCA International	E

CAFÉS, RESTAURANTS & BARS
Bukhara	M
Basil and Thyme	2
Dum Pukht	M
Soho	1

△ India Gate, Rajpath

Rajpath and around

Running across the middle of New Delhi is the majestic mall, **Rajpath**, formerly known as Kingsway, flanked by gardens and fountains that are floodlit at night. The wide grassy margins are a popular meeting place for families, picnickers and courting couples, and the location of a huge parade held every year on 26 January to mark **Republic Day**, which features military marching bands, floats from all of India's states, folk dancing, elephants, even the Bikaner Camel Corps on camelback. Tickets (grandstand seats Rs150–300, standing room Rs10–50; no cameras, bags, food or drink) can be obtained from

DTTDC and Government of India tourist offices, Dilli Haat market (see p.147) and outlets across town. Information is posted on the Press Information Bureau website (Ⓦpib.nic.in) in January. On 29 January, a ceremony called **Beating the Retreat** is held at Janpath's western end on Raisina Hill, with military bands and fireworks, and Rashtrapati Bhavan gloriously floodlit for the occasion, but tickets are scarce; there is, however, a full dress rehearsal one or two days before, for which tickets (Rs20–50) are available from the same outlets as Republic Day tickets.

At the eastern end of Rajpath is **India Gate**, which was designed by Lutyens in 1921. The 42-metre-high arch commemorates ninety thousand Indian soldiers killed fighting for the British in World War I, and bears the names of more than three thousand British and Indian soldiers who died on the Northwest frontier and in the Afghan War of 1919. The memorial beneath the arch honours those who lost their lives in the Indo-Pakistan War of 1971. Despite its solemn commemoration, India Gate has something of a carnival atmosphere at times, with sellers of balloons, ice cream and candy-floss, families enjoying a day out, and invariably lots of children running around. After sunset the gate is illuminated with floodlights, and couples come here to promenade, turning it into something of an impromptu party. The empty *chhatri* (stone canopy) to its west once housed a statue of George V, now in Coronation Park (see p.127).

Rashtrapati Bhavan

Rashtrapati Bhavan, the official residence of the president of India (before Independence, of the viceroy), is one of the largest and most grandiose of the Raj constructions built by Lutyens and his assistant Herbert Baker. Despite its classical columns, Mughal-style domes, Indian filigree work, and use of the same red sandstone so favoured by the Mughals, the whole building is unmistakably British in character. The apartments inside are strictly private (though you can visit them online, at Ⓦpresidentofindia.nic.in/scripts/rashbhav.html), but the **gardens** at the west side are open to the public for two weeks in late February (free; dates vary depending on the arrival of spring weather). Modelled by Lutyens on Mughal pleasure parks, with a typically ordered square pattern of quadrants dissected by waterways and refreshed by fountains, the gardens extend beyond the normal confines to include tennis courts, butterfly enclosures, vegetable and fruit patches and a swimming pool.

The ministry buildings and Sansad Bhawan

East of Rashtrapati Bhavan, flanking a rise called Raisina Hill, are two **Secretariat Buildings**. The North Block houses the Finance Ministry, the South Block the External Affairs Ministry. Originally they were intended to be placed further east but Baker proposed putting them on top of the hill instead, pushing Rashtrapati Bhavan westward. On seeing the finished product, Lutyens was horrified to find that Rashtrapati Bhavan was down behind the hill, which now obscured its view from India Gate, to the east. Livid and inconsolable, he blamed Baker – formerly his close friend – for the mistake, and campaigned unsuccessfully to have the hill levelled. In fact, it can be argued that the error actually enhances the approach, as the view of Rashtrapati Bhavan's dome from India Gate is often clouded nowadays by smoggy haze, through which the building rises like some wonderful apparition as you mount the hill towards it.

India's parliament, the Lok Sabha, is housed in the circular **Sansad Bhawan** (Parliament Building), north of the Rajpath at the southern end of Sansad Marg. Debates are mostly in Hindi, but some speakers use English or regional languages, and it is possible to watch. In order to do so, if you're Indian, you can obtain a permit from the visitors' reception on Raisina Road, just southeast of the Sansad Bhawan; otherwise you'll need a letter of introduction from your country's embassy or high commission (most embassies will charge for this), which you then take to the visitors' reception.

Not far away, on Talkatora Road, the **National Philatelic Museum** (Mon–Fri 10am–5pm; free) has copies of every stamp issued by India since Independence, but you'd need to be quite an enthusiast to find it interesting. The best exhibits, over by the right-hand wall, are some 1854 postal courier's accoutrements, including a lantern, bugle and a sword and spear, used as protection from bandits.

Connaught Place and around

New Delhi's commercial hub, **Connaught Place** (inevitably known as "CP"), with its classical colonnades, is radically different from the bazaars of Old Delhi, which it superseded. Named after a minor British royal of the day, it takes the form of a circle, divided by seven radial roads and three ring roads into blocks lettered A–N. The term Connaught Place originally referred to the inner circle (now renamed Rajiv Chowk after Rajiv Gandhi), the outer one being Connaught Circus (now Indira Chowk, after Rajiv's mum).

CP is crammed with restaurants, bars, shops, cinemas, banks and airline offices (there's a good online index at ⓦ www.connaughtplacemall.com), not to mention some annoying touts (trying to lure unsuspecting visitors into buying overpriced tours – their opening line is usually to inform you, quite superfluously, which block you're on) and lots of street traders. It gets especially animated in the evenings, and even on Sunday, when most of the shops are closed, there's enough going on to make it worth a stroll. On the outer circle, one of the liveliest areas is by **Super Bazaar** and **Shankar Market**, just across from Block M; it's especially buzzing in the evening when people come down to dine at the many low-priced restaurants, most famously *Kake da Hotel* (see p.139). The block opposite Palika Bazaar on the south side of the outer circle also gets very busy around nightfall, with street traders setting out their stalls, and customers jostling for position. The pavement in front of the **Regal Building**, named after a cinema in the middle of the block, is patrolled by itinerant vendors flogging sunglasses, socks and handkerchiefs. The paan-wallah who sets out his stall in front of the cinema entrance has been plying his trade here for years; notice the smouldering rope hanging from the wall by his pitch, used by passing smokers to light their cigarettes. The **central park** in the middle of the circus, now beautifully landscaped, offers a quiet retreat from the hurly-burly. If you don't fancy getting run down on the busy road above, you are advised to use the pedestrian underpasses, also favoured by beggars, who strategically place themselves at each entrance.

The street life extends onto the roads radiating off from CP too. On Baba Kharak Singh Marg, beyond **Mohan Singh Place Shopping Complex** (a hive of shops selling mostly fabric and clothing), the **Hanuman Mandir** is an old-established and a very popular place of worship among Delhiwallahs, though not of any special interest to tourists. Around its entrance traders sell religious items, old coins and small knick-knacks to devotees and passers-by, directly across the street from where the various state emporiums (see p.147) showpiece their respective crafts. On the other side of the Regal Building, **Janpath Market**, a line of stalls doing brisk business in cheap clothes, is always lively. At its western end, it meets the more touristy **Tibetan Market**, a row of shops originally established by refugees from Tibet, and a favourite stretch for souvenir shopping (see p.148).

Jantar Mantar

South of Connaught Place on Sansad Marg, the **Jantar Mantar** (daily sunrise–sunset; foreigners Rs100/$2. Indian residents Rs5) was built in 1725, the first of five open-air observatories designed by the ruler of Jaipur, Jai Singh II, and precursor to his larger one in Jaipur (see p.210). Huge red and white slanting stone structures looming over palm trees and neat flowerbeds were used to calculate time, solar and lunar calendars and astrological movements with an admirable degree of accuracy. Sadly, a lot of the instruments were damaged in the late eighteenth century when most of the original marble with its precisely carved gradations was stolen. Plaques explain how the instruments worked, but their explanations may not be too easy to follow if your trigonometry's a bit rusty. The most prominent instrument is the Samrat Yantra, which looks like a giant stairway to nowhere, but is actually a huge sundial: the position of its shadow tells the time of day, its length the sun's elevation; unfortunately, the marble scales on which these could be read off has long gone. To its south, the Ram Yantras, which resemble two mini coliseums, are for calculating the elevation of heavenly bodies such as the sun, moon and planets. The heart-shaped Misra Yantra, near the entrance, is a later addition and performed several functions, one of which was to track the progress of these objects across the sky. In recent years the Jantar Mantar has become the hub of political demonstrations in Delhi; people regularly gather here with placards and banners, or even camp out on hunger strikes, to protest about local, national or international issues.

Bangla Sahib Gurudwara

Southwest of Connaught Place, on Ashok Road by the GPO, the vast white marble structure of **Bangla Sahib Gurudwara** is Delhi's biggest Sikh temple, topped by a huge, golden, onion-shaped dome which is visible from some distance. The temple commemorates a 1664 visit to Delhi by the eighth Sikh guru, Hare Krishan, as a guest of Amber's ruler Jai Singh I, who had a haveli where the temple is now. At the time, Delhi was stricken with cholera and smallpox, and Krishan went around ministering to those stricken with illness. He also blessed a small pond at the Jai Singh's haveli so that its waters would cure sufferers of their disease. Today, devotees still drink water from the same pond, which is located to the left of the main entrance and continually replenished from the mains. The temple welcomes visitors; deposit shoes at the information centre near the main entrance, where you can also enlist the services of a free guide. Remember to cover your head and dress conservatively. Live devotional music (vocals, harmonium and tabla) is relayed throughout the complex, and everybody is invited to share a simple meal of dhal and chapatis, served three times daily.

Lakshmi Narayan Mandir

Lakshmi Narayan Mandir (daily 4am–1.30pm & 2.30–9pm; deposit cameras, shoes and mobile phones at the entrance), northwest of the GPO and directly west of Connaught Place on Mandir Marg, is a modern Hindu temple which also welcomes tourists. With its white, cream and red brick domes, it was commissioned by a wealthy merchant family, the Birlas (hence its alternative name, Birla Mandir), and was inaugurated in 1939 by Mahatma Gandhi. Its architect, Chandra Chatterjee, was founder of the Modern Indian Architectural Movement, which aimed to revive indigenous building styles in contrast to the grandiose foreign constructions of colonialists such as Lutyens. The main shrine is dedicated to Lakshmi, goddess of wealth (on the right), and her consort

Narayana, aka Vishnu, the preserver of life (on the left, holding a conch). Shrines on either side are to Durga (in the left-hand shrine, riding a tiger), and her consort Shiva (in the right-hand shrine, meditating with a cobra round his neck). At the back is a tiny ornate chamber decorated with coloured stones and mirrors and dedicated to Krishna, one of Vishnu's earthly incarnations. Devotional music is played throughout, and quotes from Hindu scriptures adorn the walls, many translated into English. Behind the temple is a pleasant garden full of fountains and kitsch statues, including dragons and other mythical beasts; if you're really brave, you can even stand inside a dragon's mouth.

Paharganj

North of Connaught Place and directly west of New Delhi railway station, **Paharganj**, centred around Main Bazaar, provides the first experience of the Subcontinent for many budget travellers. Packed with cheap hotels, restaurants, cafés and *dhabas*, and with a busy fruit and vegetable market halfway along, it's also a paradise for shoestring shoppers seeking psychedelic clothing, joss-sticks, bags, and oils of patchouli or sandalwood. A constant stream of auto- and cycle rickshaws, cars, handcarts and cows (this is the most cow-friendly part of central Delhi) squeeze through seemingly impossible gaps without the flow ever quite coming to a complete standstill, and the winding back-alleys seem worlds away from the commercial city centre just around the corner. Beware of opportunist thieves here, and the attentions of touts (see p.89). Formerly a village, Paharganj only survived the construction of New Delhi because its density of population made it difficult for the British to get away with demolishing it, and its backstreets still harbour some fine old houses with often quite imposing doorways.

There is also a less visible underside to life in Paharganj, in the shape of the **street children**. Most are runaways who've left difficult homes, often hundreds of kilometres away, and the majority sleep on the streets and inhale solvents to numb their pain. The Salaam Baalak Trust (ⓦwww.salaambaalaktrust.com) has been set up by one of the local NGOs working to help them, which organizes **walking tours** of Paharganj conducted by former street children, who will show you the district and its hidden side. Tours last for two hours and usually start at 10am, and cost Rs200. For bookings, contact ⓣ0/987 313 0383 (mobile) or ⓔsbttour@yahoo.com. Proceeds go towards providing shelter, education and healthcare for the area's street children.

National Museum

The **National Museum** (Tues–Sun 10am–5pm; foreigners Rs300, Indian residents Rs20; cameras Rs300, Indian residents Rs20; ⓦwww .nationalmuseumindia.gov.in), just south of Rajpath at 11 Janpath, provides a good overview of Indian culture and history. The entry fee includes an audio tour, but you need to leave a passport, driving licence, credit card or Rs400 (or US$40/£40/€40) as a deposit, and the exhibits it covers are rather random. At a trot, you can see the museum in a couple of hours, but to get the best out of your visit you should set aside at least half a day.

The most important exhibits are on the ground floor, kicking off in **room 4** with the Harappan civilization, which originated in the Indus Valley during the third millennium BC (contemporary with early ancient Egypt). The most impressive exhibits here are a diminutive dancing girl from Mohenjodaro in what is now Pakistan, and a bronze casting of a chariot pulled by oxen from Diamabad in Maharashtra. **Room 5** has a wonderful elephant relief from a Buddhist temple of the Shunga dynasty (second century BC) at Bharhut in

△ Cow in the streets of Paharganj

Madhya Pradesh state. The Gandhara sculptures in **room 6** betray a very
obvious Greco-Roman influence, reminding us of the trade connections that
existed between India and the European peninsula before the rise of Islam
effectively isolated Christian Europe from the rest of the world. On your left
as you enter **room 7**, two lintels of the Gupta period (sixth or seventh
century AD) with friezes of cows and other animals, plus a fifth-century AD
railing pillar, were all found embedded in the concrete roof of Sultan Ghari's
tomb near Lal Kot (see p.135). They must have come from an earlier temple
in the area, showing that it was inhabited by the fifth century. At the end of
the same room, a most impressive statue of Vishnu from Mathura in UP also
dates from that time.

Room 9 has some very fine bronzes, most especially those of the Chola period (from south India in the ninth to the thirteenth century), and a fifteenth-century statue of Devi from Vijayanagar (Hampi), in Karnataka, South India, by the left-hand wall. Among the late medieval sculptures in **room 10**, look out for a fearsome, vampire-like, late chola dvarapala (a guardian figure built to flank the doorway to a shrine), also from south India, and a couple of performing musicians from Mysore.

Room 12 is devoted to the Mughals, and in particular their miniature paintings. Outstanding in the first section of the room is the wedding of Shah Jahan's son Dara Shikoh, later killed by his pious brother Aurangzeb during wranglings for the succession while the old emperor was still alive. The second section has a wonderful painting of the great Mughal emperor Akbar on a hunt in 1595, charging on horseback at a miscellany of animals including a lion devouring a deer. In a more sexually suggestive painting, a shy young virgin is brought into the harem of a Mughal noble, who waits expectantly on a bed to receive her. Look out also for two paintings depicting a subject you wouldn't expect – the nativity of Jesus. The third section of room 12 has a portrait of Guru Nanak, first of the ten Sikh gurus, dating from the 1730s, while in the next section are representations of Udaipur's Jag Mandir (see p.339) and the legendary lovers Dhola and Maru (see p.323), as well as an action-packed painting from Kota of an elephant, ridden by two hunters, fighting a tiger.

Many of the remaining galleries, including those displaying jewellery and manuscripts, have been closed for some time, but are expected to reopen soon. Meanwhile, it's worth popping upstairs to the **textiles**, and the **musical instruments** collection on the second floor is outstanding. The **Central Asian antiquities** collection includes a large number of paintings, documents, ceramics and textiles from Eastern Turkestan (Xinjiang) and the Silk Route, dating from between the third and twelfth centuries. Finally, on your way out, take a look at the massive twelve-tiered temple chariot from Tamil Nadu, an extremely impressive piece of woodwork in a glass shelter just by the southern entrance gate.

Nehru Memorial Museum

The **Nehru Memorial Museum** (Tues–Sun 9.30am–5.30pm; free) on Teen Murti Marg was built in 1930 as the grand and sombre residence of the British commander-in-chief. After Independence it became home to India's first prime minister, Jawaharlal Nehru, and is now preserved in his memory. The rooms are full of photographs recording Nehru's life, from his childhood and student years at Harrow and Cambridge to his appointment as prime minister. One of Nehru's passions was astronomy, and the **planetarium** (Rs2; 40min astronomy shows in English Tue–Sun 11.30am & 3pm, Rs15) in the grounds of the house has a few exhibits including the descent module used by the first Indian cosmonaut in 1984, its heat-shield charred by re-entry into the atmosphere. Next to the planetarium is an old hunting lodge dating back to the time of Ghiyas-ud-din Tughluq (early fourteenth century), which you can also explore.

Indira Gandhi Memorial Museum

Nehru's daughter, Indira Gandhi, despite her excesses during the 1975–77 Emergency (see p.392), is still remembered by many with respect and affection. The **Indira Gandhi Memorial Museum** (Tues–Sun 9.30am–4.45pm; free), 1 Safdarjang Rd, was the house where she was assassinated by her Sikh bodyguards in 1984; her bloodstained sari, chemically preserved, is on display, along with letters, press cuttings, photos (many taken by her son Rajiv) and possessions, supplemented by a section devoted to Rajiv, including the clothes he was wearing when he was in turn assassinated by Sri Lankan Tamil separatists in 1991. The tastefully decorated and furnished study, drawing room and dining room conjure up images of how the family must have lived, in great style but not overt opulence. The museum is very popular, so arrive early, especially at weekends, to avoid the crowds.

Gandhi Smriti

Still more tragic than the deaths of Rajiv and Indira was the 1948 assassination of the nation's founder, Mahatma Gandhi, who shared their surname but was not related. The **Gandhi Smriti** (Tue–Sun 10am–5pm; free), 5 Tees January Marg, is the house where it happened, and where the Mahatma lived his last days. He had come to Delhi to quell the sectarian rioting that accompanied Partition, following his amazing success at ending it in Bengal, but Hindu sectarian extremists hated him for protecting Muslims, and on 30 January 1948, one of them shot him dead. His assassination so shocked the nation that sectarian murders all but ended, for which Gandhi would no doubt have considered his death a worthy sacrifice. Today, you can follow in his last footsteps and even see the spot where he died. Exhibits in the house and grounds tell more about the life and death of the man regarded by many as the twentieth century's greatest statesman.

National Gallery of Modern Art

Once the residence of the Maharaja of Jaipur, the extensive **National Gallery** (Tue–Sun 10am–5pm; foreigners Rs150, Indian residents Rs10) housed in Jaipur House near India Gate, is a rich showcase of Indian contemporary art. The permanent displays, focusing on post-1930s work, exhibit many of India's most important works of modern art, including pieces by the "Bengali Renaissance" artists Abanindranath Tagore and Nandalal Bose, the great poet and artist, Rabindranath Tagore, and Jamini Roy, whose work, reminiscent of Modigliani, reflects the influence of Indian folk art. Also on show are the romantic paintings and etchings of Thomas Daniell and his nephew William, British artists of the Bombay or Company School, which combined Indian delicacy with Western realism. The ground-floor galleries are used for temporary exhibitions.

Purana Qila

The majestic fortress of **Purana Qila** (daily sunrise–sunset; foreigners Rs100/$2, Indian residents Rs5), whose crumbling ramparts dominate busy Mathura Road, east of India Gate, is thought to stand on the site of Indraprastha, the Pandava city of Mahabharata fame. Considered the sixth city of Delhi, though actually – like Siri – it was just a citadel, it was begun by Humayun, the second Mughal emperor, as Din-Panah, and renamed Shergarh by Sher Shah, who displaced him in 1540 and oversaw most of the construction. In 1947, during Partition, Muslim refugees gathered in the fort to await transportation to Pakistan; tens of thousands of them were slaughtered en route. Purana Qila is served by **buses** between Delhi Gate and Sundernagar, including #423 and #438 (ask for the zoo, which is the same stop).

Entry is through the **western gateway**, less impressive than the north and south entries, which can be seen from opposite the Crafts Museum and from the zoo respectively. Just inside the gate, a small **Archeological Museum** (daily except Fri, 10am–5pm; included in the entry ticket) houses some interesting finds, not all from the area.

Most of the inside of the fortress is taken up by pleasant lawns and gardens, but two important buildings survive. Of them, the **Qila-i-Kuhna Masjid** is one of Sher Shah's finest monuments. Constructed in 1541 in the Afghan style, it has five elegant arches, embellished with white and black marble to complement the red sandstone. The geometric patterns and carved Arabic calligraphy around the main doorway all represent a more sophisticated degree of decorative artwork than on anything seen before in Delhi. Previous decorative carving on buildings was in plaster, but here it's in stone, a more serious affair as it's obviously much harder to work.

The Purana Qila's other main building, the **Sher Mandal**, is a red sandstone octagonal observatory and library built for Sher Shah. It was here in 1556 that the emperor Humayun died. He stumbled down its treacherously steep steps while hurrying to answer the *muezzin*'s call to prayer, just a year after he had defeated one of Sher Shah's successors, Sikander Suri and regained power.

Next door to Purana Qila, the **zoo** (Sat–Thurs summer 8am–6pm, winter 9am–5pm; foreigners Rs50/$1. Indian residents Rs10) is highly popular with Delhiites, especially young ones, and particularly at weekends. Spread over 86 hectares of land, with some two thousand animal species and lots of greenery, it is the biggest zoo in India, and one of the biggest in Asia. As well as Indian rhinos and elephants, the top attraction are the white Bengal tigers, a rarity in the wild, but bred in captivity by the zoo, which has gifted some of their siblings to zoos elsewhere in India. Neither albino nor a separate species from ordinary Bengal tigers, white tigers are rare in nature because they are the result of a recessive gene that only surfaces if both parents carry it.

The **boating lake** in front of Purana Qila (daily: summer noon–7pm, winter 11am–6pm; Rs40 per half hour for a four-person boat) is not massively exciting, but it can be a laugh, especially if you have small people in tow, and it also allows you a good view of Purana Qila's northern gateway.

Across the street are more ruins worth checking out. The **Khairul Manazil** (daily sunrise–sunset; free) was a mosque built in 1562 on the orders of Maham Angah, Akbar's faithful nurse, and an important figure in his still shaky regime when he inherited the throne from Humayun at the age of fourteen. You can climb up the eastern gateway for a view down into the courtyard with its octagonal ablutions pool. North of the Khairul Manazil, the **Lal Darwaza** gateway stands at the end of what was once an avenue of shops. You can't walk up the avenue to the gate, but you can look up it from the road. The now rather ruined but still impressive gateway is known as the **bloody gate** after a British officer, William Hodson, shot dead here three Mughal princes. He'd arrested them at Humayun's Tomb, where they'd taken refuge following the fall of Delhi in 1857, having played a particularly active part in the uprising. Hodson then had their naked bodies put on public display in Chandni Chowk. They say that during the rainy season, the gateway drips blood in their memory, though it's more likely to be rust from iron parts of the gate structure colouring the rainwater red.

Crafts Museum

Immediately north of Purana Qila on Bhairon Marg, the **Crafts Museum** (Tues–Sun 10am–5pm; free) is a dynamic exhibition of the rural arts and crafts of India, divided into three sections. The **exhibition galleries** show a range of textiles, carvings, ceramics, painting and metalwork from across India, while the **village complex** displays an assortment of traditional homes from different parts of the country. The **craft demonstrations** do feature a few artisans actually at work, but mostly they are more like shops selling crafts typical of different Indian regions. There's also a library and a fixed-price museum **shop**.

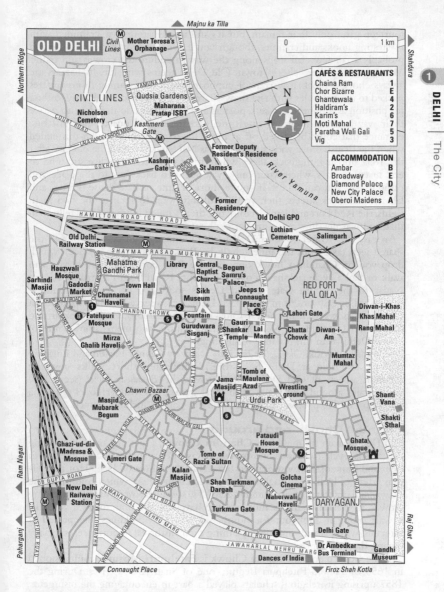

OLD DELHI

Civil Lines Ⓜ Ⓐ

Majnu ka Tilla ▲

Mother Teresa's Orphanage

Northern Ridge ◄

Shahdera ▶

0   1 km

CAFÉS & RESTAURANTS

Chaina Ram	**1**
Chor Bizarre	**E**
Ghantewala	**4**
Haldiram's	**2**
Karim's	**6**
Moti Mahal	**7**
Paratha Wali Gali	**5**
Vig	**3**

ACCOMMODATION

Ambar	**B**
Broadway	**E**
Diamond Palace	**D**
New City Palace	**C**
Oberoi Maidens	**A**

CIVIL LINES

Qudsia Gardens

Maharana Pratap ISBT

Nicholson Cemetery

Kashmere Gate Ⓜ

Former Deputy Resident's Residence

St James's

Former Residency

Kashmiri Gate

River Yamuna

Old Delhi GPO

Old Delhi Railway Station

Lothian Cemetery

Salimgarh

SHAYMA PRASAD MUKHERJI ROAD

Hauzwali Mosque

Sarhindi Masjid

Gadodia Market

Mahatma Gandhi Park

Town Hall

Chunnamal Haveli

Library

Central Baptist Church

Sikh Museum

Begum Samru's Palace

Jeeps to Connaught Place

RED FORT (LAL QILA)

Fatehpuri Mosque

Fountain

CHANDNI CHOWK

Gurudwara Sisganj

Gauri Shankar Temple

Lal Mandir

Lahori Gate

Chatta Chowk

Diwan-i-Am

Diwan-i-Khas

Khas Mahal

Rang Mahal

Mirza Ghalib Haveli

Chawri Bazaar

Jama Masjid

Tomb of Maulana Azad

Wrestling ground

Mumtaz Mahal

Shanti Vana

Masjid Mubarak Begum

Urdu Park

Shakti Sthal

Ghazi-ud-din Madrasa & Mosque

Ajmeri Gate

Tomb of Razia Sultan

Pataudi House Mosque

Ghata Mosque

Kalan Masjid

Shah Turkman Dargah

Golcha Cinema

New Delhi Railway Station

Turkman Gate

Nalverwali Haveli

DARYAGANJ

Delhi Gate

Dances of India

Dr Ambedkar Bus Terminal

Gandhi Museum

Pahargunj ◄

Ram Nagar ◄

Connaught Place ▼

Firoz Shah Kotla ▼

Raj Ghat ▶

Old Delhi (Shahjahanabad)

Though it's not in fact the oldest part of Delhi, the seventeenth-century city of **Shahjahanabad**, built for the Mughal emperor Shah Jahan, is known as **Old Delhi**. Construction began on the city in 1638, and within eleven years it was substantially complete, surrounded by over 8km of ramparts pierced by fourteen main gates. It boasted a beautiful main thoroughfare, **Chandni Chowk**, an imposing citadel, the **Red Fort** (Lal Qila), and an impressive congregational mosque, the **Jama Masjid**. Today much of the wall has crumbled, and of the fourteen gates only four remain, but it's still a fascinating area, crammed with interesting nooks and crannies, though you'll need stamina, patience, time and probably a fair few chai stops along the way to endure the crowds and traffic. More than anywhere else in town, Old Delhi teems with life. Its bazaars are always chock-a-block, a warren of cupboard-sized shops lining thoroughfares packed to the gunwales with rickshaws, barrows and hand-carts, all busy jostling for position as shoppers, hawkers, porters and pedestrians do their best to weave their way between them. At one time, each residential quarter had just one entrance that could be closed off at night for security, and though this ended when the British drove wide streets such as Nai Sarak through the old city after the 1857 uprising, the back-alleys where most of its residents live still tend to end in cul-de-sacs, where your only way out is to backtrack to the place you came in – if you can find it. If you're short of time or hate dense throngs and labyrinthine back streets, then you'll probably want to stick to the two main sights, the Red Fort and Jama Masjid, but there's much more to Old Delhi than that, and it really does repay further exploration.

An easy way to **get to Old Delhi** from Connaught Place is on one of the shared jeep taxis from the inner circle by Palika Bazaar (Rs6 a place), which drop you on Chandni Chowk opposite the Red Fort. Alternatively, you can walk or hail a cycle rickshaw along DB Gupta Road from Paharganj or Ram Nagar to the Ajmeri Gate at Old Delhi's southwest corner, and continue northward or eastward from there. Old Delhi is also served by metro stations at Chandni Chowk (actually nearer Old Delhi train station), Chawri Bazaar, and the Ajmeri Gate side of New Delhi train station (the metro stop's name of "New Delhi" is in this instance misleading).

An excellent book, *Old Delhi: Ten Easy Walks* by Gaynor Barton and Lurraine Malone (available at Delhi bookstores), details ten short **walks** covering different aspects of Old Delhi. Alternatively, the *Broadway Hotel* (see p.100) offers walks around Old Delhi with local guide, Shiv Kumar; tours require a minimum of five people, and cost Rs495 per person, including lunch.

Chandni Chowk and around

Old Delhi's main thoroughfare, **Chandni Chowk**, a seething mass of honking cars, autos, cycle rickshaws and ox carts, was once a sublime canal lined with trees and some of the most opulent bazaars in the whole of Asia. "That marvellous artery of Delhi," an English visitor called it in 1903, "which epitomises the magic and mystery of an Eastern city." To some extent, with its thronging crowds, its markets, temples, mosques and havelis, it still does today. If you take a walk along it, look out for numbered "heritage buildings" signposted at intervals, with placards outside explaining their historical importance, especially during the 1857 uprising.

At the western end of Chandni Chowk is **Fatehpuri Mosque**, commissioned in 1650 by Nawab Fatehpuri Begum, one of Shah Jahan's wives. During the 1857 uprising its religious scholars played a part in encouraging the insurgents, so when the British retook Delhi they sacked the mosque and sold it to a local businessman, though they bought it back twenty times later (for three times the price) and returned it to the Muslim community. The large courtyard contains graves of – alongside Sufi saints – some of those killed by the British in 1857. As Mughal mosques go, it isn't that impressive, but then it's up against some stiff competition in Old Delhi. To its west is **Khari Baoli** spice market (see p.121).

Though the 1857 British recapture of Delhi was a disaster for most of its residents, one or two people did well out of it. One such person was the man who bought Fatehpuri Mosque from the British, Lal Chunnamal, a Hindu merchant who had remained loyal to the East India Company, and was richly rewarded. Just how richly can be gauged from the size of his home, **Chunnamal Haveli**, a 126-room mansion just east of the mosque on Chandni Chowk. With the plunge in land prices, and his own wealth augmented and protected by the now victorious British, he was able to buy up half the north side of the street and construct this huge palace. The downstairs area has now largely been converted into shops, but Lal Chunnamal's family still live in parts of the haveli.

Almost opposite, **Ballimaran**, the shoe bazaar, leads south towards Chawri Bazaar and its metro station. Two hundred metres down on the right, opposite no. 5134, is a turning called Qasimjan Street, along which is **Mirza Ghalib Haveli** (Tues–Sun 10am–5pm; free), home from 1860 until his death nine years later of the great Urdu poet, Mirza Ghalib, who's buried in Nizamuddin (see p.129). A pioneer in Urdu literature – of which Delhi was a major centre, with its own distinct Urdu dialect – Ghalib was most famous for his *ghazals*, a poetic form consisting of rhyming couplets with a repeated refrain, nowadays very popular in songs. Part of the *haveli* has been bought up by the government and restored to its original form, with a little display about Ghalib. Though he is considered Delhi's (and the Urdu language's) greatest poet, many during his lifetime regarded his verse as pretentious and overblown. Despite being the obvious candidate, he was passed over as poet laureate by the emperor Bahadur Shah II, who instead appointed Ghalib's rival Zauq ("the Salieri to Ghalib's Mozart", as historian William Dalrymple calls him); Ghalib only inherited the post when Zauq died.

Gurudwara Sisganj and Fountain Chowk

Further east along Chandni Chowk, on the south side, is **Gurudwara Sisganj**, a Sikh temple founded in 1784, though almost all of the current building dates from the 1930s. It marks the spot where in 1675 the Mughal emperor Aurangzeb had the ninth Sikh guru, Tegh Bahadur, beheaded. The temple welcomes visitors, and has an information office to the left of the entrance, where you can leave shoes and borrow a scarf to cover your head before entering. Before he was killed, the guru was forced to see three of his followers executed in most unpleasant ways: one was sawn in half from head to foot, another wrapped in cotton and slowly burned to death, a third boiled alive in a cauldron of water. This happened across the street in what is now **Fountain Chowk** (the eponymous fountain is Victorian), where a **Sikh Museum** (daily 7am–7pm; free) contains paintings of incidents from the lives of the Sikh gurus, finishing with gory representations of the three martyrdoms. In 1857, the same spot saw further cruel deaths when the British (who had recaptured the city using a largely Sikh army) set up gallows here to hang suspected insurgents; the formality of a trial was barely followed, and sadistic British soldiers paid the hangman to let victims die slowly in order to watch them "dance".

East of Fountain Chowk, the **Central Baptist Church** was Delhi's first Christian mission when it was established in 1814, though the present building was built in 1858, after the bloody events of the previous year. Just to its east, between McDonald's and the State Bank of India, an electrical market leads up to a *chowki* (police post – from which the British slang term "chokey" is derived) and a Hindu temple. If you go past this, towards the Chitra Electric Company ("F10 Cables"), and down a turning to your right, you'll see what was once the classical facade of **Begum Samru's Palace**, now sadly crumbling away. Built in 1823 for the Indian widow of a soldier-of-fortune from Luxembourg, this is one of Delhi's oldest colonial buildings, and was once the grandest mansion in town; its front garden stretched all the way to Chandni Chowk. In 1843 it became the Delhi Bank, but the British manager was butchered by a mob of looters when insurgents took over the city during the 1857 uprising. It was subsequently taken over by Lloyds Bank, whose name can still be read above the portico. Today it's a mess of offices and workshops but some of the original interior is still visible in the Central Bank of India, which has a branch at the front of the building.

Lal Mandir and Gauri Shankar Temple

At the eastern end of Chandni Chowk, opposite the entrance to the Red Fort, is the **Lal Mandir**, a Jain temple. Though not as ornate as the Jain temples in Rajasthan, it does boast detailed carvings, and gilded paintwork in the antechambers surrounding the main shrine. Remove your shoes, and leave any leather articles at the kiosk before entering. The attached **bird hospital** (no charge but donations appreciated) puts into practice the Jain principle that all life is sacred by rescuing injured birds, with each species having its own ward. The sparrow ward is largely occupied by victims of ceiling fans, with which these poor critters apparently collide quite often. Next door, the eighteenth-century Hindu **Gauri Shankar Temple** (leave shoes in a room to the left of the entrance) is quite a warren of shrines, the biggest of which, right at the back, contains a thoroughly awesome statue of Shiva, the god of creation and destruction. The temple also boats an 800-year-old lingam, a phallic symbol representing Shiva and the primeval energy of creation.

The Red Fort (Lal Qila)

The largest of Old Delhi's monuments is Lal Qila, known in English as the **Red Fort** because of the red sandstone from which it was built (Tues–Sun sunrise–sunset, museums 10am–5pm; foreigners Rs100/$2, Indian residents Rs5). It was commissioned by Shah Jahan to be his residence, and modelled on the royal citadel at Agra. Work started in 1638, and the emperor moved in ten years later. The fort contains all the trappings you'd expect to find at the centre of Mughal government: halls of public and private audience, domed and arched marble palaces, plush private apartments, a mosque, and elaborately designed gardens. The ramparts, which stretch for over 2km, are interrupted at ninety degrees by two gates – **Lahori Gate** to the west, through which you enter, and Delhi Gate to the south. Shah Jahan's son, Aurangzeb, who kept his father captive in Agra after usurping him, added barbicans to both gates, much to the old man's disgust. In those days, the Yamuna River ran along the eastern wall, feeding both the moat and a "stream of paradise" which ran through every pavilion. Inevitably, though, as the Mughal empire declined, the fort fell into disrepair. It was attacked and plundered by the Persian emperor Nadir Shah in 1739, and then again by the British in 1857. Nevertheless, it remains an impressive testimony to Mughal grandeur. Remember to keep your ticket stub as you will have to show it several times (for example, to enter the museums).

The main entrance to the fort opens onto **Chatta Chowk**, a covered street flanked with arched cells that used to house Delhi's most talented jewellers, carpet-makers, goldsmiths and silk-weavers, but now stocks souvenirs. At the end, a path to the left leads to a **Museum of the Struggle for Independence**, whose descriptions of resistance to British rule (there are few exhibits as such) are interesting, but have more than a whiff of propaganda about them. At this point, a street ran from the northern end of the fort down to the Delhi Gate, with the soldiers, palace workers' quarters and bazaars all kept strictly to its west. Ahead, the **Naubhat Khana** (Drum House, or Musicians' Gallery)

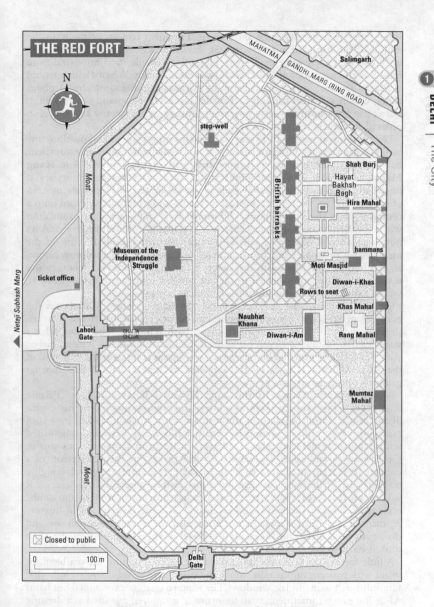

THE RED FORT

N

MAHATMA GANDHI MARG (RING ROAD)

Salimgarh

step-well

Moat

British barracks

Shah Burj

Hayat
Bakhsh
Bagh

Hira Mahal

hammans

Moti Masjid

Diwan-i-Khas

Rows to seat

Khas Mahal

Museum of the
Independence
Struggle

ticket office

Netaji Subhash Marg

Lahori
Gate

CHATTA
CHOWK

Naubhat
Khana

Diwan-i-Am

Rang Mahal

Mumtaz
Mahal

Moat

☒ Closed to public

0   100 m

Delhi
Gate

marked the entrance into the royal quarters. Today, it houses a **Military
Museum**, with swords, weapons and uniforms, but nothing worth stopping for
unless you're an enthusiast.

From the Naubhat Khana, a path leads ahead through wide lawns to the
Diwan-i-Am, or Hall of Public Audience, where the emperor used to meet
commoners and hold court. In those days it was strewn with silk carpets and
partitioned with hanging tapestries. Its centrepiece is a marble dais on which
sat the emperor's throne, surrounded by twelve panels inlaid with precious

stones, mostly depicting birds and flowers. The most famous of them, in the middle at the top (and not easy to see), shows the Greek god Orpheus with his lute. The panels were made by a Florentine jeweller and imported from Italy, but the surrounding inlay work was done locally. When British troops occupied the fort, they looted many of its treasures, including the Orpheus panel, which a British captain had made into a table-top and sent home; it wasn't put back until the early twentieth century when viceroy Lord Curzon ordered its return.

The pavilions along the fort's east wall face spacious gardens and overlook the banks of the Yamuna. Unfortunately, you can't actually go inside most of them, but you can peer into them. Immediately east of the Diwan-i-Am, **Rang Mahal**, the "Palace of Colour", housed the emperor's wives and mistresses. It once had gilded turrets, delicately painted and decorated with intricate mosaics of mirrors, and its ceiling was overlaid with gold and silver and reflected onto a central pool in the marble floor. Unfortunately, it suffered a lot of vandalism when the British used it as an Officers' Mess after the 1857 uprising, and it's now a shadow of its former self. The similar **Mumtaz Mahal**, south of the main *zenana*, or women's quarters, and probably used by princesses, now houses an **Archeological Museum**, displaying manuscripts, paintings, ceramics and textiles, with a section devoted to the last Mughal emperor, Bahadur Shah II, whose exhibits include his silk robes and silver hookah pipe.

On the northern side of Rang Mahal, the marble **Khas Mahal** was the personal palace of the emperor, split into separate apartments for worship, sleeping and sitting. The southern chamber, **Tosh Khana** ("robe room"), has a stunning marble filigree screen on its north wall, surmounted by a panel carved with the scales of justice. The octagonal tower projecting over the east wall of the Khas Mahal was used by the emperor to appear daily before throngs gathered on the riverbanks below.

North of Khas Mahal, in the large **Diwan-i-Khas** ("Hall of Private Audience"), the emperor would address the highest nobles of his court. Today it's the finest building in the fort, a marble pavilion shaded by a roof raised on stolid pillars meeting in ornate scalloped arches and embellished with exquisitely delicate inlays of flowers made from semi-precious stones. On the north and south walls you can still make out the inscription of a couplet in Persian attributed to Shah Jahan's prime minister, which roughly translates as: "If there be paradise upon this earthly sphere, / It is here, oh it is here, oh it is here". More than just a paean, the verse refers to the deliberate modelling of the fort's gardens on the Koranic description of heaven. A marble and gold Peacock Throne inlaid with rubies, sapphires and diamonds once stood on the central pedestal of the Diwan, but Nadir Shah took it back to Iran as booty in 1739.

A little further north are the **hammams**, or baths, sunk into the marble floor inlaid with patterns of precious stones, and dappled in jewel-coloured light that filters through stained-glass windows. The western chamber contained hot baths while the eastern apartment, with fountains of rosewater, was used as a dressing room. Next to the hammams, the sweetly fashioned **Moti Masjid**, or Pearl Mosque, triple-domed in white marble, was added by Aurangzeb in 1659, but unfortunately it's currently closed to the public. The northernmost pavilion in the east wall, called **Shah Burj**, was used to pump water from the river to feed the "stream of paradise". To its west, the **Hayat Bakhsh Bagh** is the only one of the formal gardens – each divided into four by water channels – that still survives. The barrack-like buildings beyond it are just that: barracks, put up by the British to house their troops after the uprising.

Sound and light shows

Each night except Monday, a **Sound and Light show** takes place in the **Red Fort**: the palaces are dramatically lit, and a historical commentary blares from crackly loudspeakers. The show starts after sunset and lasts an hour (in English Feb–April & Sept–Oct 8.30pm, May–Aug 9pm, Nov–Jan 7.30pm; Rs50; ☎011/2327 4580). The mosquitoes are ferocious, so bring repellent. Heavy monsoon rains may affect summer shows.

To the northeast of the complex is an older fort, called **Salimgarh**, commissioned by Sher Shah's son Salim Shah around 1550. It is joined to the Red Fort by a bridge, but closed to the public, though you'll pass right through it if heading east out of Old Delhi by train.

The Jama Masjid and around

A wonderful piece of Mughal pomp, the red-and-white **Jama Masjid** (8am–12.15pm, 1.45pm till half an hour before sunset; closed for half an hour in the afternoon for afternoon prayers; in summer opens earlier at 7am; free; Rs200 for cameras; no shorts, short skirts or sleeveless tops) is India's largest mosque. Soaring above the rooftops of the old city, it looks huge from a distance, and feels nothing short of immense once you've climbed the wide staircases to the arched gateways and entered the open courtyard, which is large enough to accommodate the prostrating bodies of twenty-five thousand worshippers. It was designed by Shah Jahan and built by a workforce of five thousand people between 1644 and 1656. Originally called Masjid-i-Jahanuma ("mosque commanding a view of the world"), this grand structure stands on Bho Jhala, one of Shahjahanabad's two hills, and looks east to the sprawling Red Fort, and down on the seething streets of Old Delhi. Broad red sandstone staircases lead to gateways on the east, north and southern sides, where worshippers and visitors alike must remove their shoes (the custodian will guard them for you for a small tip).

Once inside the courtyard, your eyes will be drawn to the three bulbous marble domes crowning the **main prayer hall** on the west side (facing Mecca), fronted by a series of high cusped arches, and sheltering the mihrab, the central niche in the west wall indicating the direction of prayer. The pool in the centre is used for ritual ablutions. At each corner of the square yard a slender minaret crowned with a marble dome rises to the sky, and it's well worth climbing the **tower** (Rs20; women must be accompanied by a man) south of the main sanctuary for an unrivalled view over Delhi. In the northeast corner a white shrine protects a collection of Muhammad's relics, shrouded in rose petals and watched over by keepers who will, in exchange for a tip, reveal the contents: two sections of the Koran written on deerskin by relatives of the prophet, a red beard-hair of Muhammad's, his sandals, and his "footprint" miraculously embedded in a marble slab (this isn't actually so unusual: the Prophet's footprint is quite a common exhibit in major mosques throughout the Islamic world).

The Jama Masjid is surrounded by a number of bazaars (see box, p.120), while to the east, **Urdu Park** offers a rare breather from the chaos of Old Delhi's streets, a popular spot where local residents gather for a game of cricket, cards or ludo, or to share a surreptitious chillum. Just north of the park you'll find the **tomb of Maulana Azad**, one of pre-Independence India's most important politicians. The youngest ever president of Congress, he was a prominent supporter of Gandhi (imprisoned by the British, of

Old Delhi's bazaars

Almost the whole of Old Delhi is divided into **bazaars** specializing in one type of product or another, from watches and cameras to spices and vegetables. The list below barely scratches the surface, but it does cover some of the more interesting bazaars.

Phool Mandi west of Netaji Subhash Marg. Once the flower market (which is what its name means), this is now Old Delhi's wholesale vegetable market. The market is at its most animated late at night, when goods are arriving, and early in the morning as retailers come to purchase. By about 10am, most of the selling's been done for the day.

Meena Bazaar east of the Jama Masjid. This is the area from which slum dwellers and ramshackle market stalls were cleared during the Emergency (see p.87). Today, many of the stallholders are former residents selling Muslim religious paraphernalia, including wall hangings featuring Koranic quotations or pictures of the Kaaba in Mecca, but there are some stalls selling clothes and fabrics too.

Car Parts Bazaar southwest of the Jama Masjid. Claiming to be the biggest market for spare car parts in the world, this market is very handy if you need used car parts great or small, from springs or bearings to wing mirrors, tyres, doors and even engines.

Guliyan Bazaar north of the Jama Masjid. Shops here have been selling fireworks for at least a hundred and fifty years, and possibly twice that long.

Dariba Kalan leading from Guliyan Bazaar to Chandni Chowk. Old Delhi's silver bazaar, lined with jewellers' shops, mostly selling silver, though some have gold and gemstones too.

Kinari Bazaar west off Dariba Kalan. If you're planning a wedding, this is the place to buy gold turbans (to be worn by the groom), garlands of banknotes (to bedeck the happy couple), tinsel, bridal veils and wedding paraphernalia in general. Wedding clothes can be rented too. At certain times of the year, and particularly around Holi and Dussehra, the bazaar also sells festive accessories.

Nai Sarak leading south from Chandni Chowk. This wide street was driven willy-nilly through the neighbourhood by the British after 1857 to make for easier access, and has become, especially at its southern end, Delhi's wholesale book market, each shop specializing in a different genre, though school and college textbooks predominate. At its northern end, books give way to clothes, particularly saris.

Chawri Bazaar southwest of Nai Sarak. In the nineteenth century, this street was known for its "dancing girls" (sometimes, but not always, sex workers as well). Nowadays, the northern end is a wholesale paper market selling writing paper, greetings cards and even wallpaper, while the southern end specializes in brass goods including statuettes of Hindu gods, as well as oil lamps, pots, vases and ashtrays.

Khari Baoli west of Chandni Chowk. Delhi's wholesale spice market (see opposite), encompassing not only dry spices, but also dried and crystallized fruit, pickles and chutneys, and, at its western end, tea.

course), and the most outspoken Muslim opponent of Partition. When Partition nonetheless came, he worked hard to curtail sectarian bloodshed. His tomb is surmounted by a simple white *chhatra* (canopy); visitors should remove their shoes before approaching it.

On Sundays at 4pm there's a traditional **wrestling** match in a little ground to the east of Maulana Azad's tomb, just before Netaji Subhash Marg (look for the gate with a sign in Hindi featuring a picture of two wrestlers).

Khari Baoli

The spice bazaar of **Khari Baoli**, west of the Fatehpuri Mosque in Old Delhi's northwestern corner, is even more congested than Chandni Chowk. The biggest spice market in Asia, it teems from dawn till dusk with shoppers, spice dealers, rickshaws trying to make progress through the crowds, and porters wielding barrowloads of roots, barks and seeds. Its shops are packed full of spices, teas, lentils, chutneys, pickles, and dried or crystallized fruit. **Gadodia Market**, immediately behind the Fatehpuri Mosque, is the epicentre of the whole affair, a veritable hive of spicy commerce, where untold quantities of pepper, cardamom, chutney and even the silver leaf used to cover Indian sweets are bought, sold, loaded, unloaded and haggled over all day long.

At Khari Baoli's western end, where once the Lahori Gate stood astride the road to Lahore, the **Sarhindi Masjid**, commissioned at the same time as the Fatehpuri Mosque by another of Shah Jahan's wives, Sarhindi Begum, is too hidden behind shops for you to get a decent view, but if you feel like exploring the backstreets you could seek out a more interesting if somewhat more modest mosque. Head south along Naya Bans Road and take a left at the water tank.

△ Khari Baoli spice market

After thirty metres (opposite no. 6067), turn right into a narrow street full of stalls selling namkeens (the assorted constituents and permutations of what Westerners call "Bombay mix"). Continue for 100 metres or so, until you reach a blue doorway on the left with a small Urdu sign above it, which leads into a little courtyard in front of the simple **Hauzwali Mosque**. Situated next to the original *baoli* (step-well) – now long gone – from which the spice market takes its name, this little blue-washed mosque with its three small, domed chambers, was built in the 1540s, a century before the rest of Old Delhi. Outside of Purana Qila it's one of very few buildings in Delhi dating from the Suri period (the time of Sher Shah and his family). And with its low domes, and unadorned doorways, decorated only by the simple flanging of one arch inside another, it really is quite strikingly different from all of Old Delhi's other mosques.

The street leading south from Khari Baoli road, alongside the railway line, is one of Delhi's less reputable addresses. **Shraddhanand Marg**, formerly GB Road, is the city's sleaziest red light district, and for much of the way down, particularly between nos. 53–72, the dark stairways on its east side lead mostly up to brothels.

Ajmeri Gate and around

Of Shahjahanabad's four surviving city gates, three are along Old Delhi's southern edge, on what is now Asaf Ali Road. **Ajmeri Gate**, so called because it stood astride the main road to Ajmer, was described by a British traveller in 1906 as "broad and tall and studded with sharp spikes of no friendly intent", though it looks tamer today, hived off from the street in a well-kept little garden (daily 5–8am), its spikes long gone.

Just west of the gate stand the red sandstone **Madrasa and Mosque of Ghazi-ud-din**, designed in the classic Mughal style. Built in 1692, the madrasa was commissioned by Ghazi-ud-din Bahadur Firoz Jang, a distinguished general in Aurangzeb's army. Though illness left him completely blind, Ghazi-ud-din remained one of the emperor's most important military advisors, and went on to become nawab (governor) of Gujarat. When he died in 1727, he was buried by his *madrasa*, and the mosque was built to honour his memory. In 1825, the *madrasa*, originally a Koranic school, was renamed Delhi College and became a centre for perpetuating Urdu culture, though this role was deliberately curtailed by the British after the 1857 uprising. Today, the mosque is still in use, while the *madrasa*, which has become rather run-down, is now the Anglo-Arabic Secondary School. Neither, in principle, is open to the public, but they'll almost certainly let you in to look round if you ask.

Another interesting little mosque, the **Masjid Mubarak Begum**, is on Lalkuan Bazaar Road, at Hauz Razi no. 4959, very near Chawri Bazaar metro station. The Indian wife of a British official had it built in 1823 as part of their estate, and it stands in its own terrace above the shops, accessible up a narrow staircase from the street (take off your shoes at the top).

Turkman Gate and around

Turkman Gate is named after a Sufi saint, Hazrat Shah Turkman, who died in 1240 and is buried nearby. His tomb, **Shah Turkman Durgah** – the oldest building in Old Delhi – can be found by heading north up what eventually becomes Sitaram Bazaar Road, though at these lower reaches it is officially called Mohammed Deen Ilaichi Marg. After some 200m on the right, between nos. 1900–2038, you'll pass through an enclosure painted mustard yellow. On the other side of the enclosure, straight ahead of you, is a little alley. Head down it, following it round to the right, and on your left you'll see the red and green door to the saint's tomb. The drop in floor level shows how much older it is than the surrounding streets. You may need to locate the caretaker if you want to look inside, as it's often locked up, but the tomb still attracts devotees, who leave flowers and burn incense. As with all tombs and mosques, you must take off your shoes before entering.

Some fifty metres further up Mohammed Deen Ilaichi Marg, on the left, atop a steep staircase, is a mosque called the **Kalan Masjid**, resplendent in green and blue, with a pink doorway surmounted by the name of Allah in Arabic. Like Shah Turkman's tomb, the Kalan Masjid is older than the surrounding city. It was built in 1387 on the orders of Khan-i-Jahan Junan Shah, Firoz Shah's chief minister, and is noticeably Tughluq rather than Mughal in style, with its low domes and tapering shape. Khan-i-Jahan had seven mosques built across the Delhi area, but only this one remains in use today.

Twenty metres further, Mohammed Deen Ilaichi Marg bends to the left to become Sitaram Bazaar Road. But if you take a right instead (between nos. 2045 and 2451), then turn left, opposite a little mosque, and follow the increasingly tortuous alleyway all the way to the end (bear right where it forks), you come to a little enclosure containing two graves. The one on the left is the **tomb of Razia Sultan**, who was, until Indira Gandhi, Delhi's only ever female ruler, reigning from 1236 to 1240; the other tomb belongs to her sister. The daughter of Iltutmish, and his nominee to succeed him, Razia was blocked from the throne by sexist religious and military leaders, who put her brother there instead, but he proved utterly incompetent, and seven months later she ousted him. As sultan, she threw off the veil and appeared in public dressed in a tunic and conical hat, riding into battle on horseback armed with a bow and arrows. The people of Delhi strongly supported her, but the aristocracy never accepted the rule of a woman and her reign was plagued by rebellion. Forced to flee Delhi, she was murdered by bandits at a place called Kaithal, but although she has a grave there, Delhiwallahs reckon this is where she really lies, moved by her brother and successor Behram Shah to be near Hazrat Shah Turkman, of whom she was a follower.

Delhi Gate and Daryaganj

Delhi Gate faced what had previously been the city of Delhi (Lal Kot, Jahanpanah, Firozabad and Purana Qila). Today, it marks the southern end of the district known as **Daryaganj**. To its east and south are Raj Ghat and Firoz Shah Kotla (see p.124), but if you head north up Netaji Subhash Marg, you come to the Golcha Cinema, one of Delhi's oldest movie theatres. From the car park, follow the turning round to the left and then take a right after twenty metres, and you come to a singularly unimpressive domestic courtyard called **Naherwali Haveli**. Underwhelming though it may be, this was the birthplace of Pakistan's president Pervez Musharraf, whose family fled Delhi during Partition when Musharraf was four years old. Before 1857, the same compound was home to the chief minister of Bahdur Shah II, the last Mughal emperor.

Daryaganj also has one or two interesting mosques. On its eastern edge, almost at the city wall, the 1707 **Ghata Mosque**, or Zinat al-Masjid, commissioned by Aurangzeb's daughter, is like a smaller version of the Jama Masjid. Historian William Dalrymple describes it as "the most beautiful of all the Delhi mosques", but there are other contenders. One of them can be found further north, just beyond the footbridge over Netaji Subhash Marg, where two roads lead west, signposted repectively "Pataudi House" and "Jama Masjid". The first leads to the **Pataudi House Mosque**. White with three blue-washed domes and frilly doorways (best photographed in the morning), this pretty little mosque dates from the eighteenth century, when it was part of a haveli called Kalan Mahal, a name still given to the area behind it. The mosque's own name comes from its proximity to a nearby haveli that belonged to the Nawab of Pataudi.

Raj Ghat

Riverside *ghats* (steps leading down to the water) have been used in India for centuries, for mundane things like washing clothes and bathing, but also for worship and funeral cremation. **Raj Ghat** (daily April–Sept 5am–7.30pm, Oct–Mar 5.30am–7pm; free), east of Delhi Gate – really more a park than a *ghat* – is the place where Mahatma Gandhi was cremated, on the day after his assassination in 1948. The Mahatma's *samadhi* (cremation memorial), a low black plinth inscribed with his last words, "Hai Ram" ("Oh God"), receives a steady stream of visitors, and he is remembered through prayers here every Friday evening at 5pm, and on the anniversaries of his birth and death (Oct 2 & Jan 30). Opposite Raj Ghat's southwest corner, the small **Gandhi Memorial Museum** (daily except Mon and every other Sun, 9.30am–5.30pm; free) houses some of Gandhi's photographs and writings, and at weekends you can watch films on his political and personal life (English Sat 4pm; Hindi Sun 4pm).

North of Raj Ghat, memorials also mark the places where Jawaharlal Nehru (at Shanti Vana), his daughter Indira Gandhi (at Shakti Sthal), and his grandson Rajiv Gandhi (at Vir Bhumi) were cremated. Rajiv is honoured by a striking frieze and his mother by a red-grey stone monolith. Nehru's simple memorial reproduces a section of his will asking that his ashes be scattered from an aeroplane, "so that they might mingle with the dust and soil of India and become an indistinguishable part of India." Behind this, a red granite block commemorates Rajiv's brother Sanjay, an amateur pilot who died in a 1980 plane accident; during his lifetime, he became rather unpopular, especially in Delhi, for his role in the 1975 Emergency, and his less-than-voluntary vasectomy programme.

Firoz Shah Kotla

Supposedly, Firoz Shah, sultan of Delhi from 1351 to 1358, had a whole fifth city of Delhi built – Firozabad, founded in 1354. Today few traces survive of what was in any case probably never more than a suburb of the main city, still then centred on Lal Kot (around the Qutb Minar, see p.134) and Jahanpanah (its exension to the northeast, see p.131), but what does remain is the fortified palace of **Firoz Shah Kotla** (Tues–Sun sunrise–sunset; foreigners Rs100/$2, Indian residents Rs5), now a crumbling ruin with ornamental gardens, 500m east of Delhi Gate. Its most incongruous and yet distinctive element is the third century BC polished sandstone **Ashokan pillar**, carried down the Yamuna by raft from Ambala. The 14m-high column, one of two brought by Firoz to Delhi (the other is on the Northern Ridge – see p.126), is surrounded by a building full of tiny rooms, evidently built to house it. For a reasonable view of the column, you'll need to climb to the top of the building, entering the compound through a gate on the west side, then mounting a stairway in the northeast corner. From the top you also get a view of the neighbouring mosque and *baoli* (step-well), as well as the lawns which make the site such a pleasant place to visit. On Thursday evenings, after sunset, local residents come down to burn candles and joss sticks in the building around the Ashokan pillar to placate the *djinn* (spirits) that are believed to reside here.

Small children and doll lovers may well appreciate **Shankar's International Doll Museum** (Tues–Sun 10am–6pm; Rs10), south of Firoz Shah Kotla in

Nehru House, 4 Bahadur Shah Zafar Marg (500m north of Pragati Maidan metro station). Over six thousand dolls from around the world include mannequins of John Wayne, Louis Armstrong, Henry VIII and Elizabeth I, and though none is antique, it's a prodigious collection.

North of the Red Fort

Heading north up Netaji Subhash Marg from the Red Fort, you pass under a railway bridge on the way to Old Delhi GPO. Just before the post office, on the east side of the road, **Lothian Cemetery** was the burial ground for officers of the East India Company from 1808 until just after the 1857 uprising. Today it's in a state of some disrepair, and occupied by squatters, though they don't mind curious tourists popping in for a look about. In the middle of the road in front of the post office, and still topped by an old cannon, the remains of the East India Company's **Magazine** or arsenal is now used mainly as an unofficial public toilet, so watch your step if you cross the street to explore it. Another chunk of the Magazine, on another traffic island just to the north, bears a plaque honouring the "nine resolute Englishmen" who defended it against "rebels and mutineers" for over four hours on 11 May 1857, blowing it up when all was lost to prevent it falling into enemy hands. A post-Independence plaque just below the Raj-era original points out that "The persons described as 'rebels and mutineers' in the above inscription were Indian members of the army in the service of the East India Company trying to overthrow the foreign government." Just north of the Magazine, a grey obelisk recalls the bravery of two of the Company's telegraph operators during the same episode who stayed on till the last moment to keep the army base at Ambala up to speed on the day's events.

Continuing north along Lothian Road, you'll pass another remnant of Company days on your right in the form of the old **Residency**, now the Archeology Department of Guru Gobind Singh Indraprastha University. A couple of hundred metres further is the rather fine cream and white baroque facade of **St James's Church** (daily 8.30am–1pm & 2–5pm, or whenever you can find the caretaker), commissioned in 1836 by **James Skinner**, the son of a Scottish Company-wallah and a Rajput princess. Because of his mixed ancestry, and the increasing racism of the British regime, Skinner was refused a commission in the Company's army, but set up his own irregular cavalry unit (Skinner's Horse, also called the Yellow Boys after their uniform) and made himself pretty much indispensable to the Company in northern India. Though he was continually snubbed over pay and rank, his astounding victories over the forces of the Maharajah of Jaipur and the great Sikh leader Maharajah Ranjit Singh eventually forced the Company to begrudgingly grant him the rank of Lieutenant-Colonel and absorb his cavalrymen into its ranks. Skinner died in 1842 and is buried just in front of the altar.

Immediately north of the church, Church Road leads to the offices of the Northern Railway, where the East India Company's **Deputy Resident's Residence** is now the office of the railway's chief engineer. If you ask at the gate, you'll probably be allowed in to admire the bow-fronted verandah and balustrades, but you probably won't be allowed to take photos or to venture inside. A plaque to the left of its front door explains the building's history.

The double-arched **Kashmiri Gate**, on the west side of Lothian Road just 300m north of the church, was where the Mughal court would leave Delhi every summer bound for the cool valley of Kashmir. It was also here in September 1857 that the British made their assault on the city to recapture it from the insurgents.

The Civil Lines

North of the Kashmiri Gate is Maharana Pratap Inter-state Bus Terminal, beyond which, across the busy Lala Hardev Sahai Marg, is the district known as the **Civil Lines**. This area was created after the events of 1857, when the British no longer felt safe living among the Indian residents of Old Delhi and moved up here for a more secluded location.

Immediately north of Lala Hardev Sahai Marg, the peaceful **Qudsia Gardens** are a fading remnant of the magnificent pleasure parks commissioned in the mid-eighteenth century by Queen Qudsia, wife of the Mughal emperor Muhammad Shah, and mother of Ahmed Shah. Part of it was taken over by the British Freemasons, who built a hall and banned Indians from entering the park in the afternoons. A gate in the centre and a mosque in the southeast corner still remain from Queen Qudsia's original garden.

Across Alipur Road from Qudsia Gardens is the nineteenth-century **Nicholson Cemetery**. A number of British casualties from 1857 are buried here, most prominently Brigadier-General John Nicholson, whose tomb is just beyond the entrance, to the right, surrounded by railings. An uncompromisingly violent racist responsible for ordering numerous summary killings, but also highly charismatic and extremely popular with the troops, Nicholson was just the person the British needed to lead their assault on Delhi. Shot by a sniper as his men fought their way in through the Kashmiri Gate, he took ten days to die, and when he heard that the more cautious General who had replaced him was thinking of retreating back to the gate, he said: "Thank God that I still have the strength yet to shoot him if necessary." The marble stone on his grave was looted from the gardens of the Red Fort. In 2006, a British company sponsored the cemetery's restoration, and it was reopened by the British High Commissioner, to a few raised eyebrows from those who felt that it glorified – or at the very least ignored – the horrific British war crimes of 1857, but the cemetery, once overgrown and vandalized, is now pristine and immaculate, and most would agree that this is a piece of history well preserved rather than an endorsement of imperialism and murder.

The Northern Ridge and Majnu ka Tilla

West of the Civil Lines is the **Northern Ridge**, a forested area that was previously just scrub and gave views over the city. It was here that the British army holed up in 1857 prior to their final assault on Delhi. The ridge is strewn with a miscellany of monuments, among them a very Gothic Victorian **Mutiny Monument** originally dedicated to British soldiers killed in the uprising, now rededicated to the "immortal martyrs for Indian freedom" who died fighting against them. Just to the north is an **Ashokan pillar**, the second of two brought to Delhi by Firoz Shah (the other is at Firoz Shah Kotla – see p.124); this one originally came from Meerut, which by a strange coincidence is also where the 1857 uprising began. Firoz Shah brought the pillar here to adjoin his hunting lodge, of which a ruined section, called **Pir Ghaib**, survives, in the grounds just north of the Hindu Rao Hospital. Five hundred metres north of that, the 1354 **Chauburji Mosque** is thought by some to have originally been a tomb, but the mihrab in the west wall seems to suggest that it was always used for prayer. If you still fancy a long stroll or a rickshaw ride up Ridge Road – and the woods do make it pleasant, with birds and monkeys all along the way – you'll eventually come after a kilometre and a half to its highest point, where the **Flagstaff Tower** was built in 1828 to relay signals and fly the flag (the Union Jack), unobscured by trees back then. It's also where British refugees gathered to flee the city when the 1857 insurgents first took it over. The tower is not far from Vidhan Sabha metro station.

A very different group of refugees, arriving in the 1950s following China's invasion of Tibet, set up what's now a veritable little Lhasa at **Majnu ka Tilla**, with Tibetan shops and restaurants, saffron-clad monks, and pictures of the Dalai Lama in almost every establishment. The area also has a number of good budget hotels (see p.101), but it's a bit out of the way, on the east side of Dr K.B. Hedgewar Marg, 1km northeast of Vidhan Sabha metro.

Coronation Park

Now just a windblown piece of waste ground on the city's northern fringes, 10km north of Connaught Place, **Coronation Park** once showpieced the pomp and might of the British Raj. The British held three **durbars** (huge ceremonial gatherings) here: in 1887 on Queen Victoria's assumption of the title "Empress of India"; in 1903 to mark the coronation of her successor Edward VII; and in 1911 when George V came to be crowned in person as emperor. The high point of the durbar was a procession of elephants bearing all the princes of India, headed by the Nizam of Hyderabad, to pay homage to the British ruler, in the same way that they had previously to the Mughals. All but forgotten nowadays (your auto-wallah or taxi driver won't have heard of the place so they'll need clear instructions on how to get here), the park is centred around a **granite obelisk** commemorating the 1911 coronation. In an enclosure close by, a grandiose statue of the king-emperor George, which once graced what is now the Rajpath, stands Ozymandias-like among other nameless and forgotten rulers from an empire fast receding into history. The park is located on Nirankari Marg, just south of the Outer Ring Road NH-1 bypass (Dr K.B. Hedgewar Marg) near Sant Nagar. It costs Rs60 by pre-paid auto from Connaught Place, or around Rs100 from town if you don't pre-pay.

South Delhi

Most of the early settlements of Delhi, including its first cities, are to be found not in "Old Delhi" but in **South Delhi**, the area south of Lutyens' carefully planned boulevards, where the rapid expansion of suburban Delhi has swallowed up what was previously countryside. Whole villages have been embedded within it, and the area is littered with monuments from the past. Meanwhile, as the centre becomes more and more congested, South Delhi's housing enclaves and colonies are increasingly home to the newest shopping centres and the most happening locales. There's lots to see in South Delhi if you've time to explore it, but if you need to stick with the bare minimum, don't miss the two great Mughal garden tombs – **Humayun's Tomb** and **Safdarjang's Tomb** – at either end of Lodi Road, and the **Qutb Minar complex** at Lal Kot, Delhi's first incarnation; if you can, also try to fit in the amazing lotus-shaped **Baha'i Temple**.

Humayun's Tomb

Close to the medieval Muslim centre of Nizamuddin and 2km from Purana Qila, **Humayun's Tomb** (daily sunrise–sunset; foreigners Rs250/$5, Indian residents Rs10) stands at the crossroads of the Lodi and Mathura roads, 500m from Nizamuddin railway station (one stop from New Delhi station on the suburban line), and easily accessible from Connaught Place by bus (#181, #966 and #893) or pre-paid auto (Rs50). Late afternoon is the best time to photograph it. Delhi's first Mughal mausoleum, it was constructed to house the remains of the second Mughal emperor, Humayun, who at the start of his reign lost Delhi and most of his father Babur's empire to the Afghan warlord Sher Shah Suri, but managed to regain it all from Sher Shah's son Sikander in 1555. Sher Shah had posthumous revenge, however, when Humayun died less than a year later after falling down the stairs of Sher Shah's Sher Mandal (see p.112). Humayun's tomb was built under the watchful eye of Haji Begum, his senior widow and mother of Akbar, who camped here for the duration, and is now buried here alongside her husband. The grounds were later used to inter several prominent Mughals, and served as a refuge for the last emperor, Bahadur Shah II, before his capture by the British in 1857.

The tomb's sombre, Persian-style elegance marks this as one of Delhi's finest historic sites. Constructed of red sandstone, inlaid with black and white marble, on a commanding podium looking towards the Yamuna, it stands in the centre of the formal *charbagh*, or quartered garden. The octagonal structure is crowned with a double dome that soars to a height of 38 metres. Though it was the very first Mughal garden tomb – to be followed by Akbar's at Sikander and of course the Taj Mahal at Agra, for which it can be seen as a prototype – Humayun's mausoleum has antecedents in Delhi in the form of Ghiyas-ud-din Tughluq's tomb at Tughluqabad, and that of Sikandar Lodi in Lodi Gardens. From the second of those it adopted its octagonal shape and the high central arch that was to be such a typical feature of Mughal architecture – you'll see it at the Taj, and in Delhi's Jama Masjid, for example.

Within the grounds, southeast of the main mausoleum, another impressive square mausoleum, with a double dome and two graves bearing Koranic inscriptions, is that of Humayun's barber, a man considered important because he was trusted with holding a razor to the emperor's throat. Nearby but outside the compound (so you'll have to walk right round for a closer look) stands the **Nila Gumbad** ("blue dome"), an octagonal tomb with a dome of blue tiles, supposedly built by one of Akbar's nobles to honour a faithful servant, and which may possibly predate Humayun's Tomb. The blue-domed structure in the middle of the road junction in front of the entrance to Humayun's tomb is a seventeenth-century tomb called Sabz Burj – the tiles on its dome are not original, but the result of a recent restoration. On your way round to the Nila Gumbad (depending on your route), you pass the **tomb of Khan-i-Khanan**, a Mughal general who died in 1626 (daily sunrise–sunset; foreigners Rs100/$2, Indian residents Rs5). Though originally in the same tradition of Mughal garden tombs as Humayun's and the Taj, it looks rather ragged today as the facing was all stripped for use in Safdarjang's tomb, and the garden that surrounded it has mostly gone.

Nizamuddin

Just across the busy Mathura Road from Humayun's Tomb, and now engulfed by a busy road network and plush suburbs, the self-contained *mahalla* (village) of **Nizamuddin**, with its lack of traffic, its ancient mosques and tombs, and its slow pace of life, is so different from the surrounding city that to enter it is like passing through a time warp. At its heart, surrounded by a tangle of narrow alleyways lined with shops and market stalls, lies one of Sufism's greatest shrines, the **Hazrat Nizamuddin Dargah**, which draws a constant stream of devotees from far and wide.

The marble *dargah* is the tomb of Sheikh Nizam-ud-din Aulia (1236–1325), fourth saint of the Chishtiya Sufi order, Sufism being the mystical branch of Islam, whose followers aim to bring themselves personally nearer to God, and the Chishtiya being the branch of Sufism founded by Khwaja Muin-ud-din Chishti of Ajmer (see p.268). The *dargah* was built the year the sheikh died, but has been through several renovations, and the present mausoleum dates from 1562. Lattice screens and arches in the inner sanctum surround the actual tomb (closed to women), which is surrounded by a marble rail and a canopy of mother-of-pearl. Sheikh Nizam-ud-din's disciple, the poet and chronicler **Amir Khusrau** – considered to be the first Urdu poet and the founder of *khyal*, the most common form of north Indian classical music – lies in a contrasting red sandstone tomb in front of his master's mausoleum.

Religious song and music play an important role among the Chishtiyas, as among several Sufi orders, and *qawwals* (bards) gather to sing in the evenings (especially on Thursdays and feast days). Comprising a chorus led by solo singing accompanied by clapping and usually a harmonium combined with a *dholak* (double-membraned barrel drum) and *tabla* (paired hand-drums), the hypnotic rhythm of their **qawwali music** is designed to lull its audience into a state of *mast* (spiritual intoxication), which is believed to bring the devotee closer to God.

The oldest building in the area, the red sandstone mosque of **Jamat Khana Masjid**, looms over the main *dargah* on its western side. It was commissioned in 1325 by Khizr Khan, the son of the Khalji sultan Ala-ud-din. Enclosed by marble lattice screens next to Amir Khusrau's mausoleum, the tomb of **Princess Jahanara**, Shah Jahan's favourite daughter, is topped by a hollow filled with grass in compliance with her wish to have nothing but grass covering her grave. By the compound's north gate is a holy *baoli*.

Like Amir Khusrau and Princess Jahanara, other people also wanted to be buried in the saint's vicinity. Just east of the *dargah* compound, the elegant 64-pillared white marble **Chausath Khamba** was built as a mausoleum for the family of a Mughal politician who had been governor of Gujarat, and the building, with its low, wide form and elegant marble screens, bears the unmistakable evidence of a Gujarati influence. The compound containing the Chuasath is usually locked, but the caretaker should be on hand somewhere nearby to open it up if you want to take a closer look. Just outside is the tomb of the poet Mirza Ghalib (see p.115), likewise buried here to benefit from the saint's blessing.

Lodi Gardens

Two kilometres west of Nizamuddin along Lodi Road, the leafy, pleasant **Lodi Gardens** (daily 5am–8pm; free) form part of a belt of fifteenth- and sixteenth-century monuments that now stand incongruously amid golf greens, large bungalows and elite estates. The park is especially full in the early mornings and early evenings, when fitness enthusiasts come for brisk walks or to jog through the manicured gardens against a backdrop of much-graffitied medieval monuments; it's also a popular lovers' hangout. The gardens, a Rs40 auto ride from Connaught Place, also contain the **National Bonsai Park**, which has a fine selection of diminutive trees. The best time to come is at sunset, when the light is soft and the tombs are all lit up.

Near the centre of the gardens, the imposing **Bara Gumbad** ("large dome"), is a square late-fifteenth-century tomb capped by the eponymous dome, its monotonous exterior relieved by grey and black stones and its interior adorned with painted stuccowork. **Shish Gumbad** ("glazed dome"), a similar tomb 50m north, still bears a few traces of the blue tiles liberally used to form friezes below the cornice and above the entrance. Inside, plasterwork is inscribed with ornate Koranic inscriptions.

The octagonal **tomb of Muhammad Shah** (1434–44) of the Sayyid dynasty stands 300m southwest of Bara Gumbad, surrounded by verandas and pierced by arches and sloping buttresses. Enclosed within high walls and a square garden, 300m north of Bara Gumbad, the **tomb of Sikandar Lodi** (1517–18) repeats the octagonal theme, with a central chamber encircled by a veranda. **Athpula** ("eight piers"), a sixteenth-century ornamental bridge, lies east, in the northwest corner of the park.

Safdarjang's Tomb

At the western end of Lodi Road, **Safdarjang's Tomb** (daily sunrise–sunset; foreigners Rs100/$2, Indian residents Rs5), is served by bus #505 from Ajmeri Gate or Connaught Place (Kasturba Gandhi Marg), or from Connaught Place by pre-paid auto-rickshaw (Rs50), and is at its most photogenic in the morning. Safdarjang was the Mughal nawab (governor) of Avadh who briefly became vizier before being overthrown for his Shi'ite beliefs. He died in 1753, by which time the empire was reduced to a fraction of its former size and most of the capital's grander buildings lay in ruins, and his tomb represents the last in a line of Mughal garden tombs that started with Humayun's and reached its apogee with the Taj Mahal. Compared with those two, Safdarjang's Tomb invariably gets a bad press. Where Humayun's Tomb is vigorous and solid, and the Taj is perfectly proportioned and delicately decorated, Safdarjang's Tomb is regarded as decadent and over-embellished. William Dalrymple, in *City of Djinns*, describes it as "blowzy Mughal rococo" typifying an age "not so much decaying into impoverished anonymity as one whoring and drinking itself into extinction". Certainly, its elongated proportions make it seem slender in comparison with earlier Mughal constructions, and its frills and fancies can be regarded as overdone, but for all that it has a certain feminine elegance that Humayun's Tomb lacks, and it's definitely worth the trip down Lodi Road to see it. The frills around the arches, the fussy decoration on the corner turrets, and the *chhatris* that surmount them may rouse the ire of Mughal architecture's more purist fans, but there's no denying they're pretty, and the tomb's ornate interior is filled with wonderful swirling plasterwork.

Hauz Khas

Set amid parks and woodland 4km south of Safdarjang's Tomb, the wealthy suburban development of **Hauz Khas** is typical of South Delhi in being a thoroughly modern area dotted with remnants of antiquity. The modern part takes the form of Hauz Khas village, a shopping area packed with chic boutiques and smart restaurants. There's also a very pleasant deer park and a rose garden. If you get off the #505 bus at Hauz Khas, the village is an 800m stroll to the west, on which you'll pass a whole slew of ancient tombs, but of most interest to visitors, apart from the upmarket shopping possibilities (see p.146), are the ruins of a fourteenth-century reservoir at the western end of the village.

Sultan Ala-ud-din Khalji had the reservoir (or "tank") built in 1304 to supply water to his citadel at Siri, Delhi's "second city", and it was known after him as **Hauz-i-Alai**. Half a century later, it was expanded by Firoz Shah, who added a two-storey *madrasa* (seminary), and a mosque at its northern end. Among the anonymous tombs scattered throughout the area is that of Firoz Shah himself, directly overlooking the southern corner of the tank. Its high walls, lofty dome, and doorway spanned by a lintel with a stone railing outside are fine examples of Hindu Indian traditions effectively blended with Islamic architecture. At dawn every day, the surrounding woodlands and the paths around the immense tank, once the site of Timur's camp, come alive with people out walking, practising yoga and jogging, while later in the day, the tank itself springs to life with fountains.

△ Safdarjang's Tomb

Siri, Jahanpanah and Chiragh Delhi

Ala-ud-din's citadel at **Siri** (see p.85) is a couple of kilometres east of Hauz Khas, and the remains of its ramparts can be seen from Khel Gaon Marg. Much of it has been given over to parkland, which makes it pleasant enough to visit, but short of a few very diminutive ruins and a Jat village, there isn't a lot to see.

Delhi's "fourth city", **Jahanpanah**, was built during the reign of Muhammad Tughluq to fill the space between Siri and Lal Kot (see p.132), of which it was really just a northeastward extension. All that remains of it today are some scattered mosques and tombs, mostly located south of Siri between Gamal Abdel Nasser Marg (the Outer Ring Road) and Press Enclave Road, which continues west to the Qutb Minar at Lal Kot. It isn't one of Delhi's top attractions, but it's certainly worth exploring. Starting at its junction with Gamal Abdel Nasser Marg, head south for 300m along Khel Gaon Marg, until you come to a set of traffic lights where a right turn down Geetanjali Marg brings you eventually to a turning on the right by a "Guide Map of Begampur Park". Follow that road and it leads into Begampur village, where you'll find the starkly imposing edifice of the **Begampuri Mosque** (sunrise–sunset; free), a wonderfully impressive piece of Tughluq architecture with a huge courtyard and a massive gateway into the main prayer area directly opposite the entrance. To its north (follow the street round the north side of the mosque and take a right just beyond it), the **Bijay Mandal** was almost certainly part of Muhammad Tughluq's palace. A sturdy if very ruined construction, it can be climbed for views over the area from the octagonal pavilion on its roof. Head back to the traffic lights at the start of Geetanjali Marg, and take a right turn (continuing along Khel Gaon Marg) which after 200m takes you past **Lal Gumbad** (sunrise–sunset; free), the 1397 tomb of a local Sufi saint, and reminiscent of Ghiyas-ud-din Tughluq's tomb at Tughluqabad (see p.136). Continue for another 300m until you reach Khirki Main Road, which leads south to Khirki Village and the **Khirki Masjid** (sunrise–sunset; free), a solidly imposing mosque with typically Tughluq tapering turrets, which was one of seven commissioned by Firoz Shah's chief minister Khan-i-Jahan Junan Shah. Its interior, almost completely covered, with only four small areas open to the sky, is wierdly atmospheric and partly colonized by bats. From its eastern gateway, stairs lead up to the roof, where you can check out its mass of domes.

One of Delhi's least-known attractions is the almost perfectly square village of **Chiragh Delhi**, which lies just south of Gamal Abdel Nasser Marg to the east of Jahanpanah. Like Nizamuddin, this is a village that has been swallowed whole by Delhi, but even more than Nizammudin, it retains its village atmosphere and it's a great place for a wander. Once walled, it still has the remains of gateways in the middle of each of its four sides, and at its western side a *dargah*, the tomb of Hazrat Nizam-ud-din's pupil and successor, the Chishti saint, Chiragh Delhi. Within the enclosure (take off shoes to enter) are several subsidiary tombs as well as that of the saint himself, who died in 1356. Just to its west, and worth the walk all the way round the north side of the compound to reach it, the **tomb of Bahlal Lodi**, sultan of Delhi from 1451 to 1489, is a curious castellated building, quite unlike any other royal tomb in the city.

Qutb Minar Complex

Above the foundations of **Lal Kot**, the "first city of Delhi" founded in the eleventh century by the Tomar Rajputs, stand the first monuments of Muslim India, known as the **Qutb Minar Complex** (daily sunrise–sunset; foreigners Rs250/$5, Indian residents Rs10). You'll find it 13km south of Connaught Place off Aurobindo Marg, easy to reach by bus #505 from Ajmeri Gate, Connaught Place (Super Bazaar) or Kasturba Gandhi Marg, or by pre-paid auto from Connaught Place (Rs70). One of Delhi's most famous landmarks, the fluted red sandstone tower of the **Qutb Minar** tapers upwards from the ruins, covered with intricate carvings and deeply inscribed verses from the Koran, to a height of just over 72m. In times past it was considered one of the "Wonders of the East", second only to the Taj Mahal – in the words of the Victorian historian, James Ferguson, "the most beautiful example of its class known

△ Qutb Minar tower

anywhere"; but historian John Keay was perhaps more representative of the modern eye when he claimed that the tower had "an unfortunate hint of the factory chimney and the brick kiln; a wisp of white smoke trailing from its summit would not seem out of place".

Work on the Qutb Minar started in 1202; it was Qutb-ud-din Aibak's victory tower, celebrating the advent of the Muslim dominance of Delhi (and much of the Subcontinent) that was to endure until 1857. For Qutb-ud-din, who died four years after gaining power, it marked the eastern extremity of the Islamic faith, casting the shadow of God over east and west. It was also a minaret, from which the *muezzin* called the faithful to prayer. Only the first storey has been ascribed to Qutb-ud-din's own short reign; the other four were built under his successor Iltutmish, and the top was restored in 1369 under Firoz Shah, using marble to face the red sandstone.

Adjacent to the tower lie the ruins of India's first mosque, **Quwwat-ul-Islam** ("the Might of Islam"), commissioned by Qutb-ud-din and built using the remains of 27 Hindu and Jain temples with the help of Hindu artisans whose influence can be seen in the detail of the masonry and the indigenous corbelled arches. Steps lead to an impressive courtyard flanked by cloisters and supported by pillars unmistakably taken from a Hindu temple and adapted to accord with strict Islamic law forbidding iconic worship – all the faces of the decorative figures carved into the columns have been removed. Especially fine ornamental arches, rising as high as 16m, remain of what was once the prayer hall. Beautifully carved sandstone screens, combining Koranic calligraphy with the Indian lotus, form a facade immediately to the west of the mosque, facing Mecca. Iltutmish and his successors had the building extended, enlarging the prayer hall and the cloisters and introducing geometric designs, calligraphy, glazed tiles set in brick, and squinches (arches set diagonally to a square to support a dome). In Iltutmish's tomb, on a plinth to the west of the Quwwat-ul-Islam, a relatively plain exterior with three ornate arches blending Indian and Muslim styles hides a nine-metre-square interior decorated with geometric arabesque patterns, calligraphy, and lotus and wheel motifs.

The Khalji sultan Ala-ud-din had the mosque extended to the north, and aimed to build a tower even taller than the Qutb Minar, but his **Alai Minar** never made it beyond the first storey, which still stands, and is regarded as a monument to the folly of vain ambition. Ala-ud-din also commissioned the **Alai Darwaza**, an elegant mausoleum-like gateway with stone lattice screens, just to the south of the Qutb Minar. Its inlaid marble embellishments are ascribed to an influx of Pathan artisans from Byzantine Turkey, and the import of Seljuk influences.

In complete contrast to the mainly Islamic surroundings, an **Iron Pillar** (7.2m) stands in the precincts of Qutb-ud-din's original mosque, bearing fourth-century Sanskrit inscriptions of the Gupta period attributing it to the memory of King Chandragupta II (375–415 AD). Once topped with an image of the Hindu bird god, Garuda, the extraordinarily rust-free pillar, made of 98 percent pure iron (a purity that could not be replicated until at least the end of the nineteenth century), has puzzled metallurgists. Its rust resistance is apparently due to it containing as much as one percent phosphorous, which has acted as a chemical catalyst to create a protective layer of an unusual compound called misawite (FeOOH) around the metal. The pillar's origins remain hazy; it was evidently transplanted here by the Tomars, but we do not know where from. Tradition has it that anyone who can encircle the column with their hands behind their back will have their wishes granted, but as you are not allowed to go right up to the pillar, you won't be able to test this out.

Around the Qutb Minar Complex

The area to the north, south and west of the Qutb Minar Complex was the original site of Lal Kot. To the east, encompassing the village of Lado Sarai, is the area in which the Chauhans built their extension, **Qila Rai Pithora**, though little of it survives today (part of the wall can be seen along the edge of

Qutab Golf Course, on Press Enclave Road), and the tombs you can see across Anuvrat Marg (the Mehrauli Bypass) from the Qutb Minar Complex all date from the fourteenth and fifteenth centuries.

The area south of the Qutb Minar Complex, rich with remains from all sorts of historical periods, has been turned into an **Archeological Park** (daily sunrise–sunset; free). Here, within a very pleasant stroll of each other, you'll find: the tomb of Ghiyas-ud-din Balban, one of the Slave Dynasty sultans (reigned 1265–87), believed to be the first building in India constructed with true arches; the beautiful 1528 mosque and tomb of the poet Jamali Kamali (you may need to find the caretaker to open up the tomb for you); and the octagonal Mughal tomb of Muhammad Quli Khan, one of Akbar's courtiers, which was occupied in the early nineteenth century by Sir Thomas Metcalfe, the East India Company's resident at the Mughal court, who rather bizarrely converted it into a country house. Metcalfe made his mark on the area in other ways too, restoring a Lodi-period dovecote and constructing "follies" – mock-ancient pavilions, a typical feature of English country estates of the time, except that Metcalfe's were Indian in style. The park extends over more than a hundred hectares and contains over eighty monuments, including tombs, mosques, gateways and *baolis*, dating from every century between the thirteenth and the twentieth.

West of the park, the village of **Mehrauli** was built around the *dargah* of Qutb Sahib, a disciple of Khwaja Muin-ud-din Chishti (see p.268), who died in 1235 and is considered the second great Chishti saint, after Khwaja Muin-ud-din himself. Next door is a summer palace commissioned by Akbar II early in the nineteenth century, by which time Khwaja Muin-ud-din's *dargah* at Ajmer was outside the Mughals' domains and it was easier and more politic to pay homage to his disciple instead, the palace being a handy place to stay on such occasions. At the northern edge of the village, built on the remains of Lal Kot's walls, **Adham Khan's tomb** is the last resting place of a general in Akbar's army (Mohammed Quli Khan's brother) who was hurled from the ramparts of Agra Fort on the orders of the emperor after some murderous court feuding. You can get good views of both the tomb and the Qutb complex from the roof of the **Church of St John**, an incongruous little chapel with an Anglican nave, monastic cloisters and a Hindu *chhapra* (tower), tucked down a lane opposite the tomb entrance.

Five kilometres west of the Qutb Minar, just south of the Mahalipur–Mehrauli Road at Vasant Kunj, **Sultan Ghari's tomb** (daily sunrise–sunset; foreigners Rs100/$2, Indian residents Rs5) was commissioned by Sultan Iltutmish in 1231 for his son and heir-apparent, Prince Nasir-ud-din Mahmud, who died before he could reach the throne. The oldest Islamic mausoleum in India, with its sturdy walls and domed bastions, it looks from the outside more like a fort than a tomb. Entering through the main gate, with its fine Arabic calligraphy, you come into a courtyard built around an octagonal raised platform. The tomb itself is in a crypt-like burial chamber underneath the octagonal platform – hence its nickname, "Sultan Ghari", which means "royal cave". The subterranean chamber, the octagonal platform and the mosque-like compound surrounding it are all pretty unusual for early Islamic tombs. The construction technique, using lintels rather than arches, is indigenous rather than Islamic, and the fact that pieces of earlier temples were used in the tomb's construction (see p.109), is evidence that there were settlements in this area going back to at least the fifth century. Several pieces are clearly visible embedded in the walls, and there's a yoni base from a Shiva lingam in the floor by the western wall's central mihrab.

Today, people from neighbouring villages, mostly Hindu, regard the tomb as a holy site and leave offerings every Thursday; local brides come to pray here before their wedding, and it is possible that the tomb may stand on what was originally a Hindu holy site.

Baha'i Temple

Often compared visually to the Sydney Opera House, Delhi's 1986 **Baha'i Temple** (Tues–Sun: April–Sept 9am–7pm; Oct–March 9.30am–5.30pm; you may be asked to wait briefly outside during services, which are on the hour 9am–noon & 3–5pm), on open ground atop Kalkaji Hill, 12km southeast of Connaught Place, is an iconic piece of modern architecture that attracts a steady stream of visitors – more, it is said, than the Taj Mahal or the Eiffel Tower. Dominating the surrounding suburban sprawl, 27 spectacular giant white petals of marble in the shape of an unfolding lotus spring from nine pools and walkways, to symbolize the nine unifying spiritual paths of the Baha'i faith; each petal alcove contains an extract of the Baha'i holy scriptures. You're welcome to meditate in silence inside the central hall, which rises to a height of 34 metres. Set amid well-maintained gardens, the temple is at its most impressive at sunset. It'll cost you Rs80 to get here by pre-paid auto from Connaught Place, or you can take bus #440 from New Delhi station (gate 1) or Connaught Place (the stop in Kasturba Gandhi Marg) to the Outer Ring Road by Kalkaji bus depot, a short walk from the temple. The University of Georgia's Baha'i Association has further background information about the temple online at ⓦ www.uga .edu/bahai/india.html.

Ashoka's Rock Edict

Northwest of the Baha'i Temple, just off Raja Dhirsain Marg, **Ashoka's Rock Edict** is a ten-line epigraph inscribed in ancient Brahmi script on a smooth, sloping rock. The rock, now protected by a shelter in its own little park, was used as a slide by neighbourhood kids until 1966, when local residents noticed the ancient inscription, which was promulgated by the Mauryan emperor Ashoka the Great. Ashoka ruled most of the Indian Subcontinent bar the far south in the third century BC. In the eighth year of his reign (262 BC), he became a devout Buddhist and started having edicts inscribed on prominent rocks across his empire. This one was among the earliest, and it shows there must have been an important settlement nearby. It states that the emperor's exertions in the cause of *dharma* (righteousness) had brought the people closer to the gods, and that through their efforts, irrespective of their station, this attainment could be increased even further. Later, Ashoka had his edicts inscribed on columns, of which ten survive today, including the Ashokan pillars on the Northern Ridge (see p.126) and at Firoz Shah Kotla (see p.124). Unlike those, though, this earlier rock edict still stands at its original site.

Tughluqabad

Fifteen kilometres southeast of Connaught Place on the Mehrauli–Badarpur Road (the entrance is a kilometre east of the junction with Guru Ravidas Marg), a rocky escarpment holds the crumbling 6.5-kilometre-long battlements of the third city of Delhi, **Tughluqabad** (daily sunrise–sunset; foreigners Rs100/$2, Indian residents Rs5), built during the short reign of Ghiyas-ud-din Tughluq (1320–24). After the king's death the city was deserted, probably due to the lack of a clean water source nearby, and the cyclopean ruins were almost entirely abandoned, overgrown with scrubland and occupied by rhesus monkeys and nomadic Gujar herders; according to legend, this fulfils a curse put on it by the Sufi saint, Sheikh

Nizam-ud-din Aulia (see p.128) because Ghiyas-ud-din's labourers had been moonlighting, building a *baoli* for the saint, until Ghiyas-ud-din forbade them to do so while under his employ. The most interesting area is the high-walled **citadel** in the southwestern part of the site, though only a long underground passage, the ruins of several halls and a tower now remain. The grid pattern of some of the city streets to the north is still traceable. The palace area is to the west of the entrance, and the former bazaar to the east.

The southernmost of Tughluqabad's thirteen gates still looks down on a causeway, breached by the modern road, which rises above the flood plain, to link the fortress with **Ghiyas-ud-din Tughluq's tomb** (same hours and ticket as Tughluqabad). The tomb is entered through a massive red sandstone gateway leading into a courtyard surrounded by cloisters in the defensive walls. In the middle, surrounded by a well-kept lawn, stands the distinctive mausoleum, its sloping sandstone walls topped by a marble dome, and in its small way a precursor to the fine series of garden tombs built by the Mughals, which began here in Delhi with that of Humayun (see p.127). Inside the mausoleum are the graves of Ghiyas-ud-din, his wife and their son Muhammad Shah II. Ghiyas-ud-din's chief minister Jafar Khan is buried in the eastern bastion, and interred in the cloister nearby is the sultan's favourite dog.

The later fortress of **Adilabad** (free entry), built by Muhammad Shah II in much the same style as his father's citadel, and now in ruins, stands on a hillock to the southeast.

Tughluqabad is served by buses #34, #525 and #717 along the Mehrauli–Badarpur Road from Lado Sarai near the Qutb Minar, and by #430 from Kalkaji near the Baha'i Temple. From Connaught Place, the easiest way to get here is by pre-paid auto rickshaw (around Rs100). By bus, the most direct route from New Delhi station (gate 1) or Connaught Place (the stop in Kasturba Gandhi Marg) is #440 to the junction of Guru Ravidas Marg with the Mehrauli–Badarpur Road at Hamdard Nagar, and from here you can either walk (1km) or take an eastbound bus along the Mehrauli–Badarpur Road.

Akshardham Temple

Across Nizamuddin Bridge on the east side of the Yamuna River (Rs50 by pre-paid auto from Connaught Place), the opulent **Akshardham Temple** (daily: April–Sept 9am–7pm, Oct–Mar 9am–6pm; free; Ⓦ www.akshardham .com) is Delhi's newest tourist attraction, and in terms of visitor numbers, one of its biggest. Built in 2005 by the Gujarat-based Shri Swaminarayan sect, the temple is a stunning piece of art and an eloquent reminder of the sect's wealth, embellished with wonderful carvings that were made by stone-masons employing the same tools and techniques that were used in ancient times, without the use of rivets or screws. Note that cameras, mobile phones, mirrors and any electronic equipment, including USB keys, are prohibited and should be deposited at the cloakroom outside. Visitors may not enter wearing shorts or skirts above the knee. Born in 1781, Bhagwan Shri Swaminarayan set up an ashram in Gujarat preaching non-violence and unity. He died in 1830, but his followers believe he is "eternally present on earth". His original devotees were poor Gujarati peasants, but the growth of a wealthy Gujarati diaspora has brought the sect money and influence, though it remains much respected for its spiritual values. The **main shrine** is surrounded by a pink sandstone relief (you must walk round it clockwise) whose theme is elephants: wild, domesticated or in legend. Inside, the centre-piece and main object of devotion is a three-metre-high gold statue of the sect's founder, Bhagwan Shri Swaminarayan, attended by four disciples.

Behind it are paintings depicting scenes from his life, and also some personal objects such as his sandals and even some of his hair and nail clippings. The four subsidiary shrines are devoted to Hindu gods.

National Rail Museum

The cream of India's royal coaches and oldest engines are on permanent display at the **National Rail Museum** in the Embassy enclave of Chanakyapuri, southwest of Connaught Place (Tues–Sun: April–Sept 9.30am–1pm & 1.30–7.30pm, Oct–Mar 9.30am–1pm & 1.30–5.30pm; Rs10, video Rs100); take bus #620 from Shivaji Stadium terminal by Connaught Place, or a pre-paid auto (Rs50). Some 27 locomotives and 17 carriages – including the ornate 1886 gold-painted saloon car of the Maharaja of Baroda (Rs50 to go inside), the teak carriage of the Maharaja of Mysore, trimmed in gold and ivory, and the cabin used by the Prince of Wales in 1876 – are kept in the grounds. A steam-hauled miniature "Joy Train" does a circuit of the grounds (Rs10) whenever it has enough passengers.

The covered section of the museum houses models of famous engines and coaches, displays of old tickets, and even the skull of an elephant hit by a train near Calcutta in 1894. The pride of the collection, however, is a model of India's very first train, a steam engine which made its inaugural journey of 21 miles from Mumbai to Thane in 1853.

Sulabh International Museum of Toilets

The light-hearted **Sulabh International Museum of Toilets** (Mon–Sat 10am–5pm; free; ⓦwww.sulabhtoiletmuseum.org; Rs30 by auto from Uttam Nagar East metro station), on Palam Dabri Marg in Mahavir Enclave I, in Delhi's western suburbs, belies the importance of the organization which runs it. Basing itself soundly on Gandhian principles, the Sulabh Movement aims to free members of the lowest rank of outcastes from the demeaning job of cleaning out non-flush latrines and carrying away the excrement, and to end the insanitary practice of open-air defecation by promoting hygienic, eco-friendly toilets in towns, cities and villages across India – you'll no doubt see some of their "toilet complexes" around Delhi.

The museum illustrates lavatorial history from Harappan times through to the modern day, and its grounds house examples of easy-to-build hygienic flush latrines for use in communities without sewerage or running water. Pride of place goes to the movement's machine for converting human excrement into fertilizer and fuel, an average poo yielding a cubic metre of methane gas that can be used for cooking, heating or lighting. The movement's toilet technology is self-financing, making brass from muck, while promoting caste equality and public health awareness at the same time.

Eating

Delhi has quite an eating culture, and enough prosperous foodies to sustain a large variety of **restaurants** and worldwide cuisines, while less rarified establishments cater for office workers in need of somewhere to fill up cheaply at lunchtime or after work. The result is something for every budget, with excellent food on offer at humble roadside *dhabas* and unassuming diners, and truly magnificent Indian and foreign cuisine in Delhi's more renowned restaurants. The Western junk food franchise chains are all here too, if you need them (though their hamburgers are actually lamb burgers), and there are vast buffets and superlative à la carte menus at many of the luxury hotels.

Most restaurants close around 11pm, but those with bars usually stay open until midnight. If you're looking for a **late-night** meal, you have a number of choices: eat in one of the restaurants in a top hotel, or the 24-hour coffee shops in *Le Meridien*, the *InterContinental*, the *Park* or *The Claridges*, or the *Marina* at G-59 Connaught Place; try a snack in Paharganj's round-the-clock rooftop cafés; or head to Pandara Road market (open till 1.30am). Old Delhi railway station also has a couple of 24hr places.

If you want to explore Delhi's eating places beyond those listed here, you might want to pick up a copy of the annual *Times Food Guide* (Rs100 at newsstands and bookshops), which covers just about every restaurant in the city and its suburbs, cross-referenced by district and cuisine, with reviews ranging from glowing to witheringly scathing.

Connaught Place and central New Delhi

Connaught Place ("CP") is dominated by upmarket restaurants and Western-style fast-food places, with a few cheap and cheerful eateries hidden away if you know where to look. Even if you don't want to dine here, it's sometimes nice to step into air-conditioned comfort just for a silver-service tea, cool milkshake or filter coffee; you can also get good espressos at the coffee-shops that have recently sprung up in the area. The **Bengali market**, on Tansen Marg, off Barakhamba Road, is a good place for sweets and snacks.

The restaurants and cafés listed below are marked on the Connaught Place **map** (p.96).

Anand Connaught Lane, three doors from *Sunny Guest House*. Good, cheap non-veg eats including great biryanis, with non-veg dishes at Rs70–80 a throw.

Barista N-16 Connaught Place. Popular coffee bar, the first of what is now a nationwide chain that claims to do the best espresso in India (100 percent Arabica), plus cakes and muffins to accompany.

Café Coffee Day A-35 and N-11 Connaught Place. Two branches of a new, trendy café chain (there's another down in the metro station, bright and breezy, with an upmarket clientele and the usual espresso variations, plus some very tempting chocolate cakes, and for real coffee mavens, Colombian and Ethiopian special blends.

Fire *Park Hotel*, 15 Sansad Marg ☎ 011/2374 3000. Scintillating if expensive modern restaurant whose contemporary Indian cuisine bears a strong hint of European influence, in dishes such as achari risotto or roast duck masala; what's available on the menu depends on the season. Main dishes Rs425–1100.

India Coffee House 2nd floor, Mohan Singh Place Shopping Complex, Baba Kharak Singh Marg. Not chic or trendy, but very cheap, this down-at-heel canteen, with a large roof terrace, is a workers' co-op, part of a mainly south Indian chain, serving filter and espresso coffee, snacks and basic meals (thalis at Rs30) to an eclectic cross-section of downtown New Delhi's daytime population.

Kake Da Hotel 74 Municipal Market, Outer Ring, Connaught Place. A small diner (the term 'hotel' does not imply accommodation) that's been here so long it's become a Delhi institution, known for unpretentious but reliably good Punjabi curries, mostly non-veg, such as butter chicken or sag meat (palak mutton), at Rs40–65 a plate.

Kwality 7 Regal Building, Sansad Marg. Originally set up to serve American GIs during World War Two, this is one of Connaught Place's better mid-market choices (non-veg mains Rs150–250), quite elegantly decorated with lots of mirrors and chandeliers (though the odd mouse has been spotted scurrying across the floor). Good choices include chicken tikka with green peas, and mutton shahi korma.

Parikrama Kasturba Gandhi Marg. Novel and expensive Indian (mainly tandoori) and Chinese cuisine in a revolving restaurant affording superb views over Delhi; a single rotation takes ninety minutes; main dishes cost Rs150–450. Specialities include *murg pasandey parikrama* (chicken breast stuffed with minced chicken and nuts in a cashewnut sauce) and *murg tikka parikrama* (chicken tikka in a spicy cashewnut marinade).

Q'BA E-42/3 Connaught Place. Stylish, modern, upmarket bar-restaurant on two floors and two terraces, whose "world cuisine" actually boils down to Indian, Italian and Thai, with pizza, pasta, green and red curry, and specialities such as *Q'BA raan* (char-grilled leg of lamb with herbs) and *fish tikka methi malai* (tandoori fish kebabs in a ginger and fenugreek marinade). Main courses go for Rs250–450 evenings, slightly less at lunchtime.

Sagar Ratna K-15 Connaught Place. The CP branch of the renowned Defence Colony restaurant (see p.142), great for *vadas*, *dosas* or a South Indian veg thali (Rs85).

Saravana Bhavan P-15 Connaught Place and 46 Janpath. Excellent low-priced South Indian snacks and meals, including thalis (Rs89) and quick lunches (Rs70), as well as the usual *dosas*, *iddlis* and uttapams. The mini tiffin (Rs70) has a taste of everything.

Spice Route *Hotel Imperial*, Janpath. This beautifully decorated restaurant, rarified and expensive, if perhaps a little over-priced (main dishes

Rs350–750), specializes in spicy Southeast Asian and Keralan cuisine. If you want to eat well in the CP vicinity, this is one of your best bets.

United Coffee House E-15 Connaught Place. Rather an elegant coffee room, and also a restaurant, serving Indian and European dishes (including fish and chips) for around Rs180–350, as well as great coffee and cold beer.

Veda H-27 Connaught Place ☎011/4151 3535. CP's swankiest restaurant, heavy on the "ambience" (all smoochy red and black decor with low lights), which is what you pay for here, though the food (main dishes Rs200–450) isn't at all bad.

Wenger's A-16 Connaught Place. CP's top patisserie, with a mouthwatering selection of cakes and pastries.

Zen B-25 Connaught Place. Excellent Chinese meals (plus a few Thai and Japanese dishes) served in a relaxed and traditional style, plus Western snacks (3–7pm), and a broad selection of wines, spirits and beers.

Paharganj and Ram Nagar

With so much good food on offer in Delhi, it's a shame to dine in **Paharganj**, even if that's where your hotel is. Most of the restaurants on the Main Bazaar are geared to unadventurous foreign tastebuds, offering poor imitations of Western, Israeli, Japanese, and even Thai dishes, or sloppy, insipid versions of Indian curries for foreigners who can't handle chilli. Most serve breakfasts of toast, porridge, muesli and omelettes, though they'll do you a *paratha* as well. Eating options in **Ram Nagar** are more indigenous. If you decide to eat in any of the *dhabas* opposite New Delhi station or at the eastern end of Paharganj Main Bazaar, especially those with waiters outside trying to hustle you in, and unless you can read the price list in Hindi, always ask the price of a dish before ordering, or you're likely to be overcharged.

The restaurants listed below are marked on the Paharganj **map** (p.98).

Club India 4797 Main Bazaar. First-floor and rooftop restaurant with the best views over central Paharganj, lively music, and the usual travellers' breakfast options plus Israeli, Japanese, Tibetan and even tandoori dishes. Main courses go for Rs70–150.

Darbar Restaurant and **Bikaner Sweets Corner** 9002 Multani Dhanda Chowk, just off DB Gupta Rd ☎011/2351 6666. Upstairs, it's a nononsense moderately priced veg restaurant, serving tasty thalis and Punjabi veg curries for around Rs70; it also has a takeaway service, and delivers orders over Rs100 within a kilometre radius. Downstairs, it's a wonderful sweets emporium, with all sorts of multicoloured Bengali and Rajasthani confections, stained with saffron and covered in silver leaf, plus namkeens and savouries.

Diamond Café Main Bazaar. Small, friendly restaurant with a good if typical backpackers' menu (main dishes around Rs50), a choice of set breakfasts (Continental, Indian, American, Israeli; Rs50–70), and Indian/fusion music on the sound system.

Golden Café Ramdwara Rd, opposite Sri Mahavir Mandir. Cheap and cheerful café popular with Korean and Japanese travellers, serving Chinese, Korean and European food with dishes at Rs30–80.

Malhotra Laksmi Narain Rd. One of the better restaurants in Paharganj, offering passable tandoori and Mughlai dishes at reasonable prices (Rs60–100 for non-veg dishes). There's a basement, and an air-conditioned upstairs section, plus a veg South Indian branch two doors down.

Metropolis 1634 Main Bazaar. Cosy air-conditioned ground-floor restaurant in the hotel of same name (downstairs, or on the roof terrace).

Paharganj's priciest venue serves full breakfasts, reasonable curries and tandoori specials, plus Western dishes, beer, spirits, cocktails and non-alcoholic "mocktails". Main dishes are Rs110–175 veg, Rs200–250 non-veg.

Rituraj Bhojnalya Arakashan Rd, below *Delhi Continental Hotel*. Cheap, popular *dhaba* serving excellent Indian breakfasts and South Indian snacks (Rs30–60). A great place for *chana puri* or *iddli sambar*.

Sam's Café *Vivek Hotel*, 1534–50 Main Bazaar. A small, bright café at street level and a terrace restaurant on the roof, with the usual travellers' fare (Rs50–80), plus bakery products that go for half price after nightfall.

Sonu Chat House Main Bazaar. Popular cheap diner serving noodles, soup, samosas, curries, and even masala dosa to the backpacker crowd. Main dishes around Rs50.

Sonu South Indian Restaurant Multani Dhanda Chowk, off DB Gupta Rd, Ram Nagar. Good, honest South Indian grub (masala dosa, *iddlis*, *vadas* and the like) at low prices (Rs25–35 a go, or Rs60 for a thali).

Tadka 4986 Ram Dwara Rd (Nehru Bazaar) ☎011/3291 5216. Clean, bright, modern little restaurant serving low-priced Indian veg dishes (main dishes Rs35–50, thalis Rs45–60). They'll deliver to any address within 2km.

Old Delhi

Old Delhi's crowded streets contain numerous simple food halls that serve surprisingly good, and invariably fiery, Indian dishes for as little as Rs20. Upmarket eating is thin on the ground, but some of the mid-range restaurants serve food every bit as good as the posh eateries of South Delhi, and the sweets and snacks in Old Delhi are the best in town.

The restaurants listed below are marked on the Old Delhi **map** (p.113).

Chaina Ram 6499 Fatehpuri Chowk, next to Fatehpuri Mosque. Established in Karachi in 1901, and forced to relocate in 1947, this little shop is well known for its Sindhi-style sweets; the delicately aromatic Karachi *halwa*, with almonds and pistachios, is the best in town.

Chor Bizarre *Hotel Broadway*, 4/15 Asaf Ali Rd. A wide selection of excellent Indian cuisine including specialities from around the country, but above all from Kashmir. Eccentric, delightful decor featuring a 4-poster bed, sewing table and a servery made from a 1927 vintage Fiat. Main dishes go for Rs100–400, or a set meal for Rs345. Groups of eight or more can opt for the Rs495 Kashmiri feast.

Ghantewala 1862-A Chandni Chowk. Established in 1790, this famous confectioner supplied sweets to the last Mughal emperors; its *ladoo* was already renowned in the nineteenth century, and the cashew rolls are absolutely out of this world, but their speciality is a nutty, toffee-like sweet called *sohan halwa*.

Haldiram's 1454 Chandni Chowk. Super-hygienic low-priced snack-bar and take-away with sweets and samosas downstairs, drinks, snacks (Rs22–42) and light meals (Rs70–90) upstairs, including excellent puris, lassis, lime sodas, kulfis, thalis (Rs62–70) and even toasties. If you've never tried one, check the *raj kachori* (Rs34), a crunchy shell

enclosing a tangy chickpea curry with yoghurt sauce.

Karim's Gali Kababian. A perennial Delhiite favourite, located in a passage down a side street, opposite the south gate of the Jama Masjid, consisting of four eating halls (same kitchen) offering the best meat dishes in the old city, at moderate prices, with delicious fresh kebabs, hot breads and great Mughlai curries. Full dishes cost Rs100–400, but half dishes are also available.

Moti Mahal Netaji Subhash Marg. Renowned for its tandoori chicken, this medium-priced restaurant is another local favourite – one of the first Punjabi restaurants in town – with both indoor seating and a large open-air courtyard. Main dishes go for around Rs150.

Paratha Wali Gali Off Chandni Chowk, opposite the Central Bank. Head down this alleyway by Kanwarji Raj Kumar Sweet Shop (itself pretty good), and you'll be rewarded with *parathas* filled with anything from *paneer* and *gobi* to *mutter* and *mooli*, all cooked to order and served with a small selection of curries for around Rs30. There are three *paratha*-wallahs in the alley, all good, but the most renowned is the first one, *Pandit Babu Ram*.

Vig Chandni Chowk. A small café opposite the Jain temple, serving inexpensive south Indian snacks (*iddli sambar*, *dosas*, uttapams, at Rs17–30), thalis (Rs32–40) and chow mein (Rs28–35).

South Delhi

The enclaves and villages spread across the vast area of **South Delhi** offer countless eating options, and most of its upmarket shopping zones (Hauz Khas, Defence Colony, Ansal Plaza, and the like) contain several good restaurants. **Dilli Haat**, the tourist market in Safdarjang (see p.147), has 25 food stalls offering dishes from nearly every state in India. **Pandara Road Market**'s restaurants and snack bars, just south of India Gate, stay open until 1.30 or 2am.

The restaurants listed here are among Delhi's best eating places, worth venturing out from the centre to try. Unless otherwise stated, they are marked on the Delhi **map** (pp.82–83).

Bukhara *Maurya Sheraton Hotel*, Sardar Patel Marg, Chanakyapuri ☎011/2611 2233. See map, p.103. Considered Delhi's best restaurant, specializing in succulently tender tandoori kebabs, with a menu that's short but very sweet, and a kitchen separated from the eating area by a glass partition, so you can watch the chefs at work. The *murgh malai* (chicken in curd) is wonderful, or you can get an "express platter" with three different kebabs. Bill Clinton is among the celebs who flock here. Main dishes are around Rs500, so don't expect much change out of Rs1500 for a full meal, not including drinks. The *Maurya Sheraton* also has another fine restaurant, *Dum Pukht*, which specializes in the *dum* (slow-cooked casserole) cuisine of Avadh (eastern Uttar Pradesh).

Basil & Thyme Santushti Shopping Complex. See map, p.103. Bistro-style Mediterranean eating with dishes like shitake risotto, lamb couscous and asparagus tart, and desserts including blueberry crêpes or tiramisú, mains Rs285–325. The only minus is its 6pm closing time, so it's lunch not supper, unless you want to make that tea.

Ego 4 Community Centre, Friends Colony, Mathura Rd. A saloon-style bar serving authentic and imaginative Italian food, with good beer, cocktails and loud music. Main dishes go for around Rs300. There's also a very good Thai food branch, *Ego Thai*, close by at no.53.

Flavors C-52 Defence Colony. Run by a Mizo-Italian couple, this is one of Delhi's very best Italian eateries, where you'll find excellent risotto, great pasta and pizzas, and wonderful tiramisú. Main dishes cost Rs230–430.

Park Balluchi Deer Park, Hauz Khas ☎011/2685 9369. Kebabs and Baluchi dishes (veg Rs140–190, non-veg Rs220–270) amid pleasant sylvan surroundings, with a choice of smoking (and drinking) or non-smoking (and alcohol-free) areas.

Punjabi by Nature Priya Cinema Complex, Basant Lok, Vasant Vihar ☎011/4151 6666. It's quite a haul from the centre (Rs90 by pre-paid auto from CP), but this restaurant has made a big name for itself among Delhiite foodies with its fabulous Punjabi and North Indian cuisine – expensive, but worth it (most main dishes Rs285–475). The Amritsari fish tikka is succulent, the tandoori prawns wonderful, but for something really special, try the raan-i-Punjab (leg of lamb, Rs695). They're about to open a more easily accessible branch at TF-06, third floor, Square Mall, Raja Garden (☎011/4222 5656 or 5757), by Rajaouri Garden metro.

Sagar 18 Defence Colony Market. Delicious, inexpensive south Indian vegetarian food (main dishes Rs40–65), with *vadas*, *iddlis*, *ravas* and *dosas*, plus great thalis (Rs85). They've also opened a North Indian restaurant a few doors down at no. 24, and they have branches all over town, but the original is still the best.

Swagath 14 Defence Colony Market. A non-veg off-shoot of *Sagar*, a few doors away. There are Indian and Chinese meat dishes on the menu, but ignore them and go for the Mangalore-style seafood – the *Swagath* special (chilli and tamarind), *gassi* (coconut sauce) and *sawantwadi* (green masala) dishes are all great, at around Rs185 a throw with kingfish, or Rs400–600 for versions made with pomfret, prawns or lobster.

Bars and nightclubs

With an ever-increasing number of pubs and clubs, Delhi's **nightlife** scene is in full swing. During the week, lounge and dance bars are your best bet, but come the weekend the **discos** really take off. Most, if not all, of the discos popular with Delhi's young jet-set are in the luxury hotels, and many don't allow "stag entry" (men unaccompanied by women, that is), which makes them a whole lot more comfortable for women, but is tough luck if you're male and alone; the big exception is *Elevate* – Delhi's nightclub for serious clubbers. India Gate and Rajpath attract nightly "**people's parties**" where large crowds mill about, snacking and eating ice cream; these are not advisable for women on their own, as you're likely to get hassled.

For **drinking**, the five-star hotels all have plush and expensive bars, and many of the better ones have dance floors. Lounge bars with laid-back music have become very popular of late, and there are some good ones scattered about the southern suburbs. Note that the drinking age in Delhi is 25, though there are proposals to lower it to 21.

Bars

Blues N-17 Connaught Place. See map, p.96. Snazzy bar and restaurant, offering an eclectic range of loud music (Thurs is rock night, retro on Sun). The bar staff are all pros at mixing extravagant cocktails. Happy hour (buy 1, get 1 free) is 4–8pm, after which entry is Rs200; lone males are not allowed in.

De Gem 1050 Main Bazar, Paharganj. See map, p.98. A seedier alternative to the *Hotel Gold Regency* (see below), for those who want a cheap beer but don't want to leave Paharganj to get it. You won't find many women drnking here without a male escort.

DV8 Regal Building, Connaught Place. See map, p.96. Quite old-fashioned, with a pub-like feel, music from 8pm, and live bands on Tues. Central and popular.

Hotel Gold Regency 4350 Main Bazar, Paharganj. See map, p.98. Not a place to seek out from elsewhere in town, but handy if you're in Paharganj and don't want to venture too far afield for a beer. It's open till midnight, which is just slightly later than the *De Gem* across the street; for a posher drink in Paharganj, try the *Metropolis Hotel* (see p.99).

Lizard Lounge E-5, 1st Floor, South Extension II. See map, p.83. Lounge music (what else?) and hookah pipes (21 flavours) at this well-established, but still trendy lounge bar, with Mediterranean and Middle Eastern food.

Rodeo A-12 Connaught Place. See map, p.96. Saloon-style bar with Wild West waiters, swinging-saddle bar stools, pitchers of beer, tequila slammers, and Mexican-style bar snacks (tacos, enchiladas, fajitas, quesadillas).

Shalom N-18, N-Block Market, Greater Kailash Part I ☏ 011/5163 2280 or 83. See map, p.83. An upmarket, trendy lounge bar with laid-back music, a Mediterranean theme, Spanish and Lebanese food (tapas meets mezze), hookah pipes, and

tables for all, but you'll need to book, especially at weekends.

Splash Minto Rd (Viveknand Marg), just north of the rail bridge. See map, p.96. Quite a civilized bar with food and reasonably priced beer, and quite often dance parties, a stone's throw from Connaught Place.

Soho *Ashok Hotel*, 50-B Chanakyapuri. See map, p.103. A sophisticated place with two dance floors and three bars, including one just for beers, and one for wine and cocktails. There's a huge range of spirits, including all sorts of vodkas and malt whiskies, with music and dancing from around 9pm till midnight.

Turquoise Cottage 81/3 Adh Chini, Aurobindo Marg. See map, p.83. Very popular subterranean bar, with the best rock music in town. Wed is "media night", when industry people have a night-long happy hour. Weekends attract a much younger crowd.

Nightclubs

Elevate 6th floor, Center Stage Mall, Sector 18, Noida ☏ 0120/251 3904, ⊛ www.elevateindia.com. See map, p.82. Across the river, and indeed just across the state line in UP, this is the biggest and kickingest club in town, modelled on London's Fabric, with three floors (dancefloor, chillout and VIP), a roof terrace, and Indian and international DJs playing bhangra, filmi, hip-hop, trance or techno, depending on the night. Friday and Saturday nights only (check the website for what's on), but open till 3.30am, and "stag entry" is permitted.

Royale Mirage *Crowne Plaza Hotel*, New Friends Colony ☏ 011/2683 5070. See map, p.83. A long-time favourite, with a French-Arab theme (hummus is among the snacks available), table dinner service, dancing podiums, state-of-the-art light show and a hip, young crowd. Open Wed–Sat only, 9.30pm–1am.

Cultural pursuits

A range of indoor and outdoor venues host performances of **dance**, such as Bhawai (a folk dance from Rajasthan and, typically of that state, very colourful), Bharatnatyam (the best-known classical Indian dance form, from the southern states of Karnataka, Andhra Pradesh and Tamil Nadu) and Kathakali (also from the south, but this time from the state of Kerala), as well as regular **classical music** concerts – check the listings magazines detailed on p.91 to see what's on. The **India International Centre** is a good place to catch art exhibitions, lectures and films on all aspects of Indian culture and environment, while the colossal **India Habitat Centre**, the **British Council** and the **art** and **theatre auditoriums** around India Gate are all renowned for their innovative shows and high-standard drama in both Hindi and English.

Dance and drama

Dances of India Parsi Anjuman Hall, Bahadur Shah Zafar Marg, near Delhi Gate ☎011/2328 4689 or 2642 9170. See map, p.113. Excellent classical, folk and tribal dance featuring six to seven items every night from different parts of India, usually including Bharatnatyam, Kathakali, Bhawai and the graceful dance of the northeastern state of Manipur. Daily 6.45pm. Rs200.

India Habitat Centre Lodi Rd ☎011/2468 2001 to 9, ⊛www.indiahabitat.org. See map, p.103. Popular venue for dance, music and theatre as well as talks and exhibitions.

India International Centre 40 Lodi Estate ☎011/2461 9431. See map, p.103. Films, lectures, dance and music performances.

Kamani Auditorium Copernicus Marg ☎011/2338 8084. See map, p.103. Bharatnatyam and other dance performances.

Sangeet Natak Akademi Rabindra Bhavan, 35 Firoz Shah Rd ☎011/2338 7246 to 8, ⊛www .sangeetnatak.com. See map, p.103. Delhi's premier performing arts institution.

Triveni Kala Sangam 205 Tansen Marg, just south of the Bengali Market ☎011/2371 8833. See map, p.103. Bharatnatyam dance shows, also art exhibitions.

Cultural centres and libraries

American Information Resource Center (USIS) 24 Kasturba Gandhi Marg, southeast of Connaught Place ☎011/2331 4251, ⊛newdelhi.usembassy.gov.

American newspapers and periodicals, plus books on current affairs, trade, politics and economics.

British Council 17 Kasturba Gandhi Marg, southeast of Connaught Place ☎011/2371 1401. See map, p.96. Talks, film shows and concerts, plus a good library and reading room.

Delhi Public Library SP Mukherjee Marg, opposite Old Delhi station, with branches around town ☎011/2396 2682, ⊛www.dpl.gov.in. See map, p.113. Reading rooms open to all. Daily 8.30am–8pm.

India International Centre 40 Max Mueller Marg, near Lodi Gardens ☎011/2461 9431, ⊛www .iicdelhi.nic.in. See map, p.103. Exhibitions, lectures, films and a library.

Lalit Kala Galleries Rabindra Bhawan, 35 Firoz Shah Rd, by Mandi House Chowk ☎011/2338 7241 to 3. See map, p.103. Delhi's premier art academy, with an extensive collection of paintings, sculpture, frescoes and drawings. Also shows films and stages seminars and photographic exhibitions.

Sahitya Akademi Rabindra Bhawan, 32 Firoz Shah Rd, by Mandi House Chowk ☎011/2338 6626. See map, p.103. An excellent library devoted to Indian literature through the ages, with some books and periodicals in English.

Tibet House 1 Institutional Area, Lodi Rd ☎011/2461 1515, ⊛www.tibet.net/tibethouse /eng. Mon–Fri 9.30am–5.30pm. See map, p.103. A library on all aspects of Tibetan culture, plus a small museum of Tibetan artefacts (Rs10).

Cinemas

Bollywood movies are shown at the Odeon (☎011/4151 7899), Plaza (☎011/4151 3787) and Regal (☎011/2336 2245) **cinemas**, all in Connaught Place, or the Shiela (☎011/2352 2100) on DB Gupta Road, near New Delhi railway station. Tickets cost Rs25–80. Suburban multiplexes such as those run by PVR (⊛www.pvrcinemas.com) are plusher and nowadays more popular.

Films are usually in Hindi without subtitles, though a new branch of Bollywood has recently emerged, producing films in English that ooze attitude, with sex scenes and lots of designer clothing. In addition, some of the cultural centres listed opposite occasionally run international film festivals. If you want to see Hindi films with English subtitles, your best bet is to head down to shops like Blue Bird or Planet M (see p.148), and buy them on DVD.

Sports and outdoor activities

The recreational activity most likely to appeal to visitors in the pre-monsoon months has to be a dip in one of Delhi's **swimming pools**. The main public baths are the NMDC Pool at Nehru Park in Chanakyapuri (☎011/2611 1440), and on Avenue 1, Sarojini Nagar (☎011/2412 1581) and the Talkatora Pool, Talkatora Road (☎011/2301 8178). Most luxury hotels restrict their pools to residents only, but may allow outsiders to join their health clubs.

Other local diversions include **tennis**, **golf** (there are fifteen courses in the Delhi area), **horse riding** and even **rock climbing**, on crags on the outskirts of the city during the cooler months. Spectator sports are mainly equestrian, in the form of **horse racing** and **polo**.

Army Polo & Riding Club B Squadron 61 Cavalry, Cariappa Marg ☎011/2569 9444 or 9555 or 9666, ⓦwww.armypoloclub.com. Hosts polo tournaments in winter (Nov–Feb). To watch, contact the club for an invitation.

Delhi Golf Club Dr Zakir Hussein Marg ☎011/2436 0002. Busy and beautiful 220-acre golf course on the fifteenth-century estate of the Lodi dynasty, with over two hundred varieties of trees; it also acts as a bird sanctuary. Monuments and mausoleums dot the grounds. Non-members can play for US$35 (Indian residents Rs300) weekdays, US$40 (Rs500) weekends.

Delhi Lawn Tennis Association RK Khanna Tennis Stadium, 1 Africa Avenue ☎011/2619 3955, ⓦwww.dltatennis.in. There are 21 courts and a pool at this complex near Hauz Khas village.

Delhi Riding Club Safdarjang Rd ☎011/2301 1891. Morning rides for adults at 6.30am, 7.30am, 8.30am and 9.30am, afternoon rides for children 2.45–5.45pm; open to non-members by prior arrangement.

Delhi Races Kamal Ataturk Rd ☎011/2379 2869. Regular horse racing Tues from 1.30pm, sometimes other days too. Men Rs30, women Rs10 (members' enclosure Rs50/Rs20).

Qutab Golf Course Press Enclave Rd, Lado Sarai ☎011/2696 9127, ⓦwww.dda.org.in. Run by the Delhi Development Authority, this club with an 18-hole course is open to non-members with green fees of Rs1250/$20 (Indian residents Rs230) on weekdays, or Rs1500/$30 (Rs340–400) at weekends.

Siri Fort Sports Complex Siri Fort ☎011/2649 7482, ⓦwww.dda.org.in. An Olympic-size swimming pool, a toddlers' pool, plus tennis, squash and badminton courts are among the facilities here, at the most central of the DDA's 14 sports complexes. Out-of-towners may use it for Rs100 (Indian residents Rs40) a day, or join on a temporary basis for up to three months for Rs3000 (Rs1500) plus Rs120 a month.

Children's Delhi

In addition to the sporting facilities mentioned above, children may appreciate a visit to the **Planetarium** (see p.110) or **Shankar's International Doll Museum** (see p.124). The **National Rail Museum** (see p.138), and in particular the "Joy Train" ride may also be a good diversion from Mughal architecture. At Purana Qila (see p.111), there's the **zoo** and a **boating lake**, and in Old Delhi, a visit to the Jain Temple's **bird hospital** (see p.116) is usually a winner.

The **Natural History Museum** (Tue–Sat 10am–5pm; free; ⓦnmnh.nic.in) on Barakhamba Road by Mandi House Chowk, has a rather uninspiring collection of fossils and stuffed animals that some children may find vaguely interesting, and some educational exhibitions aimed mainly at schoolchildren.

Delhi's favourite amusement park is **Appu Ghar** (Mon–Sat 1.30–9.30pm, Sun noon–9.30pm; all-rides ticket Rs150, children Rs120, one-ride ticket Rs50, children Rs40; ⓣ011/2337 1404) at Pragati Maidan, off Mathura Road north of the Crafts Museum, and has a water park called Oysters (adults Rs250, children under 85cm free), plus loads of rides including dodgems, go-karts, a roller-coaster and a giant ferris wheel. Unfortunately, the park is under threat from property developers, who want to build a Supreme Court complex on the site, and it looks set to close. The good news is that two new locations have been earmarked for it on the outskirts of town. On the southern edge of town, **Fun n Food Village** (daily: March–April 9.30am–7pm, May–June 9am–7pm, July–Oct 9.30am–8pm, Nov–Feb 9.30am–6pm; closes one hour later on Sun; Rs325, children Rs250, Sun surcharge Rs50; ⓦwww.funnfood.com) on Old Gurgaon Road at Kapashera has a water park, a snow park and lots of rides, including a ferris wheel.

Shopping

Although the traditional places to **shop** in Delhi are around **Connaught Place** (particularly the underground Palika Bazaar) and **Chandni Chowk**, a number of suburbs created by the rapid growth of the city are emerging as fashionable shopping districts. **Hauz Khas Village**, in South Delhi, has numerous boutiques, jewellery shops and galleries, while artists and artisans from all over India sell their products at the pleasant open-air **Dilli Haat** craft centre, also in South Delhi. **Old Delhi** is divided into traditional bazaars, each with its own specific trade (see p.120 for the main ones). For more hippyish wares, there's **Paharganj** and the **Tibetan Market** near Connaught Place. To check prices and quality, you can't do better than the **state emporiums** on Baba Kharak Singh Marg.

Unlike the markets of Old Delhi, most shops in New Delhi take credit cards, and beware of touts who'll try to drag you into false "government shops" for a commission. In all bazaars and street markets, the rule is to **haggle** – it's even worth asking for a discount at shops which display "fixed price" notices.

Shopping precincts

Ansal Plaza Khel Gaon Marg. See map p.83. If you want to shop in a mall, you can't get better than this, Delhi's modern and most popular plaza, geared towards middle-class Delhiites rather than tourists, with lots of department stores, plus a pub (*Geoffrey's*), cafés (*Barista*, for example), and various junk food outlets in case all that retail therapy makes you hungry.

Defence Colony Market Varum Marg, off Bhisham Pitmah Marg, Defence Colony. See map, p.83. There are shops here, but mostly you'd come to eat, at restaurants such as *Sagar* and *Swagath* (see p.142). *Moti Mahal* (see p.141) also has a branch here.

Hauz Khas Village Hauz Khas, west of Aurobindo Marg. See map p.83). An upmarket shopping "village" with some interesting art and antiques shops and galleries, including Cottage of Arts and Jewels and the Village Shop (see p.149), and Gujrat Art Gallery (see p.150). There are also stylish cafés and restaurants for a bite to eat. Most places are closed on Tuesdays.

Khan Market Subramaniam Bharti Marg. See map p.103. Upmarket open-air shopping precinct, popular with foreign expats and well-heeled Delhiites. There are good bookshops (including Bahrisons at no. 21, opposite the main gate, Faqir Chand at no. 15-A and Full Circle at no. 5-B), and lovely fabric shops (Anokhi, see p.149), as well as

The Music Shop (see p.148) and Neemrana (see p.149), plus cafés and snack bars. Closed Sundays.
M-Block Market and **N-Block Market** Greater Kailash Part I. See map p.83. Two generally upmarket shopping precincts within walking distance of each other, N-Block's being the more interesting, with great clothes shops such as Fabindia (see p.149) as well as *Shalom* lounge bar (see p.143) and cafés including a branch of *Barista* (see p.139).
Palika Bazaar Connaught Place. See map p.96. A generally downmarket subterranean shopping mall, and a good place to buy CDs, DVDs and video games, though it also has clothes shops, a bookstore (see p.148) and some interesting odd shops including Jain Super Store (see p.150) and a branch of Shaw Brothers.
Santushti Shopping Complex Panchsheel Marg. See map p.103. A fave with diplomats from nearby Chanakyapuri, this rather twee little precinct was set up by the Air Force Wives Welfare Association. Shops are upmarket and pretty classy, selling high-quality clothing, textiles and jewellery. Among them is Anokhi (see p.149), and if you're hungry you could stop for some food at *Basil & Thyme* (see p.142). Mon–Sat 10am–6pm.
South Extension I and II Mahatma Gandhi Marg (Ring Rd). See map p.83. Two upmarket shopping areas, facing each other across the busy Ring Road (there's a pedestrian underpass). Good shopping includes a number of clothes stores, lots of designer shops, and bookshops such as RS (see p.148), plus the main branch of Planet M (see p.148), and the *Lizard Lounge* bar (see p.143). Closed Mondays.
State government emporiums along Baba Kharak Singh Marg near Connaught Place. Each of India's 28 state governments has its own showroom here. Prices are fixed but fair, and browsing is hassle-free. Goods are high quality, if not very excitingly displayed, and include wooden and stone carvings, brassware, textiles, clothing and jewellery. The West Bengal emporium has high-grade Darjeeling teas, and Himachal Pradesh's sells some lesser-known tea varieties, but for Assam, you're better off going to Khari Baoli. Delhi's own emporium stocks good sandalwood carvings, as does Karnataka's, which also has some excellent *bidri* ware. The Kashmir emporium sells carpets, of course, while those of Punjab and Nagaland have lovely shawls, in rather different styles, and Orissa's has some quite jolly textiles. Between the two rows of state emporiums is Rajiv Gandhi Bhawan, whose more modern-looking shops are run mostly by NGOs. All are closed on Sundays.

Sundernagar Market off Mathura Road, south of Purana Qila. See map p.103. A row of shops, rather than a market as such, but a good if pricey place to shop for art, antiques and jewellery; try shops 5, 7, 9, 14 and 26 for the best variety. Most are closed on Sundays, but for fine Darjeeling teas, Regalia at no. 12 is open seven days a week.

Markets

Bengali Market Tansen Marg, off Barakhamba Road. See map p.103. This is really a food market, known for its sweetshops, snack stalls and and large bustling cafés.
Daryaganj Book Market north of Delhi Gate. See map p.113. Delhi's bibliophiles flock to this weekly gathering of 200 stallholders selling secondhand and remaindered books at very low prices. Sundays 10am–5pm.
Dilli Haat Aurobindo Marg, Safdarjang ⓦwww .dillihaat.org. See map p.83. You have to pay to visit this market, but it's only Rs15, and it keeps out the beggars and the touts. Other excluded undesirables are smokers, even though it's open-air. It's full of stalls selling crafts from across the country, and the range and quality is excellent. It can be a bit touristy, but it's a great place to buy souvenirs, and have a bite to eat, with food stalls from almost every Indian state, as well as Tibet (those from the northeastern states such as Assam and Meghalaya, with their delicately spiced curries, are the most popular). Open daily 10.30am–10pm.
Janpath Market Janpath Lane. See map p.96. Adjoining the Tibetan Market (see p.148), this one sells mainly clothes, and is a lot less interesting.
Karol Bagh Market around Ajmal Khan Rd. See map p.82. Mainly sells clothes and fabrics, though it has food and household goods too; this open-air market is quite busy, and handy for the metro, but not as interesting as Paharganj. The motorbike section, a few blocks west along Arya Samaj Rd, is useful if you want a bike or some spare parts.
Khari Baoli Old Delhi. See p.121. This is Delhi's wholesale spice market, but most shops will be happy to sell you retail quantities; the quality here is the best in town, and must be close to the best in the world. Unless you live where they grow, you won't find find cardamoms as big, fat and fresh as the ones you'll get here; cinnamon, cloves, black peppercorns (the spice that first attracted Europeans to India) and Assam tea are all good buys too (for the latter, look in particular around the junction of Khari Baoli Road and Naya Bans Road; try for example Jain Traders at 6050 Naya Bans).
Paharganj Main Bazaar Paharganj. See p.108. If you want to buy some joss sticks, or maybe some patchouli oil, a Shiva or Ganesh T-shirt, or even a

leather whip, then this is the place to come. It's certainly bustling, if a bit seedy (ignore the touts and their boot-polish *charas*), and it does have a great range of goods, including wall-hangings, chillums, even fruit and veg. At the junction of Rajguru Marg in particular, you'll also find itinerant vendors selling things like peacock feather fans and, yes, whips.

Sarojini Nagar (SN) Market Lane E and Cross Roads 1 & 2, Sarojini Nagar. See map p.83. A clothes market specializing in export surplus, especially seconds, at bargain-basement prices (watch out also for "Kevin Clein" and "Ralphe Lawren" labels), but give them a good look-over for flaws before you buy. The market has been a popular stomping ground for Hindu sectarian

extremists, who used to hold regular meetings here, and it was among three Delhi targets in October 2005 for their Muslim counterparts, who bombed it, killing 43 people, but did little to dent the market's popularity. It's especially crowded on Sundays, and closed on Mondays.

Tibetan Market northern end of Janpath near Connaught Place. See map p.106. Only a few stalls are still run by the Tibetan refugees who originally set this market up, and all the shops promote their goods squarely at tourists, but there's more than just the usual tat here and it is worth a browse. You can find statues, incense, shawls, T-shirts, paintings, and Tibetan artefacts including jewellery and semi-precious stones. Haggle like mad.

Books

Delhi has a wide selection of places to buy **books**. **Connaught Place** has many good general bookshops, including Amrit (N-21), Galgotia & Sons (B-17), New Book Depot (B-18), Bookworm (B-29) and Rajiv Book House (30 Palika Bazaar). RS Books & Prints at A-40 South Extension II (☎011/2625 7095) sells antiquarian books, and interesting old maps and prints. Secondhand bookstalls include Jacksons at 5106 Paharganj Main Bazaar, opposite *Vishal* hotel, and Anil Book Corner by the Plaza Cinema on Connaught Place; on Sundays there's also **Daryaganj Market** (see p.147).

Musical instruments, cassettes and CDs

Delhi is a good place to pick up classical Indian instruments as well as recorded music. The listings below include outlets for both. The music CD shops also sell DVDs of Hindi movies with English subtitles.

Blue Bird 9 Regal Building, Sansad Marg, Connaught Place ☎011/2334 2805. An excellent range of classical and modern Indian music on CD and cassette, plus Hindi movies on DVD. Also has a branch at 1279 Kashmiri Gate.

Lahore Music House Netaji Subhash Marg, Old Delhi (next-door to *Moti Mahal* restaurant) ☎011/ 2327 1305, ⊚www.lmhindia.com. Long-established north Indian musical instrument makers with a reputation for quality.

Planet M E-3 South Extension II ☎011/2625 1620 & D-3 Connaught Place. Four-storey emporium with wide-ranging stock of CDs, especially strong on Indian and Western pop, dance and lounge music, but also Indian classical music, plus DVDs of Hindi (and English) movies; there's a pleasant café on the top floor. The

Connaught Place branch is more central but has an extremely truncated range.

Rangarsons K-12, Outer Circle, Connaught Place ☎011/2341 3831. An extraordinary shop that once boasted regiments of the British Indian army among its patrons, and sells brass and other marching band instruments as well as tablas and sitars.

Rikhi Ram G-8, Outer Circle, Connaught Place ☎011/2332 7685, ⊚www.rikhiram.com. Once sitar makers to the likes of renowned musician Ravi Shankar, and still maintaining an exclusive air, with prices to match. Check out the display of their own unique instrumental inventions.

The Music Shop 18 Khan Market ☎011/2461 7797. Wide range of CDs, cassettes and DVDs, and helpful, well-informed staff.

Fabrics and clothes

Delhi's **fabric** and **clothes** shops sell everything from high-quality silks, homespun cottons, saris, Kashmiri shawls and traditional kurta pyjamas to multicoloured tie-dyed T-shirts and other hippy gear. For T-shirts and tie-dye clothing (not to mention joss–sticks and chillums), try **Paharganj** or the **Tibetan Market**. For bargain Western-style trousers, skirts and shirts the export-surplus market at **Sarojini Nagar** (see opposite) is very good. Roadside stalls behind the Tibetan Market off Janpath sell lavishly embroidered and mirrored spreads from Rajasthan and Gujarat, but silks and fine cotton are best bought in **government emporiums** on Baba Kharak Singh Marg.

Anokhi 5 & 6 Santushti Shopping Complex and 9 & 32 Khan Market ☎011/2462 8253, ⓦwww .anokhi.com. Soft cotton and raw silk clothes and soft furnishings; particularly renowned for hand-block printed cottons combining traditional and contemporary designs.

Fabindia 5, 7, 9 & 14-N, N-Block Market, Greater Kailash ☎011/2923 2183, ⓦwww.fabindia.com. Spread over several shops in the market, with a range from furnishings and interiors to chic cotton clothing for men, women and children and wearable block-printed cottons, sourced from villages across India; also sells organic spices, jams and pickles, and has branches around town including Khan Market (central hall, above nos.20 & 21) and B-28 Connaught Place.

Handloom House A-9 Connaught Place ☎011/2332 3057. Roll after roll of fine hand-woven cotton and silk textiles, plus cotton and linen shirts and silk saris.

Khadi Gramodyog Bhawan 24 Regal Building, corner of Sansad Marg and Connaught Place ☎011/2336 0902, ⓦwww.kvic.org.in. Government-run and a great place to pick up hardy, lightweight travelling clothes. Reasonably

priced, ready-made traditional Indian garments include *salwar kameez*, woollen waistcoats, pyjamas; shawls and caps, plus rugs, cloth by the metre, tea, incense, cards and tablecloths.

People Tree 8 Regal Building, Sansad Marg, Connaught Place ☎011/2334 0699, ⓦwww .peopletreeonline.com. An interesting selection of alternative designs, with an emphasis on T-shirts, ethnic chic and jewellery.

SEWA Trade Facilitation Centre 7 Rajiv Gandhi Bhawan, between the two state emporium buildings, Baba Kharak Singh Marg ☎011/3948 9374, ⓦwww.sewatfc.org. Lovely clothes, accessories and furnishings made by self-employed women, mostly working at home, and sold through their own co-operatively owned outlet.

Vedi Tailors M-60 Connaught Place ☎011/2341 6901. Originally established in Rangoon in 1926, this gents' tailor can run you up a made-to-measure suit for around Rs4500–6000, depending on fabric and cut. They usually take a week, but for Rs1500 extra they can do it in 24 hours. S.L. Kapur at G-7 is an equally reputable firm offering a similar service.

Art, antiques, crafts and jewellery

For crafts and jewellery, the **government emporiums** on Baba Kharak Singh Marg should be your first stop, especially if you want to check prices. **Pharganj** and Janpath's **Tibetan market** are good for trinkets such as cheap jewellery, decorated boxes and sandalwood carvings. For upmarket art, antiques (remember that export of anything over a hundred years old requires a permit) and jewellery, there's **Sundernagar Market** (see p.147).

Central Cottage Industries Emporium Jawahar Vyapar Bhawan, Janpath, opposite *Imperial* hotel ☎011/2372 5035, ⓦwww .cottageemporiumindia.com. Popular and convenient multistorey government-run complex, with handicrafts, carpets, leather and reproduction miniatures at fixed (if fractionally high) rates. Jewellery ranges from tribal silver anklets to costume pieces and precious stones.

Cottage of Arts and Jewels 50 Hauz Khas Village ☎011/2696 7418. Interesting, eccentric mix of jewellery, curios and papier-mâché crafts. The best of the collection, including miniatures

and precious stones, is not on display: you'll have to ask to see it.

Neemrana Shop upper floor, 12 Khan Market ☎011/2462 0262. Run by the renowned hotel group of the same name, the shop has a chic clientele and offers a range of home furnishings and knick-knacks, as well as a small collection of antiques and *objets d'art*.

The Village Shop 10 Hauz Khas Village. An attractively presented shop selling replica antiques, bronze statues and an assorted collection of silver and gold jewellery. Ethnic Silver, two doors down at 9A, has a nice selection of jewellery and silverware that's worth a browse.

Miscellaneous

Gujrat Art Gallery 22A Hauz Khas Village ℡011/5521 9649. Despite the name, old film posters – both Hollywood and Bollywood – are the speciality here, mostly in the Rs300–1000 range. You can buy them framed, but it's generally easier, if you're transporting them, to have them rolled up and slipped into in a protective tube. Sagar Art Gallery, next door, also sells film posters.

Industree 8 Rajiv Gandhi Bhawan, between the two state emporium buildings, Baba Kharak Singh Marg ℡011/6597 0850, ⓦwww.industreecrafts .com. A light, bright shop with equally light, bright designs, including mats, blinds, boxes and bags made of natural fibres such as jute, reeds and rattan, crafted by small producers mostly working from home and sold by a fair-trade NGO.

Jain Super Store 172 Palika Bazaar, Connaught Place ℡011/2332 1031, ⓦwww.jainperfumers .com. Essential oils, natural perfumes and their own in-house fragrances, as well as joss sticks, scented candles and aroma diffusers.

Nath Stationers (The Card Shop) B-38 Connaught Place. A small shop with a big selection of greetings cards featuring Indian artwork and designs.

Listings

Airlines Aeroflot, N-1 Tolstoy House, 15–17 Tolstoy Marg ℡011/2331 0426; Air Canada, 5th floor, World Trade Tower, New Barakhamba Lane ℡011/4152 8181; Air France, 7 Atma Ram Mansion, Scindia House, Janpath ℡011/2346 6262; Air Deccan (no office) ℡3900 8888 or 0/981 817 7008; Air India, Jeevan Bharati Building, Sansad Marg ℡011/2373 1225; Air Sahara, N-41 Connaught Place ℡011/5178 8888; Alitalia, 7th floor, Golf View Tower, Sector 42, Gurgaon, Haryana ℡95124/402 6000 from Delhi, or ℡0124/402 6000 from outside Delhi; American Airlines, E-9 Connaught Place ℡1800/180 7300 or 011/2341 6930; Asiana Airlines, 2 Ansal Bhawan, ground floor, 16 Kasturba Gandhi Marg ℡011/2332 9819; British Airways, DLF Plaza Tower, DLF Qutab Enclave, Gurgaon, Haryana ℡95124/254 0911 from Delhi, or ℡0124/254 0911 from outside Delhi; Cathay Pacific, airport ℡011/2565 4701; China Airlines, upper ground floor, Kanchenchunga Building, 18 Barakhamba Rd ℡011/2332 7131; Continental, 2nd floor, Belvedere Tower, Cyber Green, DLF City, Gurgaon, Haryana ℡95124/431 5500 from Delhi, or ℡0124/431 5500 from outside Delhi; Delta, 66 Janpath ℡011/2335 2257; Emirates, 7th floor, DLF Centre, Sansad Marg ℡011/5531 4444; GoAir, airport ℡011/6541 0030 to 33; Gulf Air, G-12 Marina Arcade, Connaught Place ℡011/2332 4293; Indian Airlines, Malhotra Building, Janpath, at F-Block Connaught Place ℡1800/180 1407 or 011/1407; IndiGo, 124 Thapar House, near *Imperial Hotel*, Janpath ℡0/991 038 3838 or 011/4351 3186; Indus Air, airport ℡011/2567 1370; Jet Airways, N-40 Connaught Place ℡011/3984 1111; Kingfisher Airlines, N-42 Connaught Place ℡1800/233 3131 or 1800/180 0101 or 011/2567 4841; Kenya Airways, ground floor, Amba Deep Building, 14 Kasturba Gandhi Marg ℡011/2376 6248; KLM, airport ℡011/2335 7747; Kuwait Airways, 2-C DCM Building, 16 Barakhamba Rd ℡011/2335 4373 to 77; Lufthansa, 56 Janpath ℡011/2372 4200; Malaysia Airlines, 10th floor, Ashoka Estate Building, 24 Barakhamba Rd ℡011/4102 5555; Qantas, 511 Prakash Deep Building, 7th floor, Tolstoy Marg ℡011/2331 2445; Qatar Airways, 307 Paharpur Business Centre, Nehru Place ℡011/4120 7676; Royal Jordanian, G-56 Connaught Place ℡011/2332 7418; SAA, 13 Janpath ℡011/2335 4422; Singapore Airlines, 9th Floor, Ashoka Estate Building, Barakhamba Rd ℡011/2332 6373; Spice Jet, airport ℡011/5551 5063 or 1800/180 3333; Swiss, 5th floor, World Trade Tower, New Barakhamba Lane ℡011/2341 2929; Syrian Airlines, airport ℡011/2565 3712; Thai Airways, *Park Royal Hotel*, American Plaza, Nehru Place ℡011/4149 7777; Virgin Atlantic, 8th Floor, DLF Centre, Sansad Marg ℡011/4130 3030.

Banks and exchange At the international airport, you can change money at the 24hr State Bank of India and at Thomas Cook. Almost every block on Connaught Place has ATMs that take Visa or MasterCard, as do metro stations, and there are several along Chandni Chowk and Asaf Ali Rd in Old Delhi. There's an HFDC ATM opposite the *Metropolis Hotel* on Paharganj Main Bazaar, and a couple more just up Rajguru Marg beneath the *Roxy Hotel*. You can also change money at the DTTDC office, N-36 Connaught Place, and at numerous other authorized exchange offices in Connaught Place and Paharganj (but if you're changing traveller's cheques, make sure before signing that they're not going to mess you around demanding receipts and such like, or sting you with unmentioned commissions). All major hotels have exchange facilities; the *Ajanta*, near the *Grand Godwin* on Arakashan Rd in Ram Nagar has a 24hr bureau. The central branch of Thomas Cook is upstairs at C-33 Connaught Place (☎011/2345 6585; Mon–Fri 9.30am–6pm, Sat 10am–5.30pm), and there's a 24hr branch on the Ajmeri Gate side of New Delhi station (by VIP parking, near platform 12; ☎011/2321 1819). American Express is at A-1 Connaught Place (☎011/2332 7602; Mon–Fri 9am–4pm, Sat 10am–1pm).

Car rental Avis, D-4 Shubam Gardens, near Hari Bhawan, Ram Mandir Marg, Vasant Kunj ☎011/5568 0664 or 0627, @crsdelhi@avis.co.in; Budget, 104 Ansal Bhavan, Kasturba Gandhi Marg ☎011/2331 8600; Europcar, 434 Westend Green Farm House Rd, NH-8, Rangpuri ☎011/3250 5113 (chauffeur-driven only); Hertz, c/o Carzonrent, 434 Westend Green Farm House Rd, NH-8, Rangpuri ☎1800/111 212 or 011/4184 1212, @reserve @carzonrent.com.

Courier services DHL, c/o Exel India Pvt. Ltd, 1st Floor, U&I Centre, 580 Delhi–Palam Vihar Road, Bijwasan ☎011/2806 2980 to 82; FedEx, 1/2–1/2-A, Block no III, Gopinath Bazaar, Behind Capital Restaurant, Delhi Cantonment ☎1800/226 161 or 0/981 817 0000; UPS, c/o Jetair Express, D-12/1, Okhla Industrial Area Phase II ☎011/2638 9323.

Dental treatment Delhi Dental Centre, C-56 South Extension II ☎011/2625-2398.

Embassies, high commissions & consulates Australia, 1/50-G Shanti Path, Chanakyapuri ☎011/4139 9900; Bangladesh, E-39, Dr S Radhakrishan Marg, Chanakyapuri ☎011/2412 1389; Bhutan, Chandragupta Marg, Chanakyapuri ☎011/2688 9230; Burma, 3/50-F Nyaya Marg, Chanakyapuri ☎011/2467 8822; Canada, 7/8 Shanti Path, Chanakyapuri ☎011/4178 2000; China, 50-D Shanti Path, Chanakyapuri ☎011/2611 2345, Ireland, 230 Jor Bagh (near Safdarjang's tomb) ☎011/2462 6714; Nepal, Barakhamba Rd by Mandi House Chowk, southeast of Connaught Place ☎011/2332 9218; Netherlands, 6/50-F Shanti Path, Chanakyapuri ☎011/2419 7600; New Zealand, 50-N Nyaya Marg ☎011/2688 3170; Pakistan, 2/50-G Shanti Path, Chanakyapuri ☎011/2611 0601; South Africa, B-18 Vasant Marg, Vasant Vihar, ☎011/2614 9411; Sri Lanka, 27 Kautilya Marg, Chanakyapuri ☎011/2301 0201; UK, Shanti Path, Chanakyapuri ☎011/2687 2161; USA, Shanti Path, Chanakyapuri ☎011/2419 8000.

Festivals Republic Day (26 Jan) is celebrated by a huge parade along Rajpath (see p.104), with tickets for seats to watch the parade available at travel agents, hotels and tourist offices. Beating the Retreat on 29 Jan sees military bands perform on

Vijay Chowk (see p.105). In the first two weeks of February, the state government of Haryana holds a two-week crafts fair, Suraj Kund Mela, at Suraj Kund, which is just across the state line south of Tughluqabad Fort, with transport laid on from central Delhi.

Hospitals All India Institute of Medical Sciences (AIIMS), Ansari Nagar, Aurobindo Marg (☎011/2658 8500; ambulance ☎1099) has a 24hr emergency service and good treatment as does Lok Nayak Jai Prakash Hospital, Jawaharlal Nehru Marg, Old Delhi (☎011/2323 3400) near Delhi Gate. Dr Ram Manohar Lohia Hospital, Baba Kharak Singh Marg (☎011/2336 5525) is another government hospital. Private clinics include East West Medical Centre, B-28 Greater Kailash Part I (☎011/2629 3701 to 3, @www.eastwestrescue.com). The US embassy maintains a list of hospitals and doctors on its website at @newdelhi.usembassy.gov/medical_information2.html.

Internet access Reliable places include: Sunrise and Cyber Café, N-9/II Connaught Place (Mon–Sat 9am–8pm; Rs35/hr); Friends Internet, Tooti Chowk, just off Main Bazaar, Paharganj (daily 10am–10pm; Rs20/hr). There are lots on and off Paharganj Main Bazaar.

Left luggage Located at the railway station cloakrooms (Rs10–15 per day). Most hotels in Paharganj offer a left-luggage service for their guests.

Money transfers Western Union agents include several post offices, most conveniently Old Delhi and New Delhi GPOs, but if having money sent to a post office, be sure to specify the name correctly ("Delhi GPO" means Old Delhi GPO, but specify "Old Delhi" just to be sure, and add the street name, Lothian Rd). WU agents also include the Bank of Baroda at B-3 and M-9 Connaught Place and the Centurion Bank of Punjab at L-40 and N-47. MoneyGram's agents can be found in branches of Thomas Cook (such as *Hotel Imperial*, in New Delhi station or at C-33 Connaught Place), and the South Indian Bank including 22 Regal Building, Connaught Place.

Motorcycles The Karol Bagh area has many good bike shops selling new or secondhand Enfields. Reliable dealers include Inder Motors, 1744-A/55, basement, Hardhyan Singh Nalwala St, Abdul Aziz Rd (☎011/2572 8579, @www.lallisingh.com), two blocks east of Ajmal Khan Rd, turning right at the *chowki*, then the third alley on the left, closed Mondays. Also worth trying is Ess Aar Motors, 1-E/13 Jhandewalan Extension, between Karol Bagh and Paharganj (☎011/2367 8836). In Paharganj, there's Bulletwallas on Rajguru Marg by Imperial Cinema (☎0/981 090 2872, @www.bulletwallas.com).

Opticians Lawrence & Mayo, 76 Janpath; R.K. Oberoi, H-14 Connaught Place.

Pharmacies Nearly every market has at least one pharmacy. Apollo, G-8 Connaught Place, and the pharmacy at the All India Medical Institute, Ansari Nagar, Aurobindo Marg (☎011/2696 7546), are open 24hr.

Photographic studios Delhi Photo Company, 78 Janpath, offers high-quality developing, printing, and slide processing. It's second only to Kinsey Brothers beneath the *India Today* offices at 2-A Connaught Place.

Police ☎100 (national number). If you have any problem that should involve the police, your hotel reception or the Government of India tourist office will direct you to the appropriate station. Delhi now has a dedicated squad of tourist police based at the airport, main stations and major tourist sights and hotel areas, whose aim is specifically to help tourists in trouble.

Post offices Poste restante (Mon–Fri 10am–1pm & 1.30–5pm, Sat 10am–1pm & 1.30–4pm) is available at the GPO on the roundabout at the intersection of Baba Kharak Singh Marg and Ashoka Rd (known as Gole PO). You must show your passport to claim mail, and check the register for parcels. Letters sent to "Poste Restante, Delhi", rather than to New Delhi, will probably end up in Old Delhi GPO, north of the railway line on Lothian Rd (see "money transfers" above). The GPO is open for sale of stamps Mon–Sat 8am–1pm & 1.30–8pm. There's a useful branch office at A-6 Connaught Place (Mon–Sat 10am–7.30pm).

Visa extensions and exit formalities The first place to go if you need to extend your visa is the Ministry of Home Affairs, Foreigners Division, Lok Nayak Bhawan, behind Khan Market (Mon–Fri 10am–noon). If your total stay will exceed six months, you will also need to go to the Foreigner's Regional Registration Office (FRRO), East Block 8, Level 2, Sector 1, Ramakrishna Puram (Mon–Fri 9.30am–1.30pm & 2–4pm; ☎011/2671 1443). Forms can be downloaded from ⓦwww.immigrationindia.nic.in. If you've been in India more than 120 days, before leaving you'll need to fill in a tax clearance certificate, obtainable from the Foreign Section, Income Tax Office, Central Revenue Building, Indraprastha Estate (Mon–Fri 10am–1pm & 2–5pm; ☎011/2337 9171 ext 1650); have your foreign exchange certificates to hand.

Moving on from Delhi

Delhi has very good international and domestic **travel connections**. Scores of **travel agents** (see box opposite) sell bus and air tickets, while many hotels will book private buses for you; **touts**, concentrated at the top of Janpath, waylay tourists with promises of cheap fares, but rarely give a good deal. Buses leave Delhi frequently, and tourists are usually ensured places on trains in a reserved **tourist quota**. There's an ever-expanding network of internal flights, but it's still best to book as far ahead as possible; bear in mind that at peak times such as Diwali, demand is very high.

By air

Indira Gandhi International Airport (international flight enquiries ☎011/2569 6021, domestic flight enquiries ☎011/2567 5181, ⓦwww.delhiairport.com) is 20km southwest of the city centre. Most tourists on night flights book a **taxi** to the airport in advance (around Rs200–250) through their hotel. By **auto-rickshaw** it's around Rs100–150. Otherwise, afternoons and evenings, **EATS airport buses** run from F-block on Connaught Place, by the Indian Airlines office (Rs50, plus Rs10 per item of baggage; 40min); departures are at 2pm, 5.30pm, 7pm, 9pm, 10pm and 11pm. You can book tickets in advance at the small office next to Indian Airlines (☎011/2331 6530).

    Domestic flights leave from Terminal 1 (☎011/2567 5181). Tickets can be bought through travel agents or direct from the airlines. Flights from Delhi are currently operated by Air India (AI), Air Deccan (DN), Indian Airlines (IC), Kingfisher (IT), SpiceJet (SG), Air Sahara (S2), IndiGo (6E) and Jet Airways (9W).

Travel agents and tour operators

The Rajasthan Tourism Development Corporation, Bikaner House, Pandara Road (☎011/2338 3837 or 6069) organizes **package tours** including wildlife tours and trips on the *Palace on Wheels* and *Heritage on Wheels* trains. The Delhi Tourism and Transport Development Corporation (DTTDC), N-36, Bombay Life Building, Middle Circle, Connaught Place (☎011/5152 3073) offers day-trips to Agra (Rs950) and three-day "Golden Triangle" excursions to Agra, Ajmer, Bharatpur and Jaipur (Rs3200). For competitively priced car tours around Rajasthan try *Hotel Namaskar*, Paharganj (☎011/2358 2233, ℮namaskarhotel@yahoo.com). The India Tourism Development Corporation's commercial arm, Ashok Travels, L-1 Connaught Place (☎011/2341 8039, ℮travel@attindiatourism.com) sells excursions and air tickets.

For **ticketing**, recommended operators specializing in international and domestic flights include: BTI Sita, F-12 Connaught Place (☎011/2331 1409); STA Travel, upstairs at G-55 Connaught Place (☎011/2373 1480, ℗www.statravel.co.in); and Travel Corporation of India, C-35 Connaught Place (☎011/2341 6082 to 5; ℗www .tcindia.com). Aa Bee Travel, in the lobby of *Hare Rama Guest House* (☎011/2356 2171 or 2117, ℮aabee@mail.com) at T-298 off Main Bazaar, Paharganj is a reliable firm for competitively priced air and private bus tickets. The Student Travel Information Centre, STIC Travels, 1st floor, West Wing, Chandralok Building, opposite *Imperial Hotel*, 36 Janpath (☎011/2332 1487, ℗www.stictravel.com) can issue or renew ISIC cards.

It's a very bad idea to book flights or excursions through any agency that you're directed to by a street tout, and that goes double for any agency spuriously trying to pass itself off as a tourist information office.

Generally speaking, only Indian Airlines and Jet Airways fly to Rajasthan, though IndiGo serve Jaipur, and Go Air are promising cheap flights there in the future. At present services from Delhi to Rajasthan are as follows: Jaipur (3–5 daily; 40min; IC, 6E, 9W); Jodhpur (2 daily; 55min; IC, 9W); Udaipur (3 daily; 1hr 10min; IC, 9W), though only one flight (with IC) is non-stop; stopping services take three hours.

There are direct flights from Delhi to most other Indian airports, including Bengaluru (28–29 daily; 2hr 25min–3hr; DN, IC, IT, S2, 9W); Chennai (18 daily; 2hr 30min; DN, IC, IT, S2, 9W); Kolkata (17 daily; 2hr; DN, IC, IT, S2, 9W) and of course Mumbai (45 daily; 1hr 55min; DN, IC, IT, S2, 9W).

International flights leave from Terminal 2 (☎011/2569 6021). If you don't already have a ticket for a **flight** out of India, you'll have little trouble finding one, except between December and March when it may be difficult at short notice. While you can buy tickets directly from the airlines (addresses are given on p.150), it saves time and legwork to book through an **agency** (see above). Remember that many airlines require you to reconfirm your flight between a week and 72 hours before leaving.

By train

You can check train services on line at ℗www.indianrail.gov.in (click on "Trains between Important Stations"). The most convenient trains are listed in the box on p.154.

New Delhi station (entry from Chelmsford Road or Ajmeri Gate) has a very efficient **booking office** (Mon–Sat 8am–8pm, Sun 8am–2pm; ☎011/2334 6804) for foreign and NRI tourists, on the first floor (above ground) of the main departure building. Foreigners must bring passports,

Recommended trains from Delhi to Agra and Rajasthan

The trains below are the fastest and/or most convenient. There may be others which are slower, or arrive at inconvenient times. Train timetables change frequently; check latest schedules either at your nearest station or online at ⓦ www.indianrail.gov.in before travel.

Destination	Name	No.	From	Departs	Arrives
Abu Road	Rajdhani Express*	2958	ND	7.35pm (exc Tue)	6.20am
	Ahmedabad Mail	9116	OD	10.50pm (daily)	12.46pm
Agra	Shatabdi Express*	2002	ND	6.15am (exc Fri)	8.07am
	Taj Express	2280	HN	7.15am (daily)	10.07am
	Mangala Express	2618	HN	9.20am (daily)	12.20pm
	Kerala Express	2626	HN	11.30am (daily)	2.20pm
	Sachkhand Express	2716	ND	1.35pm (daily)	4.30pm
	Gondwana Express	2415	HD	3.25pm (daily)	6.47pm
	AP Express	2724	ND	5.45pm (daily)	8.37pm
	GT Express	2616	ND	6.40pm (daily)	9.45pm
Ajmer	Shatabdi Express*	2015	ND	6.10am (exc Wed)	1pm
	Ahmedabad Mail	9106	OD	10.50pm (daily)	7.25am
Alwar	Shatabdi Express*	2015	ND	6.10am (exc Wed)	8.30am
	Kranti Express	2463	SR	8.40am (Wed, Fri, Sun)	11.39am
	Hazrat Express	4311	OD	11.50am (M, W, Thu, Su)	2.38pm
	Ashram Express	2916	OD	3.05pm (daily)	5.36pm
	Jaisalmer Express	4059	OD	5.45pm (daily)	9.03pm
Bharatpur	Golden Temple Mail	2904	ND	7.50am (daily)	10.43am
	Jan Shatabdi Express	2060	HN	1.10pm (exc Sun)	3.46pm
	Paschim Express	2926	ND	4.35pm (daily)	7.43pm
Bikaner	Sampark Kranti Express	2463	SR	8.40am (Wed, Fri, Sun)	9pm
	Assam Express	5609	OD	4.05pm (daily)	5.46am
Chittaurgarh	Dheradun Express	9020A	HN	9.45pm (daily)	12noon
Jaipur	Shatabdi Express*	2015	ND	6.10am (exc Wed)	10.45am
	Kranti Express	2463	SR	8.40am (Wed, Fri, Sun)	1.55pm
	Hazrat Express	4311	OD	11.50am (M, W, Thu, Su)	5.40pm
	Ashram Express	2916	OD	3.05pm (daily)	8.25pm
Jaisalmer	Jaisalmer Express	4059	OD	5.45pm (daily)	1pm
Jodhpur	Kranti Express	2463	SR	8.40am (Wed, Fri, Sun)	7.40pm
	Jaisalmer Express	4059	OD	5.45pm (daily)	6.05am
	Mandor Express	2461	OD	8.45pm (daily)	8am
Kota	Golden Temple Mail	2904	ND	7.50am (daily)	2.30pm
	Rajdhani Express*	2432	HN	11.05am (Tue, Sat)	3.30pm
	Rajdhani Express*	2952	ND	4.30pm (daily)	8.55pm
	Dheradun Express	9020	ND	10.40pm (daily)	7am
Sawai Madhopur					
	Golden Temple Mail	2904	ND	7.50am (daily)	1.05pm
	Jan Shatabdi Express	2060	HN	1.10pm (exc Sun)	6pm
Udaipur	Mewar Express	2963	HN	7pm (daily)	7am

OD Old Delhi **ND** New Delhi **HN** Hazrat Nizamuddin **SR** Sarai Rohilla *a/c only and in theory pay in foreign currency or in rupees backed up by exchange certificates.

The best trains tend to leave from New Delhi, but many trains to Rajasthan (except those to Bharatpur, Kota and Sawai Madhopur) leave from **Old Delhi station** (officially Delhi Junction), which is on Shayma Prasad Mukerji Marg, north of Chandni Chowk, and some trains leave from **Sarai Rohilla**, which is inconveniently situated 6km northwest of the centre (Rs50 by pre-paid auto from CP) or from **Hazrat Nizamuddin** (6km southeast of the centre near Humayun's Tomb, Rs50 by pre-paid auto from CP), so check when you buy your ticket. Bookings for all trains can be made in New Delhi station.

For **Agra** Agra (19–23 daily; 1hr 52min–5hr 5min), the most comfortable and convenient service, if you can get up in time to catch it, is the 6.15am Bhopal-bound Shatabdi Express #2002 out of New Delhi, which pulls in to Agra Cantonment shortly after 8am, well in time for a day's sightseeing; if you want to make it a day-trip, you can catch the same train back to New Delhi at 8.30pm, arriving at 10.30pm, but note that it does not run on Fridays. It is also possible to do a day's excursion on the cheaper Taj Express #2280 from Hazrat Nizamuddin at 7.15am, arriving at Agra Cantonment at 10.07am, which gives you time to see the Taj and the main sights in town – even Fatehpur Sikri if you run around like a mad thing – and still get back to Delhi that evening (it leaves Agra at 6.55pm, arriving in Hazrat Nizamuddin at 10.05pm). UP tourism even lay on a coach tour of Agra and Fatehpur Sikri especially for day-trippers using the Taj Express; see p.162. Note that trains on the Delhi–Agra route, and particularly the Taj Express, being popular with tourists, are also popular with thieves, so keep hold of your baggage at all times, especially just before departure.

For **Bikaner**, the best service was the overnight Bikaner Mail #4791, but that's currently suspended while the line is upgraded, leaving the overnight service, the Assam Express #5609 (daily; 12hr 30min). As its name suggests, this starts its journey at Guwahati in Assam, and can be hours late by the time it gets to Delhi. Failing that, there's the Sampark Kranti Express #2463 (3 weekly), or you could travel from Old Delhi to Jaipur on the Ashram Express #2916 to pick up the overnight Jaipur-Bikaner Express #4737 (arrives Bikaner 6.55am). The Jaisalmer Express #4059 (from Old Delhi) should also connect at Jaipur for the Howrah-Jammu Express #2307 (arrives Bikaner 8.30am), but it's a tight connection (fifteen minutes), though the Howrah–Jammu is coming through from Kolkata (Calcutta), so it may well be late. The Bikaner Mail should be reinstated when track work is completed.

Other **frequencies and journey times** to destinations in Rajasthan are: Abu Road (2–5 daily; 10hr 45min–13hr); Ajmer (4–7 daily; 6hr 50min–8hr 40min); Alwar (6–9 daily; 1hr 25min); Bharatpur (8–9 daily; 2hr 30min–4hr 30min); Bikaner (1–2 daily; 12hr 30min); Chittaurgarh (2 daily; 9hr 40min–14hr 15min); Jaipur (7–10 daily; 4hr 35min–5hr 45min); Jaisalmer (1 daily; 19hr 45min); Jodhpur (2–3 daily; 10hr 55min–12hr 5min); Kota (10–13 daily; 4hr 25min–9hr 20min); Sawai Madhopur (10–11 daily; 3hr 40min–7hr 30min); Udaipur (1 daily; 12hr). Recommended trains are listed in the box opposite.

If you're heading out of the region, there are plenty of trains to **Mumbai** (10–12 daily; 16hr 5min–30hr 20min), the best being the overnight #2952 Rajdhani Express from New Delhi. For **the South**, the best trains are: to Chennai (2–3 trains daily; 32hr 40min–43hr 20min), the #2434 Rajdhani Express from Hazrat Nizamuddin or the #2622 Tamil Nadu Express from New Delhi; to Bengaluru (1–2 daily; 36hr 25min–40hr 25min), the #2628 Karnataka

Express from New Delhi; and to Hyderabad (2–4 daily; 26hr 5min–30hr 10min), the #2724 AP Express from New Delhi. To Thiruvananthapuram (Trivandrum), the only direct train is the #2626 Kerala Express from New Delhi (47hr 50min). For **Kolkata** (Calcutta; 3–6 daily; 16hr 55min–35hr 20min), the most convenient trains are the #2314 Rajdhani service to Sealdah and, except on Fridays, the #2302 to Howrah. Best services for **the Northeast** are the #2424 Rajdhani Express (no service Thurs or Sun), or the #2506 Northeast Express, both from New Delhi to Guwahati (4–5 trains daily; 27hr 20min–52hr 20min).

If your destination is **Pakistan**, the #8101 Jammu Tawi Express from New Delhi on Sunday or Wednesday evening should get you into Amritsar at a bleary 5.15am the next morning, in time to catch the #4607 Samjhauta Express, which – political situation allowing – leaves Amritsar at 7am bound for Lahore. If you can't get on the #8101, then the #2903 Golden Temple Mail is a decent fall-back, though its 6.05am scheduled arrival time at Amritsar doesn't leave you so much leeway if it's running late.

By bus

Generally speaking, trains are more comfortable than buses, and most people prefer to use the train if possible. The main exception to this rule is to Pushkar, where privately-run overnight sleeper buses will take you straight there, whereas a train journey would only take you as far as Ajmer, from where you'd need to get a local bus. Some people prefer the option of a luxury state-run bus from Delhi to Jaipur too, especially as these are much more frequent than trains.

A lot of **state-run buses** depart from the **Maharana Pratap ISBT** (℡011/2386 5181; Rajasthan Roadways ℡011/2386 4470; UP Roadways ℡011/2386 8709) by Kashmere Gate metro (Rs50 from CP by auto), but buses to Agra (12 daily; 4hr), and some (rather ramshackle) buses to Jaipur (approx hourly; 7hr), Jodhpur (4 daily; 12hr) and Ajmer (9 daily; 9hr) leave from the **Sarai Kale Khan ISBT** (℡011/2435 8092, UP Roadways ℡011/2435 3359) east of Hazrat Nizamuddin. However, for Jaipur, Jodhpur, Udaipur and Ajmer, the **Rajasthan Roadways terminal** at Bikaner House, India Gate (℡011/2338 3469) has by far the best service, with comfortable deluxe Silver and Gold Line buses: to Jaipur (28 daily; 6hr); to Ajmer (11 daily; 9hr); to Jodhpur (daily; 12hr); Udaipur (daily; 14hr). If leaving from **Maharana Pratap ISBT**, be sure to arrive well before departure to allow time to find the correct counter (there are thirty or so) and book your ticket; from Maharana Pratap there are services to Agra (4 daily; 4hr); Ajmer (11 daily; 9hr); Jaipur (25 daily; 6hr 30min); Mount Abu (daily; 18hr); Udaipur (3 daily; 15hr). Ask for the numbers of both platform and licence plate to ensure you board the right bus.

Private buses usually depart from near the Ramakrishna Mission at the end of Main Bazaar, Paharganj, but some pick up passengers at hotels; you can book tickets a day or two in advance at agencies in Paharganj or Connaught Place such as Aa Bee Travel (see p.153). Private buses tend to be better than the ordinary state buses, but not as deluxe as the RSTDC Silver Line or Gold Line services. However, some overnight private buses have the option of a sleeper berth. Of most interest are the buses to Pushkar (2 daily; 10hr).

The only international bus service is to **Lahore** in Pakistan, leaving from Dr Ambedkar Terminal on Jawaharlal Nehru Marg near Delhi Gate on Tuesdays and Fridays at 6am (℡011/2331 8180; ⓦdtc.nic.in/lahorebus.htm).

2

Agra

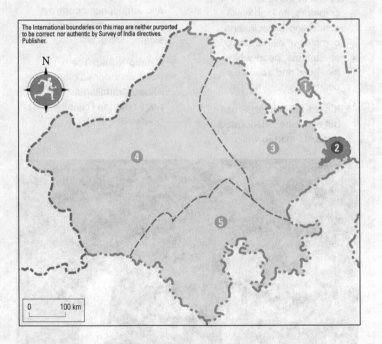

The International boundaries on this map are neither purported
to be correct nor authentic by Survey of India directives.
Publisher.

N

0   100 km

CHAPTER 2 # Highlights

* **Taj Mahal** The most beautiful building in the world: iconic, mysterious and completely unforgettable, whether you're seeing it for the first time or the fiftieth. See p.167

* **Agra Fort** Former residence of the Mughal emperors, its high walls concealing a fascinating complex of elaborate royal apartments, pearl-white mosques and spacious courtyards. See p.173

* **Itimad-ud-Daulah** Small but exquisitely decorated tomb, its marble walls covered in intricately patterned and coloured inlay work. See p.177

* **Akbar's mausoleum, Sikandra** Tucked away on the edge of Agra, the huge sandstone tomb of India's greatest Mughal emperor offers a tranquil and atmospheric contrast to the city's more touristed sights. See p.179

* **Fatehpur Sikri** The enigmatic abandoned city of Akbar, straddling an arid ridge near the Rajasthan border. See p.186

△ Diwan-i-Am, Agra Fort

Agra

The splendour of **AGRA** – capital of all India under the Mughals – remains undiminished, from the massive fort to the magnificent Taj Mahal. Along with Delhi and Jaipur, Agra forms the third apex of the "Golden Triangle", India's most popular tourist itinerary. It fully merits that status; the **Taj** effortlessly transcends all the frippery and commercialism that surrounds it, while the city's other sights – most notably **Agra Fort**, the **Itimad-ud-Daulah**, Akbar's Mausoleum at **Sikandra** and the abandoned city of **Fatehpur Sikri** – together comprise one of India's greatest architectural legacies, offering a unique insight into the opulent and cultured lives (and deaths) of the great Mughal emperors.

Mughal architecture aside, Agra city itself can be an intense experience, even for seasoned India hands. Years of corruption and political neglect have reduced its infrastructure to a shambles: filthy water and open sewers are ubiquitous, power cuts routine and the traffic pollution appalling (some mornings you can barely see the sun through the fog of fumes). Moreover, as a tourist you'll have to contend with often overwhelming crowds at the major monuments, absurdly high admission fees, and some of Asia's most persistent touts, commission merchants and rickshaw-wallahs. Don't, however, let all this put you off. Although it's possible to see Agra on a day-trip from Delhi, the Taj alone deserves so much more – a fleeting visit would miss the subtleties of its many moods, as the light changes from sunrise to sunset – while the city's other sights and Fatehpur Sikri can easily fill several days.

Some history

Little is known of the pre-Muslim history of Agra; one of the earliest chronicles, dated to the Afghan invasion under Ibrahim Ghaznavi in 1080 AD, describes a robust fort occupying a chain of hills, with a flourishing city strategically placed at the crossroads between the north and the centre of India. However, Agra remained a minor administrative centre until 1504, when the Sultan of Delhi, **Sikandar Lodi**, moved his capital here so as to keep a check on the warring factions of his empire. The ruins of the Lodis' great city can still be seen on the eastern bank of the Yamuna. After defeating the last Lodi sultan, Ibrahim Lodi, at Panipat in 1526, **Babur**, the founder of the Mughal empire, sent ahead his son **Humayun** to capture Agra. In gratitude for their benevolent treatment at his hands, the family of the Raja of Gwalior rewarded the Mughal with jewellery and precious stones – among them the legendary **Koh-i-noor Diamond**, now among the crown jewels of England. Agra's greatest days arrived during the reign of Humayun's son, **Akbar the Great** (1556–1605), with the construction of Agra Fort. The city maintained its position as the capital of the empire for

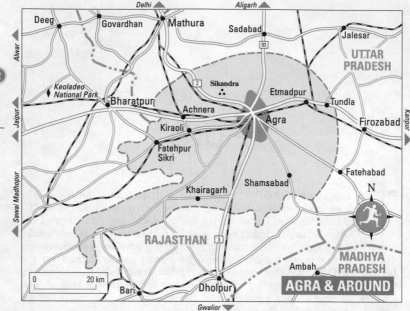

over a century; even when **Shah Jahan**, Jahangir's son and successor, built a new city in Delhi – Shahjahanabad, now known as Old Delhi – his heart remained in Agra. He pulled down many of the earlier red-sandstone structures in the fort, replacing them with his trademark – exquisite marble buildings. The empire flourished under his successor Aurangzeb (1658–1707), although his intolerance towards non-Muslims stirred up a hornets' nest. Agra was occupied successively by the Jats, the Marathas, and eventually the British.

After the uprising in 1857, the city lost the headquarters of the government of the Northwestern Provinces and the High Court to Allahabad and went into a period of decline. Its Mughal treasures have ensured its survival, and today the city is once again prospering, as an industrial and commercial centre as well as a tourist destination.

Arrival, orientation and information

Agra has no less than six **railway stations**, though visitors are only likely to use two of them. The busiest is **Agra Cantonment** ("Cantt"), in the southwest, which serves Delhi, Gwalior, Jhansi and most points south. Trains from Rajasthan pull in close to the Jama Masjid at **Agra Fort station** (a few also stop at Agra Cantt – see box, p.185). Agra Cantt is more convenient for the hotels around Sadar Bazaar, while Agra Fort Station is slightly closer to the Taj Ganj area; both are a fair way from the hotels along Fatehabad Road.

There's a prepaid auto-rickshaw/taxi booth at Agra Cantonment station (Rs50/150 to anywhere in town); cycle rickshaws wait in the forecourt outside, though if you're going to Fatehabad Road or Taj Ganj you'll probably want to use a taxi or auto, since it's a long, slow and rather smelly ride by cycle rickshaw.

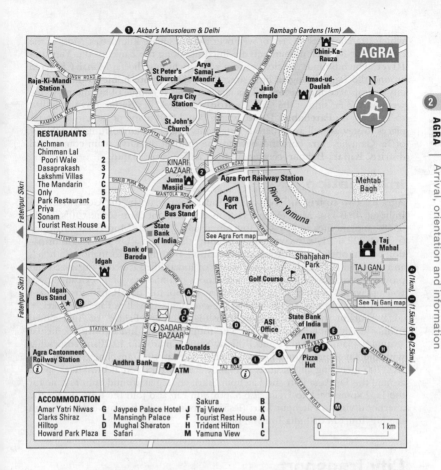

▲ ❶, Akbar's Mausoleum & Delhi Rambagh Gardens (1km) ▲

AGRA

N

Chini-Ka-Rauza

St Peter's Church
Arya Samaj Mandir
Agra City Station
St John's Church
Jain Temple
Itmad-ud-Daulah
Mehtab Bagh

Raja-Ki-Mandi Station

RESTAURANTS
Achman	1
Chimman Lal Poori Wale	2
Dasaprakash	3
Lakshmi Villas	7
The Mandarin	C
Only	5
Park Restaurant	7
Priya	4
Sonam	6
Tourist Rest House	A

KINARI BAZAAR

Juma Masjid

Agra Fort Railway Station

Agra Fort Bus Stand

Agra Fort

River Yamuna

Taj Mahal

TAJ GANJ

Fatehpur Sikri ▲

See Agra Fort map

State Bank of India

Bank of Baroda

Shahjahan Park

See Taj Ganj map

Golf Course

Idgah

Idgah Bus Stand ★

SADAR BAZAAR

ASI Office

State Bank of India

McDonalds

Andhra Bank

Agra Cantonment Railway Station

Pizza Hut

ACCOMMODATION
Amar Yatri Niwas	G	Jaypee Palace Hotel	J	Sakura	B
Clarks Shiraz	L	Mansingh Palace	F	Taj View	K
Hilltop	D	Mughal Sheraton	H	Tourist Rest House	A
Howard Park Plaza	E	Safari	M	Trident Hilton	I
				Yamuna View	C

❻ (1km), ❶ (1.5km) & ❸ (2.5km) ▲

0 — 1 km

As ever, most cycle rickshaw and auto-rickshaw drivers will try to earn commission by taking you to a hotel of their choosing, and may tell you (falsely) that the hotel of your choice is closed. **Buses** from Rajasthan and express services from Delhi terminate at **Idgah bus stand** close to Agra Cantonment station; a few services from other destinations arrive at the more chaotic **Agra Fort bus stand**, just west of the fort. In addition, some buses from Delhi stop outside the fort gate, where you'll have no trouble finding a rickshaw.

One common **scam** to look out for is as follows. Buses arriving in Agra often stop in the suburbs, about 6km out from Idgah, for locals to get off. Rickshaw drivers (sometimes in collusion with the bus drivers) may get on and insist that your vehicle has reached the end of the line, and that you need to disembark. Unfortunately, if you haven't been to Agra before it's difficult to know whether they're telling the truth, though the chances are that if there are other locals still sitting on the bus, they're not. If in doubt, sit tight.

Orientation

Agra is huge and disorienting. There's no real "centre", but rather a series of self-contained bazaar districts embedded within the formless urban sprawl, which stretches over an area of well over twenty square kilometres. Most of the city's major Mughal monuments are lined up along the banks of the **Yamuna River**, which bounds the city's eastern edge, including the Taj Mahal. Clustered around the Taj, the tangled little streets of **Taj Ganj** are home to most of the city's cheap accommodation and backpacker cafés. A couple of kilometres to the west, on the far side of the leafy **Cantonment** area, lies **Sadar Bazaar**, linked to Taj Ganj by **Fatehabad Road**, where you'll find many of the city's smarter places to stay, as well as numerous restaurants and crafts emporiums. Northwest of Taj Ganj lies Agra Fort and, beyond, the third of the city's main commercial districts, **Kinari Bazaar**, centred on the massive Jama Masjid.

Information

Agra has two **tourist offices**, one in Sadar Bazaar run by the Government of India at 191 The Mall (Mon–Fri 9am–5.30pm, Sat 9am–2pm; ☎0562/222 6378), and another run by UP Tourism at 64 Taj Road (Mon–Sat 10am–5pm; ☎0562/222 6431, ⓦwww.up-tourism.com); there's also a UP Tourism information booth (open 24hr) at Cantonment station. Both have information on hotels and local sights, though the Government of India office is better organized and provides information about other destinations in India as well. They can also set you up with a registered guide (half day Rs350, full day Rs650 for up to 4 people) who can take you around all the city sights as well as Fatehpur Sikri.

UP Tourism runs a whistlestop **tour** (daily except Friday) of Agra aimed mainly at day-trippers from Delhi. The tour leaves the India Tourism office at around 9.45am, and Agra Cantt Railway Station at around 10.20am, coinciding with the Taj Express from Delhi, which arrives at 10.07am. The full-day tour (Rs1700 including all entrance and guide fees) whisks you at breakneck speed around the Taj, Agra Fort and Fatehpur Sikri, ending at around 6pm in time for the Taj Express back to Delhi at 6.55pm; you can also join the tour just for the afternoon visit to Fatehpur Sikri (Rs550). Tours can be booked either through the UP Tourism or India Tourism offices.

City transport

Agra is very spread out and its sights too widely separated to explore on foot, so wherever you're staying you'll end up spending a fair amount of time in rickshaws or taxis. Getting from one part of the city to another can prove surprisingly time-consuming thanks to the sheer volume of traffic and the poorness of the roads, and crossing from one side of the Yamuna River to the other is particularly tedious, given the condition of the city centre's two massively over-used and under-maintained bridges.

Cycle rickshaws are good for short trips and provide a livelihood for some of the city's poorest inhabitants, as well as being cleaner and greener than autos. On the downside, they can be unbearably slow for longer journeys unless you've got a lot of time and patience and don't mind being sat amongst noisy and smelly traffic for extended periods. Unfortunately, the city's thousands of cycle rickshaw drivers are probably the single biggest source of hassle in Agra – attempt to walk anywhere, and these persistent folk will be on your case, doggedly chasing you down the street and ringing their bell in your ear. There are also a fair number of **tongas** (horse-drawn carriages) around Taj Ganj, but the sight of these skinny and near-lame horses tends to put most people off; if you do take a ride, expect to pay about the same as you would in a cycle rickshaw.

Taj Ganj exclusion zone

One of the measures introduced in recent years to protect the Taj from pollution was the creation of a 500-metre exclusion zone for motorized vehicles around the building. In practice, the exclusion zone functions in a peculiarly lopsided manner. Traffic circulates freely throughout the tiny, congested streets of Taj Ganj, almost within spitting distance of the South and West gates, but is banned from the section of road around the East Gate from just south of the *Hotel Sheela* up to near *Amarvilas*. Quite how this single random and tokenistic road closure is meant to protect the Taj is anyone's guess. It does, however, have the welcome side effect of making this side of the Taj unusually peaceful, though it also means if you want to travel across it, or to reach the *Hotel Sheela* itself, you'll have to take a cycle rickshaw or a tonga, or just walk.

Auto-rickshaws are faster and fares, including waiting time, are very reasonable if you don't mind bargaining: sample fares from Taj Ganj are Rs30–40 to Sadar Bazaar, Rs50–60 to Agra Cantt Station, and Rs15–20 to the Fort. **Taxis** are handy for longer trips to Sikandra or Fatehpur Sikri; agree a fare before you set off, since they're unlikely to have operational meters (or, if they do, to be willing to use them). Upmarket hotels have their own fleet of vehicles, and there are taxi ranks at the stations; alternatively, your guesthouse should be able to arrange a vehicle for you. There's also a cheap and environmentally friendly **electric bus** (Rs5) which shuttles back and forth between the fort and the west gate of the Taj Mahal, though you could easily spend twenty or thirty minutes waiting for it to arrive.

Whichever form of transport you choose, expect to have to haggle hard. Agra sees so many "fresh" tourists that drivers will almost always quote significantly inflated prices to start with (the best policy, if a rickshaw driver names a silly price, is simply to walk away – they'll usually chase after you and offer a more realistic fare). Also, note that the main agenda for many rickshaw- and taxi-drivers is to get you into the city's jewellers, marble shops and other such places where they can earn **commission**, often a more important source of income for them than what they earn in actual fares. Some will even quote you a lower fare if you agree to visit a couple of emporiums en route – though if you agree to this and then decide to buy anything, remember that the rickshaw driver's commission will be added to your bill.

Many locals get around the city by **bicycle**, although for foreigners unused to the anarchic traffic and treacherous road surfaces, travel on two wheels can be stressful and potentially dangerous. You're better off hiring a cycle rickshaw and getting someone else to do the pedalling for you.

Accommodation

Taj Ganj, the jumble of narrow lanes immediately south of the Taj, is where most budget travellers end up in Agra. With their unrivalled rooftop views, laid-back cafés and rock-bottom room rates, the little guesthouses here can be great places to stay, although standards are pretty basic and you'll have to contend with more or less constant hassle the moment you step out onto the street – not to mention the fact that the whole Taj Ganj backpacker scene can completely eclipse the area's traditional feel. There are more modern and

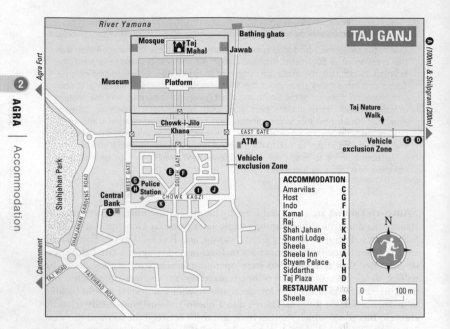

upmarket lodgings along **Fatehabad Road**, southwest of Taj Ganj, while the leafier **Cantonment** area and the adjacent **Sadar Bazaar** have places to suit every budget, as well as offering a convenient location more or less at the centre of the city.

The Taj Ganj hotels and guesthouses listed below are marked on the **map** of Taj Ganj above; all other accommodation appears on the map of Agra, p.161.

Taj Ganj

Amarvilas East Gate ☎0562/223 1515, ⓦwww.oberoihotels.com. Easily the loveliest (and most expensive) hotel in Agra, this luxurious Oberoi resort offers the closest you can get to the life of a Mughal emperor in contemporary Agra. The whole place is virtually a work of art in its own right, constructed in a serene blend of Mughal and Moorish styles around a drop-dead-gorgeous *charbagh*-style courtyard water garden – particularly magical by night. Rooms are sumptuously designed, with all mod-cons, and most have jaw-dropping Taj views (in pricier rooms you can even regard the mausoleum through large picture windows whilst lying in the bath). Facilities include a large pool (guests only), idyllic terraced gardens, a pretty spa, two very smart restaurants and a very chichi bar. From US$600. ⑨

Host West Gate ☎0562/233 1010. One of the cheapest places in town. It looks a bit run-down from the outside, but rooms – though small and

mainly windowless –- are clean and perfectly comfortable; most have air-coolers and all have cable TV, and there's also a fine view of the Taj from the roof. ①–②

Indo South Gate ☎0/981 168 3772 (mobile). Pint-sized family guesthouse with small, very basic rooms and friendly (mostly female) management. ②

Kamal South Gate ☎0562/233 0126, ⓔhotelkamal@hotmail.com. Right in the thick of the Taj Ganj action, with neat, well-maintained rooms and a great view from the rooftop restaurant. ②–③

Raj South Gate ☎0/9358 107023 (mobile). New Taj Ganj guesthouse with clean and comfortable air-cooled and a/c rooms set around a large courtyard – very good value, though the atmosphere is rather lifeless and the rooftop restaurant was still under construction at the time of writing. ②–③

Shah Jahan Chowk Kagzi ☎0562/233 1159 or 223 3071, ⓔshahjahan_hotel@hotmail.com. Centrally located, with a wildly varying selection of rooms ranging from the reasonably pleasant to the decidedly shabby – though promised renovations and improvements may have led to a general smartening up by the time you read this. There's also a rooftop restaurant and a well-equipped cybercafé downstairs. ❷–❸

Shanti Lodge South Gate ☎0562/233 1973, ✉shantilodge2000@yahoo.com. The most popular backpackers' place in Taj Ganj, with a lively atmosphere and superb Taj views from the rooftop restaurant. Rooms (some with a/c and Taj views) are a very mixed bag: those in the old block are poky and run down; those in the new annexe around the back are larger and smarter. ❷–❸

🏃 **Sheela** East Gate ☎0562/233 3074, ⓦwww.hotelsheelaagra.com. Easily the best budget hotel in Taj Ganj, in a secluded and peaceful setting inside the no-pollution zone (see p.163) and only 200m from the Taj (though you can't actually see it). The clean and spacious rooms are ranged around a lovely little garden, with fan, air-cooled and a/c options. The dependable restaurant (see p.183) is another bonus, while a friendly Alsatian dog adds to its charm. ❸–❹

Sheela Inn East Gate ☎0562/329 3437, ✉hotelsheelainn@yahoo.com. An offshoot of the excellent *Hotel Sheela*, this newish guesthouse occupies a plain modern building slightly up the road from its older relation. There's a range of fan, air-cooled and a/c rooms (some also have cable TV): all are bright, spotlessly clean and very comfortable, though the whole place is a bit lacking in atmosphere. ❸–❹

Shyam Palace West Gate ☎0562/233 1599. This rather dog-eared establishment has large but slightly shabby rooms plus a peaceful courtyard garden that doubles as a low-key restaurant. Comfortable enough, though a touch more expensive than most other places in the area. ❷–❸

Siddartha West Gate ☎0562/223 0901, ✉siddharthahotel2007@yahoo.com. After the *Sheela*, this is the nicest guesthouse in Taj Ganj, set in a central but surprisingly peaceful location near the West Gate. Rooms (fan or air-cooled) are plain but clean and spacious, arranged around a leafy courtyard with a tranquil little café in the middle. ❶–❷

Taj Plaza East Gate ☎0562/223 2515, ✉hoteltajplaza@yahoo.co.in. A slightly more upmarket alternative to the nearby Taj Ganj guest-houses, this small modern hotel has a range of clean, bright air-cooled and a/c rooms with cable TV; the more expensive ones also have good Taj views. Prices are a bit steep, though *Rough Guide* readers are promised a 40 percent discount on published rates (ask when booking). ❺–❼

Cantonment and Sadar Bazaar

Clarks Shiraz Taj Rd ☎0562/222 6221, ⓦwww.hotelclarksshiraz.com. Sprawling and rather characterless five-star in a pleasant cantonment setting with cosy and (for its class) very cheap rooms; the more expensive ones with distant Taj views. Facilities include two multi-cuisine restaurants, a bar, shopping arcade, banks and travel services, a smallish swimming pool (non-guests Rs500), basic gym, steam bath, Jacuzzi and beauty salon. ❽–❾

Hotel Hilltop (formerly the *Akbar Inn*) The Mall ☎0562/222 6836, ✉hotelhilltopagra@yahoo.com. Characterful old hotel, deep in the cantonment green-belt, with rooms in an old colonial-era building flanking a beautiful little lawn complete with a long, shady veranda for meals or idling over a book. The cheaper rooms are poky and relatively overpriced, but the smarter a/c rooms are attractively decorated and decent value. If you're utterly strapped for cash, there are also some ultra-basic cell-like cubicle rooms with shared bath for just Rs.60. *Rough Guide* readers are promised a 20 percent discount on published rates. ❷–❸

Sakura Near Idgah Bus Station ☎0562/242 0169, ✉ashu_sakura@yahoo.com. Well-run and good-value guesthouse on the west side of town. Rooms (all with air-coolers) are large, bright, spacious and nicely furnished, and the helpful owner is a mine of local information. The only drawback is the rather inconvenient location: handy for bus and train stations, but a bit of a hike from everywhere else. ❷–❸

🏃 **Tourist Rest House** Kutchery Rd ☎0562/246 3961, ✉dontworrychickencurry @hotmail.com. One of Agra's top budget options, with a range of bright, immaculately clean and very competitively priced rooms of varying sizes and standards set around a tranquil leafy courtyard – choose from smaller fan and air-cooled rooms or larger a/c rooms with fridge and TV; all have reliable 24hr hot running water. There's also a phone booth, Internet facilities, back-up generator and free pick-up from bus or train stations with a day's notice (rickshaw drivers don't get commission here, so will try to take you to one of the local "soundalikes"). ❷–❸

Yamuna View (formerly the *Agra Ashok*) The Mall ☎0562/236 1233, ⓦwww.hotelagraashok.com. A conveniently central location and very cheap rooms are the main attractions at this run-of-the-mill five-star. Rooms are rather plush but dated, while facilities include a smallish pool (non-guests Rs350), a bar and a couple of smart restaurants, including the snazzy *Mandarin* (see p.183). ❼

Fatehabad Road and around

Amar Yatri Niwas Fatehabad Rd ☎0562/223 3030, ⓦwww.amaryatriniwas.com. Very cheap – albeit utterly uninspiring – mid-range multi-storey hotel with bland but well-maintained rooms. Facilities include a gym, swimming pool (non-guests Rs.150) and multi-cuisine restaurant. ⑤–⑥

Jaypee Palace Hotel Fatehabad Rd ☎0562/233 0800, ⓦwww.jaypeehotels.com. Sprawling five-star set in a large and rather severe-looking modern red sandstone complex a few kilometres from the Taj. Rooms (prices from US$220) are comfortably plush, and the range of facilities is the best at any hotel in town, including a big pool (guest only), spa, bowling alley and games arcade, beauty salon and four restaurants. ⑨

Howard Park Plaza Fatehabad Rd ☎0562/400 1870, ⓦwww.sarovarhotels.com. Smart and central, with comfortable and spacious modern rooms, a pool (guests only) and an appealing restaurant overlooking the hotel gardens. The place is mainly aimed at business clients, and current rates make it one of the better value mid-range options in the city. ⑧

Mansingh Palace Fatehabad Rd ☎0562/233 1771, ⓦwww.mansinghhotels .com. One of Agra's most appealing mid-range options, this recently renovated hotel occupies an attractive modern sandstone building with Mughal decorative touches and plenty of shiny marble inside. Rooms (some with distant Taj views) are nicely furnished, and facilities include a good-sized pool (a very pricey Rs500 per hour for non-guests), gym, health club, multi-cuisine restaurants and the surprisingly chic little Tequila Bar. Given the quality of the place, current room rates are a snip. ⑧

Mughal Sheraton Fatehabad Rd ☎0562/233 1701, ⓦwww.sheraton.com. Run-of-the-mill five-star with all creature comforts but precious little character (despite the feeble attempts at Mughal theming which embarrass the place). A good range of in-house facilities partly compensates, including a couple of nice restaurants, bar, large pool (non-guests Rs400), beauty salon, gym, tennis courts, kids' entertainments and (most importantly) a resident astrologer. Rates are currently a bit more expensive than at the other top-end places along Fatehabad Road, with rooms from US$230 plus tax. ⑨

Safari Shaheed Nagar, Shamsabad Rd ☎0562/248 0106, ⓔhotelsafari@hotmail.com. Friendly and relaxed hotel on the southern side of town. Rooms (fan, air-cooled and a/c) are rather old, but clean and very well looked after, and there are views of the distant Taj from the rooftop café. Good value, though the location is a bit out of the way. ②–③

Taj View Fatehabad Rd ☎0562/233 2400, ⓦwww.tajhotels.com. This boxy little Taj group five-star doesn't look like much from the outside, but has lots of style within. Rooms (some with distant Taj views) are amongst the most attractive in Agra, cheerfully decorated in orange and white, while public areas are pleasantly plush and there's the usual range of amenities including a gym, salon, health club and pool (guests only). Prices from US$165. ⑨

Trident Hilton Fatehabad Rd ☎0562/233 1818, ⓦwww.trident-hilton.com. Peaceful and under-stated five-star, with low-lying buildings set around a spacious garden with a large pool (guests only). Rooms are attractively furnished in cheerful colours and come with all mod cons, while facilities include a fitness centre, kids' club, the multi-cuisine *La Brasserie* restaurant and two fully equipped rooms for disabled travellers. Room rates are superb value at present, though prices may double after planned renovations. ⑦

The City

Agra's attractions begin and end with the extraordinary collection of **Mughal monuments** which dot the city and which exemplify the finest achievements of this extraordinarily cultured, incredibly extravagant and chronically self-indulgent dynasty. The monuments in Agra date from the later phase of Mughal rule and the reigns of Akbar, Jahangir and Shah Jahan – exemplifying the ever-increasing extravagance which, by Shah Jahan's time, had already begun to strain the imperial coffers and sow the seeds of political and military decline.

The siren **Taj Mahal**, the summation and culmination of Mughal architecture in Agra – and indeed in the whole of the Subcontinent – is of course the highlight of any visit to the city, and the first point of call for many visitors (although, paradoxically, in many ways it makes better sense to leave visiting the

Agra's kabootar baz

Look up from any Taj Ganj roof terrace around 4pm, when the sun is low and the Taj's bulbous onion domes and minarets glow pale orange, and you'll see a side of local life of which few tourists are aware. Pigeons, or **kabootars**, wheel above clusters of men and boys staring skywards from their flat rooftops, shouting, whistling and waving sticks at the birds. Agra's pigeon fanciers, known as *kabootar baz*, don't race their pigeons, but fly them in flocks, controlling them with a code of high-pitched whistles and calls that are as much a feature of Muslim districts like Taj Ganj as the *muezzin*'s call to prayer. The waving of sticks is supposed to keep the lazier pigeons in the air, although a couple of sleepy specimens can usually be spotted hiding on nearby satellite dishes, waiting for their owners to scatter soaked grain for them to feed on. When this happens, the rest of the flock drops back to ground in a cloud, and pecks around the roof of their coop, or *kabootar khana*, for the grain. This five- or ten-minute cycle is then repeated for an hour or so until the pigeons have been well exercised. Four or five flocks fly above Taj Ganj each day, best watched from the area's myriad rooftop terraces and cafes.

Pigeon fancying is an established tradition in Agra, and in cities such as Old Delhi and Lucknow, where there are sizeable Muslim communities (Hindus rarely indulge in the sport). Its techniques were set down by Akbar's poet laureate, Abu'l Fazl, for the Mughal court who considered it a noble pastime, and to this day men and boys across Urdu-speaking parts of India still take their *kabootar* flying very seriously. Thoroughbred birds change hands for more than Rs5000, a fortune considering the average income of most *kabootar baz*. Owning a large flock brings with it a certain cachet, and the coveted title of *Barra Kabootar Baz*, literally "Big Pigeon Fancier". Once a man is deemed to have mastered the plethora of tricks and subtleties of this ancient sport, he may even be known among his peers as a *Khalifa*, or "Great Master". Only *Khalifas* can direct their flocks in perfect parabolic curves, or single files across the sky, or command them to encircle a neighbours' flock and drive it to ground.

Taj till after you've explored the rest of Agra, when you can more fully appreciate the constantly evolving artistic and architectural strands which went into the making of this unique monument). A short distance upriver, the myriad royal apartments, courtyards and mosques of **Agra Fort** offer a good overview of changing architectural fashions during the later days of the Mughals, as well as an insight into their fantastically opulent private lives. North of the fort stretch a sequence of outstanding monuments, most notably the imposing **Jama Masjid**, the superb little **Itimad-ud-Daulah**, and Akbar's grandiose mausoleum at **Sikandra**.

The Taj Mahal

One of the world's most famous and beautiful buildings, the **Taj Mahal** (daily except Fri 6am–7pm; foreigners Rs750, Indian residents Rs20) represents the unquestioned zenith of Mughal architecture. Described by Bengali poet Rabindranath Tagore as a "teardrop on the face of eternity" and by Kipling as "the ivory gate through which all dreams pass", the Taj has elicited astonishment and hyperbole in equal measure for four and a half centuries, while its image adorns countless glossy brochures and guidebooks, standing as an instantly recognizable symbol of the mysterious Orient. Nevertheless, however many photographs you've seen of it, the reality never fails to overwhelm.

The magic of the monument is strangely undiminished by the crowds of tourists who visit, as small and insignificant as ants in the face of the immense

△ The Taj Mahal

mausoleum. That said, the Taj is at its most alluring in the relative quiet of early morning, shrouded in mist and bathed with a soft red glow. As its vast marble surfaces fall into shadow or reflect the sun, its colour changes, from soft grey and yellow to pearly cream and dazzling white. This play of light is an important decorative device, symbolically implying the presence of Allah, who is never represented in physical form.

The secret symbolism of the Taj Mahal

Inextricably associated with the royal love legend of Shah Jahan and his wife Mumtaz, the **Taj Mahal** is regarded by most modern visitors as *the* symbol of eternal love. Recent historical research, however, suggests the world's most famous tomb complex encodes a somewhat less poetic and poignant vision – one more revealing of the Mughal emperor's megalomania and unbridled vanity than his legendary romantic disposition.

The clues to the Taj's **hidden symbolism** lie in the numerous Islamic inscriptions which play a key part in the overall design of the building. Fourteen chapters of the Koran are quoted at length here, dealing with two principal themes: the Day of Judgement, and the pleasures of Heaven. The first appears in the broad band of intricate calligraphy over the main gateway. Citing the last phrase of chapter 89, it invites the faithful to "Enter thou My Paradise". This is one of only two occasions in the Islamic scriptures when God speaks directly to man, and the quotation stresses the dual function of the Taj as both a tomb garden and replica of Heaven, complete with the four Rivers of Paradise and central Pool of Abundance.

In a dramatic break with tradition, the actual tomb is situated not in the middle of the gardens, as was customary, but at the far end of a rectangle. Recently, the theory of symbolic association has been taken a step further with the rediscovery of an enigmatic diagram contained in an **ancient Sufi text**, *The Revelations of Mecca* by renowned medieval mystic, Ibn al 'Arabi. Entitled *The Plain of Assembly on the Day of Judgement*, the diagram, which scholars know Shah Jahan's father Jahangir had a copy of in his library, corresponds exactly to the layout of the Taj Mahal complex, proving beyond doubt, they now claim, that the tomb was intended as a reproduction of God's throne. Given that the emperor's remains are enshrined within it, the inevitable conclusion is that, aside from being an extravagant romantic, Shah Jahan possessed an opinion of his own importance that knew no bounds. While scholars continue to debate the symbolism of the Taj, they are united in disbelieving the popular, but wholly apocryphal, image of Shah Jahan's last days as propounded by the tour guides. Far from spending his old age gazing whimsically down the river to the tomb of his beloved wife, the Mughals' most decadent emperor expired after a protracted bout of sex and drug-taking. His death in 1666, at the ripe old age of 74, was brought about not by grief, but by a massive overdose of opium and aphrodisiacs.

Overlooking the River Yamuna, the Taj Mahal stands at the northern end of vast gardens enclosed by walls. Though its layout follows a distinctly Islamic theme, representing Paradise, it is above all a monument to romantic love. **Shah Jahan** built the Taj to enshrine the body of his favourite wife, Arjumand Bann Begum, better known by her official palace title, **Mumtaz Mahal** ("Chosen One of the Palace"), who died shortly after giving birth to her fourteenth child in 1631 – the number of children she bore the emperor is itself a tribute to her hold on him, given the number of other wives and concubines which the emperor would have been able to call on. The emperor was devastated by her death, and set out to create an unsurpassed monument to her memory – its name, "Taj Mahal", is simply a shortened, informal version of Mumtaz Mahal's palace title. Construction by a workforce of some twenty thousand men from all over Asia commenced in 1632 and took over twenty years, not being completed until 1653. Marble was brought from Makrana (see p.273), and semi-precious stones for decoration – onyx, amethyst, lapis lazuli, turquoise, jade, crystal, coral and mother-of-pearl – were carried to Agra from Persia, Russia, Afghanistan, Tibet, China and the Indian Ocean. Eventually, Shah

Jahan's devout and austere son Aurangzeb seized power, and the former emperor was interned in Agra Fort, where as legend would have it he lived out his final years gazing wistfully at the Taj Mahal in the distance, a tragic and inconsolable figure. He died there in January 1666, with his daughter, Jahanara Begum, at his side; his body was carried across the river to lie alongside his beloved wife in his peerless tomb.

The Chowk-i-Jilo Khana and charbagh

There are three **entrances** to the Taj, via the south, east and west gates, all of which lead into the red sandstone forecourt, the **Chowk-i-Jilo Khana**. The main entrance into the Taj complex, a massive arched gateway topped with delicate domes and adorned with Koranic verses and inlaid floral designs, stands at the northern edge of Chowk-i-Jilo Khana, directly aligned with the Taj, but shielding it from the view of those who wait outside.

Once through the gateway, you'll see the Taj itself at the end of the huge **charbagh** (literally "four gardens"), an expansive, park-like garden divided into four quadrants by raised marbled walkways – a style introduced by Babur from central Asia which remained enduringly fashionable throughout the Mughal era. Dissected into four quadrants by waterways (usually dry), the gardens evoke the Islamic image of the Gardens of Paradise, where rivers flow with water, milk, wine and honey. Unlike other mausoleums in Agra such as the Itimad-ud-Daulah and Akbar's Mausoleum, the Taj doesn't stand at the centre of the *charbagh*, but at the far northern end, presumably to exploit its riverside setting; the central intersection of the four "rivers" is instead marked by a large marble tank corresponding to *al-Kawthar*, the celestial pool of abundance mentioned in the Koran.

In the western wall of the enclosure you'll find the Taj's **museum** (in theory daily except Fri 9am–5pm, although it sometimes shuts for no apparent reason; Rs5). The collection features exquisite miniature paintings, two marble pillars believed to have come from the fort, and portraits of Mughal rulers including Shah Jahan and Mumtaz Mahal. Further into the building a gallery shelters architectural drawings of the Taj Mahal, a display of elaborate porcelain, seventeenth-century coins and examples of *pietra dura* inlay work similar to those seen on the outside and inside of the Taj itself.

The mausoleum

Steps lead from the far end of the gardens up to the high square marble platform on which the **mausoleum** itself sits, each corner marked by a tall, tapering minaret. Visitors must remove their shoes before climbing to the tomb and the marble floor can get extremely hot at midday, so you may want to wear socks or use the cloth shoe-covers which foreign visitors are given free with their entrance tickets. To the west of the tomb is a domed red-sandstone **mosque** and to the east a replica **jawab**, which was probably used to house visitors, though its principal function was to complete the architectural symmetry of the whole complex – it cannot be used as a mosque, however, since it faces in the wrong direction, away from Mecca.

The Taj itself is essentially square in shape, with pointed arches cut into its sides and topped with a huge central dome which rises for over 55m, its height accentuated by a crowning brass spire which is almost 17m high. On approach, the tomb looms ever larger and grander, but not until you are close do you appreciate both its sheer size and the extraordinarily fine detail of relief carving, highlighted by floral patterns of precious stones. Arabic verses praising the glory of Paradise fringe the archways, proportioned exactly so that each letter appears to be the same size when viewed from the ground.

The Taj Mahal: a monument under threat

Despite the seemingly impregnable sense of serenity and other-worldliness which clings to the Taj, in reality, India's most famous building faces serious threats from traffic and industrial pollution, and from the millions of tourists who visit it each year. Marble is all but impervious to the onslaught of wind and rain that erodes softer sandstone, but it has no natural defence against the sulphur dioxide that lingers in a dusty haze and shrouds the monument; sometimes the smog is so dense that the tomb cannot be seen from the fort. Sulphur dioxide mixes with atmospheric moisture and settles as sulphuric acid on the surface of the tomb, making the smooth white marble yellow and flaky, and forming a subtle fungus that experts have named "marble cancer".

The main sources of pollution are the continuous flow of vehicles along the national highways that skirt the city, and the 1700 factories in and around Agra – chemical effluents belched out from their chimneys are well beyond recommended safety limits. Despite laws demanding the installation of pollution-control devices, the imposition of a ban on all petrol- and diesel-fuelled traffic within 500m of the Taj Mahal, and an exclusion zone banning new industrial plants from an area of 10,400 square kilometres around the complex, pollutants in the atmosphere have continued to rise (many blame the diesel generators of nearby hotels), and new factories have been set up illegally.

Cleaning work on the Taj Mahal rectifies the problem to some extent, but the chemicals used will themselves eventually affect the marble – attendants already shine their torches on "repaired" sections of marble to demonstrate how they've lost their translucency. Hopes for proper care of the Taj Mahal have been raised since the government turned its attention to the plight of India's greatest monument, though it now appears the UP government have more than just the threat of pollution damage to worry about. In early 2005, they launched an investigation into claims that decreased water levels in the Yamuna have led to dangerous tilts in the Taj's minarets, and fears that unless something is done to restore the Yamuna to previous levels, the entire building could collapse. It would seem that for the moment, the fate of the Taj Mahal hangs in the balance.

The south face of the tomb is the main entrance to the **interior**: a high octagonal chamber whose weirdly echoing interior is flushed with pale light. A marble screen, decorated with precious stones and cut so finely that it seems almost translucent, protects the cenotaph of Mumtaz Mahal in the centre of the tomb, perfectly aligned with the doorway and the distant gateway into the Chowk-i-Jilo Khana, and that of Shah Jahan crammed in next to it – ironically, the only object which breaks the perfect symmetry of the entire complex. The inlay work on the marble tombs is the finest in Agra, and no pains were spared in perfecting the inlay work – some of the petals and leaves are made of up to sixty separate stone fragments. Ninety-nine names of Allah adorn the top of Mumtaz's tomb, and set into Shah Jahan's is a pen box, the hallmark of a male ruler. These cenotaphs, in accordance with Mughal tradition, are only representations of the real coffins, which lie in the same positions in a crypt below.

Taj Mahal viewing practicalities

Entrance to the Taj costs a whopping Rs750 for foreign visitors (under 15s free), though despite the hiked-up price, comparatively few visitors refuse to pay it; fewer still regard the expense as money wasted once they are inside, although foreign tourists rarely visit the Taj on several consecutive days at different hours, as they used to. What is perhaps most galling about the situation is not the price itself but the fact that the ticket is valid only for one entrance, meaning that if you want to appreciate the famously changing play of light and shade on the building at dawn and dusk you'll either have to hang around inside the complex all day or buy a second ticket. Note too that the Taj is subject to extremely tight **security**, with bag and body searches (and, more often than not, long queues) at the three entrances. You're also prohibited from taking in food, cigarettes, matches, mobile phones, electronic items, tripods, bipods, alcoholic drinks and drawing materials (not to mention arms, ammunitions, explosives) – all of which further discourages long visits, since there's nowhere to buy food or drink inside.

The Taj is particularly beautiful **at night**, during the period around the full moon. It's currently possible to see the Taj by moonlight on the night of the full moon itself and on the two days before and after. Only four hundred visitors are admitted per night (in batches of fifty between 8pm and midnight). Tickets have to be purchased a day in advance from the Archeological Survey of India office, 22 Mall Rd (Mon–Sat 10am–6pm; ☎0562/222 7261). The usual admission charges apply; viewings are sometimes cancelled, in which case you'll receive a full refund.

The only ways to **see the Taj for free** are by climbing onto a Taj Ganj hotel rooftop or, better still, by heading across the Yamuna to **Mehtab Bagh** (see below). When there's sufficient water in the river, **boats** ferry passengers across from the ghats just east of the Taj at first light, charging whatever they can get away with (anything from Rs100 to Rs1000, depending on the size of your camera); the river often dries up, however, and in periods of very low rainfall you may even be able simply to walk across the riverbed. Alternatively, take a rickshaw to Mehtab Bagh, though it's a rather long, circuitous and usually extremely congested journey up to the river bridge by Agra Fort and then all the way back down again.

Mehtab Bagh and the Taj Nature Walk

The **Mehtab Bagh** (daily dawn–dusk; foreign visitors Rs100, Indian residents Rs5) sit on the north bank of the Yamuna river, directly opposite the Taj, of which it offers sublime views. The gardens themselves were laid out by Shah Jahan, probably to serve as a place from which to admire his masterpiece, though, views apart, they're now eminently forgettable, planted with tedious lines of prim ornamental shrubs, enlivened only by a few ornate scalloped tanks in various stages of disrepair and a fine riverside cupola. You can enjoy the Taj views without paying the steep admission fee simply by walking down the path to the river by the entrance to the gardens – the only advantage of going into the gardens themselves is that you escape being hassled by the opportunistic locals who hang out on the riverbank waiting to pounce on tourists. The gardens can be reached either by boat from Taj Ganj or by rickshaw; see opposite for details.

A few hundred metres up East Gate Road from the Taj, the **Taj Nature Walk** (daily 9am–6.30pm; foreign visitors Rs50, Indian residents Rs10) offers a pleasant retreat from the touts and another welcome chance to stretch one's legs in peace and quiet. A paved path loops and twists for 500m through light woodland full of birds and butterflies, with lawns for a picnic and fine Taj views from the little wooden tower at the far end of the gardens (where you'll also find drinks for sale).

Agra Fort

The high red-sandstone ramparts of **Agra Fort** (dawn to dusk; foreigners Rs300, Indian residents Rs20) dominate a bend in the Yamuna River 2km northwest of

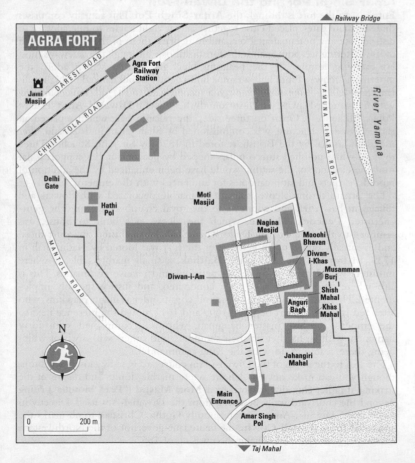

the Taj Mahal. Akbar laid the foundations of this majestic citadel, built between 1565 and 1573 in the form of a half moon, on the remains of earlier Rajput fortifications. The structure developed as the seat and stronghold of the Mughal empire for successive generations: Akbar oversaw the construction of the walls and gates, his grandson, Shah Jahan, had most of the principal buildings erected, and Aurangzeb, the last great emperor, was responsible for the ramparts.

The curved sandstone bastions reach a height of over twenty metres and stretch for around two-and-a-half kilometres, punctuated by a sequence of massive gates, (although only the **Amar Singh Pol** is currently open to visitors). The original and grandest entrance, however, was through the western side, via the **Delhi Gate** and **Hathi Pol** or "Elephant Gate", now flanked by two red-sandstone towers faced in marble, but once guarded by colossal stone elephants with riders which were destroyed by Aurangzeb in 1668. Access to much of the fort is restricted, and only those parts open to the public are described below.

Note that there's nowhere to buy drinks inside the fort, and exploring the complex can be thirsty work, so unless you're happy to take your chances at the public drinking taps, it's a good idea to take water in with you.

Amar Singh Pol and the Diwan-i-Am

Entrance to the fort is through the **Amar Singh Pol**. This actually comprises three separate gates, placed close together and at right angles to one another to disorientate any potential attackers and to deprive them of the space in which to use battering weapons against the fortifications – although the gateway's most eye-catching feature are the beautiful blue glazed tiles which adorn the innermost archway. From here a ramp climbs gently uphill flanked by high walls (another defensive measure), through a second gate to the spacious courtyard, with tree-studded lawns, which surrounds the graceful **Diwan-i-Am** ("Hall of Public Audience"). Open on three sides, the pillared hall, which replaced an earlier wooden structure, was commissioned by Shah Jahan in 1628 and, after use as an arsenal by the British, restored in 1876 by Sir John Strachey. Three rows of white polished stucco pillars topped by peacock arches support a flat roof; the elegance of the setting would have been enhanced by the addition of brocade, carpets and satin canopies for audiences with the emperor.

The ornate throne alcove is inlaid in marble decorated with flowers and foliage in bas-relief, and connects to the royal chambers within. The gem-encrusted **Peacock Throne**, which the alcove was built to house, was removed to the Red Fort in Delhi when Shah Jahan shifted his court there, and eventually ended up in Persia after the fort was looted by Nadir Shah in 1739. In front of the alcove, the **Baithak**, a small marble table, is where ministers would have sat to deliver petitions and receive commands. This is also where trials would have been conducted, and justice speedily imple-mented. The East India Company's naval commander William Hawkins, who attended Jahangir's court between 1609 and 1611, noted the presence next to the emperor of his "master hangman, who is accompanied with forty hangmen, with an hatchet on their shoulders; and others with sorts of whips being there, readie to do what the King commandeth".

The area to the north of the Diwan-i-Am courtyard is, sadly, closed to visitors, though you can make out the delicate white marble domes and *chattris* of the striking, if rather clumsily proportioned, **Moti Masjid** ("Pearl Mosque") rising beyond the courtyard walls, best seen from the Diwan-i-Am itself. Directly in front of the Diwan-i-Am an incongruously Gothic Christian tomb marks the **grave of John Russell Colvin**, the lieutenant-governor of the Northwestern Provinces, who died here during the uprising of 1857.

The Macchi Bhavan and Diwan-i-Khas

Heading through the small door to the left of the throne alcove in the Diwan-i-Am and climbing the stairs beyond brings you out onto the upper level of the **Macchi Bhavan** (Fish Palace), a large but relatively plain two-storey structure overlooking a spacious, grassy courtyard. This was once strewn with fountains and flowerbeds, interspersed with tanks and water channels stocked with fish on which the emperor and his courtiers would practise their angling skills, though the Maharaja of Bharatpur subsequently removed some of its marble fixtures to his palace in Deeg, while the zealous evangelist Lord William Bentinck (governor-general from 1828 to 1835) auctioned off much of the palace's original mosaics and fretwork, including parts of the Hammam-i-Shahi (Royal Bath).

On the north side of the courtyard (to the left as you enter) a small door leads to the exquisite little **Nagina Masjid** (Gem Mosque), made entirely of marble. Capped with three domes and approached from a marble-paved courtyard, it was built by Shah Jahan for the ladies of the *zenana* (harem). At the rear of the mosque on the right-hand side a small balcony with beautifully carved lattice screens offers a discreet viewpoint from where ladies of the harem were able to inspect luxury goods – silks, jewellery and brocade – laid out for sale by merchants in the courtyard below, without themselves being seen.

Continue to the raised terrace on the far side of the Macchi Bhavan, from where there is a superb panorama of the Yamuna river and Taj – the first of numerous such views from the various royal pavilions which line the eastern edge of the fort (though the equally prominent line of factory chimneys and industrial sprawl to the left offers a very different perspective on modern Agra). Two **thrones** adorn the terrace, one of black slate and the other of white marble. The white one was apparently used by Shah Jahan for his evening repose, while the black one – the **Takht-i-Jahangir** (Jahangir's Throne) – was fashioned in Allahabad in 1602 by the future emperor Jahangir in symbolic defiance of his father – and then emperor – Akbar. The throne was brought to Agra in 1610 and used by Jahangir as a vantage point from which to watch elephant fights in the eastern enclosure, though it now serves, somewhat less gloriously, as a favoured perch for couples posing for photos against the superb backdrop of the Taj.

To your right (as you face the river) stretches a high terrace overlooking the Yamuna, its summits topped with a sequence of lavish royal apartments designed to catch the cool breezes blowing across the waters below. The first of these is the delicate **Diwan-i-Khas** (Hall of Private Audience), where the emperor would have received kings, dignitaries and ambassadors. Erected in 1635, this is one of the most finely decorated buildings in the entire fort, with paired marble pillars and peacock arches inlaid with lapis lazuli and jasper.

The Mina Masjid to the Anguri Bagh

A passageway behind the Diwan-i-Khas leads through to the tiny **Mina Masjid**, a very plain white marble mosque – little more than an enlarged corridor – which was built by Shah Jahan and is traditionally said to have been used by him during his years of imprisonment here. Beyond here, the passageway leads to a two-storeyed pavilion known as the **Musamman Burj**, famous in Mughal legend as the spot where Shah Jahan is said to have caught his last glimpse of the Taj Mahal before he died – though the truth of the great emperor's demise is rather less edifying (see p.169). Surrounded by a veranda, the elegant pavilion is perhaps the most elaborately decorated structure in the entire fort, its lattice-screen balustrade dotted with ornamental niches and with exquisite *pietra dura* inlay covering almost every surface, while a marble *chhatri* topped by a copper dome adds a final flourish. In front of the tower a courtyard, paved with marble octagons, centres on a **pachisi board** where the emperor, following his father's example at Fatehpur Sikri, played a rather bizarre version of the game (a form of ludo) using dancing girls as pieces.

Continue past the Musamman Burj to reach another large courtyard, the **Anguri Bagh** (Grape Garden), a miniature *charbagh*, its quarters linked by wide pavements, with a marble tank at the centre. The east side of the courtyard is flanked by the marble building known as **Khas Mahal** (Private Palace), possibly used as a drawing room or the emperor's sleeping chamber. Designed essentially for comfort, it incorporates cavities in its flat roofs to insulate against the searing heat of an Agra summer, and affords soothing riverside and garden views. The palace is flanked by two so-called **Golden Pavilions**, their curved roofs (a form that would later become a staple of Rajput architecture) covered with gilded copper tiles in a style inspired by the thatched roofs of Bengali village huts, their arches framing further photogenic Taj vistas. In front of the Khas Mahal, steps descend into the northeast corner of the Anguri Bagh and the **Shish Mahal** (Glass Palace), where royal women bathed in the soft lamplight reflected from the mirror-work mosaics that covered the walls and ceiling; unfortunately the building is currently locked, so you can only peek in through the windows.

South of the Khas Mahal lies the **Shah Jahani Mahal** (Shah Jahan's Palace), a heavily graffitoed cluster of four rather sorry-looking rooms (originally painted in bright colours and embossed in gold), plus another delicate octagonal open-sided two-storey *chattri* with further Taj views.

The Jahangiri Mahal

Immediately beyond the Shah Jahani Mahal lies the huge **Jahangiri Mahal** (Jahangir's Palace), although the name is misleading since it was actually built by Jahangir's father, Akbar, and probably served not as a royal palace, but as a harem – parts of the complex are thought to have been the living quarters of Akbar's Rajput wife Jodhbai (after whom one of the major palaces at Fatehpur Sikri is named). Compared to the classic Mughal designs of the surrounding buildings, this robust sandstone structure shows striking evidence of cultural miscegenation, with adopted Hindu elements mixed up with traditional Mughal and Islamic motifs.

The first courtyard shows a rather haphazard mix of both elements, but the remarkable **central courtyard** is almost entirely Hindu in design, with characteristically Indian corbelled arches and lavishly carved columns and capitals supporting heavy overhanging eaves, above which rises a second storey of even more fantastically embellished balconies and roof brackets. The courtyard is flanked by large halls to the north and south; the ceiling of that to the north is supported on enormous stone beams embellished by fantastic mythological animals, including a serpentine form being emitted from a dragon's mouth. This whole section of the palace marks a decisive, if temporary, shift in Mughal architecture. Whereas in previous Mughal buildings essentially Islamic designs had been gently modified by the inclusion of a few Hindu motifs, here the few Islamic motifs (such as the pointed arches on the upper storeys) are more or less buried beneath a surfeit of Hindu design elements – a mix-and-match style which can also be seen throughout Akbar's palace complex at Fatehpur Sikri. The whole concept appears to be the logical architectural result of the tolerant embracing of rival faiths and cultures which Akbar achieved during his enlightened rule, although the rather random mingling of Hindu and Islamic elements exemplified by this palace would soon be eclipsed by the classic synthesis of

Persian and Subcontinental styles achieved by Shah Jahan in works such as the Taj Mahal.

From the central courtyard, a gateway leads out through the main gateway into the palace, whose impressive facade shows a characteristic mix of Mughal and Indian motifs, with Islamic pointed arches and inlaid mosaics combined with Hindu-style overhanging eaves supported by heavily carved brackets. Immediately in front of the palace sits **Jahangir's Hauz** (Jahangir's Cistern), a giant bowl with steps inside and out, made in 1611 from a single block of porphyry and inscribed in Persian. The cistern was unearthed in the nineteenth century: filled with rosewater, it would have been used by the emperor as a bathtub, whilst it's also believed that the emperor took it with him on his travels around the empire – though it seems difficult to credit this, given the bath's size and weight.

Jama Masjid and Kinari Bazaar

Opposite the fort, and overlooking Agra Fort railway station is the city's principal mosque, the soaring red-sandstone **Jama Masjid** (Friday Mosque), built by Shah Jahan in 1648 and dedicated to his favourite daughter, Jahanara Begum. The mosque was originally connected directly to the Fort's principal entrance, the Delhi Gate, by a large courtyard, though following the 1857 uprising the iconoclastic British ran a railway line between the two, leaving the mosque stranded in no-man's land on the far side of the tracks.

Standing on a high plinth above the chaotic streets of the surrounding bazaar (of which it affords fine views), the mosque is crowned by three large sandstone domes covered in distinctive zigzagging bands of marble. Five huge arches lead into the main prayer hall, topped by a prettily inlaid band of sandstone decorated in abstract floral patterns, while inside the mihrab is surrounded by delicate flourishes of Koranic script, inlaid in black, a design mirrored in the principal archway. Despite the grandeur of its design and the fineness of some of its details, however, much of the mosque is now showing the ravages of time and the depredations of the resident swarms of bats, pigeons and parakeets which nest amongst its eaves, while clusters of huge beehives dangle ominously from the summits of several of the larger arches.

The space around the base of the mosque is now filled with the crowded – but refreshingly hassle-free – streets of **Kinari Bazaar**, a fascinating little area, though the numbers of people, scooters, cycle rickshaws and cows pushing their way through the streets make exploring it a slow and tiring business. Opposite the northeast corner of the complex, look out for the **petha–wallahs**, purveyors of Agra's most famous sweets, a sickly-sweet confection made from crystallized pumpkin.

Itimad-ud-Daulah

Standing on the east bank of the Yamuna some 3km north of Agra Fort is the beautiful **Itimad-ud-Daulah** (pronounced "Artma Dollar"; daily dawn–dusk; foreign visitors Rs110, Indian residents Rs15), the tomb of Mirza Ghiyas Beg, an important member of Akbar's court and later *wazir* (chief minister) to – and father-in-law of – Emperor Jahangir, who gave him the title of Itimad-ud-Daulah, or "Pillar of the State". The tomb is popularly known amongst Agra's rickshaw-wallahs as the "Baby Taj", and though it's much smaller and less successfully proportioned than its more famous relative, it does foreshadow the Taj in being the first building in Mughal Agra to be faced entirely in marble, and in the lavish use of *pietra dura* inlay to decorate its translucent exterior walls.

△ Inlay work on Itimad-ud-Daulah

As usual, the tomb sits at the centre of a *charbagh* garden, though here entered from the eastern (rather than the usual southern) side, presumably to highlight its setting against the backdrop of the Yamuna River – another element of its design which anticipates that of the Taj. The building is rather clumsily proportioned, with an undersized rooftop pavilion replacing the usual dome, and four stocky minarets stuck onto each corner. The imperfections of the overall proportions seem relatively unimportant, however, given the superbly intricate **inlay work** which covers virtually the entire tomb – an incredible profusion of floral and geometrical patterning in muted reds, oranges, browns and greys which gives the entire tomb the appearance of an enormous, slightly hallucinogenic experiment in medieval Op-Art. Elegant inlaid designs showing characteristic Persian motifs including wine vases, trees and honeysuckles adorn the arches of the four entrances to the mausoleum. Inside, the walls are largely covered in rather eroded and clumsily restored paintings of further vases, flowers and cypresses. The replica tombs of Ghiyas Beg and his wife (the real tombs, as usual, are buried underground) stand behind an intricately carved wall, surrounded by subsidiary family tombs.

Chini-ka-Rauza

Around 1km north of Itimad-ud-Daulah is the **Chini-ka-Rauza** (open 24hr; free), built between 1628 and 1639 to serve as the mausoleum of Afzal Khan, a Persian poet from Shiraz who served as one of Shah Jahan's ministers until his death in 1639. As befits his origins, Afzal Khan's tomb is of purely Persian design, the only such building in Agra. Although now rather neglected and decaying, the exterior, topped with a bulbous dome, still retains substantial quantities of the delicate tiles that once enhanced the whole of the exterior – predominantly blue, with discreet highlights in orange, yellow, green and turquoise. Inside, the large dome is decorated with rich *muqarna* vaulting covered in fading paintwork and Koranic script.

Rambagh

A kilometre or so north of the Chini-ka-Rauza, amidst the dusty sprawl of northern Agra, the **Rambagh** gardens (daily sunrise–sunset; foreign visitors Rs100, Indian residents Rs10) are of considerable historical interest, being one of the very few surviving physical remains in India of the reign of Babur, the founder of the Mughal dynasty – although there's little left to see here now, and the site is unlikely to prove of interest to anyone but serious students of Mughal history or the unnaturally curious. The extensive gardens were originally laid out by Babur in 1526 following the Persian *charbagh* plan, which the new ruler of northern India had first seen at Samarkand and which would subsequently prove the prototype for all later Mughal gardens in the subcontinent. Their original name was Aram Bagh (Garden of Rest), subsequently corrupted to "Ram", after the Hindu god Rama. Babur himself was apparently buried here for a time before his body was exhumed and taken to its final resting place in Kabul.

The gardens originally consisted of three descending terraces, with water drawn from the Yamuna by a system of watermills, although later additions and alterations make it difficult to get much sense of how the gardens would have looked. The walkways and watercourses have been heavy-handedly restored (though, ironically, are now completely lacking in any water), leading up to a terrace high above the Yamuna, from where the crumbling remains of a trio of riverside *chattris* can be seen to the north, perched in melancholy isolation amidst the ugly industrial suburbs of the northern city.

Akbar's mausoleum: Sikandra

Given the Mughal tradition of building magnificent tombs for men and women of high status, it comes as no surprise that the mausoleum of the most distin-

Nur Jahan, Light of the World

Despite the detailed records of contemporary Mughal court historians and the efforts of modern scholars, relatively little is known about the myriad wives and concubines of the great Mughal emperors, whose personalities, ambitions and intrigues have been largely lost to history within the shadows of the imperial harem in which they spent the majority of their lives (Akbar alone had some three hundred wives, and perhaps five thousand concubines). A few emblematic figures do stand out – Akbar's formidable mother Hamida Banu Begum, for instance, and Shah Jahan's beloved wife Mumtaz Mahal – but of the very few Mughal matriarchs who suceeded in breaking through the veils of purdah and leaving their mark on the history of the empire, none had a career as dramatic or influential as **Nur Jahan**, favourite wife of Jahangir and – at least during the latter part of his reign – the de facto power behind the Mughal throne.

Nur Jahan's origins were relatively humble. She was born in 1577 in Kandahar, in present-day Afghanistan, while her family were travelling from their ancestral home in Persia to India, where her father, **Ghiyas Beg**, hoped to revive their declining fortunes. Having arrived at Akbar's court, Ghiyas Beg quickly established himself as a valued member of Mughal society, serving first Akbar and then Jahangir, who conferred the official title of Itimad-ud-Daulah, "Pillar of the State", upon him. Mehrunissa (as Nur Jahan was originally named) was married to her first husband, another Persian, Sher Afkun, at the age of 17. Sher Afkun died in 1607, however, and the 30-year-old Mehrunissa was brought to court, where Jahangir met the attractive young widow, fell in love, and married her (in 1611), making her his twentieth wife and giving her the official title first of Nur Mahal ("Light of the Palace") and subsequently Nur Jahan ("Light of the World").

Following Nur Jahan's marriage, her father's already considerable influence grew even stronger, while her brother Asaf Khan was also promoted to a senior position at court, making the family the most powerful in Mughal India, their influence significantly increased thanks to Jahangir's own frequent incapacitation due to alcohol and opium. Neither father nor brother, however, could rival the influence of Nur Jahan. As Thomas Roe, the English ambassador to the Mughal court, wrote of the empress: "[she] governs him, and wynds him up at her pleasure . . . all justice or care of any

guished Mughal ruler was one of the most ambitious structures of its time. **Akbar's mausoleum** (daily dawn–dusk; foreigners Rs110, Indian residents Rs10) borders the side of the main highway to Mathura at **SIKANDRA**, 10km northwest of Agra. Rickshaws charge at least Rs120 to make the round trip, although it's a long and smelly ride, and you might want to take a taxi instead; alternatively, hop on any bus bound for Mathura from the Agra Fort bus stand.

Although it lacks the Taj's architectural genius, Akbar's stately mausoleum possesses a serenity sometimes absent among the throngs of tourists at Agra's most visited monument. The complex is entered via its huge south gate, **Buland Darwaza** (Great Gate), so high that it obstructs any view to the tomb beyond. Surmounted by four tapering marble minarets, and overlaid with marble and coloured tiles set in repetitive geometrical patterns, it bears the Koranic inscription "These are the gardens of Eden, enter them and live forever".

Walk through to the Buland Darwaza to reach the extensive, park-like **gardens**, divided by fine raised sandstone walkways into the four equal quadrants of the typical Mughal *charbagh* design, and enclosed by high walls, with fine flanking gateways to either side (plus a ruined one to the rear). Curious langur monkeys may be seen along the path, while deer roam through thing or publique affayrs either sleepes or depends on her, who is more inaccesable than any goddesse or mystery of heathen impietye."

During the following sixteen years, Nur Jahan became the major power behind the throne of the perhaps the greatest empire in the world of its time without ever breaking the strict rules of purdah which enclosed her on every side. She issued orders and edicts, while Jahangir even had coins struck bearing her image, the first queen of India to be so honoured since the reign of Chandragupta some 1300 years earlier. By 1622, Jahangir's failing health had made her effective ruler of the empire in all but name. Nor were her energies confined to administrative dealings. When not managing affairs of state, Nur Jahan would go hunting on elephants, shooting from a closed howdah which simultaneously allowed her to enjoy the thrill of the chase whilst remaining inviolate to male eyes (and obviously developing considerable skills in marksmanship in the process, on one occasion dispatching four tigers with only six bullets). At one point she even rode into battle in a litter slung between two elephants – hardly the behaviour one would expect of a traditional seventeenth-century Indo-Islamic wife.

Ultimately, Nur Jahan's passion for intrigue and love of power was to prove her undoing. An early champion of Prince Khurram, later to become the emperor Shah Jahan, she subsequently changed her allegiances to his rival, Prince Shahriyar, although she rapidly found herself in conflict not only with Khurram, but with her own brother, Asaf Khan, who had sided with the rival prince. Following Jahangir's death in 1627 and Shah Jahan's seizure of the Mughal throne, Nur Jahan was forced finally to retire from court life. She lived for a further 18 years, during which she built the superb memorial for her father in Agra, the **Itimad-ud-Daulah**, by which she is now best remembered, as well as a fine tomb for Jahangir in Lahore, next to which she was herself interred upon her death in 1645.

The special relationship between the Mughals and the family of Ghiyas Beg did not end with Nur Jahan's fall from power, however. Shortly afterwards her niece, Asaf Khan's daughter Arjumand Banu, married the new emperor Shah Jahan, becoming in her turn the favoured Mughal consort of the age, and ultimately receiving the compliment of an even finer mausoleum: the Taj Mahal.

the tall grasses, just as they do in the Mughal miniature paintings dating from the era when the tomb was constructed, lending the whole place a magically peaceful and rural atmosphere.

The **mausoleum** itself sits in the middle of the gardens, at the centre of the *charbagh* plan and directly in front of Buland Darwaza. The entire structure is one of the strangest in Mughal Agra, its huge square base topped not by the usual dome but by a strangely haphazard superstructure, with a three-storey open-sided sandstone construction crowned by a solid-looking marble pavilion – it's sometimes suggested that the entire structure was to have been embellished with a culminating dome, though it's difficult to imagine how this would have worked. The mishmash design may be attributable to Jahangir, who ordered changes in the mausoleum's design halfway through its construction – Akbar himself having neglected to leave finished plans for his mausoleum, as was the usual custom. Judged by the standards of other Mughal buildings in India, it's an undoubted architectural failure, though the hotchpotch design isn't without a certain whimsical charm of its own, and much of the inlay work around the lower storey is exquisite.

A high marble gateway in the mausoleum's southern facade frames an elaborate lattice screen shielding a small vestibule painted with rich sea-blue frescoes and Koranic verses. From here a ramp leads down into a large, echoing and absolutely plain subterranean **crypt**, lit by a single skylight, in the centre of which stands Akbar's grave, decorated with the pen-box motif, the symbol of a male ruler, which can also be seen on Shah Jahan's tomb in the Taj Mahal.

Mariam's Tomb

Just north of Sikandra lies the altogether more modest **Mariam's Tomb** (daily sunrise–sunset; foreigners Rs100, Indian residents Rs5), the mausoleum of Mariam Zamani, a wife of Akbar and mother of Salim, the future emperor Jahangir, who ordered the construction of this large mausoleum for his mother following her death in 1623. The sandstone tomb is looking rather dilapidated nowadays, but remains impressive and also rather atmospheric, given the almost complete lack of visitors. Architecturally, the mausoleum belongs to the style embodied by Jahangir's own palace in Agra Fort, a weighty sandstone structure, with fine (though very eroded) carvings covering most of its exterior walls. The lack of the usual Mughal dome is compensated for by the large *chattris* placed at each corner and the four rectangular kiosks surmounting the centre of each facade, the whole roof enclosed by a large overhanging eave supported by heavy stepped capitals – all showing the increasingly strong Hindu influence which had begun to creep into the Mughal style during the reigns of Akbar and Jahangir. The plain interior is subdivided by a tight grid of intersecting corridors, while Mariam's own tomb sits in lonely isolation in the crypt below.

The tomb lies next to the main Mathura highway, around 1km past Sikandra (and on the opposite side of the road). If you don't have your own transport, there are plenty of buses running along the road past Sikandra which you could hop onto for the short ride, although it's probably easier just to walk.

Eating

In culinary terms, Agra is famous as the home of **Mughlai cooking**. Imitated in Indian curry houses throughout the world, the city's traditional Persian-influenced cuisine is renowned for its rich cream- and curd-based sauces, accompanied by naan and tandoori breads roasted in earthen ovens, *pulao* rice dishes and milky sweets such as *kheer*. Mughlai specialities can be sampled in many of the town's better restaurants, the majority of which can be found in **Sadar Bazaar** and along **Fatehabad Road**. There are also innumerable scruffy little travellers' cafes around **Taj Ganj**, though standards of hygiene are often suspect and the food (with the honourable exception of the *Sheela*, near the East Gate), though very cheap, is generally utterly uninspiring, with excruciatingly slow service the norm. Taj Ganj's one saving grace are the **rooftop cafes**, many with fine Taj views, which cap many of its buildings – the best views are from the *Kamal* and *Shanti Lodge* guesthouses – though of course you can't see anything after dark, except on or around full-moon days. Sadly it appears that the government is anxious to have those rooftop cafes closest to the Taj shut down for fear that they could be used to launch a terrorist attack against India's most iconic building, meaning that these places might not even exist by the time you read this.

Local **specialities** of Agra are *petha* (crystallised pumpkin) – the best is the Panchi brand, available at various outlets all over Agra, particularly in the row of *petha* shops in Kinari Bazaar along the northeast side of the Jama Masjid (past *Chimman Lal Poori Wale* cafe). Look out too for *gajjak*, a crumbly, crunchy sweet made from jaggery and sesame seeds, and *dalmoth*, a crunchy mix made with black lentils.

There's not much to get excited about when it comes to **drinking** in Agra. Easily the nicest place in town is the gorgeous bar at *Amarvilas* (see p.164), which has a good international selection of tipples at slightly less stratospheric prices than you might fear, given the sublime setting. Apart from this you're limited to surreptitious beers in the unlicensed Taj Ganj guesthouses, or the licensed but characterless bars in the various hotels along Fatehabad Road – the *Gaylord* bar and restaurant, opposite the *Park* restaurant in Sadar Bazaar, is as nice as any.

Finally, it's worth noting that Agra's restaurants – including even apparently reputable establishments – are not immune to the epidemic of **credit card fraud** (see p.184). It's best not to pay with a credit card except in the city's five-star establishments, or, if you do, to supervise the operation carefully.

Other than *Sheela*, which is shown on the Taj Ganj map (p.164), all the places listed here are marked on the Agra map, p.161.

Achman By-Pass Rd, Dayal Bagh. One of the most highly rated restaurants in the city among Agra-wallahs in the know, this place is famous for its *navratan korma* (a mildly spiced mix of nuts, dried fruit and *paneer*), *malai kofta* and chickpea masala, as well as wonderful stuffed naans. Well off the tourist trail in the north of the city, but ideally placed for dinner on your way home from Sikandra. Most mains Rs80–90.

Chimman Lal Poori Wale Opposite northeast wall of Jama Masjid. An Agra institution for five generations, this much-loved little café-restaurant looks like just another grubby tea shop from the outside (at least excepting the large "Recommended by Lonely Planet" sign), but serves delicious *puri-thalis*, with two veg dishes and melt-in-the-mouth saffron-flavoured *kheer* (Mughlai rice pudding) – all for Rs22. Ideal pit-stop after visiting the mosque.

Dasaprakash Meher Theatre Complex, 1 Gwalior Rd, near the *Hotel Yamuna View*. Offshoot of the famous Chennai restaurant, serving a limited menu of top-notch South Indian food and an extensive ice cream menu – the "hot fudge bonanza split" wins by a nose. Most mains Rs80–90.

Lakshmi Villas Sadar Bazaar. Unpretentious but deservedly popular South Indian café in the middle of Sadar Bazaar offering the usual *iddli-dosa-uttapam* menu, plus a couple of thalis – a good, and much cheaper, alternative to *Dasaprakash*, with most mains for a bargain Rs30–60.

The Mandarin Yamuna View Hotel. One of the best non-Indian restaurants in town, this rather snazzy-looking Chinese restaurant offers a possibly welcome change from Mughlai curries and masala dosas. The large (though rather expensive) menu features a good selection of delicately prepared dishes like stir-fried vegetables in almond sauce and chicken in honey chilli, with the emphasis on light ingredients and subtle flavours. Mains from Rs250.

Only Corner of The Mall and Taj Rd. One of Agra's most popular restaurants, usually packed with local families and tourist groups. It's best known for its well-prepared tandoori and Mughlai creations, though there's also a wide selection of more mainstream north Indian meat and veg standards, plus a few Chinese and Continental offerings. There's seating in an indoor a/c dining room or in the pleasant courtyard. Mains Rs60–180.

Park Restaurant Taj Rd, Sadar Bazaar. A long-established favourite with both locals and tourists, this simple a/c restaurant dishes up an excellent range of classic Mughlai chicken dishes, along with more mainstream tandooris and meat and veg curries accompanied by superb naan breads, plus a modest selection of Continental and Chinese favourites. Mains Rs70–170.

Priya Fatehabad Rd. A well-established stop on the coach-party circuit, with seating either in the unpretentious main dining hall or, in the evening, upstairs on the roof terrace. Despite the easy custom generated by crowds of day-trippers, standards remain high, with good Mughlai and other Indian dishes, including elaborate fruit-flavoured classics like *shahjanhani pullao* and *hyderabadi biryani*, plus more workaday curries and a few Chinese dishes. It's a bit pricey (and the drinks are extortionate), but portions are generous. Mains Rs110–260

Sheela East Gate, Taj Ganj. The most dependable and pleasant place to eat near the Taj, with outside seating in the shady garden or inside the narrow café. The menu features a good choice of simple (veg) Indian dishes, as well as drinks and snacks, and the fruit-and-nut lassis are a must – though they're more of a yoghurty dessert than a drink.

Sonam 51 Taj Rd. This mid-range garden restaurant and bar is an infamous tourist trap, but the food is good, including a selection of opulent Mughlai chicken and lamb classics like *murg* *shahjahani* and *murg dil bahar* along with regional specialities from the Punjab, Bengal and Kerala, plus inexpensive thalis.

Tourist Rest House Kutchery Rd. Tranquil garden restaurant serving a modest selection of (large) breakfasts and tasty Indian dishes to a sedate clientele of foreign backpackers. Try the tasty cheese *malai kofta*, rounded off with fruit custard like you never ate at school. All mains under Rs60.

Shopping

Agra is renowned for its **marble** tabletops, vases and trays, inlaid with semi-precious stones in ornate floral designs, in imitation of those found in the Taj Mahal. It's also an excellent place to buy **leather**: Agra's shoe industry supplies all India, and its tanneries export bags, briefcases and jackets. **Carpets** and **dhurries** are manufactured here too, and traditional embroidery continues to thrive. *Zari* and *zardozi* are brightly coloured, the latter building up three-dimensional patterns with fantastic motifs; *chikan* uses more delicate overlay techniques.

The biggest concentrations of crafts shops is along **Fatehabad Road**; there are also plenty of shops in **Taj Ganj**, around the east and west gates into the Taj; and around **Sadar Bazaar** (and north along the nearby General Cariappa Road). One reasonable place to start looking is the large **Cottage Industries Exposition** on Fatehabad Road, which gives a good overview of the sort of stuff you can find around the city, although at above-average prices (it's also one of the places you're likely to be taken to by a commission-seeking driver). Close to the East Gate, the **Shilpgram** crafts village hosts an annual arts and crafts festival during the second half of February. Off the tourist trail, **Kinari Bazaar**, around the Jama Masjid, is good for cheap clothes, shoes, food and a refreshingly hassle-free taste of local life.

There are literally hundreds of competing handicraft outlets, and it's well worth shopping around and comparing prices and quality – and be prepared to haggle. You should also be wary of ordering anything to be sent overseas. It's advisable never to let your credit card out of your sight, even for the transaction to be authorized, and you should make sure that all documentation is filled in correctly and fully so as not to allow unauthorized later additions. A large number of serious cases of **credit card fraud** have been reported in Agra (the problem is not confined to shops: even some popular tourist restaurants have been involved). Finally, remember that if you arrive at any shop in a **rickshaw** or **taxi**, the prices of anything you buy will be inflated to cover the driver's commission. If you're planning on buying, ask to be dropped off nearby, and then walk to the shop.

Listings

Banks and exchange The State Bank of India is just south of Taj Rd in the Cantonment (Amex traveller's cheques not accepted); Andhra Bank is over in Sadar Bazaar; and the Allahabad Bank is in the *Hotel Clarks Shiraz*. If you get caught out by a public holiday, you could always try one of the private exchange offices in the Tourist Complex Area, around *Pizza Hut* (LKP Forex, opposite the *Amar Hotel* on the Fatehabad Rd, are always reliable and fast). There are a few ATMs dotted around the city (and marked on the maps on p.160 & p.161) which accept foreign Visa and MasterCards.

Hospitals Essar (☎0562/226 5587), Namner Cross Roads; GG Nursing Home (☎0562/226 5587) at Sanjay Place; and Pushpanjali (☎0562/255 2981) at Delhi Gate are all clean and dependable, with English-speaking doctors.

Internet access There's plenty of Internet access available around town, particularly in Taj Ganj; rates virtually everywhere are Rs30–40 per hour. In Taj Ganj, try the iWay cybercafe on the ground floor of the *Shah Jahan* guesthouse; there are also a number of reasonably reliable places along East Gate Road near the *Hotel Sheela*. Elsewhere in the city, virtually all hotels and guesthouses have their own Internet connection.

Photography A number of places around Taj Ganj can download and burn digital images to disc – try the iWay cybercafe at the *Shah Jahan* guesthouse.

Police There are police stations on Chowk Kagzi in Taj Ganj (℡0562/233 1015) and on Mahatma Gandhi Road in Sadar Bazaar, slightly south of the intersection with Fatehpur Sikri Rd (℡0562/222 6561).

Post The Head Post Office is on The Mall, near the Government of India tourist office, though the poste restante service has a very poor reputation.

Swimming The pools at most of Agra's hotels are usually reserved for the use of hotel guests only, though a few places admit outsiders on payment of a fee. These currently include the *Yamuna View* (Rs350), the *Mughal Sheraton* (Rs400) and the *Clarks Shiraz* (Rs500).

Moving on from Agra

By train

Train tickets should be booked in advance at either Agra Cantonment or Agra Fort stations, both of which have fully computerized booking offices with

Recommended trains from Agra

The following services are the fastest and/or most convenient in terms of departure/arrival times; all run daily unless stated otherwise. Train timetables change frequently; check latest schedules either at your nearest station or online at ®www.indianrail.gov.in before travel.

Destination	Name	No.	From	Departs	Arrives
Bharatpur	Gwalior–Jaipur Intercity	2988	AC/AF	5.40pm/6.20pm	7.15pm
Bundi/ Chittaurgarh	Haldighati Passenger	282	AF	7.10pm	7.18am/ 10.35am
Delhi	Shatabdi Express	2001	AC	8.30pm (daily except Fri)	10.30pm
Fatehpur Sikri	Haldighati Passenger	282	AF	7.10pm	8.08pm
Jaipur	Gwalior–Jaipur Intercity	2988	AC/AF	5.40pm/6.20pm	10.20pm
	Marudhar Express	4853	AF	6.10am (Mon, Wed & Sat only)	11.30am
Jhansi	Bhopal Shatabdi	2002	AC	8.12am (daily except Fri)	10.39am
Jodhpur	Marudhar Express	4853	AF	6.10am (Mon, Wed & Sat only)	6.20pm
	Howrah–Jodhpur Express	2307	AF	7.35pm	7.20am
Kota	Avadh Express	9038	AF	5.30am (Mon, Weds, Fri & Sat only)	11.00am
Sawai Madhopur	Avadh Express	9038	AF	5.30am (Mon, Weds, Fri & Sat only)	9.25am
Varanasi	Marudhar Express	4854	AF	9.15pm	9.30am

AC = Agra Cantonment , **AF** = Agra Fort

dedicated tourist counters. Some services leave from Fort station, and some from Cantonment (and some call at both) – see box, p.185 for details. There are numerous services (roughly 18 daily; 2–3hr) from Agra Cantt to **Delhi**, the fastest being the 8.30pm Shatabdi Express. Services **into Rajasthan** are surprisingly sketchy – you might find it easier to catch a bus to Jaipur and pick up onward connections there. There are a few (inconveniently timed) services to **Jaipur** itself, plus two to **Jodhpur**, while a couple of slow passenger services run to **Sawai Madhopur** (for Ranthambore National Park) and destinations in **southern Rajasthan**. There are also two or three daily services to **Bharatpur** (but no direct connections to Alwar), plus numerous services south to **Jhansi** in Madhya Pradesh, where you can pick up onward bus connections to Orchha and Khajuraho, as well a nightly express to **Varanasi**.

By bus

Travelling by bus along the main highways, especially to the Delhi and Jaipur, can be a hair-raising experience. Accidents – most of them head-on collisions with other buses or trucks – are disconcertingly frequent, though these happen mainly at night or during the monsoon or in December and January, when the area is frequently blanketed in thick mists.

All services to Rajasthan and express buses to Delhi leave from **Idgah bus stand**, on the western side of town, or from in front of the nearby **Sakura Hotel**. There are deluxe buses to **Delhi** every half hour (plus a/c buses at 7.30am and 9am); you can buy tickets on the bus or book in advance through the *Sakura Hotel*. The journey takes four and a half to five hours and buses drop you off in Delhi at Sarai Kalekhan, near Indraprastha metro station. If you're heading into **Rajasthan**, it's simplest to take a bus to **Jaipur** and then pick up an onward connection from there. Official Rajasthan Government deluxe buses to Jaipur (5–6hr) leave hourly from the *Sakura Hotel* from 6.30am to 2.30pm (there are a/c services at 6.30am & 2.30pm from April to July) and deposit you at the Inter-State Bus Terminal in Jaipur. Tickets cost Rs174 (or Rs250 on a/c buses) and have to be booked in person at the *Sakura Hotel*. Other travel agents around town may offer alternative bus services, but these are usually less reliable or more expensive. There are also regular local services to **Bharatpur** (hourly; 1hr 30min–2hr), Fatehpur Sikri (every 30min; 1hr–1hr 30min) and Gwalior (every 2hr; 3hr 30min) from Idgah bus stand.

Chaotic **Agra Fort bus stand** is the departure point for non-express buses to Delhi and destinations within Uttar Pradesh. Tickets are sold on the buses. Getting to **Khajuraho** involves an excruciatingly long bus journey (daily at 5.30am; 12–14hr), or a train to Jhansi (2hr 45min–3hr 50min), and then a six-hour bus ride from there.

Fatehpur Sikri

The ghost city of **FATEHPUR SIKRI**, former imperial capital of the great Mughal emperor **Akbar**, straddles the crest of a rocky ridge 40km southwest of Agra at the site of the formerly obscure village of Sikri (the "Fatehpur", meaning "City of Victory", was added in 1573 following Akbar's brilliant military campaign in Gujarat). The city was built here between 1569 and 1585 as a result of the emperor's enthusiasm for the local Muslim divine **Sheikh Salim Chishti** (see p.195), though the move away from Agra may also have had something to do with Akbar's weariness with the crowds of Agra and his desire

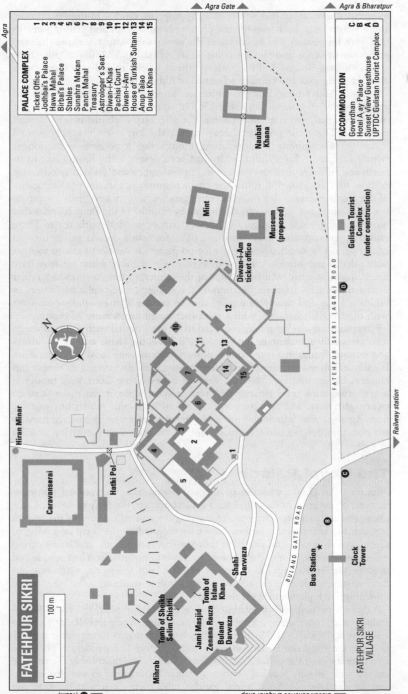

FATEHPUR SIKRI

0   100 m

PALACE COMPLEX

Ticket Office	1
Jodhbai's Palace	2
Hawa Mahal	3
Birbal's Palace	4
Stables	5
Sunahra Makan	6
Panch Mahal	7
Treasury	8
Astrologer's Seat	9
Diwan-i-Khas	10
Pachisi Court	11
Diwan-i-Am	12
House of Turkish Sultana	13
Anup Talao	14
Daulat Khana	15

ACCOMMODATION

Goverdhan	C
Hotel A ay Palace	B
Sunset View Guesthouse	A
UPTDC Gulistan Tourist Complex	D

▲ Agra Gate ▲   ▲ Agra & Bharatpur

◀ Agra

Hiran Minar

Caravanserai

Hathi Pol

Naubat Khana

Mint

Museum (proposed)

Diwan-i-Am ticket office

Gulistan Tourist Complex (under construction)

FATEHPUR SIKRI (AGRA) ROAD

▶ Railway station

BULAND GATE ROAD

Bus Station ★

Clock Tower

FATEHPUR SIKRI VILLAGE

Mihrab

Tomb of Sheikh Salim Chishti

Jami Masjid

Zenana Rauza

Tomb of Islam Khan

Buland Darwaza

Shahi Darwaza

◀ Ⓐ (100m)

▼ Biscuit bakeries & liquor shop

to create a new capital that was both an appropriate symbol of imperial power, and a sympathetic backdrop for the philosophical debates and artistic pursuits that were his passion. The buildings of the new palace would become the very embodiment of his unorthodox court, fusing Hindu and Muslim architectural traditions in a unique Indo–Islamic synthesis whose mixed styles say much about the religious and cultural tolerance of Akbar's reign.

Fatehpur Sikri's period of pre-eminence amongst the cities of the Mughal empire was brief, however, and after 1585 it would never again serve as the seat of the Mughal emperor. The reasons for the **city's abandoment** remain enigmatic. The most popular theory is that the city's water supply proved incapable of sustaining its population, though this hypothesis is no longer widely accepted – even after the city had been deserted, the nearby lake to its northwest still measured over 20km in circumference and yielded good water. A more likely explanation is that the city was simply the victim of the vagaries of the empire's day-to-day military contingencies. Shortly after the new capital was established, the empire was threatened by troubles in the Punjab, and Akbar moved to the more strategically situated Lahore to deal with them. These military preoccupations kept Akbar at Lahore for over a decade, and at the end of this period he decided, apparently for no particular reason, to return to Agra rather than Fatehpur Sikri. The demise of Fatehpur Sikri, therefore, may have been an almost accidental byproduct of the emperor's transitory mood, rather than a meaningful strategic decision. If this suggests a certain wastefulness, in building a city and then abandoning it, then it's one that is wholly consistent with the Mughal character, which was never noted for its sense of economy.

Fatehpur Sikri was originally intended to be joint capital with Agra; although it receives only a fraction of the visitors of its rival, the lavish scale of its palaces and mosque ensure that it remains as powerful a testimony to Mughal grandeur. It's also an enjoyably atmospheric place to stay, with a scattering of simple but comfortable guesthouses. Most visitors visit on a day-trip from Agra, though if you're continuing onto Bharatpur, Alwar or even Jaipur, it can make sense to **overnight here**, and avoid the rather tedious hour-plus return bus journey from Agra – a plan which also gives you the chance to give the palace remains the time they deserve, and to explore some of the little-visited outlying remains as well.

The Royal Palace

Shunning the Hindu tradition of aligning towns with the cardinal points, as dictated by the ancient canonical texts on architecture, the *Shilpa Shastras*, Akbar chose to construct his new capital following the natural features of the terrain (though the layout is also said to have been inspired by the form of a Mughal camp), which is why the principal thoroughfare, town walls, and many of the most important buildings inside it face southwest or northeast. The mosque and most private apartments, on the other hand, do not follow the main axis, but face west towards Mecca, according to Muslim tradition, with the palace crowning the highest point on the ridge.

Although unused and uninhabited since its abandonment, the main **Royal Palace** and court complex (daily sunrise–sunset; foreigners Rs260, Indian residents Rs20, video Rs25), remains largely intact, thanks to extensive restoration work carried out by British archeologists before Independence. There are two **entrances** to the palace. Independent travellers will most likely use the one on the west side, by Jodhbai's Palace; organized tours tend to use that on the east, by the Diwan-i-Am. Official **guides** offer their services at the booking office for Rs50–100. Note that there's nowhere to buy drinks in the palace, so take water in with you; you're not allowed to eat inside either.

The palace complex's myriad buildings can be rather disorienting on first acquaintance. Despite the apparent disorder, however (not helped by the various spurious and confusing names applied to buildings throughout the palace), the entire complex actually divides neatly into two: the **mardana** (or men's quarters) on the east side of the palace, and the **zenana** (women's quarters) to the west. The only exception is the Diwan-i-Am (see below), on the far eastern side of the palace, which was open to the public at large (and which was supplied with its own entrance to avoid having the hoi-polloi traipse through the main palace itself).

The Diwan-i-Am

Assuming you're entering the palace from the ticket office on the west side, by Jodhbai's Palace, follow the walkway from the ticket booth right across the palace and through the *mardana* courtyard (see below), from whose northeast corner an insignificant doorway leads into the **Diwan-i-Am**, on the far eastern edge of the main palace. The Diwan was where important festivals were held, and where citizens could exercise their right to petition the emperor. Unlike the ornate pillared Diwan-i-Am buildings at the forts in Agra and Delhi, this is basically just a large courtyard, surrounded by a continuous colonnaded walkway with Hindu-style square columns and capitals, broken only by the small pavilion, flanked by elaborately carved *jali* screens, in which the emperor himself would have sat – note the position of the royal platform in relation to the enclosure's main entrance, set at an angle which forced the emperor's subjects to approach him from the side in an attitude of humility.

The Diwan-i-Khas

Return from the Diwan-i-Am to the palace's main courtyard, the centre of the *mardana* (men's quarters), a large, irregularly shaped enclosure dotted with a strikingly eclectic range of buildings. At the far (northern) end of the enclosure stands the tall **Diwan-i-Khas** ("Hall of Private Audience"), topped with four *chattris* and embellished with the heavily carved Hindu-style brackets, large overhanging eaves and corbelled arches which are typical of the architecture of Fatehpur Sikri.

The interior of the building consists of a single high hall (despite the appearance outside of a two storey building) centred on an elaborately corbelled column known as the **Throne Pillar**, supporting a large circular platform from which four balustraded bridges radiate outwards. Seated upon this throne, the emperor held discussions with representatives of diverse religions – orthodox Muslim leaders (*ulema*), Jesuit priests from Goa, Hindu Brahmins, Jains and Zoroastrians – ranged around the walls of the balcony. Through such discussions, Akbar sought to synthesize India's religions and the pillar symbolizes this project by incorporating motifs drawn from Hinduism, Buddhism, Islam and Christianity. Eventually, however, the *ulemas* became alienated by the discussions held here and instigated an uprising, which Akbar ruthlessly crushed in 1581. Thereafter, the emperor evolved a concept of divine kingship, which the overall architecture of the Diwan-i-Khas, with its axial pillars radiating from a central point, serves to underline. Access to the pillar and balconies is via steps built inside the walls of the building.

Next to the Diwan-i-Khas lies the three-roomed **Treasury**, its brackets embellished by mythical sea creatures, guardians of the treasures of the deep; it's also known as Ankh Michauli, after the game of *ankh michauli* (hide and seek), which it's said used to be played here – in fact both names are probably just fanciful inventions, and the building most likely served as a multi-purpose pavilion which could be used for a variety of functions, as could most buildings in Mughal palaces. Attached to it is the so-called **Astrologer's Seat**, a small pavilion embellished with elaborate Jain carvings.

The Pachisi Court

In the middle of the courtyard, separating the Diwan-i-Khas from the buildings on the opposite (south) side of the complex, is the **Pachisi Court**, a giant board used to play *pachisi* (similar to ludo), with two lines of stone squares arranged in a cross, and a seat at the centre. Akbar is said to have been a fanatical player, using slave girls dressed in colourful costumes as live pieces. Abu'l Fazl, the court chronicler, related that at "times more than two hundred persons participated . . . and no one was allowed to go home until he had played sixteen rounds. This could take up to three months. If one of the players lost his patience and became restless, he was made to drink a cupful of wine. Seen superficially, this appears to be just a game. But His Majesty pursues higher objectives. He weighs up the talents of his people and teaches them to be affable."

House of the Turkish Sultana

Diagonally opposite the *pachisi* board, the **House of the Turkish Sultana** (also known as the Anup Talao Pavilion) gained its curious name thanks to the popular belief that it was once the residence of one of Akbar's favourite wives, the Sultana Ruqayya Begum – though this seems extremely unlikely, given its location in the centre of the men's quarters of the palace. The name was probably one of several made up by nineteenth-century guides to titillate early tourists, and the building was more likely to have served as a simple pleasure pavilion. The building is notable for its superbly carved stone walls, covered with a profusion of floral and geometrical designs, plus some partially vandalized animal carvings. Legend has it that the great musician Mian Tansen once sang *Deepak*, the raga of fire, here. So effective was his performance that he grew hotter and hotter, until his daughter had to come to the rescue by performing the rain raga, *Malhar*. Understandably nervous at this great responsibility, she faltered on the seventh note of the scale, thereby creating one of north India's most stirring ragas – the *Mian ki Malhar* – with its famously expressive emphasis on this ultimate note of the raga, on which Tansen's daughter had inadvertently lingered. Happily, the raga had the desired effect; rain fell, and Tansen was saved.

South of here is the **Anup Talao** (Peerless Pool), a pretty little ornamental pond divided by four walkways connected to an small "island" in the middle – a layout strangely reminiscent of the raised walkways inside the Diwan-i-Khas.

The Daulat Khana

Facing the Turkish Sultana's house from the other side of the Anup Talao are Akbar's private sleeping and living quarters, the **Daulat Khana** (Abode of Fortune). The room on the ground floor with alcoves in its walls was the emperor's library, where he would be read to (he himself was illiterate) from a collection of fifty thousand manuscripts he allegedly took everywhere with him. Behind the library is the imperial sleeping chamber, the **Khwabgah** (House of Dreams), with an enormous raised bed in its centre.

The Panch Mahal

One of Fatehpur Sikri's most famous structures, the **Panch Mahal** or "Five-Storeyed Palace", looms northwest of here, marking the beginning of the

zenana (women's quarters) which make up the entire western side of the palace complex. The palace tapers to a final single kiosk and is supported by 176 columns of varying designs; the ground floor contains 84 pillars – an auspicious number in Hindu astrology. The open spaces between the pillars were originally covered with latticed screens, so that ladies of the *zenana* could observe goings-on in the courtyard of the *mardana* below without themselves being seen.

The Sunahra Makan

Directly behind the Panch Mahal is a courtyard garden reserved for the *zenana*, the ladies of the harem. The adjoining **Sunahra Makan** ("Golden House"), also known as Mariam's House, is variously thought to have been the home of the emperor's mother or the palace of Akbar's wife Mariam, mother of Emperor Jahangir, whose mausoleum stands close to the emperor's own in Agra (see p.182). The fairly plain sandstone pavilion is enlivened by the faded remains of paintings which cover its walls (and whose now vanished golden paint gave the pavilion its name), by the lines of verse penned by Abu'l Fazl, inscribed around the ceiling in blue bands, and by the quaint little carvings tucked into the brackets supporting the roof, including several elephants and a tiny carving of Rama attended by Hanuman (on the north side of building, facing the *zenana* courtyard garden).

Jodhbai's Palace

Solemnly presiding over the whole complex is the main harem, known as **Jodhbai's Palace**. The residence of several of the emperor's senior wives, this striking building is perhaps the grandest and largest in the entire city, and looks decidedly Hindu even in the eclectic context of Fatehpur Sikri, having been modelled after Rajput palaces such as those at Gwalior and Orchha. Surrounding the central courtyard are four self-contained raised terraces; those on the north and south sides are surmounted by unusual roofs, thought to imitate the shape of bamboo and thatch, with traces of blue-glazed tile that forms an eye-catching, distinctly Persian counterpoint to the building's rich red sandstone.

On the north side of the palace, the **Hawa Mahal** (Palace of the Winds), a small screened tower with a delicately carved chamber, was designed to catch the evening breeze, while a raised covered walkway, lined with five large *chattris*, leads from here to a (now vanished) lake.

Birbal's Palace

Northwest of Jodhbai's Palace lies a third women's palace, known as **Birbal's Palace** – though this is another misnomer, as Birbal, Akbar's favourite courtier, was a man and would have been most unwelcome in the middle of the *zenana*. It's more likely to have been the residence of two of Akbar's senior wives. The palace is even more lavishly carved than Jodhbai's, covered in a profusion of decoration including a ceiling crafted to resemble a canopy of blossoms. The whole thing looks more like a South Indian temple than a Mughal palace – not that surprising, really, given that many of the sculptural features used here have been lifted straight out of Hindu temple-building traditions – though Islamic touches can be seen too in the geometrical patterns which covered parts of the facade, the two styles muddled up together in an extraordinarily lavish, if decidedly haphazard, way.

South of Birbal's Palace stretches the large rectangular enclosure, surrounded by small rooms popularly referred to as the palace **stables**, though it's unlikely that so many horses would have been quartered so close to the ladies' palaces – it's more probable that the building was used to accommodate some kind of market, or perhaps the female servants of the ladies of the *zenana*.

Outlying remains

Further significant remains of the palace complex lie scattered amongst the surrounding rocky hills. These can be visited for free and make for a pleasant ramble, especially towards sunset or early in the morning. From the main Agra road, just west of the *Gulistan* hotel, a track heads north, emerging on the sideroad up to the palace close to the **Naubat Khana**, a caravanserai-type structure flanked by an impressive pair of gateways. Follow the road west, past the small **mint** to the Diwan-i-Am ticket office. From here, a rocky little path dips downhill to your right, bringing you to the small road which runs along the northern edge of the city. Turn left and walk

△ Carving detail, Birbal's Palace

along the road, which offers fine views of its myriad *chattris* and domes before reaching the impressive **Hathi Pol** (Elephant Gate), decorated with the vandalized remains of large sculptured elephants. Head through the gate and down past the large **Caravanserai** to reach the strange **Hiran Minar**, a slender tower studded in dozens of stone protuberances, said to be modelled after elephant tusks. Retrace your steps through the Hathi Pol and continue on to the Shahi Darwaza entrance to the Jama Masjid.

Jama Masjid

At the southwestern corner of the palace complex, with the village of Fatehpur Sikri nestling at its base, stands the **Jama Masjid** (daily dawn–dusk; free) or Dargah Mosque, one of the finest in the whole of India. Unfortunately, the mosque is rife with self-appointed "guides" (around Rs20 for a tour) – it's pretty much impossible to escape their attentions, so you may as well give in gracefully and at least take your time in choosing someone who appeals.

The alignment of the entire palace complex, which faces west instead of following the ridge, was determined by the orientation of the mosque's mihrab (prayer niche) towards Mecca. The building of the mosque was apparently completed in 1571, before work on the palace itself commenced, showing the religious significance which Akbar accorded the entire site thanks to its connections with Sheikh Salim Chishti (see box opposite).

The main approach is through the neck-cricking **Buland Darwaza** (Great Gate), a spectacular entranceway scaled by an impressive flight of steps which was added to the mosque around 1576 to commemorate Akbar's brilliant campaign in Gujarat – and which offers the definitive architectural celebration of his spectacular military triumphs. Flanked by domed kiosks, the archway of the simple sandstone memorial is inscribed with a message from the Koran: "Said Jesus Son of Mary (peace be on him): The world is but a bridge – pass over without building houses on it. He who hopes for an hour hopes for eternity; the world is an hour – spend it in prayer for the rest is unseen." The

Although remembered primarily for his liberal approach to religion, Akbar was typically Mughal in his attitudes to women, whom he collected in much the same way as an obsessive philatelist amasses stamps. At its height of splendour, the **royal harem** at Fatehpur Sikri held around five thousand women, guarded by a legion of eunuchs. Its doors were closed to outsiders, but rumours permeated the sandstone walls and several notable travellers were smuggled inside the Great Mughals' seraglios, leaving for posterity often lurid accounts of the emperors' private lives.

The size of Akbar's harem grew in direct proportion to his empire. With each new conquest, he would be gifted by the defeated rulers and nobles their most beautiful daughters, who, together with their maidservants, would be installed in the luxurious royal **zenana**. In all, the emperor is thought to have kept three hundred wives; their ranks were swollen by a constant flow of concubines (*kaniz*), dancing girls (*kanchni*) and female slaves (*bandis*), or "silver bodied damsels with musky tresses" as one chronicler described them, purchased from markets across Asia. Screened from public view by ornately pierced stone *jali* windows were women from the four corners of the Mughal empire, as well as Afghanis, Turks, Iranis, Arabs, Tibetans, Russians and Abyssinians, and even one Portuguese Christian, sent as presents or tribute.

The **eunuchs** who presided over them came from similarly diverse backgrounds. While some were hermaphrodites, others had been forcibly castrated, either as punishment following defeat on the battlefield, or after having been donated by their fathers as payment of backdated revenue – an all too common custom at the time.

Akbar is said to have consumed prodigious quantities of Persian wine, local *araq* distilled from sugar cane, bhang (cannabis leaf) – often in a drink or in the form of a sweet called *majun* – and opium. The lavish dance recitals held in the harem, as well as sexual liaisons conducted on the top pavilion of the Panch Mahal and in the *zenana* itself, would have been fuelled by these substances. Over time, Akbar's hedonistic ways incurred the disapproval of his highest clerics – the *Ulema*. The Koran expressly limits the number of wives a man may take to four, but one verse also admits a lower form of marriage, known as *muta*, which was more like an informal pact, and could be entered into with non-Muslims. Akbar's abuse of this long-lapsed law was heavily criticized by his Sunni head priest during their religious disquisitions.

What life must actually have been like for the women who lived in Akbar's harem one can only imagine, but it is known that alcoholism and drug addiction were widespread, and that some also risked their lives to conduct illicit affairs with male lovers, smuggled in disguised as physicians or under heavy Muslim veils. If the reports of a couple of foreign adventurers who secretly gained access to Jahangir's seraglio are to be believed, the eunuchs were also required to intercept anything (other than the emperor) that might excite the women's passion.

In fact, the notion that the harem was a gilded prison whose inmates whiled their lifetimes away in idle vanity and dalliance is something of a myth. Many of the women in the *zenana* were immensely rich in their own right, and wielded enormous influence on the court. Jahangir's wife, Nur Jahan, virtually ran the empire from behind the screen of *purdah* during the last five years of her husband's ailing reign, while her mother-in-law owned a ship that traded between Surat and the Red Sea, a tradition continued by Shah Jahan's daughter, who grew immensely wealthy through her business enterprises.

Partly as a result of the money and power at the women's disposal, jealousies in the harem were also rife, and the work of maintaining order and calm among the thousands of foster mothers, aunties, the emperor's relatives and all his wives, minor wives, paramours, musicians, dancers, amazons and slaves, was a major preoccupation. As Akbar's court chronicler wryly observed, "the government of the kingdom is but an amusement compared with such a task, for it is within the (harem) that intrigue is enthroned".

Sheikh Salim Chishti

During the early years of Akbar's reign, the young emperor was much troubled by the fact that none of his numerous wives had succeeded in producing a male heir who survived beyond infancy. The disconsolate monarch consulted a certain elderly Muslim holy man, **Sheikh Salim**, a member of the Chishti order, who lived a reclusive life atop a hill at Sikri, west of Agra. The Sheikh Salim obligingly predicted the birth of three sons to the emperor. Soon after, one of Akbar's wives fell pregnant. She was moved to Sikri and subsequently gave birth, on 30 August 1569, to a son, the future Jahangir (though he was originally named Salim, in honour of the divine). The second and third sons were subsequently born, as predicted, and the grateful Akbar chose to show his respect by constructing a huge new mosque and palace at Sikri (significantly, the mosque preceded the palace) in the saint's honour. Sheikh Salim himself, who was already almost 90 years old, died soon after; all three sons survived to adulthood, however, though their constant rebellions against their father (and one another) were to blight Akbar's later years.

The *dargah* still attracts women who come here to pray for offspring, tying string onto the marble screen; when entering the main chamber, visitors cover their heads with cloth as a mark of respect. During Ramadan, an *urs* is held here, attracting *qawwals* (singers of Sufi songs) from all over the country.

numerous horseshoes nailed to the doors here date from the beginning of the twentieth century – an odd instance of British folk superstition in this very Islamic place.

The gate leads into a vast cloistered courtyard, far larger than any previous mosque in India. The **prayer hall**, on the west (left) side, is the focus of the mosque, punctuated by an enormous gateway. The pointed exterior arches are impeccably Islamic in design, but the inside shows the architectural miscegenation typical of Fatehpur Sikri, with the dome supported by decidedly Hindu-looking columns and pot-shaped corbels, perhaps the work of Gujarati craftsmen who were brought to work on the new mosque following Akbar's dramatic conquest of the region.

More eye-catching is the exquisite **Tomb of Sheikh Salim Chishti** (see opposite), directly ahead as one enters the courtyard. Much of this was originally crafted in red sandstone and only later faced in marble: the beautiful lattice screens – another design feature probably imported from Gujarat, though it would later become a staple of Mughal architecture – are unusually intricate, with striking serpentine exterior brackets supporting the eaves. To the right stands the lattice-screen **Tomb of Islam Khan**, housing the remains of the grandson of Sheikh Salim Chishti, who later became the Mughal governor of Bengal, along with other related nobles, while behind lies the **Zenana Rauza** (Tomb of the Royal Ladies), housing numerous tightly packed graves of various ladies of the *zenana*.

Practicalities

Buses leave either from the crowded bus station in the centre of the village or from the bus stop on the bypass near Agra Gate, about 1.5km from town (about Rs10 by tonga from the village) – it's usually quickest to pick up a bus from Agra Gate, especially if you're heading on to Bharatpur or Jaipur. Services run to Jaipur (every 30min; 4hr), Agra (every 30min; 1hr–1hr 30min), Bharatpur (every 30min–1hr; 30–45min). If you're in a rush, you can hire a Jeep at the bus stand to Agra for around Rs400–500. **Tongas** (horse-drawn carriages) are the staple means of transport around the village (there are no rickshaws at present); expect to pay about the same as you normally would for a cycle rickshaw. There are no useful **trains** from Fatehpur Sikri.

Fatehpur Sikri has a small but decent choice of **places to stay**. The best of the bunch is the *Goverdhan Guest House*, just east of the bus stand on Buland Gate Road (☎05613/282643; ❷–❹), with a range of old but spacious and well-maintained fan, air-cooled and a/c rooms arranged around a neat lawn, as well as good food (meals are made with filtered or mineral water – Fatehpur Sikri's ground water is extremely salty). Just over 1km further out of town, on the Agra Road, is the slightly more expensive UPTDC *Gulistan Tourist Complex* (☎05613/282490; ❸–❹), a rather moribund state-run complex with comfortable fan, air-cooled and a/c rooms, a run-of-the-mill restaurant and a small bar. Cheaper options include the welcoming *Ajay Palace Hotel* (☎05613/282950; ❷), right in the middle of the village, which has just four fan rooms – simple and rather small, but very clean – plus a nice little rooftop. Alternatively, the brand-new *Sunset View Guesthouse* (☎0123 84416; ❶–❷), about 250m past the Jama Masjid, has neat and clean modern fan rooms and superb views over the mosque and the countryside beyond.

You'll probably eat where you stay. If you want to go out, try the *Goverdhan* or the *Ajay Palace Hotel*. Fatehpur Sikri's delicious **biscuits** are not to be missed – you can savour them hot out of the oven each evening at the bakeries on the lane leading up from the bazaar to the Jama Masjid. A new **shopping** complex is currently under construction just beyond the *Gulistan* hotel, which it's intended will house around eighty handicrafts shops when open – which should be by the time you read this.

Jaipur and eastern Rajasthan

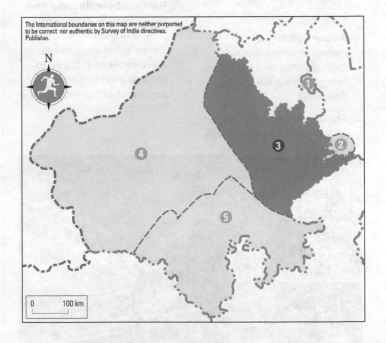

The International boundaries on this map are neither purported to be correct nor authentic by Survey of India directives. Publisher.

N

0   100 km

CHAPTER 3

Highlights

* **Jaipur City Palace** The majestic home of the maharajas of Jaipur, its sumptuously decorated courtyards and pavilions featuring an absorbing collection of historical mementoes relating to the ruling family's lavish lifestyle. See p.209

* **Shopping in Jaipur** Shop till you drop in Rajasthan's crafts capital, with endless bazaars crammed full of eye-catching local artefacts. See p.217

* **Amber Fort** One of Rajasthan's most dramatic forts, perched on a rugged hilltop on the edge of Jaipur. See p.223

* **Shekhawati** The dusty towns of Shekhawati are the unlikely home of one of India's most remarkable architectural and artistic legacies, with hundreds of ornate, crumbling havelis decorated with superb murals. See p.225

* **Keoladeo National Park, Bharatpur** Flocks of rare birds – and bird-watchers – travel from across Asia and Europe each winter to visit this remarkable wetland sanctuary. See p.250

* **Ranthambore National Park** India's most popular wildlife park, and one of the easiest places in the world to see tigers in the wild, thanks to its large and exhibitionist population of big cats. See p.255

△ Jaipur City Palace

Jaipur and eastern Rajasthan

A short journey by road or rail from either Delhi or Agra, the fascinating – if somewhat exhausting – city of **Jaipur** is most visitors' first experience of Rajasthan. The capital of the state, and easily its largest and busiest city, Jaipur is home to a rich clutch of sights, most of them built by the ruling maharajas, whose considerable military power and seemingly bottomless personal coffers are encapsulated in the flamboyant sequence of forts, palaces and other creations, from cenotaphs to observatories, which dot the city and its environs – a highlight of any visit to Rajasthan, if you can cope with the city's dense crowds and appalling traffic. North of Jaipur, the fascinating region of **Shekhawati** remains one of Rajasthan's most absorbing – and least touristed – regions, with dozens of dusty little towns filled with magnificent, decaying havelis constructed by wealthy local merchants throughout the nineteenth and early twentieth century, their walls covered with a superb array of murals showing everything from traditional religious scenes to contemporary Europeans in trains and aeroplanes.

The area east and south of Jaipur is of exceptional wildlife interest, being home to a pair of world-famous national parks: the celebrated ornithological wonderland of the **Keoladeo National Park**, just outside the engrossing little town of **Bharatpur**; and the even more popular **Ranthambore National Park** further south, which offers as good a chance of spotting tigers in the wild as anywhere on the planet. You won't, sadly, see any tigers at the region's third major national park, the **Sariska Tiger Reserve**, which despite its name is now entirely devoid of big cats. It remains well-populated with other forms of wildlife, however, and offers a peaceful and lesser-known alternative to the area's more popular parks, and an easy day-trip from the absorbing little city of **Alwar**, a rewarding destination in its own right.

Jaipur and around

A flamboyant showcase of Rajasthani architecture, **JAIPUR**, just 260km southwest of Delhi and 230km west of Agra, has long been established on tourist itineraries as the third corner of India's "Golden Triangle". At the heart of Jaipur lies the **Pink City**, the old walled quarter in the northeast of town, whose **bazaars** rank among the most vibrant in Asia, renowned above all for hand-dyed and embroidered textiles, jewellery, and the best selection of precious stones and metals in India. For all its colour, however, Jaipur's heavy traffic, dense crowds and pushy traders and touts makes it a taxing place to explore, and many visitors stay just long enough to catch a train to more laid-back destinations further west or south. Though if you can put up with the urban stress, the city's forward-looking residents and commercial hustle and bustle offer a stimulating contrast to most other places in the state.

If you're anywhere near Jaipur in March, don't miss the **Elephant Festival**, one of India's most flamboyant parades, celebrated with full Rajput pomp during Holi (March; see p.55).

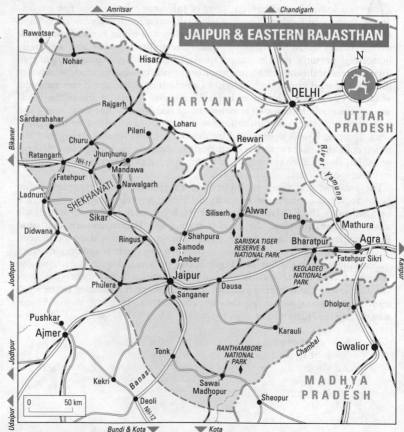

Established in 1727, Jaipur is one of Rajasthan's youngest cities, founded by (and named after) **Jai Singh II**, ruler of the **Kachchwaha** royal family, one of the leading Rajput dynasties, who ruled a sizeable portion of northern Rajasthan from their venerable palace-fort at nearby Amber. The Kachchwaha Rajputs had been the first to ally themselves with the Mughals, in 1561, and the free flow of trade, art and ideas had by the time of Jai Singh's accession won them great prosperity. Jai Singh himself excelled in battle, politics and learning, and also showed an unusual passion for astronomy, being responsible for the design of the **Jantar Mantar**, the largest stone observatory in the world (along with four other, identically named, observatories elsewhere in north India, including the well-known example in Delhi).

Jai Singh's decision to move the Kachchwaha capital from Amber to Jaipur represented a landmark in Rajput political thinking. The region's major cities had hitherto been located in positions of maximum military strength, usually occupying easily defensible positions atop craggy hilltops overlooking the surrounding plains. Jaipur was the Rajput's first city to place mercantile above military considerations, occupying a commercially strategic location on the plains next to the main Ajmer to Agra highway, one which quickly attracted traders from across the regions and led to the city's rapidly burgeoning prosperity – which continues to the present day. The city is also unusual in north India in being based on a regular grid plan, designed in accordance with the ancient Hindu treatises, the *Vastu Shashtra*s, a formal exposition on architecture written soon after the compilation of the *Vedas*.

Jai Singh's fruitful 43-year reign was followed by an inevitable battle for succession, and the state was thrown into turmoil. Much of its territory was lost to Marathas and Jats, and the British quickly moved in to take advantage of Rajput infighting. Unlike their neighbours in Delhi and Agra, the rulers of Jaipur remained loyal to the British during the 1857 uprising. Following Independence, Jaipur merged with the states of Mewar, Bikaner, Jodhpur and Jaisalmer, becoming **state capital** of Rajasthan in 1956.

Today, with a population of around 2.5 million, Jaipur is the state's most advanced commercial and business centre and its most prosperous city, drawing in workers from the depressed rural economy – some estimates put it amongst the world's 25 fastest growing cities, with an annual population growth of over 3.5 percent. More than anywhere else in Rajasthan, Jaipur evinces the jarring paradox of India's development: while glistening new shopping malls are being erected for a newly emboldened middle class, poverty from the city's poorer districts is spilling over into the streets, now dirtier than ever, and straining limited water resources, while the entire city is choked with traffic, frequently approaching gridlock during the morning and evening rush hours.

Arrival and information

Jaipur's **railway station** lies 1.5km west of the Pink City, close to the main concentration of hotels around the western end of MI Road; state buses from all over Rajasthan and further afield pull in at the **Inter-state Bus Terminal** on Station Road. Arriving from Delhi or Agra, you skirt the southern side of the city, stopping briefly first at Narain Singh Circle, where rickshaw-wallahs frequently board the bus and, with the connivance of the bus driver, announce that it's the end of the line ("bus going to yard"); this is a ploy to get you on to

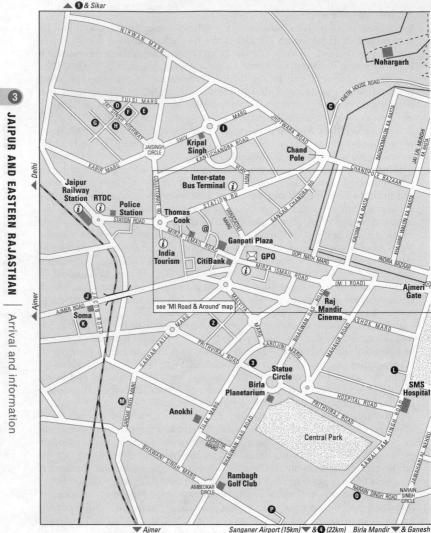

their rickshaws and into a hotel that pays generous commission. Rackets like this thrive in Jaipur, so brace yourself for a barrage of auto-rickshaw drivers wherever you arrive. The city's modern Sanganer **airport**, 15km south of the centre, is served by domestic Indian Airlines and Jet Airways flights from Delhi, Mumbai, Udaipur, Jodhpur, Ahmedebad and Kolkata (Calcutta), as well as Bangkok, Singapore, and Sharjah in the UAE. An airport bus into town costs around Rs30, a rickshaw Rs100, a taxi Rs250.

The **RTDC** has several tourist information offices around town. The most convenient are on Platform 1 of the railway station (daily 24hr; ☎0141/231 5714); at the *Tourist Hotel* on MI Road opposite the GPO (daily 8am–8pm;

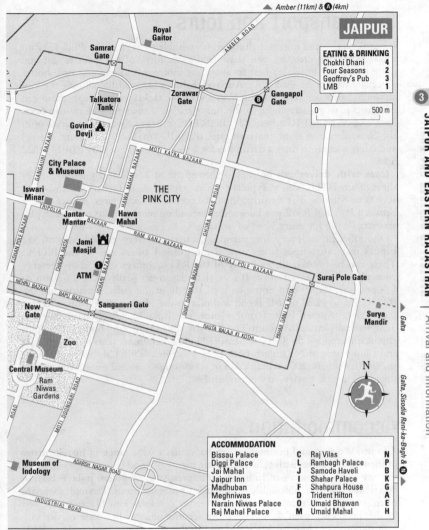

Amber (11km) & Ⓐ(4km)

JAIPUR

EATING & DRINKING
Chokhi Dhani	4
Four Seasons	2
Geoffrey's Pub	3
LMB	1

Royal Gaitor

Samrat Gate

AMBER ROAD

Zorawar Gate

Ⓑ Gangapol Gate

Talkatora Tank

0 _____ 500 m

Govind Devji

GANGAURI BAZAAR

MOTI KATRA BAZAAR

City Palace & Museum

HAWA MAHAL BAZAAR

THE PINK CITY

GHJRA NIKAS ROAD

Iswari Minar

Jantar Mantar

TRIPOLIA BAZAAR

Hawa Mahal

RAM GANJ BAZAAR

KISHAN POLE BAZAAR

CHAURA RASTA

Jami Masjid

SURAJ POLE BAZAAR

JOHARI BAZAAR

❶

ATM

GHAT DARWAJA BAZAAR

Suraj Pole Gate

NEHRU BAZAAR

BAPU BAZAAR

Sanganeri Gate

PAHAR GANJ KA RASTA

New Gate

RASTA BALAJI KI KOTHI

Surya Mandir

▶ Galta

Zoo

Central Museum

Ram Niwas Gardens

N

Galta, Sisodia Reni-ka-Bagh & Ⓝ

MOTI DOONGRI ROAD

ROAD

Museum of Indology

ADARSH NAGAR ROAD

INDUSTRIAL ROAD

ACCOMMODATION
Bissau Palace	C	Raj Vilas	N
Diggi Palace	L	Rambagh Palace	P
Jai Mahal	J	Samode Haveli	B
Jaipur Inn	I	Shahar Palace	K
Madhuban	F	Shahpura House	G
Meghniwas	D	Trident Hilton	A
Narain Niwas Palace	O	Umaid Bhawan	E
Raj Mahal Palace	M	Umaid Mahal	H

Mandir (500m)

Side tab: 3 JAIPUR AND EASTERN RAJASTHAN | Arrival and information

℡0141/237 5466); and on platform 3 at the state bus terminal (daily 9.30am–5pm). There's a third, rather difficult-to-find, office on Station Road around the back of the *Hotel Swagatam* (look for the hotel sign on the north side of the roundabout directly in front of the station); this is where you'll need to come to make bookings for the *Palace on Wheels* or *Fairy Queen* trains (see p.32). **RTDC tours** (see p.204) can be booked through any of these offices. There's an **India Tourism** office at the *Khasa Kothi* hotel (Mon–Fri 9am–6pm, Sat 9am–2pm; ℡0141/237 2200), with a good range of leaflets and countrywide information. To find out **what's on**, you're best off consulting the monthly *Jaipur City Guide* (Rs30), available at some hotels, bookshops and newspaper stalls.

203

City transport and tours

Jaipur is very spread out, and although it's possible to explore the Pink City on foot (despite the crowds), you may need some form of transport to get you there from your hotel. It's best to avoid the morning and evening rush hours, especially within the Pink City. **Auto-rickshaws** are available all over the city, although prices are relatively high, as are **cycle rickshaws**, though these can take forever to get anywhere in the heavy traffic. Unmetered yellow-top **taxis** have a stand on MI Road outside the RTDC tourist office; **radio taxis** offer the convenience of fixed, metered rates (Rs8–10/km; Rs20 minimum charge) and rarely take more than ten minutes for a pick-up; try Pink City (℡0141/222 5000).

Cars with driver can be rented through most hotels and guesthouses, or through any RTDC office. Typical costs are around Rs400 return to Amber, or Rs700 to Samode. For destinations not covered by fixed fares, expect to pay between Rs5 and Rs12 per kilometre, depending on the make of the car, plus an extra Rs100 for every hour of waiting.

One efficient and very inexpensive, though also very rushed, way to see Jaipur's main attractions is on one of the **guided tours** run by the RTDC. These can be booked through any of the RTDC offices listed above; reserve your place a day in advance. RTDC half-day tours (daily 8am, 11.30am & 1.30pm; 5hr; Rs110 plus entrance fees) start from the railway station and the RTDC *Tourist Hotel* on MI Road and take in the Hawa Mahal, Jantar Mantar, City Palace, Amber Fort, Royal Gaitor, the Birla Mandir (Laxmi Narayan Temple) and Central Museum. The full-day tour (daily 9am–6pm; Rs160 plus entrance fees) skips the Central Museum but also crams in visits to Jaigarh Fort and a lunch stop at Nahargarh Fort. They also run a "Pink City by Night" tour (6.30–10.30pm; Rs200), which takes in various sights around town, with dinner (included in ticket price) at Nahargarh Fort.

Accommodation

As a major tourist and business centre, Jaipur has a wide range of **hotels**, many of them offering excellent value. There are plenty of good budget options, while the city also boasts some of India's most impressive and opulent **palace hotels**, as well as a batch of thoroughly dilapidated former mansions, although these are often stronger on atmosphere than on creature comforts. Few places are located in the Pink City itself, however; most accommodation lies west of the city centre, along (or close to) MI Road and in the upmarket suburb of Bani Park. Wherever you choose to stay, it's a good idea to **book ahead**, particularly around the Pushkar camel *mela* (early Nov) and the Elephant Festival (first half of March).

Budget to mid-range

Arya Niwas Sansar Chandra Rd ℡0141/237 2456, ⊛www.aryaniwas.com. Dependable if uninspiring hotel – particularly popular with tour groups. Rooms (air-cooled or a/c) are a mixed bag: all are comfortable enough, though rather drab. The hotel's nicest feature is its large lawn, flanked by a spacious veranda lined with cane chairs, and a lovely little library-cum-lounge decorated with Shekhawati-style murals. There's also a small bookshop and a dull little cafeteria (but no bar or pool). ❸–❹

Atithi 1 Park House Scheme, just off MI Rd ℡0141/237 8679, ℮atithijaipur@hotmail.com. This long-established guesthouse is still one of the nicer budget places in town, with a welcoming

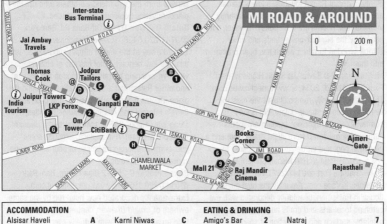

MI ROAD & AROUND

0   200 m

N

ACCOMMODATION			
Alsisar Haveli	A	Karni Niwas	C
Arya Niwas	B	Mansingh Towers	E
Atithi Guest House	D	Pearl Palace	G
Evergreen Guest House	H	Sunder Palace	F

EATING & DRINKING			
Amigo's Bar	2	Natraj	7
Barista's	9	Niro's	8
Copper Chimney	4	Om Tower Restaurant	2
Dasaprakash	6	Pearl Palace Restaurant	G
Lassiwala	3	Sankalp	5
Mediterraneo	1		

ambience and spotlessly clean tiled rooms, although at slightly higher prices than some other similar places nearby. There's also Internet access, an attractive rooftop terrace and a small garden. ❸–❹

Diggi Palace SMS Hospital Rd ☏0141/237 3091, ☝www.hoteldiggipalace.com. One of the city's best-value heritage hotels, occupying a characterful, rambling 200-year-old haveli set amidst attractive gardens. The more expensive rooms (with a/c) are nicely furnished, and some also have soothing garden views. The budget rooms (air-cooled) are smaller and plainer, though reasonable value, especially when you factor in the atmospheric setting. The very central location is another plus, and there's also Internet access, an a/c restaurant and bar, and money-changing facilities. ❹–❻

Evergreen Guest House Chameliwala Market, just off MI Rd ☏0141/236 3446, ☝www.hotel evergreen.net. This long-established place remains one of the most popular backpacker guesthouses in the city, though there are now much nicer and better-value places to stay. Ongoing renovations may improve things a bit, but for the moment rooms are bare, shabby and overpriced. Plus points include the large, tranquil gardens, the central location, and (if you like that kind of thing) the chance to hang out with dozens of young travellers. There's a small pool in summer (Rs100 for non-guests), plus Internet and money-changing facilities. Note that the guesthouse isn't signposted from

Mirza Ismail Rd, so is easily missed: to reach it, turn right by the *Moti Mahal* restaurant and head to the far end of the narrow alleys of Chameliwala Market; it can also be reached from the south via Ashok Marg. ❷–❺

Jaipur Inn Shiv Marg, Bani Park ☏0141/220 1121, ☝www.jaipurinn.com. Once the top budget option in Jaipur, this drab-looking hostel has now been left for dead by the competition, and its bare and rather overpriced rooms (and sludge-coloured concrete architecture) are unlikely to win many admirers. Having said that, the place still offers a passable fallback if you can't get in anywhere nicer, while plus points include the rooftop yoga sessions and Keralan Ayurvedic treatments, and there's also a cheap, though cramped, dorm (Rs150 per person). ❸–❹

Karni Niwas C-5 Motilal Atal Rd (behind Neelam Hotel) ☏0141/236 5433, ☝www.hotelkarniniwas .com. One of the longest-running guesthouses in Jaipur, this simple little place retains a homely ambience and sociable atmosphere, with pleasant communal seating on outside balconies overlooking a small garden. Rooms (air-cooled or a/c) aren't quite as nice, or as good value, as other places nearby, although rates are discounted by up to a third in summer. ❸–❺

Madhuban D-237 Behari Marg, Bani Park ☏0141/220 0033, ☝www.madhuban.net. Less imposing and atmospheric than the city's other "heritage" hotels (it's more of an overgrown suburban villa than a genuine palace), though with plenty of quaint Rajput touches, a lovely garden and small pool round the back, and a pleasantly intimate feel. Rooms are a bit pokey, however, not helped by the big four-poster beds and other chintzy wooden furniture which has been crammed into them. ❻

Meghniwas C-9 Sawai Jai Singh Highway, Bani Park ☎0141/220 2034, ⊛www.meghniwas.com. This modern, family-run hotel isn't the most inspiring place to stay in Jaipur, but is very comfortable, with spacious modern a/c rooms (although some suffer from slight road noise) and a nice little pool and garden around the back. ❻–❼

🏃 **Pearl Palace** Hari Kishan Somani Marg, Hathroi Fort ☎0141/237 3700, ⊛www .hotelpearlpalace.com. Arguably the best guest-house in Rajasthan, beautifully decorated with eye-catching local arts and crafts adorning every available surface and a selection of spacious, spotless and excellent-value modern air-cooled and a/c rooms. The well-drilled staff can take care of all your needs, from mailing postcards to booking bus tickets, and there's a handy in-house 24hr money exchange, Internet access, and an excellent rooftop restaurant (see p.217). Usually fills up early, so advance bookings recommended. ❸

Shahar Palace Off Ajmer Rd, Barwada Colony, Civil Lines ☎0141/222 1861, ⊛www .shaharpalace.com. Very peaceful family-run guest-house, set in a spacious, tranquil garden with large lawns to loll about on and a cute Shih-tzu dog to keep you entertained. The older air-cooled and a/c rooms are cosy and comfortable, and there are also three large but rather expensive new modern a/c rooms. Internet access available. ❸–❻

🏃 **Shahpura House** Devi Marg, Bani Park ☎0141/220 3392, ⊛www.shahpurahouse .com. The most characterful of the heritage hotels in this part of town, superbly decorated with lavish Shekhawati-style murals and with lovely Rajput architectural touches throughout. Amenities are good too, with comfortable rooms (all with a/c, minibar and bathtub) attractively furnished with old wooden furniture, plus a small pool, bar, money-changing facilities, and puppet shows and cultural dances most evenings. ❻–❼

🏃 **Sunder Palace** Sanjay Marg, Hathroi Fort, Ajmer Rd ☎0141/236 0178 or 0878 ⊛www.sunderpalace.com. Along with the *Pearl Palace*, this sparkling new guesthouse is the city's standout budget option. The spacious and spotless modern rooms are a bargain; all have deliciously crisp central air-cooling, while more expensive ones also come with a/c. There's also a choice of garden and rooftop restaurants with good food, plus reliable Internet access and outstanding

service from the two friendly brothers who run the place. Advance bookings recommended. ❸–❹

Umaid Bhawan D1-2A Off Bank Rd, Bani Park ☎0141/220 6426, ⊛www.umaidbhawan.com. Tucked away at the end of a quiet suburban street, this low-key heritage hotel has lots of character, with eye-catching murals, old wooden furnishings and other Rajasthani artefacts scattered around the place. Rooms (all a/c) are spacious and cool, and there's Internet and money exchange facilities, along with a pool, WiFi in the lobby, and a pleasant rooftop restaurant. A nice place, although some guests have reported instances of poor service and sporadic overcharging. ❺–❻

Umaid Mahal C-20/B-2 Bihari Marg, Bani Park ☎0141/220 1952, ⊛www.umaidmahal.com. Extravagantly decorated new hotel run by the same owners of *Umaid Bhawan*, centred around a pretty little arcaded atrium, with virtually every surface covered in a surfeit of flamboyant Shekhawati-style murals. The spacious a/c rooms are nicely furnished with antique-style wooden furniture, and there are also Internet and WiFi facilities, while a rooftop pool is under construction. ❻

Expensive

Alsisar Haveli Sansar Chandra Rd ☎0141/236 8290, ⊛www.alsisar.com. An unexpectedly upmarket haven in a rather ramshackle part of town, occupying a large and immaculately modern-ized century-old haveli. It's not the most atmos-pheric heritage hotel in Jaipur, though standards of service and comfort are high, and the public areas retain considerable charm, especially the superb old dining hall and the lovely Sheesh Mahal, while the pool (non-guests Rs100) is one of the prettiest in town. ❼

Bissau Palace Khetri House Rd ☎0141/230 4371, ⊛www.bissaupalace.com. Tucked away in a rather down-at-heel part of town, this attractive old heritage hotel, occupying the former summer home of the *rawas* of Bissau, is less flash than others in Jaipur but has plenty of old-world atmosphere, especially the gorgeous Sheesh Mahal and the antiquey library; modern facilities include a decent-size pool and a Jacuzzi. Good value in summer, when rates can fall by fifty percent. ❼

Jai Mahal Jacob Rd, Civil Lines ☎0141/222 3636, ⊛www.tajhotels.com. One of the smartest addresses in the city after the Rambagh Palace, this palatial former residence of the Jaipur state PM offers a genuine taste of Rajput splendour, with rambling red and yellow buildings set around beautiful gardens and elegantly furnished rooms in a stylish blend of traditional and contemporary decor. Facilities include a spa, pool (guests only), tennis court, yoga sessions and a jogging track. Prices start from US$300. ⑨

Mansingh Towers Sansar Chandra Rd ☎0141/237 8771, 🌐www.mansinghhotels.com. Modern hotel occupying an attractive red sandstone building with graceful Rajput decorative touches. Rooms are comfortable, albeit fairly characterless, and the conveniently central location is another plus. There are further rooms (same price) in the more run-of-the-mill *Mansingh Hotel* next door, which also has a pool, health club, spa and beauty salon, all of which can be used by guests at the *Tower*. Prices from around US$170. ⑨

Narain Niwas Palace Kanota Bagh, Narayan Singh Rd ☎0141/256 1291, 🌐www.hotel narainniwas.com. This grand haveli, 2km from the Pink City, has plenty of old-world charm but is looking a bit run-down and grubby in places. The pretty dining room and verandah lounge are appealingly atmospheric, but the rooms are uninspiring, with mismatched furniture and poky bathrooms. There's also a medium-sized but very shallow pool (non-guests Rs150), and a new spa should also have opened by the time you read this. Pleasant enough, but there are more attractive and better-value heritage hotels at this price, or less. ⑦

Raj Mahal Palace Sardar Patel Marg ☎0141/510 5666, 🌐www.royalfamilyjaipur.com. This elegant former palace of Jai Singh's favourite maharani has hosted notables ranging from Queen Elizabeth and Jackie Kennedy to the daughters of both General Franco and Mussolini (though not, presumably, all at the same time). The whole place has plenty of period charm, with a grand old banqueting hall, wood-panelled library and spacious lawns, plus a medium-size pool (non-guests Rs150). Rooms (all a/c) are large and old-fashioned and a bit past their best, but still good value at current rates, with further discounts in low season. ⑦

Raj Vilas Goner Rd, 7km from the city centre ☎0141/268 0101, 🌐www.oberoihotels.com. The finest accommodation in Jaipur, this dreamy resort occupies a superb fake Rajasthani fort-style complex beautifully landscaped with pools and pavilions. Accommodation is either in delectable creamy rooms (US$660) with teak four-posters and sunken Italian marble baths looking out into

your own private ornamental garden, or in luxury a/c tents (US$770) with Burma teak floors and embroidered canopies – camping out was never this much fun. There are all the mod-cons and facilities you'd expect at this price, including a beautiful spa. ⑨

🏃 **Rambagh Palace** Bhawani Singh Marg ☎0141/221 1919, 🌐www.tajhotels.com. This opulent palace complex, set amid 47 acres of beautiful gardens, is indisputably the grandest hotel in Jaipur, and one of the most romantic places to stay in India. Rooms are superbly equipped, with Rajasthani artworks, reproduction antique furniture and all mod-cons. Facilities include the suave *Swarna Mahal* restaurant featuring Indian regional specialities, and the veranda cafe with Rajasthani folk dancers every evening, while there's also a health club, indoor and outdoor pools (guests only), Ayurvedic massages and buggy rides around the grounds. Even if you can't afford a room, call in for a tea (from Rs250) and a walk around the palace. Doubles from US$500. ⑨

🏃 **Samode Haveli** Gangapole ☎0141/263 2407, 🌐www.samode.com. In an unbeatably central location amidst the tangled streets on the northeastern edge of the Pink City, this superb old haveli is brimful of atmosphere, centred on an idyllic rambling central courtyard and with the fanciest pool in town, surrounded by huge canopied loungers the size of double beds. Rooms are a mishmash: some are functional, modern and fairly characterless; other, like the richly mirrored Sheesh Mahal suites, are pure museum pieces; and others are a bit of both – ask to see several before you make a choice. Prices from around US$240. A good deal in summer (May–Sept), when rates can fall by up to 40 percent. ⑨

Trident Hilton Amber Rd, 4km from Jaipur ☎0141/257 0101, 🌐www.hilton.com. Low-key modern hotel set slightly out of town on the road to Amber – a decent choice if you prize quiet and creature comforts over atmosphere. Rooms are neat and comfortable (if on the small size) and there are all the usual five-star facilities including a medium-sized outdoor heated pool, a multi-cuisine restaurant, small gym and a kids' club. Prices start from US$225. ⑨

The city

Jaipur's attractions fall into three distinct areas. At the heart of the urban sprawl, the historic **Pink City** is where you'll find the fine City Palace, along with the Jantar Mantar observatory and Hawa Mahal, plus myriad teeming bazaars stuffed with enticing Rajasthani handicrafts. The much leafier and less hectic area **south of the Pink City** is home to the Ram Niwas Gardens, Central Museum, Birla Mandir and a handful of other low-key sights. Finally, the city's **outskirts** are dotted with a string of intriguing relics of royal rule, most notably the fort of Nahargarh, the cenotaphs at Royal Gaitor, and the temples (and monkeys) of Galta.

③ The Pink City

At the heart of Jaipur lies Jai Singh's original capital, popularly known as the **Pink City**, enclosed by lofty walls and imposing gateways which were designed to offer it some measure of protection against hostile forces, and which still serve to physically demarcate it from the sprawling modern suburbs around. One of the Pink City's most striking features is its regular **grid-plan**, with wide, dead-straight streets, laid out at right angles and broadening to spacious plazas at major intersections. The design was created in accordance with the *Vastu Shastras*, a series of ancient Hindu architectural treatises, whereby the entire layout can be read as a kind of *mandala*, or sacred diagram, in which the city becomes a divinely ordained part of the cosmic design – and also offers a notable contrast to the wildly irregular street plans of most north Indian cities (although similar divinely inspired urban grids are relatively common in the South Indian temple towns of Tamil Nadu).

The city's other striking feature is its uniform **pink colour**, intended to camouflage the poor-quality materials from which its buildings were originally constructed and lend the whole place a roseate hue reminiscent of the great imperial marble monuments of the Mughals (the design was briefly tampered with in the 1860s before being restored to its original regal pink, an event which led to the widely held but erroneous belief that the uniform colour scheme was a nineteenth-century innovation).

The neatly rectilinear streets are home to Jaipur's three most famous monuments – the **Hawa Mahal**, **City Palace** and **Jantar Mantar** observatory – as well as an extraordinary collection of **bazaars**, with different trades and crafts allotted their own streets within the grid. Johari Bazaar, for example, is full of shops selling silver, jewellery and textiles, while Chaura Rasta is the place to go for Hindi books, textbooks and stationery, and Kishanpole is devoted to bicycle shops and other types of hardware – a fascinating list detailing all the various traditional trades practised in the Pink City, and where to find them, is printed at the back of the *Jaipur City Guide* (see p.203). For more on **shopping** in Jaipur, see p.217.

Hawa Mahal

Jaipur's most acclaimed landmark, the tapering **Hawa Mahal**, or "Palace of Winds" (daily 9am–4.30pm; Rs5, camera Rs30, video Rs70), stands to the east of the City Palace. Largely gutted, it is best appreciated from the outside during the early morning, when it exudes an orangey-pink glow in the rays of the rising sun. Built in 1799 to enable the women of the court to watch street processions while remaining in strict purdah, its five-storey facade, decked out with no fewer than 593 finely screened windows and balconies, makes the building seem far larger than it really is; in fact it is little more than one room thick in most parts. You can go inside the palace itself (entrance is from the lane which runs south from Tripola Bazaar around the back of the palace, a five-minute walk from the front). It's fairly unimpressive (and there's not much of it, either), but the screened niches from which the ladies of the court would once have looked down still offer unparalleled views over the multitudinous mayhem of Jaipur far below.

Forts and palaces of Rajasthan

Few sights are as emblematic of Rajasthan as the massive forts – often perched dramatically atop craggy hilltops above the surrounding countryside – which dot the state, an image which vividly encapsulates the region's martial heritage and turbulent past. The stark simplicity and brute strength of these military strongholds presents a striking contrast to the richly decorated royal palaces which grew up within many of them, and whose fancifully decorated pavilions, apartments and gardens provide a showcase of Rajasthani architecture at its most flamboyant.

Rajput retreats

The possession of a serviceable **fort** (denoted in Hindi by the suffix -*garh*) underpinned the power and influence of all Rajput rulers – the great Mewar ruler Rana Kumbha, for instance, built or restored no less than 32, bringing his kingdom's tally to a staggering 84. Rajputana's mightiest dynasties generally boasted strategically situated and impregnable citadels, the most famous being those at **Meherangarh** (at Jodhpur), **Chittaurgarh** and **Amber**.

Some forts remained no more than military outposts from which to command the surrounding countryside. Others (such as Chittaurgarh and **Jaisalmer**) grew into self-contained fortified settlements housing sizeable towns. Still others (such as **Amber** and **Bundi**) developed into lavish palace complexes, their huge, simple exterior walls giving no hint of the beauty of the buildings and artworks inside, ranging from the delicately mirrored apartments of Amber to the exquisite murals of Bundi's City Palace – a stark contrast to the harsh desert outside.

The evolving history of Rajasthan can be read in the development of its forts and palaces. The earliest – such as Chittaurgarh, Amber, **Kumbalgarh** and the Bala Qila at **Alwar** – place the emphasis firmly on security over aesthetics, generally located in positions of maximum military strength (usually meaning the top of a hill) with sheer expanses of windowless walls, numerous strategically positioned gateways to repel attackers and enormous defensive ramparts and bastions (those at Kumbalgarh snake around the surrounding hills for an astonishing 36km). Later structures show a diminishing attention to military concerns. The City Palace at **Udaipur**, for example, is more palace than fort, while the region's city palaces, such as those at **Jaipur** and Alwar, demonstrate little concern with self-defence, reflecting the more settled times in which they were built.

Kingly pleasures

In the years since Independence, many maharajas and other Rajput royals have had problems making ends meet and in maintaining their vast ancestral family homes. The obvious solution for many has been to convert their forts, palaces and other properties into hotels, meaning that foreign hoi polloi can now stay in many of the region's finest palaces and enjoy sumptuous accommodation which was formerly the preserve of a privileged royal few. The ultimate palace stays are to be had at the *Lake Palace* and *Fateh Prakash Palace* hotels in Udaipur, at the *Rambagh Palace* in Jaipur, and at the *Umaid Bhawan Palace* in Jodhpur, but there are now dozens of heritage hotels across the region offering more intimate (and much more affordable) options.

Pieces of a palace

The layout and organization of the typical Rajput palace (in Hindi, *mahal*, pronounced "mahel") shows many similarities with those of their great Mughal adversaries, based on shared views of the nature of kingship, courtly life, and the status of women. The region's forts and palaces are typically entered through one or more gateways (*pole* or *pol*), often flanked by triumphal statues of regal elephants. Inside, palaces are divided into male and female quarters, the mardana and zenana respectively. Each usually comprises a series of constituent palaces and apartments, usually set around their own courtyard, or chowk (pronounced "chalk"). Typically these include a khas mahal, the ruler's private apartment, plus a range of other chambers usually adorned with fanciful names – *phool mahal* (flower palace), *moti mahal* (pearl palace) and *sukh mahal* (palace of bliss) are a few favoured appellations. The *zenana* sections of many palaces also include a small room covered in mirrorwork mosaics (a Mughal innovation, enthusiastically adopted by Rajput nobles) known generically as the sheesh (or shish) mahal. Imagining exactly how these apartments would originally have looked, however, requires a certain level of imagination. Private rooms and pavilions in Rajput palaces didn't normally have a fixed function or contain large pieces of heavy furniture in the manner of Western dwellings, but were filled with easily movable soft furnishings such as carpets, draperies and bolsters, enabling them to be adapted to varying functions at will.

Later Rajput palaces, including those at Amber, Jaipur and Bundi, also followed Mughal tradition in having two audience chambers, the diwan-i-am (hall of public audience), usually a large open-sided pavilion in which all classes of local society could come to lay their problems before the ruler; and the diwan-i-khas (hall of private audience), a much smaller pavilion tucked away in the depths of the palace in which the king would discuss matters of state with his ministers and advisors. Many palaces, such as those at Udaipur, Bundi and Alwar, are placed next to a lake (*sagar*) or reservoir, guaranteeing a ready supply of water – even the hilltop citadel of Chittaurgarh was supplied with several reservoirs, allowing it to withstand long sieges.

▲ Amber Fort

Five top Rajput forts and palaces

- **Amber Palace** Elegant blend of Rajasthani and Mughal architectural traditions, dramatically perched atop a craggy hill just north of Jaipur.

- **Chittaurgarh Fort** The archetypal Rajput fortress, as famous for its blood-soaked history as for its superb collection of temples, palaces and other monuments.

- **Jaisalmer Fort** Stunning desert citadel, its huge bastions enclosing a fascinating tangle of alleyways, havelis and intricately carved Jain temples.

- **Meherangarh Fort** Rajasthan's most impressive military creation, set atop a rocky outcrop overlooking the city of Jodhpur in massive, impregnable splendour.

- **Udaipur City Palace** Rajasthan's ultimate royal palace, with a labyrinthine assortment of palaces, courtyards and superbly decorated apartments in a spectacular lakeside location.

▲ Jaisalmer havelis ▼ Diwan-i-Am, Agra Fort

City Palace

The magnificent **City Palace** (daily 9.30am–5pm; Rs180, plus Rs200 for video; same ticket also valid for Jaigarh Fort at Amber if used within two days), open to the public as the **Sawai Man Singh Museum**, stands enclosed by a high wall in the centre of the city. The palace was originally built by Jai Singh, who constructed the palace to enclose the Jai Niwas pleasure gardens and hunting lodge which occupied the site before the foundation of Jaipur. Many of the apartments and halls were added by his successors, but the exhibits and interior design have lost none of the pomp and splendour of their glory days. Each door and gateway is heavily decorated, each chandelier intact and each hall guarded by turbaned retainers decked out in full royal livery, so that Jaipur's palace impresses upon the visitor the continuity of a living royal presence.

The royal family still occupies part of the palace, advancing in procession on formal occasions through the grand **Tripolia Gate** in the centre of the southern wall. Less exalted visitors must enter through the **Udaipole** gate on the northwest side of the complex. Official guides wait outside the ticket booth offering one-hour tours of the complex (Rs150 for up to four people). On the far side of the Udaipole gate lies the small **Diwan-i-Am courtyard**, with a collection of old carriages tucked into one end.

Continue straight ahead through another gate to reach the first of the palace's two main courtyards, painted a deep salmon pink and centred on the raised **Diwan-i-Khas** (Hall of Private Audience). Open-sided, with its roof raised on marble pillars, this was the place in which all important decisions of state were taken by the maharaja and his advisors. The hall contains two silver urns, or *gangajalis*, listed in the *Guinness Book of Records* as the largest crafted silver objects in the world, each more than 1.5m high with a capacity of 8182 litres. When Madho Singh II went to London to attend the coronation of King Edward VII in 1901, he was so reluctant to trust the water in the West that he had these urns filled with Ganges water and took them along with him. On the far (west) side of the Diwan-i-Khas courtyard, a small corridor leads through to the **Pritam Niwas Chowk**, known as the "Peacock Courtyard". This courtyard gives the best view of the soaring yellow **Chandra Mahal**, the residence of the royal family (and closed to the public), its heavily balconied seven-storey facade rising to a slope-shouldered summit, with the maharaja's flag (and its miniature companion – see box, p.210) flying from the topmost pavilion.

On the opposite (east) side of the Diwan-i-Khas courtyard, beneath the large clocktower, another door takes you into the ornate **Diwan-i-Am** (Hall of Public Audience; also reachable from the Diwan-i-Am courtyard near the entrance). The intricately painted walls provide perfect mounts for immense medieval Afghan and Persian carpets, while a sequence of ornate palanquins occupy the centre of the room. Miniature paintings from the Mughal and Jaipur schools, and Jai Singh's translations in Arabic and Sanskrit of the astronomical treatises of ancient scientists such

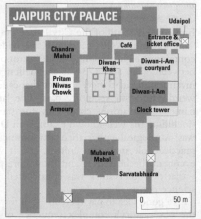

JAIPUR CITY PALACE

Udaipol

Entrance & ticket office

Café

Chandra Mahal

Diwan-i-Khas

Diwan-i-Am courtyard

Pritam Niwas Chowk

Diwan-i-Am

Armoury

Clock tower

Mubarak Mahal

Sarvatabhadra

0   50 m

Tripolia Gate

One-and-a-quarter maharajas

Prior to his accession to the throne, the young Jai Singh (see p.201) – the Kachchwaha heir apparent and future founder of Jaipur – was sent for a period to the Mughal court to demonstrate his fealty to the imperial overlords. The young Rajput's wit and sharpness so impressed the then emperor, Aurangzeb, that the crusty old Muslim potentate described him as *sawai*, or "one-and-a-quarter", implying that even as a young teenager, Jai Singh already added up to more than the average man.

The soubriquet stuck. Upon attaining the throne of Amber, the new ruler adopted *sawai* as part of his official title – Sawai Jai Singh II – and the honorific was subsequently adopted by all following rulers of Jaipur, becoming an integral part of the city's royal traditions; look up at the flag of Jaipur flying over the maharaja's apartments in the City Palace's Chandra Mahal and you'll see a miniature, *sawai*-sized replica fluttering next to it on the flagpole. It also accounts for the unusual name of the town of Sawai Madhopur, near Ranthambore National Park, named after one of Jaipur's eighteenth-century rulers, Sawai Madho Singh I.

as Euclid and Ptolemy, are displayed in glass cases, along with some superb early manuscripts, scrolls and palm-leaf books, some written in text of microscopic fineness.

An ornate elephant gateway, its southern side guarded by a pair of fine stone elephants, leads from the Diwan-i-Khas courtyard into the second main courtyard, the **Sarvatabhadra**, painted a rich red with yellow trimmings. At the centre of the courtyard lies the elegant **Mubarak Mahal**, with finely carved stone arches and a verandah encircling the whole of the upper storey. Built as a reception hall in 1899, the building now holds the museum's **textile collection**, housing examples of the tie-dyed, block-printed and elaborately woven and brocaded fabrics from the royal wardrobe. These include lavishly embroidered *chaugas* (formal long-sleeved coats), voluminous quilted *atam sukhs* for the cold winter months, plus wedding costumes, polo suits and a very fine "billiard dress" created for Ram Singh II (1835–1880), complete with fancifully decorated cue. On the north side of the courtyard, a further series of rooms is given over to the museum's **Armoury**, filled with the usual collection of blood-curdling, albeit beautifully decorated, knives, swords and guns.

Jantar Mantar

Immediately south of the City Palace lies the remarkable **Jantar Mantar** (daily 9am–4.30pm; Rs10, camera Rs50, video Rs100), a large grassy enclosure containing eighteen huge stone astronomical measuring devices constructed between 1728 and 1734 at the behest of Jai Singh, many of them his own invention, their strange, abstract shapes lending the whole place the look of a weirdly futuristic sculpture park. The Jantar Mantar is one of five identically named observatories created by the star-crazed Jai Singh across north India (including the well-known example in Delhi; see p.107), though his motivation was astrological rather than astronomical. Astrology has always played a key practical role in Indian culture, and it was in order to more accurately map events in the heavens – and thus more precisely predict their effects on earth – that the observatory was constructed, rather than from any abstract love of science per se.

It's a good idea to pay (Rs100–150) for the services of a **guide** to explain how the observatory's complex sequence of instruments work. Using Greek and

△ Jantar Mantar observatory, Jaipur

Arabic brass astronomical devices as a model, the instruments were designed so that shadows fall onto marked surfaces, identifying the position and movement of stars and planets, telling the time, and even predicting the intensity of the monsoon. The time calculated is unique to Jaipur, between ten and forty-one minutes (depending on the time of year) behind Indian standard time, but is used to calculate the Hindu (lunar) calendar.

Probably the most impressive of the observatory's constructions is the 27-metre high sundial, the **Samrat Yantra**, which can calculate the time to within two seconds. A more original device, the **Jaiprakash Yantra**, consists of two hemispheres laid in the ground, each composed of six curving marble slabs with a suspended ring in the centre, whose shadow marks the day, time and zodiac symbol – vital for the calculation of auspicious days for marriage. It's from the word *yantra* (instrument), incidentally, that the observatory gets its quirky name, "Jantar" being a slang version of *yantra*, and "mantar" from *mantra* (formula), altered to rhyme – a typical example of Hindi wordplay.

Govind Devji

North of the city palace is the Govind Devji (or Deoji), the family temple of the maharajas of Jaipur, although it also remains enduringly popular with the hoi polloi of Jaipur, who flock here in droves for the evening puja around 6pm, its popularity attested to by the dozens of shops clustered around the entrance selling religious offerings and other godly paraphernalia. The temple is dedicated to Krishna in his character of Govinda, the amorous cowherd whose dalliances with Radha and the *gopis* form one of the main subjects of Rajasthani art. The principal shrine houses an image of Govinda brought from Vrindavan (near Agra) in 1735, which is considered the guardian deity of the rulers of Jaipur.

The temple building itself occupies an unusual open-sided pavilion, more like a Mughal audience hall than a traditional Hindu temple. Local tradition states that it was originally a palace pavilion, but that Krishna appeared to Jai Singh in a dream and expressed a fondness for the building, after which the dutiful maharaja had it converted into a temple. Whatever the building's origins, the open-sided structure had the notable advantage in that Govinda's shrine could be seen by the maharaja from his rooms in the lofty Chandra Mahal in the City Palace, thus allowing him to commune with his tutelary god without the inconvenience of having to leave his private apartments.

A large shallow pool lies around the back – until quite recently home to a healthy population of crocodiles – along with further temples and a pleasant stretch of garden.

Iswari Minar Swarg Suli

Rising from the centre of the Pink City is the slender **Iswari Minar Swarg Suli** (Heaven-piercing Minaret; daily 9am–4.30pm; Rs10, camera Rs2), whose summit offers the definitive view of old Jaipur, with fascinating views down into the tangled labyrinth of alleyways and courtyards which honeycomb the city in the spaces between the major roads, and which remain largely invisible at street level. The minaret is the only significant remaining physical evidence in Jaipur of the reign of Jai Singh II's dithering son and successor, Iswari Singh, who erected this excessively grandiose monument to celebrate his army's minor victory over a combined Maratha–Rajput force in 1747 (although bazaar gossip later claimed that the tower was built so that the maharaja could spy on local girls taking their ablutions in the houses below). The triumph was short-lived, however, and a rather more accurate assessment of Iswari Singh's modest leadership abilities is provided by the fact that he poisoned himself in 1750 rather than face the returning Marathas in battle. The entrance is around the back of the minaret, which can be reached through the small arch about 50m to the west of the minaret along Tripolia Bazaar (or, alternatively, via a second arch around 100m east of the minaret).

South of the Pink City

The leafy, low-key suburbs south of the Pink City offer a welcome respite from the relentless traffic and crowds of the centre, dotted with a handful of quirky museums and temples. These include the dusty **Central Museum**, housed in the fanciful Albert Hall, one of Rajasthan's most imposing – and most kitsch – colonial buildings, and the bizarre little **Museum of Indology**. Further south, the sumptuously marbled **Birla Mandir** provides a fittingly lavish memorial to one of India's wealthiest industrial dynasties.

Central Museum

Immediately south of the Pink City, the road leading out from New Gate is flanked by the lush **Ram Niwas Gardens**, named after their creator, Ram Singh, who ruled Jaipur from 1835 to 1880. The gardens' centrepiece is the florid **Albert Hall** of 1867, designed by British architect Sir Samuel Jacob in a whimsical mix of Venetian and Mughal styles (Italian below, and Indian on top). This eye-catching structure houses the city's **Central Museum** (daily except Fri 10am–5pm; Rs30; photography prohibited inside the museum, though photos are allowed from the rooftop for an additional Rs30). The museum is a real colonial relic, from the Victorian-era decor to the mildewed exhibits themselves, which appear not to have been dusted since the nineteenth century. The **ground floor** features displays (complete with little model people) on assorted Rajasthani ethnic groups and their cultures, plus examples of the region's myriad artisanal traditions in media ranging from stone to camel hide (though the display case meant to hold objects made from gold is suspiciously empty). The first-floor **library** has a good selection of eighteenth- and nineteenth-century miniatures from the Mughal and Jaipur schools. From here you can climb up to the fancifully decorated terraces and pavilions which crown the rooftop, with breezy views out over the surrounding parkland.

Next to the museum, the city's **zoo** (daily except Tues: mid-March to mid-Oct 8.30am–5.30pm; mid-Oct to mid-March 9am–5pm; foreign visitors Rs100, Indian residents Rs10, camera Rs25, video Rs100) is a fairly depressing affair, with animals kept in grim conditions, while the hiked-up entry price for foreigners is a further turn-off.

Museum of Indology
Further south, off Jawaharlal Nehru Road, the **Museum of Indology** (daily 8am–6pm; Rs40 including guided tour, plus tip) holds assorted curiosities collected by the late writer and painter Acharya Vyakul stuffed into what is – despite the grandiose name – basically just a rambling suburban house. Exhibits include oddities such as a map of India painted on a grain of rice, letters written on a hair and a glass bed, along with enormous quantities of hopeless junk, all heaped up together in great mouldering piles – it's all fairly unedifying, and whatever one might get out of the strange little collection is largely negated by the resident caretaker, whose whistle-stop tour and largely incomprehensible "explanations" are followed by inevitable demands for further cash.

Birla Mandir and around
Flanking the roadside a kilometre south of the Museum of Indology stands the **Birla Mandir** (summer 6am–noon & 3–9pm; winter 6.30am–noon & 3–8.30pm), or Laxmi Narayan Temple, a flashy marble edifice built by the fabulously wealthy Birla family, the creators of one of India's largest industrial corporations, who originally hailed from the town of Pilani in Shekhawati. The dazzlingly white exterior is embellished with fine carvings and statues featuring an eclectic array of religious figures including Jesus, SS Anthony and Peter, Confucius, Zarathustra and Socrates. The spacious, bare interior and large stained-glass windows give the place a slightly churchy feel, while images of Lakshmi (the goddess of wealth, with whom the billionaire Birlas clearly feel a close affinity) and Narayan (a form of Vishnu) stand in the shrine at the far end, with a finely carved dome overhead; also note the Ganesh over the entrance door, whose marble has been so finely carved that it has become almost transparent. A very modest little **museum** (same hours; free) occupies one side of the temple building, housing photos of the Birla family, plus a few family mementoes. Overlooking the temple is the diminutive **Moti Dungri** fort, perched atop a steep-sided hillock and surrounded by thick walls – an eye-catching little stronghold, though sadly it's closed to visitors.

Just north of the Birla Mandir is the altogether livelier and more down-at-heel **Ganesh Mandir**. A string of little shops outside sell various offerings, including the little round sweets (*ladoos*) which are popularly offered to the rotund orange Ganesh figure inside the temple – although judging by the size of his capacious pot belly it looks as if he has had quite enough to eat already.

Outlying sights
The rocky hills which overlook Jaipur to the north and east are home to a string of spectacularly situated forts and temples, all reachable via steep paths climbing

up from the city (or, for the less energetic, via longer roads around the back of the hills). Closest to the city centre, the old royal fort and palace at **Nahargarh** offers superlative views, as does the path up past the Surya Mandir to the atmospheric temples at **Galta** – popularly known as the "Monkey Palace" thanks to its large population of engaging macaques. The grandiose marble *chhatris* at **Royal Gaitor**, last resting place of Jaipur's royal family, are also worth a visit, most easily combined with a trip to Amber.

Nahargarh

Teetering on the edge of the hills north of Jaipur, **Nahargarh**, or "Tiger Fort" (open 24hr; free), was built by Jai Singh II in 1734. The imposing walls of the fort sprawl for the best part of a kilometre along the ridgetop, although the only significant surviving structures within are the **palace apartments** (daily 10pm–5.30pm; Rs5, camera Rs30, video Rs70), built inside the old fort by Madho Singh II between 1883 and 1892 as a love nest in which he housed a selection of his most treasured concubines away from the disapproving eyes of his courtiers and four official wives. The large and rather plain pale pink structure is filled with dozens of virtually identical rooms – all retaining their simple original floral decorations, though most are now defaced by layers of modern graffiti – and a disorienting labyrinth of corridors and stairwells arranged around a large central courtyard; the perplexing layout was allegedly designed to allow the canny Madho Singh to come and go at will without anyone being aware of his movements.

The main reason for coming up here, however, is to sample the superb views of Jaipur, best enjoyed towards dusk over a beer at the *Padao* cafe, located at the far end of the complex, a five-minute walk past the palace at the highest point of the fortifications, from where there are fine vistas over the labyrinth of battlemented walls which encircle the fort, and the city below. Refreshments can also be found at the *Durg Cafeteria* right next to the palace, though it lacks views.

Vehicles of any kind can only get to the fort along a road that branches off Amber Road, a fifteen-kilometre journey from Jaipur. It's simpler to **walk** to the fort along the steep path that climbs up from the north side of the city centre, a stiff fifteen- to twenty-minute walk, although the path is a bit tricky to find, so you might want to take a rickshaw to the bottom. At the top of the path, go through the first gate and then head left, up the steps opposite a large bathing pool and through a second gate into the palace area, then head around to the left to reach the palace itself. It's best to avoid going up too late in the day or returning after dark – the fort is popular with delinquent teenagers and other unsavoury types, and the atmosphere can be a tad seedy at the best of times.

Royal Gaitor

On the northern edge of the city centre, the walled funerary complex of **Royal Gaitor** (daily 9am–4.30pm; free, camera Rs10, video Rs20) contains the stately marble *chhatris* commemorating the great, late members of Jaipur's ruling family. The compound consists of two main courtyards, each crammed full of imposing memorials to various maharajas both ancient and modern. The first (and more modern) courtyard is dominated by the grandiose though slightly shoddy-looking twentieth-century cenotaph of **Madho Singh II** (d. 1922), a ruler of famously gargantuan appetites, whose four wives and fifty-odd concubines bore him a grand total of "around 125" children (two of the wives and fourteen children are entombed in smaller *chhatris* directly behind). To the left of Madho Singh II's cenotaph lies that of **Man Singh II** (d. 1970), the most recent addition to the royal mausoleum.

The second, original, courtyard is dominated by the elaborate tomb of **Jai Singh II** (d. 1743), the founder of Jaipur and the first ruler to be interred at Gaitor. This is the finest of the *chhatris*, its base decorated with delicately carved elephant- and lion-hunting scenes, while the inside of the dome is covered in images from Hindu mythology. Immediately behind is the cenotaph of Jaipur's outstanding nineteenth-century ruler **Ram Singh II** (d. 1880), smaller but strikingly similar in design and fashioned out of finely carved white marble. To the right of Jai Singh's memorial lies that of **Madho Singh I** (d. 1768), a ruler of prodigious personal stature who (as the resident guide will fondly relate) reputedly stood seven feet tall and four feet broad – perhaps the result of a daily breakfast comprising a hundred chapatis and five litres of milk – although the poor man probably needed all the sustenance he could get given his entourage of nine wives and 350 concubines. Further memorials to Pratap Singh (d. 1803) and Jagat Singh (d. 1819) fill out the rest of the enclosure.

On the ridgetop above Gaitor (and reachable from it via a steep path) lies the **Ganesh Mandir**, the second of the city's two major Ganesh temples – a huge and eye-catching building instantly recognizable from the huge swastika painted on its side.

Galta

Nestling in a steep-sided valley 3km east of Jaipur, **Galta** (daily sunrise–sunset; free, camera Rs30, video Rs50) comprises a picturesque collection of 250-year-old temples squeezed into a narrow rocky ravine. Galta owes its sacred status in large part to a freshwater spring which seeps constantly through the rocks in the otherwise dry valley, keeping two **tanks** full. Traditionally humans bathe in the upper water tank, but except during the holy month of Kartika (usually Nov), the putrid-smelling ponds are the domain of over five thousand macaque monkeys that call Galta home and which have earned the place its nickname of the "Monkey Palace". For many tourists the sight of the splashing monkeys outstrips the attraction of the temples themselves, though the assorted shrines, dedicated variously to Krishna, Rama and Hanuman, are attractively atmospheric – a tiny shrine in the last (it's the one closest to the entrance on the north side of the path) is lit by a candle whose flame is claimed to have been kept burning continuously since a visit by Akbar more than four centuries ago. It's also worth walking up to the spectacularly situated **Surya Mandir**, perched above the tanks on the ridgetop overlooking Jaipur and commanding dramatic views of the city below.

The only way to reach Galta **by vehicle** is to drive the 10km or so along the road past Sisodia Rani-ka-Bagh (see below) around the hills behind Jaipur, passing through beautiful countryside en route – remarkably quiet and unspoilt given its proximity to the city. You can also **walk** to Galta, following the path beyond Suraj Pole gate on the eastern edge of the Pink City and climbing steeply up to the Surya Mandir on the crest of the hill above the main temple complex – a stiff thirty-minute walk.

Sisodia Rani-ka-Bagh

The road to Galta runs past a sequence of pleasure gardens, most of them now sadly dilapidated, established by the ruling nobility to serve as retreats from the city. The best preserved of these is the former royal palace and gardens of **Sisodia Rani-ka-Bagh** (Garden of the Sisodia Queen; daily 8am–6pm; free). The palace itself, built in the eighteenth century by Jai Singh II for the Udaipur princess he married to secure relations with his neighbouring Sisodia Rajputs, is a small but florid building covered in painted floral decorations and with a fine array of murals on its outer wall (facing the road to Galta) depicting scenes from the life of Krishna. Below the palace a sequence of walled and terraced gardens, dotted with small kiosks, marble fountains and water channels (usually dry), fall away down the hillside – a pleasant enough spot, though of no particular architectural or horticultural distinction. About 250m back up the main road to Jaipur is a second and similar palace and garden complex, the **Vidhyadhar-ka-Bagh**, currently closed to visitors, though it might reopen in future.

Eating, drinking and entertainment

Jaipur has Rajasthan's best selection of quality **restaurants**, both veg and non-veg, albeit at higher-than-average prices. Alternatively, if you're watching the pennies, most of the city's budget guesthouses serve up decent food – the restaurant at the *Pearl Palace* hotel is particularly good, with excellent Indian fare at bargain prices. Unless otherwise stated, all restaurants below are marked on the MI Road and around map (see p.205).

Barista's Bhagwan Das Rd, opposite the Raj Mandir cinema. Smart coffee house serving up excellent freshly ground coffee – as popular with Jaipur's affluent twenty-somethings as it is among caffeine-crazed foreigners. The well-stocked little attached bookshop is a bonus.

Chokhi Dhani 22km south of Jaipur on the Tonk Rd ☎0141/277 0554. See map, p.200. This Rajasthani theme-park-cum-restaurant attracts droves of well-heeled Jaipuris, especially at weekends, when the whole place gets wildly busy. The Rs250 entrance fee includes an evening meal plus access to a wide range of attractions (though tips are expected at many) – elephant, camel and bullock-cart rides, folk dances, drumming, puppet shows, archery, chapati-making demonstrations and a superb magician, to name just a few. When you've done with the entertainment, head off to the mud-walled restaurant where you'll be sat on the floor and served an authentically original (albeit very salty) Rajasthani village thali quite unlike anything you'll find in the restaurants of Jaipur, with lots of rustic rural delicacies like cornflour chapatis, Rajasthani special *gatta* (gram flour balls cooked in yoghurt) and unusual curried vegetables. It's all a bit hokey, but fun, in a rather kitsch way. A radio taxi charges Rs550 for the round trip, including wait (auto-rickshaw Rs300). Open Mon–Sat 6–11pm & Sun from 11am.

Copper Chimney MI Rd. Plush glass-fronted restaurant popular amongst both locals and tourists. The menu covers a good range of north Indian standards, plus a few local specialities like *laal maans* (special Rajasthani desert-style mutton) and *gatta*, as well as a few Chinese and continental dishes. Mains from around Rs85 (veg) and Rs140 (non-veg). It's also one of the few restaurants in town which is licensed.

Dasaprakash MI Rd. Another Rajasthan outpost of the well-known Chennai chain, this unpretentious a/c restaurant serves up a tasty range of classic South Indian veg fare – *iddlis*, vadas, uttapams, *upuma*, thalis, and no less than seventeen types of *dosa* – plus a selection of sweet-toothed ice-cream sundaes in various colourful combinations. Mains from around Rs70.

Four Seasons Bhagat Singh Marg. See map, p.203. The most popular veg restaurant in town among locals, and well off the tour group trail. Its South Indian *dosas* and uttapams are as good as you'll eat anywhere, and they serve a full selection of top north Indian specialities, Chinese food, and desserts. Huge portions cater to local tastes and can be a bit spicy. Expect a short wait for a table. Free delivery.

Lassiwala Opposite *Niro's*, MI Rd. A Jaipur institution (in summer you may have to wait half an hour to be served) for its sublime lassis, served in old-style, hygienic terracotta mugs. Its popularity has sparked a small lassi-wallah-war, with two impostors setting up shop to the right (as you face it) of the original. Closes early afternoon.

LMB Johari Bazaar. See map, p.203. The best-looking restaurant in town, with stylish chrome and coloured-glass fittings, and a convenient haven from the Pink City's packed bazaars. The food (mains from around Rs80) is disappointingly pedestrian, however, compensating for a lack of flavour with incendiary amounts of chili, while service is irritatingly intrusive. Alternatively, stick to the sweet counter outside, which dishes up a famous *paneer ghewar* (honeycomb cake soaked in treacle) and piping hot potato-and-cashew nut *tikkis* in spicy mango sauce.

Mediterraneo *Hotel Vijeet Palace*, off Sansar Chandra Rd next to the *Arya Niwas* hotel. One of the few places in central Jaipur specializing in non-Indian cuisine, this unpretentious rooftop Italian restaurant offers a welcome refuge for homesick European tastebuds, serving up a decent range of reasonably authentic pizzas (from Rs180) out of its real pizza oven, along with a fair selection of pastas, Italian-style meat dishes and even a few crepes.

Natraj MI Rd. Long-established pure veg restaurant offering a big range of North Indian standards, plus thalis, *dosas* and superb sweets – *rasmalai*, *barfi*, *halwa* and *ladoo* – piled up at the counter by the door. Mains from Rs75.

Niro's MI Rd. Along with Copper Chimney, this place gets the local vote for best non-veg food in Jaipur. The menu features a few excellent Rajasthani specialities including *sula* (lamb), *lal maans* (mutton) and *gatta* along with a big choice of tandooris, tikkas and other meat and veg curries, plus Western and Chinese dishes. Mains from Rs100. Licensed.

Om Tower Restaurant Om Tower, MI Rd. Rajasthan's first revolving restaurant, perched up on the 14th floor of the landmark Om Tower and offering fine views over the chaos of downtown Jaipur below. The head-spinning views, of course, are the main attraction, but the food is quite presentable, with a competently prepared selection of all the usual north Indian veg and non-veg standards – try the "revolving special" fruit curry with nuts and *paneer*. Prices, not surprisingly, are a bit above average, with mains from Rs120. No alcohol.

Pearl Palace Restaurant *Pearl Palace* hotel, Hari Kishan Somani Marg, Hathroi Fort. The lovely little rooftop restaurant at this excellent guesthouse gives the city's fancier restaurants a real run for their money. The decor is an attraction in its own right, with cute metal chairs and arty decor including a memorably quirky peacock canopy – all particularly pretty after dark, when it's illuminated with chains of fairy lights. There's a big menu of veg (most around Rs40) and non-veg (mostly Rs50–80) Indian options, all well prepared, with flavoursome sauces, crisp breads and cold beers, as well as a few Chinese dishes, western snacks and pizzas. Purified water is used to wash all fruit and veg.

Sankalp MI Rd. Recently relocated to suave new modern premises, *Sankalp* continues to dish up the best South Indian food in Jaipur. Choose from thirteen kinds of *dosa* – including the four-foot-long *Sankalp* special *dosa* – plus oodles of *iddlis*, *vadas*, uttapams and thalis, all excellently prepared and served with a mouthwatering array of sauces and pickles. Most mains Rs55–90.

Drinking and entertainment

For **drinks**, *Amigo's Bar*, on the ninth floor of the Om Tower, is a popular spot, the slightly shabby decor offset by fine city views, a reasonable drinks list (including a few cocktails) and surprisingly good Tex-Mex snacks. *Geoffrey's Pub* in the *Hotel Park Plaza* on Prithviraj Road is the city's most appealing English-style pub, complete with oak bar and sporting memorabilia, and with a good range of imported and domestic beers and spirits.

Several of the big five-star hotels, including the *Rambagh Palace*, host nightly culture **shows** (around Rs150), featuring folk dance, music and traditional puppetry. These can be a lot of fun, especially if they're held outdoors. Another music and dance venue is *Chokhi Dhani*, 22km south of the city (see opposite).

If you go to the **cinema** just once while you're in India, it should be at the Raj Mandir on Bhagwan Das Road just off MI Road, which boasts a stunning Art Deco lobby and 1,500-seat auditorium. Most movies have four daily showings (usually at noon, 3pm, 6.15pm and 9.30pm), and there's always a long queue, so get your tickets (Rs38–90) an hour or so before the show starts.

Shopping

If you come across an Indian **handicraft** object or garment abroad, chances are it will have been bought in Jaipur. Foreign buyers and wholesalers flock to the Pink City to shop for textiles, clothes, jewellery and pottery. In keeping with Maharaja Jai Singh's original city divisions, different streets are reserved for purveyors of different goods (see p.208). As a regular tourist, you'll find it harder to hunt out the best merchandise, but as a source of souvenirs, perhaps only Delhi can surpass it. The large, government-run Rajasthali emporium (Mon–Sat 11am–7.30pm), just south of Ajmer Gate, is a good place to get a sense of the range of handicrafts available and to gauge approximate costs – although you'll probably find similar items at cheaper prices in the Pink City bazaars. The stores along MI Road also tend to be pricier than those in the Pink City.

Clothes and textiles

Bapu bazaar, on the south side of the Pink City, is the best place for clothes and textiles, including Jaipur's famous **block-print** work and *bandhani* **tie-dye**. On the opposite side of town, along Amber Road just beyond Zorawar Gate, rows of emporiums are stacked with gorgeous patchwork wall hangings and **embroidery**; these places do a steady trade with bus parties of wealthy tourists, so be prepared to haggle hard.

For only a little more money, and a lot less hassle, head to the famous **Anokhi** showroom, 2 Tilak Marg, southwest of the city centre in the Civil Lines area (Mon–Sat 10am–7.30pm, Sun 10am–6pm; Ⓦwww.anokhi.com). Started by a British designer, it's the place to buy high-quality "ethnic" Indian evening wear, tastefully patterned *salwar kameez* and block-printed or batik men's shirts. They also do lovely bedspreads, quilts, tablecloths, and cushion covers. Anokhi now exports, and there are outlets across India, but this is the flagship store and has the widest selection. Slightly less expensive, but similar in style and quality, is **Soma** (Mon–Sat 10am–8pm, Sun 10am–6pm; Ⓦwww .somashop.com), at 5 Jacob Road, near the *Jai Mahal* hotel.

One of the best **tailors** in town, patronized by no less than the maharaja himself, is Jodhpur Tailors (Mon–Sat 10.30am–9.30pm, Sun 2–6pm), behind the *Neelam Hotel* near Ganpati Plaza on MI Rd. Hand-stitched suits run from around Rs7500 and up, or you could just pick up a shirt (from Rs700) or a pair of trousers (Rs1200) or jodhpurs (Rs1400).

Pottery

For old-style Persian-influenced vases, plus tiles, plates and candleholders, visit the outlets of the city's renowned **blue potteries** along Amber Road. For top-quality blue pottery, Jaipur's most famous ceramist, Kripal Singh, has a shop at B-18A Shiv Marg, Bani Park (Ⓣ0141/220 1127), in the northwest of town. Bear in mind that Jaipur's blue pottery is essentially decorative; none of it – in spite of what some shop owners tell you – should be used for hot food as the glazes are unstable and poisonous.

Jewellery and gemstones

The two best places for silver jewellery are **Johari Bazaar**, in the Pink City, and **Chameliwala Market**, just off MI Road in the tangle of alleyways by the *Evergreen Guest House*. The latter also has the city's best selection of gems, though it's also one of the hardest places to shop in peace, thanks to a particularly slippery breed of scam merchant, known locally as *lapkars* – usually smartly dressed young men speaking excellent English – whose offers of trips to local beauty spots are invariably followed by a stop at a "relative's" art studio, pottery or carpet-weaving workshop, with accompanying credit card fraud should you buy anything. If buying gemstones, be extremely suspicious of anyone offering an address in your own country where, it is claimed, you'll be able to sell them at a huge profit. This is nonsense, of course, but by the time you realize this you'll be thousands of miles away wondering where the mysterious entries on your credit card bill came from. If you're paying for gemstones or jewellery with a credit card in Jaipur, don't let it out of your sight, and certainly don't agree to leaving a docket as security.

Bookshops

Bookwise, in Mall 21, opposite the Raj Mandir cinema, has an excellent selection of English-language fiction and India-related titles; there's also a handy little bookstall attached to the *Barista* coffee house in the same building. Close by on MI Road, Books Corner (a couple of door west of *Niro's* restaurant) has a passable selection of India-related titles crammed into a poky little shop. There are lots of newspaper and magazine stalls along the south side of MI Rd east of here, heading towards Ajmer Gate. The *Arya Niwas* hotel also has a passable little bookshop.

Listings

Airlines Air France c/o Jet Air, Jaipur Towers, MI Rd ☎0141/237 5430; Air India, Ganpati Plaza ☎0141/236 8821; American Airlines c/o Jet Air (see Air France); British Airways, G-2 Usha Plaza, MI Rd, near junction with Station Rd ☎0141/231 0734; Gulf Air c/o Jet Air (see Air France); Indian Airlines, Nehru Place, Tonk Rd (the southward continuation of Sawai Ram Singh Rd) ☎0141/274 3500; Jet Airways, Umaid Nagar House, opposite Ganpati Plaza on MI Rd ☎0141/511 2222; KLM, 211 Jaipur Towers, MI Rd ☎0141/236 7772; Lufthansa, Saraogi Mansion, MI Rd ☎0141/257 6360; Royal Jordanian c/o Jet Air (see Air France); Royal Nepal Airlines, c/o Jet Air (see Air France); Virgin, c/o Inter Globe, Jaipur Towers, MI Rd ☎0141/237 0062.

Banks and exchange Changing money can be time-consuming at the city's banks, although ATM machines are common, especially along MI Road. There are plenty of private exchange places in Jaipur offering more or less the same rates as the banks. These include two branches of Thomas Cook on MI Road (both Mon–Sat 9.30am–6pm), where you can also change traveller's cheques and get cash advances on credit cards; and LKP Forex, also on MI Road, opposite Ganpati Plaza (Mon–Sat 9.30am–6pm), which also changes traveller's cheques and foreign currency.

Beauty salons Jaipur is renowned for its herbal beauty parlours. The most famous is the Shahnaz Hussain Institute, S-55 Ashok Marg, C Scheme (☎0141/237 8444), which has separate treatment areas for men and women, although both are rather shabby – don't expect any five-star spa-style luxury. Treatments include manicures, pedicures, henna-ing and various types of facial and massage; they also do haircuts.

Hospitals For emergencies, the government-run SMS Hospital (☎0141/256 0291), on Sawai Ram Singh Rd, is best; treatment is usually free for foreigners. The best private hospital is the Santokba Durlabhji Memorial Hospital (SDMH), Bhawani Singh Marg ☎0141/256 6251.

Internet access Virtually all the guesthouses and hotels listed on pp.204–207 have Internet access. If you can't get online where you're staying (or at another guesthouse), the iWay Internet cafe, just north of the *Atithi Guest House*, is one of the few reliable alternatives.

Meditation The Dhammathali Vipassana Centre (☎0141/268 0220) is one of fifty centres across the world set up to promote the practice of Vipassana meditation, a technique first practised by the Buddha, which aims to make practitioners more aware of physical sensations and mental processes. The centre is located in beautiful countryside a couple of kilometres beyond Sisodia Rani-ka-Bagh on the road to Galta. Courses (for both beginners and experienced students) last for ten days or more, and involve a strict regime, with 4am starts, no solid food after noon, segregation of the sexes and around ten hours of meditation a day. Courses are free, but a donation is expected.

Photography The well set-up Sentosa Colour Lab (daily 10am–8pm), in Ganpati Plaza (on the side facing MI Rd), can handle most photographic requirements, including downloading digital images to CD and developing print film (but not slides); they also sell a good range of film and memory cards. Goyal Colour Lab, next to *Lassiwalla* on MI Rd, can also download digital images and develop film.

Police stations The main police post is on Station Rd opposite the railway station ☎0141/220 6324.

Post For poste restante, go to the GPO on MI Rd (Mon–Sat 10am–6pm). Parcels and registered mail are kept at the sorting office behind the main desks; packages are cotton-wrapped and sewn at the concession (Mon–Sat 10am–4pm) by the main entrance. It's preferable to bring your own box. If you're sending a parcel, take it to the customs office on the first floor to have it checked before wrapping and posting; this will speed up delivery by about ten days.

Swimming pools The nicest hotel pool currently open to non-guests is at the *Alsisar Haveli* (Rs100). Non-guests can also use the rather basic pool at the *Evergreen Guest House* (Rs100), and the more attractive ones at the *Nairan Niwas* (Rs150) and *Raj Mahal* (Rs150).

Travel agents It's usually easiest to arrange something through your hotel or guesthouse. Alternatively, the reputable Rajasthan Travel Service, on the ground floor of Ganpati Plaza on MI Rd (☎0141/238 9408, ⓦ www.rajasthantravelservice .com), can arrange airline ticketing and organize local and all-India tours.

Visas For visa renewals go at least a week before it expires to the Foreigners' Registration Office (☎0141/261 8508), at the Rajasthan Police Head Office behind the Hawa Mahal.

Yoga Jaipur has several reputable yoga schools, including the Rajasthan Swasth Yog Parishad, New Police Academy Rd (☎0141/239 7330); the Rajasthan Yoga Centre, 2km north of Bani Park in Shastri Nagar; and Madhavanand Ashram (☎0141/220 0317), also in Bani Park.

Moving on from Jaipur

Jaipur is Rajasthan's main **transport hub** and has frequent bus and train services to all major destinations around the state, as well as reasonable air connections with major cities in Rajasthan and elsewhere around India. Short journeys to destinations like Bharatpur, Ajmer (for Pushkar) and towns in Shekhawati are usually best made by road; one exception is Sawai Madhopur, the jumping-off place for Ranthambore National Park, which is most easily reached by train.

By bus

RSRTC buses leave from the Inter-state Bus Station on Station Road, with frequent, direct services to pretty much every major town in Rajasthan. For longer routes, faster (but less frequent) deluxe services guarantee seats (enquiries on ☎0141/511 6031) but for express services it's less hassle to turn up at the bus stand and head for the relevant booking office; destinations are listed outside each cabin. The deluxe services have their own separate booking hatch on platform 3 (open 24hr). There's an RTDC bus for Pushkar daily at 1pm; otherwise catch one of the regular buses for Ajmer and change there, or take a private bus (see below). Other services include: Mount Abu (1 daily; 11hr); Agra (hourly; 5hr); Ahmedabad (1 daily; 16hr); Ajmer (7 daily; 2hr–2hr 30min); Alwar (hourly; 4hr); Bharatpur (every 30min; 4hr 30min); Bikaner (11 daily; 7hr 30min); Chittaurgarh (2 daily; 7hr 15min); Delhi (every 30min–1hr; 6hr); Jaisalmer (2 daily; 13–15hr); Jhunjhunu (every 30min; 5hr); Jodhpur (6 daily; 7–8hr); Kota (4 daily; 6hr); Nawalgarh (hourly; 3hr); Pushkar (1 daily; 3hr 30min–4hr); Sawai Madhopur (2 daily; 4hr 30min); Udaipur (2 daily; 10hr).

Private bus services are slightly cheaper, although they tend to cram too many passengers on board and make excessive numbers of chai stops along the way. You can book tickets for these at the string of agents on Station Road, but avoid the desperately uncomfortable video buses. A reliable company for direct buses to **Pushkar** is Jai Ambay Travels (☎0141/220 5177), on Station Rd near the junction with MI Rd, whose comfortable deluxe coaches leave at 9.30am; you can buy tickets (Rs120, or Rs180 a/c bus) just prior to departure, but it's a good idea to get them in advance (you can also book by phone). The same outfit also runs buses to

Ajmer (6 daily; 2hr 30min; Rs70), Jodhpur (3 daily, including 10.30pm sleeper; 6–7hr; Rs160, or Rs210 sleeper bus), Jaisalmer (1 nightly; 12hr; Rs200 sitting, Rs300 sleeper), Udaipur (2 nightly; 9hr; Rs150 sitting, Rs220 sleeper) and Agra (hourly, but making frequent stops; 5hr 30min; Rs100).

By train

Bookings should be made at least a day in advance at the computerized reservations hall just outside the main station (Mon–Sat 8am–8pm, Sun 8am–2pm; ☎0141/220 1401); there's a special "Foreign Tourist and Freedom Fighter" counter.

By plane

Flights are currently operated out of Jaipur's **Sanganer Airport** by Indian Airlines (IC), Jet Airways (9W), Kingfisher Airlines (IT) and Air Deccan (DN), with services to Ahmedabad (3 weekly; 1hr; IC); Delhi (daily; 45min; IC, 9W, IT); Goa (daily; 2hr 20min; IT); Jodhpur (3 weekly; 40min; DN); Kolkata

Recommended trains from Jaipur

The following daily trains are **recommended** as the fastest and/or most convenient from Jaipur. Bear in mind that timetables change, so check the departure time when you buy your ticket (it'll be printed on it), or online at ⓦ www.indianrail.gov.in before travel.

Destination	Name	No.	Departs	Arrives
Abu Road	Aravalli Express	9708	(daily) 8.45am	4.50pm
Ajmer	Shatabdi Express	2015	(daily except Wed) 10.50am	1pm
	Aravali Express	9708	(daily) 8.45am	11.15am
Agra	Jaipur–Gwalior Intercity	2987	(daily) 6.10am	10.52am
	Marudhar Express	4864/4854	(daily) 3.40pm	9.10pm
Alwar	Jaipur–Jammu Tawi Express	2413	(daily) 4.35pm	6.56pm
	Shatabdi Express	2016	(daily except Wed) 5.45pm	7.23pm
Bikaner	Jaipur–Bikaner Intercity Express	2468	(daily) 3.50pm	10.45pm
	Jaipur–Bikaner Express	4737	(daily) 10.10pm	6.55am
Chittaurgarh	Chetak Express	4715	(daily) 7.45pm	11.40pm
	Jaipur–Udaipur Express	2965	(daily) 10.25pm	5.20am
Delhi	Jaisalmer–Delhi Express	4060	(daily) 5am	11.05am
	Shatabdi Express*	2016	(daily except Wed) 5.45pm	10.40pm
Jaisalmer	Delhi–Jaisalmer Express	4059	(daily) 11.57pm	1pm
Jhunjhunu	Shekhawati Express	9734	(daily) 6.05pm	10.28pm
Jodhpur	Marudhar Express	4853	(Mon, Weds, Sat) 11.50am	6.20pm
	Intercity Express	2465	(daily) 5.40pm	11pm
	Delhi–Jaisalmer Express	4059	(daily) 11.57pm	6.05am
Kota	Jaipur–Mumbai Superfast	2956	(daily) 2.10pm	5.25pm
	Dayodaya Express	2182	(daily) 5.25pm	9.10pm
Sawai Madhopur (for **Ranthambore** National Park)	Jaipur–Mumbai Superfast	2956	(daily) 2.10pm	4pm
	Intercity Express	2466	(daily) 10.50am	1pm
Udaipur	Jaipur–Udaipur Express	2965	(daily) 10.25pm	7.45am
Varanasi	Marudhar Express	#4864/ 4854	(daily) 3.40pm	8.15am/ 9.30am

* a/c only

(Calcutta; daily except Wed; 2hr 25min; IC); Mumbai (daily; 1hr 35min; IC, 9W, IT); Udaipur (daily; 45min–1hr 50min; 9W, DN). A **rickshaw** to the airport should cost around Rs100; a taxi, Rs250.

Around Jaipur

Forts, palaces, temples and assorted ruins from a thousand years of Kachchwaha history adorn the hills and valleys near Jaipur. As big a draw as Jaipur's more modern palace complex, the superb palace at **Amber** provides the most obvious destination for a day-trip, easily combined with a visit to the impressive fort of **Jaigarh** which crowns the hills above. Many tourists also choose to travel south to search out the traditional potters, block printers and dyers of **Sanganer**. Organized tours (see p.204) visit Amber and Jaigarh in a day; Amber is accessible by public transport, and buses and minibuses run to Sanganer; see the individual accounts for details.

Amber

On the crest of a rocky hill 11km north of Jaipur, the Rajput stronghold of **AMBER** (or Amer) was the capital of the leading **Kachchwaha** clan (see p.201) from 1037 until 1728, when Jai Singh established his new city at Jaipur. Amber's palace buildings are less impressive than those at Jaipur (or many other places in Rajasthan), though the natural setting, perched high on a narrow rocky ridge above the surrounding countryside and fortified by natural hills, high ramparts and a succession of gates along a cobbled road, is unforgettably dramatic – a suitably imposing stronghold for one of Rajputana's most eminent families.

It's worth visiting Amber independently, since tour groups rarely get enough time to properly explore the entire complex. Arrive early in the day if you want to avoid the big coach parties. Regular **public buses** to Amber leave from outside Jaipur's Hawa Mahal every five to ten minutes, stopping on the main road below the palace; the journey takes around 20–30 minutes, depending on traffic. There's a small **tourist office** (daily 8am–4pm) at the bottom of the path to the palace. It's a pleasant fifteen-minute uphill walk from here up to the palace. Alternatively you could hire a Jeep (Rs200 for the return trip, including 2hr waiting time) or waddle up on the back of an elephant (Rs550 for up to four people) – though some tourists have complained that the *mahouts* are unnecessarily cruel to their animals. You may also be able to arrange cheaper elephant rides around the village (Rs250–450).

The palace complex

The path from the village leads up to Suraj Pole (Sun Gate) and the large **Jaleb Chowk** courtyard at the entrance to the main **palace complex** (daily 9am–4.30pm; foreign visitors Rs50, India residents Rs10, camera Rs25, video Rs100); this is where you'll find the ticket office and assorted official guides, who offer tours of the palace for around Rs200.

On the left-hand side of the courtyard is the **Shri Sila Devi temple**, dedicated to the goddess of war, Sila, an aspect of Kali. The revered statue of Sila Devi within ranks, along with the image of Govind Devji (see p.211), as one of the two most important in Jaipur state. The image was created in 1604 at the behest of the great Rajput general Man Singh, then serving the Mughals in Bengal. The goddess (legend runs) had appeared in a dream to Man Singh, announcing that she was trapped in a slab of stone and demanding to be released.

The relevant stone was located, carved into Sila Devi's likeness, and installed at Amber within a shrine framed by an unusual arch formed from stylized carvings of banana leaves. The goddess quickly became one of most revered of the idols under the royal family's protection, its presence at the entrance to their palace offering an important symbolic seal of divine approval to Kachchwaha rule.

Next to the Shri Sila Devi temple, a steep flight of steps leads up to **Singh Pole** (Lion Gate), the entrance to the main palace. The architectural style is distinctly Rajput, though it's clear that Mughal ideas also crept into the design – the practice of covering walls with mirrored mosaics, for example, is pure Mughal, first introduced to India at Agra and Fatehpur Sikri. Passing through Singh Pole leads one into the first of the palace's three main courtyards, on the far side of which stands the **Diwan-i-Am** (Hall of Public Audience), used by Jai Singh I and his successors from 1639. This open-sided pavilion is notably similar in its overall conception to contemporary Mughal audience halls in Delhi and Agra, even if the architectural details are essentially Rajput – the Mughal emperor Jahangir was so jealous of the building that he reputedly once declared, in a fit of artistic jealously, that he wished to have it destroyed. The decidedly Islamic-looking cusped arches of the adjacent terrace offer further architectural homage to the era's Mughal rulers.

Diagonally opposite, the exquisitely painted **Ganesh Pole** leads into a second courtyard, its right-hand side filled with a miniature fountain-studded garden, behind which lie the rooms of the **Sukh Mahal**, set into the side of the courtyard. The marble rooms here, decorated with delicate carving of blue, yellow and red vases, were cooled by water channelled through small conduits carved into the walls, an early and ingenious system of air-conditioning. The central room has a particularly finely carved example, from which water was fed through the room and back into the fountains in the gardens outside.

On the opposite side of the courtyard, the dazzling **Sheesh Mahal** houses what were the private chambers of the maharaja and his queen, its walls and ceilings decorated with intricate mosaics fashioned out of shards of mirror and coloured glass. On the far side of the courtyard beyond the Sheesh Mahal, a narrow stairwell leads up to the small **Jas Mandir**, decorated with similar mosaics and guarded from the sun by delicate marble screens.

From the rear of the Sheesh Mahal courtyard, a narrow corridor leads into a further expansive courtyard at the heart of the **Palace of Man Singh I**, the oldest part of the palace complex. The buildings here are notably plain and austere compared to later structures, though they would originally have been richly decorated and furnished. The pillared *baradari* in the centre of the courtyard was once a meeting area for the maharanis, shrouded from men's eyes by flowing curtains. This section of the palace can also be reached via various labyrinthine passages which run around the top of the **Sheesh Mahal** courtyard beyond the Jas Mandir. The impressionable Rudyard Kipling was particularly taken with this section of the complex, describing the "cramped and darkened rooms, the narrow smooth-walled passages with recesses where a man might wait for his enemy unseen, the maze of ascending and descending stairs leading no-whither, the ever-present screens of marble tracery that may hide or reveal so much – all these things breathe of plot and counter-plot, league and intrigue" – though present-day visitors are likely to suffer nothing worse than the occasional stubbed toe.

Jaigarh

Perched high on the hills behind Amber Palace, the rugged **Jaigarh** fort (daily 9am–5pm; foreign visitors Rs50, Indian residents Rs20, camera Rs40, video

Rs150; same ticket also valid for Jaipur City Palace if used within 24hr) offers incredible vistas over the hills and plains below. The fort was built in 1600, although as the Kachchwahas were on friendly terms with the Mughals, it saw few battles. Jaigarh is also renowned as the most likely hiding place of the Kachchwahas' famous **lost treasure**. A huge hoard of gemstones and jewellery disappeared after Independence, probably to prevent its confiscation by the government. Income tax officials scoured the building with metal detectors in 1977 but found nothing.

At the centre of the fort, a small **museum** has a rather dusty display of the usual old maps and photographs, plus a good little selection of cannons dating back to 1588. Jaigarh was an important centre for the manufacture of these highly-prized weapons (the buildings which once housed the fort's cannon foundry can be seen near the Awani Gate); the respect with which they were treated can be judged from the fact that all the cannons on display – even the smallest – was individually named. None of them, however, can hold a candle to the immense **Jaivana** cannon, the largest in Asia, which sits in solitary splendour at the highest point of the fort, five minutes' walk beyond the museum, commanding superlative views of the countryside below. Needing one hundred kilos of gunpowder for one shot, the Jaivana could purportedly shoot a cannonball 35km – though its true military value was never accurately gauged since it was never fired in anger.

Most people walk to Jaigarh from Amber Palace, a steep fifteen- to twenty-minute climb. The path to the fort goes from just below the entrance to the palace, branching off from near the top of the zigzagging road (the one used by elephants; not the pedestrian path). The alternative is to descend to the valley and follow the much longer road that leads to both Jaigarh and Nahargarh by vehicle; Jeeps can be hired in Amber village for the return trip to the fort (Rs400, including 2hr waiting time). If you've walked up you'll arrive at the Awani Gate – go through the gate and head left to reach the museum; if you've driven, you'll arrive on the opposite side of the fort, near the Jaivana cannon, where you'll also find several **cafes**.

Amber town

Below the palace, the atmospheric but little-visited **Amber town** is full of remnants of Kachchwaha rule including a small lake, crumbling havelis and *chhatris*, and almost four hundred temples – a good place for an idle wander. One of the most striking local landmarks is the **Jagat Shiromani Temple**, built by Man Singh after the death in battle of his son and would-have-been successor, a large and florid structure, its shrine topped by an enormous *shikhara* and fronted by an unusually large, two-storey *mandapa* with a curved roof inspired by those on Mughal pavilions. The image of Krishna within is said to have been rescued by Man Singh from Chittaurgarh after that fort had been sacked by Akbar. Behind the temple stands the small **palace** which was the original home of the Kachchwaha rulers before the construction of Amber palace proper. It's also worth hunting out the fine sixteenth-century **Gyara Mahadev Temple** dedicated to Shiva, and approached through an unusual, tranquil garden courtyard. The temple was originally built as a Jain shrine but subsequently converted to Hindu use, with three *shikhara*-topped shrines fronted by a large *mandapa* with a group of pillars at its centre arranged in an octagon – a typical Jain motif.

The town is also home to an excellent new **Anokhi Museum of Hand Printing** (daily except Mon 11am—4.30pm; closed May to mid-July; Ⓦwww .anokhimuseum.com) at Kheri Gate, a ten-minute walk from the fort. Housed in the attractive old Anokhi Haveli, the museum has an interesting collection of hand block-printed textiles and garments, along with live demonstrations of printing and carving by resident craftsmen. There's also a nice little café.

Samode

Hidden among the scrubby Aravalli Hills, **SAMODE**, on the edge of Shekhawati, is notable for its impeccably restored eighteenth-century **palace**. It became famous in the 1980s as the setting for the hit Raj-romance movie *The Far Pavilions*, and is now an award-winning heritage **hotel**, the ⚐ *Samode Palace* (☎01423/240014, ⓦ www.samode.com; from around US$270; rates drop by 40 percent May–Sept; ❾). It's possible to come here on a day-trip from Jaipur, 42km southeast, but if your budget can stretch to it, spend a night in one of the palace's uncompromisingly romantic rooms, plastered with murals and filled with antiques and ornate stonework. Non-guests have to shell out a hefty Rs100 to visit, but it's worth it just to see the beautiful **Sheesh Mahal** on the south side of the building. Three-hundred steps lead up from the palace to a hilltop **fort**, the rawal's ruined former residence, with impressive views over the surrounding countryside. Samode village itself is a centre for block printing and lacquered bangle making.

The owners of the hotel also have fifty richly appointed tents, 3km southeast of Samode at *Samode Bagh* (❽), with their own swimming pool, croquet lawns and tennis courts. **Bookings** for this and the palace can be made in Jaipur through *Samode Haveli*, Gangapole (☎0141/263 2370).

Sanganer

SANGANER, 16km south of Jaipur, is the busiest centre for handmade **textiles** in the region, and the best place to watch traditional block printers in action (much of what's on offer can be bought in Jaipur). There are a couple of large factories here, but most of the printing is done in family homes as a cottage industry. Sanganeri craftsmen and women also decorate **pottery** in Rajasthan's distinctive style – floral designs in white or deep sea-green on a traditional inky-blue glaze.

Within the town itself, there are ruined palaces and a handful of elegant Jain **temples**, most notably the Shri Digamber temple near the Tripolia Gate. Minibuses and *tempos* leave for Sanganer from Chand Pole, or you can take city bus #113 from Ajmeri Gate.

North of Jaipur: Shekhawati

North of Jaipur, small sand-blown towns nestle between sprawling expanses of parched land and dunes at the easternmost edges of the Thar Desert. Before the rise of Mumbai (Bombay) and Kolkata (Calcutta) – and the arrival of the railways – diverted the trans-Thar trade south and eastwards, this region, known as **Shekhawati**, lay on an important caravan route connecting Delhi and Sind (now in Pakistan) with the Gujarati coast. Having grown rich on trade and taxes from the through traffic, the merchant Marwari and landowning thakur castes

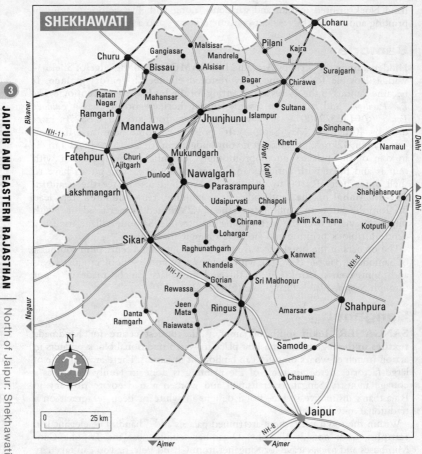

of its small market towns spent their fortunes competing with each other to build grand, ostentatiously decorated **havelis** (see box, p.229). Many have survived, and now collectively comprise one of the richest artistic and architectural legacies in all India: an incredible concentration of mansions, palaces and cenotaphs plastered inside and out with elaborate and colourful **murals**, executed between the 1770s and the 1930s.

Considering the wealth of traditional art here, and the region's proximity to Jaipur, most of Shekhawati still feels surprisingly far off the tourist trail. Precisely for these reasons it ranks among the most rewarding parts of Rajasthan to explore, and of the few independent travellers who find their way up here, most invariably stay longer than planned, using **Nawalgarh** or **Mandawa** as a base for day-trips or leisurely walks into the desert.

Shekhawati is crossed by a mainline railway, linking the major towns with Delhi, Jaipur and Bikaner, but services are hopelessly slow, unreliable and inconvenient, and you're better off travelling to and around the region by bus. Fairly regular local buses, always overcrowded, connect Shekhawati's main towns; Jeeps also shuttle between towns and villages around the region, picking up as many passengers as they can cram in. Alternatively, it's possible to hire your own Jeep or taxi through most of the region's hotels and guesthouses.

Only the main towns have been covered in the following account, but you should be able to find interesting sites in any town or village you pass through. Ilay Cooper's excellent *The Painted Towns of Shekhawati* makes an ideal guide, but unfortunately remainder copies of its last printing are hard to find.

Some history

Shekhawati's history is an intriguing blend of Muslim and Rajput influences. The district's major town, **Jhunjhunu** was ruled first by the Rajput Chauhans of Ajmer until 1450, when it was taken over by Muslim nawabs of the Khaimkani clan, who also gained control of nearby **Fatehpur**. The Khaimkanis ruled for almost three centuries, and parts of Jhunjhunu, in particular, still retain a distinctly Islamic flavour. At about the same time that the Khaimkanis were taking possession of Jhunjhunu, **Rao Shekhaji** (1433–1488), a grandson of the Kachchwaha maharaja of Amber, was carving out his own small kingdom in the region, named **Shekhawati**. After centuries of largely peaceful coexistence, Muslim Jhunjhunu was incorporated into Rajput Shekhawati in 1730 when **Sardul Singh** of the **Shekhawat** clan took over Jhunjhunu following the death of the last nawab, Rohilla Khan. Two years later he consolidated Shekhawat rule by helping his brother (already ruler of the nearby town of Sikar) to seize Fatehpur from its Muslim ruler.

Shekhawati is best known, however, not for its Rajput rulers but for its **Marwari merchants** (see p.391). Attacks by brigands against the Marwaris led to their forming an alliance with the British. In 1835 the latter, ever eager to gain a foothold in the region, despatched a small force of cavalry called the Shekhawati Brigade to control the robbers. This gave the Marwaris the security they needed to trade, using the profits to build the magnificent havelis which adorn every town in the region. Even though many of the Marwaris subsequently moved to Bombay, Madras and, especially, Calcutta, they continued to send their earnings back to Shekhawati, erecting elaborate buildings either to prove their worth as prospective bridegrooms or simply as work-creation schemes during times of famine.

Following independence, a number of Marwaris bought British industries, and Marwari families such as Birla and Poddar remain prominent in business today. Many merchant families now live outside the region, with the result that their old mansions have been allowed to fall into a state of disrepair, though renewed tourist interest in the region's heritage has encouraged some owners to embark on much-needed restoration work.

Nawalgarh

More or less at the dead centre of Shekhawati, **NAWALGARH** came into its own in 1737, when the Shekhawat Nawal Singh claimed what was then a small village as the site for a fort, erecting thick stone walls, pierced by four gateways, around it. Now a lively little market town surrounded by desert and *khejri* scrub, Nawalgarh – along with nearby Mandawa – makes the most convenient congenial base for the Shekhawati region, with a bumper crop of painted havelis and a picturesque, relatively traffic-free bazaar, along with good transport connections and a decent range of accommodation.

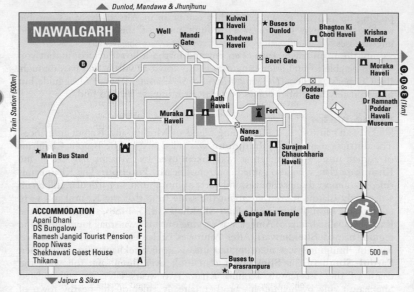

Arrival and information

Nawalgarh's **bus** and **Jeep** stand, about 2km west of town, is served by buses from Jhunjhunu (every 30min; 1hr) via Dunlod (15min); Mandawa (every 30min; 45min); and Ajmer (daily at 10am; 5hr). Travelling on to **Jaipur** there are RSRTC buses every 15min (3hr 30min) and a deluxe bus service at 8am; there are also some private buses, though these drop passengers 5km outside the centre of Jaipur. Hourly buses run to Delhi (8hr) in the morning. The **train station** is a further kilometre west from the bus station. The line between Nawalgarh and Delhi is currently being converted from metre gauge to broad gauge and there's only a single service (daily at 9.23pm) to Rewari (arriving 3.30am), where you'll have to change trains for Delhi, arriving sometime around 7am, though it's much easier to take the bus. Heading to Jaipur, there's a once-daily train departing at 6.09am and arriving at 10.20am.

For trips around the region, you can either jump on and off cheap, cramped village-to-village **Jeeps** (which leave when they're full), or rent a vehicle for the day at very reasonable rates through Ramesh Jangid at *Apani Dhani* or his son Rajesh at the *Ramesh Jangid Tourist Pension* (see p.230). Ramesh and Rajesh also run socially responsible **tours** of Shekhawati (and the rest of Rajasthan and India; see Ⓦ www.apanidhani.com). These include Jeep tours of nearby towns and other places of interest (Rs1500–2000), walking tours of Nawalgarh (Rs350 per person), tours by camel cart (Rs1500/day) and, for the adventurous, two- or three-day hiking tours in the Aravalli mountains, staying with families in local villages en route. The *Roop Niwas* hotel can also arrange short excursions on camel- (Rs400/hr) and horseback (Rs450/hr), and also runs more extended horse and camel safaris through the region – see Ⓦ www.royalridingholidays .com for full details. While exploring Nawalgarh town you may well be accosted by Bablu Sharma (he usually hangs out at the Moraka Haveli), a persistent young man who speaks reasonable English and is fairly knowledgeable about the town's havelis; he asks for around Rs300 for a full day's guiding. **Cycles** can be rented at *Apani Dhani* and the *Ramesh Jangid Tourist Pension* (Rs50 per day).

The havelis of Shekhawati

The **havelis** (after the Persian word for "enclosed space") of Shekhawati typically follow a fairly standard pattern. The **entrance** from the street is usually through a grandly decorated gateway or porch with carved brass or wooden doors; this is sometimes placed at the top of a large ramp, designed to be broad enough to be ridden up on an elephant, when the occasion required. Inside, most havelis consist of two main court-yards. Entering the haveli, you step into the first courtyard, the **mardana**, or men's, courtyard; visitors were normally received here in the **baithak**, an open-sided meeting room, usually to the left of the main entrance, often finely embellished with ornate pillars and sometimes equipped with a huge, manually operated fan, or *punkah*. From the *mardana* courtyard, a second doorway (often the most richly decorated in the entire haveli, and usually surmounted by a figure of Ganesh, the Hindu god of prosperity and good fortune) leads into the second principal courtyard, the **zenana**, or women's courtyard. This is where the ladies of the house lived in purdah, shielded from the eyes of the street, although a latticed window next to the *zenana* entrance allowed them to spy on proceedings in the *mardana*, while in some havelis there is also an upper storey above the *mardana* courtyard reserved for the use of women to observe proceedings in the *baithak* below. The *zenana* was also home to the haveli's kitchen, often recogniz-able by the areas of smoke-blackened plaster surrounding it. Although the majority of havelis consist of just these two main courtyards, some of the grander examples boast four or even six separate courtyards, while there are also occasional examples of so-called **"double havelis"**, basically two separate havelis joined together, each of which would have been used by two related families, typically those belonging to a pair of brothers. In addition, many also have a subsidiary courtyard to one side which was used for stabling animals – whether horses, camels or even elephants.

Murals

The flamboyant murals which characteristically cover both the interior and exterior walls of Shekhawati's havelis were painted by craftsmen from outside the region. Religious themes, especially episodes from the life of Krishna, were often depicted along the lintels above the main exterior doors to cultivate faith among the unedu-cated masses, as well as on walls inside the havelis. What sets the murals of Shekha-wati apart from those elsewhere in India, however, are not their religious paintings but the incongruous and often charmingly naive depictions of contemporary machines, fashions and outlandish foreigners, from pictures of early aeroplanes, steam trains and boats to Edwardian memsahibs in big hats. Quaintly old-fashioned now, at the time when they were painted these exotic images represented everything that was most modern and exotic about the outside world, one which the women and poor townsfolk of Shekhawati had no hope of ever seeing with their own eyes (nor, for that matter, the artists themselves, most of whom had probably never seen the newfangled European novelties they were asked to depict). Nowadays, most of the murals are faded, defaced, covered with posters or even just whitewashed over. In some ways this simply adds to their haunting appeal, and there are so many – and the towns are so small – that you cannot fail to see a work of art virtually everywhere you look.

Visiting Shekhawati's havelis

A small number of havelis have now been restored and opened as museums. Most, however, remain in a state of picturesque dilapidation and are still occupied by local families, while others have been abandoned, and are now empty apart from a solitary *chowkidar* (caretaker-cum-guard). Visitors are welcome to look around inside some havelis in return for a small tip (Rs10–20 is sufficient), while others remain closed to outsiders. If in doubt just stick your head in the front door and ask, but remember that you're effectively entering someone's private home, and never go in without permission.

Accommodation

Apani Dhani Northwest edge of town, on the main Jhunjhunu road ☏01594/222239, ⓦwww.apanidhani.com. Occupying a fetching cluster of mud-walled Rajasthani village-style huts, this beautiful little eco-resort is the brainchild of crusading owner Ramesh Jangid, who relies on solar energy, compost toilets and recyclable materials to create an exemplary example of sustainable tourism. Rooms (especially those in the slightly more expensive superior category) have plenty of rustic charm, and there's excellent organic food, served up in the bougainvillea-strewn garden, as well as activities including tie-dye and cookery classes. Ramesh also runs excellent tours (see p.228). Book ahead. ④

DS Bungalow Next to the *Shekhawati Guest House* on the eastern edge of town ☏01594/222703. Basic but cheerful family guesthouse, with simple air-cooled rooms decorated with quirky ornaments and knick-knacks, although dinner clocks in at a rather expensive Rs250. ③

Ramesh Jangid Tourist Pension On the western edge of town, just north of Maur Hospital ☏01594/224060, ⓦwww.apanidhani.com. Run by Rajesh Jangid, the son of local entrepreneur Ramesh Jangid (see *Apani Dhani* listing above), this homely guesthouse offers simple but good-value rooms in a sociable Brahmin family home; the more expensive rooms have solar-heated water and beautiful murals created by visiting European artists. Delicious pure-veg food is served up in the downstairs courtyard, and there's reliable Internet access, while Jeep tours, tie-dye, cooking and Hindi classes can be arranged on request. ②–④

Roop Niwas 1km east of the town centre ☏01594/222008, ⓦwww.roopniwaskothi.com. This rambling Raj-era mansion is Nawalgarh's closest thing to an upscale resort, with old-fashioned rooms and a certain faded elegance – although beds can be a bit hard. There's an attractive old dining room and bar, while evocative sepia photos from the 1930s hang on the walls, along with moth-eaten hunting trophies. Horse- and camel-riding tours can be arranged (see p.228), and guides are available for walking tours of Nawalgarh. ⑥

Shekhawati Guest House 1km east of the town centre, 200m south of the *Roop Niwas* ☏01594/224658, ⓦwww.shekhawatirestaurant .com. This friendly family guesthouse – under the management of charming hostess Kalpana Singh – is Nawalgarh's latest convert to the eco-cause, with solar heating and water-harvesting facilities, while fresh produce from the attached organic farm is used in the superb food (veg and non-veg) served up in the in-house restaurant (guests also get free cookery lessons). Accommodation is either in the clean but somewhat gloomy rooms in the main house, or in the slightly fancier cottages in the garden out the back. ③–④

Thikana 100m west of the Bhagton ki Haveli ☏01594/222152, ⓔheritagethikana@rediffmail .com. Pleasant hotel in the heart of town, with friendly female management and lovely views from the upstairs terrace. It's a nice enough spot, though the rooms, with mishmash furnishings and rather hard mattresses, are overpriced, and the slightly chintzy pink modern building doesn't really live up to its billing as a so-called "heritage" hotel. ⑤–⑥

The Town

The logical place to start a tour of Nawalgarh is on the east side of town at the magnificent Anandi Lal Poddar Haveli, now housing the **Dr Ramnath A. Poddar Haveli Museum** (daily 8.30am–5.30pm; Rs85, camera Rs30). Built in 1920 and now doubling up as a school, this is one of the few havelis in Shekhawati to have been restored to its original glory, and boasts the most vivid murals in town (although purists point out that restoration has involved repainting rather than simple cleaning and restoration). These include the usual scenes from the life of Krishna which appear on virtually every haveli throughout Shekhawati, along with more modern subjects including steam trains, soldiers drilling with rifles and well-dressed local worthies flying kites, as well as false windows with painted people staring out into the courtyard below and a clever 3D-like panel of a bull's head that transmogrifies into an elephant's as you move from left to right. The haveli also houses a mildly diverting series of **exhibits** showcasing various aspects of Rajasthani life, including musical instruments, miniature paintings (with examples of various different local schools), dolls in traditional wedding costumes and a display on local fairs, festivals and dances, though it's really the haveli itself which is the main attraction.

A short walk to the north lies the fine **Moraka Haveli** (daily 8am–6.30pm, winter until 7.30pm; Rs40), whose principal courtyard boasts murals of Shiva, Parvati and Krishna and a *baithak* complete with a fine old hand-pulled fan (*punkah*). The beautiful second courtyard is decorated with friezes showing scenes from the Ramayana and other pictures from Hindu mythology around the top of its arches, while a small portrait of Jesus can be seen on the topmost storey in the courtyard's southeast corner (on the far left-hand side as you enter). Directly opposite the Moraka Haveli lies the eye-catching **Krishna Mandir**, dating from the mid-eighteenth century, a florid mass of delicate *chhatris* housing a collection of no less than eleven lingas.

About 200m east of the Moraka Haveli, the unrestored, 150-year-old **Bhagton ki Choti Haveli** (no set hours, though the resident *chowkidar* can usually be found sitting on the doorstep waiting for visitors; Rs40) boasts an unusually varied selection of murals including a European-style angel and Queen Victoria (over the arches by the right of the main door) along with Krishna and Radha on a swing. On the left, a *trompe-l'oeil* picture shows seven women in the shape of an elephant, plus a painting of a festive stick dance, while other pictures show Europeans riding bicycles along with a steamboat and a train. A fine brass door leads into the *zenana* courtyard, from where a latticed window allowed the ladies of the house to keep an eye on events in the men's courtyard. A room overlooking the entrance to the *zenana* boasts a quirky mural showing a mournful European man smoking a pipe, while a woman plays an accordion.

A further fine pair of havelis lie west of here, side by side, due north of the Nansa Gate. The first, the **Khedwal Haveli**, is still inhabited and can usually only be viewed from the outside; look through the main entrance and you can catch a glimpse of the lovely mirrorwork (plus train) on the upper storey of the main courtyard. A few metres north, the **Kulwal Haveli** is also inhabited, though open for visitors on payment of a small baksheesh. Pictures of Gandhi and Nehru adorn the entrance porch, while a European woman sits above the main door applying her lipstick; the bizarrely ornate Italianate building opposite formerly served as the haveli's guesthouse and is slated to become a hotel in the near future. Inside the haveli, a fine door, studded with miniature peacocks, leads through to the pretty *zenana* courtyard, with pretty red and blue floral motifs covering every surface, along with the usual religious pictures, although the murals in the vicinity of the kitchen have been more or less completely obliterated by smoke from cooking fires – a common occurrence in havelis throughout Shekhawati.

The fort

Central Nawalgarh has plenty of old-fashioned, small-town charm, with dozens of tiny shops and lots of street vendors hawking piles of merchandise by the side of the road. At the heart of the town, the **fort** (Bala Qila) has more or less vanished under a clutch of modern buildings huddled around a central courtyard which now hosts the town's colourful vegetable market. The dilapidated building on the far left-hand side of the courtyard (by the Bank of Baroda) boasts a magnificent, eerily echoing **Sheesh Mahal**, covered in mirrorwork, which once served as the dressing room of the maharani of Nawalgarh, its ceiling decorated with pictorial maps of Nawalgarh and Jaipur. You'll have to pay the usual Rs10–20 baksheesh to see the room; if no one's around, ask at the sweet factory on the opposite side of the courtyard.

The havelis on the eastern side of Nawalgarh are less striking than those on the west, though this part of town is generally more peaceful, and there are fewer teenagers hanging around to annoy visitors. Heading west through the Nansa Gate (signed, confusingly, as the "Rambilas Podar Memorial Gate") and following the road around brings you to the so-called **Aath Haveli** (Eight Havelis, built by eight brothers, although only six were actually completed), a complex of heavily decorated mansions featuring murals in a range of styles depicting the usual mishmash of subjects both ancient and modern. The haveli in the southwest corner of the compound is the most interesting, sporting pictures of European ladies going for a ride in a very early motorcar and a rather odd-looking steam train whose carriages look like little houses on wheels, along with the usual horses, elephants and camels. The **Muraka Haveli** opposite also boasts a richly painted exterior, with elephants, horses and a pair of fine blue carriages, plus miniatures showing scenes from the life of Krishna, framed in a mass of florid decoration. The courtyard is usually locked, though you can peep through a gap in the gate for a glimpse of the sumptuously decorated courtyard inside.

Further havelis dot the streets south and southeast of the Nansa Gate, one of the quietest and most atmospheric parts of town. These include the **Surajmal Chhauchharia Haveli**, whose murals include a picture of Europeans floating past in a hot-air balloon. The painter took some playful licence as to the mechanics involved: the two passengers blow into the balloon to power their journey.

Dunlod and Parasrampura

The most obvious target for a day-trip from Nawalgarh is **DUNLOD**, 7km north and the site of an old fort and some large havelis. It's possible to get there by bus, but most people walk across the fields – a leisurely two-hour amble that's enjoyable save for the last couple of kilometres, which you have to cover via a rough sandy track linking the village with the main road. The musty old **fort** (Rs20) is worth a quick visit for its atmospheric Diwan-i-Khana, a fine old drawing room painted a vivid orange and filled with antique European furniture and books. Entry to the *diwan* was restricted to men; women were confined to the *duchatta*, on the storey above, whose blue-columned rooms are filled with further old bric-a-brac. The fort has been converted into a hotel, the *Dunlod Castle* (☎01594/252519 or 0141/211275; ❺), though the rather shabby and tackily restored rooms lack the atmosphere of those at Mandawa and Mahansar. Radiating from the southeastern walls of the fort, the **village** harbours several interesting havelis, painted around the start of the twentieth century, and the delicate *chhatri* of Ram Dutt Goenka, a cenotaph erected in 1888 with vibrant friezes lining its dome.

More painted buildings are dotted around the serene hamlet of **PARAS-RAMPURA**, 20km southeast of Nawalgarh, set amid rolling hills dotted with janti trees that makes for some of the most attractive desert scenery in Rajasthan. Buses run every thirty minutes or so, or you could cycle (although be warned that several stretches of the track degenerate into soft sand). Monuments include the **Gopinath temple**, built in 1742, whose murals depict the torments of hell (a common theme in the eighteenth century) alongside images of the local Rajput ruler, Sardul Singh, with his five sons. Some of the paintings are unfinished, as the artists were diverted to decorate the *chhatri* of Rajul Singh, who died that same year. The large dome of his exquisite **cenotaph**, supported by twelve pillars, contains a flourish of lively and well-preserved murals, once again including images of hell, and of Sardul Singh with his sons. Parasrampura's modest **fort**, in reasonable repair, is on the west bank of the dry riverbed.

Jhunjhunu

JHUNJHUNU is the principal entry point to Shekhawati if you're travelling from Delhi. Spreading in a mass of brick and concrete from the base of a rocky hill, it's a busy and fairly unprepossessing town, though it preserves an interesting old central bazaar and a fine collection of havelis decorated with vigorous murals – less technically accomplished than those in many other parts of Shekhawati, but possessing a distinct, naive charm all of their own. Jhunjhunu is usually visited as a day-trip from nearby Nawalgarh or Mandawa, though it has a couple of good accommodation options if you want to stay overnight.

JHUNJHUNU

ACCOMMODATION	
Fresco Palace	D
Jamuna Resort	A
Sangam	C
Shiv Shekhawati	B

Arrival, information and accommodation

Buses from the government stand in the south of town run to Nawalgarh (every 30min; 1hr) and towns throughout Shekhawati, as well as to Bikaner (hourly; 5hr 30min), Jaipur (every 30min; 4hr–4hr 30min) and Delhi (hourly; 7hr 30min). Buses to Mandawa (every 30min; 45min) also stop briefly on Mandawa Circle near the *RTDC Tourist Bungalow*. The private bus stand is east of the main bazaar, though you're unlikely to need to use it; *tempos* and shared auto–rickshaws run between the two via Gandhi Chowk. The **train** station is on the southern edge of town, though services are currently in a state of flux due to the conversion of the line to Delhi from metre gauge to broad gauge, meaning that there are no direct services to the capital at present – it's much easier to catch a bus. Heading to Jaipur, there's just one, inconveniently early train leaving at 5.06am and arriving at 10.20am.

The local **Tourist Reception Centre** (Mon–Sat 10am–5pm, closed every second Sat; ☎01592/232909), attached to the *RTDC Tourist Bungalow* on Mandawa Circle at the western edge of town, has a good stock of maps and brochures and helpful staff. Jhunjhunu is quite spread out, and walking around can be tiring, but many of the streets of the old town are too narrow for cars; **rickshaws** operate as taxis, picking up as many passengers as they can. **Taxis** gather at a rank outside the government bus stand, charging around Rs4 per kilometre. Laxmi Jangid (see below) offers full-day **tours** around Shekhawati by car or Jeep for Rs2000, as well as shorter camel tours (2hr; Rs600 per person).

Accommodation

Jhunjhunu

Fresco Palace Paramveer Path, off Station Rd ☎01592/395233, ✉fresco_palace@yahoo.com. Pleasant new modern hotel (although there aren't many frescoes in evidence), with comfortable, slightly chintzy rooms, all with a/c and TV, and a relaxing garden restaurant. The *Hotel Shekhawati Heritage* next door offers a similarly priced though less attractive fall-back if the *Fresco Palace* is full. ❺

Jamuna Resort Delhi–Sikar Rd ☎01592/232871 or 32871, ⓦwww.shivshekhawati.com. The creation of Laxmi Jangid, a government-authorized guide and avid promoter of Shekhawati's cultural heritage, this lovely village-style resort on the eastern edge of town comprises a cluster of thatch-roofed cottages (all with a/c and TV) set amid extensive grounds complete with pool and garden restaurant. The more expensive rooms are exquisitely decorated with mirrorwork and tradi- tional murals. They also run courses in Indian cooking and art (both Rs500 per person per day), plus free yoga classes. Also a good place to arrange tours. ❺–❻

Sangam Paramveer Path, opposite the government bus stand ☎01592/232544. Basic cheapie with large but bare and slightly shabby rooms – make sure you get one away from the noisy main road. ❷–❸

Shiv Shekhawati Khemi Shakti Rd, near Muni Ashram ☎01592/232651 or 32651, ⓦwww .shivshekhawati.com. Well-maintained modern sister hotel to *Jamuna Resort* with large, clean rooms (all with a/c and TV), restaurant and Internet access. ❹–❺

Around Jhunjhunu

Alsisar Mahal Alsisar Village, 15km north of Jhunjhunu ☎01595/275271, ⓦwww.alsisar.com. The ancestral home of the thakurs of Alsisar, this grand old fort has recently been spruced up and reopened as a luxurious hotel, complete with spotless traditional-style rooms, lofty courtyards and an attractive and good-sized swimming pool. Good value. ❼

Piramal Haveli Bagar Village, 15km northeast of Jhunjhunu ☎01592/221220, ⓦwww .neemranahotels.com. Intimate, self-styled "non- hotel" with just eight rooms in an unusual 1920s Rajasthani-cum-Italianate villa set in a peaceful rural location well away from the hustle and bustle of Jhunjhunu. Rooms are simple but comfortable, and there's a lovely garden, an atmospheric old lounge and good veg food. ❻

The Town

Hidden away in the alleyways behind the main bazaar is Jhunjhunu's most striking building, the magnificent **Khetri Mahal** of 1760 (entrance Rs20), a superb, open-sided sandstone palace with cusped Islamic-style arches which wouldn't look out of place amidst the great Indo-Islamic monuments of Fatehpur Sikri. The whole edifice seems incongruously grand amidst the modest streets of central Jhunjhunu and now stands empty and largely abandoned, apart from the upper terraces, which serve as impromptu open-air classrooms for local schoolchildren. A covered ramp, wide enough for horses, winds up to the roof, from where there are sweeping views over the town and across to the massive ramparts of the sturdy **Badalgarh Fort** (currently closed to the public) on a nearby hilltop.

Stretching east of the Khetri Mahal is Jhunjhunu's main bazaar, centred around **Futala Market**, a fascinating (and hopelessly confusing) tangle of narrow streets crammed with dozens of tiny, charmingly old-fashioned shops painted in pastel greens and blues, many of them owned by the town's sizeable Muslim population. On the northern edge of the bazaar, facing each other across the small square of Chabutra Chowk, lie the two so-called **Modi Havelis**. That on the eastern side is the most impressive, entered via a grand, three-metre-high ramp (a common feature of havelis in Jhunjhunu). The facade boasts symmetrical murals on either side featuring a pair of rabbits, while soldiers on horseback race a train above; the right-hand side also sports a small plane and a lady listening to a gramophone. The western haveli is less well preserved, with sections of the interior arches now blocked up with concrete and large chunks of missing plaster. Despite the encroaching dereliction, a few touchingly naive pictures remain, including various moustachioed Indian bigwigs around the door into the *zenana* courtyard, though the comic effect is perhaps the result of a lack of painterly skill rather than deliberate satirical intent.

Along Nehru Bazaar

Jhunjhunu's finest havelis are spread out along **Nehru bazaar**, immediately east of the main bazaar. Heading east, you'll first reach the striking **Kaniram Narsinghdas Tibrewala Haveli** of 1883, perched on a platform above the surrounding vegetable stalls; the entrance is around the back, on the north side of the haveli. On the west wall of the *mardana* courtyard two quaint trains chunter towards each another, one filled with livestock and the other with stylized little people – a lot more orderly than your average Indian railway carriage. On the north wall of the same courtyard a man combs his luxuriant beard in a mirror, while in adjacent panels a man and woman manipulate a puppet and another gentleman strokes a small and rather bizarre-looking dog whilst smoking a pipe.

Further east down Nehru Bazaar, entered via an impressive ramp up from street level, the **Mohanlal Ishwardas Modi Haveli** has a good selection of entertainingly naive portrait murals. Unusual oval miniatures of various Indian notables frame the entrance to the *zenana* courtyard, whose arches are topped by a quaint selection of portraits showing assorted European and Indian personages sporting a range of flouncy costumes, silly hats and magnificent moustaches (similar portraits can be seen on the ceiling of the archway separating the haveli's two courtyards). Immediately north of here, the striking little **Bihari temple** features some of the oldest murals in Shekhawati, painted in 1776 in black and brown vegetable pigments, including a dramatic depiction inside the central dome of the scene from the Ramayana in which the Hanuman's monkey army takes on the forces of the many-headed demon king Ravana; the five sons of Sardul Singh (each of whom built a fort in the town) regard the scene impassively from across the dome.

Outlying sights

West of the Khetri Mahal at the foot of the craggy Nehara Pahar lies the **Dargah of Kamaruddin Shah**, an atmospheric complex comprising a mosque and *madrasa* arranged around a pretty courtyard (still retaining some of its original murals), with the ornate *dargah* (tomb) of the Sufi saint Kamaruddin Shah in the centre. Next to the roadside immediately to the south, and now almost buried in the scrub, stands a touching monument to the infant son of Henry Forster, commander of the British-run Shekhawati Brigade (see p.227), who died in 1841 aged 1 year and 5 months.

North of the town centre lies the **Mertani Baori**, one of the region's most impressive step-wells, while further east is the extraordinary **Rani Sati Mandir**. Few foreigners ever visit this shrine, the centre of the phenomenally popular Sati Mata cult and reputedly the richest temple in the country after Tirupati (in Andhra Pradesh), receiving hundreds of thousands of pilgrims each year and millions of rupees in donations. Its immense popularity bears witness to the enduring awe with which *satis* – women who commit ritual suicide by climbing onto the funeral pyre of their husband – are regarded in the state. Although banned by the British in 1829 in areas under their rule, the practice has survived in parts of rural Rajasthan; forty cases are known to have occurred since Independence, the most infamous being that of **Roop Kanwar**, an 18-year-old Rajput girl who committed self-immolation in 1987 in the village of Deorala, near Jaipur, sparking off nationwide outrage and controversy. The *sati* commemorated here was performed by a merchant's wife in 1595. Her image, rendered in tile- and mirrorwork, adorns the ceiling of the main prayer hall, while a sequence of panels on the north wall relates the legend surrounding the events of her death.

Mandawa

Rising from a flat, featureless landscape roughly midway between Jhunjhunu and Fatehpur, **MANDAWA** was founded by the Shekhawats in 1755, though most of its paintwork dates from the early nineteenth century. The town's imposing **fort** now houses the upmarket *Castle Mandawa* hotel (see opposite), whose prominence on the tour-group trail has made this the most tourist-oriented place in Shekhawati, although the handicraft shops, touts and guides detract very little from the town's profusion of beautifully dilapidated mansions.

Arrival and information

Buses from Jhunjhunu (every 30min; 1hr) and Nawalgarh (every 30min; 45min), as well as Jaipur and Bikaner, stop at Sonthaliya Gate in the east of town. From Fatehpur, most buses pull in at a stand in the centre, just off the main bazaar. **Jeeps** ply the same routes. The town is so small that either bus stand is within walking distance of most hotels. There are various places along the main bazaar offering **Internet** access – try the Deshnok Money Changer (Rs50 per hour; open 24hr), opposite the *Mandawa Haveli* hotel; they also **change cash**, traveller's cheques and give cash advances against Visa and MasterCard.

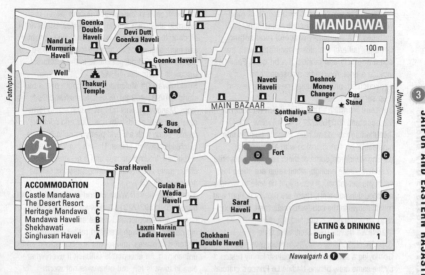

Taking a **walking tour** to see Mandawa's scattered havelis is recommended; guides can be arranged through your hotel, or at Classic Shekhawati Tours (℡01592/223144, ✉classicshekhamnd@yahoo.co.in), by the entrance to the fort. Count on around Rs200–250 for a two- to three-hour walk. Most guesthouses and hotels can also arrange Jeep tours and trips out into the surrounding desert either on horseback, camel-back or in camel-drawn carts. Prices for all these activities vary wildly, but are usually cheapest if booked through the *Hotel Shekhawati*, who also run overnight **camel safaris** camping out in the desert. Classic Shekhawati Tours arranges more upmarket day and overnight camel safaris, though you'll need to book five days in advance.

Accommodation and eating

Mandawa has the best selection of **hotels** in Shekhawati, although prices are quite steep, with only one real budget option. You'll probably **eat** at your hotel or guesthouse; meals at most places are served alongside tacky puppet shows and folk dancing. If you want to venture out, you could try the *Hotel Shekhawati* which has cheap and tasty food, along with plenty of cold beer, while the *Mandawa Haveli* serves up above-average buffets on an atmospheric rooftop terrace. Both are much better bets than the *Bungli* restaurant, whose painted advertisements disfigure walls all over town (and is also constantly touted by gangs of irritating teenage kids), which has pedestrian and overpriced food, small portions and erratic service.

Castle Mandawa ℡01592/223124, ⊛www .castlemandawa.com. Mandawa's fanciest accommodation option, set in the old town fort, with an atmospheric mishmash of buildings around a sand-filled courtyard. All rooms are different, so look at several before you decide, since standards of comfort and decor vary considerably (and the beds tend to be annoyingly small). Facilities include a spa, gym, a large but shallow pool (guests only)

and massage salon, plus spacious and attractive gardens at the rear. Nightly shows of Rajasthani music and dancing are performed during expensive (Rs700) dinners. Will exchange traveller's cheques. ⑦–⑧
The Desert Resort Mukandgarh Rd, 1.5km from Mandawa ℡01592/223151, ⊛www .mandawahotels.com. Just outside Mandawa, this attractively rustic – though surprisingly

pricey – little resort occupies a tangle of mud-walled traditional village-style Rajasthani cottages in a soothingly peaceful rural setting. Cottages (all a/c) are nicely decorated with traditional artefacts and fabrics, if a bit dark. Facilities include a pool, Ayurvedic massages and birdwatching, plus the usual camel, horse and jeep safaris. ⑦–⑧

Heritage Mandawa Off Mukandgarh Rd south of the bus stand ☎01592/223742, ⓦwww.hotelheritagemandawa.com. Brightly painted late nineteenth-century mansion with a/c rooms of varying standards, some of them absolutely covered in murals – nice enough, albeit rates are steep for what you get (although you might be able to wangle a discount in summer). There are nightly puppet and music shows in the courtyard restaurant, tours on request, and a pool is planned. ⑤–⑦

Mandawa Haveli Near Sonthaliya Gate ☎01592/223088, ⓦhttp://hotelmandawa.free.fr. Occupying a superb old haveli painstakingly restored by the same crew behind Nadine Le Prince's cultural centre in Fatehpur (see opposite), this place is rather more atmospheric and significantly better value than the *Heritage Mandawa* nearby. Rooms (all a/c in summer) are quaint, although those downstairs are a bit dark; the upstairs suites are significantly brighter and more spacious. Can arrange tours, and there are nightly music and puppet shows in the restaurant. Discounts in summer. ⑥–⑦

Shekhawati Off Mukandgarh Rd south of the bus stand ☎0/931 469 8079, ⓔhotelshekwati@sify.com. Mandawa's only budget option – and fortunately it's very good, with spacious and spotless rooms (some with a/c and pretty murals) in a eye-catchingly painted house. There's hot water, a good restaurant, Internet access and a generator, and cheap tours and henna painting sessions can be arranged. ②–④

Singhasan Haveli Western end of the main bazaar ☎01592/223137, ⓦwww.singhasanhaveli.com. Another mid-range option set in an old haveli – although it's been rather garishly restored in places, and rooms are overpriced and uninspiring. An acceptable fallback if everywhere else in town is full, but otherwise not worth bothering with. English (or the lack of) can also be a problem. ⑥

The Town

Tours usually begin with the **Naveti Haveli** (now the State Bank of Bikaner & Jaipur), on the main bazaar in the centre of town. Duck through the metal gate to the right of the bank (no charge) for a look at Mandawa's most entertaining wall of murals, including well-preserved images of a primitive flying machine, the Wright brothers' aeroplane, a man using a telephone and a strongman pulling a car.

A ten-minute walk west from here brings you to an interesting cluster of buildings centred around the **Nand Lal Murmuria Haveli**. The murals here are relatively modern, dating from the 1930s and executed in a decidedly flowery and sentimental style, perhaps influenced by contemporary European magazines, with images of various Venetian scenes (the Grand Canal, Rialto and San Marco), along with George V, Nehru riding a horse and the legendary Maratha warrior Shivaji. Next door, the sun-faded **Goenka Double Haveli** (comprising the Vishwanath Goenka Haveli and Tarkeshwar Goenka Haveli – and not to be confused with either of the town's other Goenka havelis nearby) is one of the largest and grandest in Mandawa, with two separate entrances and striking elephants and horses on the facade. The **Thakurji temple** opposite has a rather odd mural (on the right-hand side of the facade) showing soldiers being fired from the mouths of cannon, a favoured British method of executing mutinous sepoys during the 1857 uprising. Further west are a couple of *chhatris*, and a step-well, still used today and bearing paintings inside its decorative corner domes.

South of the main bazaar, the **Gulab Rai Wadia Haveli** is one of the finest in town. The south-facing exterior wall is particularly interesting, with unusually racy (albeit modestly small) murals depicting, amongst other things, a kama sutra-like scene in a railway carriage and (up in the eaves) a woman giving birth and a pair of copulating horses. Similar erotic carvings elsewhere on the building have been whitewashed over. The interior of the haveli is entered via a grand ramp, with Belgian glass mirrorwork over the finely carved door (topped by the usual Ganesh figure) leading into the *zenana* courtyard.

Immediately south of here lies the almost equally fine **Laxmi Narain Ladia Haveli**. The *zenana* courtyard boasts naive paintings of a plane and a steamship, along with a cannon being pulled by horses and a tiger attacking a centaur. Some 100m further south, the unusually large **Chokhani Double Haveli** (Rs10) consists of two separate wings built for two brothers; look for the miserable British soldiers and *chillum*-smoking sadhu facing one another in the recess at the centre of the facade.

Fatehpur

Lying just off NH-11, **FATEHPUR** is the closest town in Shekhawati to Bikaner, 116km west, and a convenient place to stop if you're taking the northern route across the Thar to or from Jaisalmer. The town itself is fairly run-down and its accommodation uninspiring, but it does boast several elaborately painted mansions, temples, wells and *chhatris*. Many of the murals here incorporate wonderful images of colonial times – the king emperor, soldiers, trains and parties of Britishers in vintage cars. Another common theme is Lakshmi, the goddess of wealth.

The most celebrated of Fatehpur's havelis is the **Nadine Le Prince Haveli** (daily 8am–7pm; Rs100), an 1802 mansion restored to its original splendour by its current owner and namesake, a French artist, who purchased the haveli in 1998. Some local aficionados complain about the manner in which the haveli has been restored – with large-scale repainting of murals, rather than the simple cleaning and preservation of existing art – but the overall effect is undeniably impressive, and the haveli as a whole is one of the few in Shekhawati where you get a real sense of how these lavish mansions would originally have looked, complete with superbly carved wooden doors and beams and a dense spread of murals, including pictures showing Lakshmi being showered by elephants. There's also a gallery showcasing local and French artists, plus a small collection of Rajasthani tribal art.

Several further fine havelis lie clustered immediately around the Nadine Le Prince Haveli. Next door on the west side, the **Saraf Haveli** boasts fine exterior murals (albeit missing large chunks of plaster – a common sight in Fatehpur) including a small Vishnu sleeping on a snake above the entrance arch, while opposite lies the expansive **Devra Lal Haveli**, fronted by an unusually elaborate sequence of arched porches, their undersides covered

Ramgarh & Mahansar ▲

0   200 m

N

Jaganath
Singania Haveli

CHURU–SIKAR ROAD

Devra Lal
Haveli

Saraf
Haveli

Nadine Le
Prince
Haveli

Geori
Shankar
Haveli

Mahavir
Prasad
Goenka
Haveli

CHURU–SIKAR ROAD

Private
Bus Stand

Roadways
Bus Stand

FATEHPUR

Lakshmangarh & RTDC Hotel Haveli (2km) ▼

with well-preserved medallion portraits. You can't go in, though you can probably get a glimpse through one of the windows of the ornately painted *mardana* courtyard inside.

Northeast of the Nadine Le Prince Haveli, the imposing **Jagannath Singania Haveli** (also closed to visitors) towers over the main road. Most of the exterior paintings have faded, though there are still some fine paintings of elephants and other subjects on the smaller western facade around the back. South from here, the **Geori Shankar Haveli** (next to an unusually fine bangle stall) is the polar opposite of the Nadine Le Prince Haveli, dilapidated but hugely atmospheric, and still inhabited by a number of impoverished local families. There's fine mirrorwork in the ceiling of the main entrance arch and around the doorway into the *zenana* courtyard, while the predominantly religious paintings of the *mardana* courtyard include a fine Narashima (Vishnu in his lion incarnation) and a panel showing legendary local folk heroes Dhola and Maru (see p.323) on a camel. It's also worth climbing up to the rooftop terrace, decorated with unusual elephant statues, for the fine views over town.

Just east of here lies the small but exquisite **Mahavir Prasad Goenka Haveli** (not to be confused with a second and relatively uninteresting Goenka Haveli signposted from opposite the Geori Shankar Haveli), built in the mid-nineteenth century by a Jain merchant, Mahavir Prasad, and currently being restored. The inner courtyard is beautifully painted, and the first-floor room is dazzling, its walls and ceiling decorated in the finest detail with myriad colours, gold leaf and mirrors. Panels to either side of the door show Krishna riding an elephant (on the right) and a horse (on the left), each animal made up of contorted female figures.

Practicalities

Fatehpur has two **bus stands**, near each other in the centre of town on the main Sikar–Churu (north–south) road. Buses from the government Roadways stand, furthest south, serve Jaipur (every 30min; 3hr 30min), Ramgarh (hourly; 30min), Bikaner (14 daily; 3hr 30min–4hr) and Delhi (5 daily; 6hr). Private buses run from the stand further north along the bazaar to Mandawa (every 30min; 45min), Jhunjhunu (every 30min; 1hr), Mahansar (4 daily; 45min) and Ramgarh (hourly; 30min). Arriving in Fatehpur, note that many buses drop passengers off at the NH-11 intersection, about 1km south of town. The **railway station**, east of town, currently has services twice-daily to Jaipur and once-daily to Bikaner, though all leave in the middle of the night.

Just off NH-11, the modern RTDC *Hotel Haveli* (☏01571/230293; ❸–❹) is the town's only plausible **hotel**, though its large and light rooms, some with a/c, don't quite compensate for the dodgy plumbing and general air of neglect; there's also a shabby little four-bed dorm (Rs75 per person). It's also a fair walk from the bazaar and bus stand; if you aim to catch the early morning (6.30am) express service to Bikaner, note that you can flag the bus down from the roadside next to the hotel. For **food**, you've a less than inspiring choice between the RTDC *Hotel Haveli*'s hit-and-miss overpriced menu, or the row of basic *dhabas* near the bus stand.

Mahansar, Ramgarh and Lakshmangarh

Some of the most outstanding murals and Hindu monuments in the region are scattered across three small towns in the far north and west of Shekhawati: **Mahansar**, **Ramgarh** and **Lakshmangarh**. Of these, only Mahansar has any accommodation, but you can reach the other two easily enough on day-trips from Fatehpur, Mandawa or Nawalgarh.

Mahansar

The relative inaccessibility of **MAHANSAR**, marooned amid a sea of scrub and drifting sand 27km northeast of Fatehpur, has ensured that its monuments, which include a fortress and some of the most accomplished interior paintings in Shekhawati, rank among the least visited in the region. A ribbon of hopelessly potholed tarmac leads out here from Mandawa, and another runs due west to Ramgarh, but aside from sporadic buses, the only traffic along them are camel carts and herds of goats. This makes Mahansar a peaceful place to hole up for a day or two, and a much more enticing prospect than touristy Mandawa, a 45-minute Jeep ride south.

Another reason to come is to **stay** at the quirky *Narayan Niwas Castle* (℡01595/264322; 5), a destination in itself. Managed by Mahansar's royal family in their crumbling 1768 abode, it consists of twelve rooms of varying standards; #1 is the most romantic, with old rugs, bolsters, ancient carved wooden doors and raised sitting alcoves with views. It's a more informal establishment than other heritage hotels in the area, but this lends it a certain charm – and affordability. Be sure to peruse the family heirlooms and sample the royal moonshine. The food is excellent, too.

Once you've explored the fort, there's little more to do other than wander around the village looking for painted buildings. Mahansar's most beautiful murals are locked away out of sight in the **Sona Ki Dukan Haveli**, next to the main crossroads (ask around the shops for the key). The ceiling of the entrance hall to this mansion is exquisitely decorated with painted and richly gilded scenes from the Ramayana and Jayaveda's classic twelfth-century life of Krishna, the *Gita Govinda*, though you'll need a torch to fully appreciate the colours and mass of detail. The *Narayan Niwas* can arrange tours.

Ramgarh

RAMGARH, 20km north of Fatehpur, was founded in 1791 and developed as something of a status symbol by disaffected members of the wealthy Poddar merchant family, who made every effort to outshine nearby Churu, which they left following a dispute with the local thakur over the wool tax. They succeeded in their aim: Ramgarh is one of the most beautiful – but also one of the least-visited – towns in Shekhawati, with the usual fine havelis along with an exceptional array of religious architecture as well.

Starting from the bus stand on the west side of town, follow either of the two roads east into the town centre. After about five minutes' walk you'll reach the **Poddar family havelis**, a superb cluster of ornate mansions which cover the entire area immediately west of the main town square. The streets here form one of the most architecturally perfect ensembles in Shekhawati, the havelis' patrician ochre facades decorated with scenes from local folk stories and a frequently repeated motif, comprising three fishes joined at the mouth, which is unique to Ramgarh.

Just beyond here lies the town's main square, centred on a two-pillared step-well surrounded by the disintegrating remains of further lavishly painted havelis. Turn left here and head through the Churu Gate, beyond which the road is lined with a dense cluster of extraordinarily ornate **temples and chhatris** erected by various members of the Poddar clan, all fantastically domed and pavilioned, while many also sport the remains of elaborate murals. Walking

△ Camel detail on a Ramgarh haveli

along the road you'll pass (on your right) the Ganga Temple (with two fine elephant statues flanking either side of entrance steps) followed by (on your left) the Hanuman and Ganesh temples (the latter with a richly painted forecourt). These are followed by a number of elaborate *chhatris* erected to commemorate assorted Poddar notables, and the diminutive Shani Mandir (dedicated to Saturn), decorated with elaborate mirrorwork.

Lakshmangarh

The small town of **LAKSHMANGARH**, 20km south of Fatehpur, is another archetypal, but seldom visited, Shekhawati destination, its neat grid of streets (a layout inspired by that of Jaipur's Pink City) dotted with dozens of ornate havelis, virtually all of them in various stages of picturesque decay. The town is dominated by its dramatic nineteenth-century **fort**, which crowns a rocky outcrop on the west side of town; it's now closed to the public, though you can walk up the steep track to the entrance to enjoy the fine views over town. Looking down from here you can also see the extensive **Char Chowk Haveli** (Four-Courtyard Haveli), off to the left, the finest in town and one of the largest in Shekhawati. Most of the haveli's exterior paintings have faded (some fine but faint elephants, horses and camels survive on the northern and eastern exterior walls) and large sections of plaster have fallen off, although the paintings under the eaves remain well preserved. The haveli remains inhabited, and the interior is generally off-limits to visitors.

Walk east from here past the attractive Radha Murlimanohar Temple to reach the **Sanganeeria Haveli**. The whole building is in a rather sorry state, and the west wall is missing large chunks of plaster, but you can still make out some entertaining details, including a Ferris wheel, a man ploughing with a buffalo and another two sawing a plank, a pair of wrestlers, women spinning cotton and a lady on a swing, as well as a curious picture showing a large number of people being pulled by an elephant in a huge cart (they look as if they're sitting in boxes in a theatre). There are several other fine havelis along the street here. Just south of here, opposite the Oriental Bank of Commerce, the **Chokhani Haveli** sports a particularly fine and colourful crop of animals, as well as rifle-wielding soldiers on horseback and a picture of Dhola and Maru (see p.323) shooting a bow and arrow from the back of a camel.

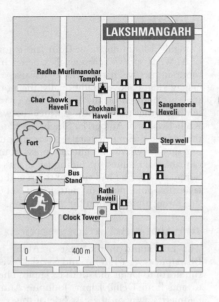

Head south to reach the town's clock tower, the centre of a lively little vegetable market; the **Rathi Haveli**, on the northeast corner of the clock tower square, has some relatively modern twentieth-century murals in kitsch Western style, with floral flourishes, classical columns and a European lady working away at a sewing machine. There's a further crop of interesting havelis in the sandy backstreets southeast of here, including a particularly fine (though apparently nameless) haveli two blocks east and one block south of the clock tower, with well-preserved murals showing Krishna being driven to his wedding in a bullock cart by Hanuman next to a fine European carriage with two musket-carrying soldiers guarding a diminutive lady and gentlemen, while a pair of bewhiskered Indian nobles follow in a camel-drawn carriage behind.

East of Jaipur

The fertile area **east of Jaipur**, interspersed with the forested slopes of the Aravalli Hills, holds an inviting mixture of historic towns and wildlife sanctuaries. To the northeast is the fortified town of **Alwar**, jumping-off point for the **Sariska Tiger Reserve and National Park**. Further east are the former princely capitals of **Deeg** and **Bharatpur**, and India's finest bird sanctuary, the **Keoladeo National Park**. The wildlife sanctuary at **Ranthambore**, in idyllic scenery southeast of Jaipur, offers the best chance in India of spotting wild tigers.

Alwar

Roughly 140km northeast from Jaipur towards Delhi, the large, bustling town of **ALWAR** sprawls across a valley beneath one of eastern Rajasthan's larger and more impressive **forts**, whose massive ramparts straggle impressively along craggy ridges above. Traditionally the northern gateway to Rajasthan, Alwar's strategic position on the Rajput border resulted in incessant warfare from the tenth to the seventeenth century between the Jats of Bharatpur and the Kachchwahas of Amber. Jai Singh, the flamboyant and eccentric great-grandfather of the present maharaja, became notorious during the British era for his outrageous behaviour. Official reports from the 1930s describe various instances of maharajal madness, including Jai Singh's habit of burying his luxury Hispano-Suiza cars once he had tired of them and the occasion on which he doused his favourite polo pony in petrol and set fire to it; rumours also circulated suggesting a predilection for young boys.

Arrival and information

The **bus stand** in the west of Alwar has services to and from Deeg and Bharatpur (every 15min), and Sariska (every 30min or so). Frequent buses also run north to Delhi and south to Jaipur. The **railway station**, which has services to and from Delhi, Jaipur, Jodhpur, Ahmedabad, Deeg and Ajmer, is a few kilometres away on the east side of town.

Just south of the station exit on the opposite side of Nehru Marg, the **tourist office** (Mon–Sat 10am–5pm; ☎0144/234 7348, ⓦwww.rajasthantourism .gov.in) has a useful range of maps and leaflets, and staff can book hotels and

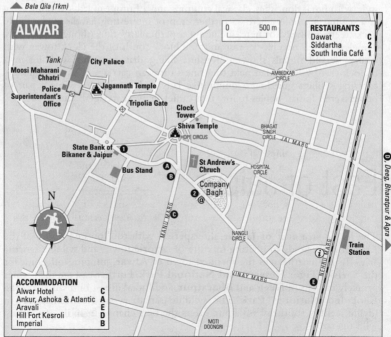

Bala Qila (1km)

ALWAR

0   500 m

RESTAURANTS
Dawat   C
Siddartha   2
South India Café   1

Tank

Moosi Maharani Chhatri

City Palace

Police Superintendant's Office

Jagannath Temple

Tripolia Gate

Clock Tower

Shiva Temple
HOPE CIRCUS

AMBEDKAR CIRCLE

BHAGAT SINGH CIRCLE   JAI MARG

State Bank of Bikaner & Jaipur ❶

Bus Stand Ⓐ
Ⓑ

St Andrew's Chruch

HOSPITAL CIRCLE

Company Bagh
❷ @

N

Ⓒ

MANU MARG

NANGLI CIRCLE

NEHRU MARG

ⓘ

Train Station

D, Deeg, Bharatpur & Agra

VINAY MARG

Ⓔ

MOTI DOONGRI

ACCOMMODATION
Alwar Hotel   C
Ankur, Ashoka & Atlantic   A
Aravali   E
Hill Fort Kesroli   D
Imperial   B

Sariska Tiger Reserve & Siliserh Palace

arrange transport (they charge Rs1000 for a full-day tour to Sariska). You can **change currency** and traveller's cheques at the State Bank of Bikaner & Jaipur, in the centre of town, which also has an intermittently functioning **ATM** which accepts foreign Visa and MasterCards. For **Internet** access, try the well-equipped Cyberlink (daily 9am–8pm; Rs20/min) on the south side of Company Bagh.

Accommodation

There's a small selection of accommodation in Alwar itself, plus a couple of seductive upmarket options in the surrounding countryside.

Alwar

Alwar Hotel 26 Manu Marg ☏ 0144/270 0012, ✆ ukrustagi@rediffmail.com. This trim little mid-range hotel is easily the nicest place to stay in Alwar itself, with smart and spacious a/c rooms set around a neat garden. The in-house *Dawat* restaurant (see below) is another major bonus. ⑤–⑥

Ankur, Ashoka, Atlantic and **Imperial** hotels. Clustered together on the corner of Manu Marg, ten minutes' rickshaw ride from the railway station or a five-minute walk from the bus station, this group of four adjacent and more or less indistinguishable hotels offers a range of simple but cheap, tolerably clean and reasonably comfortable fan and a/c rooms, and there are always plenty of vacancies – although the welcome can be slightly frostier than a medium-sized glacier. ① ④

Aravali Just south of the railway station on Nehru Marg ☏ 0144/233 2883. The town's only plausible budget alternative to the *Ankur* group of hotels. It's definitely seen better days, and the wide variety of rooms (fan, air-cooled and a/c) are all rather run-down, though reasonably clean. On the plus side, there's also a popular bar, Internet access, and a pool (guests only) in summer. ②–⑦

Around Alwar

Amanbagh Ajabgarh, around 50km from Alwar ☏ 01465/223333, ⊛ www.amanresorts.com. One of the most alluring boltholes in Rajasthan, set in a verdant oasis amidst a remote corner of the Aravalli hills. The resort has all the style you'd expect at the price (with room rates from US$720 per night and up), set in a lavish contemporary recreation of a Mughal-style palace occupying a walled compound once used for hunting camps by the maharaja of Alwar. Accommodation is in sumptuous two-storey "haveli" suites or in even more stunning (and expensive) "pool pavilions" with private swimming pools. There's also a gorgeous spa, plus a range of activities including yoga classes, trekking, horse-riding, camels safaris and jeep tours. ⑨

Hill Fort Kesroli 12km east of Alwar ☏ 01468/289352, ⊛ www.neemranahotels.com. India's oldest heritage hotel, occupying a fourteenth-century fort impeccably restored and centred on a lush inner courtyard filled with palms and bougainvillea. Rooms have great views over Kesroli village and the surrounding countryside. ⑦–⑧

Eating

The most reliable **place to eat** in town is the a/c *Dawat* restaurant, at the *Hotel Alwar* on Manu Marg, which does a good range of north Indian standards at moderate prices, plus better-than-average Chinese food. There are a couple of low-key veg restaurants in town. The *South India* café, opposite the State Bank of Bikaner & Jaipur, does crispy *dosas* and other hot snacks, or try the *Siddartha* veg restaurant, on the south side of Company Bagh. Alwar is famous throughout Rajasthan for its cavity-causing **milk cakes**, which you can buy at the stalls near the clock tower.

The town

Alwar's principal attraction is its rambling and atmospheric **City Palace**, or Vinai Vilas Mahal, a sprawling complex of ornate but now decidedly dilapidated buildings, covered in crumbling ochre plaster and studded with endless canopied balconies. Construction of the palace began under Bhaktawar Singh, Pratap

△ Alwar City Palace

Singh's successor, though most of the palace's innumerable rooms are now put to more mundane use as government offices – their dimly lit interiors piled high with musty mounds of official documents – while the courtyard in front provides open-air office space for dozens of typists, lined up behind clanking old antique metal machines, and lawyers, who prosecute their business under the trees. The whole place is marvellously atmospheric – the crumbling palace, the poky little offices and the crowds of ambling clerks lending it a genuine charm which is sometimes lacking from the region's more polished tourist attractions.

The palace's **museum** (daily except Fri 10am–4.30pm; Rs3) houses a haphazard collection of objects belonging to former maharajas – the fact that the whole place looks more like a rather dusty antique handicrafts store than a proper museum is very much in keeping with the palace's ramshackle appeal. The first room houses a medley of objects including ornately embroidered costumes, musical instruments, vases, statuettes, inlaid boxes, a quaint collection of little model people, and stuffed birds and animals including a tiger and a large bear, plus an equally fearsome bust of Queen Victoria, Empress of India. The second room is taken up by an excellent collection of seventeenth- to nineteenth-century Mughal and Rajput miniatures, including an entertaining selection of erotic scenes, while the third room is stuffed with lots of scary swords and knives (and some slightly silly helmets). The museum is on the top floor of the palace, and a bit tricky to find; look for the sign outside the ground floor of the palace (roughly in the middle of the facade) and follow the steps all the way up to the top, from where there are also fine views.

Go up the steps at the left-hand end of the main facade to reach the large **tank** which bounds this end of the palace, a beautiful spot, overlooked on one side by the palace's delicate balconies, and flanked by symmetrical *ghats* and pavilions. On the terrace overlooking the tank stands the **Moosi Maharani Chhatri**, built in memory of Bhaktawar Singh's mistress, who immolated herself on his funeral pyre. Steps lead up (take off your shoes) from the sandstone base to the ornate marble monument, with finely decorated arches and dome, decorated with a battle scene featuring elephants and horses. At the centre of the floor the former maharaja and his mistress are represented by two pairs of marble feet, strewn with flower petals.

An interesting walk leads east from the City Palace to the centre of town. Work your way round to the northeast side of the palace, then head east, past the Jagannath Temple to the large **Tripolia Gate**, which shelters a busy cross-roads at the eastern edge of Alwar's main commercial area. From here, a road arrows straight ahead to **Hope Circus** at the heart of the town's frantically busy – and wildly disorienting – central bazaar, a fascinating labyrinth of narrow alleyways packed with tiny shops selling every imaginable type of merchandise. You'll probably get lost at least a couple of times, but that's half the fun – if in doubt, the large **Shiva Temple** at the very centre of Hope Circus provides a valuable landmark, rising high above the surrounding melee on a plinth criss-crossed by symmetrical staircases.

Bala Qila

Perched high above Alwar is the **Bala Qila** fort (Mon–Fri 10am–5pm; free), whose well-preserved walls climb dramatically up and down the thickly wooded hillsides which rise above the town. There's not much actually to see inside the fort – besides a temple, a few old cannons and a radio mast – but the long climb up to the top makes a pleasant two-hour round hike from town; it's noticeably cooler up here, and the views are good. If you don't want to walk, you'll have to arrange for a taxi through your hotel or hunt out one of the town's elusive auto-rickshaws (try around the train station) – the road up is far too steep for a cycle rickshaw to tackle. Note that **police permission** is sometimes required to visit the fort. Although this regulation had been waived at the time of writing, it's worth checking before you tramp all the way up to the top; ask at the office of the Superintendant of Police, in the southwest corner of the courtyard in front of the City Palace.

Sariska Tiger Reserve and around

Alwar is the access point for **Sariska Tiger Reserve and National Park**, a former maharaja's hunting ground managed since 1979 by Project Tiger. Accustomed to being overshadowed by the more famous Ranthambore, Sariska was unwittingly thrust into the headlines in 2005 when it was discovered that its tiger population, estimated at around 28 in 2003, had all but vanished. Conservation authorities initially blamed mismanagement and a lack of resources, but after rumours surfaced that a famed taxidermist, in collusion with corrupt wardens, orchestrated a mass poisoning, Prime Minister Manmohan Singh ordered a high-profile police investigation. Regardless of where blame lies, activists see the decimation of Sariska's tiger population as one of India's biggest conservation scandals.

One silver lining from the whole affair is that the number of visitors to the sanctuary has dwindled significantly, and for birders and wildlife enthusiasts put off by the crowds and hassle of Ranthambore, Sariska's relative serenity comes as a welcome relief. The 881-square-kilometre sanctuary encompasses acres of woodland which are home to abundant **wildlife** including sambar, *chital*, wild boar, nilgai and other antelopes, jackals, mongooses, monkeys, peacocks, porcupines, and numerous birds. The park is also dotted with a number of evocative ruins and other man-made structures, including the old **Kankwari Fort**, and a **Hanuman temple** deep within the park which gets surprisingly lively on Saturdays and Tuesdays, when visitors to the temple are allowed into the park for free.

Practicalities

Sariska is **open** daily: July to mid–Sept 8am–3pm; April–June & mid–Sept to Oct 6am–4pm; Nov–March 7am–3.30pm. The park lies 35km southwest of Alwar on the main Alwar–Jaipur road; express **buses** between the two stop briefly to drop off and pick up passengers, on request, at the *Sariska Palace* hotel, a five-minute walk from the park. **Taxis** to the park can be booked through the tourist office in Alwar (see p.244) and cost Rs500 for a half-day trip, or Rs1000 for a full day, which also gives you time to visit Siliserh (see below) on the way back. Alternatively, you might be able to book transport through your hotel.

Entrance to the park costs Rs200 per person plus Rs125 per vehicle (and Rs200 for a video camera). **Jeeps with guide** can be hired at the entrance and cost Rs700 for a diesel Jeep, Rs800 for a petrol Jeep (the latter are quieter, and so less likely to scare off wildlife) for a three-hour drive around the park. The ride to Kankwari Fort costs Rs1300/1500 (diesel/petrol). Because Sariska gets so few visitors, lone travellers should be prepared for a long wait if looking for a ride-share. You can also go on **guided walks** around the entrance with reserve guides (Rs100/hr).

Most travellers choose **to stay** in Alwar, but there are a couple of places close to the reserve. Conveniently situated right next to the park entrance, the RTDC *Hotel Tiger Den* (☎0144/284 1342; ⑥) is attractive, if rather overpriced, with spacious old-fashioned fan and a/c rooms, plus a nice garden out the front, though service can be awful. A couple of minutes' drive down the main road is the far grander, but again significantly overpriced (from US$125), *Sariska Palace* (☎0144/284 1322, ⓦwww.sariska.org; ⑨). This former maharaja's residence has plenty of atmosphere, though rooms in the main building are disappointingly shabby given the price, while those in the various modern annexes scattered around the grounds are poky and boring. There's also a pool, and large swathes of manicured lawns to loll around on.

Siliserh Palace

Fifteen kilometres south of Alwar along the road to Sariska, the little-visited **Siliserh Palace** offers a sylvan escape from the hustle and bustle of Indian life, and is easily visited en route to or from Sariska if you've got your own vehicle (there's no public transport here). Maharaja Vijay Singh had the palace built in 1845 to win over a beautiful commoner, a certain Sheela, who agreed to marriage on the condition that she live within sight of her family's modest home. The whitewashed palace itself is fairly humdrum, but the Shangri-La setting, on the edge of a ten-square-kilometre lake ringed by uninhabited, jungle-clad hills, is idyllic. The lake is Alwar's water source – look out for the crumbling, sandstone aqueducts built more than a century ago. The palace now houses the RTDC *Lake Palace Hotel* (☎0144 288/6322; **④–⑥**; Fri–Sun half-board rates only; **⑥**), though rooms are disappointingly shabby and expensive, and service is haphazard, so you probably wouldn't want to stay. It's a nice spot to while away an afternoon, even so, and you can also rent out paddle-boats (Rs80/30min) and motorboats (Rs400/15min) if you want to get out onto the water – which also offers the best views of the palace itself, rising high above the lake.

Deeg

DEEG, 30km northwest of Bharatpur, is an anarchic and dust-choked little market town which, as the second capital of the local ruling Jats, was the scene of bloody encounters with the Mughal overlords in the mid-eighteenth century. The only reason you might want to come here these days is to see the town's lavish **palace** (daily 8am–5pm; Rs100) en route between Bharatpur and Alwar. Fusing Mughal and Hindu elements, it's an undeniably beautiful building, but doesn't really warrant a special day-trip.

Construction of the royal retreat began in 1730, when the Jat ruler Badan Singh established Deeg as the second capital of Bharatpur state, though most of the palace was built by his successor Surajmal in 1756. The delicate design of the complex is typical of the Jats, with the ornate buildings reflected in surrounding water tanks, and leafy gardens interspersed with myriad fountains. The extensive complex comprises a large number of finely carved buildings scattered around extensive *charbagh*-style gardens, divided into four by raised walkways, with an elaborate water tank at the centre, dotted with thirty-odd water jets – sadly, the water channels are dry, and the fountains here and throughout the complex are only switched on during local festivals.

Entering the palace, the first and largest of the various *bhawans* lies immediately ahead and to the right. This is the **Gopal Bhawan** (closed Fri), Surajmal's summer residence, a spacious and plushly furnished hall with majestic archways, sculpted pillars and intricate balconies. In front of the *bhawan* stands a marble arch which would once have supported a **swing** – popularly known as Nur Jahan's Swing – and said to have been looted from Delhi. Behind the *bhawan* (though only visible once you've walked past it) is one of the palace's two extensive tanks, the **Gopal Sagar**. Continue past the Gopal Bhawan to reach a small, subsidiary *charbagh* courtyard, popularly known as the **Queen's Palace**, flanked by a fine marble pavilion.

On the opposite side of the gardens lies the ornate **Kesav Bhawan**, or "Monsoon Palace", a square, open-sided and richly carved pavilion surrounded by a deep water channel dotted with hundreds of tiny fountains. This unusual structure was designed to recreate the cool ambience of the rainy season, with water released from rooftop pipes to imitate a shower of monsoon rain, whilst metal balls were agitated by further streams of pressurized water to simulate the sound of thunder – an extravagant entertainment, since the reservoir for the cascades took a week to fill and only a matter of hours to empty. Immediately behind here is another large **tank** (its stepped *ghats* usually covered in washing laid out by local housewives), while beyond rise the enormous walls of the town's huge fort.

At the rear of the gardens lies the third of the palace's main buildings, the **Kishan Bhawan**. A walkway here leads up to a rooftop terrace, from where there are fine views over the whole complex.

Deeg fell into decline at the beginning of the nineteenth century, and remains very small, though it is served by **bus** (every 15min; 1hr 30min) and **train** (daily; 2hr) from Alwar. Bharatpur is a one-hour bus ride away. If you get stuck, the better of the two unappealing **accommodation** options is RTDC's featureless *Motel Deeg* (℡05641/232 1203; ❷–❸), on the main road near the bus stand.

Bharatpur and Keoladeo National Park

The walled town of **BHARATPUR** is just a stone's throw from the border with Uttar Pradesh, 150km east of Jaipur, and a mere 18km from Fatehpur Sikri. The town itself has an interesting mix of traditional bazaars, temples, mosques, palaces and a massive fort, but the real reason to come here is to visit India's most famous bird sanctuary, the **Keoladeo National Park**, on the town's southern edge, one of India's, if not the world's, top ornithological destinations.

Arrival and information

Bharatpur's **bus stand** is in the west of town near Anah Gate. If you're arriving from Fatehpur Sikri, you'll save yourself time (and a rickshaw fare) by getting

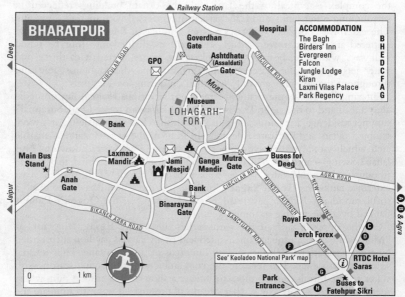

off the bus at the crossroads on the southeast side of town near the park gates and guesthouses – look out for the prominent Rajasthan government tourist office right on the crossroads, or the large *RTDC Hotel Saras* opposite. From the main bus stand, services run to Jaipur (and other major destinations in Rajasthan), Delhi, Agra and Fatehpur Sikri. Two kilometres northwest, the **railway station** lies on the main Delhi–Mumbai line. There are six services daily to Agra Fort (the most convenient being the Jaipur–Gwalior Intercity #2987 at 9.05am, arriving 10.15am, and the Barmer/Bikaner–Guwahati Express #5631/#5631A at 12.05pm, arriving 13.25pm); nine services to Sawai Madhopur (the best being the Golden Temple Mail #2904 at 10.45am, arriving 1.05pm) and two inconveniently timed services to Jaipur, for which you're better off taking the bus.

The town's informative **tourist office** (Mon–Sat 10am–5pm; ☏ 05644/222542, ⓦ www.bharatpur.nic.in) stands at the crossroads near the park entrance where Fatehpur Sikri buses pull in. You can pick up good state maps (Rs10) here, plus a useful free brochure on Bharatpur and the sanctuary, and they can also arrange transport. Nearby, on New Civil Lines, The Perch and the Royal Forex (both open till around 11pm) offer **Internet** access and also change cash and traveller's cheques, and give cash advances on credit cards.

Accommodation

Few people stay in the centre of Bharatpur town – to be well placed for an early start wildlife-viewing it's a better idea to spend the night in one of several, generally welcoming **hotels** and **guesthouses** along or near NH-11, which skirts the northern edge of the park some 4km south of the centre of town. Many of Bharatpur's hotel managers are skilled ornithologists. Bharatpur's reputation as a tourist-friendly oasis has made it an attractive base for day trippers to Agra and the Taj Mahal – a day-trip by taxi to Agra and back should cost about Rs1000. It's therefore advisable, especially in peak season (mid-Nov to late Feb), to **book rooms** in advance. Most of the guesthouses also rent bikes (Rs25–40 per day) and binoculars (Rs50–70 per day).

Budget

Evergreen ☏ 05644/225917. This basic family-run guesthouse is a convenient fallback if the other budget places nearby are full, though rooms are slightly dingy and relatively poor value compared to the competition. There's decent home cooking available, plus bikes and binoculars, at slightly inflated prices. ❷

Falcon ☏ 05644/225306, Ⓔfalconguest house@hotmail.com. Set back from the main road on a quiet suburban street, this modern guesthouse has a selection of spotless, comfortable and good-value fan, air-cooled and a/c rooms, plus a small garden restaurant with excellent food. Internet access available. ❷–❹

Jungle Lodge ☏ 05644/225622, ⓦwww .junglelodge.dk. Run by a knowledgeable naturalist, this friendly place has a range of clean and spacious modern rooms (fan, air-cooled and a/c) overlooking a tranquil flower-filled garden. The pleasant little terrace restaurant and evening fires (in winter) give it a communal feel, and there

are bikes and binoculars for rent, plus Internet access. ❶–❸

Kiran ☏ 05644/223845. Run by an extremely friendly and helpful pair of brothers, this place is tucked away 300m northeast of the park gates on a peaceful suburban backstreet and offers a range of clean and comfortable fan, air-cooled and a/c rooms at rock-bottom prices, plus good home cooking served on an intimate rooftop terrace. There's free pickup and drop-off from bus and train stations, plus bikes and binoculars for rent, and a small library. ❶–❸

Shanti Kutir Rest House 1km inside the park, ☏ 05644/222777. A downmarket alternative to the nearby *Bharatpur Ashok Hotel*, offering budget lodgings right inside the park, but note that it's only available when not occupied by government officials. Rates are cheap (full board doubles Rs600), though rooms are a bit musty and drab, and you'll also have to pay one day's park entrance fee for every night you stay. No reservations, but it's a good idea to call to check availability. Full board for 2 people ❸.

Mid-range to expensive

The Bagh Agra Rd, 1km past *Laxmi Vilas Palace* ☏05644/228333, Ⓦwww.thebagh.com. Built on the site of the Maharaja's former orchard, this idyllic upmarket hotel occupies a cluster of pink, low-rise buildings with pretty Mughal-style touches scattered around *charbagh*-style gardens which are home to over fifty species of bird. Rooms (all a/c) are cool, spacious and attractively furnished, and facilities include a decent-sized, but very shallow, pool (guests only), sauna, steam bath, Jacuzzi, gym, Ayurvedic massages (in season) and a smart multi-cuisine restaurant, coffee shop and bar. Prices from US$150. Ⓞ

Bahratpur Ashok (formerly the *Bharatpur Forest Lodge*) 1km inside park ☏0564/222760. In a pleasantly sylvan setting inside the park (note that you'll have to pay one day's park entrance fee for every night you stay here), this very sleepy hotel has spacious and comfortable old-fashioned rooms with balconies overlooking the sanctuary, a pleasant garden out the back and a passable restaurant. Relatively expensive, but the setting is pretty much unbeatable. Ⓞ

🏃 **Birders' Inn** ☏05644/227346, Ⓦwww.thebirdersinn.com. The most inviting place in town, usually full of serious bird watchers who gather nightly to compare checklists in the inviting, thatch-roofed restaurant; slideshows on the park's birds are presented most nights by the enthusiastic owner. Rooms (all a/c) are good value: large and surprisingly smart, and set well back from the traffic. Internet access available. Ⓞ

🏃 **Laxmi Vilas Palace** Agra Rd ☏05644/223523, Ⓦwww.laxmivilas.com. Former royal palace, set amid fifty acres of grounds on the eastern edge of town. It's all a trifle kitsch, but undeniably romantic, with charmingly OTT and very reasonably priced rooms (all a/c) complete with ornate cusped arches, four-poster beds and other regal decorative touches. The old-fashioned restaurant (complete with stuffed tiger head) and a medium-sized pool (guests only) are further bonuses. Ⓞ

Park Regency ☏05644/224232, Ⓔhotelpark regency@yahoo.co.uk. The newest of the mid-range hotels in this area, with large and spotless – though relatively expensive – a/c rooms and a pleasant swathe of lawn at the back. The attached a/c *Shivam Restaurant* serves up very good food prepared by retired five-star chef. Ⓞ–Ⓢ

The Town

Bharatpur was founded by the Jat king Surajmal, and quickly developed into a busy market centre, popularly known as the eastern gateway to Rajasthan. The virtually impregnable **Lohagarh** (Iron Fort) was built by Surajmal at the heart of town in 1732; the original moat, 45m wide and up to 15m deep, still encircles the fort, and time and modern development have had little effect on its magnificent eleven-kilometre-long bastions – the British spent four months in 1805 trying in vain to breach them, before suffering their heaviest defeat in Rajasthan. You're most likely to enter the fort from the south, though it's worth continuing across the fort to the impressive **Ashtdhatu** (or Eight-Metal) **Gate**, named on account of the number of different types of metal which apparently went into the making of its extremely solid-looking doors.

The fort is home to no less than three large royal palaces in various stages of dereliction, all built by the Jats between 1730 and 1850. The best preserved is the large orange **Kamra Khas Mahal**, on the west side of the fort, an atmospherically ramshackle structure, ranged around a lush garden, which now serves as the town's mildly diverting **museum** (daily except Fri 10am–4.30pm; Rs3, camera Rs10, video Rs20). Entering the palace, the first building on your right houses a large collection of finely carved sculptures, including some exquisitely detailed Jain statues, while tucked away to the rear of this section of the palace (and easily missed) is a superb little *hamman* (baths), its interior fashioned from beautifully carved marble, with ornate tiles and painted floral decorations. Head up the grand staircase on the opposite side of the courtyard to reach a further trio of rooms housing a medley of moth-eaten artefacts, including pictures of various maharajas, nineteenth-century miniatures of Krishna and Vishnu, household items ranging from fake pieces of fruit to quaint wooden children's toys, some very unpleasant stuffed animals and lots of guns and swords. From here, a further broad flight of stairs leads up to the rooftop, offering fine views over the rest of the fort.

Wonderful vistas can be had from the lofty **Jawahar Burj** next door – turn left as you exit the museum and follow the narrow road up around the edge of the palace. This small, elevated platform is topped with four delicately carved pavilions and an unusual iron pole embellished with the family tree of the maharajas of Bharatpur, though its principal attraction is the superb panorama over the fort and modern town, with bird's-eye views of the other two crumbling palaces – the **Kishori Mahal** and **Purana Mahal** – which dominate the old fort (though neither is now open to the public).

Immediately south of the fort lies the bizarre **Ganga Mandir**, a large Hindu temple dedicated to the proprietary goddess of India's most sacred river, though the elaborately carved sandstone building itself looks more like a Neoclassical French chateau than a Subcontinental temple, perhaps an expression of the Westernized sensibilities and patriarchal largesse of the maharajas of Bharatpur, who built the temple – very slowly and at enormous expense – between 1845 and 1937.

Beyond here, narrow roads snake southwest through Bharatpur's characterful bazaar district to reach the imposing **Jama Masjid**, fronted by a fine arched portal and set high on a raised platform above the densely populated surrounding streets. Work on the construction of the mosque is said to have been started on the same day in 1845 that the Ganga Mandir was begun – evidence of the ruling family's commendable even-handedness in dealing with their subjects' competing religious sympathies. A short distance further east lies the finely embellished **Laxman Mandir**, dedicated to the family deity of the maharajas of Bharatpur, Laxman, one of the brothers of Lord Rama, after whose other brother, Bharat, the town itself was named.

Keoladeo National Park

Keoladeo National Park (April–Sept 6am–6pm; Oct March 6.30am–5pm; Rs200 per visit, video Rs200) is India's premier bird-watching sanctuary – an avian wonderland that attracts vast numbers of feathered creatures thanks to its strategic location, protected status and extensive wetlands (although the last are currently much reduced - see p.254). Dedicated ornithologists also flock to the park in droves, though it's a richly rewarding place to visit even for novices who don't know one end of a pair of binoculars from the other.

Keoladeo (also known as Keoladeo-Ghana – *ghana* meaning "thick forest") was for sixty years a royal hunting reserve, a past memorialized inside the park by a

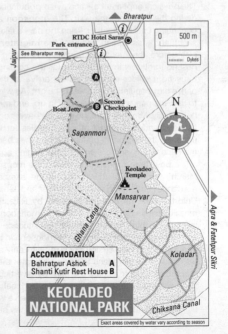

KEOLADEO NATIONAL PARK

plaque recounting the murderous exploits of former "illustrious" visitors. (On one particularly gruesome day, in 1938, the party of viceroy Lord Linlithgow bagged a staggering 4273 birds.) Despite the depredations of such trigger-happy hunters, the reserve's avian population continued to thrive. The area became a sanctuary in 1956 and a national park in 1982, and was declared a UNESCO World Heritage Site in 1985.

Today, Keoladeo's 29 square kilometres, including extensive areas of swamp and lake, constitute one of the world's most important ornithological breeding and migratory areas, with a staggering number of birds packed into a comparatively small area. Some 375 species have been recorded here, including around two hundred year-round residents along with 150-odd migratory species from as far afield as Tibet, China, Siberia and even Europe, who fly south to escape the northern winter. Keoladeo is probably best known for its stupendous array of **aquatic birds**, which descend en masse on the park's wetlands following the dramatic arrival of the monsoon in July. These include the majestic saras crane and a staggering two thousand painted storks, whose nesting cries create a constant background din, as well as snake-necked darters, spoonbills, pink flamingos, white ibis and grey pelicans (although sadly the extremely endangered Siberian cranes which were formerly one of the park's most prized visitors have not been seen in significant numbers since the early 1990s, apart from a single pair who last visited in 2002). There are also around thirty species of **birds of prey**, among them vultures, marsh harriers, peregrine falcons and ospreys, as well as smaller and more colourful exotics including hoopoes, bulbuls, bee-eaters and numerous dazzlingly coloured kingfishers. An added

Keoladeo through the seasons

The physical appearance – and avian population – of Keoladeo changes dramatically during the course of the year. The **monsoon** arrives (all being well) in July/August, continuing until September, filling the park's lakes and wetlands and turning the entire sanctuary a lush green. Many of the **migratory species** which visit the park arrive just before the monsoon breaks, competing furiously for the best perches and nesting frantically in preparation for the coming deluge. A further wave of migratory birds from colder northern climes arrive at the onset of **winter**, during which the park's bird population reaches its height. As winter draws on and temperatures begin to rise, the park's waters start drying up, and migratory visitors return to their summer homes. By May the park's wetlands have begun to evaporate, leaving turtles and fishes stranded amongst muddy puddles for those birds still in residence to feast upon. By the beginning of July the park has become dry, brown and parched, before the rains return, and the entire cycle begins again.

The **best time to visit** is following the monsoon, from around October through to March, when the weather is dry but the lakes are still full and the migratory birds in residence (although mists in December and January can hinder serious bird-watching). Unfortunately, the **drought** suffered by Rajasthan in the past decade has taken a massive toll on Keoladeo. Diminished monsoon rains over recent years have resulted in declining bird numbers, while the situation became particularly critical in 2006, when the almost total failure of the monsoon in the Bharatpur area left the park's lakes at a fraction of their customary size, with only a handful of the usual aquatic birds in residence. Whether plans to artificially water the park can be put in place (a scheme, mooted in 2004, to irrigate the park by diverting waters from surrounding agricultural land was met with furious opposition by local farmers), or whether the rains return, remains to be seen. For the time being, even a waterless Keoladeo is still an enjoyable place to visit, albeit not quite the world-class bird sanctuary of rainier seasons.

bonus is the number of large **mammals** who frequent the park, and you stand a good chance of glimpsing wild boar, mongoose, chital, nilgai and sambar along the paths, as well as hyenas, jackals and otters, and perhaps even elusive jungle cats. Rock pythons sun themselves at Python Point, just past Keoladeo temple, and in the bush land off the main road close to the entrance barrier.

Park practicalities

The park entrance is around 4km south of Bharatpur railway station. Free **maps** are available at the entrance. A single road passes through the park, while numerous small paths lined with *babul* trees cut across lakes and marshes and provide excellent cover for bird watching. If you need help identifying the birds, or finding vantage points, you can hire a **guide** at the gate (Rs70/hr for up to five people), who will probably have binoculars for you to borrow. The best way to get around is by **bike**, available at the main entrance (Rs25) if you haven't hired one at your guesthouse, or by cycle rickshaw (Rs50/hr; same price for one or two people) – drivers are trained by the park authorities and very clued up. Horse-drawn **tongas** (Rs100/hr), carrying up to six people, are also allowed in. **Cars and motorbikes** (an additional Rs50/Rs10) are allowed into the park up to the second checkpoint, but are hardly practical for bird watching. During the winter, gondola-style **boats** (Rs100) offer short rides across the wetlands, assuming there's enough water in the park, providing a superb opportunity to get really close to the birds. If you're planning a long visit, the *Bharatpur Ashok Hotel* at the north end of the park is a reliable place to get a drink or something **to eat**, although, as ever, it's a good idea to carry plenty of water with you.

Planning **when to visit** Keoladeo (see box opposite) has an important bearing on what you're likely to see. At any time of year it's best to visit at dawn and/or dusk, when the weather is coolest and the park's birds are most active. It's well worth visiting the sanctuary a couple of times, perhaps going in with a guide on the first visit for a couple of hours (you should get down to the Keoladeo temple in the centre of the park – and after which it's named), and then returning on your own later in the day to explore the wilder southern reaches of the park – although you'll have to buy a new ticket for each visit.

Ranthambore National Park

No Indian nature reserve can guarantee a tiger sighting, but at **RANTHAMBORE NATIONAL PARK** the odds are probably better than anywhere else. This has less to do with the size of the population, which is perilously small due to poaching, than because the tigers themselves are famously unperturbed by humans, hunting in broad daylight and rarely shying from cameras or Jeep-loads of tourists. Combine the big cats' bravado with the park's proximity to the Delhi–Agra–Jaipur "Golden Triangle", and you'll understand why Ranthambore attracts the numbers of visitors it does.

Arrival and information

Ranthambore National Park is reached via the small and rather grubby town of **Sawai Madhopur**, which is served by **trains** on the main Mumbai–Delhi line, and is thus easily accessible from Bharatpur, Agra, Jaipur and Delhi, as well as destinations further south, such as Kota. The **station** is right in the middle of town, close to the **bus stand** and bustling Bazriya market area. The helpful **tourist office** (Mon–Sat 10am–5pm; ☎07462/220808) in the station hands out

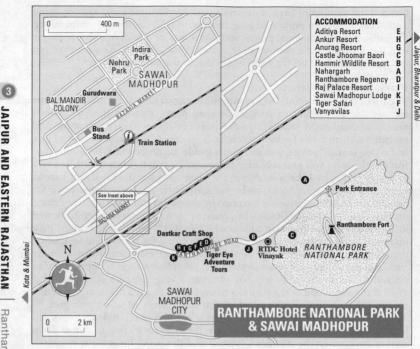

free **maps** of town and is a good place to check transport timings. There are **exchange** facilities at many hotels and in the State Bank of Bikaner & Jaipur in Sawai Madhopur. There are lots of ad hoc **Internet** places along the main road to the park, including a cluster just before you reach the *Ankur Hotel*; all charge about Rs40 per hour. The town's industrial zone, rather confusingly known as **Sawai Madhopur City**, lies south of the main town, though is of no interest to visitors except as the departure point for buses to Shivpuri in Madhya Pradesh.

Three kilometres beyond the turning for the park, near the village of Kutalpura, it's worth popping into the excellent **Dastkar Crafts Centre**, which trains local low-caste woman to make patchwork quilting and appliqué. Most of the pieces they produce are sent off to be sold in Delhi, but a small shop on site showcases their exceptional work – prices are very fair. The scheme is a laudable attempt to combat poverty in villages bordering the park, lessening the hardships that, in the past, have pushed villagers into illegal poaching. While you're in the area, have a wander around the houses on the opposite side of the road, whose walls are decorated with some wonderful traditional murals. If you can't make it to the centre, it also has an outlet in town, the Dastkar Crafts Shop, immediately north of *Ranthambore Regency Hotel*.

Accommodation and eating

Most of the area's numerous **hotels and guesthouses** are strung out along the 14km road between Sawai Madhopur and the national park; some of the better places are featured on ⓦwww.hotelsranthambhore.com. Accommodation **prices** in Ranthambore are significantly higher than average, despite the fierce competition and number of places in business (hotel owners claim that they only really see six months' business every year – and that they therefore have to charge double prices). Genuine budget accommodation is almost non-existent except for a few depressing and dingy options in Sawai Madhopur itself, although there's plenty of choice of lower mid-range places. Try bargaining hard wherever you go. Many places in town have pretty little gardens around the back surrounded by what the local hoteliers like to describe as "cottages", though in fact they're simply garden rooms.

Food in Ranthambore is very average, with lots of dull buffets and depressing dining halls, unless you want to push the boat out and go for a meal at one of the area's top-end places, like the lovely *Vanyavilas* (see below). For budget food, the rooftop restaurant at the *Tiger Safari* hotel is cheap and reasonably tasty, and usually as lively as anywhere in town.

Budget to mid-range

Aditiya Resort Ranthambore Rd, 3km north of town ☎0/941 472 8468. The best-value cheapie in Ranthambore at the time of writing, offering simple but clean and comfortable modern rooms (some with shared bath) with hot water and TV. ❷

Ankur Resort Ranthambore Rd, 2km from town ☎07462/220792, ✉ankurresort@yahoo.com. One of the most popular places in town, with a wide range of accommodation, from rather shabby budget rooms in the gloomy main building up to smart cottages in the gardens behind; the more expensive a/c cottages and rooms are relatively overpriced and worse value than the cheaper fan and air-cooled options. There's also a small square pool and decent food in the rather cheerless restaurant. ❸–❼

Anurag Resort Ranthambore Rd, 2.5 km from town ☎07462/220751, ⊛www.anuragresort.com. Sprawling pink resort with slight Rajput decorative touches and a nice big lawn out the front. Rooms are uninspiring but modern and spacious, and there are also some slightly more expensive cottages (some a/c) set around the attractively meandering gardens at the back. Reasonable value by local standards. ❺–❻

Hammir Wildlife Resort Ranthambore Rd, 7km from town ☎0/941 449 6566, ⊛www .hammirwildliferesort.com. Popular with Indian tourists, this is one of the more sensibly priced places in town (though the rooms are much better value than the garden cottages). Facilities include a pool (non-guests Rs100) and money exchange, and there are folk dances and camp fires (in winter) after dark. ❹–❻

Raj Palace Resort Ranthambore Rd, 2km from town ☎07462/224793, ⊛www.hotelraj-palace .com. Good value by Ranthambore standards, with spacious and clean (though rather bare) modern rooms with TV (some also with a/c) plus some slightly more homely a/c cottages around the gardens at the back. There's a restaurant and bar, and a pool is planned. ❸

Tiger Safari Ranthambore Rd, 2.5 km from town ☎07462/221137, ⊛www.tigersafariresort.com. The best of Ranthambore's cheaper hotels, with helpful service and well furnished and reasonable-value rooms (all with TV; some with a/c) plus spacious cottages around the rear garden – although the whole place can be a mite noisy (avoid the rooms near reception and the restaurant). There's also Internet access, free pick-up/drop-off from the station, and the rooftop restaurant is usually the liveliest place in town. ❹–❺

Expensive

Aman-i-Khás On the edge of the national park ☎07462/252052, ⊛www.amanresorts.com. Situated in a very quiet rural setting, this place rivals *Vanyavilas* for tasteful opulence (and price). Accommodation is in ten superb, cavernous luxury tents, each divided into separate "rooms" with white cotton drapes, a design loosely inspired by the travelling camps of the Mughal era. There's a traditional-style step-well for swimming, fresh produce from the on-site organic farm, and even a spa tent. Closed May to September. US$900 plus US$90 food charge per person per day; minimum two nights' stay; ❾

Nahargarh 2km south of park entrance, Khilchipur Village, Ranthambore Rd ☎07462/252281, ⊛www.alsisar.com. Superbly theatrical-looking hotel, built in the style of an old-fashioned Rajput hunting palace and looking every inch the regal retreat. Rooms are sumptuously decorated in traditional style and there's a large pool and fine views of the national park. ❽–❾

Ranthambore Regency Ranthambore Rd, 3km north of town ☎07462/223456, ⊛www .ranthambhor.com. Chintzy little pink hotel with plush, nicely furnished rooms; those around the gardens at the back are more appealing than those in the main building. It's an attractive place, though rooms (only available at full-board rates) are excessively expensive. There's also a similarly

There are virtually no **rickshaws** in Ranthambore, so you'll have to arrange transport to the bus or train station through your hotel when you come to leave.

Sawai Madhopur straddles the main Delhi–Mumbai railway line and is well served by trains. There are currently four convenient daytime services for **Jaipur** (7.20am, 10.20am, 10.45am & 3.05pm; 2hr 10min–2hr 40min) and two for **Bharatpur** (7.10am & 12.40pm; 2hr 15min–2hr 30min). For **Jodhpur** take the intercity express at 3.05pm; 8hr. Of the various trains to **Kota**, the most convenient are at 9.30am, 1.10pm, 4.10pm (1hr 20min–1hr 30min), though the morning train has a reputation for running late. There are no convenient services to **Bundi**; you can either take a train to Kota and then catch a bus, or catch a direct bus all the way from Sawai Madhopur (see below).

Ongoing improvements to the previously awful roads around Ranthambore are making **bus** travel a quicker and more comfortable option, although taking the train is still preferable for most destinations. Services run to Jaipur (every 90min; 5hr, but may have fallen to 3hr 30min by the time you read this) and, with excruciating slowness, to Bundi (4 daily; 4hr), and Ajmer (2 daily; 8hr). Buses depart from one of the two bus stands close to one another in the middle of Sawai Madhopur; check with the person who's taking you that you're at the right stand.

---

pricey Kerala Ayurvedic centre and a nice big pool (a breathtaking Rs300/hr for non-guests). US$132 full board. ⑨

RTDC Castle Jhoomar Baori. On a hillside 7km out of town ☎07462/220495, ⓦwww.hotels ranthambhore.com. Former royal hunting lodge on a lofty hilltop site inside the park, with views from a roof terrace over woodland and escarpment. The rooms are plain but comfortable enough, but the food is a lot less inspiring than the location. Book ahead; discounts April–June. ⑥

Sawai Madhopur Lodge Ranthambore Rd, 1.5km from town ☎07462/220541, ⓦwww.tajhotels .com. Stylish 1930s hunting lodge, formerly belonging to Maharaja Sawai Man Singh II but now run as a luxury heritage hotel by the Taj Group. The

whole place has a genuine leafy charm, with accommodation in a mix of rooms or in a few rather poky tents scattered around spacious grounds. Pool (non-guests Rs500). US$320 full board. ⑨

Vanyavilas Ranthambore Rd, about 7km from town ☎07462/223999, ⓦwww .oberoihotels.com. Superbly stylish and luxurious jungle resort offering a real splash of class in dusty Ranthambore – at a price. The resort is centred around a lavishly decorated building in the style of a royal hunting palace, with accommodation scattered around the rustic ground in beautifully equipped wooden-floored a/c tents. Non-guests can visit for a romantic terrace dinner around an open fire (Rs1000). Rooms US$770. ⑨

The park

In comparison to the tranquil tiger sanctuaries in the neighbouring state of Madhya Pradesh, the crowds at **Ranthambore National Park** can be off-putting, to say the least – the park is one of India's most popular, with more than eighty thousand visitors a year. And for good reason; even without the wildlife, the landscape alone would make it worth a visit. One of the last sizeable swathes of verdant bush in Rajasthan, Ranthambore is fed by several rivers that have been dammed to form **lakes**, dotted with delicate pavilions and decaying, creeper-covered Rajput palaces. At sunset or in the mists of early morning, these can be ethereal, while the ruined tenth-century **Ranthambore Fort**, towering above the forest canopy from atop a dramatic crag, is straight out of Kipling's *Jungle Book*.

The fort was conquered by Ala-ud-din Khalji's army in 1031, and Akbar in 1569, but for most of its existence Ranthambore has been controlled by the

Rajputs, and was set aside by the rulers of Jaipur for royal hunting jaunts. Soon after Independence the area was declared a sanctuary, becoming a fully fledged national park under **Project Tiger** in 1972. Over time, Ranthambore became world-renowned for its "friendly tigers", unperturbed by humans. Its reputation as Project Tiger's flagship operation, however, took a severe dent a decade later when it transpired that some of Ranthambore's own wardens were involved in **poaching**, and that, as a result, the tiger population here had plummeted to single figures (to this day, park staff deny the allegations). Since then, more rigorous policing is said to have brought the problem under control, and numbers have recovered to around 28 adult tigers and ten cubs.

In addition to tigers, Ranthambore is still home to very healthy populations of chital, nilgai, jackals, panthers, jungle cats and a wide array of birds, among which you may see crested serpent eagles, paradise flycatchers and more common peacocks and painted storks. One of the best places for bird watching is the fort, which is also the site of a temple to Ganesh; people from all over the country write to the elephant-headed god to invite him to their weddings.

Note that **Ranthambore is closed** annually from 1 July to 30 September; the **best time to visit** is during the dry season (Oct–March), when the lack of water entices the larger animals out to the lakeside. During and immediately after the monsoons, they are more likely to remain in the forest. More information can be gleaned from Project Tiger's excellent booklet, *The Ultimate Ranthambore Guide* (Rs175), on sale in local souvenir shops.

Park practicalities

Rules about **visiting Ranthambore** seem to change every couple of years, so don't be surprised if the following information has become obsolete by the time you arrive. At present, the number of vehicles allowed into the park is strictly controlled, with a maximum of around seventeen six-seater **Jeeps** (also known as "Gypsys") and twenty **Canters** (open-top buses seating twenty people) being allowed in during each morning and afternoon session. Obviously, most visitors prefer the much smaller and quieter Jeeps, although demand usually outstrips supply, and a lot of tourists find themselves having to make do with a place on a Canter instead. **Safaris** run daily every morning and afternoon, and last around three hours. Departure times vary slightly depending on sunrise, leaving between 6am and 7am and between 2pm and 3.30pm. Dress in layers: mornings can be surprisingly cool.

Seats officially cost Rs440 in a Canter and Rs533 in a Jeep (both prices include the park entrance fee which is Rs200 for foreigners and Rs20 for Indian residents). There's also a charge for video cameras of Rs200. If you want to book your own seat, the best option is to **reserve on line** at ⓦ www .rajasthantourism.gov.in. The alternative is to battle the crowds at the frequently chaotic **Tourist Reception Centre** (ticket office open 5–6.30am & noon–1.30pm) at the RTDC *Hotel Vinayak*, about 7km along Ranthambore Road, where you can buy tickets for tours on the day, though you'll be very lucky to bag a seat in a Jeep, which usually get bought up by hotels and safari operators way in advance.

A much easier option is to book a seat in a Jeep or Canter through your hotel or a local tour operator. Prices for a seat in a Canter booked like this are usually around Rs500 (ie a Rs60 surcharge on the basic government price); prices for seats in Jeeps fluctuate wildly according to demand, anything from Rs750 to Rs1200 (or frequently much more if booked through a top-end hotel). You shouldn't have any problems getting a seat in a Canter if you book the day before (except possibly on Sundays between 1 Oct and 15 April, when six

Canters are block-booked by the *Palace on Wheels*). If you want to go in a Jeep it's best to book ahead, although you might get lucky, especially in summer, when visitor numbers fall significantly. Your chances drop considerably closer to Diwali, New Year and around any other public holiday.

There are several safari operators in town. Yadvendra Singh at **Tiger Eye Adventure Tours** (T0/935 150 4600, W www.tigereyeadventuretours.com), just north of the Dastkar Craft Shop, can arrange Jeeps and Canter places for Ranthambore tours, and also runs bird-watching expeditions (3–5hr; Rs1200 per Jeep) in the Ranthambore area and tours of Ranthambore Fort (3hr; Rs1500 per Jeep).

The easiest way to **visit the fort** is to go on a tour; these can be arranged through Tiger Eye (see above) and the *Tiger Safari* hotel (Rs500–600 per person), or just ask at your hotel to see if they can arrange a Jeep. Alternatively, you could book an early morning safari and ask to be dropped at the main park entrance on the way out, from where you can climb an old paved path to the ruins. Unfortunately, once you've explored the fort, you'll be stuck without transport, and probably a considerable distance from your hotel, unless you're lucky enough to hitch a lift. Note that you don't have to pay the park entry fee if you're just going to the fort.

4

Western Rajasthan

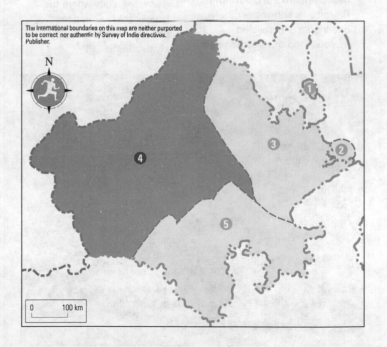

The International boundaries on this map are neither purported to be correct nor authentic by Survey of India directives. Publisher.

N

4

3

1

2

5

0   100 km

CHAPTER 4 # Highlights

✱ **Dargah Khwaja Sahib, Ajmer**
The holiest Muslim shrine
in India draws thousands of
pilgrims every day, and is the
scene of hypnotic *qawwali*
chanting every evening.
See p.267

✱ **Savitri Temple, Pushkar** For
optimum views of the famous
lake and whitewashed holy
town, climb to the hilltop
Savitri temple at sunrise.
See p.277

✱ **Meherangarh Fort, Jodhpur**
Rajasthan's showcase citadel,
offering an unparalleled
museum and maximum impact
views of the blue city below.
See p.288

✱ **Jaisalmer Fort** India's greatest
inhabited fort with more
than two thousand people
still occupying its golden
sandstone homes. See p.303

✱ **Camel trekking** There's no
better way to experience the
Thar desert than by riding
through it on camel. See p.306

✱ **Old City, Bikaner** Follow the
Heritage Route through this
warren of a city where the
havelis are built in a most
unlikely conglomeration of
styles. See p.321

△ Jaisalmer Fort

Western Rajasthan

estern Rajasthan, the region north and west of the Aravalli Hills, is a desert land rich in history, whose warrior kings built huge forts that still rise majestically out of the arid landscape. These are the strongholds of kingdoms that grew rich from taxing the caravans carrying silk, spices and precious stones across the mighty **Thar Desert** (see box below), which begins at the Aravallis and stretches west into Pakistan. Though this may conjure up images of sweeping sand dunes, most of the desert is actually scrub, inhabited by animals such as blackbuck antelope, chinkara gazelle and desert fox. Dunes do exist, however, deep in the desert – to see them, you'll generally need to go out on a **camel trek**, which is one of the region's most popular tourist activities.

Home to the most enduring images of Rajasthan, with its camels and its desert forts, western Rajasthan is unsurprisingly a major draw for tourists. The Sufi shrine at **Ajmer** has long brought pilgrims from across the Subcontinent and beyond, as has the holy lake at nearby **Pushkar**, sacred to the Hindu god Brahma, the site of Rajasthan's biggest camel fair, and a major stop on the hippy trail since the first overlanders hit the road to Kathmandu back in the 1960s. **Jodhpur**, the region's largest city, boasts its most imposing fort, dominating a walled town of houses tinged blue with indigo, while further out in the Thar, the golden city of **Jaisalmer** is the epitome of a Rajasthani desert town, with its still-inhabited fort and its beautiful havelis. **Bikaner**, to the north, is less

Legend of the Thar

Legend ascribes the **creation of the Thar** to Rama, hero of the Ramayana, one of the two great Hindu epics. In it, Rama, an earthly incarnation of the god Vishnu, has to rescue his wife Sita from the clutches of the demon Ravana, who is holding her on the island of Sri Lanka. To cross to the island, Rama loads his bow with a magical arrow that will dry up the ocean, but the sea god Sagara begs him not to shoot, offering him free passage instead. Well, says Rama, my bow is now drawn and must be shot, where shall I aim it? There is a sea to the north, replies Sagara, where evil-doers drink my water and hurt me; shoot your arrow there, and you'll be doing me a favour. So Rama takes aim and shoots, drying up the sea that Sagara has described, and creating the desert of Marwar ("Land of the Dead"). By Rama's special boon, this new land, though desert, is blessed, full of sweet herbs and fit for grazing cattle.

In fact, the legend would seem to be based on some degree of truth, for back in the Jurassic period (a mere 206–144 million years ago), the Thar was indeed covered by sea, as the fossil record shows, and you may notice that slabs of sandstone often bear tell-tale ripple marks showing that they were once part of a seabed.

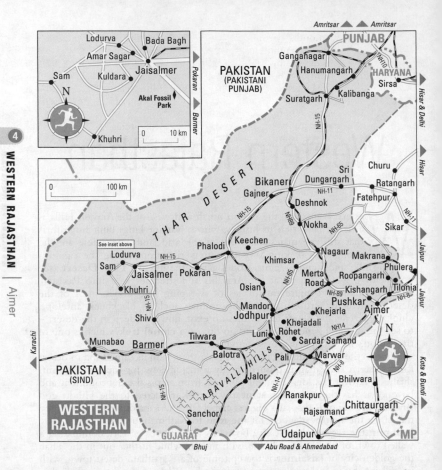

visited, but no less rewarding, its old city a maze of temples and early twentieth-century mansions built in a bizarre fusion of architectural styles.

Ajmer

The Nag Pahar ("Snake Mountain"), a steeply shelving spur of the Aravallis west of Jaipur, forms an appropriately epic backdrop for **AJMER**, home of the great Sufi saint **Khwaja Muin-ud-din Chishti**, who founded the Chishtiya Sufi order. To this day, his tomb, the **Dargah Khwaja Sahib**, remains one of the most important Islamic shrines in the world – during his 2001 visit to India even Pakistan's president, General Pervez Musharraf, scheduled a visit. The streams of pilgrims and dervishes (it is believed that seven visits here are the equivalent of one to Mecca), especially pick up during Muharram (Muslim New Year) and Id and for the saint's anniversary day, or **Urs Mela** (approximately 9 July 2008, 29 June 2009, 18 June 2010 – dates are fixed according to the lunar calendar and recede against the Western calendar by about eleven days a year).

For Hindu pilgrims and foreign travellers, Ajmer is important primarily as a jumping-off place for **Pushkar**, a twenty-minute bus ride away across the Nag Pahar, and most stay only for as long as it takes to catch a bus out, but as a day-trip from Pushkar it's a highly worthwhile excursion, and as a stronghold of Islam, Ajmer is quite unique in Hindu-dominated Rajasthan.

History

A local Rajput chieftain, Ajay Pal Chauhan, established a fort at Ajmer in the tenth century, and it became the capital of a territory carved out by his Chauhan clan. The Chauhans went on to become the dominant power in eastern Rajasthan, and even brought Delhi under their sway, but they were beaten in 1193 by Muhammad of Ghor (see p.380), who had invaded from Afghanistan. The Delhi sultans allowed the Chauhans to carry on ruling as their tributaries, but in 1365, with Delhi on the wane as a regional power, Ajmer fell to the kingdom of Mewar (Udaipur).

During the sixteenth century, the city became the object of rivalry between Mewar and the neighbouring kingdom of Marwar (Jodhpur). The Marwaris took it in 1532, but the presence of Khwaja Muin-ud-din Chishti's *dargah* (see

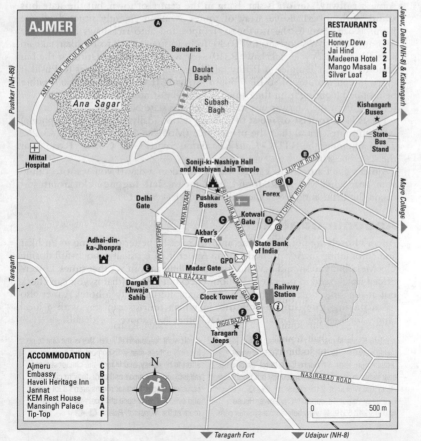

p.267) made Ajmer an important prize for the Muslim Mughals, and Akbar's forces marched in only 27 years later.

Akbar himself came on pilgrimage to the *dargah* every year, and his successor Jahangir frequently used the city as his base. It was here that Jahangir finally agreed to see England's ambassador Thomas Roe, and to give English (and subsequently British) merchants the right to trade.

The Mughals held onto Ajmer for over two centuries, but as their empire began to fragment, the neighbouring Rajput kingdoms once again started giving the city covetous looks. It was eventually taken in 1770 by the Marathas, Hindu rebels from Maharashtra (the hinterland of Mumbai), who had broken away from the Mughal empire to form their own kingdom. Even then, both Mewar and Marwar still had designs on Ajmer, which they didn't relinquish until 1818, when the Marathas sold the city to the East India Company for fifty thousand rupees. Thus, while most of Hindu-dominated Rajasthan retained internal independence during the Raj, Ajmer was a little Muslim enclave of directly-ruled British territory, only reunited with Jodhpur and Udaipur, its former overlords, when it became part of Rajasthan in 1956.

Arrival and information

Ajmer's **railway station** is slap-bang in the centre of town, but the state **bus stand**, with an exhaustive array of routes, is inconveniently situated on the Jaipur Road, 2km to the northeast. Tempos and auto-rickshaws connect the two; auto-rickshaws cost around Rs30. To head straight out to Pushkar, take an auto (Rs30) or a cycle rickshaw (Rs10) – or walk – from the station or the bus stand to the Jain Temple on Prithviraj Marg, where there are buses to Pushkar every fifteen minutes or so till 9.30pm. Arriving **from Pushkar**, you'll either be dropped (coming from the Ajmer bus stand) just north of Mahavir Circle, or (coming from the Marwar bus stand) at Ajmer's state bus stand.

The RTDC **tourist office** at the railway station (daily 10am–5pm; no phone) is much more central than the main office (Mon–Sat 10am–5pm; ☎0145/262 7426) adjoining the RTDC *Hotel Khadim* on Savitri Girls' College Road, near the state bus stand.

Ajmer's chief attractions can be easily visited in a day. If you want to dump your gear while you look around, head for the **left luggage** cloakroom just inside the main entrance at the railway station.

Accommodation

Ajmer's **hotels** are not great value, and you're really better off staying in Pushkar and commuting in. Accommodation in Ajmer itself is usually chock-full during Urs Mela, but you should have no trouble finding a room at other times. Lower-priced hotels tend to operate a 24-hour checkout system (that is, you can check out at the same time you checked in). As an alternative to a hotel, Ajmer also has a **paying guesthouse scheme**, in which tourists can stay with a local family for a set fee – contact the RTDC office (see above) for details.

Ajmeru Khailand market, off Prithviraj Marg, just inside Kotwali gate ☎0145/243 1103, ⓦwww .hotelajmeru.com. A modern, new hotel, among the best value in town, nothing sprauncy but bright, clean and well kept. 24hr checkout. ❸–❹

Embassy Jaipur Rd, opposite City Power House ☎0145/242 5519, ⓦwww.hotelembassyajmer.com.

If you want an upmarket hotel, this is the one to go for. Only a three-star, with no pool, but it makes an effort to be classy, and though the cheapest rooms (all a/c) are a bit small and dark, they're cosy and carpeted; bigger, brighter rooms aren't a lot more, and even the royal suite still costs far less than a room at the *Mansingh Palace*. ❺–❻

Haveli Heritage Inn Kutchery Rd, Phul Nawas ☏0145/262 1607, ✉haveliheritageinn@hotmail.com. It sounds grander than it is, but if you think of this as a *pension* rather than a haveli, you'll get the right idea. It's an old house from the 1870s, but the rooms are modern, and the building isn't especially interesting. The big attractions are the peaceful atmosphere, the delightful family that run it, and the great home cooking. ③–⑥

Jannat Dargah Bazaar, near Nizam Gate ☏0145/243 2494, ⊛www.ajmerhoteljannat.com. A stone's throw from the Dargah Khwaja Sahib, and the best hotel in the area, it fills up quickly on Thursdays and Fridays, but usually has space the rest of the week. There's a range of rooms, all modern and clean, some a/c, and a good restaurant. 24hr checkout. ③–④

King Edward Memorial (KEM) Rest House Station Road ☏0145/242 9936. For those who value character over comfort, or need the cheapest bed in town, this run-down colonial compound, built in 1912 as a memorial to Britain's King Edward VII, has some very cheap and grotty rooms set around a lovely big courtyard with trees and squirrels, or a few spacious if rather dusty rooms (some a/c) around a smaller courtyard at the back. 24hr checkout. ①–③

Mansingh Palace Vaishali Nagar (Ana Sagar Circular Road) ☏0145/242 5702, ⊛www .mansinghhotels.com. Three-kilometres northwest of town on the main road to Pushkar, this is Ajmer's poshest option, but it's inconveniently situated, and unless you absolutely have to take the top hotel, it isn't worth the price, though it has a go at being deluxe, with quite stately rooms and a decent restaurant, but no pool. ⑦

Tip-Top Cinema Road, off Diggi Bazaar ☏0145/510 0241 or 1241. Best of the hotels around the station, in a lively market area and good value by Ajmer standards, with a/c or non-a/c en-suite rooms. 24hr checkout. ②–④

The Town

Although Ajmer's dusty main streets are choked with traffic, the narrow lanes of the bazaars and residential quarters around the **Dargah Khwaja Sahib** retain an almost medieval character, with lines of rose-petal stalls and shops selling prayer mats, beads and lengths of gold-edged green silk offerings. Finely arched Mughal gateways still stand at the main entrances to the **old city**, whose skyscape of mosque minarets and domes is overlooked from on high by the crumbling **Taragarh** – for centuries India's most strategically important fortress.

Dargah Khwaja Sahib

The revered Sufi saint, Khwaja Muin-ud-din Chishti (see box p.268), who died in Ajmer in 1236, was buried in a small brick tomb that is today engulfed by a large marble complex known as the **Dargah Khwaja Sahib**, or Dargah Sharif (⊛www.dargahajmer.com; winter 5am–9pm, summer 4am–10pm). It is most easily reached along Nalla Bazaar from Madar Gate, or along Dargah Bazaar from Delhi Gate.

Founded in the thirteenth century and completed under the sixteenth-century Mughal emperor Humayun, the *dargah* contains structures financed by many Muslim rulers, but it was under the imperial patronage of the three great Mughals – Shah Jahan, Jahangir and, most crucially, Akbar – that this became the most important Muslim shrine in India. It remains massively popular, with thousands of pilgrims passing through the gates every day.

You enter the *dargah* through the lofty **Nizam Gate**, donated by the Nizam of Hyderabad in 1911. Once inside, you may be accosted by stern-looking young men claiming to be "official guides". In fact, they are *khadims*, hereditary priests operating in much the same way as Hindu *pujaris*, leading pilgrims through rituals in the sacred precinct in exchange for donations. Their services are not compulsory, although you may wish to employ one to point out the features of religious and historical significance inside.

Beyond the Nizam Gate is a smaller gateway, the **Shajahani Gate**, so called because it was commissioned by the Mughal emperor Shah Jahan, through which is a courtyard where, to your right, steps lead up to the **Akbari**

Masjid, a mosque donated by the emperor Akbar, who had come to the *dargah* to pray for a son; when his prayer was granted with the birth of Salim (who was to be the emperor Jahangir), Akbar had the mosque built here in gratitude.

The next gateway is the imposing, white **Buland Darwaza**, commissioned in the fifteenth century by the ruler of Malwa (now part of Gujarat), Mahmoud Khalji. After passing through it, you'll see, resting on raised platforms on either side, two immense cauldrons, known as *degs*. The one on the right, the larger of the two, was donated by Akbar after the battle of Chittaurgarh (see p.362) in 1567; the other was a gift from Jahangir upon his accession in 1605. Continuing the saint's tradition of giving succour to the needy, pilgrims throw money into them to be shared among the poor. The *degs* can hold 98 maunds (3658kg) of rice between them, and are the focus of an extraordinary ritual during Urs Mela, in which both are used to cook up the creamy Indian pudding *kheer*, paid for by wealthy patrons. When the *kheer* is ready, a mad scramble begins as the devout, dressed in protective plastic bags, dive head first into the bubbling *degs* to fill their buckets with the pudding, which is regarded by the faithful as *tabarruk* (equivalent of the Hindu *prasad*,

WESTERN RAJASTHAN | Ajmer

4

Khwaja Muin-ud-din Chishti

In 1992–3, following the demolition by Hindu fundamentalists of the mosque at Ayodha (see p.393), sectarian riots swept across India as Hindus turned on their Muslim neighbours nationwide, but Ajmer – a Muslim city in a Hindu fundamentalist state, and an obvious flashpoint – escaped unscathed. No one had any doubt that peace prevailed because of the enduring influence of the Sufi saint enshrined at the heart of the city, **Khwaja Muin-ud-din Chishti**.

Born in 1156, in Afghanistan, Muslim India's most revered saint, also known as Khwaja Sahib or Garib Nawaz, began his religious career at the age of thirteen, when he distributed his inheritance among the poor and adopted the simple, pious life of an itinerant Sufi *fakir* (the equivalent of the Hindu sadhu). On his travels, he soaked up the teachings of the great Central Asian Sufis, whose emphasis on mysticism, ecstatic states and pure devotion as a path to God were revolutionizing Islam during this period. By the time he came to India with the invading Afghan armies, Khwaja Sahib had already established a following, but his reputation as a saint and a sage only really snowballed after he and his disciples settled in Ajmer at the beginning of the thirteenth century.

Withdrawing into a life of meditation and fasting, he preached a message of renunciation, affirming that personal experience of God was attainable to anyone who relinquished their ties to the world. More radically, he also insisted on the fundamental **unity of all religions**: mosques and temples, he asserted, were merely material manifestations of a single divinity, with which all men and women could commune. In this way, Khwaja Sahib became one of the first religious figures to bridge the gap between India's two great faiths. With its wandering holy men, emphasis of mysticism and miracles, and devotional worship involving music, dance and states of trance, Sufism would have been intelligible to many Hindus. Moreover, it readily absorbed and integrated aspects of Hindu worship into its own beliefs and rituals. After Khwaja Sahib died at the age of 97, his followers lauded the Bhagavad Gita as a sacred text, and even encouraged Hindu devotees to pray using names of God familiar to them, equating Ram with "Rahman", the Merciful Aspect of Allah. The spirit of acceptance and unity central to the founder of the Chishti order's teachings explains why his shrine in Ajmer continues to be loved by adherents of all faiths.

or Christian "consecrated"). The best place from which to view this spectacle is the platform above the main entrance archway, on which you can usually gain a place by slipping a tip to one of the *khadims*.

Past the *degs*, over to the left, is the **Langer Khana**, where five maunds (some 186kg) of barley meal are cooked up every day for distribution to the poor. Shops here and in the inner courtyard sell rose petals to scatter over the saint's tomb. Opposite is the **Mehfil Khana**, which is used during the Urs Mela for the nightly recitation of *qawwali* music (11pm–4am), a soulful communal chant, accompanied by clapping, harmonium and drums, whose hypnotic rhythm lulls the participants into a trance-like state called *mast* that is believed to bring them closer to God. It is this desire to come personally nearer to God which lies at the heart of Sufism.

Beyond the *khanas* is an inner courtyard where the Tomb of Khwaja Sahib itself lies inside a domed mausoleum (the *Mazar Sharif*) made of marble, its door painted with gold leaf, green and red. The tomb inside (closed daily 3–4pm, except Thurs when it's shut 2.30–3.30pm) is surrounded by silver railings and surmounted by a large gilt dome. Devotees file past carrying brilliant *chadars*, gilt-brocaded silk covers for the saint's grave, on beds of rose petals in flat, round head-baskets. Visitors are asked by the *khadims* for donations, and are offered blessings, lightly brushed with peacock feathers and given the chance to touch the cloth covering the tomb.

Subsidiary shrines in the inner courtyard include those belonging to daughters of Khwaja Sahib and Shah Jahan, plus a handful of generals and governors, and some Afghani companions of the saint. The delicately carved marble mosque behind the saint's tomb, the **Jama Masjid** or Shahjahani Masjid, was commissioned by Shah Jahan in 1628 and took nine years to build. Despite its grand scale, the emperor deliberately had it built without a dome so as not to upstage the saint's mausoleum next door.

In March 2002, with the neighbouring state of Gujarat in the grip of sectarian strife, the *khadims* reported the image of Khwaja himself mystically appearing to them on the *Mazar Sharif*, with the aim of "spread[ing] the message of goodwill and peace after the recent rioting in Gujarat state". Police were deployed at the site to prevent a stampede when huge numbers of pilgrims arrived soon after, although many dismissed the claims as a gimmick. Things are quieter now, but the continual murmur of prayer and the heady scent of rose attar, and uplifting **qawwali** music being performed before the shrine (from an hour or so before sunset until 9pm), exactly as it has been for seven hundred years, still create an unforgettable atmosphere.

Other Islamic monuments

Often overlooked by visitors, the **Adhai-din-ka-Jhonpra**, or "two-and-a-half-day hut", 400m west of the Dargah Khwaja Sahib, is the oldest surviving monument in the city and unquestionably one of the finest examples of medieval architecture in Rajasthan. Originally built in 660 AD as a Jain temple, and converted in 1153 into a Hindu college on the orders of the Chauhan ruler Visan Dev, it was destroyed forty years later by the invading Afghan chieftain Muhammad of Ghor, who later had it renovated as a mosque. Tradition holds that its name derived from the speed with which it was constructed, but in fact the reconstruction took fifteen years, using bricks and finely sculpted panels plundered from Hindu and Jain temples; the name actually refers to a *fakirs'* festival which used to be held here in the eighteenth century, a *jhonpra* (hut) being the abode of a *fakir* (Sufi mendicant). Motifs of pre-Muslim origin are still clearly discernible on the pillars and ceilings, but

△ Baradaris on the bank of Ana Sagar, Ajmer

the mosque's most beautiful feature is the bands of Koranic calligraphy decorating its seven-arched facade.

A more recent Islamic relic is **Akbar's Fort**, a massive rectangular palace made of golden sandstone, and actually only the innermost part of a much larger fort. It was used by Akbar and his son Jahangir during their visits to the Dargah, and it was here in 1616 that Jahangir received Sir Thomas Roe, the first British ambassador to be granted an official audience, after four years of trailing between the emperor's encampments. In 1818 the palace came under British control, and after being used as an arsenal during the 1857 uprising, earned the nickname **Magazine**. Today, the old palace houses a small **museum** (daily except Fri 10am–4.30pm; Rs3, free on Mon; Rs10 for camera, Rs20 video), displaying mainly Hindu Rajasthani statues. The most impressive of them are a twelfth-century sculpture of Varaha (Vishnu in his incarnation as a boar), and a fourteenth- or fifteenth-century white marble statue of Vishnu.

Laid out in the twelfth century, the artificial lake northwest of Ajmer, known as **Ana Sagar**, is today little more than a pond – a legacy of overuse and drought. There is usually enough water to keep boat-wallahs busy, but the real reason to come out here is to stroll along the long embankment, or bund, on its southwest shore, which moderated the flow of the river through the city. It was on top of this parapet, exposed to the cooling breezes off the water, that Shah Jahan chose to erect a line of exquisite white marble pavilions called **Baradaris** as summer shelters. Modelled on the Diwan-i-Am in Delhi's Red Fort, four of the five pavilions remain beautifully preserved, standing in the shade of trees and ornamental gardens (the former **Daulat Bagh**) planted by Jahangir. The best time to visit them is an hour or so before sunset, when the colours of the lake and polished stone of the Baradaris are sublime.

Taragarh Fort

Three kilometers to the south, and just visible on the ridge high above the city, **Taragarh** (the Star Fort) was for two thousand years the most important strategic objective for invading armies in northwest India. Any ruler who successfully breached its walls, rising from a ring of forbidding escarpments, effectively controlled the region's trade. Few, however, were able to do so by mounting a siege; the fortress even repulsed the indomitable Mahmud of Ghazni in 1024. It's now badly ruined, but is still visited in large numbers by pilgrims, who come to pay their respects at what must be one of the few shrines in the world devoted to a tax inspector, the **Dargah of Miran Sayeed Hussein Khangsawar** – Muhammad of Ghor's chief revenue collector was one of many slain in the Rajput attack of 1202 when, following one of the fort's rare defeats, the entire Muslim population of the fort was put to the sword. Today, a vestigial Muslim community still survives in a tumbledown village inside the walls, clustered around his whitewashed *dargah*.

The best way of getting to Taragarh is to take a ninety-minute **hike** along the ancient paved pathway from Ajmer, which offers superb **views** across the plains and neighbouring hills. To pick up the trailhead, follow the lane behind the Khwaja Sahib Dargah, past the Adhai-din-ka-Jhonpra and on towards the saddle in the ridge visible to the south. Bring **food** as the only places to eat inside the battlements are a handful of fly-infested non-veg cafés. Alternatively, you can take one of the **Jeeps** (Rs20) which leave from the Plaza Cinema on Diggi Chowk, west of the train station; ask for the "Ta-ra-garh jeeps", pronouncing all the syllables clearly, or you may end up at the main Khwaja Sahib Dargah. To return to Ajmer, you can either follow the path back downhill, or catch a Jeep from the lot at the northeast side of the village, near the Dargah.

Other attractions

While most of Rajasthan consisted of princely states, Ajmer was under British rule, and relics of it bestrew the city, among them the **Jubilee clock tower** opposite the railway station and the **King Edward Memorial Hall** a little to the west. The famous **Mayo College**, originally built as a school for princes, and now a leading educational institution is known in society circles as the "Eton of the East".

Perhaps the most bizarre sight in Ajmer is the mirrored **Soniji-ki-Nashiya** hall adjoining the **Nashiyan Jain temple**, or "red temple" (daily summer 8am–6pm, winter 8.30am–5.30pm; Rs5, camera Rs20). Commissioned in the 1820s by an Ajmeri diamond magnate, the hall contains a huge diorama-style display commemorating the life of Rishabha (or Adinath), the first Jain *tirthankara*, believed to have lived countless aeons in the past. From the uppermost of the two storeys that surround it, you can look down on a glowing tableau featuring musicians flying above the sacred Mount Sumeru on swans, peacocks and elephants, and a huge procession of soldiers and elephants carrying the infant *tirthankara* to the mountain to be blessed. The display, sealed behind glass, contains a tonne of gold. Admission to the main temple alongside is restricted to Jains.

Eating

In addition to the snack and fruit juice places around Dargah Bazaar and Delhi Gate, Ajmer has a handful of larger **restaurants**.

Elite Station Rd, next to *KEM Rest House*. White tablecloth dining room and garden restaurant, serving moderately priced veg curries (Rs36–72) and thalis (Rs48), plus a sprinkling of vegetarian Chinese, Continental and South Indian options.

Honey Dew Station Rd, next to *KEM Rest House*. Garden restaurant with a good mixed menu (veg, non-veg, Indian, Chinese and Continental) at middling prices (Rs60–90), as well as shakes and ice cream.

Jai Hind Station Rd, tucked in an alley and directly opposite the station's main exit. Very good veg food, including delicious *alu paratha* and *raita* breakfasts, thalis (Rs38–54) and veg curries (Rs34–67).

Madeena Hotel Station Rd, by the green-and-white mosque opposite the station. Muslim establishment serving very tasty non-veg Mughlai curries, mostly involving "mutton" (ie, goat), in the form of korma, mughlai, *keema*, masala or biriani, in full or half portions

(Rs30–55) with freshly baked tandoori breads. For those who don't want mutton, there are chicken, egg and veg options.

Mango Masala Sardar Patel Marg. Popular, trendy establishment serving pizzas, snacks, veg-burgers, salads, shakes, mocktails and ice-cream sodas. If you're in need of more than a snack, there are veg set meals and thalis (Rs45–95), and lots of *paneer* curries (Rs58–68). The Rajasthani thali or the Hyderabadi biriyani are good meal options.

Silver Leaf *Embassy Hotel*, Jaipur Rd. Sedate dining, with a big selection of veg curries (Rs40–100), plus an assortment of Chinese and Continental veg dishes, as well as snacks and breakfasts.

Listings

Banks and exchange There's an ATM at the State Bank of India opposite the GPO on Prithviraj Marg, or failing that, several on Kutchery Rd and Jaipur Rd. If you need a forex bureau, UAE Money Exchange at 10 Sardar Patel Marg (Mon–Sat 9am–1.30pm & 2–6pm, Sun 9am–1.30pm) changes cash and traveller's cheques, and also receives MoneyGram money transfers.

Bookshop Bookland, 75 Kutchery Rd, opposite *Haveli Heritage Inn*.

Festival The Urs Mela, or Urs Ajmer Sharif, held on the sixth day of the Islamic month of Rajab (approximately 9 July 2008, 29 June 2009, 18 June 2010) is predominantly a religious celebration in honour of the city's Sufi saint, Khwaja Muin-ud-din Chishti (see p.267), on the anniversary of his death. Pilgrims flock to the town to honour the saint with *qawwali*

(Sufi devotional) chanting. *Kheer* (rice pudding) is cooked in huge vats at the *dargah* and distributed to visitors. At night religious gatherings called *mehfils* are held. It isn't really an affair for non-religious tourists, but the city does take on a festive air, with devotees from across the Subcontinent and beyond converging on Ajmer for the week leading up to it.

Hospital Mittal Hospital, Pushkar Rd ☎0145/260 3600 to 07 is well equipped and has a 24hr emergency department.

Internet access Satguru at 61 Kutchery Rd (daily 8am–10pm; Rs20/hr) near *Haveli Heritage Inn*, and 10 Sardar Patel Marg near Jaipur Rd (daily 11am–9pm; Rs15/hr).

Post office The main GPO is at the southern end of Prithviraj Marg, near Madar Gate (Mon–Sat 10am–8pm, Sun 10am–4pm).

Moving on from Ajmer

Ajmer station (☎0145/243 2535) is on the main Delhi–Ahmedabad **train line**, but there are considerable variations between the journey times of services passing through here (see box opposite for recommendations). The computerized **reservations** hall is on the first floor of the railway station's south wing; get there early in the morning to avoid queues, which can sometimes be very long, or alternatively shell out a little extra for a travel agent.

Ajmer has frequent **bus connections** to Agra (9 daily; 9hr), Bikaner (15 daily; 7hr), Bundi (hourly; 4–5hr), Chittaurgarh (hourly; 5hr), Delhi (38 daily; 9hr), Jaipur (7 daily; 2hr 30min), Jodhpur (half-hourly; 5hr), Kishangarh (every 15min; 30min), Kota (half-hourly; 6hr) and Udaipur (hourly; 7hr), but none direct to Jaisalmer – go to Jodhpur for onward transport. State buses depart from the **bus stand** on Jaipur Road, about 1km from Prithviraj Marg (☎0145/242 9398). Seats on private buses – many of which have connecting services from Pushkar – can be reserved at travel agents along Kutchery Road towards Prithviraj Marg.

Buses to **Pushkar**'s Ajmer bus stand leave every fifteen minutes or so from Prithviraj Marg by the Jain Temple, the last bus is at 9.30pm. There are also buses every fifteen minutes from Ajmer's main bus stand to Pushkar's Marwar bus stand.

Recommended trains from Ajmer

The following trains are recommended as the fastest or most convenient. Other services may also exist which may take longer, or arrive at inconvenient times, or not run every day. Train timetables change frequently; check latest schedules either at your nearest station or online at ⓦ www.indianrail.gov.in before travel.

To **Udaipur** there are currently no direct trains; it is possible to take the #2JA fast passenger train (departs 2.25pm) to Marwar Junction (☏ 02935/252 204; arrives 4.50pm), where there should be a connecting service to Udaipur, but this will not necessarily be direct, and it will get you in very late at night. Likewise, there are no direct trains to **Kota**; the #9769 connects at Chittaurgarh for the #2964 Mewar Express, which doesn't get in to Kota until 11.40pm. For **Agra**, there are only two direct trains a week, and no really convenient connection via Jaipur, though you could, if you don't mind travelling at odd hours, take the #2915 Ashram Express at 1.55am, arriving in Jaipur at 4.20am, where you can pick up the #2987 Gwalior Intercity at 6.10am, getting in to Agra at 10.15am. Failing that, take the bus or change at Delhi.

Destination	Name	No.	Departs	Arrives
Abu Road	Ahmedabad Mail	9106	7.40 am (daily)	12.46 pm
	Aravali Express	9708	11.25 am (daily)	4.50 pm
Agra	Ananya Express	2316	6.15 am (M only)	3.50 pm
	Ziyarat Express	2316	11.30 pm (Th only)	8.50 am
Alwar	Shatabdi Express	2016	3.50 pm (exc W)	7.23 pm
	Hazrat Express	4312	5.30 am (W,Th,S,S)	11.01 am
Chittaurgarh	Purna Express	9769	3.25 pm (daily)	7.32 pm
	Chetak Express	4707	10.41 pm (daily)	11.40 pm
Delhi	Shatabdi Express	2016	3.50 pm (exc W)	10.45 pm ND
	Rajdhani Express	2957	12.35 am (exc Tue)	7.55 am OD
	Ashram Express	2915	1.55 am (daily)	10.25 am OD
Jaipur	Shatabdi Express	2016	3.50 pm (exc W)	5.35 pm
	Ajmer-Jaipur Intercity	9652	6.40 am (daily)	9.45 am
	Link Express	2413A	1.55 pm (daily)	4.20 pm
	Aravali Express	9707	4.15 pm (daily)	6.45 pm
Jodhpur	Fast passenger train	2JA	2.25 pm (daily)	7.50 pm
Sawai Madhopur	Anyana Express	2316	6.15 am (exc Mon)	11.30 am

Kishangarh and around

You won't see many other tourists at **KISHANGARH**, the former capital of a small Rajput state founded in 1597 by Kishan Singh, a son of the then maharaja of Jodhpur, and founded as Singh's capital in 1611. Today, it's a moderate-sized town, 30km northeast of Ajmer, with an enchanting and unspoiled walled old city and a wonderful heritage hotel.

Arriving by bus or train, you'll find yourself in the new town, a centre for working the locally quarried Makrana **marble** (used to make the Taj Mahal), whose quarries are 71km to the north. You'll find marble being cut up in workshops along Ajmer Road south of the bus stand, but aside from this, the new town is pretty nondescript, and most visitors take a *tempo* or an auto-rickshaw straight to the old city's Tanga Stand.

Kishangarh's walled **old city** is a great place for an aimless wander among venerable old temples, crumbling havelis, and pastel-coloured houses. As in

Jodhpur (see p.282), the favourite colour for the outside of houses is blue, made by mixing indigo in with the whitewash, and thought to keep the interior cool and deter insects. One or two of the houses have murals, Shekhawati-style, but many of these have been whitewashed (or blue-washed) over. Motorized vehicles are notable by their absence from the old city's streets, where livestock are allowed to wander and children play without the danger of traffic.

You can take in Kishangarh on a **day-trip** from Pushkar or Ajmer but if you do decide **to stay**, your best bet is the heritage hotel just outside its walls, the *Phool Mahal Palace* (℡01463/247 405, ⓦwww.royalkishangarh .com; ❼), owned by the maharaja of Kishangarh, which is wonderfully tranquil, overlooking beautiful open countryside, and a good stop for lunch (Rs350 buffet) even if you don't stay. There are other hotels in the new town (mostly around the railway station), but they're not great value. The **fort** that looms over the *Phool Mahal Palace* is uninhabited and generally closed to the public, but guests can arrange to visit. In the eighteenth century, Kishangarh was famous throughout Rajasthan for its school of **miniature paintings**, known for their delicacy of touch and their rich colours; the tradition has now been revived, and you can buy new Kishangarh miniatures at a shop inside the entrance to the hotel, or at RK Art's by Tanga Stand, just through the gateway by the fort. The maharaja of Kishangarh maintains a second heritage hotel 25km north of Kishangarh in the fort at **Roopangarh** (℡01497/220 217, ⓦwww.royalkishangarh.com; ❼), originally built in 1648 for maharaja Roop Singh, who made it his capital. The rooms, which are spacious and elegantly done out, are in the newer section of the fort, which stands in a quiet little village.

Kishangarh can be reached from Ajmer by **bus** (every 15min from opposite the state bus stand) or by **train** (six daily, including the #9652 Intercity at 6.40am and the #2413A Link Express at 1.55pm, both taking around 30min; coming back there's the #9769 Purna Express at 2.21pm and the Intercity Express at 7.48pm, among others). Both the bus stand, on Ajmer Road, and the train station just off Ajmer Road, one kilometre north of the bus stand (℡01463/245 734), are in the new part of town, from which a *tempo* or rickshaw to Tanga Stand will cost Rs30.

Tilonia, 25km east of Kishangarh, is known for its leatherware, and is an excellent place to pick up things like wallets and slippers. More importantly, it is home to the Social Work and Research Centre (SWRC), commonly known as **Barefoot College** (ⓦwww.barefootcollege.org), established in 1972 to provide useful teaching to rural people who didn't have access to formal education. Local people built the college, and through it they have been able to set up projects to harness solar power, combat desertification and conserve drinking water. They have also been able to learn and pass on traditional craft techniques, and their products – including hand-woven, tie-dyed, appliqué, and embroidered textiles – are available at the college's crafts showroom.

Pushkar

According to legend, **PUSHKAR**, 15km northwest of Ajmer, came into existence when Lord Brahma, the Creator, dropped a lotus flower (*pushpa*) to earth from his hand (*kar*). At the three spots where the petals landed, water magically appeared in the midst of the desert to form three small blue lakes, and

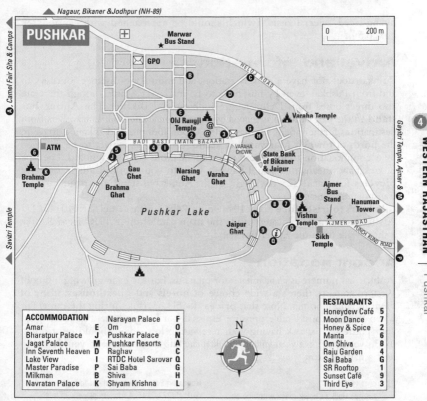

Nagaur, Bikaner &Jodhpur (NH-89)

PUSHKAR

Marwar
Bus Stand

GPO

HELOJ ROAD

Varaha Temple

Old Ranjji
Temple

ATM

BADI BASTI (MAIN BAZAAR)

VARAHA
CHOWK

State Bank
of Bikaner
& Jaipur

Brahma
Temple

Gau
Ghat

Narsing
Ghat

Varaha
Ghat

Ajmer
Bus
Stand

Hanuman
Tower

Brahma
Ghat

Pushkar Lake

Vishnu
Temple

AJMER ROAD

KUND ROAD

Jaipur
Ghat

Sikh
Temple

Savitri Temple

Camel Fair Site & Camps

Gayitri Temple, Ajmer & M

0   200 m

N

ACCOMMODATION

Amar	E	Narayan Palace	F
Bharatpur Palace	J	Om	O
Jagat Palace	M	Pushkar Palace	N
Inn Seventh Heaven	D	Pushkar Resorts	A
Lake View	I	Raghav	C
Master Paradise	P	RTDC Hotel Sarovar	Q
Milkman	B	Sai Baba	G
Navratan Palace	K	Shiva	H
		Shyam Krishna	L

RESTAURANTS

Honeydew Café	5
Moon Dance	7
Honey & Spice	2
Manta	6
Om Shiva	8
Raju Garden	4
Sai Baba	G
SR Rooftop	1
Sunset Café	9
Third Eye	3

WESTERN RAJASTHAN | Pushkar

it was on the banks of the largest of these that Brahma subsequently convened a gathering of some 900,000 celestial beings – the entire Hindu pantheon. Surrounded by whitewashed temples and bathing *ghats*, the lake is today revered as one of India's most sacred sites: *Pushkaraj Maharaj*, literally "Pushkar King of Kings". During the auspicious full-moon phase of October/November (the anniversary of the gods' mass meeting, or *yagya*), its waters are believed to cleanse the soul of all impurities, drawing pilgrims from all over the country. Alongside this annual religious festival, Rajasthani villagers also buy and sell livestock at what has become the largest **camel market** (*unt mela*) in the world, when more than 150,000 dealers, tourists and traders fill the dunes to the west of the lake.

The *mela* is a hugely colourful affair, and this combined with the beautiful desert scenery and heady religious atmosphere of the temples and *ghats* has inevitably made Pushkar a prime destination for foreign tourists; over a million domestic tourists come here every year too, but most are day-trippers. Pushkar's spiritual energy also attracted the hippy overlanders of the 1960s, and the budget hotels and cafés set up to cater for them have kept it firmly on the backpacker trail. The main bazaar, which just twenty years ago comprised a string of stalls selling traditional puja paraphernalia, is now a kilometre-long line of shops, many selling hippy trinkets, jewellery and CDs, others offering forex, Internet or international phone facilities, while the streetside cafés churn out banana pancakes, pizzas and, often, bhang-laced "special lassis" (which should be approached with caution; see box, p.59).

Arrival and information

Pushkar does not have a railway station, and most long-distance journeys to and from Pushkar, even by bus, have to be made via Ajmer, though there are also direct buses from Delhi, Jaipur, Jodhpur and Bikaner. The **Ajmer bus stand** in the east of town is served by buses from Ajmer, while travellers from destinations further afield, such as Delhi, Jaipur, Jodhpur and Bikaner, arrive in the north of town at **Marwar bus stand**. Either way, expect to be besieged by accommodation touts, whose recommendations are best ignored. The lack of rickshaws means that you'll have to walk to your hotel (though there are **bicycles** for rent (Rs25/day) right by the Ajmer bus stand, and hand-carts for transporting luggage).

Pushkar's **tourist office** (daily 10am–5pm; 24hr during camel fair; ☎0145/277 2040) is conveniently located inside the main gate of the RTDC *Hotel Sarovar*, a short walk from the Ajmer bus stand.

Accommodation

Pushkar has numerous *dharamshalas* for pilgrims. For the ever-growing influx of Western tourists, there's a wide choice of **hotels** and **guesthouses**, many of them in family homes. Note that **prices** double or triple during the camel fair when there is considerable pressure, especially at budget hotels, to pre-pay for your entire stay or risk having your reservation lost – you should resist doing this as you won't get your money back if the fair disappoints and you decide to beat a hasty retreat.

Budget

Amar Holika Chowk (back entrance on Main Bazaar) ☎0145/510 5336 or 277 2809. A delightful and very friendly place, with 20 ground-floor rooms set around a large garden, where food and drinks are served. Maintains reasonable prices during camel fair. ❶–❷

Bharatpur Palace Main Bazaar ☎0145/277 2320, ✉bharatpur_palace@yahoo.com. Rather run-down and somewhat overpriced for what you get, but the location's wonderful, right on the lake with views across the *ghats*, which some rooms overlook with multiple windows. Massive ten-fold price hike for camel fair. ❷–❸

Lake View Main Bazaar ☎0145/277 2106, ⓦwww.lakeviewpushkar.com. Pretty basic rooms (even the ones with a/c and private bathroom), and well overpriced, but you do get great views over the lake from the terrace and the rooftop restaurant (which gets crowded at sunset). ❸

Milkman Maili Mohalla ☎0145/277 3452. A little place hidden away in the backstreets which prides itself on being tranquil and family-run, with various rooms at different prices, and a rooftop café that closes at 10pm. ❶–❸

Navratan Palace near Brahma Temple ☎0145/277 2145. A modern place with fresh, spotless rooms, well-kept gardens and what they claim (quite rightly) is the best pool in town (non-guests Rs50). Great value. ❷

Narayan Palace Chhoti Basti, behind Varaha Temple ☎0145/277 3231. The rooms are decent enough, the garden pleasant, but the real attraction here is the pool, not the most pristine in town, but a boon in summer. ❶–❷

Om Ajmer Rd ☎0145/277 2672, ✉om_deepak2004 @yahoo.com. A variety of rooms, with or without bathroom, at very different prices. There's a relaxing garden with hammocks for lounging, but the pool is about as inviting as the lake. Pricey during camel fair. ❶–❹

Raghav Heloj Rd ☎0145/277 2207, ⓦwww .lakeviewpushkar.com. A quiet retreat in a huge garden on the north side of town. The rooms are plain but large, with comfy mattresses; those on the first floor have a narrow balcony, those on the roof have a/c. ❶–❸

Sai Baba On the road leading off Varaha Chowk by the post office ☎0145/510 5161. Run by a French-Indian couple in a lovely old house around a pleasant patio (with a statue of nineteenth-century holy man Sai Baba). Best rooms are on the top floor. Good restaurant (see p.281). ❷–❸

Shiva On the road leading off Varaha Chowk by the post office ☎0145/277 2120. Friendly, dependable little cheapie, with decent rooms (it's worth paying a little bit more for a larger one), set around a small courtyard with a mimosa tree and five tortoises. Does not take advance reservations. ❶–❷

Shyam Krishna Guest House Main bazaar near Vishnu temple ☎0145/277 2461. A variety of rooms with shared or private bathroom set around a garden in a lovely old blue-washed former temple compound, run by a family who live in the central court. Excellent, affordable choice during camel fair. ❶–❷

Mid-range to expensive

Inn Seventh Heaven Chhoti Basti by Mali Ka Mandir ☎0145/510 5455, ⓦ www.inn-seventh -heaven.com. Beautiful hotel in a lovely old haveli, with a range of rooms, each with its own style of decor, all at different prices, some very affordable. ❷–❻

Jagat Palace Ajmer Rd ☎0145/277 2953, ⓦ www.hotelpushkarpalace.com. Wonderful decor at this well-run luxury hotel on the outskirts of town, incorporating masonry plundered from an old fort, but superbly reconstructed with elaborate wall paintings, gilt inlay and period fittings. Sweeping views, huge pool, steam bath, Jacuzzi and walled garden. ❼

Master Paradise Punch Kund Rd ☎0145/277 3933. Spotless, well-kept three-star with lovely gardens, a pool, steam bath and Jacuzzi, but a fifteen-minute walk from town. Prices quoted are bed-only, but B&B, half-board and full-board rates are available; prices quadruple during the camel fair. ❺–❻

Pushkar Palace ☎0145/277 3001, ⓦ www .hotelpushkarpalace.com. A poor second-best to its sister hotel the *Jagat Palace*, well worn around the edges with rather unenthusiastic staff. It still has a lot of charm and a great location in a former maharaja's palace overlooking the lake, but only a few rooms actually have lake views, and to get to it you have to run the gauntlet of annoying shopkeepers and stallholders trying to grab your attention every time you go past. ❼

Pushkar Resorts Motisar Rd, Ganehara ☎0145/277 2017 or 277 2944, ⓦ www .pushkarresorts.com. Modern resort, inconveniently situated 5km (a Rs100 taxi ride) out of town in the desert, with 40 swish a/c cottages in pristine gardens and a kidney-shaped pool. Their restaurant is the only one hereabouts with a non-veg menu, and an alcohol licence. Booking recommended. ❼

RTDC Hotel Sarovar ☎0145/277 2040. The state-run option, a bit institutional, but in a pleasantly ramshackle kind of way, with big rooms and an Indian rather than touristy feel, overlooking the lake. You get a choice of ordinary, air-cooled or a/c rooms. ❸–❹

The Town

There are more than five hundred **temples** in and around Pushkar; many had to be rebuilt after pillaging during the merciless rule of Mughal emperor Aurangzeb (1656–1708), while others are recent additions. Some, like the splendid **Vishnu Temple**, on your right as you enter the village from Ajmer, are out of bounds to non-Hindus. Pushkar's most important temple, **Brahma Temple**, houses a four-headed image of Brahma in its main sanctuary, and is one of the few temples in India devoted to him. The Mughal emperor Aurangzeb had the original structure demolished in 1679, but Maharaja Jai Singh II of Jaipur ordered its reconstruction in 1727. Raised on a stepped platform in the centre of a courtyard, the always crowded chamber is surrounded on three sides by smaller subsidiary shrines topped with flat roofs providing views across the desert to **Savitri Temple** on the summit of a nearby hill. The one-hour climb to the top of that hill is rewarded by matchless vistas over the town, surrounded on all sides by desert, and is best done at dawn, to reach the summit for sunrise, though it's also a great spot to watch the sun set. The temple itself is modern, but the image of Savitri is supposed to date back to the seventh century. **Gayitri Temple** (Pap Mochini Mandir), set on a hill east of the town, also offers great views, but especially at sunrise.

Brahma, Savitri and Gayitri

Although **Brahma**, the Creator, is one of the trinity of top Hindu gods, along with Vishnu (the Preserver) and Shiva (the Destroyer), his importance has dwindled since Vedic times, and he has nothing like the following of the other two, featuring nowadays more in Hindu legend than in Hindu devotion. The story behind his temple here in Pushkar serves to explain why this is so, and also reveals the significance of the temples here named after Brahma's wives, **Savitri** and **Gayitri**.

The story goes that Lord Brahma was to marry Savitri, a river goddess, at a sacrificial ritual called a *yagna*, which had to be performed at a specific, astrologically auspicious moment. But Savitri, busy dressing for the ceremony, failed to show up on time. Without a wife, the Creator could not perform the *yagna* at the right moment, so he had to find another consort quickly. The only unmarried woman available was a shepherdess of the untouchable Gujar caste named Gayitri, whom the gods hastily purified by passing her through the mouth of a cow (*gaya* means "cow", and *tri*, "passed through"). When Savitri finally arrived, she was furious that Brahma had married someone else and cursed him, saying that henceforth he would be worshipped only at Pushkar. She also proclaimed that the Gujar caste would gain liberation after death only if their ashes were scattered on Pushkar lake – a belief which has persisted to this day. After casting her curses, disgruntled Savitri flew off to the highest hill above the town. To placate her, it was agreed that she should have her temple on that hilltop, while Gayitri occupied the lower hill on the opposite, eastern side of the lake, and that Savitri would always be worshipped before Gayitri, which is exactly how pilgrims do it, visiting Savitri's temple first, and Gayitri's temple afterwards.

The lake and ghats

Pushkar **lake** is ringed by five hundred beautiful whitewashed temples, connected to the water by 52 *ghats* – one for each of Rajasthan's maharajas, who built separate guesthouses and employed their own private *pujaris* (priests) to perform rituals during their stays here. Each is named after an event or person, and three in particular bear special significance. Primary among them is **Gau Ghat,** sometimes called Main Ghat, where visiting ministers and politicians come to worship, and from which ashes of Mahatma Gandhi, Jawaharlal Nehru and Shri Lal Bahadur Shastri were sprinkled into the lake. **Brahma Ghat** marks the spot where Brahma himself is said to have worshipped, while at the large **Varaha Ghat**, just off the market square, Vishnu is believed to have appeared in the form of Varaha (a boar), the third of his nine earthly incarnations. At all the *ghats*, it is a respected and unspoken request that visitors should remove their shoes at a reverential distance from the lake, and refrain from smoking and taking photos.

Indian and Western tourists alike are urged by local Brahmin priests to worship at the lake; that is, to make **Pushkar Puja**. This involves the repetition of prayers while scattering rose petals into the lake, and then being asked for a donation, which usually goes to temple funds, or to the priest who depends on such benefaction. On completion of the puja, a red thread taken from a temple is tied around your wrist. Labelled the "Pushkar passport" by locals, this simple token means that you'll no longer attract pushy Pushkar priests and can wander unhindered onto the *ghats*. Indians usually give a sum of Rs21 or Rs31; Rs51 should suffice for a foreign tourist. A favourite trick of (usually phoney) priests is to ask how much you want to pay, then say a blessing for assorted members of your family, and demand the amount you stated times the number of family members blessed, but you needn't be bullied by such cheap tricks into giving

△ Pushkar's camel *mela*

any more than you agreed. Indeed, you should really report anyone impersonating a priest to the RTDC office or the tourist police.

In years past, the lake used to be prowled by dozens of man-eating **crocodiles** that would often pick off unwary pilgrims. Elderly Brahmins can still recall the days when they regularly had to beat the rapacious reptiles on the head with long sticks before entering the water, but their strict vegetarian principles prevented them from doing anything about the problem. Eventually, the British intervened by fishing the crocodiles out with nets and transporting them to a nearby reservoir. Nart Singh Ghat, a few steps down from Varaha Ghat, still has on display one rather dusty stuffed crocodile, which didn't make it as far as the reservoir.

Eating

As Pushkar is sacred to Lord Brahma, all food within city limits is strictly veg: meat, eggs and alcohol are banned, as are drugs other than bhang (though *charas* is easy enough to find if you want it, and you should think twice before downing a bhang lassi, for reasons explained on p.59). Most **restaurants** tend to cater for foreign rather than Indian palates, offering "lo-chilli" curries as well as pizza, falafel and chow mein, but be wary of the many buffets offering tempting all-you-can-eat menus; with the highly recommended exception of *Om Shiva*, most are likely to consist of terribly unhealthy reheated food. Pushkar's sweet speciality is **malpua**, which is basically a chapati fried in syrup, sold at sweetshops around town, and on Halwai Gali, the street directly opposite Gau Ghat.

Honeydew Café Main Bazaar near *Bharatpur Palace Hotel*. A hole-in-the-wall place that's been a hippy hang-out since the days of the overland trail. It still knocks out a decent breakfast, especially if you like filter coffee, and its pasta dishes (Rs30–50) aren't bad either.

Honey & Spice Laxmi Market, Main Bazaar. Slightly pricier but much more imaginative than Pushkar's other tourist eateries, offering good filter coffee, and a short but sweet menu of tasty vegetarian dishes (Rs60–90) including garlic tofu steak, or tangy tofu with brown rice. Closes 5.30pm.

Hindus visit Pushkar year-round to take a dip in the redemptory waters of the lake, but there is one particular day when bathing here is believed to relieve devotees of all their sins, and ultimately free them from the endless cycle of death and reincarnation. That day is the full moon (*purnima*) of the **Kartika** month (usually Nov). The five days leading up to and including the full moon, Pushkar hosts thousands of celebrating devotees, following prescribed rituals on the lakeside and in the Brahma Temple. To add to the flurry of colour and activity, a large week-long **camel fair** is held at around the same time in the sand dunes west of the town, with hordes of herders from all over Rajasthan gathering to parade, race and trade over 25,000 animals. The transformation of Pushkar from a peaceful, if touristy, desert town is overwhelming – the streets are packed with swarms of pilgrims, hawkers and thousands of tourists; hotels and restaurants are chock-a-block, and prices soar.

Once trading is under way, camels and cattle are meticulously groomed and auctioned, while women dressed in mirrored skirts and vivid shawls lay out embroidered cloth, jewellery, pots and ornaments beside the herds. Cattle, poultry, sheep and goats are entered for competitions, and prizes given for the best displays of fruit and vegetables. Away from the main activity, the dusty ground is stirred up by vigorous **camel races**, urged on by gamblers. Aside from its overwhelming size, the most striking feature of the fair from a foreign visitor's point of view is that it is attended by equal numbers of men and women. With the harvest safely in the bag and the surplus livestock sold, the villagers, for this brief week or so, have a little money to spend enjoying themselves, which creates a lighthearted atmosphere that's generally absent from most other Rajasthani livestock fairs.

The popularity of Pushkar's fair has – inevitably – had an effect on the event. The number of foreign tourists crossed the ten thousand mark for the first time in 2004, with zoom lens-saddled package tourists now bumping elbows with the event's traditional pilgrims, camel traders and backpackers. But while the commercialism can be off-putting, the festive environment and coming together of cultures does produce some spontaneous mirth: the second prize in the moustache contest was recently won by a Mancunian. To avoid the worst of the tomfoolery **come at least a week before the final weekend**, when most of the buying and selling is done. By the full moon, the bulk of the herders have packed up and gone home (unless the government has managed to induce them to stick around with the lure of free fodder, as it has done for the past few fairs), leaving Pushkar with the stale feeling of a party the morning after.

Practicalities

Hotels hike their rates sometimes a fortnight before the full moon and still fill up quickly. Though it's best to book a room as far ahead as possible, if you arrive early in the day – and with a bit of hunting – securing **accommodation** shouldn't be a problem. RTDC usually sends its package guests out to **tented compounds** close to the fairgrounds, where there's a choice between dormitory beds (Rs300), deluxe tents (⑨), or huts (④) complete with private bathrooms. Book well ahead by contacting the RTDC office in Jaipur (☏0141/511 4768, ✉cro@rajasthantourism.gov.in). The tent village has an information counter, exchange facilities, safes, shops, medical centre, and a **Shilpgram** artisans' village, where you can buy crafts directly from the artists. For more details, check RTDC's website at ⊛www.rajasthantourism.gov.in. Additional luxury camping, complete with carpets, furniture, running water and Western toilets, is offered by the maharaja of Jodhpur's *Royal Camp* (for reservations contact WelcomHeritage ☏0291/257 2321 to 7, ⊛www.welcomheritagehotels.com; ⑨), or *Royal Desert Camp* (for reservations contact the *Pushkar Palace* or *Jagat Palace* hotels; ⑨).

The **dates** of the next few camel fairs are: 17–24 Nov 2007, 5–13 Nov 2008, 25 Oct–2 Nov 2009, and 13–21 Nov 2010. It's best to get here for the first two or three days to see the *mela* in full swing.

Manta near Brahma Temple. This is where a lot of Pushkar's Indian visitors come to eat, not surprisingly as it serves up the best veg curries (Rs25–50) and thalis (Rs45–55) in town. What's available depends on what vegetables are in season, but there's always a good selection.

Moon Dance Opposite the Vishnu temple. Pizzas, pasta, Chinese dishes and a reasonable range of Indian food too (main dishes Rs30–110). Eat at tables or on floor mattresses which are ideal for reclining after a filling meal. There's also a great bakery.

🏃 Om Shiva On the lane heading down to *Pushkar Palace* from Main Bazaar. With the feel of a beach bar, the all-you-can-eat buffets here (different for breakfast, lunch and supper) are superb considering the Rs50 price tag, unchanged in over a decade. Avoid copycats with similar names.

Raju Garden Main Bazaar, near Ram Ghat. Delicious Indian, Chinese and Western food of a standard rarely matched by other restaurants, though service could be improved. Particularly renowned for its veg shepherd's pie and baked potatoes with peanut butter, garlic cheese or Marmite, but a good range of veg curries too. Main dishes Rs30–65.

Sai Baba On the road leading off Varaha Chowk by the post office. As well as Indian veg curries (Rs36–60), the restaurant here does great pasta and the best pizzas in Pushkar (the tandoor doubles as a pizza oven). You can sit out front or, more atmospherically, in the garden. There's Rajasthani Gypsy dancing on Saturdays at 8pm, when there's a Rs100 buffet.

SR Rooftop Restaurant Main Bazaar. Grimy but reliable *dhaba*-style restaurant, with first-floor and sometimes rooftop eating. Serves delicious north Indian thalis (Rs35–60), and can get crowded.

Sunset Café East side of the lake near the *Pushkar Palace*. As its name implies, an ideal spot to enjoy Pushkar's legendary lakeside sunsets; big crowds gather here for this daily event. There's an impressive selection of juices, lassis, shakes, and even non-alcoholic beer and organic tea. Inevitably, there are also pizzas and a German Bakery. Service is swift, mains Rs50–100.

Third Eye Varaha Chowk. An Israeli backpacker hang-out that's more like the chill-out at a Tel Aviv trance party than a restaurant in India, it has going for it a pleasantly laid-back atmosphere, great views over the street below, a pool table, and the best hummus and falafel in town. Main dishes around Rs50.

Shopping

Though it isn't a craft centre as such, Pushkar is a good place to pick up **touristy souvenirs**, with its shops conveniently strung out along the Main Bazaar. As well as lots of hippy-type clothes, T-shirts and silver jewellery, not to mention ceramic chillums (Pushkar's rival those of Hampi and Pondicherry in the south), you'll find lac bangles, Rajasthani textiles, incense, essential oils and – always handy for a paint fight – Holi dyes. For new and used **books**, there's a slew of shops on the Main Bazaar just south of Varaha Chowk.

Antique Boutique Main Bazaar, opposite *Lake View Hotel*. Silver jewellery – the best selection in town.

Kamna Handicraft Main Bazaar (north side), west of Varaha Ghat. Kitschy wooden toys, including folded-in miniature wooden temples from Bassi.

Shiva Silk Emporium Main Bazaar, just east of Gau Ghat ☎0145/277 2150. Lovely silk and cotton garments, which they make themselves for export.

Raj Shree Bangles Brahma Temple Rd, two doors east of *Navratan Palace Hotel*. Certainly not the only place in town that sells lac bangles, but it does stock the biggest range.

Ram Crafts Main Bazaar (north side), west of Varaha Ghat ☎0145/277 2890. Lots of miniature paintings of various sizes and qualities that you can browse through at leisure.

Moving on from Pushkar

State and private intercity **buses** leave from Marwar bus stand (☎0145/242 9398), north of town for Delhi (2 daily; 8hr), Jaipur (up to 14 daily; 3hr 30min), Bikaner (12 daily; 6hr 30min), Udaipur (3 daily; 7hr), Jodhpur (3 daily; 4hr 30min–6hr 30min) and Jaisalmer (1 daily; 9hr). Intercity services leave from Marwar bus stand, north of town (☎0145/242 9398). The **Delhi** buses are overnight with sleeper accommodation available. For **Jodhpur**, the best service is the state bus (currently leaving Pushkar at 9am), which is faster than the two private services. A shuttle service takes passengers from Pushkar to meet the Jaipur–Jaisalmer overnight bus. Many more destinations are served from Ajmer, and connecting services are available, but it is not unknown for people who have bought tickets at agencies in Pushkar to find their seats double-booked when they try boarding in Ajmer. To avoid mishaps, it's best to make bookings for bus journeys from Ajmer in Ajmer itself. Services to Delhi in particular are often reserved days ahead. Leaving for **Ajmer**, use the Marwar bus stand for Ajmer bus station and Ajmer bus stand (every 15min; 20min journey) for Ajmer train station (same frequency and journey time; you get dropped just north of Mahavir Circle, Rs10–15 by rickshaw from the station, or a 1km walk).

A list of recommended **trains from Ajmer** appears on p.273. EKTA Travels (by Marwar bus stand ☎0145/277 2131; by Ajmer bus stand ☎0145/277 2888) are the Indian Railways agents in Pushkar and can arrange tickets for train journeys out of Ajmer for a small charge, and book, cancel or confirm air tickets.

Listings

Banks and exchange The State Bank of Bikaner & Jaipur has an ATM near the Brahma Temple. Their branch in town near Varaha Chowk (Mon–Sat 10am–4pm) offers currency exchange, but you can change cash or traveller's cheques more quickly at any of the forex offices in the main bazaar, though you should check the rate of commission first. LKP Forex on the Main Bazaar near *Shyam Krishna Guest House* (Mon–Sat 9.30am–6.30pm) changes cash and traveller's cheques and gives cash advances (Visa or MasterCard). NL Forex in Laxmi Market, by *Honey & Spice* café (daily 9.30am–7pm) is open Sundays.

Bicycle rental Malakar Bicycle Shop, by Ajmer bus stand ☎0145/277 2888 (Rs25 a day).

Festival Pushkar Camel Fair, held in October or November (see box p.280).

Hospital Government Hospital, opposite the GPO near Marwar bus stand ☎0145/277 2029.

Internet access Most places are small and charge Rs20–30 per hour. One of the best is KK Internet by the Old Rangji Temple (daily 11am–

3pm & 5–11pm). For longer hours, try the office in Shri Raghu Bhajnashram, directly opposite Narsing Ghat on the Main Bazaar (daily 8.30am–midnight).

Laundry Chhotu just off Varaha Chowk ☎0145/277 2453 (daily 7am–9pm). Bring clothes early if you want same-day service.

Motorcycle rental and repairs Bhagwati, nearly opposite Ajmer bus stand ☎0/982 923 8180, ⓔkrishparashar@yahoo.co.in (Rs100–200 a day). For repairs, there's Shree Ram Bullet Garage and Royal Enfield Bullet Workshop, at 13 and 32 Prem Parkash Ashram, on Ajmer Road near Hanuman Tower.

Police Next to the GPO ☎0145/277 2046.

Post office The GPO (Mon–Sat 9am–5pm) for parcels, poste restante and Western Union money transfers, is in the north of town near Marwar bus stand. There's a smaller branch (Mon–Sat 9.30am–5pm) in the middle of town, at Varaha Chowk on the Main Bazaar.

Swimming pools The *Navratan Palace Hotel* charges non-guests Rs50 to use theirs.

Jodhpur and around

On the eastern fringe of the Thar Desert, **JODHPUR**, dubbed "the Blue City" after the colour-wash of its old town houses, sprawls across the arid terrain, overlooked by the mighty **Meherangarh Fort**, the best maintained fort in Rajasthan, whose ramparts rise from a sheer-sided sandstone outcrop. It was once the centre of Marwar, the largest princely state in Rajputana, and today has a population of around a million. But despite its size and importance, Jodhpur is barely a pit-stop for most travellers en route between Jaisalmer, 300km to the west, and Udaipur or Jaipur to the east, and only that by virtue of the fort. It's a shame to rush the place, though. Getting lost in the blue maze of the old city you'll stumble across Muslim tie-dyers, puppet-makers and

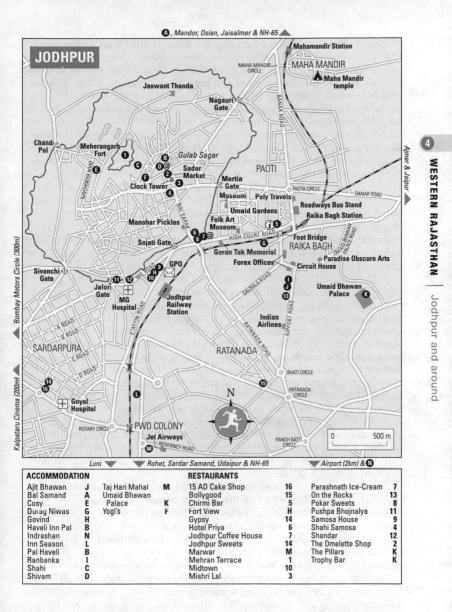

JODHPUR

A, Mandor, Osian, Jaisalmer & NH-65

Mahamandir Station

MAHA MANDIR

Maha Mandir temple

MAHA MANDIR CIRCLE

Jaswant Thanda

Nagauri Gate

BANAR ROAD

Ajmer & Jaipur

Chand Pol

Meherangarh Fort

Gulab Sagar

PAOTI

Sadar Market

Mertia Gate

Museum

Poly Travels

PAOTA CIRCLE

BANAR ROAD

Clock Tower

Umaid Gardens

Roadways Bus Stand

Raika Bagh Station

Manohar Pickles

Folk Art Museum

Sojati Gate

HIGH COURT ROAD

Foot Bridge

RAIKA BAGH

Goran Tak Memorial

Forex Offices

Paradise Obscure Arts

Sivanchi Gate

GPO

Circuit House

Umaid Bhawan Palace

Jalori Gate

MG Hospital

Jodhpur Railway Station

Indian Airlines

Umaid Bhawan Palace

K

SARDARPURA

RATANADA

BHATI CIRCLE

Goyal Hospital

N

RATANADA CIRCLE

ROTARY CIRCLE

PWD COLONY

Jet Airways

PANCH BATTI CIRCLE

500 m

Luni

Rohet, Sardar Samand, Udaipur & NH-65

Airport (2km) & N

ACCOMMODATION				RESTAURANTS			
Ajit Bhawan	J	Taj Hari Mahal	M	15 AD Cake Shop	16	Parashnath Ice-Cream	7
Bal Samand	A	Umaid Bhawan		Bollygood	15	On the Rocks	13
Cosy	E	Palace	K	Chirmi Bar	5	Pokar Sweets	8
Durag Niwas	G	Yogi's	F	Fort View	H	Pushpa Bhojnalya	11
Govind	H			Gypsy	14	Samosa House	9
Haveli Inn Pal	B			Hotel Priya	6	Shahi Samosa	4
Indrashan	N			Jodhpur Coffee House	7	Shandar	12
Inn Season	L			Jodhpur Sweets	14	The Omelette Shop	2
Pal Haveli	B			Marwar	M	The Pillars	K
Ranbanka	I			Mehran Terrace	1	Trophy Bar	K
Shahi	C			Midtown	10		
Shivam	D			Mishri Lal	3		

traditional spice markets, while Jodhpur's famed cubic roofscape, best viewed at sunset, is a photographer's dream. In addition, the encroaching desert beyond the blue city is dotted with small settlements where you can escape the congestion for a taste of rural Rajasthan.

Some history

The **kingdom of Marwar** came into existence in 1381 when Rao Chanda, chief of the **Rathore** Rajput clan seized the fort of Mandor (see p.295) from its former rulers, the Parihars. In 1459, the Rathore chief **Rao Jodha** moved from the exposed site at Mandor to a massive steep-sided escarpment, naming his new capital Jodhpur after himself. His high barricaded fort proved virtually impregnable, and the city soon amassed great wealth from trade. The Mughals were keen to take over Jodhpur, and **Akbar** got his hands on the city in 1561, but he eventuallly allowed Marwar to keep its internal independence so long as the Rathore maharajas allied themselves to him.

This alliance was shaken in the mid-seventeenth century, when **Jaswant Singh I** supported Shah Jahan's elder son Dara Shikoh in an unsuccessful power struggle against his brother Aurangzeb. Furious, but unable to subdue Jodhpur, Aurangzeb eventually had to be content with sending Jaswant Singh to battle in Afghanistan, where he was killed, and procuring the death of his son, leaving him, or so he thought, without an heir. But Jaswant Singh's wife was pregnant, and defying a summons to Delhi, went into hiding. Her son, **Ajit Singh**, was swapped by his wet-nurse, Goran Tak, with her own son to protect him (a 1711 monument on the south side of High Court Road commemorates Goran Tak's selfless deed). Ajit Singh lived to recapture his kingdom, which he ruled until murdered in 1724 by his son, Bakhat Singh.

In the eighteenth century, Marwar, Mewar (Udaipur) and Jaipur sealed a triple alliance to retain their independence against the Mughals, and revived the tradition (dropped during Marwar's alliance with the Mughals) that every maharaja of Marwar would marry a Mewari princess, but this led to dynastic squabbles, and the three states were as often at each other's throats as allied together. At the end of the century, maharaja **Man Singh**, best known for his patronage of the arts, found himself in conflict with Jaipur, first when his step-mother attempted with Jaipuri support to gain the throne for her own son, and then because he and the maharaja of Jaipur both wanted to marry the same Mewari princess. Man Singh also found himself under pressure from the Maratha empire to his south, to which he already had to pay an annual tribute, so in 1818 he turned for help to a new power, the **British**. Under the terms of his deal with them – not unlike Marwar's old arrangement with the Mughals – the kingdom retained its internal independence, but had to pay the East India Company an annual tribute equivalent to the one previously enforced by the Marathas.

In 1880, under maharaja **Jaswant Singh II**, Marwar got its own train line, the **Jodhpur Railway**, brainchild of **Sir Pratap Singh**, the maharaja's younger brother and prime minister, and the brains behind the throne, most famous abroad for his invention of Jodhpur britches (see p.292).

The last but one maharaja before Independence, **Umaid Singh**, is commemorated by his immense Umaid Bhawan Palace. In 1930 he agreed in principle with the British to incorporate Marwar into an independent India. When that eventually came, his son and successor, Hanuwant Singh, attended the Independence ceremony wearing a black turban. "Today," he explained, "the 500-year-old reign of my family has come to end, so I am in mourning." Nonetheless, his descendants retain much of their wealth, and a great deal of influence and genuine respect in Jodhpur, of whose culture the present maharaja remains a great patron.

Arrival, orientation and information

The heart of Jodhpur is its walled **old city**, a maze of higgledy-piggledy streets hugging the base of **Meherangarh Fort** on three sides, and almost impossible to navigate on your first visit, but most easily approached up **Nai Sarak**, the broad, modern street that connects Jodhpur's modern centre with **Sardar Market**, the old city's commercial hub with its landmark **clock tower**.

Jodhpur's main **railway station** is pretty central, just south of the old city on Station Road. If you're heading for the old city, you can walk to the clock tower (turn right out of the station) in fifteen minutes, or take an auto-rickshaw for Rs20. The state (Road ways) **bus stand** is east of the old city and a longish walk (1km) from the clock tower, or Rs30 by auto. **Private buses from Jaisalmer** drop you by Bombay Motors Circle at the western end of Sardarpura, 4km southwest of town, or Rs50 by auto. **Other private buses** deposit you nearby at Kalpataru Cinema. From the **airport**, 4km south, an auto-rickshaw into town costs Rs80; taxis charge a fixed rate of Rs220.

The **tourist office** (Mon–Sat 10am–5pm, but closed on the second Sat of each month; ☎0291/254 5083), in the RTDC *Goomar Hotel* on High Court Road, has timetables for private bus services and keeps lists of families offering homestays. They also run **village safaris** (see p.295) and excursions to Osian (see p.296).

Online, there are two good **websites** worth checking for further information about Jodhpur: the district office of the National Informatics Centre runs a site at ⓦjodhpur.nic.in which has facts and figures aplenty, plus information about things to see and do in and around Jodhpur, while the maharaja's site at ⓦwww .maharajajodhpur.com has some very informative pages about the history of Jodhpur and its places of interest.

Accommodation

Jodhpur has plenty of pleasant places to stay in all brackets (budget and mid-range hotels tend to have a 10am checkout time), but auto-wallahs will invariably find ways to avoid taking you to any hotel that doesn't pay them commission. If you phone ahead and book a room, some guesthouses will pick you up from your arrival point, or you take an auto to a point nearby, such as the clock tower if your hotel is in the old city. If looking for a particular hotel, watch out for imitators: whenever one place gets popular, five more appear on the same block with nearly identical names, and obviously those are the ones your auto-wallah will want to take you to, swearing blind that they're the place you asked for.

Budget

Cosy Bhram Puri, Chuna ki Choki, Navchokiya ☎0291/261 2066, ⓦwww.cosyguesthouse.com. It's a steep climb (signposted) from Navchokiya Road, and the rooms are slightly overpriced, but it's friendly and fun, and the upper terraces have killer views of the fort, and tents where you can stay cheaply, if you reserve far enough ahead to bag them. ❷–❸

Durag Niwas 1 Old Public Park, Raika Bagh ☎0291/251 2385, ⓦwww.durag-niwas.com. Very friendly and well-run little place, great value and socially responsible too, with a volunteer programme teaching English, literacy and crafts to disadvantaged local women, but the plumbing is highly temperamental, so check you have a hot shower that works before taking a room. ❷–❸

Govind Station Rd, opposite the GPO ☎0291/262 2758, ⓦwww.govindhotel .com. A long-standing travellers' favourite, 200m from the station and now upgraded, with jolly rooms in pretty colours, clean dorms (Rs80–90), a good rooftop restaurant and a very helpful owner. He doesn't pay commission, so auto-wallahs won't want to bring you here, but it's a piece of cake to find – look for the trees outside. ❷–❸

Shivam Makrana Mohalla ☎0291/262 0688, ⓔshivamgh@hotmail.com. Easy to find from the clock tower (out of the northern gateway from Sardar Market, turn left then first right), it's got a selection of rooms at different prices and great views of the fort and old city from its rooftop. The owner is due to open a second guesthouse nearby, the *Ganpati*, with slightly posher rooms ❷–❸

Yogi's Rajpurohitji ki Haveli, Manak Chowk, Nayabas ☎0291/264 3436, ⓔyogiguesthouse@hotmail .com. Very blue, with lovely decor and a variety of nice, fresh rooms. The mosaic-laid rooftop terrace has excellent views of the fort and sunrise, and is among Rajasthan's best chill-out spaces. ❶–❷

Mid-range

Haveli Inn Pal near Gulab Sagar Lake, 200m north of the clock tower (out of the north gate of Sardar Market, turn right and first left) ☎0291/261 2519, ⓦwww.haveliinnpal.com. Large, well-appointed rooms in an eighteenth-century haveli formerly belonging to the thakur of Pal, and still owned by the same family. The best room is huge with a fort view, but even the cheapest rooms are pretty spacious. Reservation is recommended. ❺–❻

Indrashan 593 High Court Colony, 3km south of town ☎0291/244 0665, ⓦwww.rajputanadiscovery .com. Eight thoroughly comfortable rooms in an

Heritage hotels in the Jodhpur region

There are quite a few very attractive **heritage hotels** in the region around Jodhpur. Often, they're in the middle of nowhere, but you can usually arrange a pick-up from Jodhpur, and taxi rates from Jodhpur airport are fixed (expect to pay up to a thousand rupees or so, depending on the exact distance involved).

Fort Chanwa Luni (36km south of Jodhpur) ☎02931/284216, ⓦwww.fortchanwa.com. Though it's an 1895 red-sandstone fort, the standard rooms aren't all that old-fashioned, and it's worth forking out more to get one that's a bit special. The usual deluxe heritage hotel trappings are here (a pool, sauna, Jacuzzi, croquet lawn), and there's entertainment in the form of Rajasthani folk dancing every evening. The endearingly named village of Luni, in which the fort stands, is also rather pretty, with some interesting old houses and temples, and is quite renowned for its *rasgulla*. ❼–❽

Fort Khejarla Khejarla (84km east of Jodhpur) ☎02930/258311. A mightily imposing fort with lots of carved red sandstone, tastefully furnished rooms and views over the surrounding countryside. Best rooms are in the turrets. ❼

Jhalamand Garh Jhalamand (7km south of Jodhpur) ☎0291/274 0481. The late eighteenth-century palace of the thakurs (barons) of the village of Jhalamand is close enough to Jodhpur that you can actually see the city from it. The whole building is rather elegant, and the lobby was formerly the thakur's Diwan-i-Am (audience hall). The meals are set menus of traditional Rajput cuisine, with dance performances by a Kalbelia Gypsy troupe held around an outdoor fire every night. ❼

Khimsar Fort Khimsar (80km northeast of Jodhpur) ☎01585/262345, ⓦwww .khimsarfort.com. There's a variety of rooms in different styles – some traditional, some Art Deco – plus a pool, tennis courts, a croquet lawn and golf practising facilities at this former sixteenth-century fort. Antelope-spotting safaris are available, and the location is also handy for Nagaur (see p.327), just 40km away. ❽

Rohet Garh Rohet (39km south of Jodhpur) ☎02936/268231 or 531, ⓦwww .rohetgarh.com. This rather sleek hotel was a palace given in 1622 by the maharaja of Jodhpur to the thakur of Rohet, whose heirs still live in it. There are cool, spacious rooms, candle-lit poolside dinners, royal-style picnics with liveried attendants, and for those interested, culinary workshops, horse riding and bird-watching expeditions. The local village isn't tremendously exciting, but it does offer a taste of everyday India just outside the hotel gates. ❽

Sardar Samand Palace Sardar Samand Lake (65km southeast of Jodhpur) ☎02960/245001 to 3, ⓦwww.welcomheritagehotels.com. Bird-watchers and fans of Art Deco will love this hunting lodge built in 1930 for the maharaja of Jodhpur (the same one who commissioned Umaid Bhawan Palace). On the highest piece of land for miles, with magnificent panoramic views over the neighbouring lake and surrounding countryside, the palace has retained many of its original features, fittings and furniture, including stuffed animal heads gazing down from the dining room walls. Activities include bird-watching, nature walks, village safaris, or just laze by the pool. The current maharaja still holds a suite here for his personal use. ❽ authentic homestay. The husband/wife team offer sumptuous food and cooking classes that draw amateur chefs from around the world. Non-guests are welcome for dinner if they call ahead (Rs350). The owner also arranges homestays in other parts of the state, and in Delhi and Agra. ④–⑤

Inn Season PWD Rd ☎ 0291/261 6400, ⓦ www .innseasonjodhpur.com. Boutique hotel whose Art Deco rooms pay homage to the owner's love affair with vintage cars. A loyal clientele of handicraft exporters chill out at night to vinyl on a vintage gramophone. One drawback: it's noisy during wedding season (approx Oct–March) due to the wedding ground next door. Book ahead. ⑥

Pal Haveli near Gulab Sagar Lake ☎ 0291/329 3328, ⓦ www.palhaveli.com. In the same compound as *Haveli Inn Pal*, and owned by the same family, this is a more upmarket affair, with statelier rooms – a low-priced heritage hotel rather than a guesthouse. ⑥

Shahi Gandhi St, City Police district, off Katla Bazaar opposite Narsingh Temple ☎ 0291/262 3802, ⓔ shahigh@rediffmail.com. Quirky 350-year-old haveli buried deep in the warren of lanes beneath the fort's southwest wall. Three cavernous, atmospheric rooms offer little in the way of plush comfort but a whole lot of tranquillity and bags of character. Queen Palace room can sleep up to five comfortably. Call for directions. ③–④

Expensive

Ajit Bhawan Airport Rd ☎ 0291/251 1410, ⓦ www.ajitbhawan.com. Despite the Flintstones-like theme park design, this self-contained resort – built to resemble a *dhani* village – gets rave reviews for its try-hard attitude and relaxing environment. All guests have access to a waterfall-fed pool, thatch-roofed outdoor restaurant and spa,

and there are vintage cars to admire or even rent, but the rooms are chic rather than palatial. ⑧–⑨

Bal Samand Lake Palace off Mandor Rd, 8km north of town ☎ 0291/257 2321 to 6, ⓦ www .welcomheritagehotels.com. Among the most attractive heritage hotels of its kind in the state, converted from the maharaja's lakeside summer palace. The standard rooms, in former stables, are nothing special, but if your budget can stretch to Rs12,100, go for one of the nine suites in the main building: they're huge, airy and exquisitely furnished. Either way, you get the run of a lush, monkey-filled garden with a pool and croquet lawn. Prices quoted in rupees from Rs6270. ⑨

Ranbanka Airport Rd ☎ 0291/251 0162, ⓦ ranbankahotels.com. In the other half of the palace occupied by *Ajit Bhawan*, this is more authentic in some ways (the rooms are actually inside the palace, and have wood floors), but less professional and a bit creakier, though it has a nice pool, a health spa and a garden restaurant. ⑦–⑧

Taj Hari Mahal 5 Residency Rd, less than 1km south of town ☎ 0291/243 9700, ⓦ www.tajhotels.com. All the luxury you'd expect from a five-star Taj hotel, including good restaurants and a huge pool, but it lacks the charm and personality of the heritage and boutique alternatives. Rooms from US$247.50. ⑨

Umaid Bhawan Palace southeast of town ☎ 0291/251 0101 or 1600/111 825, ⓦ www .tajhotels.com. The Maharaja of Jodhpur's princely pile (see p.289) ranks among the world's grandest hotels, with celebrity guests and lashings of trendy Art Deco. But being king or queen for a day can be a solitary experience – some find the oversized suites, stately salons and dark, marbled passage-ways a bit foreboding. Rooms start at US$506, or US$4400 for the presidential suite in the former royal apartment. ⑨

The City

Life in Jodhpur focuses very much around the fort, which dominates the walled old city. The blue wash applied to most of the houses huddled like a Cubist painting beneath it originally denoted high-caste Brahmin residences, and resulted from the addition to their lime-based whitewash of indigo, thought to protect buildings from insect pests, and to keep them cool in summer. Over time the distinctive colour caught on – there's now even a blue-wash mosque on the road from the Jalori Gate, west of the fort.

The bazaars of the old city, with different areas assigned to different trades, radiate out from the 1910 **Sardar Market** with its tall **clock tower**, a distinctive local landmark marking the centre of town. Most of the ramparts on the south side of the old city have been dismantled, leaving **Jalori Gate** and **Sojati Gate** looking rather forlorn as gates without a wall. South of the old city, the **train station** was constructed in 1880 as part of Marwar's own Jodhpur Railway.

Meherangarh Fort

Jodhpur's **Meherangarh Fort** (daily: summer 8.30am–5.30pm; winter 9am–5pm; Rs250 entry includes audio tour if you leave ID, credit card or deposit; camera Rs50, video Rs200; elevator Rs15; guide Rs100 for up to four people, Rs150 for five to fifteen; Ⓦ www.mehrangarh.org), provides a taste of the war, honour and extravagance that characterized Rajputana. Huge and imposing, it dominates the city, but for decades it was locked up, caked in bat droppings, until 1972, when the current, Oxford-educated maharaja – who was born a midnight child in the year of India's Independence and took office at the age of four – created a foundation to rescue the derelict edifice. Unlike the fort in Jaisalmer it is uninhabited, its paths trodden only by visitors.

The walk up to the fort from the old city is pretty steep, but you can reach the entrance by taxi or auto along the road from Nagauri Gate. The audio tour is outstanding and highly recommended; it takes about two hours to complete. You enter the fort through **Jai Pol**, the first of seven defensive gates on the way up to the fort's living quarters, and constructed in 1806 to celebrate Meherangarh's successful holdout against a siege mounted by the Jaipuri and Mewari armies during a dispute over the hand of a Mewari princess.

The sixth of the seven gates, **Loha Pol**, has a sharp right-angle turn and sharper iron spikes to hinder the ascent of charging enemy elephants. On the wall just inside it you can see the handprints of Maharaja Man Singh's widows, placed there in 1843 as they left the palace to commit *sati* on his funeral pyre according to the Rajput code of honour; *sati* had already been banned by the East India Company in British India but, although the Company's writ didn't run in Marwar, this was the last mass *sati* by wives of a Marwari maharaja.

Beyond the final gate, the massive **Suraj Pol**, lies the **Coronation Courtyard** (Shangar Chowk), where maharajas are crowned on a special marble throne. Looking up from the courtyard, you can see the fantastic *jali* (lattice) work that almost entirely covers the surrounding sandstone walls. The adjoining apartments now serve as a **museum** in which solid silver *howdahs* (elephant seats) and palanquins are on display, as well as assorted armaments including Akbar's own sword. One prize exhibit is a very grand glass palanquin seized in battle from the Mughal governor of Gujarat. Upstairs (though sometimes moved during temporary exhibitions) are some fine **miniature paintings** of the Marwari school, mostly featuring maharaja Man Singh, who greatly encouraged miniature painting during his reign.

The most elaborate of the royal apartments, the magnificent 1724 **Phool Mahal** (Flower Palace), with its jewel-like stained-glass windows and gold filigree ceiling, was a pleasure hall used by the maharajas to listen to music or poetry, or watch dancers perform. Maharaja Takhat Singh, on the other hand, preferred his own nineteenth-century apartment, **Takhat Vilas**, its ceiling hung with huge Christmas tree balls, while the walls are painted with murals reminiscent of those in Shekhawati (see p.229).

In the **Jhanki Mahal**, or Queen's Palace, there's a colourful array of cradles of former rulers. The *jali* screens on either side of the room allowed the women of the palace to look out onto the courtyards on both sides without themselves being seen. This was important, for purdah, usually thought of as a Muslim custom, was strictly applied in the Hindu Rajput kingdoms.

The **Moti Mahal** (Pearl Palace – so called because crushed seashells were added to the lime plaster of the walls to give them a pearly sheen) holds the nine cushions reserved for the nine heads of the Marwari state, and one central cushion for the maharaja. It was used for councils of state. The five alcoves in the wall opposite the entrance are in fact concealed balconies where the maharaja's wives could listen in secretly on the proceedings, perhaps overhearing and reporting private conversations between those attending which the maharaja wasn't meant to know about. In the courtyard just before the Moti Mahal, the royal **astrologer**, who doubles as a palmist, provides "consultations" for a Rs200–350 fee, but his powers don't work if you're wearing nail polish (call ☎0291/553 6506 for an appointment; he also holds nightly evening consultations at the *Umaid Bhawan Palace* at 7–9pm).

Beyond the Moti Mahal is the **Zenana**, or women's quarters, otherwise known as the harem, and formerly guarded by eunuchs. From here, you descend to the **Temple of Chamunda**, the city's oldest temple, dedicated to Jodhpur's patron goddess, an incarnation of Durga. In 1965, during one of India's frequent set-tos with its sibling state of Pakistan, three hundred Pakistani bombs fell on the city, but the only thing hit was a wall of the city jail, and nobody was hurt; Jodhpuris ascribe this luck to the goddess's intervention, and she is even said to have appeared in the form of a kite (a large bird of prey) to intercept a bomb destined for the fort.

Jaswant Thanda

Some 500m north of the fort, and connected to it by road, **Jaswant Thanda** (daily 9am–5pm; Rs20, camera Rs25, video Rs50) is a pillared marble memorial to the popular ruler Jaswant Singh II (1878–95), who purged Jodhpur of bandits, initiated irrigation systems and boosted the economy. The cenotaphs of members of the royal family who have died since Jaswant are close to his memorial; those who preceded him are remembered by *chhatris* at Mandor (see p.295). In the morning, this southwest-facing spot is also a top place from which to photograph the fort.

Umaid Bhawan Palace

Dominating the city's southeast horizon is the **Umaid Bhawan Palace**, a colossal Indo-Saracenic heap commissioned by Maharaja Umaid Singh in 1929 as a famine relief project. It kept three thousand labourers gainfully employed for sixteen years, used a hundred wagon-loads of marble from the quarries at Makrana (see p.273), and its 26-acre garden needed half a million donkey-loads of soil. The project cost nearly 95 lakh (nine and a half million) rupees. When completed in 1944, it boasted 347 rooms, including a cinema and indoor swimming pool. Its furniture and fittings, ordered from Maples in London at the height of World War II, were sunk by a U-boat en route to India, and the maharaja had to turn instead to a wartime Polish refugee, Stephen Norblin, who gave the palace its fabulous Art Deco interiors. Umaid Singh unfortunately had little time to enjoy his new home; only three years after it was finished he died.

The present incumbent, Maharaja Gaj Singh, occupies only one-third of the palace; the rest is given over to a luxury **hotel** (see p.287) and a **museum** (daily: April–Sept 8.30am–5.30pm, Oct–March 9am–5pm; Rs50; no photography). The museum contains an exhibition on the building of the palace, including a video presentation showing some of its opulent interiors. There's also a gallery of crockery and glassware, a salon with a peeling gold gilt ceiling and some of Stephen Norblin's murals to give a taster of the palace's splendour (though it's in bad need of patching up), and a gallery of clocks and barometers, some in the form of railway locomotives, lighthouses and windmills. Far more interesting than the museum is the palace itself, its Art Deco furniture and fittings nearly all original, enlivened with lashings of typically Rajasthani gilt and sweeping staircases. To see them, unless you stay at the hotel, you'll need to spend at least Rs1500 to visit the bar, coffee shop or restaurants (see p.291).

Umaid Gardens

Umaid Gardens is a little park on High Court Road about which is scattered a small **zoo** (daily except Tues 8am–5.30pm; Rs4, camera Rs10, video Rs40). It also has a rather dark and sombre **museum** (daily 10am–4.30pm; Rs3) with a few mildly interesting exhibits including (in the natural history gallery) a pickled scorpion with two stings, and (in the last gallery) some lovely miniature paintings, notably one featuring a rather inebriated-looking Rajput eating goat heads and trotters. Just outside the gardens, the Rajasthan Sangeet Natak Akademi runs a **Folk Art Museum** (Mon–Sat 11am–5pm; Rs5) with a good if slightly moth-eaten collection of Rajasthani musical instruments.

Maha Mandir

In a bustling suburb northeast of town, once a village in its own right, the **Maha Mandir** temple was commissioned in 1804 by maharaja Man Singh. As a prince, Man Singh was in hiding from Bhim Singh, the previous maharaja, who wanted him killed, and he was considering making a getaway. A Nath yogi guru by the name of Aayas Deonath told him to hold out for five more days, at the end of which Bhim Singh died and Man Singh emerged to take the throne. He commissioned the temple in gratitude to the yogi.

The temple is supported by 84 pillars, and the main shrine, dedicated to Aayas Deonath, is decorated with murals depicting the 84 positions of Nath yoga. Like many medieval churches in Europe, the temple was once a sanctuary for criminals. Today it's used as a school, but members of the public are allowed in. To reach it take an auto from town (Rs50) or a bus (#1, #5, #7 or #15) to Maha Mandir circle, walk over the level crossing and through the arch (one of four gates into the formerly walled Brahmin settlement around the temple), and turn left after 300m or so.

Eating and drinking

Jodhpur's **restaurants** cater for all tastes and all budgets, though most of them are outside the old city. Local **specialities** include *mirchi bada*, a chilli in wheatgerm and potato, which is deep-fried like a *pakora*. Jodhpuri sweets, often made with *mawa* (milk that's been boiled down until solid), include *makhan wada* (a sweet made of wheatflour, semolina and sugar, fried in ghee) and *mawa kachori* (a *kachori* filled with *mawa* and dizzled with syrup). In winter, there's *doodh feni*, consisting of wheat strands (sweet or plain) in hot milk.

Bars are pretty thin on the ground in Jodhpur. If you don't want to pay Rs1500 to visit the *Umaid Bhawan Palace Hotel*'s Trophy Bar, you could try the uninspiring but quiet *Chirmi Bar* at the *RTDC Hotel Goomar*, next to the tourist office, or the bars around the *Midtown* restaurant on Station Road.

Cafés, sweets and snacks

Jodhpur Coffee House High Court Rd. The locale is a bit dingy and the service a bit dopey, but it's cheap (curries Rs26–50) and they do reasonable filter coffee, plus toast, bhajis, *pakoras*, *alu paratha*, South Indian staples such as vada, *dosa* and uttapam, ice cream (including rose-flavoured), and even the odd Chinese and Continental dish.

Jodhpur Sweets C Rd, Sardarpura, next to *Gipsy*. The best sweet shop in town, and an excellent place to try *makhan wada*, *mawa kachori*, or any other Rajasthani or Bengali sweets. Very near by (west, at the next corner), *15 AD Cake Shop* does Jodhpur's best Western-style gateaux and pastries.

Mishri Lal in the eastern arch of the south gate to Sardar Market. The most famous purveyor of *makhania lassi*, made with cream, saffron and cardamom, very rich and thick, but those with delicate stomachs should take note that they use crushed ice made from tap water. They also do good *doodh feni*.

Parashnath Ice-Cream High Court Rd. Jodhpur's best address for juices and ice creams. Their

Marwari *kulfi* (kulfi with nuts and saffron) is outstanding.

Pokar Sweets corner of Nai Sarak with High Court Rd. Not all their sweets are good, but they're known for their *makhan wada*, and their *mirchi bada*'s pretty hot too. This is also a good place to try *doodh feni*.

Samosa House Station Rd, 50m north of *Govind Hotel*. Lightly spiced but very tasty veg samosas, and sweet *mawa* samosas, plus syrupy Bengali sweets including excellent *rasgullas* and *gulab jamuns*.

Shahi Samosa 95B Nai Sarak, by the south gate to Sardar Market. Great veg samosas, if you like them spicy, and excellent *mirchi badas*, if you like them even spicier. They sell like hot cakes, so they're always freshly made.

The Omelette Shop just outside the north gate to Sardar Market. Since foreign guidebooks started recommending it, this shack selling eggy snacks (omelette sandwiches in particular) has become extremely popular with tourists, and spawned a cluster of imitators trying to cash in on its name. The original *Omelette Shop* is the ramshackle little affair between the central and western arches on the north side of the gate.

Restaurants

Bollygood Khaas Bagh, Ratanada. A fun, movie-themed restaurant with medium-priced indoor or garden dining, veg or non-veg. Tandoori dishes are the mainstay. Main courses around Rs100–150.

Fort View On the roof of the *Govind Hotel*, Station Rd. A cut above the usual tourist places, with good, reasonably priced veg curries (Rs30–60), thalis, local specialities such as *makhania lassi*, *doodh feni* and *gulab jamun* (not the Bengali sweet, but a savoury Rajasthani dish made with *mawa*), plus some Chinese items, good breakfast options, including real coffee (though no eggs as it's strictly veg), Wi-Fi coverage, and a view of the fort. You can hang out here while waiting for a bus or train (baggage storage facilities are available).

Gypsy C Rd, Sardarpura. Downstairs it's a diner selling South Indian, Chinese and Continental snacks (Rs30–60). Upstairs it's an immaculate restaurant serving one thing only: an unlimited and very delicious veg thali (Rs90) which they keep refilling for as long as you can keep eating. There's another branch on PWD Rd, next to *Inn Season* hotel.

Hotel Priya 181–2 Nai Sarak. A good place for breakfast, with *parathas*, chai and good curd. It's

also not a bad spot for lunch or even supper, serving low-priced veg curries (Rs30–47) and thalis (Rs55).

Marwar At the *Taj Hari Mahal* hotel ☎0291/243 9700. Pricey, but the best place in town to sample traditional Marwari cuisine, such as *Jodhpuri mas* (a spicy mutton dish) or *gatta di subzi* (its veg equivalent), rounded off with *kulfi*. Main dishes are Rs210 275 vcg, Rs375–400 non-veg.

Mehran Terrace in the fort ☎0291/254 8790. You'll need to book ahead to eat up here, atop the fort with great views all round. The only choice is between a veg thali (Rs411) or a non-veg one (Rs470), but it's the location rather than the food that you come here for. Open daily 7.30–10pm only.

Midtown on a branch off Station Rd leading from opposite the station to Raj Ranchodji Temple. Bright, clean and friendly, with a good menu of pure-veg options (curries Rs55–65), South Indian dishes, Gujarati and Rajasthani thalis (Rs90–100), pizza and pasta.

On the Rocks Next to *Ajit Bhawan* hotel, Airport Rd ☎0291/230 2701. A renowned upmarket non-veg garden restaurant specializing in kebabs and tandoori cuisine. Though the service is slow, and the buffet no great shakes, it's fun and festive at night. The lunch crowd is mostly tour groups. Mains Rs60–105 veg, Rs110–270 non-veg.

Pushpa Bhojnalya MG Rd by Jalori Gate. A small, cheap diner known in particular for its *dal bati* (Rs50).

Shandar off MG Rd, 100m up a street directly opposite MG Hospital. A grimy little vegetarian *dhaba* with a sweet shop outside, where women in particular won't feel comfortable, but the food is great and very cheap (main dishes Rs20–40), though rich, with lots of ghee. The *malai kofta* is definitely worth trying.

The Pillars *Umaid Bhawan Palace Hotel* ☎0291/251 0101. (Rs1500 minimum charge, payable on entry). Taking a drink or a bite to eat at the verandah café of the maharaja's palace gives you the excuse to wander around the hotel's opulent Art Deco interior. It's also a great place for a sundowner, with peacocks on the well-manicured lawn and sweeping views of the distant city. Sandwiches are available all day and there's a dinner menu of mostly Western food from 7.30pm. You could also sit yourself down on an elephant-foot footstool and have a drink in the *Trophy Bar*.

Shopping

Jodhpur's first-rate **antique reproductions** – everything from chests of drawers to sculptures of Jain *tirthankaras* – attract dealers from around the world. There's a

The city of Jodhpur gives its name to a type of trouser – baggy around the thigh but narrow around the calf – designed for horseback riding. They were invented for his own personal use by Sir Pratap Singh, brother of Maharaja Jaswant Singh II and effectively his prime minister. In 1887, Sir Pratap went to London as the maharaja's emissary to attend Queen Victoria's golden jubilee celebrations. En route, the ship carrying his clothes and jewellery sank. Divers managed to rescue his jewels, but his clothes, including his riding britches, were lost, so Sir Pratap went to a Savile Row tailor, who managed to replicate his design, and his custom-made riding trousers caught on big-time among Britain's aristocracy, who were soon flocking to Savile Row to get their own jodhpurs made. So successful was the design that a new type of boot – the jodhpur boot – was invented specifically to go with them.

line of shops selling them along Umaid Bhawan Palace Road east of the Circuit House. Other good buys in town are **textiles**, including mirrorwork dresses, patchwork bedcovers, and *Bandhani* (tie-dye) fabric and saris, not to mention **Jodhpur riding britches** (see box above). For bookshops see opposite.

India Tailors High Court Rd, 200m east of the junction with Nai Sarak ☏ 0291/255 0214. For custom-made suits or Jodhpur riding britches, none can beat this tailor, used by the maharaja and the royal family.

Khadi Shop Station Rd opposite *Govind Hotel*. The federal government's official outlet for handloom cloth and cottage-produced clothing. If you need a pukka Nehru jacket or Congress-wallah hat, this is the place.

Manohar Pickles 16 Nai Sarak, in a group of shops set slightly back, 100m north of the junction with MG Rd (sign in Hindi only). If you like Indian pickles, check out this locally renowned purveyor and manufacturer; their range isn't huge (green chilli, mango, lime or mixed), but the quality's excellent, the prices are low, and you can get them in tough plastic packets as well as glass jars.

Mohanlal Verhomal's (MV) Spice Shop 209-B Kirana Merchant Vegetable Market, west of the clock tower, and also at the fort entrance ☏ 0291/261 5846, ⊛ www.mvspices.com. Lots of spices, whole and ground, including pukka saffron, masalas and teas. Has a reliable pay-on-receipt

mail-order service, though in fact you can buy many of the same spices more cheaply at open stalls in the adjoining spice market.

Paradise Obscure Arts Umaid Bhawan Palace Road ☏ 0291/251 0838, ⓔ rajobscure@yahoo .co.in. A treasure trove of superior bric-a-brac, including old tin boxes, enamel signs, silverware, glassware, little brass gods, metal toys, doorknobs and all kinds of collectables. Definitely worth a browse.

Raju's MG Rd, almost opposite Sojati Gate, and also on C Rd, Sardarpura ☏ 0291/262 7723. Embroidered and *bandhani* saris and *salwar kameez* suits: very classy, very colourful, very Rajasthani. Also worth checking is their competitor, Lucky Silk Stores, a few doors away on MG Rd.

Shriganesham Pal Haveli, north of Sardar Market, opposite the eastern arch of the north gate ☏ 0291/264 5857, ⓔ arjunshah@satyam .net.in. Wonderful Rajasthani fabrics, old and new, including *dhurries*, mirrorwork dresses, patchwork bedspreads made from recycled garments, and some sumptuous embroidered coats and dresses.

Listings

Airlines Indian Airlines, East Patel Nagar, Airport Rd ☏ 0291/251 0758; Jet Airways, Osho Apartments, Residency Rd ☏ 0291/510 3333.

Banks and exchange There are ATMs at 151 and 157 Nai Sarak, and on MG Rd 100m east of Sojati Gate, and on the little street off MG Rd opposite Sojati Gate, and also on Station Road near *Govind Hotel*, and next to the tourist office. Forex offices can

be found in Sadar Market, north of the clock tower in Sardar Market, there's also a cluster of them on Hanwant Vihar just north of Circuit House, plus one on the corner of Airport Rd, so you can compare rates and commission before changing your cash.

Bicycle rental Hind Silk Store, 30m west of *Midtown* restaurant on Station Road (☏ 0291/261 2953), rents bicycles for Rs25–35 a day.

Bookshops Sarvodaya Bookstall, opposite Raj Ranchodji Temple on the same branch of Station Rd as *Midtown* restaurant, has a good selection of English-language books. Krishna Book Depot, upstairs at Krishna Art and Export in Sardar Market, just east of the north gate, has a wide selection of used books at reasonable (but unmarked) prices.

Festival Jodhpur's annual two-day Marwar Festival, held at the full moon of the Hindu month of Ashvina (25–26 Oct 2007, 13–14 Oct 2008, 3–4 Oct 2009, 21–22 Oct 2010) is a showcase of performing arts, mainly music and dance.

Hospital The best private hospital is the Goyal on Residency Rd in the Sindhi Colony, 2km south of town (℡ 0291/243 2144). The government infirmary is Mahatma Gandhi Hospital on MG Rd, near Jalori Gate (℡ 0291/263 9851).

Internet access Internet (usually Rs30–40 an hour) is widely available, even amid the medieval labyrinth of the old city. Handy Internet stations include The Net (daily 9am–10pm) on High Court Rd by *Parashnath Ice-Cream*, *Govind Hotel*'s Internet office on Station Rd (daily 9am–10pm) and Sify I-Way (daily 9am–11pm), opposite the north gate from Sardar Market.

Motorcycle rental If you're prepared to risk it on Jodhpur's roads, you can rent motorbikes and mopeds at a couple of travel agencies on Station Road, a few doors south of *Govind Hotel*. Prices start at Rs200 a day.

Police ℡ 0291/265 0777. There's a police tourist assistance booth by the Clock Tower in Sardar Market.

Post office The GPO is opposite the *Govind Hotel* on Station Road for sale of stamps (right-hand entrance; Mon–Sat 8am–4pm, Sun 10am–2pm) or for poste restante and parcel packing (left-hand entrance; Mon–Sat 10am–3pm).

Moving on from Jodhpur

Jodhpur stands at the nexus of Rajasthan's main **tourist routes**, with connections northeast to Jaipur, Pushkar and Delhi, south to Udaipur and Ahmedabad, and west to Jaisalmer. Buses for most destinations are faster than the train. The five-hour journey to **Jaisalmer** is certainly more rewarding by road, as it allows for stops at Osian (see p.296), Keechen (see p.315) and Pokaran (see p.313), though most travellers end up on the freezing cold sleeper rail service across the Thar instead. If you do end up taking the train, take plenty of warm clothes and a blanket, and stay alert for thieves and con merchants – well-spoken *lapkars* from Jaisalmer routinely bribe the conductors to be allowed on board, where they attempt to lure customers to their "uncle's" dodgy hotels and desert safaris.

By train

The **railway station** (℡ 0291/243 2956) is on Station Road, 300m south of Sojati Gate. Train tickets should be booked at least a day in advance at the computerized **reservations office** (Mon–Sat 8am–8pm, Sun 8am–2pm), just north of the station behind the GPO. If you're a foreigner or NRI, you're entitled to use the musty International Tourist Waiting Room on the ground floor of the main station building. *Govind Hotel* will also allow customers at its *Fort View* restaurant (see p.291) to leave baggage free of charge and use toilet facilities while waiting for a train. Recommended services are listed in the box on p.294.

The weekly Thar Express to Karachi in **Pakistan**, a service inaugurated early in 2006, but derailed by floods later that year, should now be back on track, but only Indian and Pakistani nationals have so far been allowed to use the service, though this may change. All being well, the train should leave Jodhpur at 11.30pm on Friday night for Munabao, where passengers disembark for lengthy border formalities before boarding another train to Karachi. Total journey time should be around 25 hours.

By bus

Destinations served by bus include: Abu Road (12 daily; 6–9hr), Agra (3 daily; 14hr), Ajmer (half-hourly; 5hr), Bharatpur (2 daily; 10hr), Bikaner (17 daily; 6hr),

Recommended trains from Jodhpur

The following trains from Jodhpur are recommended as the fastest or most convenient; all run daily. Other services may also exist, which take longer, arrive at inconvenient times, or do not run every day. Train timetables change frequently; check latest schedules either at your nearest station or online at ⓦ www.indianrail. gov.in before travel.

To **Udaipur** there are no direct trains; it is possible to go by rail if you take the #4707 Ranakpur Express at 3.10am to Marwar Junction (enquiries ☎02935/252204), where there should be a connecting service to Udaipur, but this will involve long waits and currently another change of train en route, and will get you into Udaipur very late at night. There are likewise no direct trains to **Chittaurgarh**, but it is possible to take the 7.15am passenger train to Ajmer (arrives 12.50pm), have lunch there, and then get the #9769 Purna Express at 3.25pm, arriving in Chittor at 7.32pm.

Destination	Name	No.	Departs	Arrives
Abu Road	Ahmedabad Express	9224	6.15am	11.25am
	Ranakpur Express	4707	3.10pm	8pm
Agra	Howrah Superfast	2308	7.45pm	6.35am
Ajmer	Fast passenger train	1JA	7.15am	12.50pm
Alwar	Jaisalmer–Delhi Express	4060	10.30pm	7.23am
Bikaner	Ranakpur Express	4708	10.10am	4pm
	Barmer-Howrah Express	4888	10.45am	4.30pm
	Bhatinda passenger train	340	1.45pm	8.40pm
Delhi	Mandor Express	2462	7.30pm	5.50am
	Jaisalmer–Delhi Express	4060	10.30pm	10.23am
Jaipur	Jaipur Intercity Express	2466	5.45am	10.43am
	Marudhar Express	4854	9.15am	3.20pm
Jaisalmer	Delhi–Jaisalmer Express	4059	6.45am	1pm
	Jaisalmer Express	4810	11.30pm	5.20am
Kota	Bhopal passenger train	492	7.30am	10.40pm
Sawai Madhopur	Intercity Express	2466	5.45am	1pm
	Bhopal passenger train	492	7.30am	8.25pm

Bundi (3 daily; 10hr), Chittaurgarh (5 daily; 9hr), Delhi (7 daily; 11–12hr), Jaipur (9 daily; 7–8hr), Jaisalmer (27 daily; 5hr 30min), Mount Abu (1 daily; 6–9hr 30min), Osian (every 30–45min; 2hr), Pushkar (3 daily; 4hr 30min–6hr 30min), Ranakpur (5–6 daily; 4–5hr) and Udaipur (14 daily; 7–9hr). **Private buses** for most destinations leave from Kalpataru Cinema, 4km southwest of town, reached by auto for Rs30; private buses for Jaisalmer (of which there are a dozen a day) leave nearby, from Bombay Motors Circle. You can book private buses at most travel agents and a lot of hotels (for a Rs50 fee). **Government buses** leave from the Roadways Bus Stand just east of town – turn up an hour or so before departure to buy a ticket. For timetable information, it's best to ask your hotel or guesthouse to ring on your behalf (☎0291/254 4686). There are Silver and Gold Line buses to Delhi, Agra, Ajmer, Jaipur and Udaipur. Whether going state or private, keep an eye on your valuables around the bus stands and on night buses.

By air
The **airport** (☎0291/251 2617) is 4km south of town, reached by auto (Rs50) or taxi (Rs220). Indian Airlines and Jet Airways (see p.292 for contact details) each have one daily flight to Delhi (1hr 20min) and one to Mumbai (2hr 20min); Indian Airlines also have one flight a day to Udaipur (40min).

Mandor

The royal cenotaphs, or *dewals*, at **MANDOR**, 9km north of the city, are set in a little park full of monkeys, and can be reached on minibuses #1, #5, #7 and #15 from Sojati Gate. Between the sixth and fourteenth centuries, Mandor was capital of the Parihar Rajputs, who were ousted by Rathore Rao Chauhan in 1381. His successors moved their capital to Jodhpur in1459, but once they had been cremated their cenotaphs were erected here in Mandor. Temple-like in their sombre dark red sandstone (the canopy-like *chhatris* next to them are for lesser royals), the cenotaphs grew in size and grandeur as the Rathore kingdom prospered. The largest is Ajit Singh's, built in 1724. His six queens, along with assorted mistresses, concubines, maids and entertainers – 84 women in all – committed *sati* on his funeral pyre.

At the end of the gardens, over to the left of the *chhatris*, you'll find the **Hall of Heroes**, a strange display of life-sized gods and Rajput fighters hewn out of the rock face early in the eighteenth century and covered with lime plaster and paint. Nearby is the octagonal **Ek Thamba Mahal** (Single Pillared Palace), a three-storey pagoda-like affair in red sandstone with filigree *jali* screens for windows. It was built at the beginning of the eighteenth century for royal ladies to watch public events without breaking their purdah. Behind it is a small **museum** (daily except Fri 10am–4pm; Rs3), whose main item of interest is a twelfth-century pornographic sculpture from Kiradu, alongside a ninth-century "amorous couple" from Mandor itself, and, also of local origin, a rather contorted thirteenth-century statue of Kichak (a character in the Mahabharata).

Steps behind the gardens lead up to the old **Mandor Fort**, citadel of the Parihar and Rathore Rajputs when Mandor was their capital. From here, a path leads over the hill to a set of **queens' cenotaphs** commemorating the ranis of Jodhpur. Though smaller than those of the men, they are more stately, with exquisitely detailed carving on the pillars and domed roofs.

If you'd like to **stay** in Mandor, you could try the *Mandore Guest House* on Dadawari Lane (☎0291/254 5210, ⊛www.mandore.com; ❹), which has clean and pleasant a/c attached huts and cottages set around a garden full of trees. It can also be booked via Poly Travels in Jodhpur (see p.296).

The Bishnoi villages

Jodhpur's surroundings can be explored on organized "**village safaris**", which take small groups of tourists out into rural Rajasthan, usually stopping at four or five **Bishnoi villages** where you can taste traditional food, drink opium tea, and watch crafts such as spinning and carpet-making.

The Bishnois – a religious sect rather than an ethnic group in the usual sense – are among the world's earliest tree huggers. Their origins go back to a drought in the year 1485. Observing that this was caused largely by deforestation, a guru by the name of Jambeshwar Bhagavan formulated 29 rules for living in harmony with nature and the environment – his followers are called Bishnoi after the Marwari word for twenty-nine. As well as enforcing strict vegetarianism, Jambeshwar's rules forbid the killing of animals or felling of live trees. In particular, Bishnoi hold the *khejri* tree sacred. In 1730, at the village of **Khejadali**, workers sent by the maharaja of Marwar to make lime for the construction of a palace started felling *khejri* trees to burn the local limestone. A woman by the name of Amrita Devi put her arms around a tree and declared that if they wanted to cut it down, they would have to cut her head off first. The leader of the working party ordered her decapitation, upon which her three daughters followed her example, and were similarly beheaded. Bishnoi people from the

△ Making opium tea at one of the Bishnoi villages

whole of the surrounding region then converged on the site to defend the trees – 363 of them gave their lives doing so. When news reached the maharaja, he ordered the felling to cease and banned cutting down trees and hunting animals in Bishnoi territory. Today, a small temple marks the place where all this happened, while in its grounds, 363 *khejri* trees commemorate the martyrs. Although it is possible to go to Khejadali by bus, you'll be hard put to find a villager who speaks English, and it's a lot better to go with a tour group, which will also visit other villages. Most tours stop at Khejadali for lunch. This is usually followed by an **opium ceremony** in which opium is dissolved in water in a specially designed wooden vessel, and poured through a strainer into a second receptacle. The process is repeated twice more, and the resulting tea is drunk from the palm of a hand. Strictly speaking, it's illegal, but blind eyes are turned to this kind of traditional opium use, though in fact opium addiction is something of a social problem in rural Rajasthan.

On most village safaris you'll spot nilgai (bluebull) antelopes, gazelles, and countless varieties of birds. Though the invasiveness of the tours can prove unsettling, they are almost always fascinating. However, a lot depends on the integrity of the operators and the relations they have with the villagers. Four inexpensive, commendable **companies** are RTDC, based at the tourist office on High Court Road (☎0291/254 5083); Poly Travels, just north of the Roadways Bus Stand at 10-D Near Government Bus Stand, Paola (☎0291/254 5210); *Govind Hotel* on Station Road (☎0291/262 2758); and *Yogi's Guest House* (☎0291/264 3436). Rates start at around Rs400 per head and usually include a home-made meal, though sharing a Jeep tour booked by RTDC (Rs1200 for up to 7 people, including guide) brings down the cost considerably. Book at least one day in advance.

Osian

Rajasthan's largest group of early Jain and Hindu temples lies on the outskirts of the small town of **OSIAN**, 64km north of Jodhpur. RSTDC buses take a

Tilwara Cattle Fair

Tilwara Cattle Fair, also known as Mallinath Fair, is one of Rajasthan's biggest livestock markets. Held annually over a fortnight in March or April at Tilwara near **Balotra**, 93km southwest of Jodhpur, it's been going since 1374, and was originally held in honour of a local holy man, Rawal Mallinath; offerings are still made at his shrine nearby. Today it attracts some eighty thousand head of livestock – goats, sheep, camels and horses as well as cattle – plus buyers and sellers from all over Rajasthan and the neighbouring states of Gujarat and Madhya Pradesh. So far it remains largely undiscovered by tourists, and there's no accommodation; visitors are advised to bring a tent. As well as cattle trading, and animal races, there's also a crafts market, and sale of cattle fodder and agricultural implements.

scenic route that drops you at a bus stand on the main road just south of town; the railway station (served by the Jodhpur–Jaisalmer train, 1hr 15min trip from Jodhpur) is 1km west. Alternatively, book a Jeep through Jodhpur's tourist office (Rs1200 for up to six people with a guide). The temples date from the eighth to the twelfth centuries when Osian was a regional trading centre. The town's ruler and population apparently converted to Jainism in the eleventh century, and Osian gives its name to the Oswal sect, which originated in the town. Today, though many Jain pilgrims come to visit, none actually lives in Osian.

The oldest collection of temples, just south of the bus stop, centres on the **Vishnu and Harihara temples**, built in the Pratihara period (eighth and ninth centuries). The nine temples in this group retain a considerable amount of decorative carving, particularly in the surrounding friezes.

In the opposite direction from the bus stop, where the main Jodhpur–Phalodi road bends round to the right, the smaller road straight ahead leads to the town centre, where you'll find the twelfth-century **Sachiya Mata Temple**, overlooking the whole of Osian, which is still used for worship. The main shrine, to Sachiya, an incarnation of Durga, is surrounded by smaller, earlier ones to Ganesh and Shankar (an aspect of Shiva) and, on the right, to Surya and Vishnu.

As you leave the Sachiya Mata temple, the third group of temples lies roughly straight ahead. The first is the **Mahavira Jain Temple** (Rs5, Rs40 camera, Rs100 video; usual rules apply, no leather, don't enter during menstruation), built in the eighth century, renovated in the tenth, and restored quite recently. Its main portico is held up by twenty elegantly carved pillars. Fifty metres beyond is the **Surya (Sun) Temple**, surrounded by gargoyle-like projecting elephants, and whose inner sanctum contains an image of Surya, flanked by Ganesh and Durga. A little way behind the temple is a massive Pratihara-period step-well.

For **accommodation**, most people stay at the very basic *Priest Bhanu Sarma Guesthouse* (☎02922/274 029; ❷), opposite the Mahavira temple, a welcoming place run by the (Hindu) priest who looks after the (Jain) temple, and who can also provide information and arrange camel safaris, or just short camel rides. There's also a simple restaurant in town, the *Maishuri Bhajnale* between the bus stop and the Sachiya Mata temple.

More upmarket accommodation can be found at the luxury *Camel Camp*, perched on a sand dune overlooking the railway line west of town (book in advance through the *Safari Club* in Jodhpur on ☎0291/243 7023, ⓦwww .camelcamposian.com; ❾), with carpeted tents and a pool; rates include three meals and a camel ride. Two or three times over the winter, the Camp organizes **camel races**, details of which can be found on their website.

Jaisalmer and around

In the remote westernmost corner of Rajasthan, **JAISALMER** is your quintessential desert town, its sand–yellow ramparts rising out of the arid Thar like a scene from the *Arabian Nights*. Rampant commercialism has dampened the romantic vision somewhat, but even with all the touts, hustling merchants and tour buses, the town deservedly remains one of India's most popular destinations. Villagers from outlying settlements, dressed in dazzling red and orange *odhnis* or voluminous turbans, still outnumber foreigners in the bazaar, while the exquisite sandstone architecture of the "Golden City" is quite unlike anything else in India.

Some history

Rawal Jaisal of the Bhati clan founded Jaisalmer in 1156 as a replacement for his less easily defensible capital at Lodurva (see p.312). Constant wars with the neighbouring Rajput states of Jodhpur and Bikaner followed, as did conflict with the Muslim sultans of Delhi. In 1298, a seven-year siege of the fort by the forces of Ala-ud-din Khalji (see p.381) ended when the male survivors – bar two infant princes who were smuggled out to continue the Bhati line – burned

Jaisalmer in jeopardy

Signboards, banners and electric wires may have horribly disfigured Jaisalmer, but the tourist boom has created a far more serious, potentially irreversible threat to the town's survival. Erected on a base of soft bantonite clay, sand and sandstone, the **foundations** of Rajasthan's most picturesque citadel are rapidly eroding because of huge increases in water consumption. At the height of the tourist season, around 120 litres per head are pumped into the area – twelve times the quantity used only a couple of decades ago. Many believe the troubles started in the late 1980s when the city spent Rs9million on replacing the open sewers with covered drainage; unfortunately this backfired and large quantities of water ended up seeping into the soil, weakening the citadel's foundations. Compounding the problem has been the increased planting of trees, which keeps the ground moist. The result has been disastrous; houses have collapsed and significant damage has been done to the sixteenth-century Maharani's Palace. In 1998 six people died when an exterior wall gave way, and five more bastions fell in 2000 and 2001. (Ironically, since then, drought in Rajasthan has dried the fort out and no great damage has been reported since – although a normal monsoon could change that quickly.) Jaisalmer is now listed among the World Monument Fund's 100 Most Endangered Sites.

The Indian National Trust for Art and Cultural Heritage (INTACH; ⊛www.intach.org) has spent more than $100,000 restoring the Maharani's Palace, and an international campaign, **Jaisalmer in Jeopardy** (JiJ), has been set up to facilitate repairs throughout the fort. JiJ has already upgraded more than half of the 350 homes in the fort with underground sewerage, plus restored their facades and replaced grey cement with traditional material. Despite the repairs, city authorities still think the best way to save the fort is to evacuate the two thousand people who live there and start the drainage repairs over from scratch, an expensive and time-consuming venture much opposed by the thirty-plus hotel owners inside whose earnings depend on tourism. The JiJ campaign relies substantially on donations. If you'd like to help, contact JiJ at 3 Brickbarn Close, London SW10 0UJ, UK (☎+44(0)20/7352 4336, ⊛www.jaisalmer-in-jeopardy.org). Bear in mind, too, that you can make a small difference by not staying in the fort or, if you do, by conserving water as much as possible while you're there.

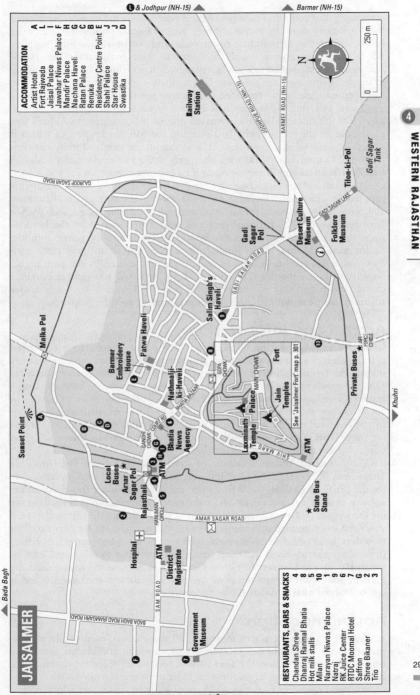

JAISALMER

ACCOMMODATION

Artist Hotel	A
Fort Rajwada	L
Jaisal Palace	I
Jawahar Niwas Palace	F
Mandir Palace	H
Nachana Haveli	C
Ratan Palace	B
Renuka	K
Residency Centre Point	E
Shahi Palace	J
Star House	J
Swastika	D

RESTAURANTS, BARS & SNACKS

Chandan Shree	4
Dhanraj Ranmal Bhatia	8
Hot milk stalls	5
Milan	10
Natraj	1
Narayan Niwas Palace	9
RK Juice Center	6
RTDC Moomal Hotel	7
Saffron	G
Shree Bikaner	2
Trio	3

▲ & Jodhpur (NH-15)   ▲ Barmer (NH-15)

N

0   250 m

GAJROOP SAGAR ROAD

Railway Station

JODHPUR ROAD (NH-15)

BARMER ROAD (NH-15)

Gadi Sagar Tank

Melka Pol

Sunset Point

Barmer Embroidery House

Patwa Haveli

Salim Singh's Haveli   9

GADI SAGAR ROAD

Gadi Sagar Pol

Desert Culture Museum

Folklore Museum

Tilon-ki-Pol

Gadi Sagar Lake

i

E

Nathmalji-ki-Haveli

BHATIA BAZAAR

Bhatia News Agency

COOPER RD

GANDHI CHOWK

8

GOPA CHOWK

Fort

See 'Jaisalmer Fort map p. 301

Jain Temples

MAIN CHOWK

Palace

Laxminath Temple

J

SHIV MARG

ATM

10

AIR FORCE CIRCLE

Private Buses

▲ Khuhri

Local Buses

Amar Sagar Pol

Rajasthali

HANUMAN CIRCLE

ATM

4   G   H

B   I

3

2

5

State Bus Stand

AMAR SAGAR ROAD

Hospital

ATM

District Magistrate

SAM ROAD

BADA BAGH ROAD (RAMGARH ROAD)

Government Museum

7

F

▲ Bada Bagh

▲ Amar Sagar, Lodurva & Sam

everything they could and rode out to their deaths while the women committed *johar* (voluntary death by sword and fire). Rajput forces continued to harry the Muslims from the surrounding countryside, and with no local food supplies, Ala-ud-din's forces were unable to continue their occupation. The Bhatis resumed their rule but were again besieged by Sultanate forces in 1326, resulting in another desperate act of *johar*, but Gharsi Bhati – one of the two princes who had been smuggled out – managed to negotiate the return of his kingdom as a vassal state of Delhi, and it remained in Bhati hands from then on.

In 1570 the ruler of Jaisalmer married one of his daughters to Akbar's son, cementing an alliance between Jaisalmer and the Mughal Empire, of which it nonetheless remained a vassal state. Its position on the overland route between Delhi and Central Asia – which led ultimately to the vast markets of the Middle East, North Africa and Europe – made it an important entrepôt for goods such as silk, opium and spices, and the city grew rich on the proceeds, as the magnificent havelis of its merchants bear witness. However, the emergence of Bombay and Surat as major ports meant that overland trade diminished, and with it Jaisalmer's wealth. The financial problems were compounded by the burdensome taxes imposed on merchants by a particularly greedy prime minister, **Salim Singh Mehta**, in the nineteenth century. The death blow came with Partition, when Jaisalmer's life-line trade route was severed by the new, highly sensitive Pakistani border. The city took on renewed strategic importance during the Indo-Pakistani wars of 1965 and 1971, and it is now a major **military outpost**, with jet aircraft regularly roaring past the ramparts.

Arrival and information

Jaisalmer's **railway station** is 2km east of the city. Thanks to a concerted crackdown by local authorities, touts and rickshaw drivers are now held at bay outside the terminal. Instead of being accosted by aggressive hawkers, reservationless travellers can calmly enquire among the sandwich-board toting hoteliers lined up in the parking lot. The majority offer free rides; otherwise an auto-rickshaw into town will cost around Rs20–30. **Government buses** stop briefly at a stand near the railway station before continuing to the more convenient new **RSRTC bus stand** southwest of the fort. **Private buses** will drop you at Air Force Circle south of the fort.

RTDC's **tourist office,** southeast of town near Gadi Sagar Pol (Mon–Sat 10am–5pm; ☎02992/252406) is of little use, and its "recommended" operators pay for the privilege. **Online**, you'll find some travellers' tips and a run-down of the sights at ⓦwww.jaisalmer.org.uk, and more general information at ⓦjaisalmer.nic .in, the website of the Jaisalmer district unit of the National Informatics Centre. If you need more detailed information about Jaisalmer, look out for two excellent **booklets**: *Jaisalmer: Folklore, History and Architecture*, by local shopkeeper L.N. Khatri (if nowhere else, try his shop, Desert Arts, a few doors east of *RN Juice Center* on Court Road); and *Jaisalmer: the Golden City* by N.K. Sharma, the man behind the Folklore and Desert Culture museums (see p.305), available at the museums and at city bookshops such as Bhatia News Agency (see p.309).

Accommodation

Jaisalmer has plenty of places to stay in all categories. Traditionally, visitors preferred the atmospheric guesthouses among the jumble of sandstone houses and havelis within the **fort**, whose roofs offer splendid desert vistas. But that's changing fast, in response to the campaign to make tourists aware of structural problems to the citadel caused by increased water consumption

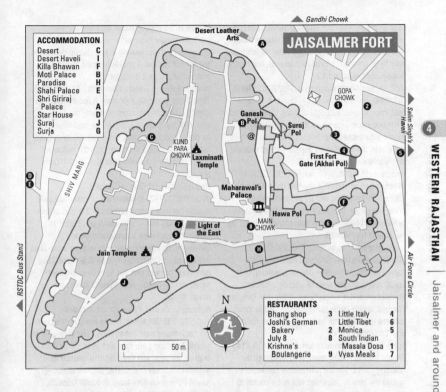

ACCOMMODATION

Desert	C
Desert Haveli	I
Killa Bhawan	F
Moti Palace	B
Paradise	H
Shahi Palace	E
Shri Giriraj	
Palace	A
Star House	D
Suraj	J
Surja	G

JAISALMER FORT

RESTAURANTS

Bhang shop	3	Little Italy	4
Joshi's German		Little Tibet	6
Bakery	2	Monica	5
July 8	8	South Indian	
Krishna's		Masala Dosa	1
Boulangerie	9	Vyas Meals	7

(see box, p.298). Do think twice before staying here. Not only do you often pay a premium to do so, but so does the fort itself. You'll be doing Jaisalmer a favour if you stay elsewhere. Fearing their days are numbered, many hoteliers inside the fort have neglected upkeep of their properties. Meanwhile, there are some very stylish hotels in the old city around the fort, many with lovely terraces offering fort views. Mass-produced three-star hotels and luxury resorts have also appeared on the fringes of Jaisalmer to service tour groups, but offer discounts of 20–30 percent off-season (April–Aug) when they may be worthwhile, especially if you need air-conditioning and a pool (which you probably will at that time of year). Note that most hotels in Jaisalmer have a very early 9am checkout time.

Almost all accommodation offers **camel treks**, which vary in standard and price, and some managers at even the recommended hotels can be uncomfortably pushy if you don't want to arrange a safari through them, suddenly hiking room rates or turfing you out in the middle of the night. Shop around and bargain before committing.

In the fort

The hotels listed below are shown on the Jaisalmer Fort map, above.

Desert Northwest side of the fort
☎02992/250602, ✉ajitdeserthotel@yahoo.com. Friendly little budget place with cheaper rooms downstairs, brighter, airier rooms upstairs. ❷

Desert Haveli near the Jain temples
☎02992/251555. A slightly grungy but popular budget guesthouse. Variously sized stone-walled rooms, with old *dhurries* on the floor, tiny windows and attached bathrooms. The friendly owner offers free pick-ups from bus or railway station. ❷–❹

Killa Bhawan 445 Kotri Badda ℡02992/251204, ⊛www.killabhawan.com. Lovers of interior design give high ratings to this boutique hotel, which tries hard to be chic, and generally succeeds, but is still ridiculously overpriced. ⑥

Moti Palace Above Surya gate ℡02992/254693, ✉kailash_bissa@yahoo.co.uk. One of the friendliest, most laid-back budget choices inside the fort, with unbeatable views over the main gate. All rooms are attached with hot showers, five of them are across the street in an annexe shared with the family who run the hotel. ①–②

Paradise off the Main Chowk ℡02992/252674, ✉hotelparadise_jsm2001@yahoo.co.in. Old haveli with a leafy courtyard and 23 rooms ranging in price. The larger ones have views and bathrooms, or there are budget options with common baths on the ground floor. ①–④

Suraj near the Jain temples ℡02992/251623, ✉hotelsurajjaisalmer@hotmail.com. Superbly carved sandstone haveli – one of Jaisalmer's finest, with a simple, tasteful interior, a family atmosphere and a rooftop view of the Jain temples. The best choice is the painted room, with original features including wall paintings; cheaper rooms aren't attached. ③–④

Surja Southeast corner of fort ℡0/941 439 1149. Simple, budget rooms, some with shared bath. Relaxing rooftop terrace with alcove seating area is among the best in Jaisalmer. Not to be confused with the initially alluring but ultimately disappointing *Surya* next door. ①–④

In town

Unless otherwise stated, the hotels listed below are shown on the Jaisalmer map, p.299.

Artist Hotel Manganyar colony at Suly Dungri ℡02992/252082, ✉artisthotel @yahoo.com. Immaculate hotel run by an Austrian expat as a co-op for members of the Manganyar (minstrel musician) caste, who live in the surrounding neighbourhood and host evening jam sessions at the hotel. The rooftop restaurant, where they play, has excellent coffee, good Indian and European food, and great views over the old city to the fort. ②

Jaisal Palace Behind the royal palace ℡02992/252717, ✉hoteljaisalpalace@yahoo.com. Modern and a bit bland, with smallish, simply furnished rooms; upstairs rooms are better, and have balconies, and the view of the fort and palace from the rooftop and restaurant are magnificent. ④

Mandir Palace Gandhi Chowk ℡02992/252788 or 951, ✉mandirpalace@hotmail.com. Richly carved palace (the maharawal still lives in part of it) with lots of character, whose most prominent feature is the striking Badal Vilas tower – one of the town's main landmarks. However, the rooms are unexciting and lacking in any classic decor, and the service is slow. A pool is planned. Worth a try if you can negotiate a discount. ⑦

Nachana Haveli Gandhi Chowk ℡02992/251910, ✉nachana_haveli@yahoo.com. A recent refurbishment makes this atmospheric haveli, run by a cousin of the maharaja, one of the best choices in its class. Rooms are dark but enlivened by original features and period antiques. Only the suites get 24hr hot water – for everyone else, it's 7–10am/pm. ⑥–⑦

Ratan Palace Off Gandhi Chowk ℡02992/252757, ✉hotelrenuka@rediffmail.com. Among the best budget options in this part of town, with a friendly owner who takes great pride in spotless, hassle-free accommodation for foreigners. Spacious rooms with large, marble-lined bathrooms (hot water 8am–noon & 6–9pm). They offer good camel treks and have even cheaper rooms in the slightly older *Renuka* across the street. ①–②

Residency Centre Point Khumbara Para ℡02992/252883. Small, family-run guesthouse in the backstreets near Patwa Haveli and Nathamal ki Haveli. The rooms are nice and fresh, some with original features, and there's home-cooked food available, but only five rooms, so book ahead. ③

Shahi Palace off Shiv Marg ℡02992/255920, ⊛www.shahipalacehotel.com. See also Fort map p.301. It can be hard to find this hotel, just west of the fort, but it's worth seeking out. The rooftop terrace restaurant with stunning views is alternately festive or romantic, and the spotless rooms are handsome, all attached, with high ceilings and lots of sandstone. The same people also run a sister hotel, the *Star House*, next door. ②–⑤

Shri Giriraj Palace Near Gopa Chowk ℡02992/252268. See Fort map p.301. Small, ornately carved haveli near the first fort gate, with pleasant rooms and courteous management. A dependable and very cheap budget choice in the very heart of the bazaar. ①

Swastika Off Gandhi Chowk ℡02992/252152 or 483, ✉swastikahotel@yahoo.com. Great budget hotel, with a helpful owner and a name that could only be inoffensive in India. Good value, but still marginally second-best to the neighbouring *Ratan Palace*, though it does have 24hr hot water. ②

Out of town

Fort Rajwada off Jodhpur Rd, 3.5km east of town ℡02992/253233 or 533, ⊛www.fortrajwada.com. Best by a long chalk of the new resort hotels on the outskirts of town. Its massive marble lobby includes chunks of richly filigreed sandstone plundered from havelis in the old city. Has all the facilities of a five-star (pool, bar, good restaurant and grand coffee shop), with a 25 percent discount off-season; otherwise, double rooms start at US$176. **⑨**

The Town

Getting lost in the narrow winding streets of Jaisalmer is both easy and enjoyable, though the town is so small that it never takes long to find a familiar landmark. Main roads lead around the base of the fort from the central market square, **Gopa Chowk**, east to **Gadi Sagar Tank**, and west to **Gandhi Chowk**. Within the fort the streets are narrower still, but orientation is simple: head west from the main *chowk* and **Maharawal's Palace** to reach the **Jain temples**. For optimum **sunset views**, head for "Sunset Point" north of the main bazaar area, or the northwest corner of the fort.

Jaisalmer Fort

Every part of **Jaisalmer Fort**, from its outer walls to the palace, temples and houses within, is made of soft yellow Jurassic sandstone. The medieval fort, founded by Rawal Jaisal in 1156, so inspired Bengali filmmaker Satyajit Ray that he wrote a story about it called *Shonar Kella* (The Golden Fortress), which he later made into a movie. Inside, the narrow winding streets are flanked with carved golden facades, and from the barrel-sided bastions, some of which still bear cannons, you can see the thick walls that drop almost 100m to the town below. Two thousand people live within its walls; seventy percent of them are Brahmins and the rest, living primarily on the east side, are predominantly Rajput.

A paved road punctuated by four huge gateways winds up to the fort. On the ramparts above the entrance road sit large round stones, waiting to be pushed down onto any enemy army trying to force its way in. The first gate, **Akhai Pol**, dating from the eighteenth century, opens into a large plaza that narrows at its far end to funnel you up through to the second gate, **Suraj Pol** (Surya Pol), which was the original entrance to the fort. Next to it is a deep trench called **Berisal Burj**, the "death well" into which traitors and criminals were once thrown. A steep, enemy-deterring sharp bend, almost doubling back on itself, takes you through to the third gate, **Ganesh Pol**.

The fourth gateway, **Hawa Pol**, leads into **Main Chowk**, where terrible acts of *johar* once took place. Choosing death rather than dishonour for themselves and their children if their husbands were ever defeated on the battlefield, the women of the royal palace, which overlooks the *chowk*, had a huge fire built, and jumped from the palace walls into it. This happened three times during the fourteenth and fifteenth centuries, when Jaisalmer frequently had to fight bloody wars against the Delhi sultans and its Rajput neighbours.

Palace of the Maharawal

The *chowk* is dominated by the **Palace of the Maharawal** (daily: summer 8am–6pm; winter 9am–6pm; Rs250 entry includes audio tour if you leave ID, credit card or deposit; Rs150 video). The palace's five-storey facade of balconies and windows displays some of the finest masonry in Jaisalmer. The monarch (known in Jaisalmer as the maharawal rather than the maharaja) would address his troops and issue orders from the large ornate marble throne to the left of the palace entrance. In the armoury, a silver **coronation throne** surmounted with lions and peacocks is used only for crowning the maharawal on his accession.

Beyond the armoury, the Tripolia Mahal features portraits of the maharawals, and a family tree tracing their ancestry all the way back to Krishna, incarnation of Vishnu and hero of the great Hindu epic the Mahabharata. In **Gaj Vilas**, the quarters of a nineteenth-century maharawal, you can see his bed and silver thali dish in a room decorated with blue and white Delft tiles from the Netherlands. Philatelists will enjoy the exhibition of **stamps and banknotes** in **Akhai Vilas**, the apartment of Maharawal Akhai Singh (1722–61), which were issued by Rajputana's 22 princely states as a statement of their continuing independence while the rest of India was mostly under British rule. The beautifully preserved **fifteenth-century sculptures** in the next gallery include an unusual one of Ramayana hero Rama depicted – most unconventionally – with a beard, and flanking him, a belly-dancer, and a courtesan looking into a hand-mirror. The sculpture gallery leads into the **Rang Mahal**, private bedroom of Maharawal Mool Raj II (1761–1819), its walls lovingly painted with wonderful murals, including depictions of Jaisalmer, Jaipur and Udaipur. Strikingly incongruous among them, in an alcove over the second window, is a very European portrait of a European woman. Who she was, and why the maharawal had her picture in his bedroom remain a mystery. Upstairs, in **Servottam Vilas**, more Delft tiles, and a ceiling painted to match, decorate the Akhai Singh's bedroom, while the **rooftop terrace** gives unrivalled views over the city and the surrounding countryside. The tour ends with the *zenana* (women's quarters), known as **Rani ka Mahal**, which was little more than a pile of rubble a few years ago. The reopening of this richly filigreed edifice is thanks to restoration work supported by Jaisalmer in Jeopardy (see p.298).

Hindu and Jain temples

The Fort has a number of Hindu temples, the most venerable of which is the 1494 **Laxminath Temple**, dedicated to Laxmi, the goddess of wealth, and her consort Vishnu (Nath), the preserver of life. However, none is as impressive as the complex of **Jain temples** (daily 7.30am–12.30pm; Rs10, plus Rs50 for camera, Rs100 video, Rs30 camera phone; usual entry restrictions apply). Built between the twelfth and fifteenth centuries in the familiar Jurassic sandstone, with yellow and white marble shrines and exquisite sculpted motifs covering the walls, ceilings and pillars, the temples are connected by small corridors and stairways. In a vault beneath the Sambhavnath temple, the **Gyan Bhandar** (daily 10–11am) contains Jain manuscripts, paintings and astrological charts dating back to the eleventh century, among them one of India's oldest surviving palm-leaf books, a 1060 copy of Dronacharya's *Oghaniryaktivritti*.

The havelis

The streets of Jaisalmer are flanked with numerous pale-honey facades, covered with latticework and floral designs, but the city's real showpieces are its **havelis**. Each of these extravagant mansions, comprising three or more storeys around a central courtyard, was commissioned by a wealthy merchant during the eighteenth or nineteenth century. Their stonework was the art of *silavats*, a community of masons responsible for much of Jaisalmer's unique sculpture.

Just off Court Road, on the road to Malka Pol, the **Nathmalji-ki-Haveli** was built in 1885 for the prime minister of the state of Jaisalmer by two brother stonemasons, one of whom built the left half, the other the right, as a result of which the two sides are subtly different. It's guarded by two elephants, and if you look carefully at the intricate carvings around the first-floor bay window above the main doorway, you'll see that it's surmounted by a frieze of little figures. Among them, above the smaller window to the right of the central one, the figures include not only elephants and horses, but also a steam train (on the left), and a bicycle and a horse-drawn carriage (towards the right). It's free to pop in and see the patio, which has a gift shop, but it's the outside that impresses.

Even more finely decorated, the large **Patwa Haveli**, or Patwon-ki-Haveli (daily 8am–6.30pm; Rs20), down a street to the right a couple of blocks north from the Nathmalji-ki-Haveli, was constructed in the first half of the nineteenth century by the Patwa merchants – five brothers from a Jain family who were bankers and traders in brocade and opium. Five separate suites with individual entrances facing a narrow street are connected from within, and all have flat roof areas – the views are excellent. Traces of stylish wall paintings survive in some rooms, but the building's most striking features are its exuberantly carved *jharokhas*, or protruding balconies. As well as visiting the interior of the Patwa Haveli, it's worth taking a little stroll down the street whose entrance it bridges, to check out the stonework on four impressive neighbouring havelis.

Salim Singh's Haveli (daily summer 8am–7pm, winter 8am–6pm; Rs15) provides Jaisalmer's only favourable memory of the tyrannical Salim Singh Mohta, who became prime minister in 1800 after his father was murdered for publicly challenging a Rajput prince to repay a loan. From an early age, Salim seemed hell-bent on avenging this crime, impoverishing Jaisalmer's citizens through vigorous taxation and extortion rackets, and holding the royal family to ransom by raising interest rates on their huge loans. He was eventually stabbed by a furious Rajput, and his wife made sure the wound wouldn't heal by infecting it with poison. Their curious family home is topped with small bluish domes; its upper floor, enclosed by an overhanging balcony, is best seen from the roof of *Natraj Restaurant*.

In addition to these three famous havelis, parts of the **Mandir Palace**, still inhabited by the maharawal, but partly converted into a heritage hotel (see p.302) can be visited (daily 10am–5pm; Rs10), but its most striking feature, the elegant Badal Vilas tower, is best seen from the west, just outside Amar Sagar Pol.

Gadi Sagar Tank and museums

South of town through an imposing triple gateway, **Gadi Sagar Tank**, built in 1367 and flanked with sandstone *ghats* and temples, was once Jaisalmer's sole water supply. This peaceful place staring out on the desert hosts the festival of **Gangaur** in March, when single women fling flowers into the lake and pray for a good husband, and the maharawal heads a procession amid pomp and splendour unchanged for generations. It's possible to rent boats the rest of the year (daily 8am–9pm; 30min; Rs50–100 for 2–4 people). The gateway over the *ghat* leading down to the lake, **Tilon-ki-Pol**, was commissioned in 1909 by a rich courtesan named Tilon, who was famed for her beauty. While it was being built, a group of town prudes went to the maharawal to persuade him that it would be inauspicious to have to access the lake through a gate built with the earnings of a prostitute. The maharawal ordered it dismantled, but Tilon was smarter than him: she had incorporated into the top of the structure a shrine to Vishnu, so that its destruction would be an insult to the god. She won the day and her gate still stands.

The little **Folklore Museum** (daily 8am–6pm; Rs10) near the tank's main gate has displays of folk art, textiles and opium and betel nut paraphernalia from the personal collection of its proprietor, a one-time school teacher. You'll find a slightly larger selection of local curiosities, including musical instruments, fossils, manuscripts, tools and utensils, at the **Desert Culture Museum** (daily 10am–1.30pm & 3.30–8pm; Rs10), opened by the same person, next to the tourist office on the main road. The main exhibit (though other museums seem to have identical ones), right at the back, is a cloth painting depicting the life of

Few visitors who make it as far as Jaisalmer pass up the opportunity to go on a **camel trek**, which provides an irresistibly romantic chance to cross the barren sands and to sleep under one of the starriest skies in the world. Sandstorms, sore backsides and camel farts aside, the safaris are usually great fun.

Although you can travel for up to two weeks by camel from Jaisalmer to Bikaner, treks normally last from one to four days, at **prices** varying from Rs400 to Rs1500 per night. For most travellers, the highlight is the evening spent under the desert stars and you usually find that departing around 3pm one day and returning the next at noon is sufficient. Unfortunately, the price you pay is not an adequate gauge of the quality of services you get. Hotels are notorious for sizing up potential clients and charging prices on a whim, and it pays to shop around, ask other travellers for recommendations and bargain appropriately. We've listed a few dependable operators below, though the list is far from exhaustive and not every trip they offer is the same. A lot depends on what expectations you have, whether the guides are friendly and how big the group is. Make sure you'll be provided with your own camel, an adequate supply of blankets (it can get very cold at night), food cooked with mineral water, a quota of fruit if you're paying anything over the average, and a campfire. As a precaution, have the deal fixed on paper, giving the maximum size of the group, details of the food you'll be getting, transport and anything else you've arranged. If you're only going for a day, none of this applies, but wear a broad-brimmed hat and take high-factor sun-protection lotion and plenty of water, especially in summer.

Following government restrictions on **routes**, most safaris head out to the assorted villages west of Jaisalmer, typically visiting Amar Sagar, Bada Bagh, Lodurva, Sam and Kuldera. Some visitors find these places, especially the dunes at Sam, overrun with other tourists and barely more than a scenic trash pit. However, it's possible to arrange a few days' amble through the desert without stopping at the popular sights. Taking a **Jeep** at the start or end of the trek enables you to go further in a short time, and some travellers prefer to begin their trek at Khuhri (see p.313). Longer treks to Pokaran, Jodhpur or Bikaner can also be arranged. Firms running treks into restricted areas (see p.310) should fix the necessary permits for you, but check in advance.

However much you intend to spend on a trek, don't book anything until you get to Jaisalmer. Touts trawl the train from Jodhpur, but they, and the barrage of operators combing the streets, usually represent dodgy outfits, most of which are based at one or other of the small budget hotels north of the fort. Some offer absurdly cheap rooms if you agree to book a camel trek with them, but guesthouse notice boards (not to mention our postbags) are filled with sorry stories by tourists who accepted. As a rule of thumb, any firm that has to tout for business – and that includes hotels – is worth avoiding.

Recommended operators

Adventure Travel (T02992/252558, Wwww.adventurecamels.com), just south of the First Fort Gate, gets rave reviews for seeking out remote locations and providing fringe amenities, like real mattresses and sheets, at low prices. Slightly cheaper, but equally dependable, is **Sahara Travels** in Gopa Chowk (T02992/252609, Wwww .mrdesertjaisalmer.com), run by the instantly identifiable "Mr. Desert," a former truck driver turned Rajasthani model and movie star. "Don't make a booking until you see the face," is his motto.

Of the **hotels** which organize camel safaris, *Shahi Palace* has a deservedly good reputation and virtually guarantees you won't see another tourist, though their prices are known to fluctuate. Among the budget alternatives, the friendly *Ratan Palace* offers excellent value for money. They've been running trips for more than a decade into a stretch of drifting dunes south of Sam that only a couple of other operators are allowed into.

local folk hero Pabuji (see p.400), a legendary figure credited with introducing the camel to Rajasthan. The museum puts on a half-hour puppet show (Rs30) at 6.30pm and 7.30pm each evening, using traditional Rajasthani puppets. If, after that, you still haven't had your fill of little local museums, you could pay a visit to the **government museum** (daily 10am–4.30pm; Rs3) by the *RTDC Moomal Hotel* on the western edge of town. Among the assorted fossils, sculptures and folk artefacts is a twelfth-century statue of a Jain dancer from Kiradu, and next to her, from the same period and location, a bearded man in drag.

Eating and drinking

Jaisalmer's tourist **restaurants**, usually rooftop affairs with fort views, offer pizza, pancakes, apple pie and cakes on their menus alongside Indian dishes, and some of them are pretty good, as are some hotel restaurants (the *Artist*, for example, which has a few Austrian dishes in among the usual Indian and European fare), but there are decent Indian eateries in town as well, and there's no reason at all why tourists should confine themselves to tourist restaurants.

The only licensed **bars** in town are to be found in the bigger hotels, though most restaurants will in fact serve you beer if you ask for it. The *Narayan Niwas Palace*, between Nathmalji-ki-Haveli and Malka Pol, has one of the better bars in town, or for somewhere posher still, you could head out to the *Fort Rajwada*. The *RTDC Moomal Hotel* on the western edge of town, on the other hand, has a less refined (and less expensive) bar. Right in the heart of town, *Nachana Haveli* on Gandhi Chowk is about to open a bar in its former stables, which should be a cut above Jaisalmer's other drinking spots.

Unless otherwise indicated, the restaurants and snack bars listed here are shown on the Jaisalmer map on p.299.

Restaurants

Chandan Shree Restaurant on the outside of the city wall, just south of Amar Sagar Pol. Popular low-priced diner for veg curries (Rs20–75) and thalis (choice of five, Rs50–100), as well as Rajasthani specialities such as *govind gatta* and *malai jamun*.

July 8 Main Chowk, in the fort. See Fort map p.301. Recommended for its privileged terrace view of the bustling *chowk* and palace rather than for its service or food (dishes Rs30–75), though it does have smoothies, jaffels, and toast with Vegemite or Marmite. It's a good spot for breakfast, when you can watch the fort wake up before it's invaded by tourists.

Little Italy just inside first fort gate. See Fort map p.301. Italian restaurant with great pasta dishes (Rs90–125), served in heaped portions at reasonable prices (the pizzas have a stab at authenticity, but don't really cut it). The indoor eating area is very atmospheric, but better still is the terrace, on the fort's outer wall, directly opposite the main ramparts – wonderful when they're floodlit at night.

Little Tibet In the Fort. See map p.301. Travellers' café-restaurant run by a team of young Tibetans. Their extensive menu includes all the usual Indian/Chinese choices, plus enchiladas, pasta and Tibetan *momos* (main dishes Rs30–60). They wash all their veg in iodized water, and it's a good venue for breakfast, but slow service is a drawback.

Milan south of Gopa Chowk. Really just a big tent with a dirt floor, and Indian, not Italian, despite the name, the *Milan* serves up some pretty tasty medium-priced veg and non-veg grub (main dishes Rs50–100). The tandoori chicken dishes, such as butter chicken, are particularly good, and the veg korma isn't bad either.

Monica Near the first Fort gate. See Fort map p.301. Moderately priced Rajasthani and tandoori dishes include delicious veg and non-veg Rajasthani thalis. The special (*malai*) *kofta* is a veritable festival of flavours. Main dishes Rs70–125.

Natraj Facing the top floor of Salim Singh's haveli. Pleasant rooftop and indoor non-veg restaurant, famous for its Mughlai chicken and *malai kofta*. The food is soft on spices and moderately priced (main dishes Rs50–80).

Saffron Gandhi Chowk, in the entrance to *Nachana Haveli* ☎02992/251910. Stylish upmarket restaurant with fine tandoori food, or Continental if you prefer, prices that won't break the bank (main dishes at Rs50–150), and musical entertainment in the evenings.

Shree Bikaner Restaurant north of Hanuman Circle, near Geeta Ashram. There are Punjabi veg

curries (Rs35–80) and a choice of thalis (Rajasthani, Gujarati or Bengali, at Rs50–90), but what
this place is really known for is its wonderful *dal
bati churma* (Rs90), which they'll keep refilling till
you've had enough.

Trio Gandhi Chowk ☏ 02992/252733. The grand-
daddy of Jaisalmer's upscale choices is no longer
unrivalled, but retains a loyal clientele for its
sumptuous tandoori and Mughlai food (there's a
very non-veg tandoori thali for Rs274, but most
meat dishes cost half that). Book early for the best
tables overlooking *Mandir Palace* and the fort.

Vyas Meals In the fort by the handicraft shops on
the way to the Jain temples. See Fort map p.301.
Hole-in-the-wall place run by an elderly couple
who do superb home-style veg thalis and snacks at
unbeatable prices (Rs20–40). Eat-in or take away.
Expect a long wait.

Drinks and snacks

Bhang shop Gopa Chowk. See Fort map p.301. If
you like bhang (and be warned that it doesn't
agree with everybody – see p.59), this is one of the
best places in the country to get it, with a whole
menu of bhang-laced drinks and sweets, and a
choice of different strengths.

Dhanraj Ranmal Bhatia Court Rd. Wonderful,
moist milk-based sweets (*ladoo*, *barfi* and the like),
plus great samosas and *mirchi badas*, and you can

even watch them being made, as they do it all out
front.

Hot milk stalls Hanuman Circle. From nightfall till
around midnight, the chai- and paan-wallahs just
east of Hanuman Circle sell glasses of hot sweet
milk boiled with saffron and almonds, ladled from
huge bubbling vats outside their shops.

Joshi's German Bakery Gopa Chowk. See Fort
map p.301.One of the few European-inspired
pastry shops in Rajasthan to live up to its name,
with a scrumptious, diet-busting range of fresh
cakes, croissants and cookies, especially in the
morning. Too bad the coffee's instant.

Krishna's Boulangerie in the fort, near the Jain
temples. See Fort map p.301. A handy place to
stop for a breather in the fort, with excellent coffee,
reasonable cakes, and more substantial food (such
as pizza) if you need it.

RK Juice Center Bhatia Bazaar. Wonderful, vitamin-
filled, freshly pressed juices including pomegranate,
pineapple and banana, or carrot and ginger; not on
the menu as such, but it's worth asking for. They
promise not to add ice or tap water (though they do
use it to rinse out the juice extractor).

South Indian Masala Dosa Gopa Chowk,
opposite *Joshi's German Bakery*. See Fort map
p.301. Very cheap South Indian snacks, not only
masala dosa, but also *iddli sambar* and *vadas*.
Evenings only, 4–9pm.

Shopping

Jaisalmer's flourishing tourist trade has made it one of the best places in India
to **shop** for souvenirs. Prices are comparatively high and the salesmen push
hard, but the choice of goods puts the town on a par with Pushkar and Jaipur.
As well as embroidered patchwork tapestries and other Rajasthani textiles, good
buys include woven jackets, tie-dyed cloth, puppets, wooden boxes and
ornaments, camel-leather slippers (*jutties*) and Western-style (or at least, hippy-
style) clothes made from Indian fabrics with Indian designs. **Bhatia Bazaar**,
between Gandhi Chowk and Gopa Chowk, is the prime shopping street, but
the little streets off Gopa Chowk are also worth exploring.

Barmer Embroidery House near Patwa Haveli
☏ 02992/252 270, ✉ bmrembrhouse@hotmail.com.
A good place to look for textiles. Stock ranges from
standard Jaipuri block-printed bedspreads and
mirrorwork or appliqué cushion covers to rare door-
hangings (*torans*), ornately embroidered cradle
covers, sari blouses (*choli*), Lamani chillum pouches
and silk-woven *mashru* skirts from remote Muslim
villages of Kutch in Gujarat.

Desert Leather Arts near Gopa Chowk, opposite
Shri Giriraj Palace hotel ☏ 02992/254 495. See
map, p.299. Camel leather goods made on the spot
– they claim to be able to make up anything in
leather to order.

Light of the East Tewata Para, in the fort, near
Vyas Meals ☏ 02992/253 237. See map, p.299.
Rocks, minerals and crystals, including amethyst
and rose quartz marbles, crystal balls, and all
sorts of semi-precious stones. One item is not for
sale – a football-sized apophyllite crystal, which
the owner keeps under lock in a glass case
behind a curtain.

Rajasthali outside Amar Sagar Pol. The official
Rajasthan state crafts emporium, rather dry and
unattractively arranged, and not always the very
best quality, but handy for checking prices as
they're fixed and marked.

Listings

Banks and exchange There's an ATM just inside Amar Sagar Pol, one directly opposite the gate on the outside, one by the District Magistrate's office on Sam Road, and one on Shiv Chowk south of the *Shahi Palace Hotel*. Forex bureaux are clustered in Gandhi Chowk, where you'll find at least four of them, making it easy to compare rates and commission before converting your currency.

Bicycle rental Naran Thaker, in the street directly opposite *Nachana Haveli* hotel (no sign in English but it's 100m up on the left, just where the street starts to bend) ☏0/921 483 8746; Rs5/hr.

Bookshops Bhatia News agency on Court Rd, just beyond Gandhi Chowk, has guidebooks and English-language novels. There are also a few shops in the fort selling new and used English books.

Doctor Dr S.K. Dube (☏02992/251560) is well liked and speaks good English; he charges Rs500 for a consultation at your hotel.

Festival Jaisalmer's Desert Festival is held over three days at the full moon in the lunar month of Magha (19–21 Feb 2008, 7–9 Feb 2009, 28–30 Jan 2010). Unlike many of the region's other festivals, this is not a livestock fair, but a festival of performing arts, and generally a fun occasion, with folk dancing, turban-tying and moustache competitions, camel racing, camel-back polo matches, and craft bazaars. Main events are held at Dedansar Polo Ground. Hotels tend to get full at this time, but they don't generally increase their prices. The Jaisalmer unit of the National Informatics Centre usually posts a programme of events in advance on their website (🌐 jaisalmer.nic.in).

Hospital The government hospital is on Sam Road, west of Hanuman Circle (☏02992/252495), but a better bet is the small, private Maheshwari Hospital off Sam Road opposite the court and District Magistrate's office (☏02992/250024).

Internet access Internet is widely available but mostly slow. The *Chai Bar*, inside the fort just beyond Ganesh gate, has the best PCs of the bunch (Rs40/hr). Nearby, slower and cheaper, there's *Joshi Cyber Café* (Rs20/hr) in the *Joshi's German Bakery* at Gopa Chowk.

Motorbike rental south of Gopa Chowk, opposite *Milan* restaurant ☏0/941 415 0033. Bikes and scooters for Rs300/day; helmet provided.

Police Amar Sagar Rd ☏02992/252322.

Post office The main post office, with poste restante, is on Amar Sagar Rd 200m south of Hanuman Circle (Mon–Sat 9am–3.30pm); there's a smaller office opposite the fort wall behind Gopa Chowk (Mon–Sat 10am–5pm).

Swimming pool There's a trio of package hotels 2km west of town on the Sam road, all of which allow outsiders to use their pools for a price. The best value is *Rang Mahal*, the westernmost of the three, which charges Rs165.

Moving on from Jaisalmer

The **train station** (☏02992/252354) is east of town on the Jodhpur road, and shouldn't cost you more than Rs40 to get to from town by auto. The #4060 **Jaisalmer–Delhi** Express, which departs at 4pm, stops at, among other places, Pokaran (5.30pm), Phalodi (6.41pm), Osian (7.56pm), Jodhpur (9.50pm), Jaipur (4.50am), Alwar (7.23am) and Old Delhi (11.05am). The overnight #4809 **Jaisalmer-Jodhpur** Express departs at 11.15pm, arriving in Jodhpur nice and early at 5.20am, and is obviously less convenient for stops in between. If you do take the night train, make sure you have something to keep you warm as it can get very cold on the journey (close to freezing in winter). There should also be a direct daily service to Bikaner by the time you read this, but full details were not available at time of writing.

Buses serve Abu Road (1 daily; 12hr), Bikaner (9 daily; 6hr 30min–8hr), Jaipur (3 daily; 12–15hr), Jodhpur (27 daily; 5hr 30min), Khuhri (4 daily; 1hr 30min), Lodurva (4 daily; 40min), Pushkar (1 daily; 9hr), Sam (3 daily; 1hr 30min) and Udaipur (1 daily; 12–14hr). The **bus stands** are both just south of the old city, the RSTDC Roadways bus stand at the southern end of Amar Sagar Road (☏02992/251541), while private buses leave from Air Force Circle, directly south of the fort. An auto to either from town shouldn't cost more than Rs30. There are plenty of state and private buses to Jodhpur, both equally fast but the private buses are more comfortable. Jaipur has two state buses a day including one deluxe service, plus one private departure. For Bikaner, the best services are the three daily private buses that travel via Pokaran (services via Mohangarh are slower). Abu Road is served by one state bus a day, Udaipur and Pushkar by one private bus each. **Tickets** for private buses can be purchased from agents such as Swagat Travels (℡02992/252557) or Hanuman Travels (℡02992/250340), just north of Hanuman Circle; for RSTDC services you'll have to buy your ticket at the state bus stand. **Local buses**, serving places like Lodurva, Khuhri and Sam, leave from a stand to the northeast of Hanuman Circle.

Jaisalmer does have an **airport**, 9km west of town off the Sam Road, but there are no passenger flights at present.

Around Jaisalmer

The sandy, barren terrain around Jaisalmer harbours some unexpected monuments, dating from the Rajput era when the area lay on busy caravan routes. Infrequent buses negotiate the dusty roads, or you can rent a Jeep through RTDC or through your hotel; the best way to visit these places, however, and see villages and abandoned towns inaccessible by road, is on a **camel trek** (see box, p.306). Being close to the Pakistani border, the area west of Highway NH-15 is **restricted**. Tourists are currently allowed to visit **Bada Bagh**, **Amar Sagar**, **Lodurva**, **Sam**, **Kuldara** and **Khuhri**, but if you want to travel beyond those areas, you'll need a **permit**, for which you apply to the District Magistrate's Office, just west of Hanuman Circle in Jaisalmer (℡02992/252201; Mon–Fri 10am–5pm). On the few camel treks where permits are necessary, however, the organizers should obtain them for you.

Bada Bagh, Amar Sagar and Lodurva

Six kilometres north of Jaisalmer, in the fertile area of **Bada Bagh** (daily summer 6am–8pm, winter 6am–7pm; Rs50, plus Rs20 for camera or video), a cluster of

△ Detail found on Jain temple, Lodurva

Moomal and Mahendra

Though not as famous as the story of Dhola and Maru (see p.323), the tale of Moomal and Mahendra – Rajasthan's Romeo and Juliet – has inspired countless storytellers, poets and painters, and is guaranteed to bring a tear or two to the eye.

Moomal was a princess of Lodurva, famed for her beauty. Her suitors were many, but not one had gained her hand. Mahendra was a prince of Umerkot (now in Pakistan), Lodurva's deadly enemy. Curious to see the famous princess, he arranged a hunting expedition *incognito* to bring him down to the sacred River Kak, which ran alongside the palace at Lodurva. When she saw him from her palace chamber, Moomal was smitten with love, and sent out a servant to invite him in. As soon as he met her, Mahendra too fell immediately in love, but when he told her who he was, she knew that their relationship must be kept a secret.

So every night, Mahendra, who already had seven wives, rode hot-foot upon his trusty camel to the river, and swam across to the palace, returning each morning at dawn. Thus the lovers stole their precious time together, but others were becoming suspicious. Mahendra's father, the king of Umerkot, who was blind – but only physically so – wanted to know why none of the prince's wives had borne him an heir. "Mahendra doesn't spend the night with us," they explained. "Every night, as soon as darkness falls, he leaves us, returning each morning with his hair wet." So the king asked them to keep some of the water from Mahendra's hair when it was combed, which they did, and when the king dropped some of it on his eyes he was immediately cured of his blindness. Instantly he knew where Mahendra had been, for only water from the River Kak could have done this, and he ordered that Mahendra be given a lame camel to impede his journey.

Meanwhile, Moomal's sister Soomal also got wind of her sister having a secret lover. "Who is he?" she demanded to know, "I want to see him." So Moomal arranged for her to masquerade as a minstrel boy, to attend in her room. They waited and waited, but Mahendra didn't come. Eventually, they fell asleep in each other's arms. When Mahendra finally arrived, delayed by the lameness of his camel, he saw his love asleep in the arms of – as he thought – a young rival, and left in bitter sorrow, swearing never to see her again.

Moomal sent him message after message but all were in vain. Finally, completely distraught, she disguised herself as a male itinerant salesman, and managed to gain an audience with him. They sat down for a game of *chopar* (similar to backgammon), when suddenly he began to cry. "What is it?" she asked. "It's the birthmark on your hand," he said. "My lost love had one just the same. If only I could see her again."

Throwing aside her disguise, the princess cried, "Oh my love, it is me, your Moomal. Truly I have never loved anyone but you." And so the couple were reunited, but already weak with pining, they expired in each other's arms, and at the very moment of their deaths, the sacred River Kak ceased to flow, and has never done so since.

cenotaphs built in memory of Jaisalmer's rulers stands on a hill, looking rather incongruous amidst a very modern field of electricity-generating wind turbines. Domed roofs shade small marble or sandstone slabs bearing inscriptions and equestrian statues. The green oasis below is where most of the fruit and vegetables of the region used to be grown – a surreal sight amid the sand and scrub.

Seven kilometres northwest of Jaisalmer is **AMAR SAGAR**, a peaceful small town set around a large artificial lake (empty during the dry season). On the edge of this are the eighteenth-century Amar Singh Palace and a Jain temple complex (Rs10 entry, Rs50 camera), recently restored to their former magnificence. The biggest of the three Jain temples, the Adeshwar Nath Temple, was commissioned in 1928 by a member of the same family who put up the Patwa Haveli in town (see p.305).

A further 10km northwest of Amar Sagar, **LODURVA** was the capital of the Bhati Rajputs from the eighth century until the twelfth, when it was sacked by Mohammed Ghori, after which the Bhatis moved their capital to Jaisalmer. Of the city's fine buildings, only a few **Jain temples**, rebuilt in the seventeenth century, remain. The main temple (daily 6am–8pm; Rs20, Rs50 camera, Rs100 video) is dedicated to Parshvanath, the 23rd Jain *tirthankara*. The ornately carved eight-metre *toran* (arch), just inside the entrance to the main temple compound, is the most exquisite in Rajasthan. The temple itself has detailed tracery work in the stone walls and a finely carved exterior. Inside are images of Parshvanath in black and white stone. To the right of the temple is a structure built in a series of diminishing square platforms, out of which springs the Kalpataru tree, made from an alloy of eight metals, with copper leaves. There are four daily **buses** to Lodurva, but taking a **taxi** is a better, more leisurely option (Rs400 including stops at Amar Sagar and Bada Bagh). More intrepid tourists might consider getting here by bicycle.

Kuldara

South of the Sam road, around 25km west of Jaisalmer, the ghost village of **Kuldara** (daily sunrise–sunset; Rs10, vehicles Rs50) was one of 84 villages abandoned simultaneously one night in 1825 by the Paliwal Brahmin community, which had settled here in the thirteenth century. Stories vary as to why the villages were deserted, but the consensus is that the onerous taxes imposed by the rapacious Prime Minister Salim Singh (see p.305), and his brutal methods of collecting them, forced the Paliwals to complain to the maharawal. When he ignored them, they upped and left in protest, en masse.

Close-knit and industrious, the Paliwals had prospered. Their sense of order is attested by their homes, each with its living quarters, guest room, kitchen and stables, plus a parking space for the camel, and you can take an atmospheric stroll through them to the temple at the heart of the village. A story that they buried their wealth before leaving – which probably stems from the fact that each house had an underground safe – led a group of foreigners in 1997 to scour the place with metal detectors in search of the alleged treasure. Following this, the village was made a protected area and some of its houses have been restored, along with its temple. It has also featured as a backdrop in a number of Hindi movies such as Milan Luthria's 1999 *Kachhe Dhaage*, with Ajay Devgan and Manisha Koirala, and John Matthan's *Sarfarosh*, released the same year, with Aamir Khan and Sonali Bendre.

Sam

The huge, rolling sand dunes 40km west of Jaisalmer are known as **SAM**, though strictly this is the name of a small village further west. The dunes are a prime attraction for tourists, who come here in droves to watch the sunset. But though this event can be breathtaking, the drink-sellers, musicians, piles of plastic rubbish and numerous camel trains and bus parties somewhat dilute the romance. Most camel safaris decamp nearby, but there are a few **accommodation** options inside the town itself. The RTDC *Hotel Sam Dhani* (reservations via RTDC *Moomal Hotel* in Jaisalmer ☎02992/252392; ⑤) offers simple rooms with supper and breakfast, plus bucket hot water. In contrast, the *Royal Desert Camp* is decidedly plush (reservations through *Nachana Haveli in* Jaisalmer ☎02992/251910, ✉nachana_haveli@yahoo.com; ⑧); the Rs4500 nightly rate includes meals, evening performances and a camel ride. If you come here under your own steam and don't stay the night, you can arrange half-hour **camel rides** for Rs80 per person per camel, plus Rs70 for a camel driver and Rs10 local development charge. Jeeps pay Rs20 to enter the dunes area. Three **buses** run to Sam (12.30pm, 3pm & 5pm); the last one returns in the morning but it's easy enough to hitch a ride back after the ritual sunset viewing.

Khuhri

Another superior place to watch the sun set over the dunes is the village of **KHUHRI**, 42km south of Jaisalmer. Some people prefer to begin their camel safari at Khuhri too, as it's already out in the desert. Most safaris time their arrival so tourists can see women, dressed in flamboyantly coloured dress, arriving with large jugs on their heads to fill up with water at caste-specific wells. The village is also quite a charming, sleepy little place to stay, many of its homes still made of mud and thatch rather than concrete, their exterior surfaces beautifully decorated with ornate white murals. If you're lucky enough to be invited inside one, you'll see some superb moulded mud shelves and fireplaces, inlaid with mica and mirrorwork.

Khuhri can be reached by four daily **buses** (10.30am, 1.30pm, 3pm & 5.30pm) from the local bus stand in Jaisalmer, or by jeep (Rs500 for the round trip from Jaisalmer) or taxi (Rs250 round trip). There's a large and growing number of guesthouses, including some rather fly-by-night operations, and the older, established places tend to be the best. Hotel prices in Khuhri include supper and breakfast. The oldest **guesthouse** is *Mama* (℡953014/274042, ✉gajendra_sodha2003@yahoo.com; ❸–❺), hosted by the charismatic former mayor, and slap bang in the middle of the village. Some of its rooms have private bathrooms but they're all pretty simple, and hot water comes in a bucket. Across the street is the peaceful and relaxed *Badal House* (℡935014/274120; ❷), which is much more like staying with a local family, and a good place to choose if you want to chill out for a few days and get a feel of village life. *Khuhri Guest House* (℡935014/274044; ❺–❼), near the bus stand, throws in an evening camel ride and a performance of Rajasthani dancing, but a better bet is *Fort Khuhri* (℡953014/274123, ✉mairtanesinghsodha@yahoo.com; ❺–❺), a kilometre out of town, where all the rooms are attached with hot showers, some a/c, and there's an unimpeded view of the dunes, to which this is the nearest hotel (it isn't actually a fort, but a fort-style compound). All these hotels can arrange camel safaris. Note that the **phone code** if calling from Jaisalmer is ℡935014; from anywhere else it is ℡03014.

Akal Wood Fossil Park

A 21-hectare slice of desert off the Barmer road, 17km east of Jaisalmer, the **Akal Wood Fossil Park** (daily 8am–5pm; foreign visitors Rs20, Indian residents Rs2, vehicle Rs10) is less exciting than it sounds. There are some fossilized trees here from the Jurassic period (dinosaur times, in other words), but don't expect to be meandering among a stone forest: the trees are just fallen trunks which lie on the ground, protected by mesh cages under metal shelters. That said these petrified logs – 25 of them in all – are impressive in their own way. The largest measures thirteen metres in length, and they all date from around 180 million years ago, when the whole region was rainforest, which is hard to imagine looking around at the barren landscape today. You'll pay around Rs200 to get here and back from town by auto, around Rs 300 by jeep.

Pokaran

POKARAN, with its red-sandstone fort and superb havelis, is a quiet, seldom-visited desert pit stop 110km east of Jaisalmer, situated at the road and rail junctions between Jodhpur, Bikaner and the west. Once included in the

The Pokaran N-tests

At around 3.45pm on May 11, 1998, three massive explosions erupted 200m beneath the sands of the Thar Desert, 20km northwest of **Pokaran**, a stone's throw north of the main Bikaner–Jaisalmer highway. The bombs were small by modern standards – 20 kilotonnes, like the bomb that destroyed Hiroshima – but their political shock-waves resounded from western Rajasthan to Islamabad, Beijing and Washington. By May 13, after two more detonations, India's transition from so-called "threshold state" to fully-fledged atomic power was complete.

In the Indian press, the tests were hailed as "A Moment of Pride", and celebratory fireworks lit the skies of the capital. The widespread euphoria, however, temporarily faltered when the scale of the international outcry became apparent. Caught completely unawares by the explosions, the US immediately announced that it was suspending all aid to India, and recommended a freeze in IMF and World Bank loans. These threats alone were enough to sober up the Delhi government, which owes US$40 billion to the US, and had been promised a further US$3 billion in aid that year. The country's barely disguised triumphalism took a further battering when, two weeks after the tests at Pokaran, Pakistan detonated its own thermo-nuclear devices in reply. India was suddenly locked into a spiralling nuclear arms race in one of the most geopolitically sensitive parts of the world. The rupee took a severe tumble, plummeting to an all-time low against the dollar, as did tourist bookings.

Yet within India, few dissenting voices were heard. Among the only high-profile critics of the government was Booker prize-winner Arundhati Roy, who compared India's pride at the tests with its poor track record on tackling poverty. Lesser-known opponents of the N-tests are to be found in the villages surrounding the site of the explosions, where hundreds of poor farmers and their families fell ill soon after the detonations. Although no fatalities have been directly attributed to the blast, scientists warn public health and environmental hazards may take years to materialize.

territory of Jodhpur, it passed into the huge state of Jaisalmer after Independence. Pokaran became the unlikely object of world attention in May 1998, when five nuclear bombs were detonated at the army test range 20km northwest of town (see box above). Despite this incongruous fifteen minutes of fame, Pokaran remains something of an outpost, but it does offer excellent **accommodation** at the sixteenth-century **fort** (T02994/222274, Wwww .fortpokaran.com; ⑥), a wonderful old sandstone building that feels more authentic for having only been partly restored. The fort now houses a **museum** (daily 8am–6pm; Rs50, Rs30 camera, Rs50 video) featuring a dusty collection of medieval weapons and clothing, plus a hand-cranked air-conditioning system. The only other accommodation is the RTDC *Motel* at the road junction on the edge of town (T02994/222275; ❸–❹). Should you need cash, the State Bank of Bikaner and Jaipur in the middle of town has an **ATM**.

Phalodi and Keechen

The main highway and broad-gauge train wind in tandem east from Jaisalmer across the desert, separating at the small junction settlement of **PHALODI**, almost exactly midway between Jaisalmer and Bikaner. This scruffy salt-extraction colony would be entirely forgettable were it not the jumping-off place for one of Rajasthan's most beautiful natural sights, one that shouldn't be missed if you're passing. Sheltered by a rise of soft yellow dunes, the village of **Keechen**, 4km east on the opposite side of the main road, hosts a four thousand-strong flock of **demoiselle cranes** (*Anthropoides virgo*), that migrate here each winter from their breeding grounds on the Central Asian steppes. Known locally as *kurja*, the birds are encouraged to return by the villagers, who scatter specially donated grain for them to feed on twice a day – a custom which has persisted for 150 years or more. At feeding times (6.30am & 3.30–4pm), the flock descends en masse on a fenced-off area just outside the village, where you can watch and photograph them at close quarters. At other times, the birds usually congregate just outside the fenced-off area on the nearby dunes, or at a small reservoir north of town; they're easy to spot.

From Phalodi, the best way to **get to Keechen** is to rent a bicycle from one of the stalls near the bus stand – a pleasant, mostly flat four-kilometre ride on well-surfaced roads. Alternatively, jump in an auto-rickshaw (Rs100) or taxi (Rs200); Ambassador taxis queue outside the railway station. For **accommodation**, *Hotel Chetnya Palace* (℡02925/223945; ❷–❹), next to the bus stand serving Jaisalmer, is the best budget option, with a decent restaurant and a variety of rooms, though the cheaper ones look a bit moth-eaten. Your other option is ⚵ *Lal Niwas* (℡02925/223813, Ⓦwww.lalniwas.com; ❻), a three hundred-year-old red-sandstone haveli converted into a top-notch heritage hotel, with a pool, thirteen prettily furnished rooms and two suites. The hotel also has an interesting **museum** (daily 10.30am–7pm; Rs50), with a well-presented collection of ivory carvings, coins, jewels, manuscripts and miniatures. The town's other attraction is the 1847 **Gori Pashnar Jain Temple** (daily 6.30am–noon & 6–8pm; free, camera Rs20, video Rs30, usual entry restrictions apply), with its fine mirror-work and old Belgian glass, which attracts Jain pilgrims from across the state. If you're only stopping for a couple of hours, **check bus times** before you head off to Keechen, as services can be sporadic, though theoretically there's a bus roughly every hour to Jaisalmer and Bikaner. For Jaisalmer, **trains** depart at 9.10am and 1.53am; to Jodhpur departure times are 6.43pm and 2.30am. There should also be a service to Bikaner (and the other way, a third departure to Jaisalmer), but details were unavailable at time of writing.

Bikaner and around

The smog-filled commercial city of **BIKANER** has none of the aesthetic magic of its more venerable neighbour, Jaisalmer, over 300km southwest, but travellers who make it here are usually surprised by the abundance of attractions. In addition to a spectacular **fort** – Junagarh – Bikaner boasts an atmospheric old city dotted with havelis and artisan shops and enclosed by 7km of high walls. And because Rajasthan's fourth largest city receives fewer visitors than other major settlements, it has a certain unspoilt feel – most residents go out of their way to be friendly, their curiosity not yet stamped out by mass tourism. Foreign tourists usually only spend one night here en route to or from Jaisalmer, but extend your stay and you will have time to visit the unforgettable **rat temple** at nearby Deshnok – one of India's most intriguing attractions – and the government **camel-breeding farm**, 10km south. If you're around in January, Bikaner's **camel fair** – smaller than Pushkar's – is an added bonus.

The city was founded in 1486 by **Bika**, one of fourteen sons of Rao Jodha, the Rathore king who established Jodhpur, as a link in the overland trading route. Rai Singh came to the throne in 1573, and during his reign ordered the construction of **Junagarh Fort** and forged closer ties with the Mughals; Rai Singh gave his daughter in marriage to one of Akbar's sons. In the early 1900s, new agricultural schemes, irrigation work, town planning and the construction of a rail link with Delhi helped Bikaner's economic advance; it has long since

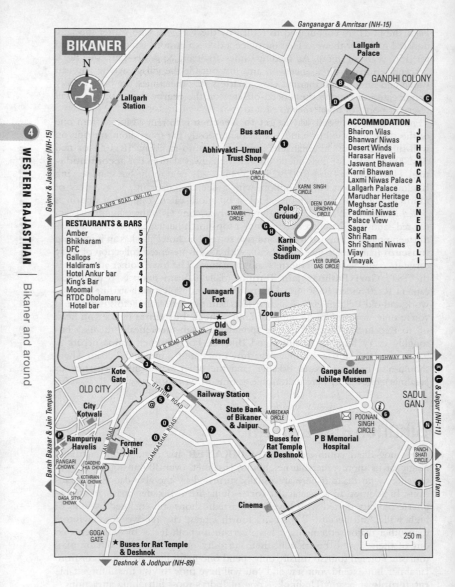

BIKANER

N

Ganganagar & Amritsar (NH-15)

Gajner & Jaisalmer (NH-15)

Lallgarh
Palace

Lallgarh
Station

GANDHI COLONY

Bus stand

Abhivyakti–Urmul
Trust Shop

URMUL
CIRCLE

KARNI SINGH
CIRCLE

ACCOMMODATION

Bhairon Vilas	J
Bhanwar Niwas	P
Desert Winds	H
Harasar Haveli	G
Jaswant Bhawan	M
Karni Bhawan	C
Laxmi Niwas Palace	A
Lallgarh Palace	B
Marudhar Heritage	Q
Meghsar Castle	F
Padmini Niwas	N
Palace View	E
Sagar	D
Shri Ram	K
Shri Shanti Niwas	O
Vijay	L
Vinayak	I

GAJNER ROAD (NH-15)

KIRTI
STAMBH
CIRCLE

DEEN DAYAL
UPADHYA
CIRCLE

Polo
Ground

RESTAURANTS & BARS

Amber	5
Bhikharam	3
DFC	7
Gallops	2
Haldiram's	3
Hotel Ankur bar	4
King's Bar	1
Moomal	8
RTDC Dholamaru	
Hotel bar	6

Karni
Singh
Stadium

VEER DURGA
DAS CIRCLE

Junagarh
Fort

Courts

Zoo

Old
Bus
stand

M G ROAD (KEM ROAD)

JAIPUR HIGHWAY (NH-11)

Kote
Gate

OLD CITY

Ganga Golden
Jubilee Museum

SADUL
GANJ

STATION ROAD

City
Kotwali

M

Railway Station

State Bank
of Bikaner
& Jaipur

AMBEDKAR
CIRCLE

POONAN
SINGH
CIRCLE

P B Memorial
Hospital

Rampuriya
Havelis

Former
Jail

JAIL ROAD

GANGASHAR ROAD

Buses for
Rat Temple
& Deshnok

PANCH
SHATI
CIRCLE

RANGARI
CHOWK

DADDHO
KA CHOWK

2. KOTHRIAN
KA CHOWK

DAGA SITYA
CHOWK

Cinema

GOGA
GATE

★ Buses for Rat Temple
& Deshnok

Deshnok & Jodhpur (NH-89)

K, L & Jaipur (NH-11)

Camel farm

0   250 m

outgrown the confines of the city wall, and the population has more than tripled in size since 1947 to over six hundred thousand.

Arrival and information

Auto-wallahs working on commission are a nuisance in Bikaner, especially if you've just arrived after a tiring journey and want to get to your hotel with the minimum of hassle. They'll employ all the usual tricks to avoid taking you to any establishment that doesn't pay them, and even if you ask to be dropped at a location nearby, they may try to second-guess you, hot-footing it to the hotel

Although lacking Jaisalmer's edge-of-the-desert feel, **camel treks** in Bikaner can be just as rewarding. This eastern part of the desert, while just as scenic as the western Thar, is not nearly as congested with fellow trekkers, with the result that local people in the villages along the route don't wait around all day for the chance to sell Pepsi to tourists. Wildlife is also abundant, and during a three-day safari you can be pretty sure of spotting demoiselle cranes, blackbuck, nilgai, desert foxes, monitor lizards and, if you look hard enough, the odd chameleon.

Since safaris are less established here your choices of **operator** are somewhat limited, but the same advice applies as that outlined in the "Camel safaris from Jaisalmer" box on p.306. Most hotels work with a single guide, who usually hails from one of the villages you'll visit. Currently offering the best all-round value safaris out of Bikaner is Vijay Singh Rathore (aka "Camel Man"), based at *Vijay Guest House*, 5km out of town along the Jaipur Road (☎0151/223 1244, ⓦwww.camelman.com). His basic daily rate, which includes all meals, mattresses and travel to and from starting and finishing points, is Rs550, but pricier treks are available (rates are posted on his website). Another similarly affordable and dependable operator is Dilip Singh Rathore's Thar Camel Safari (contacted via the *Meghsar Castle* or ☎0/935 120 6093). Both offer itineraries ranging from half-day trips and village visits to full-blown fourteen-day treks to Jaisalmer, complete with camel carts for carrying luggage and mattresses. One operator to watch out for is Vino Desert Safari, whose representatives comb the bus stations and tourist attractions to tap up clients for their massively overpriced (though otherwise not bad) treks. As usual, it's a rule of thumb that people who have to tout for business are worth avoiding.

they reckon you're bound for, and informing the manager that you're their mark and they're therefore due commission on your room rent. A ride across town from the **state bus stand**, near Lallgarh Palace a few kilometres north of the centre, to the **railway station** should cost around Rs30. From the **old bus stand**, just south of the fort, used by some private firms, the fare is Rs20. Auto-wallahs frequently offer Rs10 rides to arriving passengers; the trick is to take the ride without having the commission added to your room rent.

The helpful **tourist office** (daily 10am–5pm; ☎0151/222 6701), in the RTDC *Dholamaru Hotel* at Pooran Singh Circle, can suggest **homestays**. There's **online information** on Bikaner at ⓦwww.realbikaner.com, including details on hotels, recreational facilities, history and geography.

Accommodation

Bikaner boasts a surprisingly large selection of **hotels**, and because competition is cut-throat, some of the best-value accommodation in Rajasthan, though the shoestring-priced flophouses along the congested and trash-strewn Station Road are insalubrious and best avoided. Air-conditioning in summer tends to jack prices up slightly.

Budget

Desert Winds 200 metres east of Kirti Stambh Circle ☎0151/254 2202, ⓦwww.hoteldesertwinds .in. Excellent value at this immaculate little place run by a retired RTDC director of tourism. Not as brash as its neighbour (see next entry), but more homely, with a decent veg (plus eggs) restaurant in the basement. ②–③

Harasar Haveli next to *Desert Winds* ☎0151/220 9891, ⓦwww.harasar.com. Notorious for paying hefty commissions (so contrive to arrive without an auto-wallah in tow), but there's no denying the ambition of this pink four-storey edifice or its politician owner. Thirty-eight stylish rooms run the gamut from basic to garish, but all are spotless and offer great value. The terrace restaurant serves good veg and non-veg food and has panoramic views. ②–③

Marudhar Heritage Gangashahar Rd ☎0151/252 2524, ✉hmheritage2000@yahoo.co.in. A variety of rooms from semi-deluxe to a/c "royal", all attached, in this friendly, tranquil hotel near the station. Hot water 6am–noon only. ②–⑤

Meghsar Castle 9 Gajner Rd, 300m west of Urmul Circle ☎0151/252 7315, ⓦwww.hotel meghsarcastle.com. Well-equipped, comfortable rooms and a very friendly owner who goes out of his way to assist independent travellers. Well worth the hike from the city centre, even if the location on the busy Jaisalmer road (NH-15) lacks tranquillity. Buses from Jaisalmer will drop you off upon request. If it's full, the *Kishan Palace* next door is a pretty good fall-back. ②–④

Shri Shanti Niwas Gangashahar Rd ☎0151/252 4231, ✉hemantdaga@sancharnet.in. A bit institutional-looking, and often full, but of all the ultra-cheapies near the station, this is by far the cleanest and the most inviting. Has a variety of rooms at different prices, including some very inexpensive non-attached singles. Doubles are all attached. 24hr checkout. ①–③

🏃 **Vijay** Opposite Sophia School, 5km east of centre along the Jaipur Highway ☎0151/223 1244, ⓦwww.camelman.com. Slightly eccentric, pleasantly scruffy and affordable family guesthouse that's been serving backpackers since 1983. Eight rooms, some huge, all have attached shower-toilets, and there's camping/parking space, plus a nice garden, and free use of bicycles. ②

Vinayak Old Ginani ☎0151/220 2634. Hidden away in the backstreets north of the fort, this little homestay is run by the same people as the Abhivyakti handicrafts shop. It's all very folksy, and they offer free pick-ups (worth taking up as it's hard to find), and some very cheap and simple non-attached singles as well as attached doubles (hot water is provided in a bucket). ②

Mid-range

Bhairon Vilas Next to Junagarh Fort ☎0151/254 4751, ⓦhotelbhaironvilas.tripod.com. Delightful owner Harsh, cosmopolitan cousin of the maharaja, has stylishly employed family curios and antiques to convert this terracotta- and ochre-coloured royal haveli into a very stylish heritage hotel with funky decor – one of Rajasthan's most unique. Evening bonfires and the occasional dance party take place in the lovely garden. Room 101 has a great view of the fort. Book ahead. ④–⑤

Jaswant Bhawan Alakhsagar Rd ☎0151/254 8848, ⓦwww.hoteljaswantbhawan.com. Head out of the back exit from the rail station to find this

quiet hotel in a lovely old house, just across the tracks but a world away from the doss-houses on Station Road. ③–⑤

Padmini Niwas 148 Sadul Ganj, off Jaipur Rd 1.5 km east of the city centre ☎0151/252 2794, ✉padmini_hotel@rediffmail.com. A little bit out of the way, but – and never mind that it's quiet and good-value, with carpeted rooms, all with TV, a/c and a minibar – this hotel has a pool, which alone makes it worth considering, especially in summer. ③

Palace View Lallgarh Palace Campus ☎0151/254 3625, ✉opnain_jp1@sancharnet.in. Quiet location and homely rooms at various sizes and prices, with unrivalled views of Lallgarh Palce from the veranda. ③–④

Sagar Lallgarh Palace Campus ☎0151/252 0677, ⓦwww.sagarhotelbikaner.com. Attractive hotel with well-appointed rooms and several conveniences (TV, exchange, travel agency, credit card advances). You'll need a mosquito net if you stay in the Rajasthani cottages in the rear garden. ③–⑤

Shri Ram A-228 Sadul Ganj, 1.5 km east of the city centre ☎0151/252 2651 or 252 1320, ⓦwww.hotelshriram.com. This suburban guesthouse doubles as Bikaner's youth hostel. Second-floor suite rooms are preferable to the cramped rooms out back, or there are 5-bed dorms (Rs100). ③–⑤

Expensive

Bhanwar Niwas In the old city ☎0151/220 1043, ⓦwww.bhanwarniwas.com. The run-down exterior makes it easy to miss Bikaner's most ostentatious haveli, built for a textile tycoon in the late 1920s and now run as an independent heritage hotel. Crammed with original fittings and furniture, it's a Versailles-like kitsch piece, complete with Italian tiles and a 1927 Buick (with a klaxon in the form of a snake) in the lobby. Rs395 for veg meal in the *fin-de-siècle* restaurant. Rooms Rs3888. ⑦

Karni Bhawan Palace Gandhi Colony, 1km east of Lallgarh Palace ☎0151/252 4701 to 5, or 1800/180 2933 or 2944, ⓦwww.hrhindia.com. On the outside it looks like an oversized 1930s suburban English house, but the interior is period and wonderful. There are two ordinary rooms in an annexe, but you might as well splash out on one of the (admittedly, well overpriced) Art Deco suites in the main building, with their original 1930s furniture – why else would you be staying here after all. ⑨

Laxmi Niwas Palace Lallgarh Palace ☎0151/220 2777, ⓦwww.laxminiwaspalace.com. The better and more tranquil choice of two palatial hotels in the Lallgarh Palace complex boasts a beautifully carved exterior and large rooms with period English furniture – the best is #108, which has hosted British monarchs Queen Victoria, George V, and Elizabeth II. Rooms start at Rs6480, which is pretty good value compared to other heritage hotels in the state (though the neighbouring, and not as nice, *Lallgarh Palace Hotel* is about a third cheaper). ⑨

The City

Bikaner's main sight is its **fort**, but there's also a **palace** and a couple of **museums** to check out while you're in town. Most rewarding of all is a wander through the **old city**, where you'll find a wealth of early twentieth-century architecture, not to mention a couple of **temples** with half a millennium more on the clock.

Junagarh Fort

Built on ground level, defended only by high walls and a wide moat, **Junagarh Fort** (daily 10am–4.30pm; foreign visitors Rs100, Indian residents Rs20, includes 1hr compulsory guided tour; Rs30 camera, Rs100 video) is not as

△ Anup Mahal, Junagarh Fort

immediately imposing as the mighty hill forts elsewhere in Rajasthan. But the decorative interiors and sculpted stone of the palaces, temples and 37 pavilions within its walls are almost unrivalled in their magnificence.

The fort was built between 1587 and 1593 during the rule of Rai Singh, and embellished by later rulers, who added their own palatial suites, temples and plush courtyards. Although never conquered, the bastion was attacked – handprints set in stone near the second gate, **Daulat Pol**, bear witness to the voluntary deaths of royal women, remembered as *satis*, whose menfolk had lost their lives in battle.

Opening onto the main courtyard, the **Karan Mahal**, with gold-leaf painting adorning its pillars and walls, was built in the seventeenth century to commemorate a victory over the Mughal emperor Aurangzeb. From the ceiling still hangs a punkah, a huge back-and-forth fan which would have been worked with a string pulled by a specially designated servant called a punkah-wallah, who was hidden behind the scenes. The **Phool Mahal** (Rai Niwas) is the oldest part of the palace, built for Rai Singh himself. Among the items on display are Maharaja Gai Singh's ivory slippers, one of Akbar's swords, and a set of regal insignia including a representation of the Pisces zodiac sign which looks remarkably like a dinosaur in a headscarf.

The **Anup Mahal** (Diwan-i-Khas) is the grandest room in the palace, with stunning red and gold filigree *usta* (decorative painting). The red satin throne sits in a niche surmounted by an arc of glass and mirrors like a huge jewelled tiara. The carpet was made by inmates of Bikaner jail, who were famous for them – a manufacturing tradition that has only recently ceased. The room was used by the maharajas for public audiences. After such a hectic display of opulence, the **Badal Mahal** (Sardar Mahal), painted with blue sky and clouds (*badal mahal* means "cloud palace"), is pleasantly relaxing by contrast. It was built in the mid-nineteenth century for Maharaja Sardar Singh (1851–72).

Upstairs, in a room adjoining the terrace, beds of nails, sword blades and spear heads were used by sadhus to demonstrate their immunity to pain, as shown in photos on display. Across the terrace, in the **Gaj Mandar**, you can see the maharaja's single bed, and the maharani's double bed, where he would join her whenever he so fancied. Unfortunately, the mirror tiles on the walls are much eroded, reducing the glitter of the room.

The next part of the palace, **Ganga Niwas**, belonging to maharaja Ganga Singh (1887–1943) takes you into the twentieth century. A 1914 elevator here was the first in Rajasthan, as were the rather twisted electric ceiling fans that signalled the end of employment for India's punkah-wallahs. Among the display of arms and powder bottles, a German machine gun was among items seized during World War One, when Bikaner troops fought in Europe alongside the British. Going way back in time, the sandalwood throne in the **throne room** dates from 1212, whose sandstone walls, carved with reliefs of trees and animals, are much more recent, dating from 1937. In the adjacent Ganga Singh's office, with its early twentieth-century furniture, a painting depicts Britain's George V awarding the maharaja a medal at the 1911 Durbar (see p.389). While next door in the **Diwan-i-Am**, there's a World War One biplane, still in tip-top condition, which was a present from the British to Bikaner's state forces, who had supported them during the war.

Before leaving the fort, it's worth looking at the **Prachina Museum**, (daily 9am–6pm; foreign visitors Rs30, Indian residents Rs10, Rs30 camera, Rs100 video). It houses a pretty collection of objects (glassware, crockery, cutlery and walking sticks) demonstrating the growing influence of Europe on Rajasthani

Rajasthani Crafts

Rajasthan is renowned for its abundance of exquisitely made crafts, and you'll be lucky to get through the state without buying far more than you ever intended. Textiles and jewellery are Rajasthan's most famous products, but woodwork, metalwork, ceramics, and almost anything they make, has that special Rajasthani touch of shimmering colour and delicate application.

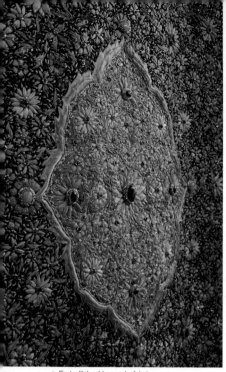

▲ Embellished brocade fabric

Textiles and clothing

Rajasthani textiles are known for their vibrant colours, and they come in a splendid variety. The most characteristic of all Rajasthani fabrics are rich **brocades**, embellished with embroidery, appliqué, quilting and patchwork, and sometimes with gold and silver thread added. Mirror-work, in which small mirrors are stitched into the cloth, was originally a speciality of Jaisalmer, but you'll find it state-wide. Worth looking out for in Shekhawati, particularly Sikar and Jhunjhunu, are skirts embroidered around the edges with motifs of plants or animals.

Saris are wonderfully bright items of clothing, in cotton for everyday use, silk for special occasions. Foreigners usually find it easier to wear a **salwar kameez** (a tunic with a pair of baggy pyjama-like trousers, typically worn by Sikh or Muslim women), or a *dupatta* (a large shawl, worn over a sari or *shalwar-kameez*), or to have local cloth made up into Western-style clothes. Some of the heavier fabrics and brocades make excellent coats, jackets or waistcoats. You can also buy large spreads that can be used as bedcovers, tablecloths or wall hangings.

A very popular method of colouring textiles is **tie-dyeing**. Many of Rajasthani fabrics are made this way; flaming with primary colours they make great saris and *dupattas*. *Bandhani* tie-dyed fabrics are enlivened with huge splashes of bold dyes, especially reds, yellows and greens, and are regularly designed for specific festivals or times of the year. *Odhni* or

chunri fabric has lots of little dots on it, formed by impressing the fabric with a nail, then tying off and blocking the raised spot of material before dyeing. More sophisticated are *lehariya* tie-dyes, with long lines or bands of colour, generally more subdued than those of *bandhani* fabrics.

Block printing is another common method of adding a pattern to a cloth. In principle it is simple enough: a pattern is carved into a wooden block, which is dipped into dye and impressed on the fabric. Most block-printed cloth will be printed on one side only, but the best is printed on both sides. Block-printing may also be accompanied by resist printing in which a dye-resistant material such as wax or gum is painted onto the fabric, which is then dyed. Once dry, the resist is washed away with hot water leaving that part of the fabric undyed, ready to be block-printed. Nowadays, much apparently block-printed fabric is in fact machine-printed, so check carefully before buying.

▲ Wooden-block printing

◀◀ Sari garment factory, Rajasthan

Metalware and jewellery

The decorative metalwork most typical of Rajasthan is **meenakari**, made with enamel inlays on silver or gold. The technique was introduced from the Punjab in the eighteenth century, and is used to make pillboxes, caskets and jewellery, among other things. At its best, *meenakari* work is a feast of glowing colour, especially blues and greens. Jaipur in particular is a centre for it.

Jewellery is big in Rajasthan, in all senses. Earrings, nose-rings, finger rings, toe rings, anklets, bangles and necklaces are not just decorative, but can also indicate people's caste, religion, ethnic group or social standing. Along with *meenakari* enamelwork, the other main jewellery-making technique is *kundan*, which means embedding gemstones into precious metal, especially gold. Some pieces will have *kundan* on one side, and *meenakari* on the reverse. Very traditional in *kundan* are *navratan* pieces, which have nine gemstones (traditionally: ruby, pearl, coral, emerald, yellow sapphire, blue sapphire, diamond, cat's eye, and gomed, aka hessonite). These are supposed to correspond to the nine planets of Indian astrology, so they are auspicious on any occasion, no matter which planet rules it. A very popular piece of jewellery among Rajasthani men is the *karanphool jhumka* ("flower of the ear") ear stud, made in the form of a flower, with different coloured petals.

Bangles are usually decorated with gold leaf and often studded with mirrors or glass chatons. They are made from lac (shellac), a red resin secreted by a plant-sucking bug (*Laccifer lacca*), known as the lac insect. Other bangles, not so typical of Rajasthan, are made from glass, which makes them clatter with a satisfying noise, but also makes them break easily (which is considered very bad luck). Rajasthani women wear their bangles by the armload and buy them in shops that usually stock them by the myriad (or by the lakh). You can buy them in most towns, but the top place is Tripolia Bazaar in Jaipur.

▼ Lac Bangles

Other crafts to buy

Wooden furniture can be a real bargain, but heavy to cart around, let alone take home, though you could have it shipped. A lot of shops in Jodhpur sell reproduction antique carvings and chests.

One very typical Rajasthani souvenir are the **puppets** traditionally used in staging dramatizations of popular folk tales such as Dhola and Maru (see p.323) or Moomal and Mahendra (see p.311). The puppets have a wooden head and are clothed, and double as dolls. Udaipur and Jaipur are the best places to get them, but you'll find them in Jodhpur and Jaisalmer too. Udaipur is also known for its painted **toys**, made from a softwood called doodhia (the same techniques are used to make kitchen utensils). Bassi, near Chittaurgarh, is famous for special little wooden statues of Parvati, used to celebrate the festival of Gangaur. Another popular Bassi product are cleverly folded-in miniature wooden temples painted with scenes from the Hindu epics, which gradually unfold to recount the story, and were once used by travelling bards to illustrate their tales.

Rajasthan's finest **ceramic** work is the blue glazed pottery of Jaipur and Delhi. Unusually, the pottery itself is made with quartz and fuller's earth rather than clay. The cobalt blue of the glaze really is cobalt oxide, supplemented by oxides of copper (light blue), manganese (yellow) and chromium (green). Jaipur is the best place to buy it (see p.218).

Miniature paintings, on cotton, silk or paper, are a tradition in Rajasthan, and almost every Rajput principality at one time had its own style of miniature painting. Udaipur and Kishangarh in particular are known for their miniatures, though almost every tourist centre in the state will sell them. Things to look out for are fineness and detail.

◄ Rajasthani puppets

style in the early twentieth century. A whole circa-1900 salon has been recreated, plus there's also an interesting collection of Rajasthani textiles and clothing.

The old city

Bikaner's labyrinthine **old city** is not easy to navigate, so accept getting lost as part of the experience. The attractions include a cluster of **temples** in the south, and a profusion of extraordinary **havelis** whose idiosyncratic architecture is an unlikely fusion of indigenous sandstone carving with *fin-de-siècle* Art Nouveau and red-brick municipal Britain. The tourist office have designated a "Heritage Route" through the old city, but it isn't easy to follow, even using their map; the route described here covers the most rewarding section of it.

Entering the old city through Kote Gate, bear left (south) down Jail Road to follow the tourist office's "Heritage Route". After 300m, a right turn just before a strikingly fort-like pink and white girls' school (look for the "Heritage Route" sign) takes you to the City Kotwali, which is the old city's central police station. More-or-less straight ahead, along the left-hand (south) wall of the Kotwali, Rampuriya Street leads after 300m to a small chowk with a little shrine, overlooked by two of the **Rampuriya Havelis**, three mansions commissioned by three brothers from a Jain trading family. The first, on the left, built in 1924, is faced with reliefs of Bikaner's Maharaja Ganga Singh, and Britain's King (India's Emperor) George V and Queen Mary. The second, directly ahead, on the right-hand side of the street, is bigger and generally more impressive, but no royalty graces its facade. The third, a little way further along on the left, is decorated with medallions above its main windows featuring Krishna and Radha, and pastoral scenes. Sadly, no one lives in these impressive buildings, and all three havelis are currently boarded up, as, unfortunately, are many of the old city's fine mansions.

If you continue ahead, the next haveli on your right is *Bhanwar Niwas Hotel* (see p.318; the entrance is round the other side of the building). Otherwise the "Heritage Route" turns left (south) just before the third Rampuriya Haveli, and emerges by the boarded-up 1918 **Golchha Haveli**, its three ground-floor windows topped with flowery rosettes. Continue roughly straight ahead (you'll need to take two dog-legs to the right), and you emerge after 100m onto a street full of ironmongers selling buckets, pots, pans and tiffin boxes. A left here would take you back to the City Kotwali, whereas the "Heritage Route" takes a right which after 300m takes you out onto a square called **Rangari Chowk**, in the middle of which is an odd little building with four painted figures in relief between its first-floor windows. Proceed along the right-hand side of the building and straight ahead is **Kothrion ka Chowk**, where handsome havelis look down on you from both sides – check the balcony of the one to your left, and the fine carving on the building facing it. The "Heritage Route" now continues round to the left, and takes the first right, and then the first right again, but before you do so, it's worth taking a little detour. Before the first right turn, carry straight on, past the **Kothari Building** (actually spelt "Bilding"), on your right, with five wonderfully extravagant Art Nouveau balconies, surmounted by carvings including an elephant flanked by cherubs, two peacocks holding three strings of pearls, and George V between a lion and a unicorn. Beyond here is a little square called **Daga Sitya Chowk**, where a house on the left still has fading murals of steam trains on each side of its front door, while Diamond House, on the right with pretty tiles and a first-floor verandah, gets wider as it goes up, each storey overhanging the one below it.

Before the second right turn from Kothrion ka Chowk, continue straight ahead for 50m and you'll come across the amazingly carved, almost psychedelic, floral facade of the **Punan Chand Haveli** – and while you're there, you might as well take a quick look at the decorative facade of the smaller and less spectacular building behind it too.

Back on the "Heritage Route" you come to a large square called **Daddho ka Chowk** (Dhadha Chowk), surrounded by fine havelis. Cross the square, to where the street ends at a T-junction; a left turn here takes you out of the old city at Goga Gate (straight on for 400m, then right at the end), passing more havelis on the way – in particular, check the one on the right at 200m, with lovely carving, cast-iron banisters on its upper-floor balcony, and murals round the side. A right turn at the T-junction, on the other hand, leads after 400m to **Barah Bazaar**, where the orange, white and green pillar in the middle appears to sprout out of a gaggle of auto-rickshaws, whose drivers will be eager to nab you as you pass. Follow the street round to the left (you'll pass a "Heritage Route" sign after 20m), and you'll eventually reach a square with two **Jain temples** (daily 5am–7pm). Commissioned by two merchant brothers, both are remarkable for their mass of colour and intricate wall paintings. The ground floor of the **Bhandreshwar (Bhandasar) Temple** has a cluster of pillars, some decorated with gilded floral designs, others with embossed male and female sculptures. Porcelain tiles imported from Victorian England decorate the main altar, and steps lead up the tower, where you get a great view over the old city. Building started in 1468, before Bikaner itself was founded, but the temple wasn't finished until 1504. The mortar for the foundations was apparently made with ghee instead of water. Next door, the 1536 **Sandeshwar Temple**, dedicated to Neminath, the 22nd *tirthankara*, houses rows of saints shaped from solid marble, and has enamel and gold-leaf paintings on the walls. To the right of the two Jain temples, the Hindu **Laxminath Temple** was commissioned in the early sixteenth century by Lunkaran Singh, the third ruler of Bikaner, on the edge of the high city wall. In the early twentieth century, Maharaja Ganga Singh gave the temple a grant of five villages and a number of city shops, whose rent ensures its upkeep.

Lallgarh Palace and Ganga Golden Jubilee Museum

The sturdy red-sandstone **Lallgarh Palace** in the north of the town is home to the royal family of Bikaner, although parts now serve as a hotel (see p.318). It was built during the reign of Ganga Singh, who lived here from 1902, and despite some detailed carving, its modern aspect makes it fairly mundane compared to other Rajasthani palaces. The **Shri Sadul Museum** (Mon–Sat 10am–5pm; Rs20) houses an enormous collection of old photographs showing various viceregal visits, pictures of Ganga Singh at the signing of the Versailles Treaty and royal processions that will fascinate Rajophiles. If you still have reserves left, you could go and see the small **Ganga Golden Jubilee Museum** (daily except Tue 10am–4.30pm; Rs3), east of the centre on NH-8, which offers much of the same, plus terracottas from the Gupta period (fourth and fifth centuries).

The camel farm

What claims to be Asia's largest camel-breeding farm, the **National Research Centre on Camels** (daily 2–5pm; foreign visitors Rs10, Indian residents Rs5, Rs20 camera; camel ride foreign visitors Rs40, Indian residents Rs30; guided tour Rs100) lies out in the desert 10km south of Bikaner, an easy round trip by rickshaw that should cost around Rs80 (including 30min waiting time). Although Bikaner has long been renowned for its famously sturdy beasts – the camel corps was a much-feared component of the imperial battle formation – growing proliferation of the internal combustion engine has severely reduced the

The tale of Dhola and Maru is a typical Rajasthani romantic folk tale and, even more than the story of Moomal and Mahendra (see p.311), it is a favourite theme of miniature paintings, poems, ballads and puppet shows. Numerous versions of the tale exist, and every poet, songster or storyteller adds their own details, but usually it follows something like: Once upon a time, the king of Pugal, near Bikaner, had a daughter called Maru. While she was still a little girl, as was then the custom, he married her to Dhola, the infant son of his good friend, the king of neighbouring Narwar. Unfortunately the king died before his son was old enough to know that he had been married off, and when he grew up, he married another bride, by the name of Malwani. But Maru grew up knowing that she had a husband, and to him she remained faithful, sending a series of letters by different means to Dhola. The letters were intercepted by Malwani, however, who destroyed them, and Dhola remained in ignorance.

Finally, Maru arranged for a troupe of balladeers to visit Dhola and sing to him of their marriage. Dhola set off immediately for Pugal to see for himself. Despite numerous obstacles and red herrings strewn in his way by Malwani – and by a bandit chief or, in some versions, a Sindhi prince, who fancied Maru himself – Dhola reached Pugal and when he met Maru, he realized that she had always been his true love. In most versions of the tale, Malwani accepts the situation and they all live happily ever after. In some permutations, it is Dhola's faithful camel, a present to the king of Narwar from Maru's father, whose undaunting efforts bring the two lovers together, and invariably in paintings, the couple are shown riding on the camel.

"desert ship's" traditional role as a means of rural transport. It's best to take a guided tour of the farm; aim to be here at 3.30–4pm, when you'll be wowed by the sight of three hundred stampeding dromedaries arriving from the desert for their daily chow. The small **museum** has little of interest, bar a stuffed aborted camel foetus, and a photo of two camels copulating, but the camel milk parlour next door sells an assortment of camel milk-based products such as lassis and even kulfi. Researchers at the farm are busy studying the properties of camel milk, which is purportedly effective in staving off tuberculosis and diabetes.

Eating and drinking

Restaurants are thin on the ground in Bikaner and most visitors eat at their hotels, but there are a few good eating places scattered around town should you need them.

Bikaner's **sweets** are as ubiquitous as they're famous. Try *kaju katli*, made with cashew nuts (its taste and texture are somewhere between *barfi* and marzipan), and *tirangi*, a three-coloured sweet made with cashews, almonds and pistachios. A heavenly seasonal sweet if you're in town during December or January is *malai ghaver*, a fried honeycomb ring moistened with syrup and filled with saffron cream.

For a **drink**, the sleazy bar of the *Hotel Ankur*, down an alley opposite *Amber* restaurant, is not a place where women will feel comfortable, and neither is *King's Bar*, opposite the bus stand, but the bar of the RTDC *Dholamaru Hotel* at Pooran Singh Circle isn't too bad. Otherwise, you can drink without hassle at the bar of the *Lallgarh Palace Hotel*, but don't expect the cheapest beers in town.

Amber Station Rd. A cleaner than average (though dark) Indian place that's popular with Westerners. Full veg menu and refreshing masala chai. Main dishes Rs50–100.

Bhikharam Chandmal Bhujiwala just off Station Rd on the road to Kote Gate. There's always a line at this top *mithai* shop, known for its excellent Bengali and Rajasthani sweets, though it also has a good range of savoury snacks. *Haldiram's*, next door, is almost as renowned.

DFC (Dwarika Food Cuisine) Station Rd, south of the station, by Silver Square mall. A clean and pleasant restaurant with a bakery next door. The special thali (Rs75) is pretty good, or there are more economical thalis, and even train tiffins to take with you on a rail journey. They also do an excellent salted lassi laced with cumin; their sweet lassi is more like what would be called makhania lassi elsewhere.

Gallops Court Rd, directly opposite the fort. It may look posh, and feel it, but the food here (veg and non-veg) is very moderately priced, not to mention very good. Try the *kaju kumb* (mild and creamy mushroom and cashew curry) or the *gatta Bikaner*, a local version of the pan-Rajasthani dish. There's also espresso coffee, but they don't open till 10am, so it's only good for late breakfasts. Main dishes Rs70–150.

Moomal Tucked away behind the south side of Panch Shati circle, this white linen restaurant serves sumptuous South Indian veg food that's popular with well-heeled locals. The punchy cashew and cherry Moomal Special alone is worth the trip. Prices around Rs90–180.

Shopping

Bikaner is famous for its skilled lacquer work and handicrafts, sold in the bazaar for a fraction of Jaisalmer's inflated "tourist prices", and for its hand-woven woollen shawls and blankets. The best place to buy the latter is the **Abhivyakti** handicrafts shop, established with the aid of funding from the local Urmul Trust and from Oxfam in Britain. There's a small outlet at the camel-breeding farm, but serious shoppers will want to visit the main store (℡0151/252 2139) on Ganganar Road, near the bus stand. The store manager can even arrange visits to villages to see how the textiles are woven by the charity-supported women's co-ops. **Vichitra Arts**, at *Bhairon Vilas*, sells vintage royal garb and miniature paintings.

Listings

Banks and exchange ATMs include one directly opposite the station, and another just 100m south, one on Station Rd almost opposite the road from Kote Gate, one about halfway along MG Rd on the south side, and one between RTDC *Hotel Dhola Maru* and Panch Shati Circle. For changing cash or traveller's cheques, there's a forex bureau (LKP Forex) on Lallgarh Palace Rd between the fort and Kirti Stambh Circle, and one just inside the fort entrance.

Bicycle rental Available from a row of shacks just south of the main post office, opposite the southwest corner of the fort.

Festival Bikaner's camel fair (21–22 Jan 2008, 10–11 Jan & 30–31 Dec 2009, 18–19 Jan 2011), not as renowned, nor as touristed as those of Pushkar or Jaisalmer, still has plenty of colour, with camel races, razor-cut camel hairstyle competitions, camel milking and camel acrobatics, not to mention Gair dancing, fire dancing and fireworks. Most of the action takes place at the polo ground, which is north of town near *Desert Winds* and *Harasar Haveli* hotels. Accommodation prices don't rocket like they do in Pushkar, but it might be as well to book ahead if you're going to be in Bikaner at this time.

Hospital PB Memorial Hospital by Ambedkar Circle ℡0151/222 6334.

Internet access Internet is widely available but generally slow. The best-equipped cyber café is New Horizons behind the *Amber Restaurant* on Station Road (daily 10.30am–9pm; Rs20/hr).

Police Station Rd ℡0151/252 2225.

Post office The main post office is just west of the fort (Mon–Fri 10am–3pm, Sat 10am–1pm).

Swimming pool The *Padmini Niwas Hotel* allows non-guests to use theirs for Rs100.

Moving on from Bikaner

Destinations served by **bus** include Ajmer (15 daily; 7hr), Chittaurgarh (1 daily; 10hr 30min), Delhi (6 daily; 10hr), Fatehpur (14 daily; 3hr 30min–4hr), Jaipur (11 daily; 7hr 30min), Jaisalmer (8 daily; 7hr), Jodhpur (8 daily; 6hr), Kota (2 daily; 10hr), Pushkar (12 daily; 6hr 30min) and Udaipur (4 daily; 12hr). RSTRC buses operate out of the main bus stand on the north side of town

The following trains are recommended as the fastest or most convenient; other services may exist, take longer or arrive at inconvenient times. Train timetables change frequently; check latest schedules either at your nearest station or online at Ⓦ www.indianrail.gov.in before travel.

For **Delhi**, the #2464A Sampark Kranti Express to Sarai Rohilla station runs on Tuesdays, Thursdays and Sundays only; on other days, you'll have to get the #2308 Howrah Superfast to Merta Road (arrives 9.40pm) and wait there till 12.10am for the #4060 Jaisalmer–Delhi Express, which gets you in to Old Delhi at 11.05am. The only train to Fatehpur is the daily #4738 Jaipur Express, which leaves Bikaner at 9.20pm and pulls in to Fatehpur at a rather inconvenient 2.06am. There are no direct trains **to Ajmer**, but if you take the #2467 Jaipur Intercity at 5am, you can change at Phulera (arrive 10.45am) for the #2414A Link Express, which leaves for Ajmer at 11.11am, getting in at 12.45pm. For Sawai Madhopur, Kota and Chittaurgarh, get #2467 and change at Jaipur. All the Nagaur trains listed, except the #2464A, stop at **Deshnok**.

Destination	Name	No.	Departs	Arrives
Abu Road	Ranakpur Express	4707	9.45am (daily)	8pm
	Ahmedabad Express	9224	12.55am (daily)	11.25am
Agra	Howrah Superfast	2308A	6.30pm (daily)	6.35am
Delhi (SR)	Sampark Kranti Express	2464A	5.20pm (T, Th ,S)	5.45am
Jaipur	Jaipur Intercity	2467	5am (daily)	11.35am
	Jaipur Express	4854	9.20pm (daily)	5.45am
Jodhpur	Ranakpur Express	4707	9.45am (daily)	2.45pm
	Kalka–Barmer Express	4887	11 20am (daily)	4.50pm
	Ahmedabad Express	9224	12.55am (daily)	5.40am
Nagaur	Jaipur Intercity	2467	5am (daily)	6.40am
	passenger train	339	6am (daily)	8.11am
	Ranakpur Express	4707	9.45am (daily)	11.25am
	Kalka–Barmer Express	4887	11.20am (daily)	1pm
	Sampark Kranti Express	2464A	5.20pm (T, Th, S)	6.56pm
	Howrah Superfast	2308A	6.30pm (daily)	8.25pm
	Ahmedabad Express	9224	12.55am (daily)	5.40am

(Ⓣ0151/252 3800). Buses to Deshnok and Nagaur start at the state bus stand but can be picked up at Ambedkar Circle and Goga Gate Circle. Private buses are run by a handful of firms, all using different departure points. One of the best and most dependable is Chandra Travels on Gajner Road near *Meghsar Castle* hotel (Ⓣ0151/512 0011), who serve Delhi, Ajmer, Pushkar, Jodhpur and Jaisalmer. Others include Milan Travels on MG Road (Ⓣ0151/252 5105), Sharma Travels at Rani Bazaar (Ⓣ0151/220 2581 to 3), MS Travels at Teerth Stumbh near Karni Singh Stadium (Ⓣ0151/220 9902), and, all at the old bus stand just south of the fort, Neelam Travels (Ⓣ0151/254 7851), Rathore Travels (Ⓣ0151/252 5347), UK Travels (Ⓣ0151/220 9924) and BK Travels (Ⓣ0151/220 9895; to Jaisalmer only). You can buy tickets for most of these services at the old bus stand, and details of most private services out of Bikaner can be found online at Ⓦ www.rajb2b.com (click on "private bus route"). UK, Milan and Sharma run overnight services to Delhi, the last two with sleepers, and BK and Rathore run overnight services to Jaisalmer, though the journey can be pretty exhausting. Rathore, Sharm and MS do overnight services to Jaipur.

The **railway** station is on Station Road, just east of the old city. Recommended services are listed in the box on p.325. Following the completion of a new track between Kolayat and Phalodi, there should now be a direct train service between Bikaner and Jaisalmer, but details are unavailable as we go to press.

Deshnok

The **Karni Mata temple** (daily 6am–10pm; free; Rs20 camera, Rs50 video; Ⓦ www.karnimata.com) in **DESHNOK**, 30km south of Bikaner, is definitely one of India's more bizarre attractions. Step inside the Italian marble arched doorway and everywhere you'll see free-roaming rats, known as *kabas*, which devotees believe are reincarnated souls saved from the wrath of Yama, the god of death. Around the temple, bowls of milk are put out daily for the holy rodents. The innermost shrine, made of rough stone and logs cut from sacred jal trees, houses the yellow marble image of the folk hero turned goddess Karniji (see box below). This in turn is encased by a much grander marble building erected by Rao Bika's grandson after he defeated the Mughals. Pilgrims bring food offerings for the rats to eat inside the main shrine (they seem rather partial to *ladoo*), and it's customary to eat this *prasad* (blessed food) after it has been nibbled by the *kabas*. Ashes from a fire in the shrine are also daubed on pilgrims' foreheads. Some spend hours searching for a glimpse of the white rat, which is believed to be highly auspicious. It's also considered a blessing for a rat to run over your feet (this would require you to stand still for a while, and preferably next to some

> ### The Deshnok Devi
>
> Members of the Charan caste of bardic musicians believe that incarnations of the goddess Durga periodically appear among them, sometimes as *sagats*, who are blessed with healing powers, and less commonly as more powerful *purn* avatars. **Karni Mata**, born into a Charan family at a village near Phalodi in 1387, exhibited from birth traits associated with this latter incarnation of the *Devi* (goddess). She went on to perform such miracles as water divination and bringing the dead back to life, eventually becoming the region's most powerful cult leader, worshipped by Jats and low-caste farmers.
>
> According to legend, one of Karni Mata's followers, a Charan woman, came to her because her son was grievously ill, but by the time they got to him, he had died, so Karni Mata went to Yama, the god of the underworld, to ask for him back. On this occasion, however, Yama refused. Knowing therefore that of all the creatures upon the earth, only rats were outside of Yama's dominion, Karni Mata decreed that all Charans would be henceforth reincarnated as rats, thus escaping Yama's power, and when they died as rats, they would be reincarnated into the Chamar caste again. It is these sacred rats (*kabas*) which inhabit the Deshnok Temple.
>
> The rise in Karni's popularity, dating from her family's move north to Deshnok, mirrored that of the Rathore clan, whose constant raids were causing great instability in the region at the end of the fourteenth century. **Rao Bika**, the founder of Bikaner, realized that he and Karni could forge a formidable alliance to rid the area of the Rathores, and wooed her with promises of tax exemptions and tutelary deity status if she gave his clan her stamp of approval. When her eventual endorsement came it turned Bika's fortunes, quadrupling the size of his army. After he finally defeated the local warlords, Karni was accorded the honour of laying the foundation stone of Junagarh fort, and Bika regularly consulted her throughout his reign – a connection with the ruling family that has endured to this day. The Bikaner flag sports Karni's colours, and she is the patron goddess of the Bikaner camel corps, who still march into battle crying "Shree Karniji!".

food), but whatever you do don't step on one, or you'll have to donate a gold model of a rat to placate the deity. Shoes have to be removed at the gate (a guardian looks after them for a small tip), leaving you to wander among the rat droppings barefoot or in your socks. A net over the shrine protects the rodents from birds of prey, but it doesn't seem to keep out the "rats with wings" (pigeons), which are almost as prolific as their terrestrial counterparts.

Directly in front of the temple, the easily overlooked **Shri Karni Sixth Centenary Auditorium** contains a collection of oil paintings recounting the major events in Karniji's life, with English captions. A few kilometres away on the edge of town, the rarely visited **Nahrij Temple**, although lacking in rodents, has encased in marble the tree where Karniji in her last years came to make butter and await nirvana.

Buses from Bikaner leave for Deshnok every fifteen minutes (journey time 40min) or so from the main bus stand, stopping on the east side of Ambedkar Circle near PB Memorial Hospital, and just south of Goga Gate Circle, near the southeast corner of the old city. There are also five trains a day, but only the 10.25am and 11.20am departures from Bikaner are convenient if you want to make Deshnok a day-trip, or stop en-route to somewhere else.

Gajner wildlife sanctuary

You're unlikely to go to **Gajner wildlife sanctuary** (Rs100, vehicles Rs1000), 32km southwest of Bikaner on the way to Jaisalmer, just to look at the wildlife (which despite its name is sadly lacking), though it does harbour a number of gazelle and antelope species, including chinkara (Indian gazelle), nilgai (bluebull) and blackbuck, as well as wild boar and desert foxes, and its lake attracts large numbers of waterfowl, especially in the winter, when there are also imperial sandgrouse. Most people come to stay at the *Gajner Palace Hotel* (☎01534/275 061 to 9, ⓦwww.hrhindia.com; ⓞ), a rather grand affair in red sandstone, built in the early twentieth century as a hunting lodge for the maharajas of Bikaner, where deluxe double rooms start at Rs6750. The hotel overlooks the lake, and can arrange jaunts around the sanctuary, which otherwise has no transport or accommodation.

Nagaur

Almost equidistant between Bikaner, Ajmer and Jodhpur, the ancient city of **NAGAUR** (sometimes spelt Nagore, which is how it's pronounced) is dominated by its magnificent **fort**, called Ahhichatragarh (Fort of the Cobra's Hood), accessed from Gandhi Chowk at the very centre of Nagaur's old city (daily 9am–5pm; foreign visitors Rs50, Indian residents Rs15, camera Rs25, video Rs100, guide Rs100 for 1–4 people or Rs150 for 5 or more). A huge, rambling place covering nearly fifteen hectares and surrounded by over 2km of ramparts, the fort was originally constructed around 1120, on the site of an earthwork predecessor dating back to the fourth century. Over the years, it was added to by successive maharajas and Mughal emperors. Though it fell into disrepair after the eighteenth century, the fort was the object of a major conservation project in 1998–2001, whose fruits you can now enjoy. The guided tour is worth taking to get an explanation of what's what. Highlights include the Hadi Rani Mahal (Queen's Palace), with its wonderful murals of Krishna dancing (on the downstairs ceiling) and ladies desporting (upstairs in the queen's bedroom), and the Amar Singh Mahal, which has some beautifully restored murals and a water system that supplied a *hammam* with hot and cold water. The Mughal emperor Akbar had his own apartment in the fort, near the

Deepak Mahal (Lamp Palace), where alcove-lined walls were furnished with a multitude of oil lamps, making it a palace of light in the evenings. Outside the fort, Nagaur's sights include the sixteenth-century **Akbari Mosque**, east of Gandhi Chowk, its tapering minarets recalling the style of the Tughluqs of Delhi (see p.381), though it is in fact Mughal.

Nagaur's main event is its **cattle fair** (Ramdev Pashu Mela), held in late January or early February each year (13–16 Feb 2008, 2–5 Feb 2009, 22–25 Jan 2010). Not as big as the camel fair at Pushkar, Nagaur's event still brings in thousands of visitors, not to mention some seventy thousand steers, cows and bullocks to be bought, sold, raced or just shown off. The region's own breed of cattle is much sought-after, and the state government has moved in to protect it by banning the sale of animals under three years old to buyers from outside Rajasthan. The fair is enlivened by less commercial events such as moustache and turban-tying competitions, as well as cattle races and tug-of-war contests.

The **train station** and **bus stands** are at opposite ends of town, with the old city and fort in between. Five trains a day serve Bikaner and Merta Road (change at the latter for Jodhpur and Delhi), including the #2308A Howrah Express, which trundles through at 8.32pm bound for Jaipur and eventually Kolkata. Frequent bus departures from the Roadways Bus Stand (for state buses) serve Bikaner, Jodhpur and Ajmer. Private buses, from a smaller stand just outside Delhi Gate, include an overnight sleeper service to Delhi. In Bikaner, the same buses that serve Deshnok continue to Nagaur, and can be picked up at the same stops (see p.325).

There's a limited choice of **accommodation** in Nagaur, though from October through March you can stay in the fort, in one of the twenty luxury tents (US$165, rising to US$275 during cattle fair) at the *Royal Camp* (for reservations, contact WelcomHeritage ☎0291/257 2321 to 7, ⓦwww .welcomheritagehotels.com; ➒). Of the hotels in town, the best is *Hotel Bhaskar* on the Bikaner Road near the train station (☎01582/240100; ➋–➌), which has a variety of rooms at different prices, as does the more run-down but still respectable *Hotel Mahaveer International*, at Vijay Vallabh Chowk, near the bus stands (☎01582/243158; ➋–➌). The *Bhaskar* is the best place in town to **eat**, though there are some reasonable *dhabas* between it and the station. Bicycles can be rented just across the square from the private bus stand outside Delhi Gate. There are two **ATMs** on Fort Road, southwest of Gandhi Chowk on the way to the train station.

5

Southern Rajasthan

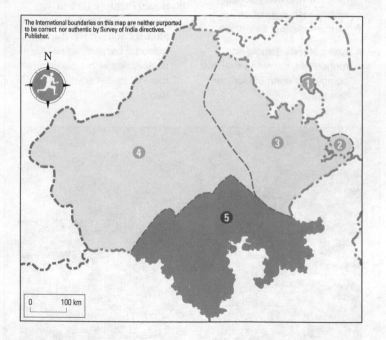

The International boundaries on this map are neither purported to be correct nor authentic by Survey of India directives. Publisher.

N

0   100 km

CHAPTER 5 # Highlights

✱ **Udaipur** Rajasthan's – if not India's – most romantic city: a fairy-tale ensemble of lakes, floating palaces and sumptuous Rajput architecture ringed by dramatic green hills. See p.331

✱ **Ranakpur** Home to possibly the most magical Jain temple in the Subcontinent, a marvellous sculptural tour de force with every surface embellished in a riot of intricate carving. See p.350

✱ **Kumbalgarh** Remote and rugged fort, sprawling over the craggy hills north of Udaipur. See p.352

✱ **Mount Abu and Dilwara temples** Rajasthan's only hill resort, with a scenic setting, a laid-back holiday atmosphere and some of the finest Jain temples in India. See p.353

✱ **Chittaurgarh** One of Rajasthan's most dramatic and historic forts, filled with a fascinating array of temples, towers and palaces. See p.361

✱ **Bundi** Picturesque and peaceful little town, full of atmospheric old havelis, colourful bazaars, a fine palace, and with a pleasantly low-key tourist scene. See p.366

△ Udaipur overlooking Lake Pichola

Southern Rajasthan

outhern Rajasthan has a notably different flavour from the rest of the
state. Shot through with the heavily forested southern outliers of the
Aravalli hills, the region is markedly greener and cooler than the desert
areas to the north, while its distance from Delhi and Jaipur lends it a
pleasantly laid-back atmosphere which can be bliss for those sated on crowds
and traffic. Highlight of the region is the marvellous city of **Udaipur**, whose
palace-fringed lake (now restored to its full watery glory after years of drought)
offers one of Rajasthan's most quintessentially romantic experiences – still
unforgettable, despite the city's increasingly rampant tourist development and
vast crowds of Western visitors.

Udaipur's tourist hordes are the exception rather than the norm in southern
Rajasthan, however, and the region's other major destinations still remain
relatively unexplored, despite good transport connections. North of Udaipur,
and easily visited as a day-trip from it, are the superb fort of **Kumbalgarh** and
the eye-popping Jain temples at **Ranakpur**, while there are further lavishly
embellished Jain shrines at breezy **Mount Abu**, Rajasthan's only hill station,
whose scenic location and throngs of cheerful Gujarati tourists and dreamy-
eyed local honeymooners offer a pleasantly cheerful and low-brow contrast to
the state's more established tourist destinations. Northeast of Udaipur, the
picturesque little town of **Bundi** is becoming an increasingly popular destination amongst budget travellers, with an engaging old town full of lively bazaars
and characterful havelis, as well as an intriguing fort and palace, home to one of
the state's finest collections of murals. Nearby **Kota** is one of the few cities in
southern Rajasthan to have experienced any kind of significant industrialization
and development, though it compensates with another fine palace and a further
collection of outstanding paintings. Finally, midway between Bundi and
Udaipur, the legendary fort at **Chittaurgarh** is one of southern Rajasthan's
most compelling attractions, whose glorious but ill-starred legacy of heroic
defeats and ritual mass suicides encapsulates the region's history at its –
depending on your point of view – goriest or most glorious.

Udaipur

The valley of Oodipur, the most diversified and most romantic spot on the continent
of India

Col. James Tod, *Annals and Antiquities of Rajasthan* (1829)

Few people forget their first sight of **UDAIPUR**. Spreading around the shores
of the idyllic Lake Pichola and backdropped by a majestic ring of craggy green

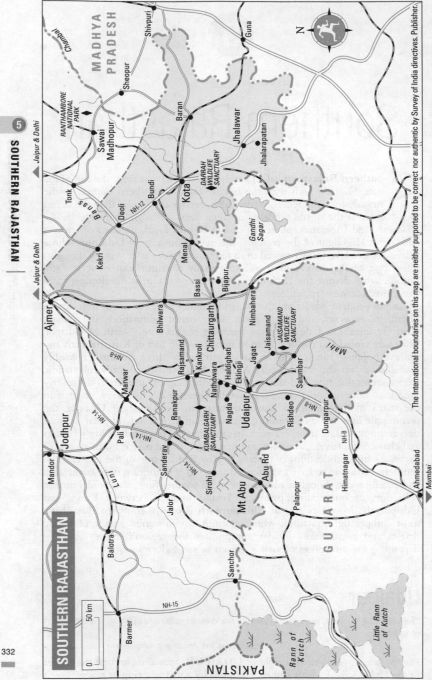

SOUTHERN RAJASTHAN

0   50 km

The International boundaries on this map are neither purported to be correct nor authentic by Survey of India directives. Publisher.

N

hills, the city seems to encapsulate everything that's most quintessentially romantic about Rajasthan and India, with its intricate sequence of ornately turreted and balconied palaces, whitewashed havelis and bathing *ghats* clustered around the waters of the lake – or, in the case of the *Lake Palace Hotel* and Jag Mandir, floating magically upon them. Not that the city is quite as perfect as the publicity would have you believe. The drought which recently emptied Lake Pichola for several years has mercifully ended, and water levels have now been restored to their original levels, but insensitive modern lakeside development, appalling traffic and vast hordes of tourists mean that the city is far from unspoilt or undiscovered. Even so, Udaipur remains a richly rewarding place to visit, and although it's possible to take in most of the sights in a few days, many people spend at least a week exploring the city and the various attractions scattered about the surrounding countryside.

Some history

Udaipur is a relatively young city by Indian standards, having been established in the mid-sixteenth century by Udai Singh II (see p.335) of the **Sisodia** family, rulers of the state of **Mewar**. The Sisodias are traditionally considered the foremost of all the Rajput royal dynasties, boasting the longest uninterrupted lineage and being the only one to have succeeded in resisting – symbolically, at least – the onslaught of the Mughals. The present maharana is the seventy-sixth in the unbroken line of Mewar suzerains, which makes the Mewar household the longest-lasting of all ruling powers in Rajasthan, and perhaps the oldest surviving dynasty in the world.

The state of Mewar was established by Guhil, the first Sisodia maharana, in 568 AD. His successors set up their capital first at **Nagda**, north of Udaipur, and then, in 734, at the mighty fort of Chittaurgarh, from where they established control over much of present-day southern Rajasthan. By the time Udai Singh II inherited the throne of Mewar in 1537, it was clear that Chittaurgarh was doomed and that a change of location was required. Udai chose a swampy site beside Lake Pichola for his new city, Udaipur, protected on all sides by outcrops of the Aravalli range. On his death in 1572 Udai was succeeded by his son Pratap, a legendary hero whose refusal to recognize the Mughal Akbar as emperor led to the battle of Haldighati, in which Akbar's forces were outwitted and peace in Udaipur was guaranteed.

As the city prospered, the arts flourished: Mewar became home to a flourishing school of miniature painting, while imposing palaces were constructed around and even in the lake. However, in 1736 Mewar was attacked by the destructive Marathas and by the end of the century the city had been reduced to poverty and ruin. The British stepped in to pick up the pieces, and this helped to put Udaipur on the road to recovery. Yet the principle of refusing to bow down to a foreign power persisted and the maharanas never allowed the British to displace them. When Britain withdrew from India in 1947, the maharana of Udaipur spearheaded the movement by the princely states to join the new democratic and independent India. Congress was, however, determined to reduce the Rajput princes to the status of normal citizens, and political recognition of royalty came to an end in 1969.

Centuries of loyalty between rulers and subjects have been kept alive by songs, stories and paintings; the maharana may now lack political power, but he remains as respected by the people of Udaipur as were his forefathers. His personal funding and income from tourism are invested in the Maharana of Mewar Trust, which subsidizes local hospitals and educational institutions, and supports environmental projects.

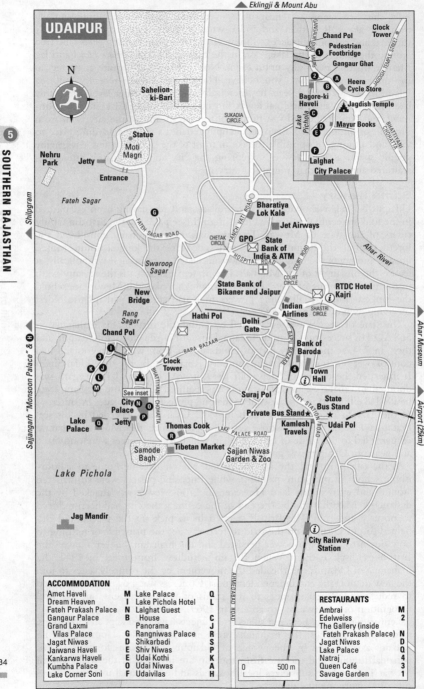

UDAIPUR

▲ Eklingji & Mount Abu

N

Sahelion-ki-Bari

SUKADIA CIRCLE

Chand Pol
Clock Tower
Pedestrian Footbridge
Gangaur Ghat
Heera Cycle Store
Bagore-ki Haveli
Jagdish Temple
Mayur Books
Lalghat
City Palace

Statue
Moti Magri

Nehru Park
Jetty
Entrance

Fateh Sagar

Shilpgram ►

SOUTHERN RAJASTHAN

5

Bharatiya Lok Kala
Jet Airways

FATEH SAGAR ROAD
CHETAK CIRCLE
GPO
State Bank of India & ATM

Swaroop Sagar

PANCH VATI ROAD
HOSPITAL ROAD
COURT ROAD

New Bridge

State Bank of Bikaner and Jaipur
COURT CIRCLE

Rang Sagar

RTDC Hotel Kajri
SHASTRI CIRCLE

Hathi Pol
Delhi Gate
Indian Airlines

Chand Pol

Sajjangarh "Monsoon Palace" ◄

BARA BAZAAR
Clock Tower

Bank of Baroda

BHATTIYANI CHOHATA

Town Hall

See inset

City Palace
Jetty

Suraj Pol
Private Bus Stand ★
State Bus Stand ★
Udai Pol

Lake Palace

Thomas Cook
Kamlesh Travels

CITY STATION ROAD

Tibetan Market
LAKE PALACE ROAD
Sajjan Niwas Garden & Zoo

Ahar Museum ►

Airport (25km) ►

Samode Bagh

Lake Pichola

BAPU BAZAAR

Jag Mandir

City Railway Station

AHMEDABAD ROAD

Ahar River

ACCOMMODATION

Amet Haveli	M	Lake Palace	Q
Dream Heaven	I	Lake Pichola Hotel	L
Fateh Prakash Palace	B	Lalghat Guest	
Gangaur Palace	J	House	C
Grand Laxmi		Panorama	J
Vilas Palace	G	Rangniwas Palace	R
Jagat Niwas	D	Shikarbadi	S
Jaiwana Haveli	E	Shiv Niwas	P
Kankarwa Haveli	O	Udai Kothi	K
Kumbha Palace	O	Udai Niwas	A
Lake Corner Soni	F	Udaivilas	H

RESTAURANTS

Ambrai	M
Edelweiss	2
The Gallery (inside	
Fateh Prakash Palace)	N
Jagat Niwas	D
Lake Palace	Q
Natraj	4
Queen Café	3
Savage Garden	1

0   500 m

334

S & Ahmedabad ▼

The founder of Udaipur, **Udai Singh II** (1522–72, reigned from 1540), is one of the most intriguing of all Rajput rulers, alternately vilified as the leader who abandoned his kingdom's ancestral capital at Chittaurgarh (Chittor) to the Mughals and celebrated as the founder of the new city which bears his name. Udai's accession to the throne of Mewar is itself the stuff of Rajput legend. The youngest of four brothers, it was never expected that he would succeed to the throne, but by the time Udai had reached the age of fifteen his three elder brothers had all met violent deaths – the last at the hands of Udai's cousin Banbir, who had determined to seize the throne for himself. Anxious to eliminate the final surviving brother, Banbir set out to murder the young Udai while he slept in the fort at Chittor. Udai's nurse, **Panna Dhai**, hid the young heir and put her own son in Udai's bed and looked on while he was murdered by Banbir, who promptly declared himself king of Mewar, believing that he had extinguished all rival claimants to the throne. Panna Dhai spirited the young Udai away from Chittor and, following an arduous journey of several weeks, eventually found refuge at the fort of Kumbalgarh, where Udai Singh lived incognito for the next two years until old enough to march upon Chittor and reclaim his rightful inheritance. Banbir was driven into exile, never to be heard of again.

Having seen off rival Mewari claimants to his kingdom, Udai Singh faced an even greater challenge to his rule in the form of the great Mughal emperor **Akbar** (1542–1605), who had determined to subjugate the various independent kingdoms of Rajasthan and bring them into the Mughal fold. Previous Mughal rulers had been unable to subdue the fiery Rajputs, but Akbar's more subtle approach – using intermarriage and the forging of alliances with the region's ruling families rather than attempts at outright military conquest – had already borne considerable fruit. All such attempts to coerce Udai Singh into an alliance with the Mughal empire, however, were steadily rebuffed, while Udai Singh poured scorn on those Rajput rulers (such as the Kachchwahas of Amber) who had come to terms with the Muslim invaders.

The scene for a decisive clash between Akbar, the ruler of Muslim India, and Udai Singh, the figurehead of Hindu resistance in the north, was thus set. Akbar determined to attack Chittor and bring the kingdom of Mewar to heel once and for all. Hearing of the planned attack, Udai Singh, instead of defending the fort against whatever odds, in time-honoured Rajput-style, simply abandoned Chittor to the care of eight thousand soldiers and ran off to the fledgling city of Udaipur, in which he had already established a palace back in 1559. This act of apparently brazen cowardice called down the wrath of centuries of commentators upon Udai Singh's unsuspecting head. The British historian Colonel Tod, in his celebrated *Annals and Antiquities of Rajasthan* (1829), described Udai Singh as "a coward succeeding a bastard to guide the destinies of the Sesodias." Others echoed his view, characterizing Udai Singh as a "craven prince", "the unworthy son of a noble sire" and so forth. Modern historians have seen the matter somewhat differently, however. Realizing the impossibility of defending Chittor against the armies of Akbar, it is argued, Udai Singh made a strategic withdrawal to a more secure position from which the independence of the state of Mewar could be far more easily guaranteed. In this respect, history has proved him right. Chittor duly fell in 1568, after a protracted and bloody siege, though by that time Udai Singh was safely established in his new capital, from where he continued to defy Akbar up until his death in 1572. Udaipur itself has flourished since its foundation right up to the present day, while, interestingly, the city founded by his adversary Akbar at Fatehpur Sikri lasted barely two decades before falling into terminal decline.

Arrival, information and city transport

The **bus stand** is on the east side of the centre, a Rs20–30 rickshaw ride from the City Palace area. **Trains** pull in at Udaipur City Station, southeast of the city centre (don't get off at Udaipur Station, much further north). **Flights** arrive at **Dabok Airport** (☎0294/265 5453), 25km east of Udaipur; taxis run from here to the city for around Rs200.

The grand but largely ineffectual **tourist office** (Mon–Sat 10am–5pm; ☎0294/241 1535) is inconveniently situated on the east side of the city just north of the bus stand; there's another utterly useless branch office (daily 10am–4pm) next to the Bagore-ki-Haveli in the city centre, plus offices at the airport, and railway station.

City transport and tours

Auto-rickshaws and **taxis** are the usual means of transport, though rickshaw prices are relatively high. Renting a **bicycle** is another possibility (see Listings on p.346), although traffic around the city is fairly awful.

The RTDC office, based in the *RTDC Hotel Kajri* on Shastri Circle, arranges city sightseeing trips (Rs90) and other **tours**, including cheap day-trips to Ranakpur and Kumbalgarh (Rs330), Haldighati, Nathdwara and Eklingji (Rs130), and Chittaurgarh (Rs330). Similar tours are offered by some of the innumerable **travel agents** dotted around the city centre (see Listings, p.347), as well as car rental for day-trips and longer tours. Count on around Rs1200 for a full-day trip of up to 300km.

Accommodation

Most accommodation in Udaipur is clustered around the City Palace and Jagdish Temple on the **east side of Lake Pichola**, where countless guesthouses vie with elegant havelis and royal palaces for views of the water. Cut-throat competition has meant perennially low tariffs for punters in most categories, but has also sparked off a destructive building boom as hoteliers scramble to attract customers with better views from ever loftier roof terraces; the result is a mass of hideous concrete that threatens to engulf the very skyline tourists flock here to see. A more appealing option is to head to the enclave of guesthouses and hotels on the **west side of Lake Pichola**, just across the bridge by Chand Pol. Many of the places here occupy prime spots with optimum views of the palace complex, and this entire area also has the added benefit of being much more peaceful than the area around the City Palace. There are also a few places dotted around other parts of the city and along **Lake Palace Road**; these usually have larger rooms and gardens but lack the views.

Jagdish temple area/east side of Lake Pichola

Fateh Prakash Palace City Palace ☎0294/252 8016, ⓦwww.hrhindia.com. The best location in the city, right in the heart of the City Palace complex, with prices to match. Most of the rooms and suites (from US$350) have superb lake views, although some are rather small and characterless for the price. Even so, it's a more appealing – and better-value – option than the nearby *Shiv Niwas* (see opposite), whose lovely pool and other facilities guests can use for free. Note that the hotel's numerous stairs can present problems to those with limited mobility. ❾

Gangaur Palace Gangaur Ghat Marg ☎0294/242 2303, ⓦwww.ashokahaveli.com. Popular budget

hotel in an atmospheric traditional haveli (albeit now buried under the usual crass rooftop expansion). There's a wide range of rooms of varying standards, including some with lake views and a few with original, 250-year-old frescoes. Prices for the smarter rooms can be a bit steep – try bargaining. Facilities include a resident palm reader, in-house painting lessons and good little European-style bakery. ❷–❹

Jagat Niwas 23–25 Lalghat ☎0294/242 2860, ⓦwww.jagatniwaspalace.com. Beautifully restored seventeenth-century haveli right on the lakeside, with shady courtyards, rooftop lake views, pleasant a/c rooms (the more expensive ones with lake views) and a good restaurant (see p.345), though not as peaceful or as good value as the nearby

Kankarwa and *Jaiwana* havelis. Popular with tour groups. ⑤–⑦

🏃 **Jaiwana Haveli** 14 Lalghat ☎0294/241 1103, ⓦwww.jaiwanahaveli.com. Inexpensive lakeside haveli accommodation with a range of spotless modern rooms; some have a/c, and the more expensive ones have fine lake views, as does the good rooftop restaurant. Excellent value. ③–⑥

🏃 **Kankarwa Haveli** 26 Lalghat ☎0294/241 1457, ⓔkhaveli@yahoo.com. Romantically restored haveli right on the waterfront. Not quite as pristine as the nearby *Jagat Niwas*, but more atmospheric and much better value, with colourful, antiquey rooms from as little as Rs650; the more expensive ones have superb lake views and a/c. There's also excellent veg food (see p.345) and Internet access. ③–⑥

Lake Corner Soni Paying Guest House Lalghat ☎0294/252 5712. This simple little guesthouse, run by a charming elderly couple, offers some of the cheapest lodgings in Udaipur. Rooms (some with shared bathroom) are basic but clean, peaceful and very cheap, and there are fine lake views from the rooftop terrace. ①–②

🏃 **Lake Palace** Lake Pichola ☎0294/252 8800, ⓦwww.tajhotels.com. One of the most famous and spectacular hotels in India, sailing in magnificent isolation on its own island amidst the serene waters of Lake Pichola, with marvellous city views and an incomparably romantic ambience. Accommodation is in a selection of rooms and suites which range from the merely luxurious to the opulently theatrical, while facilities include a spa, pool, butler service and limousine rental. Non-guests can visit for a pricey lunch or dinner (see p.345). Room rates start at US$630, though check the website for discounts. ⑨

Lalghat Guest House Lalghat ☎0294/252 5301, ⓔlalghat@hotmail.com. One of the oldest budget guesthouses in Udaipur, and still going strong thanks to its cheap room rates and superb lakeside position. The whole place is beginning to look a mite shabby, but it remains peaceful and atmospheric, with rooms arranged around a spacious courtyard and the sight and sound of water lapping against the outside walls. There's a mix of rooms: the cheapest with shared bath, the most expensive with a/c; some also have superb lakeside views, and there's a nicer-than-average ten-person dorm (Rs75pp) with curtained beds, as well as Internet access and a well-stocked in-house shop. ②–⑤

Shiv Niwas City Palace ☎0294/252 8016, ⓦwww.hrhindia.com. This upmarket heritage hotel trades on its superb location inside the City Palace complex, with grand public areas (although they're

also surprisingly shabby in places) and a dreamy pool (non-guests Rs300). The standard ("palace") rooms lack any sort of lake view and are disappointingly small and ordinary given the US$275 price tag; suites (from US$525) are far more memorable, with genuine old-world atmosphere and marvellous lake views. Discounts of around 20 percent in summer. ⑨

Udai Niwas Gangaur Ghat Marg ☎0294/512 0789, ⓦwww.hoteludainiwas.com. Bright modern high-rise hotel with a range of smart rooms in various price categories (the more expensive ones with a/c). The three-tier rooftop restaurant is one of the highest in town, and there's a well-equipped Internet cafe and a good in-house travel agents, although road noise and the periodic outbursts of massively amplified music from the nearby Jagdish Temple mean that it's not particularly peaceful. ②–⑤

North side of Lake Pichola

🏃 **Amet Haveli** Chand Pole ☎0294/243 4009, ⓔregiudr@datainfosys.net. This fine old white haveli is one of the best lakefront properties in town. All rooms are beautifully decorated with old wooden furniture and other traditional touches and come with a/c, TV and fine lake views, though you might want to spend the small extra amount to get one of the superb suites, with big windows and window seats right over the water. Also has the bonus of the excellent *Ambrai* restaurant (see p.345). ⑦

Dream Heaven Chand Pole ☎0294/243 1038, ⓔdeep_rg@yahoo.co.uk. A decent fallback if the nearby *Panorama* is full, with a good range of small but clean and cheap rooms, some with superb lake views – excellent value at the price. The rooftop restaurant has great views so long as you don't mind the vertigo-inducing spiral staircase up to it, or the annoying music. ①–③

Lake Pichola Hotel Chand Pole ☎0294/243 1197, ⓦwww.lakepicholahotel.com. This long-established hotel won't win any design awards (and boasts some of the ugliest furniture in Udaipur) but the lakeside location and City Palace views are just about perfect, and prices quite reasonable. Don't bother with the viewless (and only slightly cheaper) economy rooms, though. All rooms with a/c and TV. ⑥

🏃 **Panorama** Chand Pole ☎0294/243 1027, ⓔkrishna2311@rediffmail.com. The best budget hotel in Udaipur, very efficiently run and with cheap, cosy and excellent-value rooms (some with slight lake views and pretty murals). There's also a nice rooftop restaurant with superb lake views, plus cooking lessons if you feel like making your own dinner. Book ahead. ❶–❷

Udai Kothi Chand Pole ☎0294/243 2810, ⓦwww.udaikothi.com. Smart and spotless modern hotel in traditional style, with lots of flowery murals and chintzy little architectural touches. Rooms all come with TV, a/c and plenty of slightly twee furnishings; there's also a pool (non-guests Rs300) and a lovely garden, though no real lake views except from the rooftop restaurant. ❽

Along Lake Palace Road

Kumbha Palace 104 Bhatiyani Chohatta ☎0294/242 2702, ⓔkumbha01@hotmail.com. Friendly, Dutch-owned guesthouse hidden under the east walls of City Palace. Rooms are simple but bright and clean, and the whole place is a lot more peaceful than most budget options, while the bougainvillea-strewn garden and pleasant rooftop restaurant are further pluses. ❷

Rangniwas Palace Lake Palace Rd ☎0294/252 3890, ⓦwww.rangniwaspalace.com. Pleasant and peaceful old hotel retaining some vestiges of period charm at a relatively affordable price. There's a huge spread of accommodation (most of it a/c) from simple rooms with shared bath up to large luxurious suites, plus a small pool (Rs125 for non-guests), attentive staff and a nice lawn to sit out on. ❷–❼

Around Fateh Sagar

Grand Laxmi Vilas Palace Off Fateh Sagar Rd ☎0294/252 9711, ⓦwww.thegrandhotels.net. Luxury hotel occupying Gopal Singh's nineteenth-century hilltop guesthouse, set high above Fateh Sagar Lake. Immaculately restored and sumptuously furnished, the hotel is strong on creature comforts and five-star pizzazz – including well-equipped rooms (US$350), a huge pool, and acres of shiny marble – although the whole place is rather lacking in atmosphere compared to the similarly priced *Shiv Niwas* and *Fateh Prakash Palace* hotels in the City Palace complex. ❾

Outside the city centre

Shikarbadi Goverdhan Vilas, 5km south of Udaipur on the NH-8 to Ahmedabad ☎0294/258 3201, ⓦwww.hrhindia.com. Former royal hunting lodge set in the lower Aravallis, with its own pool, lake, deer park and stud farm – less ostentatious and more peaceful (and significantly cheaper) than the palaces in town. Suites in the old 1930s block have more character than the newer a/c rooms. ❽

🏃 **Udaivilas** ☎0294/243 3300, ⓦwww .oberoihotels.com. Udaipur's most opulent hotel, on the west side of Lake Pichola, is more regal even than anything the Rajputs ever built, occupying a sprawling palace, topped with innumerable cupolas and embellished with acres of marble, a magnificent courtyard, a wonderful Sheesh Mahal and a novel "moated pool" which flows around the outside of the main building. Rooms start at US$600, climbing up to a cool US$3300 for the massive Kohinoor Suite. Suites come with their own infinity swimming pools and private butler, and the spa is pure indulgence. ❾

Around Udaipur

🏃 **Devi Garh** Delwara Village, 25km north of Udaipur ☎02953/289211, ⓦwww .deviresorts.com. Hidden away in the Aravalli hills a 40-minute drive north of Udaipur, this luxury all-suite hotel occupies the magnificent eighteenth-century Devi Garh palace, mixing traditional Rajasthani palace opulence with contemporary style to memorable effect. Well placed for excursions either into Udaipur or to other local attractions (both Eklingji and Nagda are just 5km away) – or just relax in the superb spa, one of the finest in Rajasthan, if not India. Rooms from around US$440. ❾

The City

The original settlement of Udaipur grew up around the grand **City Palace**, bordering the east shore of **Lake Pichola**, while immediately north is the maze of tightly winding streets that constitute the **old city**. North of here stretches the second of Udaipur's two major lakes, **Fateh Sagar**, surrounded by a cluster of more low-key sights including **Moti Magri** park and the gardens of **Sahelion-ki-Bari**. Further afield, most visitors make the trip out (often by bicycle – a pleasant little ride) to the crafts village of **Shilpgram**, while many also make it up to the so-called "Monsoon Palace", **Sajjangarh** – from where there are fantastic views over Udaipur and the surrounding countryside.

Lake Pichola

Udaipur's idyllic **Lake Pichola** provides the city with virtually all of its most memorable views, offering a beautiful frame for the superb City Palace buildings, havelis, *ghats*, temple towers and myriad other structures which crowd its eastern side – best seen from a boat trip around the lake (see below). The lake – which covers eight square kilometres and draws water from mountains up to 160km away – was enlarged by Udai Singh, while subsequent rulers added dams and canals to prevent flooding during the monsoon. The lake's two **island palaces** are amongst Udaipur's most familiar and photogenic features. **Jag Niwas**, now the *Lake Palace* hotel, is the larger of the two, built in amalgamated Rajput–Mughal style as a summer palace during the reign of Jagat Singh (1628–52), after whom it was named. Unfortunately, if you aren't staying here, the only way of visiting the island is to splash out on lunch or dinner (see p.345). The larger **Jag Mandir**, on the island to the south, has changed little since its construction (which was begun by Karan Singh in 1615, and finished by Jagat Singh, who, once again, named it after himself). The main building on the Jag Mandir, the **Gol Mahal**, houses a small exhibition on history of the island. Karan Singh offered refuge here to the Mughal Prince Khurum (later Emperor Shah Jahan), who had been exiled by his father, Emperor Jahangir, in the 1620s. Khurum succeeded his father while still in Udaipur, and the Mughal gathering for the occasion defied the established code of Rajput–Mughal enmity. According to tradition, Prince Khurum was so impressed by the architecture of the Gol Mahal that he later used elements of its design in the Taj Mahal, although it's difficult to see much resemblance between the two buildings. During the 1857 uprising the island once again served as a safe haven, this time for European women and children. The Gol Mahal has detailed stone inlay work within its domed roof. In front of it a green marble *chhatri* carved with vines and flowers stands at the centre of a garden guarded by stone elephants. Jag Mandir's only inhabitants other than flocks of birds are three royal servants who tend the gardens and grow flowers for the maharana's celebrations.

Boat rides around the lake depart from the jetty below the City Palace, below the *Fateh Prakash Palace* hotel, offering unforgettable views of the palaces and shoreline from the lake (note that you'll have to buy a Rs25 general entrance ticket to the City Palace complex to reach the jetty; see p.340). Choose between a quick thirty-minute circuit of the lake (Rs130) or the same trip with an additional twenty-minute stop at the Jag Mandir (Rs250). Both tours depart hourly on the hour from 10am to 5pm. You can also hire boats (seating up to 7 people) for Rs2000. To make the most of them by boat, sit on the side facing the palace (they usually run anticlockwise around the lake, so check when you get on).

City Palace

Udaipur's fascinating **City Palace** stands moulded in soft yellow stone on the northeast side of Lake Pichola, its thick windowless base crowned with ornate turrets and cupolas. The largest royal complex in Rajasthan, the building comprises eleven different *mahals* (palaces) constructed by successive maharanas during the three hundred years that followed the foundation of Udaipur in 1559. Part of the palace is now a **museum** (daily 9.30am–4.30pm; Rs50, camera Rs200, video Rs200). **Guided tours** (Rs100–150) serve to illuminate the chronology of the palace buildings, the significance of the paintings, and details of the lives of the maharanas. Narrow low-roofed passages connect the different *mahals* and courtyards, creating a haphazard effect, designed to prevent surprise intrusion by armed enemies – the layout of the whole complex is incredibly labyrinthine and confusing, although fortunately visitors are directed around a clearly signed and easy-to-follow one-way circuit, so your opportunities for getting lost are pretty limited.

Toran Pol to the Badi Mahal

To reach the palace museum, first buy your ticket at the kiosk at the main entrance then walk across the massive courtyard bounding the eastern side of the palace where elephants once lined up for inspection before battle. At the far end of this courtyard, head to the right through a large gate, the **Toran Pol**, and then turn right again across the **Moti Chowk** courtyard (look out for the large portable tiger trap in the middle of the courtyard). The entrance to the museum is on the far side of the courtyard, past the palace's small **armoury**.

Go in, past propitious statues of Ganesh and Lakshmi set amidst rich wall tiling, and head up some steep stairs to reach the first of the palace's myriad courtyards, the **Rajya Angan**. A room off on one side is devoted to the exploits of Pratap Singh (see p.343), including some of his own weapons, as well as a model of his famous horse, Chetak.

Steps lead up to the **Nav Chowki Palace** and past a small railed shrine ("fire pit") dedicated to Goswami Prem Giri, who in 1559 advised the founder of Udaipur, Udai Singh, to build his new palace on this spot. Further steps lead up to the **Chandra Mahal**, home to a huge basin carved from a single block of marble which was filled with one hundred thousand silver coins on the occasion of Maharana Karan Singh's wedding, the coins were then distributed amongst the citizens of Udaipur. A finely carved balcony with the remains of stained glass overlooks the lake from here. More steps lead up to pleasantly sylvan **Badi Mahal** (Garden Palace; also known as Amar Vilas after its creator, Amar Singh II, who reigned 1695–1755), its main courtyard embellished with finely carved pillars and a marble pool and dotted with trees which flourish despite being built some 30m above ground level.

The Dilkushal Mahal to the Surya Choupad

From the Badi Mahal, a twisting passageway leads down to the **Dilkushal Mahal**, whose rooms house a superb selection of small- and large-scale paintings depicting festive events in the life of the Udaipur court and portraits of the maharanas, as well as the superb **Kanch ki Burj**, a tiny little chamber eye-catchingly walled with red zigzag mirrors and capped with a reflective dome. This is the first of three exquisitely mirrored rooms in the palace built by Karan Singh I (reigned 1620–28), who was responsible for many of its most striking buildings, including the Chandra Mahal, Mor Chowk and Zenana Mahal, as well as the Jag Mandir in Lake Pichola. Immediately past here, the courtyard of the **Madan Vilas** (built by Bhim Singh, who reigned 1778–1828) offers fine lake and city views; the lakeside wall is decorated with quaint inlaid mirrorwork pictures.

Stairs lead down to the **Moti Mahal** (Pearl Palace), another of Karan Singh's oddly futuristic-looking little mirrored chambers, flanked by a pair of old ivory doors, its walls entirely covered in plain mirrors, the only colour being supplied by its stained-glass windows. Steps leads around the top of the Mor Chowk courtyard (see opposite) to the **Pitam Niwas** (built by Jagat Singh II, who reigned 1734–1790) and down to the small **Surya Choupad**, dominated by a striking image showing a kingly-looking Rajput face enclosed by a huge

Note that to reach certain parts of the City Palace, including the *Fateh Prakash Palace* and *Shiv Niwas* hotels, the Durbar Hall, Crystal Gallery, and the jetty for boats around Lake Pichola and over to the *Lake Palace* hotel, you'll have to fork out Rs25 for a **general entrance ticket** to the City Palace complex. You don't have to buy this ticket, however, if you're just visiting the City Palace Museum or the courtyard outside, or if you're actually staying at any of the three aforementioned hotels.

golden halo – a reference to the belief that the rulers of the house of Mewar are descended from the sun.

Mor Chowk to Laxmi Chowk

Next to here, the wall of the fine **Mor Chowk** courtyard is embellished with one of the palace's most flamboyant artworks, a trio of superb mosaic peacocks (*mor*), commissioned by Sajjan Singh in 1874, each made from around five thousand pieces of glass and coloured stone. On the other side of the courtyard is Karan Singh's opulent little **Manak Mahal** (Ruby Palace), its walls mirrored in rich reds and greens.

From here a long corridor winds past the kitschly decorated apartments of Rajmata Shri Gulabkunwar (reigned 1928–73) and through the **Zenana Mahal** (women's palace), whose long sequence of rooms now house a huge array of paintings depicting royal fun and frolics in Mewar. Continue onwards to emerge, finally, into the last and largest of the palace's internal courtyards, **Lakshmi Chowk**, the centrepiece of the *Zenana Mahal*. The exit is at the far end of this.

The rest of the City Palace complex

In the unlikely event that you have energy for more after going around the City Palace museum, the small **Government Museum** (daily 10am–4.30pm; Rs3; no photography), entered through a doorway opposite the entrance to the Palace Museum, is mainly of interest for its impressive sculpture gallery of pieces from Kumbalgarh, including some outstanding works in black marble, along with various stone inscriptions and the inevitable token assortment of miniature paintings, stuffed animals, weapons and faded bits of cloth.

More interesting in many ways – and certainly far more atmospheric – is the vast **Durbar Hall** in the Fateh Prakash Palace (the building immediately behind the main City Palace building which now houses the *Fateh Prakash Palace* hotel). Originally named Minto Hall after the British viceroy who laid the foundation stone, this huge, wonderfully time-warped Edwardian-era ballroom was built to host state banquets, royal functions and the like, and remains brimful of (rather solemn) period character, complete with huge chandeliers, creaky old furniture and fusty portraits. You can have afternoon tea here as part of a visit to *The Gallery* cafe (see p.345). In a gallery overlooking the hall is the eccentric **Crystal Gallery**, housing a collection of fine European crystal ordered by Sajjan Singh in the 1880s and featuring an outlandish array of crystal beds, chairs, tables and the like. Entrance to the Crystal Gallery costs a rather pricey Rs300 (plus the Rs25 general entrance charge; see opposite), though this also gets you a drink at *The Gallery* cafe.

Jagdish Temple

Raised above the main crossroads a little north of the City Palace, **Jagdish Temple** is a centre of constant activity. Built in 1652 and dedicated to Lord Jagannath, an aspect of Vishnu, its outer walls and towering *shikhara* are heavily carved with figures of Vishnu, scenes from the life of Krishna, and dancing *apsaras* (nymphs). The spacious *mandapa* leads to the sanctuary where a black stone image of Jagannath sits shrouded in flowers, while a small raised shrine in front of the temple protects a bronze Garuda, the half-man, half-bird vehicle of Vishnu. Smaller shrines to Shiva and Hanuman stand to either side of the main temple.

Bagore-ki-Haveli

North of the temple, a lane leads past a series of guesthouses to Gangaur Ghat and the **Bagore-ki-Haveli**, a 138-room lakeside haveli built in 1751 by the prime minister, Amarchand Barwa, and now nicely restored. A section of the building has been converted into a worthwhile museum (daily 10am–5.30pm; Rs25, camera Rs10, video Rs50), arranged on two floors around one of the rambling haveli's several courtyards. The upper floor has several immaculately restored rooms with original furnishings and artworks, plus some fine original murals. The lower floor has rooms full of women's clothes, musical instruments, kitchen equipment and – the undisputed highlight – what is claimed to be the world's largest turban, an enormous baggy pile of cloth which is probably big enough to fit an elephant. Steps lead down to an art gallery containing an eclectic (though completely unlabelled) collection of works by contemporary Indian artists, plus a few old colonial photos. Traditional **music and dance** shows (Rs60, camera Rs50, video Rs50) are staged here nightly at 7pm.

Bharatiya Lok Kala

Just north of Chetak Circle in the new city, the hoary old **Bharatiya Lok Kala** museum (daily 9am–6pm; foreign visitors Rs35, Indian residents Rs20, camera Rs10, video Rs50) is home to a mildly interesting collection of exhibits covering the folk traditions of Rajasthan and India, with dusty displays of colourful masks, musical instruments and models of folk dances, plus some interesting photos of Rajasthani and other Indian indigenous tribes such as the Bhils and Garasias, and an entertaining roomful of quaint puppets from around the world. Short, amusing **puppet shows** (tip expected) are staged throughout the day on demand (the performers will probably hunt you down and drag you into the theatre shortly after your arrival), while there's an hour-long show, with music, dancing and more puppets, daily at 6pm (Rs50, camera Rs10, video Rs50).

Moti Magri

The northeast side of the city is bounded by the expansive **Fateh Sagar** lake, connected to Lake Pichola by a canal built in the early 1900s and fringed with rugged hills. On the eastern side of the lake is the pleasantly peaceful **Moti Magri** (Pearl Hill; daily 7.30am–7pm, summer until 7.30pm; Rs20, camera Rs10, video Rs25), a steep-sided hillock covered in a mix of light woodland and ornamental gardens, and offering fine views over Fateh Sagar. Paths lead up to the ruins of the modest **Moti Mahal**, the original palace of Udai Singh, where he and his family lived while the City Palace was under construction. Close by, at the highest point of the hill, stands a large equestrian statue of **Pratap Singh** (see box opposite) astride his famous mount Chetak, decorated with friezes showing scenes from the battle of Haldighati, scene of Pratap Singh's greatest triumph. Further Pratap Singh memorabilia can be found in the **Hall of Heroes Museum** (Rs5), a short distance back down the hill, featuring a few dull paintings of various rulers of Mewar and scenes from the state's history (Hindi signs only), along with a couple of big models of Chittaurgarh Fort and the battlefield at Haldighati.

Just past the entrance to Moti Magri, a small jetty marks the departure point for boats to **Nehru Park**, on an island in the centre of the lake (daily: March–Oct 8am–7.30pm; Nov–Feb 8.30am–6.30pm; Rs112, including return boat trip to park) – nothing special, but a pleasant enough escape from the bustle of the town. You can also hire pedaloes, rowing boats, water scooters and motor boats at the jetty for trips out onto the lake.

Sahelion-ki-Bari

Northeast of Moti Magri, **Sahelion-ki-Bari** (daily 9am–7.30pm; Rs5), the "garden of the maids of honour", was laid out by Sangram Singh (1710–34) as

Pratap Singh: Rajput freedom fighter

There is not a pass in the alpine Aravalli that is not sanctified by some deed of the great freedom fighter, Maharana Pratap Singh, some brilliant victory or, more often, more glorious defeat.

Colonel James Tod, *Annals and Antiquities of Rajasthan*

The first son and successor of the founder of Udaipur, Udai Singh (see p.335), the feisty **Pratap Singh** (1540–97, reigned from 1572) is still revered as the original Mewari freedom fighter who defied the odds to take on the might of the Mughal empire and emerge bloody but unbowed. Born at Kumbalgarh in the year in which Udai Singh officially recaptured the mantle of King of Mewar, Pratap Singh continued his father's lifelong struggle against the forces of the Mughal emperor Akbar. Following his father's example, Pratap Singh met all of Akbar's numerous attempts to reach a diplomatic compromise with stubborn resistance, refusing to cede sovereignty to the Mughals and constantly rebutting their envoys – the last of the Rajput rulers to hold out against the might of the Mughals. Anticipating the inevitable attack, Pratap Singh put the kingdom on a war footing, in whose austerities he took full part, promising to eat off nothing but plates of leaves, to sleep on straw mattresses and not to shave his beard until the war was finished.

The promised attack finally arrived in 1576. Akbar massed an army of some eighty thousand soldiers at Ajmer, which marched into Mewar under the command of the rival Rajput ruler, Man Singh of Amber. On June 18, 1576, a short but intense pitched battle was fought at the narrow mountain pass at **Haldighati** between Pratap Singh's modest forces and the numerically far superior Mughal army. The outcome was inconclusive, though the encounter has been celebrated ever since as a moral triumph for the hopelessly outnumbered Mewari forces. Pratap Singh himself led from the thick of the action, saved only by his legendary steed **Chetak**, who bore him to safety before succumbing to his own wounds, and by his own previously estranged brother Sakta, formerly in the pay of the Mughal forces, who switched sides at the last minute to save Pratap from pursuing horsemen.

Following the battle of Haldighati, Pratap Singh retired to the Aravalli hills where, in time-honoured guerrilla fashion, he continued to harry the forces of Akbar over the following years until the Mughal emperor finally gave up the pursuit of Mewar in 1587 in order to concentrate on new campaigns in the Punjab. Pratap Singh was thus able to spend the final years of his reign unmolested, albeit the ruler of a kingdom which, though still independent, had been largely bankrupted by continual warfare.

a summer retreat for the diversion and entertainment of the ladies of the royal household – though the eye-catching fountains weren't installed until the reign of Fateh Singh (1884–1930). The gardens are centred on a peaceful courtyard enclosing a large pool and surrounded by attractive formal walled gardens, at the back of which four elephant statues surround Udaipur's most striking fountain – a fanciful tiered creation which looks a bit like a huge, multi-coloured cake stand.

Shilpgram

The road running around the south of Fateh Sagar leads to the rural arts and crafts centre of **Shilpgram** (daily 11am–7pm; Rs25, camera Rs10, video Rs50), near the village of Havala, 5km out from town. Shilpgram was set up by Rajiv Gandhi as a crafts village to promote and preserve the traditional architecture, music and crafts of the tribal people of western India, and holds displays dedicated to the diverse traditional lifestyles and customs of the Subcontinent's rural population. Around thirty replica houses and huts in traditional style are arranged in a village-like compound, with examples of buildings from Gujarat, Maharastra, Goa, Madhya Pradesh and, of course, Rajasthan (including a fine desert-style courtyard house modelled after buildings from the Sam region, near Jaisalmer). Musicians, puppeteers and dancers – *hijras* (see p.69) among them – hang out around the houses and strike up on the approach of visitors (a tip will be expected if you stay to watch or listen), while you may also see people weaving, potting, and embroidering as they would in their original homes – although most of the actual handicrafts on sale are fifth-rate, if that.

Despite its honourable origins, many tourists find the whole atmosphere contrived and resent the hustling by musicians and their ilk at what's supposed to be a non-commercial venue. But the scenic journey to get there by bike is a definite plus, and the week-long crafts fair around Christmas gets quite festive drawing more than six hundred artisans from across India. It's possible to breeze through the village in less than half an hour. Guides charge Rs50; the return journey by auto-rickshaw from Udaipur costs around Rs100 including waiting time.

Sajjangarh

High on a hill 5km west of the city, the so-called "Monsoon Palace", **Sajjan-garh**, was begun in 1883 by Maharana Sajjan Singh to serve as a summer retreat, complete with a nine-storey observatory from which the royal family proposed to watch the monsoon clouds travelling across the countryside below – hence the building's nickname. Unfortunately, the maharana's untimely death the following year put paid to the planned observatory, and although the palace itself was finished by Singh's successor, Maharana Fateh Singh, it was found to be impossible to pump water up to it, and the whole place was abandoned shortly afterwards. The large but rather plain building is now a somewhat melancholy sight, but the views over Udaipur, more than 300m below, are unrivalled. The journey up to the palace takes a good fifteen minutes by rickshaw or taxi, and costs around Rs200 for the round trip; the climb is too steep to tackle comfortably by bicycle. The palace is located inside the **Sajjan-garh Wildlife Sanctuary** (foreign visitors Rs80, Indian residents Rs10, plus Rs20 for a rickshaw or Rs65 for car). It's open daily from 9am, with last entry at 5.30pm, although you can come down after sunset.

Royal cenotaphs and Ahar museum

Across the narrow River Ahar, 2km east of Udaipur, domed **cenotaphs** huddle together on the site of the royal cremation ground. The cenotaphs are raised on platforms, some of which are decorated with shiva lingams, although many of the *chhatris* are falling into disrepair and the site is pretty dirty. Even so, it's a good place to pick up on local history, featuring an ornate memorial to the prodigious builder Jagat Singh (1628–52) and the cenotaph, embellished with friezes depicting the immolation of his wives, of Amar Singh (d. 1620) who contributed so much to the City Palace.

Less than 1km south of here, archeological exhibits at the **Ahar Museum** (daily except Fri 10am–5pm; Rs5) include locally unearthed pottery from the Ahar Civilization, which is believed to have come into existence around 2000 BC, making it one of India's earliest cultures. Among more recent statues is a handsome tenth-century Surya image.

Eating, drinking and entertainment

The place to eat in Udaipur has long been the *Lake Palace's* romantic dining terrace. The closest most visitors get to it, however, are the rooftop **restaurants** stacked behind Lalghat and Gangaur Ghat, whose gastronomic shortcomings and generally inflated prices are more than offset by spellbinding views over Lake Pichola to the distant Aravallis. Many of them also have free screenings (*ad nauseam*) of the James Bond movie *Octopussy*, with its manic boat and auto-rickshaw chases around the city's landmarks, beginning every evening, sharply at 7pm.

Live music can be found at many of the more expensive restaurants in town and everyday at 7.30pm at the Sunset View Terrace overlooking the boat jetty on Lake Pichola below the *Fateh Prakash Palace* hotel. Bagore-ki-Haveli (see p.341) also has nightly dance performances, while Shilpgram (see p.343) routinely invites out-of-town performers. Hour-long displays of traditional Rajasthani **folk dances** are staged at the Meera Kala Mandir, Meera Bhawan, Sector 11, on the Ahmedabad Road (Mon–Sat 7pm; Rs60; ☎0294/258 3176); call ahead for tickets.

Restaurants and cafes

Ambrai *Amet Haveli*, Chand Pole. In a super-lative setting on a spit of land facing the City Palace, this is one of the few lakeside restaurants whose cooking lives up to its location. The menu features an extensive selection of north Indian veg and non-veg dishes (including top-notch tandooris) prepared by the royal family's former chef, as well as a few Chinese and European offerings. Or just come for a sundowner and watch the sun set over the lake. Mains from around Rs110.

Edelweiss 71 Gangaur Ghat Marg, next to *Gangaur Palace*. Excellent hole-in-the-wall bakery and pastry shop that receives a steady stream of customers thanks to its tasty home-baked apple pie, chocolate cake and fresh ground coffee.

The Gallery *Fateh Pakash Palace*, City Palace. Buried away in the innards of the *Fateh Prakash Palace* hotel (just finding it is half the fun) this is Rajasthan's most memorable spot for a classic English-style high tea (daily 3–6pm), served either on a sunny terrace overlooking the lake or in the memorably grandiose nineteenth-century Durbar Hall (see p.341) inside. A full cream tea with cakes and scones will set you back Rs255, or just come for a tea or coffee.

Jagat Niwas 23–25 Lalghat. Popular restaurant in the hotel of the same name, serving up well-prepared north Indian standards (mains around Rs100) in a beautifully restored haveli, with nice views over the lake from its comfy window seats and discreet live sitar music in the background.

Kankarwa Haveli 26 Lalghat. The low-key rooftop restaurant at this excellent hotel offers a welcome alternative to the stereotypical tourist menus which characterize most of the eating establishments in this part of town. The evening menu comprises a choice of just two thalis featuring authentic and delicious home-cooked dishes like sweet aubergine and pumpkin curries served with crisp breads and flavoursome little side dishes. Opt either for the basic Rs150 thali or slightly more elaborate Rs250 thali with unlimited refills. Cold beer and panoramic lake views complete the ambience.

Lake Palace Lake Pichola ☎0294/252 8800. If your budget won't stretch to a stay at the iconic *Lake Palace Hotel*, the next best thing is to book in for lunch (Rs2000) or the four-course à la carte dinner (Rs3000) at what must rank among the world's most romantic restaurants. Reserve a table at least a day in advance at the reception desk at the jetty beneath the City Palace – dressing smartly will improve your chances of getting a reservation. As a one-off extravagance, the whole experience is hard to beat.

Natraj New Bapu Bazaar, behind Ashok Cinema. Udaipur's top thali joint for over twenty years, but well off the tourist trail because it's fiendishly hard to find (head to Suraj Pol and then ask for directions). Easily the best cheap meal in town: Rs50 for unlimited portions of five different vegetables, dhal, rice, *papad*, fresh chapatis and pickle.

Queen Café Chand Pol. This homely and unpretentious little cafe offers a refreshing alternative to Udaipur's mainstream tourist restaurants, with an authentic taste of home-style vegetarian Indian cooking served up by a charming elderly couple. The menu features a delicious selection of delicately spiced dishes including coconut-flavoured banana, mango and pumpkin curries, and some of the best vegetable pakoras in Rajasthan – all at giveaway prices, with most mains at around Rs45.

Savage Garden Chand Pol. Stylish restaurant set in an old haveli given a funky modern makeover, with loads of blue and white paint and minimalist decor. Food is mainly Indian (both veg and non-veg), with slight gourmet pretensions, plus a few European dishes including good pastas, salads and soups. Mains Rs110–210.

Shopping

Udaipur rivals Jaipur, Pushkar and Jaisalmer as one of Rajasthan's top shopping destinations, with an extremely eclectic array of local artisanal specialities along with other crafts from across the state. The city's particular speciality is **miniature painting**, with numerous shops selling traditional Mewari-style works on paper and silk (while a few galleries around town stock more contemporary Indian artworks). Many places also do a good local line in attractive leather- and cloth-bound **stationery** using hand-made paper – diaries, notebooks, photo albums and the like. Udaipur is well known for its **silver jewellery** – Bara Bazaar, running east from the clock tower, is a good place to explore. Generic **Rajasthani crafts** can be found all over town, including plenty of Jaisalmer-style patchwork fabrics, block-printed cloth, wood and stone carvings, and cheap, colourful clothes, while you'll also find plenty of little shops devoted to spices, perfumes and jewellery. The city is home to probably the best selection of **bookshops** in the state too (see the Listings below for details).

The obvious place to start looking is the area **around the Jagdish Temple and City Palace**, whose streets are stuffed with literally hundreds of little shops offering a bewildering array of colourful merchandise, often at bargain prices, especially if you're prepared to haggle. Outlets become progressively more upmarket as you head south down **Bhattiyani Chohatta** and along **Lake Palace road** – the latter, in particular, is home to a string of emporiums selling heirloom-quality Hindu bronzes and wood carvings, amongst many other things. It's also a significantly more relaxed and less traffic-plagued place to shop, and you'll generally suffer less hassle and sales patter as well. The main courtyard outside the **City Palace** also has a good, though expensive, range of shops, including a small branch of the excellent Jaipur-based Anokhi clothes shop (see p.218), tucked away opposite Toran Pol.

Listings

Airlines Indian Airlines, LIC Building, Delhi Gate (Mon–Sat 10am–5pm; ☎0294/241 0999); Jet Airways, Blue Circle Business Centre, 1C Madhuban (Mon–Sat 9.30am–6pm, Sun 10am–3pm; ☎0294/256 1105); Kingfisher Airlines, airport ☎0294/510 2468.

Banks and exchange There are ATMs all over the city, including a particularly handy 24hr machine (Visa and MasterCard) on the street leading to the City Palace (it's on left as you walk up). Other useful machines can be found at the State Bank of Bikaner and Jaipur on Panch Vati Rd; at the HDFC Bank immediately south of the GPO; at the HDFC ATM at the entrance to the State Bus Stand; and at the State Bank of India on Hospital Rd. All these machines accept both Visa and MasterCard and are open 24hr. The handily located Mewar International (daily 8am–11pm), on Lalghat behind the Jagdish Temple, changes cash and all brands of traveller's cheques, as well as giving cash advances on Visa and MasterCard. Thomas Cook (Mon–Sat 9am–6pm), near the *Rang Niwas Palace* on Lake Palace Rd, changes cash and all traveller's cheques. The State Bank of Bikaner and

Jaipur (Mon–Fri 10am–3.30pm) on Panch Vati Rd in the new city also changes all types of traveller's cheque at their foreign exchange desk upstairs. The nearby State Bank of India (Mon–Fri 10am–4pm) on Hospital Road changes Thomas Cook and Amex traveller's cheques only.

Bicycle and motorbike rental Heera Cycle Store (daily 7.30am–9pm; ☎0/982 852 0466), at 86 Gangaur Ghat Marg by the Jagdish Temple, rents out basic bicycles for Rs25 per day, and mountain bikes for Rs50 per day. They also have mopeds (Rs150–200/day), 150cc Vespa motorcycles (Rs300/day) and 350cc Enfield Bullets (Rs500/day). Crash helmets are included in the hire prices. You'll need to show a driving licence and leave your passport or US$500 cash as a deposit.

Bookshops There are dozens of places around the city offering a good stock of Indian and Western titles. One of the best places is Mayur Book Paradise, on a small side road behind the Jagdish Temple, while the bookshop on the main courtyard outside the City Palace complex (no ticket required) has a particularly good selection of India-related cultural and historical titles. Mewar International, on Lalghat behind the Jagdish Temple, buys and exchanges secondhand books.

Cooking lessons Available at numerous places around town. Try the homely little *Queen Cafe* (see p.345), which runs four-hour classes (Rs900) during which you'll be taught how to make no less than 14 dishes. Cheaper lessons can be had at the excellent *Panorama Guest House* (see p.337; Rs400 per person for three hours).

Horse riding Various places around town offer horse-riding expeditions into the surrounding countryside. One of the best places to arrange a trip is at the *Hotel Kumbha Palace* (see p.338) which runs half- and full-day excursions (Rs700/Rs1300) from its *Krishna Ranch* property, 7km from Udaipur, exploring local Rajasthani villages and the Aravallis. The safaris are suitable for both beginners and experienced riders, and longer stays at farm-style cottages can also be arranged. For more details, see ⓦ www.krishnaranch.da.ru. Another well-regarded operator is Princess Trails (☎ 0/982 904 2012, ⓦ www.princesstrails.com), which specializes in more extended, 4- to 8-day safaris on thoroughbred Mawari mounts.

Hospital The (private) Aravalli Hospital, 332 Ambamata Rd (☎ 0294/242 0222 or 241 8787), has a 24hr emergency room and a doctor permanently on call.

Internet access There are dozens of places offering Internet around Lalghat and Gangaur Ghat; most of the hotels and guesthouses we list also have Internet facilities. The going rate is Rs30 per hour. Two of the best-equipped places are Mewar International, on Lalghat near the Jagdish Temple, which also allows you to upload material; and the well-equipped cybercafe on the ground floor of the *Udai Niwas* hotel.

Music The enthusiastic Rajesh Prajapat at the Prem Musical Instrument shop (☎ 0294/243 0599), opposite the *Gangaur Palace* hotel, offers sitar and tabla lessons (Rs250 for 90min) and can also arrange flute lessons with his brother, or musical appreciation classes if you just want to learn more

about Indian music without actually trying to play anything yourself. Count on around Rs250 for a 90min lesson.

Pharmacies There are numerous pharmacies along Hospital Rd near the entrance to the main city hospital.

Photography The well set-up Mewar International, on Lalghat behind the Jagdish Temple, burn CDs and DVDs, sell memory cards and have equipment to download photos from most types of digital cameras; they also offer backup and photo recovery from defective memory cards.

Post office Parcels are best sent from the GPO (Mon–Fri 10am–4pm & Sat 10am–3pm), located at Chetak Circle. Note that poste restante mail is held at the post office at Shastri Circle, not at the GPO. Mewar International, on Lalghat behind the Jagdish Temple, sells stamps and will mail your postcards for free.

Travel agents Virtually every shop and guesthouse around the Jagdish Temple seems to offer bus and rail ticketing (see p.348 for more details). Reliable agents include Mewar International, on Lalghat behind the Jagdish Temple; Gangaur Tour 'n' Travels, close by on Gangaur Ghat Marg; and the travel agency inside the *Udai Niwas* hotel. All can arrange bus and railway tickets, car hire and tours, and hotel bookings, while Gangaur Tour 'n' Travels also offers domestic and international air ticketing. One day's car hire normally goes for around Rs1200 for up to 300km

Volunteer work The Animal Aid Society (☎ 0294/251 3359, ⓦ www.animalaidsociety.org), run by a friendly American ex-pat couple, maintains a pet hospital about 1km from Shilpgram. Volunteers and visitors are encouraged and no special skills are required – just a willingness to work with animals, usually including street dogs, cows, donkeys, cats, and monkeys.

Yoga Ashtanga Yoga Ashram (aka "Raiba House"), Chand Pol (☎ 0294/252 4872). Daily hatha yoga classes; free, but donations appreciated (proceeds go to the local Animal Aid hospital).

Moving on from Udaipur

By bus

Government buses leave from the main RSTRC bus stand at Udai Pol, with services to Agra (2 daily; 14hr); Ahmedabad (hourly; 7hr); Ajmer (hourly; 7hr); Bikaner (1 nightly; 12hr); Bundi (10 daily; 7hr); Chittaurgarh (hourly; 3hr–3hr 30min); Delhi (3 daily; 15hr); Jaipur (hourly; 10hr); Jodhpur (11 daily; 9–10hr); Kota (10 daily; 6hr); Mount Abu (10 daily; 7hr); and Mumbai (1 daily; 15hr). Make sure when you buy your ticket that you're booked on an express bus, not a slow passenger service.

Private buses depart from Udai Pol, opposite the government bus stand, and run to a similar range of destinations, plus Jaisalmer and Pushkar. Private buses are often a bit faster and more comfortable than government services, and are probably a better option for longer and (especially) overnight journeys – most night buses are sleepers. Destinations include Mount Abu (2 daily; 5hr); Jodhpur (3 daily; 6hr); Ahmedabad (4 daily; 4–6hr); Jaisalmer (1 nightly; 12hr); Pushkar (1 nightly; 6hr 30min); Delhi (1 nightly; 13hr); Mumbai (2 nightly; 13hr 30min–15hr 30min); Agra (1 nightly; 14hr); and Bundi (1 nightly; 7hr 30min). It's easiest to book **tickets** for private buses through one of the many travel agents in town (usually for a modest surcharge of around Rs20). If you want to book your own ticket you'll need to make a reservation with one of the various bus company offices clustered around Udai Pol – the reliable Kamlesh Travels (℡0294/248 5823) is a decent bet.

Local buses to destinations such as Nagda, Eklingji, Nathdwara and Kankroli leave from the main government bus stand at regular intervals throughout the day.

By train

Train services from Udaipur are surprisingly poor; those listed below are the best of a very bad bunch. Note that there are no direct services to Jodhpur, Ajmer, Bundi (change at Kota) or Mumbai (change at Ahmedabad). There are a couple of direct services to Sawai Madhopur, but both at horrible times; it's better to break the journey at Kota. Note that you can save yourself a trip to the station by booking railway tickets through any of the numerous travel agents in town (see Listings p.347) for a surcharge of around Rs50–75, which is about what you'd pay to make the return journey to the station by rickshaw.

By air

At the time of writing, flights were being operated out of Udaipur's Dabok Airport by Jet Airways (9W), Indian Airlines (IC), Kingfisher Airlines (IT) and Air Deccan (DN), with daily services to **Delhi** (1hr 10min; 9W, IC, IT, DN); **Mumbai** (1hr 15min; 9W; IC); **Jaipur** (45min; 9W, DN), and **Jodhpur** (40min; IC). Fares usually run from around US$70 to Jodhpur, US$90 to Jaipur, US$100 to Delhi and US$110 to Mumbai (although Air Deccan flights can be significantly cheaper) -- it's worth checking latest fares online with all the relevant airlines. Local contact details are given in the Listings on p.346.

Recommended trains from Udaipur

The following trains are recommended as the fastest or most convenient. Other services may also exist which may take longer, or arrive at inconvenient times, or not run every day. Train timetables change frequently; check latest schedules either at your nearest station or online at ⓦ www.indianrail.gov.in before travel.

Destination	Name	No.	Departs	Arrives
Ahmedabad	Ahmedabad Fast Passenger	431	9.20am daily	8.55pm
	Ahmedabad Express	9943	7.45pm daily	4.20am
Chittaurgarh	Mewar Express	2964	6.35pm daily	8.30pm
Delhi (Hazrat Nizamuddin)	Mewar Express	2964	6.35pm daily	6.15am
Jaipur	Jaipur Superfast Express	2966	9.40pm daily	7.10am
Kota	Mewar Express	2964	6.35pm daily	11.40pm

Around Udaipur

The rugged landscapes around Udaipur are some of the most scenic in Rajasthan, and you'd need a lot of time to see more than a fraction of the area's myriad ruins, palaces, temples, forts and lakes. North of the city are the historic temples of **Nagda**, **Eklingji**, **Nathdwara** and **Kankroli**, while to the northwest, en route to Jodhpur, lie the superb Jain temples of **Ranakpur** and the rambling fort at **Kumbalgarh**. Renting a car or motorcycle saves time and roads are generally empty, though local buses, as well as private tour companies, serve both routes.

Nagda and Eklingji

The ragged remnants of the ancient capital of Mewar, **NAGDA**, which date back to 626 AD, stand next to a lake 20km northeast of Udaipur, a couple of kilometres short of Eklingji. Buses from Udaipur set down passengers for Nagda shortly before the road drops into the valley that shelters the Eklingji Temple, beside a chai stall and bicycle shop (bike rental Rs5/hr). Nagda itself is about 1km away, west of the lake. Most of the buildings here were either destroyed by Mughal zealots or submerged by the lake, which has expanded naturally over the centuries. All that survives is a majestic pair of tenth-century Vaishnavite temples known as **Saas-Bahu** – literally "mother-in-law" and "daughter-in-law". The larger (mother-in-law) has a wealth of carving in its interior, while within the *mandapa*, a marriage area is marked by four pillars bearing images of the gods Brahma, Vishnu, Shiva and Surya to whom couples must pay homage. On the northeast pillar you can make out representations of Sita's trial by fire, a favourite episode from the Ramayana, while scenes from the Mahabharata cover the ceilings. The outer walls of both temples display images of the entire Hindu pantheon, nubile *apsaras* (heavenly maidens), and even a few couples engaged in erotic acts.

Returning to the main road, you can continue down to **EKLINGJI** via the paved road or along a path that leads behind the old protective walls and downhill, passing shaded water tanks and half-preserved muddy-brown temples. Ask for directions to the trailhead at the bike shop. The god **Eklingji**, a manifestation of Shiva, has been the protective deity of the rulers of Mewar ever since the eighth century, when Bappa Rawal was bestowed with the title *darwan* (servant) of Eklingji by his guru. To this day, the maharana of Udaipur still visits the 108-temple complex every Monday evening – the day traditionally celebrated all over India as being sacred to Shiva. Lesser mortals can make the straightforward half-hour trip northeast of Udaipur by taxi, or on one of the frequent buses from the main bus stand. Dominating the compound, the milky-white marble main temple (daily 5.30am–8.30pm), is crowned by an elaborate two-storey *mandapa* guarded by stone elephants; inside, a four-faced black marble lingam marks the precise spot where Bappa Rawal received his accolade. Images of Shiva and his fellow deities, *apsaras* and musicians are etched into the walls both outside and within. The temple had to be rebuilt under Maharana Raimal at the end of the fifteenth century, and again two hundred years later after the ravages of the iconoclastic forces of the Mughal emperor Aurangzeb.

Nathdwara

The temple dedicated to Krishna – known also as **Nath**, the favourite avatar (incarnation) of Vishnu – at **NATHDWARA**, "Gateway to God", is said to be the second-richest temple in India after Tirupati (in Andhra Pradesh). The site was known as Sihar until the moment in the seventeenth century when a chariot laden with an image of Krishna became stuck in the mud 26km north of Eklingji. The idol was being carried from Krishna's birthplace Mathura to Udaipur to spare it almost certain destruction by Aurangzeb; its bearers interpreted the event as a divine sign and established a new temple where it had stopped.

Nathdwara is on NH-8, and sees a constant flow of buses en route north and south. Although the area around the bus stand is grim, a short ride west on a rickshaw brings you to narrow streets where stalls display incense, beads, perfumes and small Krishna statues. In the centre of town the **Shri Nathji Temple** opens for worship eight times daily, when the image is woken, dressed, washed, fed and put to bed. The most elaborate session, *aarti*, takes place between 5pm and 6pm. Don't miss the radiant *pichwai* paintings in the main sanctuary, made of hand-spun cloth and coloured with strong vegetable pigments; these original hangings possess a brilliance unmatched by the numerous copies available all over Rajasthan. You could also ask a guide to show you the "footsteps of Krishna", a process that requires rubbing rose petals on the marble floor.

Kankroli and Rajsamand

Northeast of Nathdwara, NH-8 winds through another 17km of undulating scrub before reaching **KANKROLI**, 65km from Udaipur. This dusty little market town stands on the shores of the vast **Rajsamand Lake**, whose construction was commissioned by Maharana Raj Singh in the seventeenth century after a terrible drought swept Rajasthan. On the lake's western shore, a few kilometres out of town, is **Nauchowki**, a collection of nine *chowks* (pavilions) erected by Raj Singh on platforms above the steps leading to the water. The **Dwarkadish Temple** overlooking the southern shore houses an image of Krishna installed by Raj Singh in 1676, and has a sanctuary similar to that at Nathdwara. You can buy grain to feed the local flocks of pigeons beside the lake. The best views of the lake are to be had from the **Digambara Jain Temple**, dedicated to Adinath, which crowns a steep hill between Nauchowki and the bus stand. From here you can see the Dwarkadish Temple, Nauchowki, scattered old palaces on the nearby hills, and the Aravalli landscape rolling south as far as the eye can see.

With your own car or a lot of patience (local buses are painfully slow), it's possible to travel from here for two hours on empty country roads to **Kumbalgarh** (see p.352).

Ranakpur

Some 90km north of Udaipur, the spectacular **Jain temples** at **RANAKPUR** boast marble work on a par with that of the more famous Dilwara shrines at Mount Abu (see p.353). The temples are hidden away in a beautiful wooded valley, deep in the Aravalli hills, that was originally gifted to the Jain community in the fifteenth century by Rana Kumbha, the Hindu ruler of Mewar. Ranakpur's isolated position has long kept it well off the foreign tourist trail, but word is spreading fast about the area's bucolic beauty and a modest cluster of hotels is helping it to develop into a destination in its own right. If you're working your way between Jodhpur and Udaipur, it's an excellent place to break the journey.

The **main temple** (noon–5pm; free, camera Rs50, video Rs100) was built in 1439 according to a strict system of measurement based on the number 72 (the age at which the founder of Jainism, Mahavira, achieved nirvana). The entire temple sits on a pedestal measuring 72 yards square and is held up by 1440 (= 72 x 20) individually carved pillars. Inside, there are 72 elaborately carved shrines, some octagonal in shape, along with the main deity (a 72-inch tall image of the four-faced Adinath, the first *tirthankara*) encased in the central sanctum. The carving on the walls, columns and the domed ceilings is superb. Friezes depicting the life of the *tirthankara* are etched into the walls, while musicians and dancers have been modelled out of brackets between the pillars and the ceiling.

Three smaller temples nestle among the trees in the enclosure in front of the main temple. The most impressive is the **Parshwanath Temple**, around 100m from the main temple, with a small but finely carved shrine, while a further 100m walk brings you to the simpler **Neminath Temple**. Close by, a short walk across the car park, is a contemporary Hindu temple dedicated to **Surya**.

Practicalities

Ranakpur is a bumpy three-hour journey on regular **buses** from Udaipur (around six daily). You can also get here by bus from Jodhpur (5–6 daily; 4–5hr) via the market town of Falna (the nearest railway station) on the NH-14, and there are a couple of express buses daily to Abu Road (5–6hr). Getting from the bus stop to the village's hotels can be tricky. Buses stop right outside the Jain temples, between 2km and 4km away from the various hotels. If you're lucky, you might find a rickshaw or jeep available for hire at the bus stop; if not you'll have to ring your hotel and ask to be picked up or (worst-case scenario) walk.

Ranakpur can also be visited as a day-trip from Udaipur, either on its own or in combination with nearby Kumbalgarh; count on around Rs1000–1200 for the round trip by **car**. If you're intending to visit Kumbalgarh as well, though, think about **trekking** between the two sites, a beautiful hike through an unspoilt section of the Aravalli hills. As Kumbalgarh is on the top of the range, it's much easier to hike from there down to Ranakpur (for more on this route see p.352), but guides may be arranged through any of the hotels listed below for the six-hour uphill climb in the other direction.

Accommodation

For budget **accommodation** in Ranakpur, you can stay for a Rs10 donation with the Jain pilgrims at the temple complex, but don't expect anything more than a mattress on a cold, cement floor; dinner, costing Rs20, is served at 5pm to satisfy Jain proscription from eating after sunset. This option excepted, accommodation in the village is relatively expensive.

Aranyawas 10km from Ranakpur on the road to Kumbalgarh, near the village of Maga ☎0294/258 3148, ✉aranyawas@hotmail.com. Small jungle lodge with rustically elegant cottages overlooking a watering hole frequented by leopards – an ideal place to recharge your batteries in complete isolation. ⓻

Fateh Bagh 4km south of the temples ☎02934/286186, ⓦwww.hrhindia.com. Ranakpur's top accommodation option, this 200-year-old palace was painstakingly disassembled piece by piece, transported 50km, and then rebuilt here with all the corresponding pomp you'd expect. Rooms have plenty of comfort and character,

and facilities include a pool, spa and Ayurveda centre. ⓼

Maharani Bagh Orchard 3.5km south of the temples ☎02934/285105, ✉mbor@sancharnet.in. Pleasantly low-key resort, with attractively furnished rooms (all with a/c and fridge) in red-brick cottages around rambling gardens. There's also a (very shallow) pool. ⓼

Ranakpur Hill Resort 3km south of the temples ☎02934/286411, ⓦwww.ranakpurhillresort.com. Chintzy pink little resort with a range of rooms (air-cooled and a/c; the latter also with TV) of varying standards, and some less appealing tents (available Oct–March only), including a couple pitched, rather bizarrely, on the hotel roof. Also has a decent-size pool, a small Ayurveda centre, and can arrange half-day horse safaris. Rooms ④–⑦, tents ⑥–⑦ **Shivika Lake Hotel** 2km south of the temples ☎02934/285078. The only real budget option in

Ranakpur, although the cheaper rooms are disappointingly basic and shabby for the price; the more expensive rooms (some with a/c) are relatively better value. Local treks (Rs300pp) and jeep safaris (Rs600pp) can be arranged here. ③–⑤

Kumbalgarh

The remote hilltop fort of **KUMBALGARH** (daily 9am–6pm; foreign visitors Rs100, Indian residents Rs5), 80km north of Udaipur, is the most formidable of the 32 constructed or restored by Rana Kumbha of Chittaurgarh in the fifteenth century. Protected by a series of seven thick ramparts, it was only successfully besieged once, when a confederacy led by Akbar poisoned the water supply. Aside from the impressive fortifications and the ancient monuments they enclose, the main reason to venture out here is to experience the idyllic Aravalli countryside. Winding through a string of tribal villages and picturesque valleys, the Udaipur road alone more than repays the effort, and once you've reached the top of the range the views are superb.

The most memorable panorama of all is from the pinnacle of Kumbalgarh **palace**, crowning the summit of the fort – the finest views are from the Cloud Palace (which really does sit in the clouds during the monsoon) at the very top, restored and furnished by Udaipur's Fateh Singh in the early twentieth century. The palace buildings themselves are plain and uninteresting, though if you like one of the resident staff will show you (for a tip) to the room where Udai Singh was raised by his nurse Panna Dhai after fleeing Chittaurgarh (see p.335). From the rooftops, there are striking bird's-eye views over the numerous Jain and Hindu **temples** clustered around the main gate and scattered over the hills below. The oldest are thought to date from the second century; the **tombs** of the great Rana Kumbha himself (murdered by his eldest son) and his grandson Prithviraj (poisoned by his brother-in-law) stand to the east.

Provided you're equipped with good shoes and ample provisions, the best way to explore these more remote monuments is on foot, via the old walls. Some 36km of crenellated ramparts wind around the rim of the hilltop, and it's possible to complete a circuit in two comfortable days, sleeping rough midway around. You won't need a guide, but be sure to take food and water as there are no permanent settlements.

Lining the deep valley that plunges west from the fort down to the plains, the **Kumbalgarh Wildlife Sanctuary** comprises a dense area of woodland which offers a refuge for wolves and leopards. With a local guide, you can trek through it to Ranakpur, a rewarding and easy hike of between four and five hours (the alternative is a long journey on an infrequent country bus). Entry to the sanctuary costs Rs80 (plus Rs200 for camera); foreigners need **permits**, obtainable from the District Forest Officer at nearby **Kelwara**. Local guides, contactable through the hotels listed below, can also obtain your permit for you – and stop you getting lost – for around Rs600–1000. To save money you can try to find a guide on your own – it's not easy, but if you ask around at the café just inside the fort gates you might get lucky.

Practicalities

Kumbalgarh and Ranakpur can easily be visited as a (longish) day-trip from Udaipur (count on around Rs1000–1200 for the round trip by taxi), but it's best to take your time and travel at a more leisurely pace, staying for a night or two. A direct **bus** currently leaves Udaipur's RSRTC stand at 12.45am, arriving at the *Aodhi* hotel in Kumbalgarh around 5pm; there are also jeeps and slow local buses (roughly every hour) either from Udaipur's RSRTC stand or from Chetak Circle to the town of **Kelwara**, 7km down the road, from where you should be able to pick up a Jeep or rickshaw to Kumbalgarh. Competent motorcyclists could consider riding out here on a rented **bike**.

Accommodaton

There's a cluster of mid-range and top-end **places to stay** close to one another below the fort, though no budget options.

Aodhi 1km below the fort ☏02954/242341, ⓦwww.hrhindia.com. This peaceful and welcoming heritage hotel, occupying a former hunting lodge of the maharana of Udaipur, is easily the nicest (and most expensive) place to stay in Kumbalgarh. Accommodation is in stylishly furnished rooms set in a cluster of attractive little thatched granite buildings, and there's nightly folk dancing and music during dinner in the multi-cuisine restaurant, plus Internet and money-changing facilities, a big pool, coffee shop and a nice bar serving "heritage liquors" originally concocted for the maharana himself; you can also arrange Jeep safaris (Rs1200) to local villages here. ⑥

The Dera 1.5km below the fort ☏02954/242200, ⓔjsameta@yahoo.com. Occupying a scenic hillside location, with accommodation in spacious, if rather hot and overpriced, tents with basic bathrooms and floor fans. ⑧

Kumbalgarh Fort Hotel 5km along the Kelwara road ☏02954/242057. Upmarket modern hotel with superb views from its garden terrace and pool. Closed for refurbishment at the time of writing, though should have reopened by the time this book is published. April–July 50 percent discounts. ⑦–⑧

Kumbhal Castle 1.5km below the fort ☏02954/242171, ⓦwww.kumbhalcastle.com. Pleasant, run-of-the-mill modern hotel, with spacious and nicely furnished air-cooled and a/c doubles, plus a pool. You can also arrange Jeep and car hire here. ⑥

Mount Abu

As Rajasthan's only bona fide hill station, **MOUNT ABU** (1220m) is a major Indian resort, popular above all with honeymooners who flock here during the winter wedding season (November to March) and with visiting holiday-makers from Gujarat, a short distance south across the state border, whose importance to Mount Abu's economic health is evidenced by the myriad signs in Gujarati script which adorn virtually every restaurant and hotel in town. Mount Abu's hokey commercialism is aimed squarely at these local vacationers rather than foreign tourists, but the sight of lovestruck honeymooners shyly holding hands and jolly parties of Gujarati tourists on the loose lends the whole place a charmingly idiosyncratic holiday atmosphere quite unlike anywhere else in Rajasthan – and the fresh air is exhilarating after the heat of the desert plains.

One attraction that draws foreigners and Indians alike are the **Jain Temples** at **Dilwara**. Hidden in thick woodland north of the town, the temples are decorated with what is considered by some to be the most intricate marble carving in the world. Anyone happy to rock hop and follow unmarked trails will also find plenty of scope for **hikes** and scrambles amid the granite boulders and wooded ridges high above the town, where dozens of tiny caves, connected by a tangle of dirt paths, shelter a transient community of semi-nomadic, chillum-smoking sadhus – a reminder of the area's great religious importance.

According to Hindu mythology, the focal point of Mount Abu, **Nakki Lake**, was formed when the gods scratched away at the mountain with their fingernails (*nakh*). These days, the waterside is cluttered by far more pedaloes and ice-cream parlours than pilgrims, but the temple marking the site of the famous *yagna agnikund* – a powerful fire ceremony conducted in the eighth century AD,

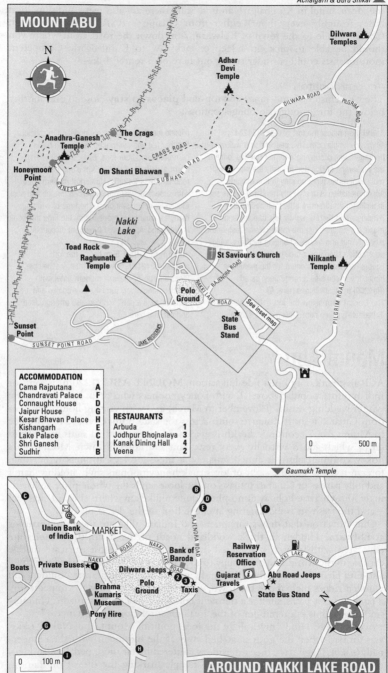

MOUNT ABU

N

Dilwara Temples

Adhar Devi Temple

DILWARA ROAD

PILGRIM ROAD

Anadhra-Ganesh Temple

The Crags

CRAGS ROAD

SUBHASH ROAD

Honeymoon Point

Om Shanti Bhawan

A

GANESH ROAD

Nakki Lake

St Saviour's Church

Nilkanth Temple

Toad Rock

RAJENDRA ROAD

Raghunath Temple

PILGRIM ROAD

Polo Ground

NAKKI LAKE ROAD

State Bus Stand

Sunset Point

SUNSET POINT ROAD

LAKE RESERVOIR

See inset map

Abu Road (28km)

ACCOMMODATION

Cama Rajputana	A
Chandravati Palace	F
Connaught House	D
Jaipur House	G
Kesar Bhavan Palace	H
Kishangarh	E
Lake Palace	C
Shri Ganesh	I
Sudhir	B

RESTAURANTS

Arbuda	1
Jodhpur Bhojnalaya	3
Kanak Dining Hall	4
Veena	2

0   500 m

Gaumukh Temple

C

@

Union Bank of India

MARKET

B

D

E

F

RAJENDRA ROAD

Railway Reservation Office

Boats

Private Buses

NAKKI LAKE ROAD

Bank of Baroda

NAKKI LAKE ROAD

Gujarat Travels

i

Abu Road Jeeps

Dilwara Jeeps

2 3

Taxis

State Bus Stand

Polo Ground

Brahma Kumaris Museum

Pony Hire

4

N

G

I

H

0   100 m

AROUND NAKKI LAKE ROAD

which Rajasthan's ruling caste, the "twice-born" Rajputs, trace their mythological origins back to – at Gaumukh, 7km south of Mount Abu, still sees streams of devotees. In addition, around Mount Abu itself you'll come across many white-clad **Brahma Kumaris**, members of an international spiritual movement whose headquarters are situated in a quiet valley behind the lake.

In order to get the most benefit from Mount Abu's scenery and climate, it's essential to **time your visit** carefully. During the peak months of April–June, and at almost any major festival time (especially Diwali in November) the town's thirty thousand population mushrooms, room rates skyrocket and peace and quiet are at a premium.

Arrival, information and accommodation

Mount Abu is accessible only by road. Aim to spend as little time as possible in the grim bazaar town of **Abu Road**, the nearest railhead, where travellers pick up buses for the 45-minute ascent from the plains. Entering Mount Abu itself, you have to pay a Rs10 fee (or Rs21 if entering in your own vehicle). Passengers arriving at the main **bus stand**, on Nakki Lake Road in the southeast of Mount Abu, are swamped by hotel touts and would-be luggage porters.

The **tourist office** (Mon–Sat 10am–1.30pm & 2–5pm), opposite the main bus stand, has wildly inaccurate maps of local sights but not much else. For information on hotels, try Ⓦwww.mountsabu.com. To **change traveller's cheques** the best bet is the Union Bank of India, hidden away in the bazaar just behind the **post office**. There's a handy State Bank of India **ATM** (24hr; Visa and MasterCard) in front of the tourist office. For **Internet** access try the *Shri Ganesh* guesthouse, the Yani-Ya Cyber Zone, just south of the post office, or the Shree Krishna Cybercafe in the lane just behind the Yani-Ya (all Rs30/hr).

Pony rides are available from next to the Brahma Kumaris Museum (Rs150/hr), or you can hire various types of boat for a cruise around Nakki Lake from around Rs50 for 30min. Longer **tours** can be arranged through the *Shri Ganesh* guesthouse, whose owner organizes Jeep tours (Rs400 for the vehicle for a half-day trip) out to places like Achalgarh and Guru Shikar.

Accommodation

The steady stream of pilgrims and honeymoon couples ensures that Mount Abu has plenty of **hotels**, lots of them offering luxuries for newlyweds in special "couple rooms". Though in **low season** you can live in stylish comfort for little more than you might otherwise pay for rock-bottom accommodation, prices rocket in **high season** (April–June & Nov–Dec), reaching their peak during Diwali (Oct & Nov). The price codes given below are for high season.

Budget

Chandravati Palace 9 Janta Colony ☎02974/238219. Excellent little guesthouse (though staff's English is limited) on a quiet side road. The small, bright modern rooms are impeccably maintained and have good-sized balconies and hill views. Best alternative if *Shri Ganesh* is full. ❷

🏃 **Shri Ganesh** Southwest of the polo ground, near Sophia High School ☎02974/237292, Ⓔlalit_ganesh@yahoo.co.in. By far the best-value budget hotel in town and the only one geared towards foreign budget travellers. There are plenty of simple, clean rooms with TV (the cheaper ones with shared bathroom), plus a handy little in-house shop and good home-cooked food. Lalit and his Irish wife offer Indian cooking lessons and guided walks. Free pick-up from bus stand. ❷–❸

Sudhir Opposite *Connaught House*, Rajendra Rd ☎02974/235120. Functional modern hotel with bright and spacious rooms: choose between the rather bare "semi-deluxe" and the significantly nicer "deluxe" categories. Rather expensive during high season (May–July & Oct–Dec), but good value at other times of the year. ❹–❻

Mid-range to expensive

Cama Rajputana Adhar Devi Rd ☎02974/238205, ⒲www.camahotelsindia.com. The largest of Mount Abu's upscale offerings, occupying a neatly refurbished granite colonial building located in sprawling grounds. The cool and spacious rooms (all a/c) overlook an immaculate garden, while extensive facilities include squash and tennis courts, gym, sauna and steam bath, Ayurveda massage centre and a big pool (guests only). Popular with foreign tour groups. ❼

Connaught House Rajendra Rd ☎02974/238560, ⒲www.welcomheritage .com. Set in the former maharaja of Jodhpur's bolthole, this is Mount Abu's most memorable accommodation option, occupying a typically British-era retreat, boasting beautifully preserved rooms (all a/c), complete with period furniture and decor, and an intensely atmospheric old photo-filled lounge and dining room. There are some newer but less atmospheric rooms in the modern block on the hill above, plus a sunny veranda, flower-filled garden and sweeping views over the surrounding hills. ❼

Jaipur House South of the lake ☎02974/235176, ⒲www.royalfamilyjaipur.com. Perched on a hilltop above town, this fine old summer palace (owned by the maharaja of Jaipur) offers some of the town's most atmospheric accommodation in tastefully decorated suites with wooden furnishings, high ceilings and sweeping views – although the so-called "deluxe" rooms, occupying an ugly modern block halfway down the drive, are dull and overpriced. The restaurant has some of the best views in town, though the food is very ordinary. ❼

Kesar Bhavan Palace Sunset Rd ☎02974/238647, ⒲www.kesarpalace.com. Functional modern hotel rather than the promised "palace", though rooms (some with a/c) are pleasantly spacious and sunny, with views over the tree tops from large individual verandas. The rooms in the new annexe (same price) are darker and less appealing. ❼

Kishangarh House Rajendra Rd ☎02974/238092, ⒲www.royalkishangarh.com. Recently opened heritage hotel occupying a former country residence of the rulers of Kishangarh (near Ajmer). It's not as memorable as the neighbouring *Connaught House*, but still offers a modest helping of colonial-era charm, with accommodation in neatly furnished rooms (most a/c) in the old building itself (or in cheaper but relatively characterless "cottage" rooms in a new block outside), plus a prettily painted lounge and dining areas and fine views over town from the lovely lawn out the front. Cottages ❺, rooms ❼

Lake Palace Nakki Lake Rd ☎02974/237154, ⒲www.savshantihotels.com. One of the town's best mid-range options, in a scenic position facing Nakki Lake, with good service and a range of well-maintained modern rooms (all a/c, the more expensive ones with lake view and balcony). Reasonable value, especially in low season, when prices fall by a third or more. ❺–❻

The town and around

Mount Abu has a significant number of religious sites. All are some way out of town, although virtually all foreign visitors make their way sooner or later to the superb Jain temples at **Dilwara**, the highlight of any visit here. Nearer the centre, **Nakki Lake** is where everyone converges in the late afternoon for pony and pedalo rides. Of several panoramic viewpoints on the fringes of town above the plains, **Sunset Point** is the favourite – though the hordes of holiday-makers, peanut sellers, camel drivers, cart pushers and horse owners also make it one of the noisiest and least romantic. **Honeymoon Point**, also known as Ganesh Point (after the adjacent temple), and **Anadhra Point** offer breath-taking views over the plain at any time of day, and tend to be more peaceful; 4pm is a good time to visit.

Dilwara temples

Jains consider temple building to be an act of devotion, and their houses of worship are always lovingly adorned and embellished, but even by Jain standards the **Dilwara temples** (daily noon–6pm; free, but donation requested; no photography, leather, phones, radios, tape recorders, or menstruating women), 3km northeast of Mount Abu, are some of the most beautiful in India. All five are made purely from marble, and the carving, especially in the two main shrines, is breathtakingly intricate, unparalleled in its lightness and delicacy. For sheer aesthetic splendour, only the main temple at Ranakpur comes close. Entrance to

The views over the plains from the hilltops around Mount Abu town are a revelation. Down in the market area, you gain little sense of the wonderfully wild **landscape** enfolding the town, but head for a few minutes up one of the many trails threading through the rocks and undergrowth around the sides of the plateau, and it is easy to see why the area has inspired sages, saints and pilgrims for centuries.

After decades of deforestation by woodcutters, a strictly enforced ban on wood gathering seems to be heralding a recovery in the forests around town. Abu's other **environmental menace** is the lantana plant, an introduced flower which has squeezed out many of the eighteen highly prized medicinal herbs listed as growing here in ancient Hindu scriptures. Also under pressure are the fragile populations of bear and leopard. Sightings of both, however, are still not uncommon and you should take great care while trekking not to disturb any you may encounter aong the trails. **Bears**, in particular, can be dangerous if surprised, or when with young.

Unfortunately **hiking alone** is no longer recommended and tourist police will turn back anyone spotted heading out on their own. The cause for alarm is well founded. The same, extended drought that has pushed emaciated bears towards the city has also denied peasant farmers their traditional livelihood and a few unscrupulous characters have taken to highway robbery. In 2002 a group of foreign tourists were seriously injured after being ambushed by stone-throwing bandits. As a result, more remote locations are considered off-limits even by locals. Two good local **guides** are Lalit Kanojia at the *Shri Ganesh Hotel*, who leads 3–4hr treks every morning (Rs100 per person); and Mahendra Dan, better known as "Charles" (@www.mount-abu-treks.blogspot.com), who runs a range of half-day (Rs300) and full-day (Rs450) walking tours focusing on village life, wildlife spotting and local Ayurvedic plants, as well as overnight camping expeditions. He can be contacted via the *Lake Palace* hotel or on ℡0/941 415 1854.

the temples is by guided tour only – you'll have to wait until sufficient people have arrived to make up a group – though once inside it's easy enough to slip away and look around on your own and at your own pace.

The oldest temple, the **Vimala Vasahi**, named after the Gujarati minister who funded its construction in 1031, is dedicated to Adinath, the first *tirthankara*, whose image sits cross-legged in the central sanctuary guarded by tall statues of Parshvanath (the 23rd *tirthankara*). Although the exterior is simple – as, indeed, are the exteriors of all the temples here – inside not one wall, column or ceiling is unadorned, a prodigious feat of artistry which took almost two thousand labourers and sculptors fourteen years to complete. There are forty-eight intricately carved pillars inside, eight of them supporting a domed ceiling arranged in eleven concentric circles alive with dancers, musicians, elephants and horses. A sequence of 57 subsidiary shrines run around the edge of the enclosure, each containing a figure of a *tirthankara*; while in front of the entrance to the temple the so-called "Elephant Cell" (added after the construction of the temple itself in 1147) contains ten impressively large stone pachyderms. A more modest pair of painted elephants, along with an unusual carving showing stacked-up tiers of *tirthankaras*, flank the entrance to the diminutive **Mahaveerswami Temple**, built in 1582, which sits by the entrance to the Vimala Vasahi; a white marble image of Mahavira can be seen inside.

The second of the two great temples at Dilwara, the **Luna Vasahi Temple** was built in 1231 at a cost of over 125 million rupees and is dedicated to Neminath, the 22nd *tirthankara*. The temple follows a similar plan to the Vimala Vasahi, with a central shrine fronted by a minutely carved dome and surrounded by a long sequence of shrines (a mere 48 this time) running around the edge of the enclosure.

△ Marble elephants at Dilwara temple, Mount Abu

The carvings, however, are perhaps even more precise and detailed, especially so in the magnificently intricate dome covering the entrance hall. Friezes etched into the walls depict cosmological themes, stories of the *tirthankaras* and grand processions, while sculptures near the entrance porch commemorate the temple's patrons, the two brothers Vastupala and Tejapala. Said in legend to have discovered a huge treasure, they were advised by their wives – also portrayed here – to build temples, and funded many on the holy hill of Shatrunjaya in Gujarat.

The remaining two temples, both dating from the fifteenth century, are less spectacular. The **Bhimasah Pittalhar Temple** houses a huge gilded image of the first *tirthankara*, Adinath, installed in 1468, which was made out of five different types of metal, measures over eight foot high and weighs in at around 4.5 tons. The shrine sports some detailed carving, much of it unfinished, though compared to the Luna Vasahi and Vimala Vasahi it all looks decidedly plain.

The large three-storey **Khartar Vasahi Temple** (near the entrance to the temples) was built in 1458 and is also consecrated to Parshvanath. The temple is topped by a high grey stone tower and has ornate ceilings and carvings of Jain saints etched into the outer walls, while inside there's some intricate carving around the central shrine and in the dome in front of the shrine. Overall, however, it's only a pale shadow of the earlier temples

To **get to Dilwara**, you can charter a Jeep (Rs50 one way or Rs150 return) from the corner by the *Jodhpur Bhojnalaya* restaurant, or take a place in a shared one (Rs5); the latter leave from in front of the large Chacha Museum (a shop, incidentally, not a museum), a few doors down from the *Veena* restaurant. The hour-long walk up there is also pleasant, though many prefer to save their energies for the downhill walk back into town.

Hindu temples

On the north side of town, en route to the Dilwara temples, a flight of more than four hundred steps climbs up to the **Adhar Devi Temple** (dedicated to Durga). The small main shrine is cut into the rocky hilltop and entered by

Brahma Kumaris

The spiritual sect **Brahma Kumaris** ("children of Brahma") preaches that all religions reach for the same goal, but label it differently. Based at about five thousand centres around the world they teach *raja* yoga – meditation that directs people to knowledge of an inner light, the "divine spark" or soul, that is part of, and one with, the all-encompassing soul, Shiva. Belief in the five evils – anger, ego, attachment, greed and lust – is shared with Buddhism and Hinduism, with the ultimate goal being their elimination, and the advent of a **Golden Age** of peace, prosperity and purity.

The **Brahma Kumaris Spiritual University** at **Om Shanti Bhawan** (☏02974/238268) to the north of Nakki Lake aims to foster awareness, tolerance, love and "God-consciousness" in a meditative atmosphere where smoking, alcohol, meat and sex are avoided. Classes range from three-day *raja* yoga camps to advanced six-month courses; lectures are translated into eighteen languages. The **Brahma Kumaris Museum** (daily 8am–8pm; free) by the private bus stand between the polo ground and the lake holds daily meditation classes and makes a worthwhile detour. Once through the "Gateway to Paradise," you'll be greeted by freakish, life-size manne-quins including blue monsters wielding long knives. Each personifies greed, sex-lust and other vestiges of the so-called "iron age" that temple leaders promise deliver-ance from. If it all sounds somewhat cultish you'll understand why many locals try to keep foreigners from entering into the sect's clutches.

clambering under a very low overhang. There are fine views from the terrace above, where there's another tiny shrine cut out of solid rock. The milk-coloured water of the **Doodh Baori** well at the foot of the steps is considered to be a source of pure milk (*doodh*) for gods and sages.

A further 8km northeast, the temple complex at **ACHALGARH** is dominated by the **Achaleshwar Mahadeo Temple**, believed to have been created when Lord Shiva placed his toe on the spot to still an earthquake. Its sanctuary holds neither an image of Shiva nor a lingam, however, but only a yoni with a hole in it which is said to reach into the netherworld, watched over by figures of Parvati and Ganesh on the walls. Statues of Parvati flank the entrance, faced by an unusually large metal Nandi bull. Subsidiary shrines include one dedicated to Vishnu, in which detailed plaques depict the familiar reclining Vishnu and his nine incarnations. The large tank lined with stone buffaloes outside the temple, intended to contain purifying water, is the legendary scene of the slaying of demons disguised as buffaloes who stole purifying ghee from the tank. Nearby, the **Jamadagni Ashram** is site of the **Agnikund**, where the sage Vashishtha presided over the fire ritual that produced the four Rajput clans (the Parmars, Parihars, Solankis and Chauhans).

The lesser visited, but more dramatically situated, **Gaumukh Temple** lies 7km south of the market area. Reached via a steep flight of 750 steps, the small pool inside the shrine – which continues to flow even during times of drought – is believed to hold water from the sacred Sarawati Ganga River. Pilgrims come here to perform puja, to invoke the blessings of India's two greatest *rishis* (sages), Vashishtha and Vishwamitra, who are thought to have meditated and conducted a famous metaphysical debate on the spot.

The last important Hindu pilgrimage site on Mount Abu is the Atri Rishi temple at **Guru Shikar**, 15km northeast of town, which at 1772m above sea level marks the highest point in Rajasthan. Depending on how energetic you're feeling, you can enjoy superb panoramic vistas either from the temple itself, or from the drinks stall at the bottom of the steps leading up to it. There's no public transport there, however, so you'll have to hire a Jeep (around Rs400).

Eating and drinking

Mount Abu's predominantly middle-class Gujarati visitors are typically hard to please when it comes to food, so standards are exceptionally high and prices low in the numerous **restaurants** dotted along Nakki Road – competition is stiffest between the squeaky-clean pure-veg Gujarati thali joints. Meat is fairly rare in Mount Abu; if you get carniverous cravings, there are a couple of Punjabi restaurants in the bazaar. The classier hotels serve **alcohol**, also available at the wine and beer shops opposite the *Veena* restaurant on the east side of the polo ground.

Arbuda Nakki Lake Rd. Perennially popular spot with a huge veggie menu ranging from pizzas, burgers and sandwiches through to Chinese and Indian, as well as good fresh juices. Lightning-fast, friendly service and a popular, airy terrace.

Jodhpur Bhojnalaya Nakki Lake Rd. The only place in town where you can eat authentic Rajasthani food, very heavy on ghee and spices. It's famous for its definitive *dhal bati churma*, and also has the usual big list of veg north and south Indian dishes.

Kanak Dining Hall Nakki Lake Rd. Friendly place offering arguably the best Gujarati thalis in town – a superb array of subtly spiced veg delicacies for a very modest Rs60 per head. Come hungry – portions are literally limitless. They also have a big range of north and south Indian veg dishes, plus a few Chinese options

Veena Nakki Lake Rd. Open-air seating next to the main road. Quintessentially tacky Mount Abu (bright lights and the latest *filmi* hits blaring out), but the fast food is second to none, and they have a welcome open fire on the terrace most evenings. Try a tangy *pau bhaji* or melt-in-the-mouth *dosas*.

Moving on from Mount Abu

By bus

Government **buses** run from the state bus stand on Nakki Lake Road. There are services to Udaipur (4 daily; 5hr), Jaipur via Ajmer (1 nightly; 7hr to Ajmer, 11hr to Jaipur), Chittaurgarh (1 daily; 10hr), and Jodhpur (1 daily; 6hr). **Private buses** run to Ahmedabad (3 daily; 6hr), Udaipur (2 daily; 5–6hr), Jaipur via Ajmer (1 nightly; 7hr to Ajmer, 11hr to Jaipur), and Jodhpur (1 daily; 6hr). For timings and information, check at the *Shri Ganesh* guesthouse or at one of the numerous bus and travel agents along Nakki Lake Road west of the State Bus Stand (Gujarat Travels is a reliable option).

By train

There's a computerized **train booking office** (daily 8am–2pm) upstairs at the tourist office. Buses leave Mount Abu for **Abu Road**, the nearest railhead, every

Recommended trains from Abu Road

Destination	Name	No.	Departs	Arrives
Ajmer	Aravali Express	9707	9.58am (daily)	4.05pm
	Haridwar Mail	9105	2.05pm (daily)	8.10pm
Ahmedabad	Jammu Tawi–Ahmedabad Express	9224	11.45am (daily)	4.30pm
	Haridwar–Ahmedabad Mail	9106	12.48pm (daily)	5.35pm
Delhi	Ashram Express	2915	9.20pm (daily)	10.25am
Jaipur	Aravali Express	9707	9.58am (daily)	6.45pm
	Haridwar Mail	9105	2.05pm (daily)	10.45pm
Jodhpur	Ahmedabad–Jammu Tawi Express	9223	3.27pm (daily)	8.05pm
Mumbai	Ahmadebad–Mumbai Express	2990	00.25am (M, Th & S only)	1.05pm

hour until 9pm; Jeeps leave when full (from opposite the bus stand), and taxis can be hired at the corner by the *Jodhpur Bhojnalaya* restaurant for Rs250.

Chittaurgarh, Kota and Bundi

The belt of hilly land east of Udaipur is the most fertile in Rajasthan, watered by several perennial rivers and guarded by a sequence of imposing forts perched atop the craggy ridges which criss-cross the region. Heading east, the first major settlement is the historic town of **Chittaurgarh**, capital of the kingdom of Mewar before Udaipur and site of one of Rajasthan's most spectacular and historic forts. Further east, the tranquil town of **Bundi** boasts another atmospheric fort and picturesque old bazaars and havelis, while an hour away by bus, **Kota** is home to another impressive palace, if not much else.

A prime crop in this area for centuries has been **opium.** Although grown for the pharmaceutical industry according to strict government quotas, the legal cultivation masks a much larger illicit production overseen by Mumbai drug barons. An estimated one in five men in the area are addicts.

Chittaurgarh

Of all the former Rajput capitals, **CHITTAURGARH** (or Chittor), 115km northeast of Udaipur, was the strongest bastion of Hindu resistance against the Muslim invaders. No less than three mass suicides (*johars*) were committed over the centuries by the female inhabitants of its **fort**, whose husbands watched their wives, sisters and mothers burn alive before smearing ash from the sacred funeral pyres over their bodies and riding to their deaths on the battlefield below. An air of desolation still hangs over the honey-coloured ramparts, temples, towers and ruined palaces of the old citadel. It seems impossible to fathom that such an imposing structure, towering 180m over the Mewar valley on a rocky plateau, could have ever been taken, yet alone three times. As a symbol of Rajput chivalry and militarism only Jodhpur's Meherangarh Fort compares.

Below the fort, the modern **town**, spread over both banks of the River Ghambiri, holds little to detain travellers beyond the narrow bazaars of its old quarter, and some tourists choose to squeeze a tour of Chittaurgarh into a daytrip, or en route between Bundi and Udaipur. A one-night stop, however, leaves time for a more leisurely visit to the fort and a stroll through the town.

Some history

The origins of Chittor fort are obscure. According to legend it was founded by Bhim, one of the Pandava heroes of the Mahabharata, although it probably actually dates from around the 7th century. The fort was seized by **Bappa Rawal**, founder of the Mewar dynasty, in 734, and remained the Mewar capital thereafter for the next 834 years, bar a couple of brief interruptions.

Despite its commanding position and formidable appearance, however, Chittor was far from invincible, as proved by the three catastrophic attacks which blighted the city's later history and led to its eventual abandonment. The first sack of Chittor occurred in 1303, during the reign of **Rana Ratan Singh**, a devastating attack was launched by **Ala-ud-din-Khalji**, the fiercest of the Delhi sultans. Having besieged the city, he offered to withdraw on condition that he be allowed a glimpse of Ratan's famously beautiful queen, **Padmini**. After admitting him alone into the palace to view the queen's reflection in a

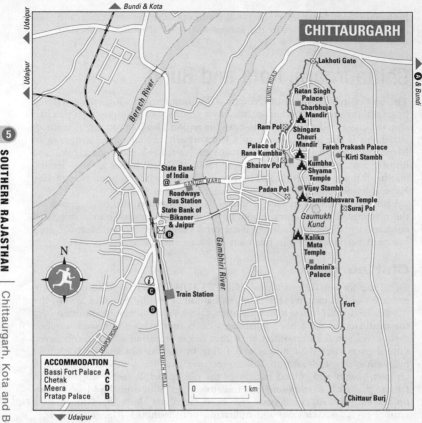

CHITTAURGARH

Bundi & Kota

Udaipur

Lakhoti Gate

Ratan Singh
Palace
Charbhuja
Mandir

Ram Pol

Shingara
Chauri
Mandir

Palace of
Rana Kumbha

Fateh Prakash Palace

Kirti Stambh

Bhairov Pol

Kumbha
Shyama
Temple

State Bank
of India

GANDHI MARG

Vijay Stambh

Roadways
Bus Station

Padan Pol

Samiddhesvara Temple

Suraj Pol

State Bank of
Bikaner
& Jaipur

Gaumukh
Kund

N

Kalika
Mata
Temple

Padmini's
Palace

Train Station

Fort

ACCOMMODATION
Bassi Fort Palace   A
Chetak   C
Meera   D
Pratap Palace   B

0   1 km

Chittaur Burj

Udaipur

Berach River

Gambhiri River

BUNDI ROAD

JODHPUR ROAD

NEEMUCH ROAD

lake, however, the sultan contrived to have Ratan ambushed just as he was showing him out of the door. Padmini devised a plan to recapture him. Sending word that she would give herself up to the sultan, the queen left the fort accompanied by troops disguised as maids of honour. As in the Greek story of the Trojan horse, once inside the Muslim camp the sari-clad commandos unveiled themselves and managed to rescue Rana Ratan, but not before seven thousand of them were killed in the process. As a result, the defence of the fort foundered and the Rajputs lost the ensuing battle. Thirteen thousand women, led by Padmini, committed *johar* by throwing themselves and their children onto a huge funeral pyre, whereupon the angry sultan destroyed most of the fort's temples and palaces.

After returning to Rajput hands in 1326, Chittaurgarh enjoyed two hundred years of prosperity. However, in 1535, an unexpected onslaught led by **Sultan Bahadur Shah** from Gujarat once again decimated the Rajput ranks, and the women surrendered their lives in another ghastly act of *johar*. Aware of Chittaurgarh's vulnerability, the young ruler of Mewar **Udai Singh** (see box, p.335) searched for a new site for his capital and, in 1559, established a new palace at Udaipur on the shore of Lake Pichola. This proved to be a prescient decision. **Akbar** laid siege to Chittaurgarh in 1567 and, after one of the longest, bloodiest and most famous sieges in Indian history, finally breached its defences the following year. Once more the fort's Rajput defenders sallied forth to death and glory, while the women sacrificed themselves on a raging pyre. Having finally gained the fort, Akbar devastated many of the buildings within it, and – in an action which rather undermines his reputation as the most humane and tolerant of the great Mughals – massacred at least twenty thousand non-combatant local villagers who had sought refuge within it. Chittaurgarh was eventually ceded back to the Rajputs in 1616 on condition that it was never refortified, but the royal family of Mewar, by now firmly ensconced in Udaipur, never resettled there, and the entire fort, which once boasted a population of many thousands, is now home to no more than a few hundred people.

The fort

The entire fort is 5km long and 1km wide, and you could easily spend a whole day up here nosing around the myriad remains, although most visitors content themselves with a few hours. **Tours** of the fort are most easily made by rickshaw (Rs200 for around 3hr); many hang out at the bus station awaiting tourists, though note that rickshaw drivers tend to take visitors to only the most famous monuments rather than around the entire fort, unless specifically requested. An alternative is to just take a rickshaw up to the entrance, and then explore on foot or, perhaps best, to rent a **bike** from the shop on the road leading west from the crossroads outside the station. It's a long and steep climb up to the fort, but most of the roads on the plateau itself are flat.

The Palace of Rana Kumbha to the Kumbha Shyama temple

The ascent to the fort (daily 7am–6pm), protected by massive bastions, begins at **Padan Pol** in the east of town and winds upwards through a further six gateways. About 100m uphill from the second gateway, Bhairov Pol, stand the memorial *chhatris* of Jaimal and his cousin Kalla, who carried the injured Jaimal piggyback into battle in the final sacking of 1568. The houses of the few people who still inhabit the fort are huddled together near the final gate, Rama Pol, where the foreign visitors (Rs100) and Indian residents (Rs5) **entry fee** is payable (plus Rs5 extra per rickshaw).

Entering the fort, you first reach the slowly deteriorating fifteenth-century **Palace of Rana Kumbha** (reigned 1433–68), built by the ruler who presided over the period of Mewar's greatest prosperity on the spot where Padmini (see opposite) is said to have committed *johar* in 1303. The main palace building still stands five-storeys high, though it's difficult to now make much sense of the confusing tangle of partially ruined walls, cupolas and towers which surround it, the general dereliction concealing a few finely carved balconies, pillars and friezes. Opposite the palace stands the intricately carved fifteenth-century **Shingara Chauri Mandir**, dedicated to Shantinath, the sixteenth *tirthankara*, a small but lavishly adorned Jain temple, though many of the faces around the main door have been obliterated, possibly by Islamic iconoclasts. Another, even smaller, Jain temple stands directly behind.

Nearby, the modern **Fateh Prakash Palace**, a large, plain edifice built for the maharana in the 1920s, is home to a small **archeological museum** (daily except Fri 10am–5pm; Rs3), filled with a forgettable display of weapons, costumes and pictures, plus a fine array of Jain and Hindu carvings recovered from various places around the fort.

A couple of hundred metres further on lies the imposing **Kumbha Shyama Temple**, the first of several superb Hindu temples which dot the fort and another creation of Rana Kumbha, after whom it's named. Crowned by a pyramidal roof and lofty tower, with every interior and exterior surface embellished in a riot of carved decoration, this marvellously ornate structure wouldn't look out of place amongst the famous temples of Khajuraho in Madhya Pradesh, and its sinuous, purely Indian outlines offer a striking architectural contrast to the more Islamic-influenced styles of the fort's palace buildings. A black statue of Garuda stands in its own pavilion in front of the shrine, while an image of Varaha, the boar incarnation of Vishnu, occupies a niche at the rear of the temple, surrounded by an open-side ambulatory from where there are fine views back to Rana Kumbha's palace. A second shrine stands close by within the small walled enclosure, also constructed by Rana Kumbha and dedicated to **Meerabai**, a Jodhpur princess and poet famed for her devotion to Krishna – smaller but almost equally finely decorated, with a similarly delicate curved tower.

The Vijay Stambh and beyond

The main road within the fort continues south to its focal point, **Vijay Stambh**, the soaring "tower of victory", erected by Rana Kumbha to commemorate his 1440 victory over the Muslim Sultan Mehmud Khilji of Malwa. This magnificent sand-coloured tower, whose nine storeys rise 36m, took a decade to build; its walls are lavishly carved with mythological scenes and images from all Indian religions, including Arabic inscriptions in praise of Allah. You can climb the dark narrow stairs to the very summit for free.

The area around the Vijay Stambh is littered with an impressive number of further remains, including a pair of monumental gateways and a number of florid temples, including the superb **Samiddhesvara Temple**, its *shikhara* tower honeycombed with deeply incised, geometrical carvings, while a frieze of busty celestial nymphs runs around the walls and a statue of a lion sits guard on the roof. The shrine inside houses an image of the three-headed *trimurti*, a composite, three-headed image of Shiva, Brahma and Vishnu. A path leads from here down to the **Gaumukh Kund**, a large reservoir fed by an underground stream that trickles through carved mouths (*mukh*) of cows (*gau*) and commands superb views across the plains. On the other side of the enclosure, clusters of small *chhatris* and red-painted stones commemorate some of the acts of *sati* performed by women of the fort.

Buildings further south include the **Kalika Mata Temple**, originally dedicated to Surya in the eighth century, but rededicated to the Mother Goddess, Mahadevi, after renovations in 1568. Carvings on the outer wall include a frieze depicting the churning of the ocean by the gods and demons, a popular creation myth, and (next to it) another image of Varaha, the boar-headed incarnation of Vishnu. Some 200m beyond the Kalika Mata Temple lies **Padmini's Palace**, its rather plain buildings enclosing a series of attractive little walled gardens leading to a tower overlooking the small lake in which Ala-ud-din Khalji was allegedly allowed to glimpse the reflection of the beautiful princess after whom the palace is named (see p.361).

The road continues south past the deer park to the point once used for hurling traitors to their deaths, and returns north along the eastern ridge to **Suraj Pol** gate, with spectacular vistas across a patchwork of farmland. Several temples line the route, but the most impressive monument is **Kirti Stambh**. The inspiration for the tower of victory, this smaller "tower of fame" was built by Digambaras as a monument to the first *tirthankara* Adinath, whose unclad image appears throughout its six storeys.

△ Vijay Stambh at Chittaurgarh

Practicalities

Chittaurgarh's **railway station** is in the western corner of the city. From here it's about 2km north to the **Roadways** (aka "**Kothwali**") **bus stand** on the west bank of the Ghambiri, and a further 2km east to the base of the fort. The RTDC **tourist office** (Mon–Sat 10am–5pm; ☎01472/241089), where you can obtain free maps of the town and hire government-registered guides (Rs230 for up to 4hr), stands just north of the railway station on Station Road. There are **ATM**s at the State Bank of India and the State Bank of Bikaner & Jaipur. **Internet** access is available at both the *Pratap Palace* and *Meera* hotels; alternatively try Megavista Internet, on the way into town.

Accommodation and eating

While Chittaurgarh's mid- and upper-range **hotels** cost a little more than elsewhere, places at the lower end of the price scale are pretty dingy – this is one place budget travellers might want to splash out (if you don't, there are a few cheap but fairly grim hotels around the train station and in town). Outside Chittor, the peaceful *Castle Bijaipur* makes an appealing alternative to staying in the town itself.

Bassi Fort Palace Bassi, 24km east of Chittaurgarh ☎ 01472/225321, ⓦ www.bassifortpalace.com. Attractive heritage hotel, occupying the town's florid palace, with sixteen comfortable rooms and spacious grounds where you'll find a sacred tree which is believed to grant all one's wishes ... allegedly. The hotel also runs a tented camp close to the nearby Bassi Wildlife Sanctuary, home to leopards and other indigenous wildlife. ❼

Castle Bijaipur ☎ 01472/240099, ⓦ www.castlebijaipur.com. This lovely hotel occupies a superb 350-year-old castle set in a tranquil and unspoilt rural location a 45-minute (32km) drive east of Chittor. Rooms are decorated with traditional Rajasthani wooden furniture and artefacts, and there's a pool, Ayurvedic massages, daily group yoga and meditation sessions (and individual tuition on request), plus cycle, jeep and horse safaris to nearby villages. Day-trips to Chittor can be arranged for Rs700. They also have tented accommodation (❼) a few kilometres away in an even more remote rural location at Pangarh Lake. ❼

Chetak Neemuch Road, immediately outside the railway station ☎ 01472/241679. Passable budget option, with spotless modern rooms (though avoid the noisy ones next to the main road) and a busy little restaurant downstairs. ❸–❺

Meera Neemuch Road ☎ 01472/240266. The best option in town for budget travellers, with a wide selection of fan and a/c rooms, plus some very quirkily decorated suites; facilities include an inexpensive restaurant and bar, plus Internet access. ❸–❺

Pratap Palace Opposite the GPO on Shri Gurukul Road ☎ 01472/240099, ⓦ www.castlebijaipur.com. This pleasant mid-range hotel is a bit shabby in places, but boasts an attractive garden, good food and Internet access. The smarter deluxe and super-deluxe a/c rooms are the nicest in town (though rather expensive); the cheaper rooms are relatively unappealing and overpriced. They can also arrange horse, jeep and cycle safaris in the surrounding countryside, starting from their sister property, *Castle Bijaipur* (see left). ❺–❻

Moving on from Chittaurgarh

There are regular **buses** (but no trains) to Ajmer (hourly; 5hr), as well as services to Udaipur (hourly; 3hr–3hr 30min); Kota (6 daily; 4hr 30min); and Bundi (4 daily; 5hr). For other destinations you're better off catching one of the **trains** listed in the box below.

Bundi

The walled town of **BUNDI**, 37km north of Kota, lies in the north of the former Hadaoti state, shielded on the north, east and west by jagged outcrops of the Vindhya Range. Visible only from the south and guarded by the tremendous

Recommended trains from Chittaurgarh				
Destination	**Name**	**No.**	**Departs (daily)**	**Arrives**
Bundi	Nimach–Kota Express	9019A	2.55pm	5.10pm
Delhi (Hazrat Nizamuddin)	Mewar Express	2964	8.50pm	6.15am
Jaipur	Udaipur–Jaipur Superfast Express	2966	11.50pm	7.10am
Kota	Nimach–Kota Express	9019A	2.55pm	6pm
Udaipur	Mewar Express	2963	5am	7am
	Jaipur–Udaipur Express	2965	5.40am	7.45am

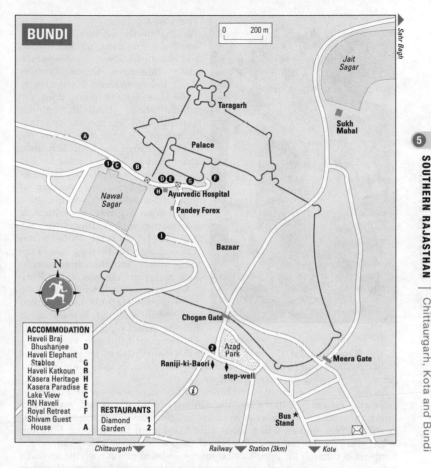

BUNDI

0   200 m

Sahr Bagh

Jait Sagar

Taragarh

Sukh Mahal

Palace

Ⓐ

❶ⒸⒷ

ⒹⒺⒼ Ⓕ

Ⓗ **Ayurvedic Hospital**

Nawal Sagar

■ **Pandey Forex**

Ⓘ

Bazaar

N

Chogan Gate

ACCOMMODATION

Haveli Braj Bhushanjee	D
Haveli Elephant Stabloo	G
Haveli Katkoun	B
Kasera Heritage	H
Kasera Paradise	E
Lake View	C
RN Haveli	I
Royal Retreat	F
Shivam Guest House	A

❷ **Azad Park**

Ranjji-ki-Baori ◆

◆ **step-well**

ⓘ

RESTAURANTS

Diamond	1
Garden	2

Bus Stand ★

Meera Gate

✉

Chittaurgarh ▼   *Railway* ▼ *Station (3km)*   ▼ *Kota*

Taragarh or "star fort" high in the north of town, the site made a perfect capital for the Hadachauhans, perched in their immense turreted **palace** beneath the lofty walls of the fort. Although settled in 1241, 25 years before Kota, Bundi never amounted to more than a modest market centre, and remains relatively untouched by modern developments. The palace alone justifies a visit thanks to its superb collection of **murals**, while the almost complete absence of intrusive modern structures within the **old walled town**, crammed with crumbling stucco havelis, makes this one of southern Rajasthan's most laid-back and appealing destinations – a fact recognized by the increasing numbers of foreign tourists who are now visiting the place.

The town

Bundi is small, and easily explored on foot. Dominating the town, the craggy **Taragarh** fort is home to the town's **palace**. South of here the narrow streets of the old town run gently downhill through a sequence of lively bazaars to reach Chogan Gate and the superb **Ranjji-ki-Baori** (step-well). Further low-key attractions lie dotted around the surrounding countryside, including the fine old **Sukh Mahal** and the evocative **Sahr Bagh** gardens.

The Palace

Walking north through the bazaar, you'll see the stone domes, cupolas and bleached walls of Bundi's **palace** (daily 7am–5pm, foreign visitors Rs50, Indian residents Rs10; camera Rs50, video Rs100) spilling down the hillside ahead. Built during the sixteenth and seventeenth centuries in authentic Rajput style, it was one of the few royal abodes in Rajasthan untouched by Mughal influence and its appearance is surprisingly homogeneous considering the number of times it was added to over the years. If you want a **guide**, the extremely informative Keshav Bhati (☎0/941 439 4241, ⓔbharat_bhati@yahoo .com) charges Rs200 for a tour of the entire palace, and also offers visits to local rock paintings sites and of Kota.

A short steep path winds up to the main gateway, **Hathi Pol**, surmounted by elephant carvings, beyond which lies the palace's principal courtyard.

△ Chogan Gate, Bundi

On the right-hand side, steps lead up to the **Ratan Daulat**, the early seventeenth-century Diwan-i-Am, or Hall of Public Audience, an open terrace with a few naive murals and a simple marble throne overlooking the courtyard below.

At the far end of the Ratan Daulat, further steps lead up to the *zenana* (women's quarters), entered via the **Chhatra Mahal**, centred on a small courtyard with a marble pool at its centre and fine views over the town and its numerous blue houses, which looks a bit like a miniature Jodhpur from this angle; you can also make out the **Nawal Sagar** tank with its half-submerged temple. Go through the open-sided turquoise-painted pavilion on the southern side of the courtyard and the room beyond to reach a superb little **antechamber** (usually described as a "dressing room"). This is one of the most beautiful rooms in the palace, every surface covered in finely detailed murals including scenes showing Krishna playing his flute amidst cows and *gopis*; a spectacular procession with hundreds of horses, soldiers and some superb elephants; scenes of courtly life; and (in a niche by the window) a stirring battle scene. The opposite side of the courtyard is flanked by a pavilion with columns supported on the backs of quaint black trumpeting elephants, at the back of which you'll find a well-preserved old squat toilet (still in occasional use, judging by the smell), offering possibly the best view from any public convenience in Rajasthan.

From the Chattra Mahal courtyard, a narrow flight of steps leads up to the **Phool Mahal** (1607), with an even smaller courtyard flanked by another superbly decorated room, its murals including a vast procession featuring regiments of soldiers in European dress, a camel corps and yet more elephants and horses. From here further narrow steps ascend to the **Badal Mahal** (Cloud Palace; also built 1607), home to what are often regarded as the finest paintings in Bundi, if not the whole of southern Rajasthan. A vividly coloured ring of Krishnas and Radhas dance around the highest part of the vaulted dome, flanked in the two subsidiary domes by murals showing Krishna being driven to his wedding by Ganesh, and Rama returning from Sri Lanka to Ayodhya following the battle against Ravana described in the Ramayana; the god is shown travelling through the sky in his air-chariot, borne on the shoulders of four winged angels, while Hanuman looks on, brandishing a palm frond. The ten various human and animal incarnations of Vishnu are shown around the base of the dome.

The Chittra Sala

There are further outstanding murals in the **Chittra Sala** (sunrise–sunset; free), just above the palace (to reach it, exit the palace, go downhill for 20m then head up the signed ramp on your left, up the hill and in past the sign saying VEDIOGRAPHY PROBIBIRED). At the rear left-hand corner of the garden inside, steps lead up to a small courtyard embellished with an outstanding sequence of murals painted in an unusual muted palette of turquoises, blues and blacks. The main panels are (as usual) devoted to scenes from the life of Krishna, with successive murals showing the divine young shepherd boy dancing in a ring with the *gopis* (while various deities hover overhead in floating palanquins); lifting Mount Goverdhan with the little finger of his fourth arm while simultaneously playing the flute and brandishing a lotus; and sitting in a tree playing his flute after having stolen the clothes of the *gopis*, who splash around in the river below. On the opposite wall is a fine mural showing a panorama of eighteenth-century Bundi, with a stylized map on the right.

A steep, twenty-minute climb up from the Chittra Sala, the monkey-infested **Taragarh** offers even more spectacular views over Bundi, its palace and the surrounding countryside.

The rest of the town

On the south side of town lies one of Rajasthan's most spectacular step-wells, the **Raniji-ki-Baori**, built in 1699 by Nathwati, wife of Rao Raja Singh. One of fifty step-wells in Bundi, the well is reached by a flight of steps punctuated by platforms and pillars embellished with sinuous S-shaped brackets and elephant capitals. As you descend, look for the beautifully carved panels showing the ten avatars of Lord Vishnu which line the side walls. Note that there are no formal opening hours for the well, which often closes around lunchtime. A **second step-well** sits next to the road immediately to the east – impressively deep, but now choked with rubbish.

Northeast of the town, the beautiful **Sukh Mahal** – Rao Raja Vishnu Singh's summer palace – on the southern shore of **Jait Sagar** tank, is where Rudyard Kipling (who stayed here for a few months at the invitation of the raja) wrote parts of *Kim* and the *Jungle Book*; it's now the regional water authority's resthouse and generally closed to visitors, but you can take a pleasant stroll in the gardens. Further along the northwest side of the lake, 1.5km beyond the RTDC hotel, the **Sahr Bagh** encloses sixty crumbling royal cenotaphs. If the door is locked, ask for the key at the *chowkidar*'s hut on your left just after the gateway over the main road. You can rent paddleboats to splash around on the Jait Sagar at the RTDC hotel (Rs50/hr).

Practicalities

Buses arrive in the southeast part of town near the post office, from where it's about five minutes by rickshaw (Rs20–30) to the palace and most guest-houses; the train station is around 5km south of town (Rs40–50 by rickshaw). Bundi's **tourist office** (Mon–Sat 10am–5pm; ☏0747/244 3697) is south of town near the *Ishwari Niwas* hotel. You can **change money** at Pandey Forex, about 100m south of the palace, and at the *Kasera Heritage* guesthouse. There are dozens of places in the main tourist area offering Internet access for around Rs40 per hour. Lots of places also rent out **motorbikes** (around Rs250/day), and a few also have **bicycles** (or try *Kasera Heritage*, which has both; bikes for just Rs10/day).

If you're in the area around mid-November try to arrive for the annual **Bundi Festival**, a celebration of Hadaoti heritage with a very local, country-fair feel.

Accommodation and eating

Much of Bundi's **accommodation** is in old havelis, with a big selection of budget rooms – standards are often rather basic, but rates are among the cheapest in Rajasthan. The vast majority of places are lined up along the (seemingly nameless) road that runs directly below the castle along the north side of Nawal Sagar. Most people **eat** where they're staying; otherwise, the pleasant garden restaurant at the *Haveli Katkoun* is usually the liveliest place in town.

Haveli Braj Bhushanjee ℡0747/244 2322, Ⓦwww.kiplingsbundi.com. Bundi's most appealing mid-range option, this 150-year-old haveli is full of character, with original murals, antiques and assorted other artworks adorning virtually every surface. Rooms (the more expensive ones with a/c and TV) are similarly characterful, and immaculately maintained. There's also delicious, if rather pricey, home-cooked food (though no meat or beer) and Internet access. The attached *Badi Haveli* at the back (same rates) has larger and quieter rooms, though less atmosphere. ❹–❼

Haveli Elephant Stables ℡0/992 815 4064. Just three rooms (2 doubles and 1 single) in the palace's former elephant stables, which occupy a pretty and very peaceful spot underneath the huge walls which flank the path up to the entrance. Rooms are fairly basic, but at this price and in this location you can't really complain. ❶–❷

Haveli Katkoun Near Gopal Mandir Balchand para ℡0747/244 4311, Ⓦwww.haveli-katkoun.com. The most popular budget guesthouse in town at present, with four immaculate, newly furnished rooms overlooking the leafy garden, plus two more basic and noisier ones right next to the pleasant and lively garden restaurant. ❷–❸

Kasera Heritage ℡0/982 917 0982, Ⓦwww.kaseraparadise.com. Budget offshoot of the nearby *Kasera Paradise*, with inexpensive but clean and attractive rooms in an old haveli – even the cheapest have attached bath and hot water, and there's also the inevitable rooftop restaurant. ❶–❸

Kasera Paradise ℡0747/244 4679, Ⓦwww.kaseraparadise.com. Tucked away in a tiny lane just behind the *Braj Bhushanjee*, this attractive guesthouse occupies a meticulously restored

sixteenth-century haveli with old stone pillars and balconies set around a small interior courtyard. There's a big selection of variously priced rooms (some with a/c and TV) – all are refreshingly quiet and peaceful, while the more expensive ones boast attractive murals and nice furnishings. ❷–❻

Lake View ℡0747/244 2326, Ⓔlakeviewbundi @yahoo.com. Scruffy old guesthouse in the haveli once occupied by the *diwan* (prime minister) of Bundi, whose family still run the place. It's not the cleanest guesthouse in town, but has one of Bundi's best views, with a huge terrace overlooking Nawal Sagar tank, and inexpensive rates. The cheapest rooms are out in the garden and are pretty basic – the more expensive ones in the haveli itself have faded old murals and lake views. Decent food, with a good selection of cheap veg options from Rs30 (try the "Rajasthani pizza" or the "Excrmbal egg with chees"). ❶–❸

RN Haveli ℡0747/512 0098, Ⓔrnhavelibundi@yahoo.co.in. By some accounts the best guesthouse in Rajasthan, if only because it's run entirely by women – the delightfully cheeky sisters Rachana and Archana and their mother Kamla, who have managed to keep their guesthouse going despite persistent bad-mouthing from certain of their bigoted male rivals in town and suffering a series of dirty tricks ranging from seeing their signs defaced to having raw sewage diverted into their garden. The 200-year-old haveli itself is a bit run-down and the rooms are basic, but they're cheap and clean, and the home-cooked meals are excellent. ❶–❷

Royal Retreat ℡0747/244 4426. Just five rooms (all air-cooled) in a superb and peaceful location in a courtyard in the lower part of the palace complex (formerly home to the palace's printing and dyeing works) – although the place can feel a mite lonely after dark, especially if there's no one else staying. Rooms are nicely furnished, and the cheaper ones (especially the two Rs300 rooms) are surprisingly good value given the location. There's decent food in the attached restaurant, which is also a superb place for a sunset beer. ❷–❺

Shivam Tourist Guesthouse ☎0/946 030 0272, @shivam_pg@yahoo.com. Friendly and intimate little family guesthouse with four clean and good-sized en-suite rooms (and two more planned), decorated with traditional Rajasthani murals. Good home cooking too. ❶–❷

Moving on from Bundi

Heading south, there are regular buses to **Kota** (every 30min; 45min–1hr), but no convenient trains. There are two fast trains to **Chittaurgarh** daily at 7.20am (#282 Haldighati Passenger) and 9.20am (#9020A Dehra Dun Express), arriving at 10.35am and noon respectively; Chittaurgarh is also served by four buses daily (5hr, though road improvements may have reduced the journey time to 3hr by the time you read this). There are two buses daily to **Udaipur** via Chittor but no trains; the journey currently takes around eight hours, though improvements to the road to Chittor may have knocked a couple of hours off this by the time this book is published.

Heading north, **Sawai Madhopur** (for Ranthambore National Park) is most easily reached by catching a bus to Kota and then picking up a train (see p.374 for details). Alternatively there are a few direct buses daily, currently taking an agonizingly slow and bumpy 4–5 hours, though ongoing road improvements may have knocked around an hour off the journey by the time you read this. Buses are also the best way of reaching **Ajmer** (hourly; 4hr), **Jaipur** (hourly; 5hr), **Jodhpur** (three daily; 10hr) and **Pushkar** (3 daily; 5hr).

Kota

KOTA, 230km south of Jaipur on a fertile plain fed by Rajasthan's largest river, the Chambal, is one of the state's dirtier and less appealing cities. With a population nudging 700,000, it is one of Rajasthan's major commercial and industrial hubs, with hydro, atomic and thermal power stations lining the banks of the Chambal, alongside Asia's largest fertilizer plant, whose enormous chimneys provide a not-very-scenic backdrop to many views of the town. Foreign visitors are sufficiently unusual here to attract stares in the street, but Kota is worth a visit if only for its city palace, which houses one of the better museums in Rajasthan, while the old town has a pleasantly stimulating commercial hustle and bustle which makes a nice contrast to somnolent Bundi, just down the road.

Greatly prized **saris** from the village of **Kaithoon**, 20km southeast of Kota, are sold in all the bazaars. Made of tightly woven cotton or silk, and often highlighted with golden thread, they are known here as *masooria* and elsewhere as *Kota doria* saris.

The City Palace

The huge walls of Kota's **fort**, built in 1264 by Rajkumar Jait Singh of Bundi, rise above the flat eastern bank of the Chambal, encircling the old town centre (although they've now been largely swallowed up by modern buildings). At the southern end of the fort, around 2km from the bus station, lies the **City Palace**, a well-preserved cluster of royal residences painted an incongruous mixture of very pale sky-blue and fleshy salmon pink; construction on them began in 1625 and continued sporadically until the early years of this century. The palace now houses the excellent **Maharao Madho Singh Museum** (daily except Fri 10am–4.30pm; combined entrance to museum and palace foreign visitors Rs100, Indian residents Rs10, camera Rs50, video Rs100). The first room is

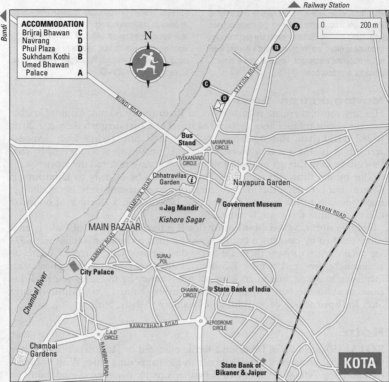

ACCOMMODATION
Brijraj Bhawan	C
Navrang	D
Phul Plaza	D
Sukhdam Kothi	B
Umed Bhawan	
Palace	A

Railway Station

0   200 m

N

BUNDI ROAD

STATION ROAD

Bus Stand

NAYAPURA CIRCLE

VIVEKANAND CIRCLE

Chhatravilas Garden

Nayapura Garden

RAMPURA ROAD

Jag Mandir

Kishore Sagar

Goverment Museum

BARAN ROAD

MAIN BAZAAR

BARRAGE ROAD

SURAJ POL

Chambal River

City Palace

CHAWNI CIRCLE

State Bank of India

RAWATBHATA ROAD

AERODROME CIRCLE

C.A.D CIRCLE

Chambal Gardens

RANGBARI ROAD

State Bank of Bikaner & Jaipur

KOTA

filled with a selection of the usual luxury items which were considered *de rigueur* by any status-conscious Indian ruler, including elaborate howdahs and palanquins, silver hookah pipes, a gem-studded chair and a magnificent silver painted throne. Walk diagonally across the courtyard to reach the dazzling **Raj Mahal**, built by Rao Madho Singh (ruled 1625–49), though the lavish paintings and mirrorwork date from the nineteenth and twentieth centuries, which served as the ruler's public audience hall. An attached room is decorated with religious miniatures and further mirrors.

From the Raj Mahal, a corridor leads into a further sequence of rooms. These begin with a well-stocked **armoury**, home to an unusual golden fish emblem, the Mahi Maratib, awarded by the Mughals to high-ranking rajas and carried aloft in procession. Beyond here a large room is filled with rather dull photos of the rulers of Kota and their nearest and dearest, along with the occasional Britisher. The next room contains a small art gallery containing a few fine (but poorly displayed) **miniatures**, mainly of various maharajas on horseback, complete with shiny little halos, a visual combination designed to emphasize both their military prowess and kingly virtues. The depressing **wildlife gallery** downstairs is mainly filled with the mothy remains of various leopards and tigers.

Exit the museum then follow the steps up past the Raj Mahal to reach a series of finely painted palace buildings. Two storeys up, the red-pillared **Barah Dari** offers good town views. A storey above is the **Barah Mahal**, one of whose rooms is richly decorated with dozens of square miniatures placed together on the wall like tiles and depicting a range of religious and contemporary scenes, from Krishna lifting Mount Goverdhan to exotic-looking European ladies and gentlemen.

The rest of the city

Kishore Sagar, an artificial lake built in 1346, gives some visual relief from the city's grim industrial backdrop; the red-and-white palace in its centre, **Jag Mandir**, was commissioned by Prince Dher Deh of Bundi in 1346. On the northern edge of the lake the dusty **Government Museum** (daily 10am–5pm; Rs3) serves as the dispiriting home for an excellent collection of local stone carvings (signs in Hindi only, if at all), including a few voluptuous heavenly nymphs and four-armed Vishnus carved in a dark, coppery stone, plus a fine sequence of miniatures showing scenes from the life of Krishna.

On the edge of the river a few kilometres south of the fort, crocodiles and gharial sun themselves in a shallow pond in the **Chambal Gardens** (Rs2); boats depart from here for fifteen minute tours (Rs15) of the crocodile-infested River Chambal.

Practicalities

Kota's **railway station** is in the north of town, a few kilometres from the central **bus stand** on Bundi Road. The **tourist office** (Mon–Sat 10am–5pm; ☎0744/232 7695) is in the RTDC *Chambal Hotel*, just north of the Kishor Sagar. The best place for changing **traveller's cheques** is the inconveniently located State Bank of Bikaner & Jaipur in the south of town; alternatively try the State Bank of India (Amex only) on Chawni Circle. There are no less than four 24hr **ATMs** scattered around the road intersection by the *Navrang* hotel; all accept both Visa and MasterCard. The **post office** is northeast of the bus stand on Station Road.

Accommodation and eating

Kota's **hotels** cater mainly for passing business travellers, and the cheaper places reflect the neglect that prevails in the town; if you can't afford to stay in one of the places below, it's better to base yourself in Bundi. For **eating**, the modern *Venue* pure veg restaurant, attached to the *Navrang* hotel, has a good selection of north Indian veg mains (most around Rs50) plus *dosas*, pizzas and Chinese dishes.

Brijraj Bhawan Civil Lines ☎0744/245 0529, ✉brijraj@datainfosys.net. An idyllic retreat in the heart of noisy Kota, occupying a lovely old yellow colonial mansion set in a very peaceful spot overlooking the river amidst beautiful gardens. Rooms are pure period pieces, with old Victorian wooden furniture, and fetching old paintings and prints on the walls, all scrupulously maintained and very comfortable. **❼**

Navrang Station Rd ☎0744/232 3294. A cut above the other cheap hotels in town for cleanliness and service, with a mix of simple air-cooled and more attractively furnished a/c rooms, all with TV. **❸–❹**

Phul Plaza Station Rd ☎0744/232 9351. Inexpensive, functional business hotel. The rooms here are actually fractionally nicer (and cheaper) than the air-cooled ones at the adjacent *Navrang*, though

the overall atmosphere is drabber and less appealing. There's also a passable veg restaurant and a gloomy bar downstairs. **❸**

Sukhdam Kothi Civil Lines ☎0744/232 0081 or 233 2661, ✉sukhdam@datainfosys.net. Marvellously atmospheric guesthouse located in a hundred-year-old stone mansion set amid three acres of gardens. Rooms are comfy and atmospheric, with old wooden furniture, paintings and other nineteenth-century bits and pieces. **❻**

Umed Bhawan Palace Station Road, Khelri Phatak ☎0744/232 5262, ⓦwww.welcomeritage.com. Occupying a huge and rather ugly former royal residence, this fancy hotel offers upmarket comforts (and a fair bit of chintz) at a reasonable price, though it lacks the atmosphere of the *Brijraj Bhawan* and *Sukhdam Kothi*. **❼**

Moving on from Kota

Buses leave regularly from the stand near Nayapura Circle to Bundi (every 30min; 45min–1hr); Ajmer (every 30min; 6hr); Chittor (6 daily; 4hr 30min); Jaipur (12 daily; 6hr); and Udaipur (10 daily; 6hr). Kota also has good **train** connections, the most convenient of which are listed in the box.

Recommended trains from Kota

Destination	Name	No.	Departs	Arrives
Agra (Agra Fort)	Avadh Express	9037	2.55pm (M, W, Th & Sa)	9.45pm
Bundi	Dehra Dun Express	9020A	9.05am (daily)	9.18am
Chittaurgarh	Dehra Dun Express	9020A	9.05am (daily)	noon
Delhi (Hazrat Nizamuddin)	Kota Jan Shatabdi	2059	6am (except Sun)	12.25pm
	Rajdhani Express	2431	7.05am (Thu & Sat)	12.35pm
	Golden Temple Mail	2903	11.25am (daily)	6.23pm (New Delhi 6.05pm)
	Mewar Express	2964	11.55pm (daily)	6.15am
Jaipur	Dayodaya Express	2181	8.35am (daily)	12.30pm
	Mumbai–Jaipur Express	2955	8.55am (daily)	12.55pm
Mumbai	Mumbai Rajdhani	2952	9.05pm (daily)	8.35am
	Kranti Rajdhani	2954	9.55pm (daily)	10.15am
Sawai Madhopur (for Ranthambore National Park)	Dayodaya Express	2181	8.35am (daily)	10am
	Golden Temple Mail	2903	11.25am (daily)	12.35pm
	Avadh Express	9037	2.55pm (M, W, Th & Sa)	4.20pm

Contexts

Contexts

History

T he history of **northwestern India** – the region containing modern Rajasthan, Delhi and Agra – has played a seminal role in the development of the Subcontinent. South Asia's first great civilization developed in the valley of the Indus river, just west of Rajasthan in what is now Pakistan, and the region was also the first to experience the impact of the endless waves of invaders who swept down from the mountains of Central Asia into the Subcontinent over the succeeding centuries. These invaders – ranging from the first Indo-Aryans through successive waves of Greeks, Persians, Huns, Scythians, Parthians, Afghans, Mongols and Mughals – each helped shape the history, culture and ethnic make-up of the region, sometimes in ways which are now so buried in the past that they have become almost impossible to decipher.

It's no coincidence, therefore, that India's most historically important city, **Delhi**, should be located at this cultural crossroads between Central Asia and the wide-open plains of the Subcontinent. The city has been home to a remarkable array of dynasties, ranging from the semi-legendary heroes of the Mahabharata through to twentieth-century British imperialists, and also served for centuries as the principal meeting place between India's Hindu majority and roving Muslim empire builders. The latter were also responsible for the most glorious days of nearby **Agra**, the Mughal capital *par excellence* and home to its most memorable monuments, including the unforgettable Taj Mahal. Interlopers from Central Asia are also central to the early history of **Rajasthan**, though for much of its subsequent history the region has remained somewhat isolated and introspective, protected by its expanses of desert and craggy fortresses and enjoying a political and physical separation which has fostered the development of one of India's most colourful and staunchly Hindu cultures.

Prehistory

The earliest human activity in the Indian Subcontinent can be traced back to the **Stone Age** (400,000–200,000 BC). Implements from this period have been found all over India, from Rajasthan and Gujarat in the west to Bihar in the east. These Paleolithic peoples were semi-nomadic **hunters and gatherers** for many millennia.

Around 2500 BC, one of the world's earliest civilizations – roughly contemporary with those of Sumer and ancient Egypt – began to develop, centred around the Indus Valley (now in Pakistan) and its tributaries. Known variously as the **Indus Valley Civilization** or the **Harappan Civilization**, this first great Subcontinental culture spread across a sizeable proportion of what is now southern Pakistan and the periphery of western India; archeological remains of Harappan-style culture have been discovered as far afield as Lothal in Gujarat and at several places in Rajasthan. The most celebrated of these is at the town of **Kalibangan**, in a remote spot in northern Rajasthan close to the Pakistan border (some 205km from Bikaner), where the remains of a town have been uncovered, built on a grid plan, with temples devoted to the worship of fire and relics of a well-developed agricultural society, including what is claimed to be the remains of the world's oldest ploughed field.

The Vedic Age

The written history of India begins with the arrival of the charioteering **Indo-European** or **Aryan** tribes, who emerged from the steppes of Central Asia at around the start of the second millennium BC and proceeded to raid and conquer their way across the length and breadth of the Eurasian continent, eventually settling in Europe, the Middle East and the Indian Subcontinent, where they rapidly overwhelmed the remains of the Indus Valley civilization. This period of Indian history is usually known as the **Vedic Age**, after the earliest Indian literature, the **Vedas**, collections of Aryan religious hymns composed in Sanskrit. By 1000 BC, the Aryans had become integrated with the indigenous inhabitants of India, establishing a fourfold division of society based on the **varnas** (see p.398), the origin of the caste system which persists to this day.

The first Aryan settlements were concentrated in northwest India and the Punjab, though during the later Vedic period, between 1000 and 600 BC, the centre of Aryan culture and power shifted to the Doab, the region between the Ganges and Yamuna rivers in modern Uttar Pradesh (including the area around modern Agra), whence their influence continued to spread eastwards and southwards. Many **sacred texts** including the Upanishads, Mahabharata and the Ramayana (see p.397), date from this period. Though they are unreliable as historical sources, being overlaid with accretions from later centuries, it's possible to extract some of the facts entwined with the martial myths and legends. The great battle of **Kurukshetra** – the central theme of the Mahabharata – is certainly historical, and took place near modern Delhi some time in the ninth and eighth centuries BC. Archeological evidence has been found of the two main settlements mentioned in the epic: Indraprastha (Delhi) and Hastinapura, further north on the Ganges.

Invaders from the west

For the thousand years following the arrival of the Aryans, the regions which would later become Rajasthan and Delhi remained at the periphery of northern Indian history, which largely developed along the fertile **Ganges valley**, where a string of important new cities such as Magadha, Ayodhya and Pataliputra (modern Patna) were established, and where the new Buddhist and Jain religions first emerged. This period of steady internal development was interrupted by further invaders arriving in the northwest including, most importantly, **Alexander the Great**, who crossed the Indus in 326 BC, and overran the Punjab. He stayed in India for just two years and although he left garrisons and appointed satraps to govern the conquered territories, his death in 323 BC made their position untenable.

The ensuing political vacuum was quickly exploited by Chandragupta Maurya, who around 321 BC seized control of the major city of Magadha, in the Ganges valley in central northern India, and rapidly overran large portions of north India, thus establishing the **Mauryan Empire**, the first great Indian dynasty. From about 297 BC onwards, Chandragupta's son Bindusara and grandson Ashoka successively extended the empire south to Mysore, east to Assam and west to Afghanistan, though it appears to have had little influence on

Rajasthan, which remained a peripheral area of small kingdoms contested by local tribes such as the Bhils and Minas, who still survive in isolated pockets of the state to this day.

After Ashoka's death in 232 BC, the empire began to fall apart and India became politically fragmented. Successive **invasions** followed as different ethnic groups from Central Asia poured down into the Subcontinent, fighting with and displacing one another in turn. This deeply confused historical period is impossible to follow in any detail, though is important in the context of Rajasthan since it is probable that at least some of these invaders would become the ancestors of people who were later to become the celebrated Rajput clans who loom so large in the history of India.

The Bactrian Greeks of Gandhara were the first to arrive, followed by Parthians from Iran, Yueh-Chi Central Asian nomads and – most importantly in the light of the subsequent history of Rajasthan – the Scythians, or **Shakas**, from the Aral Sea area. This chaotic period was interrupted by the emergence of the **Guptas** (320–550 AD), during which north India was once again reunified into a single empire. The first great Gupta ruler, Chandra Gupta I (no relation to the Mauryan Guptas), established a powerful kingdom centred on Magadha in the Ganges valley in central northern India. His son and heir, Samudra Gupta (c.335–376 AD), expanded the empire from the Punjab to Assam and, according to an inscription in Allahabad, "violently uprooted" nine kings of northern India and temporarily incorporated parts of Rajasthan into the Gupta empire.

By the mid-fifth century, however, western India was again threatened by invasions from Central Asia. The last major Gupta ruler, Skanda Gupta (reigned 455–467 AD), managed to repel repeated raids by the **Huns**, another nomadic people who had wandered into India from Central Asia, but after his death their disruption of Central Asian trade seriously destabilized the empire. By the end of the fifth century, the Huns had wrested the Punjab from Gupta control, and further incursions early in the sixth century dealt the death blow to the empire, which had completely disintegrated by 550 AD. At around the same time, another wave of Central Asian tribes, the **Gurjaras**, also arrived in west India, and established themselves in Gujarat and parts of what is now southern Rajasthan.

The emergence of the Rajputs

During the sixth and seventh centuries, a new warrior class emerged in northern and western India who described themselves as **Rajputs** (a corruption of *Raj-puteras*, meaning "son of a raja" – raja being translated variously as "prince" or "king") and who gradually seized control of large areas of northern India. Exactly who this new warrior class was and where they came from remains a mystery, although it seems most likely that the Rajputs were largely or entirely of foreign origin, the descendants of the waves of invaders who poured into northwest India from Central Asia between the third and sixth centuries AD, and who were gradually integrated into Indian society. The Huns, Shakas (Scythians) and Gurjaras have all been named as possible progenitors, and quite possibly all three (and probably quite a few other) ethnic groups all played a part in establishing this new bloodline in Indian society. It's worth noting that the name originally had no particular ethnic or geographical connotations, and that even today self-professed Rajputs can be found not only in Rajasthan, but also in several other states in India, as well as in Pakistan and Nepal. Only in the Mughal era did the name Rajput come to be applied to the warlike inhabitants of the area which later became the modern state of Rajasthan. The Rajputs also formed a minority of the overall population (and still make up under ten percent of the population of contemporary Rajasthan) – a ruling aristocracy bound, like the medieval European knights to which they are frequently compared, by strict codes of honour and ties of loyalty to the family clan.

The theory that the Rajputs are descended from people of foreign origin is supported by the efforts that were made to give them a suitably grandiose royal lineage and to incorporate them within India's caste system – and by their own unusually dogged insistence on their *kshatriya* (warrior) status. The various Rajput clans can be divided into three main groups. The four clans of the **Agnikula** ("Fire Family", comprising the Chauhans, Solankis, Paramaras and Pratiharas), claiming descent from a mythical figure who emerged from a vast fire pit near Mount Abu, were the dominant force in early Rajput affairs. Later clans subsequently emerged belonging to the **Suryavansa** or **Induvansa** Rajput branches and claiming descent from either the sun or moon respectively – these included the Guhilas (later the Sisodias) of Mewar in southern Rajasthan and the Chandellas of Khajuraho in modern Madhya Pradesh. By the tenth century, Rajput clans could be found controlling many parts of northern India – not only in present-day Rajasthan, but also in Gujarat, Madhya Pradesh and Haryana. Some of the best known include the Chauhans of Ajmer, the Sisodias of Chittaurgarh, the Chandellas of Khajuraho, and the Tomars of Haryana, who (according to tradition) founded the modern city of Delhi in 736.

The Delhi Sultanate

Despite their military prowess and newly acquired genealogical credentials, incessant Rajput infighting fatally undermined their ability to counter a powerful new threat from the northwest. Between 1000 and 1027 the Turkish chieftain Mahmud of Ghazni, founder of the **Ghaznavid** dynasty in Afghanistan, launched no less than seventeen raids into northwest India in search of plunder – the first of the incessant Muslim raids from Central Asia which were to convulse northwest India right through until the eighteenth century. A long period of calm followed Mahmud's demise, though Mahmud's descendants were subsequently ousted by another Afghan Turk, Muhammad of Ghor, who seized Ghaznavid possessions in the Punjab at the end of the twelfth century and then turned towards the wealthy lands further east. Prithviraj III, ruler of the Chauhans of Ajmer, the most important of the early Rajput dynasties, patched together an alliance to defeat the Turkish warlord at Tarain (near Thanesvar) in 1191, but Muhammad returned the next year with a superior force and defeated the combined Rajput forces. He had Prithviraj executed before returning home, leaving his generals to complete the conquest of northern India and seize Delhi from the Chauhans (who had themselves wrested it from the Rajput Tomars barely a decade earlier).

Muhammad of Ghor was assassinated in 1206 and his empire rapidly disintegrated. The Turkish slave general **Qutb-ud-din Aiback**, whom Muhammad had left behind in Delhi to superintend the newly conquered Indian territories, thus suddenly found himself the independent ruler of a sizeable kingdom. These fortuitous events led to the creation of one of north India's most important states, the **Delhi Sultanate**, which would prove to be the major political force in the region from the thirteenth to the sixteenth century, and under which Delhi would first assume pre-eminence amongst the cities of north India.

Aiback's son-in-law **Iltutmish** (1211–36) extended the sultanate's territories from the Sind in Pakistan to Bengal, though shortly after his death another and even more deadly Central Asian force, the **Mongols**, arrived on the Indian scene, sending raiding parties into the Punjab and even laying siege to Delhi for two months in 1303 before being decisively beaten off by the implacable **Ala-ud-din Khalji** (1296–1316), generally regarded as the greatest – or at least the most fearsome – of the Delhi Sultans. Ala-ud-din went on to energetically enforce Islamic rule over the northern Hindu states, conquering Gujarat and assorted Rajput fortresses in a series of expeditions between 1299 and 1311 – including, most famously, the sack of Chittaurgarh in 1303 (see p.361) – before turning his attention to the Deccan and the south, although his hopes of building a stable empire were dashed when Gujarat and Chittaurgarh re-asserted their independence before his death in 1316.

A fresh imperial impetus came from the **Tughluq** dynasty, which succeeded the Khaljis in 1320. Under Muhammed Tughluq (1325–51), the sultanate reached its maximum extent, although the end of his reign was marred by a series of revolts sparked by the burden of taxation imposed thanks to his endless campaigns – as well as his aborted attempt to relocate the capital to Daulatabad in the Deccan. Firoz Shah Tughluq (1351–88) re-established the capital at Delhi and reasserted Tughluq control, though the degeneracy of his successors made the sultanate increasingly vulnerable to external predators. When **Timur**, the Central Asian conqueror known to the West as Tamerlaine, sacked Delhi in 1398, the Delhi Sultanate was reduced to just one of several competing Muslim states in northern India.

The Sultanate experienced a modest revival under the energetic rule of the Afghan **Lodis**, especially Sikandar Lodi (1489–1517), who established a new, subsidiary capital at the hitherto relatively unimportant city of **Agra**, a move whose full significance would only be realized under the subsequent Mughal dynasty. His successor, Ibrahim (1517–26), however, was unable to overcome the dissension among his Afghan feudatories, and would eventually fall to yet another Central Asian invader, Babur, the first of the Mughals, at the Battle of Panipat.

The rise of Mewar, Marwar and Amber

The fluctuating efforts of the Delhi sultans to subdue the independent kingdoms of northern India made little lasting impression on Rajasthan, where a trio of important Rajput Hindu statelets had emerged during the centuries of Islamic rule in the north; these three kingdoms would henceforth dominate the political and military landscape of Rajasthan. Despite the temporary setback of the sack of Chittaurgarh by Ala-ud-din-Khalji in 1303, the kingdom of **Mewar** in southern Rajasthan had become an increasingly powerful player in the affairs of Rajasthan. Chittaurgarh itself had been retaken by the ruling **Sisodia** family in 1326 and subsequently refortified by **Rana Kumbha** (reigned 1433–68), traditionally regarded as one of the greatest of Mewar's rulers. Kumbha also established a massive new citadel at Kumbalgarh (north of Udaipur), as well as refortifying existing settlements throughout Mewar, consolidating the Sisodias' hold over southern Rajasthan – one which would survive largely intact, despite ferocious Mughal challenges, until Independence.

Meanwhile, in northern Rajasthan, the **Rathore** clan had established themselves as rulers of the state of **Marwar** (the area around Jodhpur). The Rathores were originally from Kanauj, near Kanpur in Uttar Pradesh. Having lost control of that city to Muhammad of Ghor in 1193, they established themselves as rulers of Pali, south of Jodhpur, before ousting another local dynasty, the Parihars, from Mandor, to the north, in 1381. In 1459 Rao Jodha (reigned 1438–89) moved his capital to a new site at Jodhpur, where he built the virtually impregnable Meherangarh fort. His second son, Bika, subsequently established himself as ruler of the desert city of **Bikaner**.

The Rathores' near neighbours, the **Kachchwahas of Amber**, had originally hailed from Gwalior in Madhya Pradesh. In 1128 a prince named Dulha Rai married a daughter of the Rajput chief of Dausa, east of Jaipur, whose throne he subsequently inherited, thus founding the Kachchwaha dynasty. Around 1150 a descendant of Dulha Rai wrested Amber from the Susawat Minas, and it was here that the Kachchwahas constructed the imposing fort and palace which would serve as the Kachchwaha capital for six centuries until Jai Singh II moved it to Jaipur in 1727.

Babur and the arrival of the Mughals

The fall of the Delhi Sultanate was to usher in an even more famous dynasty – indeed probably the most famous in Indian history – the **Mughals**. The founder of the Mughal dynasty, **Babur** (reigned 1526–30) was a descendant of the ferocious Mongol adventurers Timur and Genghis Khan (his dynastic name, "Mughal", being simply a variant of "Mongol") – indeed it was Timur's sack of Delhi in 1398 which gave Babur his extremely tenuous claim to sovereignty in north India. The ruler of Kabul in Afghanistan, Babur spent much of his life attempting to recapture his ancestral home of Samarkand, in modern Uzbekistan – India appears to have been something of an afterthought. In 1526, his small but battle-hardened and well-armed forces descended on the squabbling remnants of Ibrahim Lodi's Delhi Sultanate and, despite being outnumbered ten to one, routed them at the **Battle of Panipat**, during which Ibrahim, the last of the Delhi Sultans, was killed.

Babur thence claimed control of Delhi, while his son Humayun rode off to take control of the Lodi's new fort and treasury at **Agra**. Despite having gained control of Delhi and Agra Babur found his position threatened by a Rajput confederacy led by Rana Sanga of Mewar and the Afghan chiefs, who had united under the Sultan of Bengal – the first of innumerable Rajput–Mughal clashes over the coming years. Facing defeat, Babur reacted vigorously by declaring a religious war (*jihad*) against the rana and annihilating the Mewar forces at the **Battle of Kanwaha** (close to Fatehpur Sikri) in 1527, before turning his attention to the Afghan uprisings in the east. Although he crushed the allied armies of the Afghans and the Sultan of Bengal in 1529, his failing health forced him to retire to Agra, where he died in 1530.

Humayun (reigned1530–56), Babur's son and successor, was a volatile character, alternating between bursts of enthusiastic activity and hedonistic indolence. He subdued Malwa and Gujarat, only to lose both while he took his pleasure in his harem in Agra. Humayun's empire was soon threatened by the redoubtable Afghan warrior **Sher Shah Suri** (also known as Sher Khan), based in south Bihar, and after two resounding defeats at his hands, Humayun had to seek refuge in Persia in 1539. A much cleverer politician than Humayun, Sher Shah later subjugated several of the Rajput dynasties which had proved troublesome for the Mughals, though it was during a siege against one of these dynasties, at Kalinjar in modern Uttar Pradesh, that the Afghan was killed, when a rocket rebounded off the fort's walls and exploded a pile of weapons next to him.

Akbar

After Sher Shah's death in 1545 Humayun took advantage of the ensuing chaos to stage a return. His armies, led by Bairam Khan and Prince Akbar, crushed Sikander Suri at Sirhund in 1555; but Humayun died the following year after a fall in the Purana Qila in Delhi leaving his young son **Akbar** to succeed where he had failed. Akbar, aged only thirteen, faced an immediate crisis when Delhi was briefly stormed and occupied by the brilliant Hindu general **Hemu** (a remarkable figure who despite his tiny stature and feeble physique had risen from hawking saltpetre in a bazaar to commanding the united armies of northern India in a sequence of 23 consecutive victories). Akbar's own generals favoured a retreat to Afghanistan, but Bairam Khan encouraged Akbar to stand firm. The advice bore fruit when Akbar and Hemu's forces met at a second Battle of Panipat, the site of Babur's earlier victory over Ibrahim Lodi, in 1556, during which Hemu was killed, and his army put to flight. Khan subsequently recovered Gwalior and Jaunpur, and handed over a consolidated north Indian kingdom to Akbar in 1560.

It was during Akbar's reign that the Rajputs – or at least almost all the Rajputs – were finally subdued and brought into the Mughal fold (Akbar, coincidentally, was actually born in a Rajput fort not far from Jaisalmer, at Umarkot, just over the border in present-day Pakistan). Akbar succeeded where his predecessors had failed thanks to a notable change of tactic, introducing a carrot-and-stick-style strategy based on a combination of military might and diplomatic overtures. Establishing a large garrison in Ajmer, Akbar set out to woo the Rajputs. His first notable "conquest" was his **marriage**, in 1562, to Mariam, the daughter of the maharaja of Amber (Mariam, in turn, would become the mother of the next Mughal emperor, Jahangir, thus binding the Mughals and Amber even closer, while it was on lands donated by the maharaja of Amber that Shah Jahan would subsequently construct the Taj Mahal). The raja of Amber and his progeny were inducted into the Mughal hierarchy and given high offices – indeed the raja's grandson, **Man Singh**, would become one of Akbar's most trusted generals and headed many campaigns on behalf of the emperor, including several against fellow Rajputs, such as that against Pratap Singh which led to the Battle of Haldighati (see p.343). Subsequent treaties were soon brokered with many of Rajasthan's other rulers, signalling a new and peaceable alliance between the empire's Islamic centre and the Hindu hinterlands. Mughals would thenceforth be able to count on the Rajput loyalty and military assistance, while the Rajputs were able to reap the rewards of holding high offices within the mighty Mughal empire – by 1580, 43 of the 222 Mughal *umrah* (nobility) were Rajput.

Unfortunately for Akbar, the Sisodia rulers of the pre-eminent Rajput state, Mewar, still holed up in the mighty fort at **Chittaurgarh**, were unpersuaded by Akbar's advances or promises of elevated official Mughal status – and indeed publicly derided the maharaja of Amber for his perceived sell-out. The carrot having therefore failed, Akbar resorted to the stick, launching a huge offensive against Chittaurgarh (see p.362), which he finally captured after a long and brutal siege in 1568. The siege marked the end of Chittaurgarh's illustrious history – although by then the ruler of Mewar, Udai Singh II (see p.335), had absconded to his newly founded capital of **Udaipur**, from where he and his successor Pratap Singh (see p.343) continued to defy Akbar.

Akbar, meanwhile, was indulging in his own spate of city-building. In 1565 he had the small fort built by Sikander Lodi in **Agra** demolished and replaced by the magnificent new Agra Fort, the centrepiece of a newly revitalized city which would henceforth rival Delhi as the major centre of Mughal power. Not content with this, in the early 1570s he embarked on the creation of an entire new city, the remarkable but short-lived **Fatehpur Sikri**, which served for a brief period as the capital of the empire, before the court's return to Agra, and thence, ultimately, back to Delhi.

Akbar possessed the personal magnetism of his grandfather and was a brilliant general, and by the end of his reign in 1605 he controlled a broad sweep of territory from the Bay of Bengal to Kandahar in Afghanistan. Akbar was as clever a politician and administrator as he was a successful general. In addition to involving Hindu land-owners and nobles in economic and political life, Akbar adopted a conscious policy of religious toleration aimed at widening the base of his power. In particular, he abolished the despised poll tax on non-Muslims (*jizya*), and tolls on Hindu pilgrimages. A mystical experience in about 1575 inspired him to instigate a series of discussions with orthodox Muslim leaders (*ulema*), Portuguese priests from Goa, Hindu Brahmins, Jains and Zoroastrians at his famous Diwan-i-Khas in Fatehpur Sikri. The discussions culminated in a politico-religious crisis and a revolt, organized by the alienated *ulema*, which Akbar ruthlessly crushed in 1581. He subsequently evolved a theory of divine kingship incorporating the toleration of all religions, and thereby restored the concept of imperial sanctity with which the early Hindu emperors had surrounded themselves, while declaring his nonsectarian credentials. Akbar was a liberal patron of the arts and his eclecticism encouraged a fruitful Muslim-Hindu dialogue.

Jahangir and Shah Jahan

The reign of **Jahangir** (1605–27) was a time of brisk economic and expansionist activity conjoined with artistic and architectural brilliance – as well as some notable excesses of imperial indulgence. Jahangir was a contradictory character: an alcoholic and a sadist, but also a notable connoisseur of art and loving husband of his famous queen, **Nur Jahan** (see pp.180–181). He was also an able and determined military commander who succeeded in extending the bounds of the already very considerable domains bequeathed to him by Akbar. One of his principal targets was the recalcitrant state of Mewar, against which he launched repeated expeditions. The new ruler of Mewar, Pratap Singh's son **Amar Singh**, continued to fight for as long as he could, but sheer weight of Mughal offensives gradually rendered him helpless. In 1615 he was finally forced to sign a treaty recognizing Mughal overlordship. His son, Karan Singh, presented himself at the Mughal court, where he was showered with honours and became firm friends with Prince Khurram – who would himself later seek refuge in Udaipur (see p.339), an ironic turnaround in Mughal-Mewari relations.

Jahangir's son **Shah Jahan** (1628–57) came to power in 1628 after the by-now traditional military contest between rival brothers, followed by the exile or (if they could be caught) execution of the losing parties. The bloodbath which generally preceded the emergence of a new emperor at least ensured that only the fittest were able to survive and claim the Mughal throne, and in this respect Shah Jahan – who had already proved himself an outstanding military commander during his father's reign – was no exception, displaying all the traditional Mughal qualities of administrative and military élan. It is as perhaps the greatest patron of architecture the world has ever known that Shah Jahan is best remembered, however. In 1648 he officially moved the Mughal capital from Agra back to Delhi, celebrating the translocation with the construction of the new city of **Shahjahanabad** (now better known as Old Delhi), complete with its huge new Red Fort and Jama Masjid, though it was in Agra that he left his greatest mark, with his myriad embellishments to the city's fort and, pre-eminently, in the creation of the **Taj Mahal**, arguably the most beautiful building on the planet.

Aurangzeb

Shah Jahan's reign witnessed the entry of a new force into Indian history: the **Marathas**, a potent military power in central India who would loom large in the later history of north India in general and Rajasthan in particular. A group of militant Hindus from Maharastra in central India, the Marathas had carved out a kingdom of their own under their inspirational chief, **Shivaji**, and soon began to turn their attentions northwards. Shah Jahan had responded to the Maratha threat by sending his third son, an ambitious young prince named **Aurangzeb**, to the Deccan to take charge of Mughal interests in the region, although his military successes were repeatedly undermined by Shah Jahan's oldest son and preferred heir **Dara Shikoh**, who was anxious to destabilize Aurangzeb's military exploits lest they create a threat to his own prestige. The anticipated struggle between the two brothers erupted in 1657 when Shah Jahan fell suddenly and seriously ill with acute constipation (bowel problems appear to have been a recurrent feature of Mughal rule – Akbar himself apparently perished of acute diarrhoea). Shah Jahan recovered, but not before Aurangzeb had seen off Dara Shikoh, wiping out his army in a series of encounters that culminated in a rout at Ajmer. The thirty-year reign of the ailing emperor ended ignominiously. Aurangzeb had him incarcerated in Agra Fort, where he lived out his remaining days in an opium-induced stupor gazing wistfully down the Yamuna at the mausoleum of his beloved Mumtaz.

Though lacking the charisma of Akbar or Babur, Aurangzeb (reigned 1658–1707) evoked an awe of his own and proved to be a firm and capable administrator, who retained his grip on the increasingly unsettled empire until his death at the age of 88. In contrast to the extravagance of the other Mughals, Aurangzeb's lifestyle was pious and disciplined. However, his religious dogmatism ultimately alienated the Hindu community whose leaders had been so carefully cultivated by Akbar. Hindu places of worship were again the object of iconoclasm, the *jizya* tax on non-Muslims was reintroduced and discriminatory duties were imposed on Hindu merchants. The Jats of the Agra-Delhi region rebelled, and elsewhere peasant farmers rallied behind Maratha and Sikh leaders.

Disintegrating relations between the Hindu populace and Muslim rulers across the empire were mirrored by events in Rajasthan. In 1678 the ruler of the leading Rajput state of **Marwar** (Jodhpur) died without leaving an heir. Pending the election of a successor, Aurangzeb seized control of the state and garrisoned it with Mughal troops, who passed the time by vandalizing local Hindu temples, an activity hardly calculated to please local Rajput sensibilities. By the time the succession had come to be decided, two of the deceased ruler's wives had given birth to male heirs (although one soon died), though ignoring the surviving infant's claims Aurangzeb conferred the throne on an unpopular relative, whereupon revolt erupted. The infant's mother decamped post-haste to Udaipur, whereupon the rulers of Mewar joined the fray, launching their army against various Mughal targets. Aurangzeb was forced to despatch a large military expedition to the region in 1680. An inconclusive series of battles ensued, before a tenuous peace was reimposed, but not before Udaipur had been sacked by Mughal troops, who followed up their conquest with a further spate of temple bashing.

Aurangzeb's attention, however, was turning steadily south. In 1681 he transferred his base to the Deccan, where he spent the rest of his extremely long life overseeing the subjugation of the Bijapur and Golconda kingdoms and trying to contain the Maratha rebellion. In 1689, he succeeded in capturing and executing Shivaji's son, and by 1698 the Mughals had overrun almost the whole of the peninsula. The Rajputs had been left in peace and the Marathas had been temporarily suppressed – though they would increasingly re-emerge in the next century to harass the remnants of Mughal and Rajput power.

Maratha threats and the rise of Jaipur

Aurangzeb's death was followed by the rapid disintegration of the empire, and although a succession of Mughal "emperors" continued to rule in Delhi right through until the uprising of 1857, their actual powers were increasingly limited. By the 1720s Hyderabad, Avadh and Bengal were effectively independent, while closer to Delhi the **Jats** succeeded in creating their own independent statelet in Bharatpur out of a slice of previously Mughal territory. In 1737 the Marathas raided Delhi and the following year overwhelmed the rich province of Malwa (in Madyha Pradesh). Two years later, Nadir Shah of Persia dealt a fatal blow to the Mughal Empire's prestige when he invaded India, defeated the Mughal army and sacked Delhi in 1739.

In the midst of the general chaos, one forward-looking development was occurring in Rajasthan. In 1727, the Kachchwaha ruler Jai Singh had taken the momentous decision to relocate his capital from the hoary old fortress of Amber to a brand new city to be named (after himself) as **Jaipur**. Major Rajput towns and fortresses had hitherto always been sited in places which offered the greatest defensive security – the summits of craggy, sheer-sided hills, for example, as at Chittaurgarh, Meherangarh (Jodhpur) and, indeed, Amber itself. For his new capital, however, Jai Singh, for the first time in Rajputana history, put mercantile above military considerations, locating his new city on the plains in a commercially strategic position directly beside the major highway between Ajmer and Agra, and inviting tradesmen and craftspeople to settle in it – a far-sighted decision which largely explains why it is that Jaipur, rather than Udaipur (the capital of the pre-eminent Rajput kingdom of Mewar), is now the most important city in Rajasthan.

The city immediately flourished, though Jai Singh's failure to provide an heir meant that his death in 1743, and subsequent arguments over the royal succession, opened the door to **Maratha interference**, with disastrous consequences. The rival pretenders to the throne each enlisted Maratha mercenaries to back up their claims, though the successful contender, Madho Singh, upon attaining the throne found himself at the mercy of the Maratha troops who had put him there. In 1753 the Marathas returned in numbers and were only bought off with a substantial bribe, a pattern which continued on and off for the next forty years. Attempts to take on the Marathas on the battlefield met with mixed results. In 1787 Pratap Singh narrowly defeated a combined Mughal–Maratha force at the Battle of Tunga by bribing the Mughal contingent to switch sides at the beginning of the fighting, though Pratap's subsequent attempt to engage a purely Maratha force, at the Battle of Malpura in 1800, backfired when 27,000 Rajputs were put to flight by a far smaller but superior force of Maratha troops.

Similar events unfolded at Jodhpur and Udaipur, and at many other places around Rajasthan, during the second half of the eighteenth century, with Maratha armies roaming around the countryside demanding huge amounts of tribute from whoever they felt was vulnerable to attack, until they had effectively bled the treasuries of Rajputana dry. Things were little better in **Delhi**. Following a murderous spate of looting by Nadir Shah in 1739, it was again ransacked in 1757, this time by an independent Afghan force led by Ahmad Shah Durrani. Mughal ministers called in the Marathas to rescue the situation. The Marathas drove the Afghans back to the Punjab; but Ahmad Shah advanced again in 1761 and overwhelmed them at the third battle of Panipat. Any designs he had on the imperial throne were dashed, however, when his soldiers mutinied over arrears of pay.

The rise of the British

The scourge of the Marathas was finally arrested, not by any of the royal houses of Rajasthan, but by an entirely new breed of interlopers: the British. India's trading potential had attracted European interest ever since 1498, when Vasco da Gama landed on the Malabar coast. During the ensuing century Portuguese, Dutch, English, French and Danish companies had all set up coastal trading centres. British interests in India were formalized by the creation of the **East India Company**, granted a royal charter by Elizabeth I in 1600, whose representatives arrived at Surat in Gujarat in 1608, quickly establishing 27 trading posts around the country, including those at the nascent cities of Bombay, Madras and Calcutta. In 1717 the Company (as it was generally known) finally wheedled an imperial *firman* (decree) out of the Mughal emperor Farrukhsiyar formalizing their trading rights in the country – a document which would underpin the gradual British rise to pre-eminence over the following century.

The War of the Austrian Succession in Europe in 1740 led to armed conflict between the French and English trading companies along the South Indian coast, which soon developed into a minor war over the succession of the Nizam of Hyderabad. Sporadic fighting continued until the end of the Seven Years' War in Europe and the Treaty of Paris in 1763 put an effective end to French ambitions in India. Meanwhile, **Robert Clive**'s defeat of the rebellious young nawab of Bengal at Plassey in 1757 had decisively augmented British power; by 1765 the enervated Mughal emperor legally recognized the Company by granting it the revenue management of Bengal, Bihar and Orissa.

For the next thirty years, the British in India contented themselves with developing trade and repulsing Indian offensives against their three provinces in Calcutta, Bombay and Madras, though by the end of the century the defeat of Tipu Sultan of Mysore, the Company's best-organized and most resolute enemy, and the subjugation of the Nizam of Hyderabad resulted in the annexation of considerable territories, and by 1805 nearly all the other rulers in India recognized British suzerainty. A long-drawn out series of conflicts between the British and Marathas (the so-called three "Marathas Wars" of 1774–1818) finally extinguished the Marathas as an effective military threat.

Following the subjugation of the Marathas, the British established a series of treaties with the rulers of Rajasthan – or **Rajputana**, as it became known during the colonial era. Under these treaties, the various kingdoms of Rajputana retained their autonomy more or less intact and received a guarantee of military protection in exchange for pledging their loyalty to the British crown and agreeing to certain political, mercantile and financial concessions. Similar arrangements were reached with most of India's other surviving independent kingdoms, collectively known as the so-called "**princely states**", stretching from Hyderabad in the south to Kashmir in the north; although some were gradually swallowed up and incorporated into British-ruled India, many were to survive until Independence. The much-abused city of Delhi, the traditional capital of north India, fared less well, as the British established their capital at the burgeoning new city of Calcutta. Not until 1911 would Delhi recapture its mantle as the north's imperial city.

The 1857 uprising

The new British colony, however, was in a state of social and economic collapse as a result of the almost incessant conflicts of the previous hundred years. The controversial "Doctrine of Lapse", whereby autonomous states were gradually annexed, caused widespread resentment. In addition, the Company's policy, after 1835, of promoting European literature and science (with English replacing Persian as the official state language), the suppression of local customs such as *sati* and child marriage, and the deployment of Indian troops overseas (causing them to lose caste) all caused resentment and were increasingly perceived as part of a covert but systematic British attack on traditional Hindu and Muslim religious and cultural practices.

The final spark which ignited a full-blown uprising by the Indian army was supplied when troops were issued with cartridges for a new Enfield rifle smeared in cows' and pigs' grease (polluting to both Hindus and Muslims). The resultant **1857 uprising** (traditionally referred to by the British as the Indian Mutiny or Sepoy Rebellion, and also described by Indian historians as the First War of Independence) began with a rebellion at Meerut on May 10, 1857, and Delhi was seized the next day. The last Mughal emperor Bahadur Shah in Delhi, the dispossessed court at Lucknow, and the exiled members of the Maratha court at Kanpur all supported the cause (albeit possibly under duress) and some landlords participated in the rebellion – though, crucially, the Sikh regiments in the Punjab chose to side with the British. The rebellion quickly spread across most of central northern India, where mutineers seized Lucknow and Kanpur and threatened Agra, whose rebellious citizens forced the European community to flee into the city's fort for safety. The states of Rajasthan, which remained nominally independent and had benefited more than other parts of the country by the British presence, remained relatively unaffected, with the maharajas of Jaipur and Udaipur both remaining loyal – the latter offered shelter to fleeing British women and children on the island of Jag Mandir, remarking that "war is only for men".

The British authorities were caught by surprise, though control was gradually reasserted. Delhi and Kanpur were both retaken in September, Agra was relieved soon afterwards, and the final recapture of Lucknow in March 1858 effectively broke the back of the Mutiny.

The Raj and Indian nationalism

The uprising had important consequences for subsequent British rule in the Subcontinent. The governing powers of the East India Company were abolished and the British crown assumed the direct administration of India in the same year. Henceforth, British India was no longer merely a massive trade operation, but a fully-fledged independent kingdom, or **Raj**. As a British colony, India assumed a new position in the world economy. Its trade benefited from the railways developed by the British, and Indian businessmen began to invest in a range of manufacturing industries, including textiles, iron and steel – among them the remarkable Marwari trading families from Rajasthan (see p.391) who would come to dominate Indian manufacturing in the twentieth century. However, India subsidized the British economy as a source of cheap raw materials and as a market for manufactured goods, and its own economy and agriculture remained underdeveloped.

British civil servants dominated the higher echelons of the administration, imposing Western notions of progress on the indigenous social structure and often introducing policies contrary to Indian interests. At the same time, the propagation of the English language and the Western knowledge to which it gave access resulted in the emergence of a new **middle class** of civil servants, landlords and professionals, whose consciousness of an Indian national identity steadily increased. Public demonstrations eventually forced the British to sanction the creation of the **Indian National Congress** party (usually known simply as "Congress") in 1885, and by 1905 Congress had adopted self-government as a political aim – while in 1906, concerns about the predominantly Hindu Congress led to the foundation of the **All-India Muslim League** to represent the country's Muslims. The Morley-Minto Reforms of 1909 paved the way for Indian participation in provincial executive councils and made allowance for separate Muslim representation.

At the **Great Durbar** of 1911, held in honour of the new king, George V, the capital was moved back to **Delhi**, with the construction of yet another imperial city, so-called "New" Delhi, to celebrate the relocation (though it wasn't completed and officially inaugurated until 1931). A few years later, the Royal Proclamation of 1917 promised a gradual development of dominion-style self-government; and two years later the Montagu-Chelmsford Reforms attempted to implement the declaration. At this point an England-educated lawyer, **Mohandas Karamchand Gandhi** – better known as the Mahatma, or "Great Soul" – took up the initiative, espousing a political philosophy based on non-violence (*ahimsa*), the pursuit of truth (satyagraha) and the championing of the untouchables (see p.398), whom he renamed the Children of God (*Harijan*).

Gandhi began by organizing India-wide one-day strikes and protests, though these were mercilessly crushed by the government – as in the infamous incident in 1919 when General Dyer dispersed a meeting at Jallianwalla Bagh Amritsar by firing on the unarmed crowd, killing 379 and wounding 1200.

By 1928 Congress was demanding complete independence. The government offered talks, but the more radical elements in Congress, now led by the young **Jawaharlal Nehru**, were in a confrontational mood. Gandhi, in turn, led a well-publicized 240-mile "salt march" from his ashram in Sabarmati to make salt illegally at Dandi in Gujarat in defiance of a particularly unpopular British tax. This demonstration of nonviolent civil disobedience (*satyagrah*) fired the popular imagination, leading to more processions, strikes, and mass imprisonments.

The idea of a **separate Muslim state** was first raised in 1930 by the celebrated Indian Muslim poet and writer Muhammad Iqbal. **Mohammed Ali Jinnah**, a lawyer from Bombay who assumed the leadership of the Muslim League in 1935, initially promoted Muslim-Hindu co-operation, but he soon despaired of influencing Congress and by 1940 the League passed a resolution demanding an independent Pakistan.

Another problem faced in the run-up to Independence was the question of what was to become of the numerous **princely states** scattered over many parts of India – nowhere more so than in Rajputana – which were still technically independent and autonomously run. The states still covered two-fifths of the country's total area and represented a huge potential stumbling block to future independence should their rulers (most of whom were deeply suspicious of Congress) choose not to join the newly independent country. The question was never to be properly solved and even at Independence rulers of several of the major states had yet to decide which country they were going to join (with enduringly disastrous consequences in Kashmir).

Confrontations between the government, Congress and the Muslim League continued throughout World War II, despite the promise, in 1942, by a Britain increasingly reliant on Indian troops, of post-war Independence (an offer which Gandhi compared to "a post-dated cheque on a failing bank"). British attempts to find a solution that would preserve a united India and allay Muslim fears after the war disintegrated in the face of continued intransigence from both sides, and they gradually realized that the division – or so-called **Partition** – of the existing country of India into separate Muslim and Hindu states was inevitable.

Independence

India achieved **Independence** (and the newly created state of Pakistan came into official existence) on August 14 and 15, 1947. Celebrations over Independence were overshadowed by events in the newly partitioned Punjab, where five million Hindus and Sikhs from Pakistan and a similar number of Muslims from India fled from India to Pakistan or vice-versa, accompanied by an enormous outbreak of reciprocal communal atrocities which cost half a million lives. The fighting even spread as far as **Delhi**. Most of the Urdu-speaking Muslims who had lived there since the time of the Mughals fled to Pakistan, while numerous Punjabi Sikhs travelled in the opposite exchange, dramatically altering the city's ethnic demographic, while post-Partition, towns like Jaisalmer and Bikaner suddenly found themselves marooned at the country's western extremity and

One of Rajasthan's major contributions to modern India has been the business skills of its **Marwari merchant** community. Originally hailing from the region around Jaipur – Shekhawati in particular – Marwari merchants have long been famous as traders in Rajasthan, and have been venturing further afield since perhaps as far back as the sixteenth century, accompanying local princes who had been appointed as governors to distant provinces by the Mughals. In the nineteenth century, many Marwari merchants left Rajasthan and moved out to India's burgeoning new cities, Bombay and Calcutta in particular, where they established commercial dynasties which in many cases have survived to this day – most notably the great **Birla** group in Calcutta, one of India's largest industrial conglomerates, which was established (and is still owned) by a Marwari family from Pilani in Shekhawati. Marwari businessmen such as GD Birla were also closely associated with the Independence struggle, and gave generous financial support to Congress and other opponents of British rule – and also played a vital role in the country's rapid industrialization following Independence in 1947.

severed from traditional trans-Thar trading routes which had previously connected them to places in what had suddenly become Pakistan.

The modern state of **Rajasthan** was slightly longer in the making. Following Independence, the rulers of the region's princely states finally agreed to merge with India, and the new state – the largest in the country – was formally inaugurated on March 30, 1949 (though it didn't reach its current dimension until November 1956, when Ajmer and a few areas in the south were added). Jaipur was named the new capital, and its maharaja, Man Singh II, given the honorary title of *Rajpramukh*, a kind of ceremonial head of state. Many centuries of proud independence were thus erased at a single administrative stroke. Their rulers – who had suddenly become ex-rulers – were allowed to retain their titles and property, and were to be solaced by generous allowances, the so-called "privy purses", to be funded in perpetuity by the national government.

Nehru and Indira Gandhi

Jawaharlal Nehru, India's first and longest serving prime minister, proved a dynamic and popular leader, establishing a democratic, secular nation and overseeing the first stages of its agricultural and industrial development, while the country's first elections, in 1951, involving 173 million voters, made India the **world's largest democracy**. Interestingly, many of the Rajput rulers who had lost their hereditary powers at Independence now began to enter the democratic fray, often with considerable success thanks to the esteem in which they continued to be held by their former subjects. Female candidates of aristocratic lineage have also enjoyed an unexpected level of popularity in a very conservative and male-dominated state, a tradition which began with the legendarily beautiful Gayatri Devi, wife of Man Singh II of Jaipur, who won three separate elections between 1962 and 1971, and which has continued right up to the present day, exemplified by the case of Vasundhara Raje (see box, p.394), current chief minister of Rajasthan and wife of the former ruler of Dholpur.

On the economic front, Nehru engineered the first three of India's Five-Year Plans, inaugurating a programme of rapid industrialization whose productive (if unaesthetic) results can be seen in the massive factories and chimney stacks which ring cities like Agra and Kota. In foreign policy, Nehru became closely associated with the widespread post war pan-Asian policy of **nonalignment**, which sought to keep a healthy distance from both the US and USSR, though this had to be speedily abandoned (and replaced with desperate appeals for US military aid) in 1962 following a brief Chinese invasion of Assam. Nehru died in 1964, which prevented him from witnessing the restoration of India's military prestige in the **Indo-Pakistan War** of 1965, during which Indian tanks advanced to within five kilometres of a virtually defenceless Lahore before a UN ceasefire was agreed.

Nehru's daughter **Indira Gandhi** succeeded her father as leader of Congress in 1966 and continued his policy of rapid industrialization and agricultural development – the latter, the so-called "Green Revolution", led to the enviable position of India becoming entirely self-sufficient in food production by the 1970s. She also introduced a series of socialist reforms which included abolishing the generous annual allowances which had been granted to the rulers of the princely states, including the maharajas of Rajasthan, at Independence. In a final indignity, the state's increasingly impoverished former masters were thus forced to either sell off their assets or convert their superb ancestral palaces into luxury hotels in order to get by.

After widespread unrest against the rate of inflation and corruption within the Congress in 1975, Mrs Gandhi declared a **State of Emergency**, which suspended all civil rights and silenced all opposition, using strict press censorship. Her administrative and economic reforms had the desired effect of cutting inflation and curbing corruption, but the enforced sterilization of men with two or more children, and brutal slum-clearances in Delhi supervised by her son Sanjay, created a widespread legacy of bitterness. When she finally released her opponents and called off the Emergency in January 1977, the widespread anger she had engendered resulted in her ignominious defeat in the March elections. The ensuing **Janata** coalition fell apart within two years and Mrs Gandhi, who had rebuilt her Congress (I) Party with Sanjay's help, swept back into office in 1980. Their joint triumph was short-lived, however. Sanjay died in a plane crash soon afterwards, and in 1984 Mrs Gandhi was assassinated in Delhi by her Sikh bodyguards in retaliation for her decision to send the Indian Army into Amritsar's Golden Temple to flush out Sikh militants holed up in the shrine. Delhi was subsequently convulsed by another wave of communal rioting during which thousands of Sikhs were murdered.

The rise of the BJP

Mrs Gandhi's other son, **Rajiv Gandhi**, a former airline pilot, came to power in 1984 on a wave of sympathy boosted by his reputation as "Mr Clean". The honeymoon was short-lived, however. The political accords he reached with the Punjab, Assam and Mizoram deteriorated into armed conflict; more than two years of "peacekeeping" by the Indian army failed to disarm Tamil guerrillas in Sri Lanka; and allegations of corruption tarnished his image. In December 1989 elections, V.P. Singh's ousted Janata Party formed a coalition government with the support of the "Hindu first" **Bharatiya Janata Party** (BJP), led by L. K. Advani. Founded in 1980, the BJP was to prove a massive new force in Indian politics, and the only nationwide challenger to Congress. The BJP has been widely criticized for being anti-Muslim and for stirring up communal tensions, though its formidable electoral success is based on a wide-ranging appeal to India's more traditional voters. The party has done particularly well in Rajasthan, and has provided all but one of the state ministers since 1990, including the present incumbent, Vasundhara Raje.

Singh's government lasted less than a year thanks to the first and most contro-versial of all the BJP's policies, led by Advani, who argued that the Babri Masjid mosque in **Ayodhya**, built by Babur in the sixteenth century on the supposed site of the birthplace of Rama, god-hero of the epic Ramayana, should be torn down and replaced with a Hindu temple. The building rapidly became a deeply contentious symbol of the increasingly rocky relationship between India's two largest religious groups. Singh, utterly committed to secularism, pleaded with Advani to desist but, undeterred, Advani set off towards Ayodhya in October 1990. Singh had Advani arrested before he could reach Ayodhya, but saw his own coalition immediately collapse as a result. Fresh elections were called, in the lead-up to which Congress were doing well, promising a return to power for Rajiv Gandhi, until he was assassinated by Tamil Tigers seeking revenge for India's intervention in the civil war in Sri Lanka.

It was left to **P.V. Narasimha Rao** to steer Congress to electoral victory, though the BJP also increased its parliamentary representation, with Advani becoming leader of the opposition. Simmering tensions at Ayodhya final boiled over in December 1992, when extremists incited crowds of fanatical devotees to tear down the Babri Masjid in a blaze of publicity. Nationwide riots ensued, and the BJP-led state governments (including those of Rajasthan and Delhi) were suspended. Subsequent elections in these states in late 1993 showed that the popularity of the BJP, and its call for the creation of **Hindutva**, a Hindu homeland, was fading. They re-asserted control of Delhi, which has always been a stronghold of the Hindu right, barely hung on in Rajasthan, and lost the rest.

National morale during this post-Ayodhya period was shaky. After a year blighted by riots and the rise of religious extremism, it seemed as if India's era as a secular state was doomed. Against this backdrop of uncertainty, the rise of right-wing Hindu-fundamentalist parties gathered pace. Temporarily cowed by the Babri Masjid debacle, the BJP took advantage of the power struggle in the Congress Party to rekindle regional support. Expediently sidelining the contentious Hindutva agenda, the new rallying cry was **Swadeshi** – a campaign against the Congress-led programme of economic liberalization and, in particular, the activities of multinationals such as Coca-Cola, Pepsi and KFC (one of whose branches was forced to close by the BJP-controlled Delhi municipality).

After the general election of May 1996. The BJP emerged as the single largest party and attempted to form a government but was unable to muster a majority and was ousted by the hastily formed Unified Front coalition. Another general election followed in March 1998, after which the BJP struggled to power as the head of a new conservative coalition government under **Atal Behari Vajpayee**. The BJP had promised change and the restoration of national pride, and one of its early acts in government was to conduct five underground **nuclear tests** in May 1998 in Pokaran near Jaisalmer (see box, p.314), provoking Pakistan to respond in kind.

Following its defeat in the 1998 elections, the Congress Party emerged as a stronger political force with **Sonia Gandhi**, the Italian-born widow of Rajiv Gandhi, at the helm. Congress helped to bring about the downfall of the BJP in April 1999, but were unable to form a coalition government. As a conse-quence, India faced a third **general election** in as many years. At the start of the campaign, Congress hopes were high that, with a Gandhi once again as party leader, it could revive the popular support lost after years of infighting and corruption scandals. However a decisive victory against Pakistan in a border conflict at Kargil was a godsend for Vajpayee. Riding high on the feel-good factor, his party inflicted the biggest defeat Congress had sustained since Independence.

The new millennium

Figures from the **millennium census** revealed that the population of India stood at around 1.1 billion (with a literacy rate of 66 percent and an average life expectancy of 68 years – a significant increase on those of 1947). This measure of national progress, however, was eclipsed by a succession of catastrophic natural disasters which wracked the country in mid-2000, including a savage **drought** in parts of Rajasthan and Gujarat, during which high summer temperatures and the third failure of the monsoon in as many years forced tens of thousands of poor farming families off their land in search of fodder and drinking water. Water, or the lack of it, has remained a chronic problem in the state in recent years, with the persistent failure of the monsoon in many areas, symbolized by the complete (although fortunately only temporary) disappearance of Udaipur's Lake Pichola, and the sight of its famous Lake Palace Hotel sitting amongst a sea of mud.

A new wave of **communal riots** engulfed the country in the spring of 2002, following the massacre by a Muslim mob in Godhra, Gujarat, of a train-load of Hindu pilgrims returning from Ayodhya, while in 2003, renewed tensions in

Out from under the veil

You don't have to be long in Rajasthan to realize that **women** are rarely seen or heard. As part of the state's feudal legacy, the purdah system, by which married women are kept isolated and under veil by their husbands, is still widespread in rural areas. Ditto for the dowry system and the age-old practice by which girls are denied an education. But it's not all chauvinism and second-class status. In India's male-dominated political system, where women have an abysmally low representation, it's striking that the state's top three political offices – Chief Minister, Governor, and Speaker of the Rajasthan Assembly – are all held by women.

Of the three, the most prominent is Chief Minister **Vasundhara Raje**, who hails from a politically powerful family that has long monopolized power in the state. Key to her 2003 victory as the head of the BJP slate was her marriage to the former ruler of Dholpur. Her decision to play the role of maharani during the campaign – trading in her chiffons for bright ethnic garb and a *rath* (chariot) – certainly endeared her to a local populace nostalgic for Rajputana's glorious past. But many feminists were uncomfortable with Raje's actions and asserted that she, along with Governor Pratibha Patil and Assembly speaker Sumitra Singh rose to the top of their field by playing as rough and dirty as the boys and carefully avoiding the suicidal tag of "feminist".

Still, there is modest hope that the triumvirate will circumspectly and in their own way elevate the political agenda of Rajasthani women. Certainly they have their work cut out for them. The literacy rate of women in Rajasthan is one of the worst in India: 25 percent, versus more than double that for men. Women living in the state's rural areas are arguably the most repressed in all of India. By one account half are forced into marriage by the age of fifteen, and despite the intense work of internationally supported NGOs like the Urmul Trust and Barefoot College (see p.274), which work to valorize the contributions of women to rural life, economic independence remains at best a distant dream for most.

Kashmir led to a massive deployment of troops along the Pakistan border. **Elections in 2004** brought Congress back to power under the leadership of Sonia Gandhi, although constant BJP sniping over her foreign origins led to the appointment of the low-key former finance mininster **Manmohan Singh** as prime minister. The steady growth of **regionalism** in recent years has been underpinned by a marked weakening of New Delhi's grip as the nation's political capital. Rotten to its core with corruption, the city no longer commands the respect and power it used to.

As it struggles to balance the ambitions of its privileged elite with the basic needs of its poor, Indian society at the start of the twenty-first century is rife with ironies. The country chosen as the site of Microsoft's new Hi-Tech City and capable of launching satellites, nuclear rockets and manned-space programmes is also unable to provide clean drinking water, adequate nutrition and basic education for millions of its inhabitants. Not until the country's politicians are able to deliver stable government and to curb the corruption and self-interest which have come to dominate public is this situation likely to change.

Religion

T he region encompassing modern Delhi, Agra and Rajasthan is one of the country's most religiously diverse areas, predominantly **Hindu**, though also including a large **Muslim** community, as well as a considerable number of **Sikhs**. **Delhi** and **Agra** have traditionally been amongst India's most Islamicized cities thanks to their history as the seat of power of the country's two most important Muslim dynasties (although many of Delhi's Muslims left the city during Partition in 1947, their places taken by incoming Sikhs from the Punjab). **Rajasthan**, by contrast, has always been staunchly Hindu, though its people have espoused a variety of gods, ranging from the ruling Rajputs' devotion to the cult of Krishna through to the flourishing array of local deities worshipped in the state's rural villages. The **Jain** religion has also added another small but colourful thread to the region's cultural fabric.

Hinduism

Contemporary **Hinduism** – the religion of over 85 percent of Indians – is the product of several thousand years of evolution and assimilation, and for most Indians its influence permeates every aspect of life, from commonplace daily chores to education and politics. It has no founder or prophet, no single creed, and no single prescribed practice or doctrine; it takes in hundreds of gods, goddesses, beliefs and practices, and widely variant cults and philosophies. Some deities are recognized by only two or three villages, others are popular right across the Subcontinent. Hindus (a term derived from the name of the Indus river, the cradle of South Asian civilization) call their beliefs and practices **dharma**, which envelops natural and moral law to define a way of living in harmony with a natural order, while achieving personal goals and meeting the requirements of society.

Early developments

The foundations of Hinduism were laid by the **Aryans**, semi-nomads who entered northwest India during the second millennium BC, and mixed with the indigenous Dravidian population. They brought a number of gods with them, including **Agni**, the god of fire and sacrifice, **Surya**, the sun-god, and **Indra**, the chief god. Most of these deities subsequently faded in importance, though Indra is still regarded as the father of the gods, and Surya was widely worshipped until the medieval period – he still has particular significance in Rajasthan, given that certain of the ruling families (including the Sisodias of Udaipur) claim direct descent from the sun.

Aryan religious beliefs were set out in the **Vedas**, a collection of hymns, prayers and directions for ceremonial rituals; transmitted orally for centuries, they were finally written down in Sanskrit between 1600 BC and 1000 BC. The second group of core Hindu religious writings, the **Upanishads**, written between 800 BC and 400 BC, describe in beautiful verse the mystic experience of unity of the soul (*atman*) with **Brahma**, the supreme god, ideally attained through asceticism, renunciation of worldly values and meditation. The Upanishads also introduce the concepts of **samsara**, a cyclic round of death and rebirth characterized by suffering and perpetuated by desire, and **moksha**, liberation from *samsara*. These fundamental aspects of the Hindu world view are accepted by all but a handful of Hindus today, along with the belief in **karma**, the certainty that one's present position in society is determined by the effect of one's previous actions in this and past lives.

Hindu society

The stratification of Hindu society is rooted in a series of texts called the Dharma Shastras and Dharma Sutras, written at the same time as the Vedas.

The Mahabharata and the Ramayana

Eight times as long as the *Iliad* and *Odyssey* combined, the **Mahabharata** was written around 400 AD and tells of a feuding *kshatriya* family in northern India during the fourth millennium BC. The chief character is **Arjuna**, who, with his four brothers, represent the **Pandava** clan, supreme fighters and upholders of righteousness. The Pandava clan are resented by their cousins, the evil **Kauravas**, led by Duryodhana, the eldest son of Dhrtarashtra, ruler of the Kuru kingdom.

When Dhrtarashtra hands his kingdom over to the Pandavas, the Kauravas are understandably less than overjoyed. The subsequent battle between the Pandavas and Kauravas is described in the sixth book, the famous **Bhagavad Gita**. Krishna steps into battle as Arjuna's charioteer. Arjuna is in a dilemma, unable to justify the killing of his own kin in pursuit of a rightful kingdom. Krishna consoles him, reminding him that his principal duty is as a warrior, and convincing him that by fulfilling his dharma he not only upholds law and order by saving the kingdom from the grasp of unrighteous rulers, he also serves the gods in the spirit of devotion, and thus guarantees himself eternal union with the divine in the blissful state of *moksha*.

The Pandavas finally win the battle and Yudhishtra, eldest of the five Pandava brothers, is crowned king. Eventually Arjuna's grandson, Pariksit, inherits the throne, and the Pandavas trek to Mount Meru, the mythical centre of the universe and the abode of the gods, where Arjuna finds Krishna's promised *moksha*.

The Ramayana

The Ramayana tells the story of **Rama**, the seventh of Vishnu's eight incarnations. Although possibly based on a historic figure, Rama is seen essentially as a representation of Vishnu's heroic qualities. Rama is the oldest of four sons born to Dasaratha, the king of Ayodhya, and heir to the throne. When the time comes for Rama's coronation, Dasaratha's scheming third wife Kaikeyi has her own son Bharata crowned instead, and has Rama banished to the forest for fourteen years. In an exemplary show of filial piety, Rama accepts the loss of his throne and leaves the city with his wife Sita and brother Laksmana.

One day, Suparnakhi, the sister of the demon **Ravana**, spots Rama in the woods and instantly falls in love with him. Being a virtuous, loyal husband, Rama rebuffs her advances, while Laksmana cuts off her nose and ears in retaliation. In revenge, Ravana kidnaps Sita, who is borne away to one of Ravana's palaces on the island of **Lanka**.

Determined to find Sita, Rama enlists the help of the monkey god **Hanuman**, and the two of them gather an army and prepare to attack. After much fighting, Sita is rescued and reunited with her husband. On the long journey back to Ayodhya, Sita's honour is brought into question. To prove her innocence, she asks Laksmana to build a funeral pyre and steps into the flames, praying to Agni, the fire god. Agni walks her through the fire into the arms of a delighted Rama. They march into Ayodhya guided by a trail of lights laid out by the local people. Today, this illuminated homecoming is commemorated by Hindus all over the world during **Diwali**, the festival of lights. At the end of the epic, Rama's younger brother gladly steps down, allowing Rama to be crowned as the rightful king.

These defined four hierarchical classes, or **varnas**, each of which was assigned specific religious and social duties. In descending order the *varnas* are: **brahmins** (priests and teachers), **kshatriyas** (rulers and warriors), **vaishyas** (merchants and cultivators) and **shudras** (menials). Below the four *varnas* are the casteless **untouchables**, whose jobs involve contact with dirt or death (such as undertakers, leather-workers and cleaners). Though discrimination against untouchables is now a criminal offence, in part thanks to the campaigns of Gandhi (who rechristened them the "Harijans", or "Children of God"), the lowest stratum of society has by no means disappeared.

Within the four *varnas*, social status is further defined by **jati**, in which each individual is classified according to family and occupation (for example, a *vaishya* may belong to any one of hundreds of groups – anything from a jewellery seller or cloth merchant to a cowherd or farmer). A person's *jati* determines his **caste**, and lays restrictions on all aspects of life ranging from

Hindu gods and goddesses

Vishnu

The chief function of **Vishnu**, **"preserver"**, is to maintain the balance of the universe. With four arms holding a conch, discus, lotus and mace, Vishnu is blue-skinned, and often shaded by a serpent, or resting on its coils, afloat on an ocean. He is usually seen alongside his half-man-half-eagle vehicle, **Garuda**. According to tradition, Vishnu has descended to earth nine times in various forms (avatars) in order to fight the forces of evil and chaos and preserve the harmony of the cosmos: as a fish (Matsya), tortoise (Kurma), boar (Varaha), man-lion (Narsingh), dwarf (Vamana), axe-wielding Brahmin (Parsuram), Rama, Krishna and the Buddha (though others claim that Krishna's brother, Balaram, was also an avatar of Vishnu). The most important of these nine avatars are Rama and Krishna. **Rama**, Vishnu's seventh incarnation, is the chief character in the Ramayana (see p.397); for more on **Krishna**, see the separate box on p.401. Vishnu's tenth appearance on earth as Kalki, the saviour who will come to restore purity and destroy the wicked, is eagerly awaited. Followers of Vishnu, or **Vaishnavites**, are often recognizable by two vertical lines of paste on their foreheads.

Shiva

Shaivism, the cult of **Shiva**, was inspired by *bhakti*, requiring selfless love from devotees in a quest for divine communion, though unlike Vishnu, Shiva has never been incarnate on earth. He is presented in many different aspects, such as **Nataraja**, Lord of the Dance; **Mahadev**, Great God; **Maheshvar**, Divine Lord and source of all knowledge; and the terrible **Bhairav**, the god of the Shaivite ascetics who renounce family and caste ties and perform extreme meditative and yogic practices. Though he does have terrifying aspects, his role extends beyond that of destroyer, and he is revered as the source of the whole universe. He is often depicted with four or five faces, holding a trident, draped with serpents, and bearing a third eye in his forehead. In temples, he is identified with the lingam, or phallic symbol, resting in the yoni, a representation of female sexuality. Whether as statue or lingam, Shiva is guarded by his bull-mount, Nandi, and often accompanied by a consort, who also assumes various forms, and is looked upon as the vital energy, **shakti**, that empowers him.

Other gods and goddesses

Chubby and smiling, **Ganesh** acquired his unmistakable elephant head when he was mistakenly beheaded by his father, Shiva. The first son of Shiva and Parvati, Ganesh is invoked before every undertaking (except funerals). Seated on a throne or lotus, his image is often placed above temple gateways, in shops and houses; in his four arms he holds a conch, discus, bowl of sweets (or club) and a water lily, and he's always the types of food they can eat, their religious obligations and their relations with other castes. It also determines possible marriage partners, since Hindus generally only marry members of the same *jati* – marrying someone of a different *varna* often results in ostracism from both family and caste, leaving the couple stranded in a society where caste affiliation takes primacy over all other aspects of individual identity. There are almost three thousand *jatis*; the divisions and restrictions they have enforced have repeatedly become the subject of reform movements and the target of critics – though, equally, they also ensure a valuable but easily overlooked degree of social cohesion and economic support.

A Hindu has three aims in life: **dharma**, fulfilling one's duty to family and caste and acquiring religious merit through right living; **artha**, the lawful making of wealth; and **karma**, the satisfaction of desires.

attended by his vehicle, a rat. Credited with writing the Mahabharata as it was dictated by the sage Vyasa, Ganesh is regarded by many as the god of learning, the lord of success, prosperity and peace.

The great mother goddess, or **Mahadevi**, is represented in various forms. The most important is **Durga**, the fiercest of the female deities, an aspect of Shiva's more conservative consort, **Parvati** (also known as Uma), who is remarkable only for her beauty and fidelity. Statues show her with ten arms, holding the head of a demon, a spear, and other weapons; she tramples demons underfoot, or dances upon Shiva's body. A garland of skulls drapes her neck, and her tongue hangs from her mouth, dripping with blood; animal sacrifices are a crucial element of worship, to satisfy her thirst for blood and deter her ruthless anger. Amongst Durga's many terrifying aspects is the famous demon-slaying goddess **Kali**.

Vishnu's consort **Lakshmi**, usually shown sitting or standing on a lotus flower, and sometimes called Padma (lotus), is the embodiment of loveliness, grace and charm, and the goddess of prosperity and wealth (and thus enduringly popular with India's commercial classes). Lakshmi appears in different aspects alongside each of his avatars; the most important are Sita, wife of Rama, and Radha, Krishna's favourite *gopi*. In many temples she is shown as one with Vishnu, in the form of the composite male-female Lakshmi Narayan.

India's great monkey god, **Hanuman**, features in the Ramayana as Rama's chief aide in the fight against the demon-king of Lanka. Depicted as a giant monkey clasping a mace, Hanuman is the deity of acrobats and wrestlers, but is also seen as Rama and Sita's greatest devotee, and an author of Sanskrit grammar. As his representatives, monkeys find sanctuary in temples all over India.

The most beautiful Hindu goddess, **Saraswati**, the wife of Brahma, is revered as the goddess of music, creativity and learning. She is usually shown with a flawless milk-white complexion, sitting or standing on a water lily or peacock, playing a lute, sitar or *vina*.

Mention must also be made of the **sacred cow**, Kamdhenu, who receives devotion through the respect shown to all cows, left to amble through streets and temples all over India. The origin of the cow's sanctity is uncertain; some myths record that Brahma created cows at the same time as Brahmins, to provide ghee (clarified butter) for use in priestly ceremonies. To this day cow dung and urine are used to purify houses (in fact the urine keeps insects at bay), and the killing or harming of cows by any Hindu is a grave offence. The cow is often referred to as mother of the gods, and each part of its body is significant: its horns symbolize the gods, its face the sun and moon, its shoulders Agni (god of fire) and its legs the Himalayas.

The principal Hindu deities

Surpassing even the Vedas and Upanishads in cultural influence and popularity are Hinduism's two great epics, the **Mahabharata** and **Ramayana** (see box, p.397), thought to have been completed by the fourth century AD at the latest, though subsequently retold, modified and embellished on numerous occasions and in various different regional languages. The two epics helped crystalize the basic framework of Hindu religious belief which survives to this day, based on a supreme triumvirate of deities. **Brahma**, the original Aryan godhead, or "creator", was joined by two gods who had begun to achieve increasing significance in the evolving Hindu worldview. The first, **Vishnu**, "the preserver", was seen as the force responsible for maintaining the balance of the cosmos whenever it was threatened by disruptive forces, incarnating himself on earth nine times in various animal and human forms, or avatars, to fight the forces of evil and chaos, most famously as Rama (the god-hero whose exploits are described in the Ramayana) and as Krishna (who appears at the most significant juncture of the Mahabharata). The second, **Shiva**, "the destroyer" (a development of the Aryan god Rudra, who had played a minor role in the Vedas), was charged with destroying and renewing the universe at periodic intervals, though his powers are not merely destructive, and he is worshipped in myriad forms with various attributes (see box, p.398 for more). The three supreme gods are often depicted in a trinity, or *trimurti*, though in time Brahma's importance declined, and Shiva and Vishnu became the most popular deities – the famous Brahma temple at Pushkar is now one of the few in India dedicated to this venerable but rather esoteric god.

Local Rajasthani deities

In addition to the major Hindu gods (see box, p.398), most of Rajasthan's tribal people and rural villagers worship various deities associated with the natural world; there are sacred trees in every village (a belief particularly strong amongst the Bishnois of Jodhpur; see p.295), while animals including cows, monkeys, peacocks, deer and snakes – as well as the famous rats of the Deshnok temple near Bikaner – all have various religious associations.

A number of folk heroes have also achieved quasi-divine status and are widely worshipped throughout the state (and in other parts of India), the pre-eminent being Gogaji and Pabuji. **Gogaji** (or Gugga, also worshipped by Muslims, who call him Jahar Pir) was an eleventh-century Chauhan Rajput from the Churu region in Shekhawati. According to legend he was chasing bandits who had stolen a relative's cows when he was confronted by a hostile snake. Gogaji pleaded with the snake to allow him to pass, promising to return later. The snake granted this wish, and Gogaji – having bested the dacoits – returned to the snake as promised. The snake, impressed by the warrior's honesty, promised that Gogaji would henceforth have the power to cure his followers of snakebite, for which he is revered today throughout Rajasthan (and also in neighbouring states). Many villages have shrines to him, to which victims of snake-bite are taken; carvings show him mounted on horseback with a serpent in attendance.

Rajasthan's other principal folk deity, **Pabuji**, was another warrior-like figure who has achieved immortality thanks to his devotion to cows. The historical Pabuji appears to have been a minor fourteenth-century noble belonging to the Rathore clan of the Jodhpur region, although he has since become embroiled in a tangled skein of legend, existing in various confusing versions (in one he

Krishna

Krishna, the penultimate incarnation of Vishnu (see box, p.398), is perhaps the single most important Hindu deity in the Rajasthani pantheon, occupying a pre-eminent place in the affections of maharajas and commoners. The Induvansa (moon-descended) Rajput dynasties (see p.380) claim direct descent from him, while he is also considered the tutelary deity of the rulers of Jaipur, as well as occupying an important place in the religious worship of the house of Mewar, the rulers of Udaipur.

Krishna (literally "black" – paintings usually show him with blue skin, often with a flute in hand) was according to some historians based on a historical figure who lived around 3200–3000 BC. He was born into the ruling family of the kingdom of **Mathura**, close to modern Agra, then under the rule of the tyrant Kamsa, who had usurped the throne of his father, Ugrasena. A prophecy had predicted that Kamsa would meet his death at the hands of the eighth son of his sister Devaki. This son was Krishna, though he was magically spirited away from court before Kamsa could do away with him and brought up in secret as the adopted son of the cowherd Nanda, growing up in a rural village in the countryside of **Vrindavan**, in the hinterlands of Mathura. Here the young Krishna (along with his brother Balarama, who had also escaped Kamsa's clutches) spent his time sporting with the local maidens, or **gopis**, in particular his favourite, **Radha** (considered an incarnation of Vishnu's consort, Lakshmi), whilst periodically demonstrating his divine powers in warding off attacks by demons dispatched by Kamsa (who had discovered the young prince's escape and subsequent whereabouts) and other assaults, such as when he saved his village from a catastrophic flood released by the god Indra by lifting Mount Goverdhan above his head to serve as a protective shield.

In due course Krishna grew to manhood and, fulfilling the prophecy, returned to Mathura where he slew Kamsa and placed Ugrasena back on the throne. He also became friendly with his cousins, the **Pandavas**, the heroes of the Mahabharata (see p.397), serving as Arjuna's charioteer during that epic's climactic battle and offering him the advice which forms the core of the celebrated **Bhagavad Gita**. He later established a kingdom at **Dwarka**, on the coast of modern Gujarat, where he eventually died, accidentally shot by a hunter whilst meditating in the forest.

Part of the reason for Krishna's local importance is geographical. The proximity of the sacred region of Vrindavan meant that certain Rajput rulers (particularly the Kachchwahas of Amber) became directly involved in preserving temples and religious artefacts in the area – the images worshipped by the rulers of Udaipur at Nathdwara (see p.350) and the rulers of Jaipur at the city's Govind Devji temple were both rescued from Vrindavan during the long period of Mughal iconoclasm which characterized the reign of Aurangzeb. In addition, Krishna's uncompromising military ethos, encapsulated by his advice to Arjuna which forms the basis of the Bhagavad Gita, is very much of a piece with the traditional Rajput warrior values.

It is Krishna's amatory exploits as the young flute-playing cowherd Govinda, however, which continue to inspire the greatest devotion in his followers. The love of Radha and the *gopis* for Krishna equates physical and spiritual love – a form of personal devotion, or **bhakti**, which makes it possible to achieve union with the divine without the ritualized intercession of Brahmin priests or the asceticism and renunciation which had previously been considered essential elements in traditional Hindu worship, and which lies at the heart of Krishna's enduring appeal, both to Indians and to Krishna devotees worldwide.

even travels to Lanka and, Rama-like, kills the demon king Ravana). The various Pabuji legends are all characterized by his superhuman fighting prowess and his long struggles to prevent the cattle-rustling villain Khici from making off with the herds of Deval (perhaps a form of the mother goddess Devi), during which Pabuji is assisted by his magical horse, Kesar Kalami (who, it turns out, is a reincarnation of his own mother). Interestingly, Pabuji's divine status is not accepted by higher-caste Hindus, and his shrines are attended not by Brahmins, but by low-caste Nayaks.

Another remarkable example of how local agricultural and environmental concerns have merged with the religious is supplied by the **Bishnois** of the Jodhpur region, who under their inspirational guru Jambeshwar Bhagavan espoused a pantheistic creed in which all forms are natural life are considered sacred – for their full story, see p.295.

Female deities and folk heroes also have an important place in the Rajasthan pantheon; most are considered manifestation of the Mother God, or Mahadevi. Various local incarnations of the Devi (or, according to other interpretations, Durga) are widely worshipped, most famously **Karni Mata** (see p.326), the miracle-working medieval divine whose bizarre rat temple just outside Bikaner still attracts hordes of pilgrims. Woman who have voluntarily performed **sati** are widely venerated – most famously at the immensely popular Sati Mata temple at Jhunjhunu in Shekhawati, though shrines to *satis* can be seen throughout the region, especially at Chittaurgarh Fort, the place most closely associated with this gruesome act.

Hindu religious practice

The primary concern of most Hindus is to reduce bad karma and acquire merit by honest and charitable living in the hope of attaining a higher status of rebirth. Strict rules address purity and pollution, the most obvious of them requiring high-caste Hindus to limit their contact with "polluting" lower castes. All bodily excretions are polluting (hence the strange looks Westerners receive when they blow their noses and return their handkerchiefs to their pockets). Above all else, **water** is the agent of purification, used in ablutions before prayer, and revered in all rivers, especially Ganga (the Ganges).

In most Hindu homes, a chosen deity is worshipped daily in a shrine room, and scriptures are read. Outside the home, worship takes place in temples, and consists of **puja**, or devotion to god – sometimes a simple act of prayer, but more commonly a complex process when the god's image is circumambulated, offered flowers, rice, sugar and incense, and anointed with water, milk or sandalwood paste (which is usually done on behalf of the devotee by the temple priest). The aim in puja is to take **darshan** – glimpse the god – and thus receive his or her blessing. Whether devotees simply worship the deity in prayer, or make requests – for a healthy crop, a son, good results in exams, a vigorous monsoon or a cure for illness – they leave the temple with *prasad*, an offering of food or flowers taken from the holy sanctuary.

Communal worship and get-togethers en route to pilgrimage sites are celebrated with the singing of hymns, perhaps verses in praise of Krishna taken from the Bhagavad Purana, or repetitive cries of "Jai Shankar!" (Praise to Shiva). Temple ceremonies are conducted in Sanskrit by *pujaris* who tend the image in daily rituals that symbolically wake, bathe, feed and dress the god, and finish each day by preparing the god for sleep during the elaborate evening ritual, or *aarti*. In many villages, shrines to *devatas*, village deities who function as protectors and may bring disaster if neglected, are more important than temples.

The most significant event in a Hindu's life is **marriage**, which symbolizes ritual purity, and for women is so important that it takes the place of initiation. Feasting, dancing, and singing, usually lasting for a week or more before and after the marriage, are the order of the day.

Festivals and pilgrimages

The Hindu year is marked by **festivals** devoted to deities, re-enacting mythological stories and commemorating sacred sites. The grandest festivals are held at places made holy by association with gods, goddesses, miracles, and great teachers, or rivers and mountains; throughout the year these are important **pilgrimage** sites, visited by devotees eager to receive *darshan*, glimpse the world of the gods, and attain merit. Important Hindu pilgrimage sites in Rajasthan include the Karni Mata temple near Bikaner; the town of Pushkar and its Brahma temple; the Sati Mata temple in Jhunjhunu, Shekhawati; and the Dargah in Ajmer, the most important place of Muslim pilgrimage in India, though also much-visited by devout Hindus; as well as the various Jain and Hindu temples of Mount Abu.

For a full list of religious festivals in Rajasthan, Delhi and Agra, see pp.55–57.

Islam

Muslims – making up some twelve percent of India's population – form a significant presence in almost every town, city and village, even in determinedly Hindu Rajasthan. The belief in only one god, Allah, the condemnation of idol worship, and the observance of their own strict dietary laws and specific festivals set Muslims apart from their Hindu neighbours, with whom they have coexisted for centuries. The coexistence hasn't always been peaceful, though in recent times Delhi and Rajasthan have largely avoided the communal fighting which has engulfed other parts of the country, even in potential flashpoints such as Ajmer (thanks, it is said, to the presence of the tomb of the great Muslim divine Khwaja Muin-ud-din Chishti – see p.267)

Islam (literally, "submission to God"), was founded by **Mohammed** (570–632 AD), who transmitted God's final and perfected revelation to mankind through the **Koran** (Qur'an). The true beginning of Islam is dated to 622 AD, when Mohammed and his followers, exiled from Mecca, made the *hijra*, or migration, north to Medina. From Medina, Mohammed led his community in battles against the Meccans. When **Mecca** was peacefully surrendered to Mohammed in 630, he cleared the sacred shrine, the Kaa'ba, of idols, and proclaimed it the pilgrimage centre of Islam.

The first Muslims to settle in India were traders who arrived on the south coast in the seventh century, probably in search of timber for shipbuilding. Much more significant was the invasion of north India under **Mahmud of Ghazni** (see p.380) and successive Turkish invaders from Afghanistan who set themselves up in Delhi as **sultans**, the forerunners of the **Mughals** (see p.382). The first Muslim presence in Rajasthan also dates back to this time: Ajmer became part of the Ghaznivid empire – and remains the pre-eminent Muslim town in the state to this day – while Muslims also established a subsidiary statelet further north at Jhunjhunu in Shekhawati, where they continue to live in considerable numbers. The fruits of this invasion can be seen today in the superb Islamic monuments of Delhi, Agra, Fatehpur Sikri and Ajmer – the finest architectural legacy of Islam anywhere in the Subcontinent.

Many Muslims who settled in India intermarried with Hindus and Jains, and the community spread. A further factor in its growth was missionary activity by **Sufis**, who emphasized abstinence and self-denial in service to God, and stressed the attainment of inner knowledge of God through meditation and mystical experience. Sufi teachings also spread among Hindus – their use of music (particularly *qawwali* singing) and dance, shunned by orthodox Muslims, appealed to Hindus, for whom *kirtan* (singing) played an important role in religious practice. Some of India's most important Sufi **shrines** are located in Delhi, Agra and Rajasthan, including (most famously) the shrine of Khwaja Muin-ud-din Chishti in Ajmer, along with the shrines of his fellow Chishti saints, Sheikh Nizamuddin Aulia in Delhi and Sheikh Salim at Fatehpur Sikri.

Sikhism

Sikhism, India's youngest religion, remains dominant in the Punjab, while its adherents have spread throughout northern India; Delhi has a particularly large Sikh community, and there are significant numbers of Sikhs across Rajasthan, especially in Jaipur.

The movement was founded by **Guru Nanak** (1469–1539). Born into an orthodox Hindu *kshatriya* family near Lahore (in present-day Pakistan), he was among many sixteenth-century poet-philosophers who formed emotional cults, drawing elements from both Hinduism and Islam. Nanak declared that "God is neither Hindu nor Muslim" and regarded God as **Sat**, or truth. In common with Hindus, Nanak believed in a cyclic process of death and rebirth caused by worldly attachment, but also asserted that liberation (*moksha*) was attainable in this life by all women and men regardless of caste. Though he condemned ancestor worship, astrology, caste distinction, sex discrimination, auspicious days, and the rituals of Brahmins, Nanak did not attack Islam or Hinduism – he simply regarded the many deities as names for one supreme God, and encouraged his followers to shift religious emphasis from ritual to meditation.

Following Nanak's death, nine successive Sikh gurus acted as leaders of the faith, each introducing new elements into their increasingly powerful religious movement. Throughout their history, the Sikhs have had to battle to protect their faith and their people, especially against the Mughals; Guru Arjan Dev became Sikhism's first martyr when he was executed by Jahangir, while Guru Teg Bahadur was beheaded by Aurangzeb in 1675.

Teg Bahadur's son and successor, and the last Sikh guru, **Guru Gobind Singh**, revolutionized the entire movement, giving it a notably more muscular and militaristic ethos. In 1699 Gobind Singh founded the militant Sikh brotherhood known as the **Khalsa**, which was designed to protect the faithful from persecution and fight oppression. The Khalsa requires members to renounce tobacco, halal meat and sexual relations with Muslims, and to adopt the **five Ks**: *kesh* (unshorn hair – hence the distinctive Sikh turban), *kangha* (comb), *kirpan* (sword), *kara* (steel bracelet) and *kachcha* (short trousers). This code, together with the replacement of caste names with Singh ("lion") for men and Kaur ("princess") for women, created a distinct cultural identity. Guru Gobind Singh also compiled a standardized version of the Adi Granth, which contains the hymns of the first nine gurus as well as poems written by Hindus and Muslims, and installed it as his successor, naming it **Guru Granth Sahib**. This became the Sikhs' spiritual guide, while political authority rested with the Khalsa.

Militant Sikh demands for a separate state – **Khalistan** – have burdened Sikhs with a reputation as military activists, but Sikhs regard their religion as one devoted to egalitarianism, democracy and social awareness. Though to die fighting for the cause of religious freedom is considered to lead to liberation, the use of force is officially sanctioned only when other methods have failed. Due to their martial traditions and emphasis on valour, Sikhs continue to provide an essential element of the Indian army.

Sikh **worship** takes place in a **gurudwara** ("door to the guru") or in the home, providing a copy of the Guru Granth Sahib is present. There are no priests, and no fixed time for worship, but congregations often meet in the mornings and evenings, and always on the eleventh day of each lunar month, and on the first day of the year. During **Kirtan**, or hymn singing, a feature of every Sikh service, verses from the Guru Granth Sahib or Janam Sakhis (stories of Guru Nanak's life), are sung to rhythmic clapping. The communal meal, *langar*, following prayers and singing, reinforces the practice laid down by Guru Nanak that openly flaunted caste and religious differences. *Gurudwaras* – often schools, clinics or hostels as well as houses of prayer – are usually whitewashed and surmounted by a dome, and are always distinguishable by the *nishan sahib*, a yellow flag introduced by Guru Hargobind (1606–44). As in Islam, God is never depicted in pictorial form. Instead, the representative symbol Ek Onkar is etched into a canopy that shades the Guru Granth Sahib, which always stands in the main prayer room.

Jainism

India's **Jain** population in India is relatively small, accounting for less than one percent of the population, but has been tremendously influential throughout the north of the country. Jain traders have played an important part in the economic life of Rajasthan, and the state is home to two of the world's finest complexes of Jain temples (at Ranakpur and Mount Abu). Similarities to Hindu worship, and a shared respect for nature and non-violence, have contributed to the decline of the Jain community through conversion to Hinduism, but there is no antagonism between the two sects.

Focused on the practice of **ahimsa** (non-violence), Jains follow a rigorous discipline to avoid harm to all living substances – including humans, animals, plants, water, fire, earth and air. Their world-view is similar to that of Hinduism, believing that the original purity of the soul is obscured by *karma* created by worldly actions, and that the only way to escape the wheel of death and rebirth is to follow the path of asceticism and meditation, rejecting passion, attachment and impure action.

The Jain doctrine is based upon the teachings of **Mahavira**, or "Great Hero", the last in a succession of 24 **tirthankaras** ("crossing-makers") said to appear on earth every three hundred million years. Mahavira (c.599–527 BC) was born as Vardhamana Jnatrputra into a *kshatriya* family near modern Patna in northeast India. Like the Buddha, Mahavira rejected family life at the age of thirty, and spent years wandering as an ascetic, renouncing all possessions in an attempt to conquer attachment to worldly values. Firmly opposed to sacrificial rites and caste distinctions, after gaining complete understanding and detachment, he began teaching others, not about Vedic gods and divine heroes, but about the true nature of the world, and the means required for release, *moksha*, from an endless cycle of rebirth.

His teachings were written down in the first millennium BC, and Jainism prospered throughout India. Not long after, there was a schism, in part based on linguistic and geographical divisions, but mostly due to differences in monastic practice. On the one hand the **Digambara** ("sky-clad") Jains believed that nudity was an essential part of world renunciation, and that women are incapable of achieving liberation from worldly existence. The ("white-clad") **Svetambaras**, however, disregarded the extremes of nudity, incorporated nuns into monastic communities, and even acknowledged a female *tirthankara*. Today the two sects worship at different temples, but the number of naked Digambaras is minimal. Many Svetambara monks and nuns wear white masks to avoid breathing in insects, and carry a "fly-whisk", sometimes used to brush their path; none will use public transport, and they often spend days or weeks walking barefoot to a pilgrimage site.

Jain **temples** are wonderfully ornate, with pillars, brackets and spires carved by *silavats* into voluptuous maidens, musicians, saints, and even Hindu deities; the *swastika* symbol commonly set into the marble floors is central to Jainism, representing the four states of rebirth as gods, humans, "hell beings", or animals and plants. Worship in temples consists of prayer and puja before images of the *tirthankaras*; the devotee circumambulates the image, chants sacred verses and makes offerings of flowers, sandalwood paste, rice, sweets and incense. It's common to fast four times a month on *parvan* (holy) days, the eighth and fourteenth days of the moon's waxing and waning periods. While reducing attachment to the body, this emulates the fast to death (while in meditation), or *sallekhana*, accepted by Jain mendicants as a final rejection of attachment, and a relatively harmless way to end worldly life.

Art and architecture

The area covered by Rajasthan, Delhi and Agra boasts an extraordinary wealth of art and architecture, exemplified by world-famous monuments such as the Taj Mahal, the lakeside palace of Udaipur, the desert citadel of Jaisalmer and the doughty Meherangarh Fort in Jodhpur. Two distinct strands run through the region's artistic history: the Islamic monuments of the Delhi Sultanate and their Mughal successors, and the great forts and palaces of Hindu Rajasthan, and it is these two diverse traditions – and the constant interactions between them over the centuries – which have shaped almost all the region's range of artistic achievements.

Early Islamic architecture

The region's first great architectural monuments date from the beginning of Islamic rule in the Subcontinent, starting with the **Qutb Minar** complex in Delhi, which was erected following the establishment of the Slave Dynasty by Qutb-ud-din Aiback in 1206. The complex is best known for the soaring **Qutb Minar**, a massive minaret whose monumentally simple outline, decorated with bands of Koranic calligraphy, was inspired by the funeral towers of Persia. More interesting in the context of Indo-Islamic architecture, however, is the **Quwwat-ul-Islam** ("Might of Islam"), India's first mosque, which stands at the heart of the complex and which neatly demonstrates the creative interplay between imported Islamic styles and local Hindu traditions which was to remain a defining feature of north Indian architecture right through to the Taj Mahal. Obviously preferring speed of construction to artistic purity, Aiback's architects constructed the mosque using a mass of columns recycled from the numerous Hindu and Jain shrines which had previously stood on the site, sometimes piled on top of one another to achieve the necessary height, though many of the original images were defaced to satisfy traditional Islamic strictures forbidding the representation of human and animal forms. In addition, the mosque is placed on a raised platform (a Hindu temple tradition, physically separating the sacred from the secular) and topped by a flat roof (another Hindu influence, since local architects were unfamiliar with the use of true arches which form such an important feature of traditional Islamic architecture). In sum, the mosque offers an early and telling example of the way in which local traditions were to challenge the architectural and even theological credentials of all the subsequent Muslim rulers of north India.

The Qutb complex is the finest architectural achievement of the Delhi Sultanate. The sultans' subsequent architectural creations, though numerous, follow no discernible evolutionary pattern, although they do introduce many of the architectural motifs which are usually thought of as being the preserve of the later Mughal dynasty, such as the combination of red sandstone decorated with white marble inlay, a stock-in-trade of Mughal design, which was actually first used at Ala-ud-din Khalji's **Alai Darwaza** gateway at the Qutb complex. The Indo-Islamic tradition of constructing grandiose **tombs** was also already well-established under the Delhi Sultans. The first notable mausoleum built in the Subcontinent was the (now ruined) **tomb of Iltimush** at the Qutb complex, while further notable examples were erected by the **Tughluq** dynasty (such as the plain, almost cubist Tomb of Ghiyas ud-din Tughluq at Tughluqabad) and the later **Lodi** rulers, whose elegant mausoleums, surmounted by domes and fronted by high arches, were to exert a significant influence on Mughal architects.

Mughal architecture

For many people, the great monuments of the Mughal period represent the pinnacle of Indian architecture, although to what extent they can be properly regarded as "Indian" at all remains a subject of considerable debate, and Hindu nationalists have always felt uncomfortable with the way in which Indian culture is often symbolized by the "Islamic" Taj Mahal rather than, for example, by the temples of Khajuraho or Tamil Nadu (conversely, during Partition, some Muslim nationalists claimed that the Taj Mahal should have been taken to pieces and moved to the Islamic state of Pakistan, where – they claimed – it more properly belonged).

In fact, despite its Muslim provenance and superficially Persian-influenced design, the sources of Mughal architecture are surprisingly varied, and include not only the Islamic styles which they brought with them from their original Central Asian homelands but many Indian features as well, ranging from local Hindu sculptural traditions through to the important (but easily overlooked) influence of the numerous Indo-Islamic works already constructed in the Subcontinent by the Delhi Sultans. Different styles come to the fore in different buildings, ranging from the largely Persian-style Humayun's Tomb through to the almost entirely Hindu buildings constructed during Akbar's reign at Fatehpur Sikri and Agra Fort – a constant interaction between conflicting styles which only achieved a kind of synthesis towards the end of the great Mughal period during the reign of Shah Jahan.

The early Mughals

The first two Mughal rulers, Babur and Humayun, were more concerned with establishing their hold on the empire, and left little in the way of physical remains. **Babur** appears to have been happy to live in tents during his four brief years in power, and channelled his creative energies into commissioning a modest sequence of Persian-style gardens inspired by his Central Asian homeland, such as the much-modified Rambagh at Agra. **Humayun** spent most of his life in exile, and had only just begun work on a new citadel in Delhi, now known as the **Purana Qila**, when he was deposed by the Afghan warlord **Sher Shah** (reigned 1540–55). Sher Shah continued Humayun's building works at the Purana Qila, commissioning the Sher Mandal pavilion and Qila-i-Kuhna mosque. The elegantly simple designs of these two buildings, with large masses of red sandstone delineated by towering pointed arches and bands of white marble, are the first buildings to display the essential hallmarks of what would later be called the "Mughal" style – a notable irony, given that they were created by the man who very nearly extinguished Mughal rule in India before it had even properly begun.

Akbar and Jahangir

Following Sher Shah's death, Humayun briefly reclaimed his Indian empire before tumbling to his death down a steep flight of steps in the Sher Mandal –

Sher Shah's architectural legacy wreaking an unintentional posthumous revenge on his former adversary. It was thus left to **Akbar** to initiate the golden era of Mughal architecture (and art; see p.410).

Akbar and his successors embarked on an unprecedented architectural spree, the lavishness of their buildings intended to symbolize the dynasty's glory and imperial status, and thus to buttress its legitimacy in the eyes of their Hindu subjects. Fittingly enough, the first great Mughal monument is an imperial mausoleum, **Humayun's Tomb** in Delhi, a type of building with which the Mughals would become inextricably associated, and which would eventually reach its apotheosis in the peerless Taj Mahal – though the fact that the Koran expressly forbids the construction of extravagant funerary monuments suggests just how shaky the Mughals' Islamic credentials really were, and how much they owed to local Indian cultural circumstances, including those of the recently vanquished Delhi Sultans, whose own funerary monuments can still be seen scattered across Delhi.

Humayun's Tomb established a pattern which would henceforth be followed in virtually all Mughal mausoleums, with a monumental square or rectangular tomb chamber (usually – but not always – topped by a dome) set on a raised plinth within a *charbagh*-style Persian garden, divided into four quadrants by walkways and water channels – a symbolic representation of the gardens and rivers of paradise. Some of the tomb's design features had already appeared in mausolea erected by the Delhi Sultans, though never before on this epic scale, with a huge but simple sandstone tomb, its monumental mass artfully broken up by symmetrical arched portals (*iwans*) and decorative bands of coloured inlay work, the whole combining simplicity with subtlety on an epic scale – a classic example of the Mughal style.

Humayun's Tomb is, however, quite untypical of most of the architecture of Akbar's reign. Far more representative are the great abandoned city of **Fatehpur Sikri** and **Agra Fort**, which Akbar comprehensively remodelled. Both these sites are characterized by their extraordinarily eclectic medley of architectural styles – from the chastely Islamic to the exuberantly Indian – a physical expression of the emperor's famous cultural and political tolerance. Many of the buildings at both sites are architectural one-offs, such as the strange Diwan-i-Khas at Fatehpur Sikri and the flamboyant, Gujarati-influenced Jahangiri Mahal at Agra Fort – not to mention the great mosque at Fatehpur Sikri which, in an odd echo of Qutb-ud-din Aiback's Quwwat-ul-Islam mosque in Delhi, uses Hindu-style temple columns to support the arcades of an otherwise traditional Islamic place of worship.

Akbar's successor, **Jahangir**, was more interested in painting (and opium) than architecture. The major monument from his reign is another tomb, the enormous mausoleum built for Akbar at **Sikandra** near Agra, though it suffers from a rather hotpotch design – possibly the result of the emperor's own interference in ongoing designs. More successful is the exquisite **Itimad-ud-daulah** mausoleum commissioned for her father by Jahangir's remarkable wife, Nur Jahan (see pp.180–181), the dynasty's first purely marble structure, beautifully decorated with inlay work – a combination that was to become one of the defining features of the culminating phase of Mughal architecture.

Shah Jahan

The pinnacle of Mughal architecture was reached during the reign of **Shah Jahan**, one of the greatest patrons of architecture the world has known, whose massive sequence of building projects in Delhi and Agra has done much, for good or ill, to colour foreign perceptions of the nature of Indian art and culture. Many of Shah Jahan's creative energies were expended in comprehensively remodelling the old imperial capital at **Delhi**, where he created both the Red Fort and the new city of Shahjahanabad (now better known as Old Delhi) – a gargantuan undertaking with which the self-styled King of the World (as his imperial moniker translates) intended to thoroughly eclipse all the creations of his illustrious forebears and stamp his mark on posterity once and for all. Unfortunately, both have suffered major depredations since their construction, and the only part of the plan which survives intact is the magnificent Jama Masjid, a vast sandstone edifice whose masterfully proportioned ensemble of *iwans*, domes and minarets encapsulates the Mughal style at its most massively simple and severe.

It is with **Agra**, however, that Shah Jahan is now most closely associated, most obviously the Taj Mahal, though he also made significant embellishments to the city's fort, creating a fine new sequence of sumptuous apartments within Akbar's original palace. Whereas previous Mughal architecture had been built largely in sandstone, Shah Jahan's new palace architecture employed pristine white marble, typically decorated with beautiful *pietra dura* inlay, in which semi-precious stones were inlaid into the marble in graceful floral patterns and abstract geometrical designs, a type of rich but understated decoration which is subordinated to overall architectural schemes of chaste simplicity.

Besides the sumptuous use of marble and *pietra dura*, Shah Jahan's buildings at Agra Fort also exemplify a new phase in Mughal architecture. Compared to the stylistic free-for-all of Akbar's reign, the elegantly simple outlines of Shah Jahan's palace buildings appear, superficially at least, to represent a return to a purer and more obviously Islamic style of architecture. Despite their ostensibly Persian appearance, however, Shah Jahan's creations also incorporate many of the Hindu features – chhatris, *chajjas*, *bangaldar*-style roofs and Hindu temple-style columns – which had crept into Mughal architecture during the reign of Akbar, though they are now incorporated into the overall design in a more subtle and considered form, achieving a genuine synthesis of Islamic and Indian motifs which is perhaps the true definition of the Mughal style.

This new-found synthesis is also present in Shah Jahan's **Taj Mahal**. Most obviously, the Taj represents the culmination of the great Mughal tradition of tomb building – an etherealized version of Humayun's Tomb, its proportions reworked in a more satisfyingly compact form and clad in a translucent coat of white marble. Again, however, the overall Islamic design is blended with specifically Indian elements, such as the four chhatris which surround the main dome, while even the four minarets which flank the mausoleum are topped by decidedly Indian-looking cupolas.

Not that the Taj was the end of the Mughal tomb-building tradition. The Mughal emperor Aurangzeb subsequently built a decidedly Taj-like tomb for one of his wives in Aurangabad, the Bibi-ka-Maqbara, while **Safdardang's Tomb** in Delhi offers a rather kitsch later take on the same theme.

Mughal painting

Although the Mughals are now best remembered for their architectural creations, they also oversaw a golden era in Indian painting thanks to their assiduous patronage of both local and foreign artists (although sadly many of the finest Mughal-era artworks are now in foreign collections). Mughal art grew out of the traditions of Persian painting, though, as with their buildings, a host of foreign influences soon enriched the original style. The painting of Persian-style miniatures had already been encouraged by Muslim rulers in various parts of India since the fifteenth century, such as the sultan of Mandu, in modern Madhya Pradesh, who around 1500 had commissioned the celebrated *Ni'mat-nama* ("Book of Delectation"), an illustrated recipe book.

The second Mughal emperor, **Humayun**, probably had painters working for him before his exile from India in 1539 (the loss of several illustrated manuscripts whilst on campaign is recorded by his court biographer). The effective foundation of the school of Mughal painting, however, can be dated to 1549, when Humayun, in temporary exile in Kabul, recruited the painters Mir Sayyid Ali and Abd al-Samad. Both subsequently travelled to India with Humayan, where they oversaw a creative explosion of Mughal art, as well as giving painting lessons to both Humayun and his son Akbar.

Akbar greatly increased production and established a state atelier, employing around a hundred mainly Hindu artists working under the supervision of Mir Sayyid Ali and Abd al-Samad, who trained these local artists in the Persian manner – whilst the Indian painters in turn introduced aspects of their own pictorial traditions. Akbar-era paintings were predominantly historical or political in nature; many depict famous events from various legends, showing a sense of drama and action quite unlike the more sedate style of the traditional Persian miniature. Most of these paintings were found in the enormous illustrated books which the emperor commissioned, including the *Akbarnama*, the official court history of his reign, along with other works of Muslim history, poetry and legend, most famously the *Romance of Amir Hamza* (or *Hamza-nama),* an account of the legendary struggles of the Prophet's uncle, comprising around fourteen hundred large (over 2ft high) illustrations painted on pieces of cotton. Richly illustrated translations of the Hindu classics the Mahabharata and Ramayana were also produced – a typical example of Akbar's tolerance and curiosity.

The increasing presence of European diplomats and merchants at Akbar's court also introduced local painters to contemporary Western art (a selection of illustrated Bibles presented to the emperor by a Jesuit mission in 1580 proved particularly influential). Europeans subsequently began to crop up occasionally in Mughal painting, as did Western stylistic features such as halos, cherubs and angels. In addition, a new Western-style emphasis on realism and the greater use of perspective began to creep into Mughal art; figures become more three-dimensional, with the introduction of shading on faces (though these developments were perhaps also partly influenced by Indian artists, who had been brought up in the much more sculptural traditions of Hindu art).

Mughal painting reached its apogee during the reign of **Jahangir**, who had a particular passion for the pictorial arts. Jahangir reduced the number of artists working for him and encouraged a cult of technical excellence, whereby individual painters became fully responsible for particular works (many Akbar-era works had been produced on an assembly-line principle, so that different artists were responsible for colouring, outlines, the painting of figures and faces, and for overall composition). The emphasis shifted from the massive illustrated historical books and dramatic action scenes favoured by Akbar to much more restrained style, with far fewer figures, often arranged in carefully stylized poses. The most frequent subject is, not surprisingly, the emperor himself, who features in a long line of hagiographic portraits, some of them featuring an outlandish array of allegorical symbols (perhaps influenced by Western mannerist art) intended to emphasize Jahangir's secular and spiritual credentials. A famous painting by the leading artist Bichitr, for example, shows the emperor engulfed in a vast halo (composed of a combined sun and moon) while sitting on an hourglass throne and presenting a book to a Sufi holy man. The Ottoman sultan and James I of England look on reverentially, while a pair of winged angels at the bottom polish a laudatory inscription. Not that all Jahangir-era paintings are similarly overblown. Natural history was another of the emperor's pet themes, and there are dozens of paintings, such as those by the famous artist Mansur, showing pictures of exotic creatures which had been brought to court, ranging from turkeys to zebras.

The production of miniatures continued under Shah Jahan, though he was less interested in painting than in jewellery and architecture. The pious Aurangzeb had even less concern with artistic matters, and his declining patronage meant that most of the painters of the Mughal atelier left court to work for Hindu nobles – a considerable number appear to have ended up in Rajasthan.

Rajput secular architecture

Rajput architecture developed out of a completely different set of cultural traditions to those which informed Mughal art, and although Mughal stylistic innovations had an important influence on Rajput designs (just as Rajput styles, in turn, influenced Mughal craftsmen), the art and architecture of the state evolved in its own distinct way, and out of an essentially Indian, rather than Islamic, tradition.

Despite the state's strong Hindu culture, Rajasthan's major monuments are almost all secular, either the great Rajput forts or the lavish palaces that were often built alongside or within them, or the flamboyant havelis constructed by wealthy merchants. The finest expressions of Rajput architecture can be found in the region's sumptuous **palaces** (for more on which, see the *Rajasthan forts and palaces* colour insert). Like their Mughal equivalents, these creations were intended to symbolize the glory of the ruling dynasty, and were frequently expanded and embellished by subsequent rulers, as in the remarkable City Palace at Udaipur, where over a dozen individual mini-palaces created by successive Mewari maharanas are squeezed into a single building. Rajput palaces also reflect the Indian traditions shared by both Indian and Mughal rulers, both in their division into male and female quarters (the *mardana* and *zenana*, respectively – a division also seen in the region's havelis), and by their configuration of private and public spaces, exemplified by the diwan-i-am and diwan-i-khas (private and public audience halls) found in Mughal and Rajput palaces alike. The region's remarkable collection of **havelis** (the best of which can be found in Jaisalmer and Shekhawati) also share many of these features (see p.229 for a fuller description), with a similar division into *mardana* and *zenana* quarters, and a homespun version of the diwan-i-khas, known as the *baithak*, in which local merchants would meet to transact business and swap news.

Although Mughal architecture had a strong influence on Rajput styles – leading to the introduction of features like mirrored Sheesh Mahals and cusped arches – most features of Rajput architecture spring from Hindu architectural traditions, with features drawn from temple and vernacular architecture. These include the **jarokha**, or projecting balcony, often containing a small window seat, which is one of the classic features of Rajput architecture; **chajjas**, a type of large overhanging eave, designed to protect against monsoonal downpours, also found its way into many Mughal buildings; along with other elements such as finely carved stone screens (*jalis*), cusped arches fringed with stylized lotus buds, coloured tiles and traditional decorative patterns. Another characteristic architectural motif is the **bangaldar** pavilion, topped with a distinctively curved roof inspired by the roof of Bengali village huts (a notable pair of copper-roofed *bangaldar* pavilions can even be seen flanking the Khas Mahal in Agra Fort).

Perhaps the classic Rajasthani architectural feature, however, is the **chhatris** (literally "umbrella", though often referred to as "pavilions"), usually a simple dome supported by four columns, although far more lavish examples are common. These were originally erected as memorials to deceased royals or other notables (as at Royal Gaitor in Jaipur, or the extraordinary chhatris of Ramgarh in Shekhawati), though in time they also appeared as purely decorative features lining the rooftops of buildings across the region, as well as in numerous Mughal buildings – four octagonal chhatris even appear on the roof of the Taj Mahal, flanking the main dome.

One final notable Rajasthani architectural form is the **step-well** (*baori* or *baoli*). Examples of step-wells can be found throughout the region, especially in Shekhawati. Most are modest structures, surrounded by a raised plinth topped by a pair of pillars, though there are also a number of remarkably elaborate versions, such as the Raniji-ki-Baori in Bundi and the Mertaini Baori in Jhunjhunu: huge and lavishly decorated wells approached via grand flights of steps descending deep into the bowels of the earth, whose architectural splendour attests to the crucial role water has always played in this desert state.

Rajput temple architecture

Rajasthan's **Hindu religious architecture** is not particularly well known compared to other places in the country, though the state boasts plenty of fine examples of Hindu sacred architecture, such as those at the remote complex of Osian in western Rajasthan and the temples in the fort at Chittaurgarh, which rival those at more celebrated north Indian sites such as Khajuraho in the lavishness of their ornamentation.

There could scarcely be a greater contrast between the region's Hindu temples and Mughal mosques. Mosques are essentially places of communal worship, enclosing large open courtyards in which the faithful can gather to pray together. The Hindu temple, by contrast, is considered the home of the god whose image it enshrines, and its architecture emphasises the mysterious, personal encounter with god – a sense of being in the presence of the divine, known as *darshan*, which is central to Hindu worship. At the heart of every temple is the principal shrine, or *garbhagriha* ("womb chamber"), housing the image of the temple's principal deity. This main shrine is generally topped by a large stone tower, or *shikhara*, and fronted by a small pillared hall, the *mandapa*, while subsidiary shrines are placed into the exterior walls, the whole complex set on a raised plinth (a scheme which was copied in Indo-Islamic mosques and mausoleums).

If the state's Hindu temples remain relatively unappreciated, its **Jain temples** are amongst the most celebrated in the country – most obviously those at Ranakpur and Dilwara (at Mount Abu), though there are further outstanding examples at Jaisalmer, Osian and Chittaurgarh. Jain temples share many common features with Hindu places of worship, except that the shrines within are dedicated to one of the religion's various *tirthankaras* (see p.405) rather than a

Hindu god. They are usually relatively small in scale, but compensate with the extraordinary detail of their decorative carving – the examples at Ranakpur and Dilwara are particularly remarkable, with fine white marble columns and vaults fretted into extraordinary three-dimensional sculptural design, while the larger examples also display some idiosyncratic architectural features, such as the richly carved domes supported on an octagonal arrangement of columns (a Jain variant of the classic Hindu *mandapa*) which front the main shrines in temples at both Ranakpur and Dilwara.

Rajasthani painting

Rajasthani painting is one of the most vivid expressions of the state's artistic heritage, and (unlike Mughal painting) many fine works remain in situ, with at least a few works of interest on display in virtually every major museum or palace in the region – the collections at the city palaces of Bundi, Kota and Udaipur are particularly fine. Despite the intermittent influence of Mughal art, painting in Rajasthan developed in a quite different manner to that of its Islamic counterpart. Whereas most Mughal art was more or less realistic, Rajasthani painting was essentially symbolic. Much of the reason for this is the far greater concentration on **religious subjects** – particularly those connected with the life of Krishna, an enduring source of fascination for local artists. Such paintings were one result of the popularization of religion and increasing emphasis on personal devotion to god (*bhakti*) rather than on formal Brahmin-led rituals, which for many Hindus took the form of ecstatic Krishna worship. Rajasthani paintings also tend to be far larger than their Mughal equivalents, and although meticulously detailed Persian-style minia-tures remain popular, many of the finest Rajasthani paintings are executed on a much larger scale, exemplified by the magnificent murals which became something of a regional speciality.

Unlike their Mughal contemporaries, Rajasthani painters were not usually looking to depict contemporary or historical events or to explore the person-ality of their subjects, but to create a poetic mood, and there is relatively little concern with realism, perspective or the three-dimensional modelling of figures. These qualities give many Rajasthani paintings a wonderfully fairy-tale, and often an also strangely modern, appearance – a kind of slightly surreal, magical realism which frequently suggests the work of much later Western artists like Douanier Rousseau or Chagall. Part of this quality is created by the use of intense colours, which are sometimes used in an explicitly symbolic way – red for anger, brown for the erotic, yellow for the miraculous, and so on. Colour is also a key element in the remarkable Rajasthani **ragamala** ("garland of melody") pictorial style, in which individual paintings are designed to evoke the mood of one of the classical modes of Indian music (either the six "male" ragas or their five musical "wives", called raginis), with different colours used to represent specific musical notes from the raga or ragini.

Different schools of painting flourished in various parts of the region from the sixteenth to eighteenth centuries, each developing its own idiosyncratic characteristics (although many of the subtle nuances of style which distinguish the various schools are generally discernible only to the eyes of professional art historians). Rajasthani painting first flourished in **Udaipur** (which remains the state's largest contemporary producer of traditional-style miniatures). Early paintings from the state are marked by their simple designs and vivid colours, almost like folk art, though later paintings – such as the numerous examples on display at Udaipur's City Palace – tend to concentrate on courtly subjects. Rajasthani painting reached its apogee, however, in the relatively minor state of **Bundi**, whose painters showed an almost obsessive fascination with various aspects of the Krishna legend – the lifting of Mount Goverdhan is a popular subject, as are Krishna's dalliances with the *gopis*, whether in the celebrated scene showing Krishna making off with the *gopis*' clothes while they are bathing, or the popular round dance (the Mandalanritya or Rasamandala), showing a circle of *gopis* dancing in a ring around Krishna and Radha, most memorably depicted in the marvellous mural which crowns the Badal Mahal in Bundi's City Palace. A similar, if slightly cruder, style flourished at nearby **Kota**, while another striking regional school of painting emerged at **Kishangarh**, near Ajmer, whose artists specialized in elegantly elongated figures with huge eyes.

A later and hugely idiosyncratic development of Rajasthani painting occurred during the nineteenth and early twentieth centuries in the towns of **Shekhawati**, whose magnificent havelis were decorated by local artists in a vast assortment of colourful murals depicting both traditional and contemporary themes – a remarkable kind of public street-art designed for the entertainment and edification of the masses, rather than for the private delectation of a cultured elite. Although technically amateurish compared to earlier Rajasthani paintings, the engagingly naive style of these Shekhawati murals, with their fantastical depictions of modern European inventions like planes, trains and motor cars, is hugely entertaining, and adds a final, quaint flourish to the region's remarkable artistic traditions.

Colonial architecture

Local art and architecture continued to develop during the **British colonial period**, although the new European masters did little to distinguish themselves artistically beyond inflicting a variety of bastardized Gothic, Neoclassical and other European styles on the cities of north India, exemplified by buildings such as the Central Museum in Jaipur – a bizarre miscegenation of Venetian and Mughal forms which is typical of so-called **Indo–Saracenic** school, which attempted to blend European and Indian traditions, often with surprisingly little success. The major British contribution to the region's architectural heritage was the city of **New Delhi**, whose bombastic monuments are more interesting for what they say about the self-regard of the British Empire rather than for their rather modest artistic qualities, at least with the notable exception of Edwin Lutyens' monumental Rashtrapati Bhavan, whose smooth sandstone lines, mammoth dome and subtle Mughal-cum-Hindu styling achieves an oddly memorable synthesis of modern and traditional.

Wildlife

Rajasthan's wide-open spaces are home to a plentiful array of wildlife, ranging from magnificent tigers and leopards through to local curiosities such as the nilgai (blue bull) and four-horned chowsingha (swamp deer) – not to mention a rich selection of colourful birdlife. The state's relatively low population density compared to other parts of India and the presence of numerous nature reserves (some first established as hunting grounds by former rulers) have both contributed to the state's abundant wildlife, as have the attitudes of traditional rural communities closely attuned to the natural world, exemplified by the celebrated Bishnois of the Jodhpur region (see p.295), India's original eco-warriors. Habitat loss due to human encroachment remains a problem, however, as does the often catastrophic attentions of wildlife poachers, who have succeeded in reducing Rajasthan's tiger population to the verge of extinction, as well as targeting species ranging from sambar deer to the great Indian bustard.

Rajasthan's wildlife highlights are the world-famous **Keoladeo National Park** at Bharatpur and **Ranthambore National Park**. The former is one of Asia's most celebrated ornithological destinations, home – recent periods of drought excepted – to an extraordinary array of aquatic (and other) birdlife. Ranthambore is one of India's – indeed the planet's – foremost tiger-spotting destinations, offering excellent odds of seeing these magnificent beasts in the wild. The state's other main park, the peaceful **Sariska Tiger Reserve**, is home to pretty much every sort of wildlife found in the region apart from (whatever its name suggests) tigers.

Elephants

The Indian **elephant**, distinguished from its African cousin by its long front legs and smaller ears and body, and the fact that not all male elephants have tusks, is still widely used as a beast of burden throughout Rajasthan. Elephants have worked and been tamed in India for three thousand years, but it is through the battle legends of the sixteenth and seventeenth centuries that they earned their loyal and stoic reputation, both as great mounts in the imperial armies of the Mughals and as bejewelled bearers of rajas and nawabs. Elephants are also of great religious significance – they're a common sight in temple processions and ceremonies, often sporting a brightly painted trunk and forehead, and throughout the Subcontinent, stone elephants stand guard with bells in their trunks as a sign of welcome in medieval forts and palaces.

Wild elephants are now no longer found in Rajasthan, though captive elephants are a common sight around the region, especially at Amber and during the famous elephant festival in nearby Jaipur.

Tigers

India is one of the very few places where **tigers** can still be glimpsed in the wild, stalking through the teak forests and terai grass. As recently as the beginning of the last century, up to one hundred thousand tigers still roamed the Subcontinent, even though *shikar* (tiger hunting) had long been the "sport of kings". An ancient dictum held it auspicious for a ruler to notch up a tally of 109 dead tigers, and nawabs, maharajas and Mughal emperors all indulged their prerogative to devastating effect. But it was the trigger-happy British who

Tigers on the Web

ⓦ **www.savethetigerfund.org**
Homepage of the Save The Tiger Fund, with everything you ever wanted to know about tigers, in India and elsewhere.

ⓦ **www.wwfindia.org**
Home page of the Worldwide Fund for Nature, India, dedicated to conservation and environmental protection in the Subcontinent. Useful source of volunteer work opportunities and news.

ⓦ **www.projecttiger.nic.in**
Home page of Project Tiger.

ⓦ **www.tigersincrisis.com**
US-based tiger conservation group.

ⓦ **www.wpsi-india.org**
The Wildlife Protection Society of India was set up to provide support in the struggle against poaching, and its site holds a wealth of information, links and news on everything connected to tigers in India.

brought tiger hunting to its most gratuitous excesses. Photographs of pith-helmeted, bare-kneed *burra-sahibs* posing behind mountains of striped carcasses became a hackneyed image of the Raj. Even Britain's Prince Philip (who subsequently served as president of the Worldwide Fund for Nature) couldn't resist bagging one during a royal visit in 1961.

In the years following Independence, demographic pressures nudged the Indian tiger perilously close to extinction. As the human population increased in rural districts, more and more forest was cleared for farming, depriving large carnivores of their main source of game and of the cover they needed to hunt. Forced to turn on farm cattle as an alternative, tigers were drawn into direct conflict with humans; some animals, out of sheer desperation, even turned man-eater and attacked human settlements. **Poaching** has taken an even greater toll. The black market has always paid high prices for live animals – a whole tiger can fetch up to US$100,000 – and for the various body parts believed to hold magical or medicinal properties. The meat is used to ward off snakes, the brain to cure acne, the nose to promote the birth of a son and the fat of the kidney – applied liberally to the afflicted organ – as an antidote to male impotence.

By the time an all-India moratorium on tiger shooting was declared in the 1972 Wildlife Protection Act, numbers had plummeted to below two thousand. A dramatic response geared to fire public imagination came the following year, with the inauguration of **Project Tiger**, created at the personal behest of Indira Gandhi. Nine areas of pristine forest were set aside for the last remaining tigers, displaced farming communities were resettled and compensated, and armed rangers employed to discourage poachers. Demand for tiger parts did not end with Project Tiger, however, and the poachers remained in business, aided by organized smuggling rings.

One of the problems facing conservationists is that even if poachers are caught, they are unlikely to be adequately punished – the maximum fine for tiger poaching is US$125, or one year in prison. Well-organized guerrilla groups thus operate with virtual impunity out of remote national parks, where inadequate numbers of poorly armed and paid wardens offer little more than token

417

resistance. Project Tiger officials are understandably reluctant to jeopardize lucrative tourist traffic by admitting that sightings are getting rarer, but the prognosis looks very gloomy indeed.

Today, though there are 27 Project Tiger sites, numbers continue to fall. Official figures optimistically claim a national **population** of over 3500, but independent evidence is less encouraging, putting the figure at under two thousand. It was estimated in 1996 that one tiger was being poached every eighteen hours and the situation is believed to be just as depressing today. In 2005 it was discovered that there was no longer a single tiger left in the Sariska Tiger Reserve, in eastern Rajasthan, presumably due to the ravages of poaching, and the resultant national scandal prompted a government enquiry and has cast a long shadow over Project Tiger's activities and credibility. There have been suggestions that park wardens at both at Sariska and Ranthambore National Park have been implicated in poaching, and although such allegations have been vehemently denied (indeed one of Ranthambore's park trackers was actually murdered in 1992, possibly in a confrontation with poachers), suspicions remain. Whatever the details, the most pessimistic experts claim that at the present rate of destruction, India's most exotic animal could face extinction within the next decade.

Other wild cats

Some of India's other **big cats** have fared even worse than the tiger. The cheetah is now extinct in India, while the Asiatic lion is now found only in one tiny patch of Gujarat. **Leopards** (often referred to as "panthers") survive in larger numbers, favouring forested areas near human settlement where domestic animals make easy prey. In Rajasthan they are mainly confined to hilly districts, such as the forested slopes around Mount Abu, and sightings are uncommon, although they can sometimes be spotted in Ranthambore National Park. Other indigenous felines include the **fishing cat** (occasionally spotted at Keoladeo National Park), the miniature **leopard cat**, the **jungle cat** (with a distinct ridge of hair running down its back), and a kind of lynx called the **caracal**. All these species are present in Rajasthan, though very rarely seen.

Deer and antelope

Deer and antelope, the larger cats' prey, are abundant throughout Rajasthan. The often solitary sambar is the largest of the **deer**, weighing up to 300kg and bearing antlers known to reach 120cm long (for which they are sometimes targeted by poachers). Smaller and more gregarious are chital (spotted deer), usually seen in herds skulking around langur monkey or human habitats looking for discarded fruit and vegetables. In Ranthambore you may hear the high-pitched call of the chital and the gruff reply bark of the langur warning of the presence of a tiger in the vicinity. Other deer include the elusive mountain-loving muntjac (barking deer) and the para (hog deer), which fall victim annually to flooding in the low grasslands. The smallest deer in India is the nocturnal chevrotain, known from its size (only 30cm high) as the mouse deer.

Antelopes include the endangered blackbuck, or "Indian antelope", revered by the Bishnoi (see p.295), along with the nilgai (bluebull; a curious creature halfway between an antelope and a cow), and the unique forest-dwelling four-horned chowsingha (swamp deer) – the last two are most easily spotted at Sariska Tiger Reserve. The desert-loving gazelle is known as the *chinkara* ("the one who sneezes") due to its alarm call, which sounds like a sneeze.

Monkeys

The two most common monkeys found in Rajasthan are the feisty red-bottomed Rhesus macaque and the shyer and more skittish grey-furred, black-faced common (or "Hanuman") langur, often found around temples. Monkeys are protected by the Hindu belief in their divine status as noble servants of the gods, a sentiment that derives from the epic Ramayana, where the herculean Hanuman leads his monkey army to assist Rama in fighting the demon Ravana. Wild monkeys live in large troupes in the forests.

Other mammals

Among other wild animals you might see in Rajasthan, the shaggy **sloth bear** is hard to spot in the wild, being shy and mainly nocturnal, although you may see captive specimens being forced to "dance" at tourist spots, which is actually illegal under the Wildlife Protection Act, and should not be encouraged. If you do happen to see this barbaric spectacle you should walk away. For further information about freeing India's dancing bears go to ⓦ www.wildlifesos.com. Other bears include the black and brown varieties, distinguishable by the colour of their fur. Of the **canines**, the scavenging striped hyena, the jackal and the small Indian fox are all fairly common. The Indian wolf lives in both desert and forest (particularly in that around Kumbalgarh), though it is threatened due to vigorous culling by humans protecting their domestic animals. The wild **buffalo** has a close genetic relationship with the common domesticated water buffalo.

Asia's answer to the armadillo is a scaly anteater called a **pangolin**, whose tough plate-like scales run the length of its back and tail; this armour is believed to contain magical healing properties, for which the pangolin is hunted. The three-striped **palm squirrel**, common around towns, is said to have been marked as such by the gentle stroke of Rama. The **common mongoose** is frequently seen in Rajasthan's national parks and elsewhere, as is the snouty **wild boar**.

Reptiles

The 238 species of **snake** in India (of which fifty are poisonous) extend from the 10cm-long worm snake to nest-building king cobras and massive pythons. While the mangy and languid cobra or python wrapped around the snake-charmer's neck is tame and non-venomous, poisonous snakes you might meet in the wild are the majestically hooded cobra, the yellow-brown Russell's viper, the small krait and the saw-scaled viper.

Crocodiles and **gharial** (a species of freshwater crocodile with a curious and instantly recognizable bump on the end of its snout) are common throughout the Subcontinent and can be seen in Rajasthan in locations ranging from Sariska National Park to the banks of the River Chambal on the edge of Kota. **Lizards** are also common – every hotel room seems to have a resident gecko to keep the place free of insects, while the colourful garden lizard and Sita's lizard are both found throughout the country.

Birds

You don't have to be an aficionado to enjoy India's abundant **birdlife**. Travelling around the country, you'll see breathtaking birds regularly flash between the branches of trees or appear on overhead wires at the roadside, and even complete novices will enjoy a visit to the superb Keoladeo National Park at Bharatpur. Serious birders should consult ⓦwww.camacdonald.com/birding/asiaindia.htm, which has exhaustive reviews of India's bird-watching hotspots, online resources and printed material, with dozens of pictures and reports from recent field trips by real enthusiasts.

The wealth of different aquatic feeding and nesting habitats at Keoladeo National Park in Bharatpur draws exotic waterfowl such as flamingoes, spoon-bills and pelicans. Stately **eagles** swoop among the Himalayas and peacocks flounce around forts and palaces.

Three common species of **kingfisher** are frequently spotted, as often perched on telephone wires as on the branches of a tree. Other common and brightly coloured species include the grass-green, blue and yellow **bee-eaters**, the stunning **golden oriole**, and the **Indian roller**, celebrated for its brilliant blue flight feathers and exuberant aerobatic mating displays. **Hoopoes**, recognizable by their elegant black-and-white tipped crests, fawn plumage and distinctive "*hoo...po...po*" call, also flit around fields and villages, as do several kinds of **bulbuls**, **babblers** and **drongos**, including the fork-tailed black drongo - a winter visitor that, like local kingfishers, can often be seen perched on telegraph wires. If you're lucky, you may also catch a glimpse of the **paradise flycatcher**, which is among the Subcontinent's most exquisite birds, with a thick black crest and long silver tail streamers.

Paddy fields, ponds and saline mud flats often teem with water birds. The most ubiquitous of these is the snowy white **cattle egret**, which can usually be seen wherever there are cows and buffalo, feeding off the grubs, insects and other parasites that live on them. Look out too for the mud-brown **paddy bird**, India's most common heron, distinguished by its pale green legs, speckled breast and hunched posture.

Common birds of prey such as the **brahminy kite** – recognizable by its white breast and chestnut head markings – and the **pariah kite** – a dark-brown buzzard with a fork tail – are widespread around towns, where they vie with raucous gangs of house **crows** and **white-eyed jackdaws** for scraps. Gigantic pink-headed **king vultures** and the **white-backed vulture**, which has a white ruff around its bare neck and head, also show up whenever there are carcasses to pick clean, although in recent years a mysterious virus has decimated numbers.

Rajasthan's abundant **forest birds** include the magnificent **hornbill**, with its huge yellow beak with a long curved casque on top. Several species of **woodpecker** also inhabit the wooded ranges of the Aravallis, among them the rare Indian great black woodpecker, which makes loud drumming noises on tree trunks between December and March.

The secretive but vibrantly coloured **red jungle fowl**, the wild ancestor of the domestic chicken, sports golden neck feathers and a metallic black tail. You're most likely to come across one of these scavenging for food on the verges of forest roads.

Books

ndia is one of the most written-about places on earth, and there are a bewildering number of titles available covering virtually every aspect of the country, ranging from scholarly historical dissertations to racy travelogues – although you might have trouble tracking some of them down outside India itself. Books marked 🏃 are particularly recommended.

History

Jad Adams and Phillip Whitehead *The Dynasty: The Nehru-Gandhi Story* (Penguin). A brilliant and intriguing account of India's most famous family and the way its various personalities have shaped post-Independence India, although Sonia Gandhi's recent rise to prominence rather begs an update.

A.L. Basham *The Wonder That Was India* (Picador). A veritable encyclopedia by India's foremost authority on his country's ancient history. Every page bristles with the author's erudition. A companion volume by S.A. Rizvi (see p.422) brings it up to the arrival of the British.

David Burton *The Raj at Table* (Faber). Few books evoke the quirky world of British India quite as vividly as this unlikely masterpiece – commendable both for its extraordinary recipes and as a marvellous piece of social history, compiled over years of travel, archival research and interviews.

Larry Collins and Dominique Lapierre *Freedom at Midnight* (HarperCollins). Readable, if shallow, account of Independence, highly sympathetic to the British and, particularly, to Mountbatten, who was the authors' main source of information.

🏃 **William Dalrymple** *The Last Mughal* (Bloomsbury/Knopf). Dalrymple surpasses himself in this masterful account of Delhi's part in the 1857 uprising. Using Urdu as

well as English sources, he tells us what it was like for the insurgents, the British, the Mughal court and – most importantly – the ordinary people of Delhi. A great read, and a great piece of historical research.

Gurcharan Das *India Unbound* (Knopf). Political economy doesn't tend to make for riveting prose, but Gurcharan Das (a former industrialist turned writer, government advisor and management guru) brings the economic history of post-Independence India compellingly to life with this mix of autobiographical anecdote and essay.

Patrick French *Liberty or Death* (Flamingo/HarperCollins). The definitive account (and a damning indictment) of the last years of the British Raj. Material from hitherto unreleased intelligence files shows how Churchill's "florid incompetence" and Atlee's "feeble incomprehension" contributed to the debacle that was Partition.

🏃 **Bamber Gascoigne** *The Great Moghuls* (Constable & Robinson). Concise, entertaining and eminently readable account of the lives of the first six great Mughals, offering a fascinating glimpse into both the imperial ambitions and private lives of India's most remarkable dynasty.

Christopher Hibbert *The Great Mutiny* (Penguin). Account of the 1857 uprising, told entirely from the British point of view, in easy prose and with some excellent first-hand material from the British side, but little about how the uprising was seen by the insurgents, or by ordinary civilians caught up in it.

Dilip Hiro *The Rough Guide History of India*. Crams a huge amount of background material on India into handy pocket-sized format, complete with literary extracts, potted biographies, quotations and black-and-white photos. An excellent travelling companion.

Lawrence James *Raj: the Making and Unmaking of British India* (Abacus/St Martin's Griffin). A doorstopping 700-page history of British rule in India, drawing on official papers and private memoirs. The most up-to-date, erudite survey of its kind, and unlikely to be bettered as a general introduction.

John Keay *The Honourable Company: A History of the English East India Company* (HarperCollins). In characteristically fluent style, Keay strikes the right balance between those who regard the East India Company as a rapacious institution with malevolent intentions and others who present its acquisition of the Indian empire as an unintended, almost accidental process.

John Keay *India: A History* (HarperCollins/Grove Press). The best single-volume history currently in print. Keay manages to coax clear, impartial and highly readable narrative from five thousand years of fragmented events, spiced up with plenty of quirky asides.

Geoffrey Moorhouse *India Britannica* (Harvill Press/Academy Chicago). A balanced, lively survey of the rise and fall of the British Raj, with lots of illustrations. Recommended if this is your first foray into the period, as it's a lot more concise and readable than Lawrence James' *Raj* (though correspondingly less detailed).

S.A.A. Rizvi *The Wonder That Was India: Part II* (Picador). Rizvi's follow-up to A. L. Basham's classic study (see p.421) looks at Indian history and culture from the arrival of Islam until colonial times, with thorough coverage of the Delhi Sultanate and Mughal Empire, though relatively little on Rajasthan.

Romila Thapar *History of India Volume I* (Penguin). Concise paperback account of early Indian history, ending with the Delhi Sultanate. Percival Spear's *History of India Volume II* covers the period from the Mughal era to the 1970s.

Giles Tillotson *Jaipur Nama: Tales from the Pink City* (Penguin India). Engaging portrait of Jaipur through the ages, entertainingly presented using extensive eye-witness accounts from past visitors.

Society

Zia Jaffrey *The Invisibles* (Random House/Vintage). An investigation into the hidden world of Delhi's *hijras*, or eunuchs. Using anthropological and journalistic research techniques, Jaffrey unravels the layers of myth and mystique surrounding this secretive subculture.

John Keay *Into India* (John Murray/South Asia Books). As an all-round introduction to India, this book – originally written in 1973 but reissued in 1999 – is the one most often recommended by old hands, presenting a wide spread of history and cultural background, interspersed with lucid personal observations.

V.S. Naipaul *An Area of Darkness* (Picador/Vintage). One of the finest (and bleakest) books ever written about India: a darkly comic portrait of the country based on a year of travel around the Subcontinent in the early 1960s – dated, but still essential reading. Naipaul followed this up with *India: A Wounded Civilisation* (Vintage), a damning analysis of Indian society written during the Emergency of 1975–77, and the altogether sunnier *India: A Million Mutinies Now* (Vintage), published in 1990.

Mark Tully *No Full Stops in India* (Penguin). Earnest dissection of contemporary India by the former BBC correspondent, incorporating anecdotes and first-hand accounts of political events. His latest book, *India in Slow Motion*, covers a similarly diverse range of subjects, from Hindu extremism, child labour and Sufi mysticism to the crisis in agriculture.

Travel

William Dalrymple *City of Djinns* (Flamingo/Penguin). Dalrymple's award-winning account of a year in Delhi sifts through successive layers of the city's past. Each is vividly brought to life with a blend of inspired historical sleuth work and encounters with living vestiges of different eras: Urdu calligraphers, Sufi clerics, eunuchs, pigeon fanciers and the last surviving descendant of the Mughal emperors. A real gem. *The Age of Kali* (published in India as *In the Court of the Fish-Eyed Goddess*) is a collection of essays drawn from ten years' travel in India.

Robyn Davidson *Desert Places* (Penguin). Absorbing account of Davidson's long and difficult journey through Rajasthan and Gujarat in company with the nomadic, camel-herding Rabari tribe, giving a rare insight into a way of life which has now virtually disappeared.

Royina Grewal *In Rajasthan* (Lonely Planet). Interesting contemporary travelogue exploring Rajasthan's folk music, architecture, feudal traditions and regional cuisine through encounters with a range of interviewees ranging from maharajahs to itinerant snake charmers.

Tim Mackintosh-Smith *The Hall of a Thousand Columns* (John Murray). Quirky, learned and entertaining travelogue following the footsteps of the famous fourteenth-century Moroccan traveller Ibn Battuta through the Delhi of the Tughluq sultan Muhammad Shah and thence south to Kerala, with lashings of offbeat Subcontinental Islamic (and other) history en route.

Jeremy Seabrook *Notes from Another India* (Pluto Press). Life histories and interviews – compiled over a year's travelling and skilfully contextualized – reveal the everyday problems faced by Indians from a variety of backgrounds. One of the soundest and most engaging overviews of Indian development issues ever written.

Trevor Fishlock *Cobra Road* (John Murray). Former *Times* correspondent Fishlock's 1999 account of a journey from the Khyber to Cape Comorin (with a stop at Delhi en route), a classic all-round introduction to the Subcontinent. Sympathetic yet balanced, it looks at many of the ironies and absurdities inherent in modern India, whilst retaining a sense of humour and adventure.

Fiction

Anita Desai *Fasting, Feasting* (Phoenix/Mariner Books). One of India's leading female authors' eloquent portrayal of the frustration of a sensitive young woman stuck in the stifling atmosphere of home while her spoilt brother is packed off to study in America.

Ruth Prawer Jhabvala *Out of India* (Penguin). One of many short-story collections by long-term Delhi resident Ruth Prawer Jhabvala, showing India in its full colours: amusing, shocking and thought-provoking. Other titles include *How I Became a Holy Mother*; *Like Birds, Like Fishes*; *Heat and Dust*; and *In Search of Love and Beauty*.

Rudyard Kipling *Kim* (Penguin). Partly written at Bundi in southern Rajasthan, this classic Raj tale can be cringingly colonialist at times, but the atmosphere of India and Kipling's love of it shine through in this subtle story of an orphaned white boy. Kipling's other key works on India are two books of short stories: *Soldiers Three* and *In Black and White*.

Rohinton Mistry *A Fine Balance* (Faber/Vintage). Two friends seek promotion from their lower-caste rural lives to the opportunities of the big smoke (in this case a fictionalized Mumbai). A compelling and savage triumph-of-the-human-spirit novel detailing the evils of the caste system and of Indira Gandhi's brutal policies during the Emergency.

R.K. Narayan *Gods, Demons and Others* (Vintage/Chicago UP). Classic Indian folk tales and popular myths told through the voice of a village storyteller.

Salman Rushdie *Midnight's Children* (Vintage). This story of a man born at the very moment of Independence, whose life mirrors that of modern India itself, won Rushdie the Booker Prize and the enmity of Indira Gandhi, who had it banned in India.

Vikram Seth *A Suitable Boy* (Phoenix/Harper Perennial). Vast, all-embracing tome set in UP shortly after Independence; wonderful characterization and an impeccable sense of place and time make this an essential read for those long train journeys.

Khushwant Singh *Delhi: a Novel* (Penguin India). A jaded Delhiwallah and his *hijra* lover contemplate the accounts of characters from key moments in Delhi's past in this odd but compelling mix of serious history and bawdy humour by one of India's most distinguished and popular writers. Singh's other works include *Train to Pakistan*, a chillingly realistic portrayal of life in a village on the Partition line, set in the summer of 1947; and *Sex, Scotch and Scholarship*, a collection of wry short stories.

William Sutcliffe *Are You Experienced?* (Penguin). Hilarious novel sending up the backpacker scene in India (including the inevitable stint in Pushkar). Wickedly perceptive and very readable.

Biography and autobiography

Charles Allen *Plain Tales from the Raj* (Abacus). First-hand accounts from erstwhile *sahibs* and *memsahibs* of everyday British India, organized thematically.

James Cameron *An Indian Summer* (Penguin). Affectionate and humorous description of the veteran British journalist's visit to India in 1972, and his marriage to an Indian woman. Somewhat dated, but an enduring classic.

Gayatri Devi *A Princess Remembers* (Rupa). The nostalgic reminiscences of the multi-talented Gayatri Devi, maharani of Jaipur and global style icon – widely regarded as one of the most beautiful women of her era – who later became an immensely popular Rajasthani politician.

Louis Fischer *The Life of Mahatma Gandhi* (HarperCollins). First published in 1950, this biography has been re-issued several times since, and quite rightly – veteran American journalist Louis Fischer knew his subject personally, and his book provides an engaging account of Gandhi as a man, politician and propagandist.

M.K. Gandhi *The Story of My Experiments with Truth* (Penguin). Gandhi's fascinating record of his life, including his spiritual and moral quests, changing relationship with the British Government in India, and gradual emergence to the fore of national politics.

Women

Elizabeth Bumiller *May You Be the Mother of a Hundred Sons* (South Asia Books). Lucid exploration of the Indian woman's lot, drawn from dozens of first-hand encounters by an American journalist.

Lucy Moore *Maharanis: The Lives and Times of Three Generations of Indian Princesses* (Penguin). Rip-roaring saga following the lives and love of the maharanis of Jaipur (the legendary Gayatri Devi), Cooch Behar and Baroda in the later days of the Raj.

Vrinda Nabar *Caste as Woman* (Penguin India). Conceived as an Indian counterpart to Greer's *The Female Eunuch*, this wry study of the pressures experienced during various stages of womanhood draws on scripture and popular culture to explore issues of identity and cultural conditioning.

Sakuntala Narasimhan *Sati: Widow Burning in India* (Anchor Books). Definitive and engaging exploration of *sati* and its significance throughout history, including an account of the infamous Roop Kanwar case.

Mala Sen *Death By Fire* (Phoenix). Later made into a controversial movie, this book uses the Roop Kanwar case as a springboard to explore some of the wider issues affecting women in contemporary Indian society – a bleak read, but one that shows up the hollow triumphalism of the country's right-wing politicians in its true colours.

The arts and architecture

Milo Cleveland Beach *Mughal and Rajput Painting (New Cambridge History of India)* (Cambridge University Press). Definitive academic overview of the pictorial arts of the Mughals and Rajputs.

Roy Craven *Indian Art* (Thames & Hudson). Concise general introduction to Indian art, from Harappan seals to Mughal miniatures, with lots of illustrations.

Pauline van Lynden *Rajasthan* (Editions Assouline). Attractive coffee-table book showcasing photographs of Rajasthan's arts, crafts and cultural traditions amassed over the author's fifteen years of travel throughout the region.

George Michell *The Hindu Temple* (Chicago University Press). A fine primer, introducing Hindu temples, their significance, and architectural development.

George Michell and Antonio Martinelli *Princely Rajasthan: Rajput Palaces and Mansions* (Vendome Press). George Michell provides a solid, if pedestrian, account of Rajasthan's royal history and architectural heritage, accompanied by Antonio Martinelli's evocative photographs. Also published in hardcover by Frances Lincoln as *The Palaces of Rajasthan*

Giles Tillotson *Mughal India* (Penguin). Excellent architectural guide to the great Mughal monuments of Delhi, Agra and Fatehpur Sikri, academic but accessible, and with interesting snippets of historical and biographical information thrown in to flesh out the descriptions of the buildings themselves.

Giles Tillotson *The Rajput Palaces* (Yale University Press). Definitive, though expensive, study of Rajasthan's palace architecture, with an erudite but readable blend of history and architecture.

Giles Tillotson (ed) *Stones in the Sand: the Architecture of Rajasthan* (Marg Publications India). Refreshingly original overview of Rajasthani architecture, edited by one of the foremost authorities in the field, examining a range of local creations from forts and palaces through to havelis, temples and tanks.

Religion

Dolf Hartsuiker *Sadhus: Holy Men of India* (Thames & Hudson). The weird world of India's itinerant ascetics exposed in glossy colour photographs and erudite but accessible text.

Stephen P. Huyler *Meeting God* (Yale University Press). This acclaimed introduction provides an unrivalled overview of the beliefs and practices of contemporary Hinduism. The text evokes general principles by focusing on individual acts of worship, accompanied by Huyler's sublime photographs.

Wendy O'Flaherty (transl.) *Hindu Myths* (Penguin Classics). Translations of key myths from the original Sanskrit texts, providing an insight into the foundations of Hinduism.

Language

Language

Language

The principal language of the Rajasthan, Delhi and Agra region is **Hindi**, the most important of India's eighteen official languages, spoken by over two hundred million people across north of the country. Hindi, like all the major north Indian languages, is derived from the ancient Indo-Aryan language of Sanskrit and is written using a modified form of Sanskrit's classic devanagari script (variants of which are also used to write Bengali, Punjabi and other Indian languages). It first developed around the markets and army camps of Delhi during the establishment of Muslim rule at the start of the second millennium AD. Hindi is closely related to **Urdu**, the principal language of Pakistan, which developed at the same time and subsequently became the lingua franca of the Mughal Empire. Urdu later became culturally more closely associated with Islam, being written in its own **Perso–Arabic** script. Delhi boasted a sizeable Urdu-speaking population right up until Independence, when many native speakers migrated to Pakistan.

Many people in Rajasthan also speak one of the various **local Rajasthani languages**, such as Marwari, Mewari, Mewati, Shekhawati, Dhundhari, Bagri, Wagri and Harauti. All these are closely related to Hindi – indeed it is only fairly recently that they have been accepted as separate languages in their own right, rather than dialects of Hindi. Rajasthani languages are also spoken by a few people in the neighbouring states of Gujarat, Haryana, Madhya Pradesh and Punjab, and in the Pakistani provinces of Punjab and Sind. **Other languages** spoken in Rajasthan include Sindhi, Gujarati, and Punjabi.

Not surprisingly, given India's linguistic diversity and colonial heritage, English still plays an important role as a link language between Indians from different

Indian English

During the British Raj, **Indian English** developed its own characteristics, which have survived to the present day. It was during this period that many Indian words entered the **vocabulary** of everyday English, including words like verandah, bungalow, sandal, pyjamas, shampoo, jungle, turban, caste, chariot, chilli, cardamom, pundit and yoga. The traveller to India soon becomes familiar with other terms in common usage that have not spread so widely outside the Subcontinent: *dacoit, dhoti, panchayat, lakh* and *crore* are but a few (see the Glossary on p.437 for definitions) – a full list of Anglo-Indianisms can be found in the famous *Hobson-Jobson* dictionary. Perhaps the most endearing aspect of Indian English is the way it has preserved forms now regarded as highly **old-fashioned** in Britain. Addresses such as "Good sir" and questions like "May I know your good name?" are commonplace, as are terms like "tiffin" and "cantonment". This type of usage reaches its apogee in the more flowery expressions of the media, which regularly feature in the vast array of daily newspapers published in English. Thus headlines often appear such as "37 perish in mishap", referring to a train crash, or passages like this splendid report of a bank robbery: "The miscreants absconded with the loot in great haste. They repaired immediately to their hideaway, whereupon they divided the iniquitous spoils before vanishing into thin air."

areas, and is still the preferred language of law, higher education, much of commerce and the media, and to some degree political dialogue. Indeed for many educated Indians, not just those living abroad, English is actually their first language, and it's not unusual to hear Indians talking together in English, especially in the larger and more Westernized cities, particularly Delhi and Mumbai.

It's well worth attempting to pick up a bit of Hindi to use on your travels – the language is relatively straightforward compared to many others in Asia, at least at a basic level. There are plenty of **tutorial aids** available. Hugo's *Hindi in Three Months* by Mark Allerton is brilliantly direct and will get you talking (almost) like a native in no time at all. Rupert Snell's *Teach Yourself Beginner's Hindi* offers a rather more detailed, but still commendably practical, course of study, with excellent audio materials. *The Rough Guide Hindi & Urdu* **phrasebook** makes a good on-the-road companion, with an extensive dictionary, thematically presented vocabulary lists and scenarios, and a run-down of the grammatical basics. The scenarios can also be downloaded free as audio files from Ⓦwww .roughguides.com.

Useful Hindi words and phrases

Greetings

Namaste/Namaskar (slightly formal; not used for Muslims)	Hello	**Kya hal hai?** (familiar)	How are you?
As salaam alaykum (formal; to a Muslim)		**bhaaii** (informal; not to be used to older men)	brother
(in reply) **Alaykum as salaam**		**diidi** (informal; not to be used to older women)	sister
Namaste	Goodbye		
Phir mileynge	See you later	**sahib**	sir
Khudaa haafiz	Goodbye (to a Muslim)	**hazur** (Muslims only)	sir
Aap kaise hai? (formal)	How are you?		

Basic words

haa or **ji haa**	yes (informal/more formal)	**dhanyavad/shukriya**	thank you (formal; Indians don't usually say thank you during everyday transactions, eg when buying something. Note that there's also no direct Hindi equivalent to the English word "please".)
nahi or **ji nahi**	no (informal/more formal)		
acha or **tiika**	OK		
mai	I/me		
aap	you (formal)	**acha**	good
tum	you (familiar; and to children)	**bahut acha**	very good
		buraa	bad
aur	and/more	**barra**	big
kaise?	how?	**chhota**	small
Kitna?	How much?	**garam**	hot

mirchi	hot (spicy)	aao	come
thanda	cold	aiiye	please come
saaf	clean	jaao	go
gandaa	dirty	bhaago	run (also "take a run" or "scram")
khulaa	open		
mehngaa	expensive	bas	enough

Basic phrases

Mera naam . . . hai	My name is . . .	Ma'af kiijiye	Sorry
Aapka naam kya hai?	What is your name? (formal)	Tiika hai?	It is OK?
		Kitna paisa?	How much?
Tumhara naam kya hai?	What is your name? (familiar, and to children)	Yeh kya hai?	How much is this?
		Nahi chai'iya	I don't need it (literally "not needed"); useful response to persistent touts
Mai . . . se hu	I'm from . . .		
Hum . . . se hai	We're from . . .		
Aap kaha se aate hai?	Where do you come from?	. . . hai?	Do you have . . . ?
		Acha lugta hai	I/we like it
Samaj gayaa	I understand	Kya haal hai?	How are you?
Samaj nahin aayaa	I don't understand	Tiika hai	I'm fine
Maluum nahi	I don't know	Kya kam karte hai?	What work do you do?
Mai Hindi nahi bol sakta hu	I don't speak Hindi	Bhaai behan hai?	Do you have any brothers or sisters?
Dhiire se boliye	Please speak slowly	Arey!	Oh dear!

Getting around

. . . kaha hai?	Where is the . . . ?	Agra ka bas kaha hai?	Which is the bus for Agra?
Mai . . . jaana chaata hu	I want to go to . . .	Gaarii kab jayegi?	What time does the train leave?
Kaha hai?	Where is it?		
Kitna duur?	How far?	Ruko!	Stop!
		Thehero!	Wait!

Accommodation

Mujhe kamra chai'eeya	I need a room	Mai ek raat ke liiye theheroonga	I am staying for one night
Kamra kitne ka hai ?	How much is the room?		

Medicinal

Sir me dard hai	I have a headache	Daktar ka clinic kaha hai?	Where is the doctor's surgery?
Mere pate me dard hai	I have a pain in my stomach	Haspital kaha hai?	Where is the hospital?
Dard yaha hai	The pain is here		

Dawaaii khana kaha hai?	Where is the pharmacy?	aank	eye
dawaaii	medicine	naakh	nose
bimar	ill	kaan	ear
dard	pain	piith	back
pate	stomach	paao	foot

Numbers and time

shunya	zero	saath	sixty
ek	one	sattar	seventy
do	two	assii	eighty
tiin	three	nabbe	ninety
char	four	ek sau	one hundred
paanch	five	ek hazaar	one thousand
che	six	ek lakh	one hundred thousand
saat	seven	ek crore	ten million
aat	eight	aaj	today
nau	nine	kal	tomorrow/yesterday
das	ten	din	day
gyaarah	eleven	dopahar	afternoon
baarah	twelve	shaam	evening
terah	thirteen	raat	night
chaudah	fourteen	haftaah	week
pandrah	fifteen	mahiinaa	month
solah	sixteen	saal	year
satrah	seventeen	somvaar	Monday
ataarah	eighteen	mangalvaar	Tuesday
unniis	nineteen	budhvaar	Wednesday
biis	twenty	viirvaar	Thursday
tiis	thirty	shukravaar	Friday
chaaliis	forty	shanivaar	Saturday
pachaas	fifty	ravivaar	Sunday

Food and drink glossary

Basics

khaana	food	kali mirch	black pepper
chawaal	rice	jaggery	unrefined sugar
chamach	spoon	namak	salt
chhoori	knife	mirch	pepper
kanta	fork	mirchi	chilli hot
plate	plate	mirchi kam	less hot
chini	sugar	garam	hot
chini nahi	no sugar (eg in tea)	thanda	cold

dahi	yoghurt	gravy	any kind of curry sauce; nothing to do with British gravy
dhal	curried lentils, usually reduced to a kind of broth; traditionally served as an accompaniment to all Indian meals	jeera	cumin
		lal mirch	red pepper
		masala	generic term indicating either a spice mixture or something spicy
garam masala	any kind of spice mixture added to give flavour to dishes (literally "hot spices")	methi	fenugreek
		paan	digestif; see p.440
		paneer	unfermented cheese
ghee	clarified butter; often used instead of cooking oil, or to flavour food	sabji	any vegetable curry

Drinks

bhang lassi	lassi flavoured with bhang (cannabis)	kavhaa or kaafi	coffee
botal vaala paani	mineral water	lassi	yoghurt drink, served either plain or flavoured with salt or fruit
chai	tea		
doodh	milk	pani	water
falooda	traditional Muslim drink, made with milk, ice, cream, nuts and sweets	peenay ka pani	drinking water (not mineral water)

Meat and fish

chingri	prawns	macchi	fish
gosht	meat, usually mutton	murg	chicken
keema	minced meat		

Vegetables and fruit

aam	mango	kela	banana
alu	potatoes	muttar	peas
baingan	eggplant (aubergine) or brinjal	piaz	onions
		sabji	vegetables (literally, "greens")
bhindi	okra (ladies finger)		
chana	chickpeas	santaraa	orange
gaajar	carrot	sev	apple
gobi	cauliflower	tamatar	tomato
kaddoo	pumpkin		

Dishes and cooking terms

alu baingan   potato and aubergine; usually mild to medium

alu gobi   potato and cauliflower; usually mild

alu methi   potato with fenugreek leaves, usually medium-hot

alu muttar   potato and peas curry; usually mild

baingan bharta   baked and mashed aubergine mixed with onion

bhindi bhaji   gently spiced fried okra

bhuna   roasted and then thickened-down medium-hot curry sauce

biriyani   rice baked with saffron or turmeric, whole spices, and meat (sometimes vegetables), and often hard-boiled egg; rich

channa masala   spicy chickpeas; usually medium-hot

chop   minced meat or vegetable served with breaded mashed potato

cutlet   fried cutlet of minced meat or vegetable

dhal bati churma   classic Rajasthani dish comprising dhal, *bati* (a baked wheatflour ball with a tough crust) and *churma* (a sweet made of coarse-ground wheat flour cooked with ghee and sugar)

dhal gosht   meat cooked in lentils; usually hot

dhal makhania   lentils cooked with cream

dhansak   curry sauce made from reduced lentils; usually medium-hot

dopiaza   onion-based sauce; medium-mild

dum   steamed in a casserole; the most common dish is *dum aloo*, with potatoes

gatta   small dumplings of gram flour cooked in a masala sauce

jalfrezi   dish cooked with tomatoes and green chilli; medium-hot to hot

karahi   cast-iron wok which has given its name to a method of cooking with dry spices to create dishes of medium strength

karhi   dhal-like dish made from *dahi* and gram flour

kofta   balls of minced vegetables or meat in a curried sauce

korma   mild sauce made with curd (and perhaps cream)

lal maas (or laal maans)   literally "red meat": a spicy dish of lamb marinated in chilli

malai kofta   vegetable balls in a rich cream sauce; usually medium-mild

mughlai masala   Mughal-style mild, creamy sauce

mulligatawny   classic Anglo-Indian-style vegetable soup; moderately spicy

murg makhani   butter chicken

muttar paneer   paneer and peas curry

palak paneer   paneer and spinach

pathia   thickened curry with lemon juice; hot

pulau   rice, gently spiced and pre-fried

raita   chilled yoghurt flavoured with mild spices, sometimes with the addition of small pieces of cucumber and tomato; usually eaten as an accompaniment to a main course

rasam   South Indian-style spicy soup

rogan josh   deep-red lamb curry, a classic Mughlai dish; medium-hot

sambar	soupy lentil and vegetable curry with asafoetida and tamarind		tarka dhal	lentils with a masala of fried garlic, onions and spices
shahi paneer	"royal" paneer; slightly more elaborate version of standard paneer curry, sometimes including fruit and nuts		thali	combination of vegetarian dishes, chutneys, pickles, rice and bread served as an all-in-one meal
seekh kebab	minced lamb grilled on a skewer		vindaloo	Goan vinegared meat (sometimes fish) curry, originally pork; very hot (but not as hot as the kamikaze UK version)
shami kebab	small minced lamb cutlets			

Breads and pancakes

appam	South Indian-style rice pancake speckled with holes, soft in the middle		naan	white leavened bread kneaded with yoghurt and baked in a tandoor
bhatura	soft bread made of white flour and traditionally accompanying *chana*; common in Delhi		papad or poppadum	crisp, thin, chick-pea flour cracker
chapati	unleavened bread made of wholewheat flour and baked on a round griddle-dish called a *tawa*		paratha or parantha	wholewheat bread made with butter, rolled thin and griddle-fried; a little bit like a chewy pancake, sometimes stuffed with meat or vegetables
dosa	crispy South Indian rice pancake; can be served in various forms, the best known of which is the *masala dosa*, when the *dosa* is wrapped around a filling of spicy potato curry		phulka	a chapati that has been made to puff out by being placed directly on the fire
iddli	South Indian steamed rice cake, usually served with *sambar*		puri	crispy, puffed-up, deep-fried wholewheat bread
kachori	small thick cakes of salty deep-fried bread		roti	loosely used term; often just another name for chapati, though it should be thicker, chewier, and baked in a tandoor
Mughlai paratha	paratha with egg		uttapam	thick, South Indian-style rice pancake often cooked with onions

Snacks (chaat), sweets and desserts

barfi (or burfi)	traditional sweet made with milk; a bit like fudge		bhel puri	mix of puffed rice, deep-fried vermicelli, potato, crunchy puri with tamarind sauce; a Mumbai speciality, though now popular nationwide
bhaji (or bhajia)	pieces of vegetable deep-fried in chickpea batter, served as a main course or a street snack			

gulab jamun	classic Indian sweet made from deep-fried dough balls served in syrup
halwa	traditional sweet made from lentils, nuts and fruit, baked in a large tray and cut into small squares
jalebi	deep-fried whorls of brightly coloured orange sugar-syrup; one of India's most popular street snacks
raj kachori	a crisp puri usually filled with chickpeas and doused in curd and sauce
kheer	delicate, Mughal-style rice pudding
kulfi	Indian-style ice cream, often flavoured with pistachio
ladoo (or ladu)	sweets made from small balls of gram flour and semolina
mirchi bada	large chilli fried in a thick batter of wheatgerm and potato; a speciality of Jodhpur
pakora	pieces of vegetable deep-fried in chickpea batter; a popular street snack
rasgulla	cheese balls flavoured with rosewater; a popular dessert
samosa	parcels of vegetable and potato (and sometimes meat) wrapped up in triangles of pastry and deep-fried
vada	doughnut-shaped, deep-fried lentil cake

Glossary

aarti evening temple puja of lights

acharya religious teacher

adivasi official term for tribal person

ahimsa non-violence

akhandpath continuous reading of the Sikh holy book, the Guru Granth Sahib

amalaka repeating decorative motif based on the fluted shape of a gourd, lining and crowning temple towers: a distinctive feature of north Indian architecture

angrez general term for Westerners

apsara heavenly nymph

arak liquor distilled from rice or coconut

ashram centre for spiritual learning and religious practice

asura demon

atman soul

avatar reincarnation of Vishnu on earth, in human or animal form

Ayurveda ancient system of medicine employing herbs, minerals and massage

baba respectful term for a sadhu

bagh garden, park

baithak reception area in private house

baksheesh tip, donation or alms

bandhani tie-dye

banyan vast fig tree, used traditionally as a meeting place, or shade for teaching and meditating

baoli or baori step-well

beedi Indian-style cigarette, with tobacco rolled in a leaf

begum Muslim princess; Muslim woman of high status

betel leaf chewed in *paan*, with the nut of the areca tree; loosely applies to the nut, also

bhajan song in praise of god

bhakti religious devotion expressed in a personalized or emotional relationship with the deity

bhang pounded marijuana, often mixed in lassi

bhawan (or *bhavan*) building, house, palace or residence

bindu seed, or the red dot (also *bindi*) worn by women on their foreheads as decoration

brahmin priest; a member of the highest caste group

burj tower or bastion

burkha body-covering shawl worn by orthodox Muslim women

burra-sahib colonial official, boss or a man of great importance

cantonment area of town occupied by military quarters

caste social status acquired at birth

cella chamber, often housing the image of a deity

cenotaph ornate tomb

chaat snack

chaddar large head-cover or shawl

chajja sloping dripstone eave

chakra discus; focus of power; energy point in the body; wheel, often representing the cycle of death and rebirth

chandra moon

chappal sandals or flip-flops (thongs)

charas hashish

charbagh Persian-style garden divided into quadrants

charpoi string bed with wooden frame

chaumukh image of four faces placed back to back

chauri fly whisk; a symbol of royalty

chhatri domed stone pavilion, often erected over a tomb

chillum cylindrical clay or wood pipe for smoking *charas* or ganja

choli short, tight-fitting blouse worn with a sari

chowk crossroads or courtyard

chowki police post

chowkidar watchman/caretaker

coolie porter/labourer

crore ten million

dacoit bandit

dalit "oppressed", "out-caste". The term, introduced by Dr Ambedkar, is preferred by so-called "untouchables" as a description of their social position

dargah tomb of a Muslim saint

darshan vision of a deity or saint; receiving religious teachings darwaza gateway; door

deva god

devadasi temple dancer

devi goddess

dhaba food hall selling local dishes

dham important religious site, or a theological college

dharamshala rest house for pilgrims

dharma sense of religious and social duty (Hindu); the law of nature, teachings, truth (Buddhist)

dhobi laundry

dhoti white ankle-length cloth worn by males, tied around the waist, and sometimes hitched up through the legs

dhurrie woollen rug

digambara literally "sky-clad": a Jain sect, known for the habit of nudity among monks, though this is no longer commonplace

diwan (*dewan*) chief minister

diwan-i-am public audience hall

diwan-i-khas hall of private audience

dowry payment or gift offered in marriage

Dravidian of the south

dupatta veil worn by Muslim women with *salwar kameez*

durbar royal audience or council of state

dvarpala guardian image placed at sanctuary door

eve-teasing sexual harassment of women, either physical or verbal

fakir ascetic Muslim mendicant

finial capping motif on temple pinnacle

ganj market

ganja marijuana buds

garbhagriha temple sanctuary, literally "womb-chamber"

garh fort

gari vehicle, or car

ghat mountain, landing platform, or steps leading to water

ghazal melancholy Urdu songs

ghee clarified butter

gopi young cattle-tending maidens who feature as Krishna's playmates and lovers in popular mythology

gopura towered temple gateway, common in south India

guru teacher of religion, music, dance, astrology etc

gurudwara Sikh place of worship

haj Muslim pilgrimage to Mecca

hajji Muslim engaged upon, or who has performed, the *haj*

hammam sunken Persian-style bath

harijan title – "Children of God" – given to "untouchables" by Gandhi

haveli elaborately decorated mansion

hijra eunuch or transvestite

hookah water pipe for smoking strong tobacco or marijuana

howdah bulky elephant-saddle, sometimes made of pure silver, and often shaded by a canopy

hypostyle a building or room in which the roof is supported by columns (usually numerous) rather than walls, arches or vaulting

idgah area laid aside in the west of town for prayers during the Muslim festival id-ul-zuha

imam Muslim leader or teacher

imambara tomb of a Shi'ite saint

imfl Indian-made foreign liquor

Indo-Saracenic overblown Raj-era architecture that combines Muslim, Hindu, Jain and western elements

ishwara god; shiva

iwan the main (often central) arch in a mosque

jagirdar landowner

jali latticework in stone, or a pierced screen

jama or jami Friday, as in Jama masjid, or "Friday mosque"

janapadas small republics and monarchies; literally "territory of the clan"

jangha the body of a temple

jarokha small canopied balcony, often containing a window seat

jat major north Indian ethnic group; particularly numerous in eastern Rajasthan around Bharatpur

jati caste, determined by family and occupation

jawan soldier

jhuta soiled by lips: food or drink polluted by touch

-ji suffix added to names as a term of respect

jihad striving by Muslims, through battle, to spread their faith

jina another term for the Jain *tirthankaras*

johar old practice of self-immolation by women in times of war

jyotirlinga twelve sacred sites associated with Shiva's unbounded lingam of light

kabutar khana pigeon coop

kama satisfaction

karma weight of good and bad actions that determine status of rebirth

katcha the opposite of pukka

kavad small decorated box that unfolds to serve as a travelling temple

khadi home-spun cotton; Gandhi's symbol of Indian self-sufficiency

khan honorific Muslim title

khana dwelling or house

khejri small tree found throughout the desert regions of Rajasthan

khol black eye-liner

kirtan hymn-singing

kot fort

kothi residence

kotla citadel

kshatriya the warrior and ruling caste

kumkum red mark on a Hindu woman's forehead (widows are not supposed to wear it)

kund tank, lake, reservoir

kurta long men's shirt worn over baggy pajamas

lakh one hundred thousand

lingam phallic symbol in places of worship representing the god Shiva

liwan prayer hall or covered area of a mosque

loka realm or world, eg *devaloka*, world of the gods

lunghi male garment; long wraparound cloth, like a *dhoti*, but usually coloured

madrasa Islamic school

maha- great or large

mahadeva literally "great god", and a common epithet for Shiva

maharaja (maharana, Maharawal) king

maharani queen

mahal palace; mansion

mahatma great soul

mahout elephant driver or keeper

maidan large open space or field

makara crocodile-like animal featuring on temple doorways, and symbolizing the river Ganges. Also the vehicle of Varuna, the Vedic god of the sea

mandala religious diagram

mandapa hall, often with many pillars, used for various purposes: eg *kalyana mandapa* for wedding ceremonies and *nata mandapa* for dance performances

mandi market

mandir temple

mantra sacred verse, often repeated as an aid to meditation

mardana area for use of men in a haveli or palace

marg road

masjid mosque

mataji polite form of address to an older women or a female sadhu

math Hindu or Jain monastery

mayur peacock

mehendi henna

mela festival

memsahib respectful address to European woman

mihrab niche in the wall of a mosque indicating the direction of Mecca. In India the mihrab is thus in the west wall

minbar pulpit in a mosque from which the Friday sermon is read

minaret high slender tower, characteristic of mosques

mithuna amorous couples in Hindu and Buddhist figurative art

moksha blissful state of freedom from rebirth aspired to by Hindus, Sikhs and Jains

mor peacock

mudra hand gesture used in Vedic rituals, featuring in Hindu, Buddhist and Jain art and dance, and symbolizing teachings and life stages of the Buddha

muezzin man behind the voice calling Muslims to prayer from a mosque

mullah Muslim teacher and scholar

muqarna a style of Islamic moulded vaulting

naga mythical serpent; alternatively a person from Nagaland

nautch performance by dancing girls

nawab Muslim landowner or prince

nilgai blue bull

NRI non-resident Indian, someone entitled to Indian nationality but resident abroad

om (aka **aum**) symbol denoting the origin of all things, and ultimate divine essence, used in meditation by Hindus and Buddhists

paan betel nut, lime, calcium and aniseed wrapped in a leaf and chewed as a digestive. Mildly addictive

padma lotus; another name for the goddess Lakshmi

paise there are a hundred paisa in a rupee

pajama men's baggy trousers

panchayat village council

parikrama ritual circumambulation around a temple, shrine or mountain

Parsi Zoroastrian

pietra dura inlay work, traditionally consisting of semi-precious stones set in marble; particularly associated with Agra

pir Muslim holy man

pol fortified gate

pradakshina patha processional path circling a monument or sanctuary

pranayama breath control, used in meditation

prasad food blessed in temple sanctuaries and shared among devotees

prayag auspicious confluence of two or more rivers

purdah literally "curtain"; the enforced segregation and isolation of women within a haveli or palace or, more figuratively, within society in general. General term for wearing a veil

puja worship

pujari priest

pukka correct and acceptable, in the very English sense of "proper"

punya religious merit

qawwali devotional singing popular among sufis

qibla wall in a mosque indicating the direction of Mecca

qila fort

raag or **raga** series of notes forming the basis of a melody

raj rule; monarchy; in particular the period of British imperial rule 1857–1947

raja king

Rajput An Indian of the *kshatriya* caste, famous for their martial traditions and keen sense of honour. Rajputs make up around ten percent of the population of Rajasthan, and form the state's traditional ruling elite. They can also found in many other states in northern India. See also p.379.

rakshasa demon

rangoli geometrical pattern of rice powder laid before houses and temples

rawal chieftain or ruler of a minor principality

rishi "seer"; philosophical sage or poet

rudraksha beads used to make Shiva rosaries

sadar "main"; eg Sadar Bazaar

sadhu Hindu holy man with no caste or family ties

sagar lake

sahib respectful title for gentlemen; general term of address for European men

salwar kameez long shirt and baggy ankle-hugging trousers worn by Indian women

sambar a small Asian deer

samsara cyclic process of death and rebirth

sangam sacred confluence of two or more rivers, or an academy

sangeet music

sannyasin homeless, possessionless ascetic (Hindu)

sarai resting place for caravans and travellers who once followed the trade routes through Asia

sari usual dress for Indian women: a length of cloth wound around the waist and draped over one shoulder

sati one who sacrifices her life on her husband's funeral pyre in emulation of Shiva's wife. No longer a common practice, and officially illegal

satyagraha Gandhi's campaign of nonviolent protest, literally "grasping truth"

scheduled castes official name for "untouchables"

sepoy infantry private, an Indian soldier in the British army during the colonial period shaikh Muslim holy man or saint

shaivite Hindu recognizing Shiva as the supreme god

shankha conch, symbol of Vishnu

shastra treatise

sheesh mahal "glass palace"; usually a small room or apartment decorated with mirrorwork mosaics

shikar hunting

shikhara temple tower or spire common in northern Indian architecture

sri respectful prefix

shudra the lowest of the four *varnas*; servant

singh or singha lion

sit-out veranda

soma medicinal herb with hallucinogenic properties used in early Vedic and Zoroastrian rituals

stambha pillar, or flagstaff

Surya the sun, or sun god

sutra (aka sutta) verse in Sanskrit and Pali texts (literally "thread")

svetambara "white-clad" sect of Jainism, that accepts nuns and shuns nudity

swami title for a holy man

swaraj "self rule"; synonym for independence, coined by Gandhi

tandoor clay oven

tank square or rectangular water pool in a temple complex, for ritual bathing

tanpura the twangy drone which accompanies all classical music

tempo three-wheeled taxi

thakur landowner

thug member of a north Indian cult of professional robbers and murderers

tiffin light meal

tiffin carrier stainless steel set of tins used for carrying meals

tilak red dot smeared on the forehead during worship, and often used cosmetically

tirtha river crossing considered sacred by Hindus, or the transition from the mundane world to heaven; a place of pilgrimage for Jains

tirthankara "ford-maker" or "crossing-maker": an enlightened Jain teacher who is deified – 24 appear every 300 million years

tola the weight of a silver rupee: 180 grains, or approximately 11g

tonga two-wheeled horse-drawn cart

topi cap

torana arch, or freestanding gateway of two pillars linked by an elaborate arch

trimurti the Hindu trinity

trishula Shiva's trident

untouchables members of the lowest strata of society, considered polluting to all higher castes

urs Muslim saint's day festival

vahana the "vehicle" of a deity: the bull Nandi is Shiva's *vahana*

vaishya member of the merchant and trading caste group

varna literally "colour"; one of four hierarchical social categories: brahmins, *kshatriyas*, *vaishyas* and *shudras*

vedas sacred texts of early Hinduism

vihara Jain or Buddhist monastery

vimana tower over temple sanctuary

-wallah suffix implying occupation, eg: dhobi, rickshaw-wallah

wazir chief minister to the king

yaksha pre-Vedic folklore figure connected with fertility and incorporated into later Hindu iconography

yakshi female *yaksha*

yantra cosmological pictogram, or instrument used in an observatory

yatra pilgrimage

yatri pilgrim

yogi sadhu or priestly figure possessing occult powers gained through the practice of yoga (female: *yogini*)

yoni symbol of the female sexual organ, set around the base of the lingam in temple shrines

yuga aeon: the present age is the last in a cycle of four yugas, *kali-yuga*, a "black-age" of degeneration and spiritual decline

zamindar landowner

zenana women's quarters; segregated area for women in a mosque, haveli or palace

Travel store

D: Rough Guide
DIRECTIONS for
short breaks

Available from all good bookstores

Kenya
Marrakesh **D**
Morocco
South Africa, Lesotho
& Swaziland
Syria
Tanzania
Tunisia
West Africa
Zanzibar

Travel Specials
First-Time Africa
First-Time Around
the World
First-Time Asia
First-Time Europe
First-Time Latin
America
Travel Health
Travel Online
Travel Survival
Walks in London
& SE England
Women Travel
World Party

Maps
Algarve
Amsterdam
Andalucia
& Costa del Sol
Argentina
Athens
Australia
Barcelona
Berlin
Boston & Cambridge
Brittany
Brussels
California
Chicago
Chile
Corsica
Costa Rica
& Panama
Crete
Croatia
Cuba
Cyprus
Czech Republic
Dominican Republic
Dubai & UAE
Dublin
Egypt

Florence & Siena
Florida
France
Frankfurt
Germany
Greece
Guatemala & Belize
Iceland
India
Ireland
Italy
Kenya & Northern
Tanzania
Lisbon
London
Los Angeles
Madrid
Malaysia
Mallorca
Marrakesh
Mexico
Miami & Key West
Morocco
New England
New York City
New Zealand
Northern Spain
Paris
Peru
Portugal
Prague
Pyrenees & Andorra
Rome
San Francisco
Sicily
South Africa
South India
Spain & Portugal
Sri Lanka
Tenerife
Thailand
Toronto
Trinidad & Tobago
Tunisia
Turkey
Tuscany
Venice
Vietnam, Laos
& Cambodia
Washington DC
Yucatán Peninsula

**Dictionary
Phrasebooks**
Croatian
Czech
Dutch
Egyptian Arabic
French
German
Greek
Hindi & Urdu
Italian
Japanese
Latin American
Spanish
Mandarin Chinese
Mexican Spanish
Polish
Portuguese
Russian
Spanish
Swahili
Thai
Turkish
Vietnamese

Computers
Blogging
eBay
iPhone
iPods, iTunes
& music online
The Internet
Macs & OS X
MySpace
PCs and Windows
PlayStation Portable
Website Directory

Film & TV
American
Independent Film
British Cult Comedy
Chick Flicks
Comedy Movies
Cult Movies
Film
Film Musicals
Film Noir
Gangster Movies
Horror Movies
Kids' Movies
Sci-Fi Movies
Westerns

Lifestyle
Babies
Ethical Living
Pregnancy & Birth
Running

Music Guides
The Beatles
Blues
Bob Dylan
Book of Playlists
Classical Music
Elvis
Frank Sinatra
Heavy Metal
Hip-Hop
Jazz
Led Zeppelin
Opera
Pink Floyd
Punk
Reggae
Rock
The Rolling Stones
Soul and R&B
Velvet Underground
World Music
(2 vols)

Popular Culture
Books for Teenagers
Children's Books,
5-11
Conspiracy Theories
Crime Fiction
Cult Fiction
The Da Vinci Code
His Dark Materials
Lord of the Rings
Shakespeare
Superheroes
The Templars
Unexplained
Phenomena

Science
The Brain
Climate Change
The Earth
Genes & Cloning
The Universe
Weather

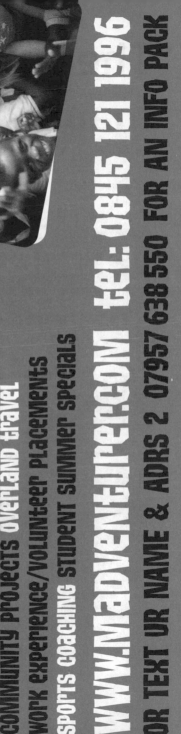

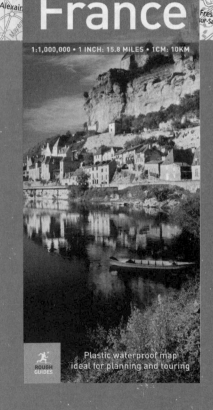

Small print and
Index

A Rough Guide to Rough Guides

Published in 1982, the first Rough Guide – to Greece – was a student scheme that became a publishing phenomenon. Mark Ellingham, a recent graduate in English from Bristol University, had been travelling in Greece the previous summer and couldn't find the right guidebook. With a small group of friends he wrote his own guide, combining a highly contemporary, journalistic style with a thoroughly practical approach to travellers' needs.

The immediate success of the book spawned a series that rapidly covered dozens of destinations. And, in addition to impecunious backpackers, Rough Guides soon acquired a much broader and older readership that relished the guides' wit and inquisitiveness as much as their enthusiastic, critical approach and value-for-money ethos.

These days, Rough Guides include recommendations from shoestring to luxury and cover more than 200 destinations around the globe, including almost every country in the Americas and Europe, more than half of Africa and most of Asia and Australasia. Our ever-growing team of authors and photographers is spread all over the world, particularly in Europe, the USA and Australia.

In the early 1990s, Rough Guides branched out of travel, with the publication of Rough Guides to World Music, Classical Music and the Internet. All three have become benchmark titles in their fields, spearheading the publication of a wide range of books under the Rough Guide name.

Including the travel series, Rough Guides now number more than 350 titles, covering: phrasebooks, waterproof maps, music guides from Opera to Heavy Metal, reference works as diverse as Conspiracy Theories and Shakespeare, and popular culture books from iPods to Poker. Rough Guides also produce a series of more than 120 World Music CDs in partnership with World Music Network.

Visit www.roughguides.com to see our latest publications.

Rough Guide travel images are available for commercial licensing at www.roughguidespictures.com

Rough Guide credits

Text editor: Karoline Densley
Layout: Umesh Aggarwal
Cartography: Jasbir Sandhu and Maxine Repath
Picture editor: Harriet Mills
Production: Aimee Hampson
Proofreader: Stewart Wild
Cover design: Chloë Roberts
Photographer: Simon Bracken and
Gavin Thomas
Editorial: **London** Kate Berens, Claire
Saunders, Ruth Blackmore, Polly Thomas,
Alison Murchie, Andy Turner, Keith Drew,
Edward Aves, Nikki Birrell, Alice Park, Sarah
Eno, Lucy White, Jo Kirby, Samantha Cook,
James Smart, Natasha Foges, Róisín Cameron,
Emma Traynor, Emma Gibbs, Joe Staines,
Duncan Clark, Peter Buckley, Matthew Milton,
Tracy Hopkins, Ruth Tidball; **New York** Andrew
Rosenberg, Steven Horak, AnneLise Sorensen,
Amy Hegarty, April Isaacs, Ella Steim, Anna
Owens, Joseph Petta, Sean Mahoney
Design & Pictures: **London** Scott Stickland,
Dan May, Diana Jarvis, Mark Thomas,
Jj Luck, Chloë Roberts, Nicole Newman,
Sarah Cummins; **Delhi** Ajay Verma, Jessica
Subramanian, Ankur Guha, Pradeep Thapliyal,
Sachin Tanwar, Anita Singh, Madhavi Singh,
Karen D'Souza
Production: Vicky Baldwin
Cartography: **London** Ed Wright, Katie Lloyd-
Jones; **Delhi** Jai Prakash Mishra, Rajesh
Chhibber, Ashutosh Bharti, Rajesh Mishra,
Animesh Pathak, Karobi Gogoi, Amod Singh,
Alakananda Bhattacharya, Swati Handoo
Online: **New York** Jennifer Gold, Kristin
Mingrono; **Delhi** Manik Chauhan, Narender
Kumar, Rakesh Kumar, Amit Kumar, Amit Verma,
Rahul Kumar, Ganesh Sharma, Debojit Borah
Marketing & Publicity: **London** Liz Statham,
Niki Hanmer, Louise Maher, Jess Carter,
Vanessa Godden, Vivienne Watton, Anna
Paynton, Rachel Sprackett, Lenalisa Fornberg;
New York Geoff Colquitt, Megan Kennedy, Katy
Ball; **Delhi** Reem Khokhar
Manager India: Punita Singh
Series Editor: Mark Ellingham
Reference Director: Andrew Lockett
Publishing Director: Martin Dunford
Publishing Coordinator: Helen Phillips
Commercial Manager: Gino Magnotta
Managing Director: John Duhigg

Publishing information

This first edition published September 2007 by
Rough Guides Ltd,
80 Strand, London WC2R 0RL
345 Hudson St, 4th Floor,
New York, NY 10014, USA
14 Local Shopping Centre, Panchsheel Park,
New Delhi 110017, India
Distributed by the Penguin Group
Penguin Books Ltd,
80 Strand, London WC2R 0RL
Penguin Group (USA)
375 Hudson Street, NY 10014, USA
Penguin Group (Australia)
250 Camberwell Road, Camberwell,
Victoria 3124, Australia
Penguin Books Canada Ltd,
10 Alcorn Avenue, Toronto, Ontario,
Canada M4V 1E4
Penguin Group (NZ)
67 Apollo Drive, Mairangi Bay, Auckland 1310,
New Zealand

Cover concept by Peter Dyer.
Typeset in Bembo and Helvetica to an original
design by Henry Iles.
Printed in Italy by LegoPrint S.p.A
© Daniel Jacobs and Gavin Thomas 2007
No part of this book may be reproduced in any
form without permission from the publisher except
for the quotation of brief passages in reviews.
464pp includes index
A catalogue record for this book is available from
the British Library
ISBN: 978-1-84353-864-6

The publishers and authors have done their best
to ensure the accuracy and currency of all the
information in **The Rough Guide to Rajasthan,
Delhi and Agra**, however, they can accept no
responsibility for any loss, injury, or inconvenience
sustained by any traveller as a result of
information or advice contained in the guide.

1   3   5   7   9   8   6   4   2

Help us update

We've gone to a lot of effort to ensure that
the first edition of **The Rough Guide to
Rajasthan, Delhi and Agra** is accurate and up
to date. However, things change – places get
"discovered", opening hours are notoriously
fickle, restaurants and rooms raise prices or lower
standards. If you feel we've got it wrong or left
something out, we'd like to know, and if you can
remember the address, the price, the time, the
phone number, so much the better.
We'll credit all contributions, and send a copy of
the next edition (or any other Rough Guide if you
prefer) for the best letters. Everyone who writes
to us and isn't already a subscriber will receive
a copy of our full-colour thrice-yearly newsletter.
Please mark letters: "**Rough Guide Rajasthan,
Delhi and Agra Update**" and send to: Rough
Guides, 80 Strand, London WC2R 0RL, or Rough
Guides, 345 Hudson St, 4th Floor, New York,
NY 10014. Or send an email to
mail@roughguides.com
Have your questions answered and tell others
about your trip at
www.roughguides.atinfopop.com

SMALL PRINT

451

Acknowledgements

Daniel Jacobs would like to thank: Reem Khokhar, Manik Chauhan, Karen D'Souza, Madhavi Singh, Punita Singh, Amit Verma and the team at Rough Guides in Delhi for their input, advice, corrections, comments and suggestions, and also to Sanjay Khandelwal (Narrowcasters, Delhi), Anoop Sherma (EKTA Travels, Pushkar), Jaggi and Sohel Sadarangani (*Govind Hotel*, Jodhpur), Mal Singh, Sankar Zoya, Mahindra Joshi (*Cosy Guest House*, Jodhpur), Helmut Pachler (*Artist Hotel*, Jaisalmer), Vikram Singh Shokawat (*Meghsar Castle*, Bikaner), Ashkumar Vyas (RTDC Bikaner) and Chris Wroblewski. Special thanks to Claire Saunders for getting me involved in the project, to Kate Berens for overseeing it, and to Karoline Densley for her sound editing and staunch support. Thanks also to Stewart Wild for proofreading, Jasbir Sandhu for the maps, Harriet Mills for the picture selection, Umesh Aggarwal for the layout, and Karoline and Gavin for being such a pleasure to work with on this book.

Gavin Thomas would like to thank: in India, Sudhir Kumar; Sanjeev Bharti Sinha (Ashu); Ramesh at the *Hotel Safari* in Agra; Umakant Rustagi (Rusty); Rishi Singh; Rajesh Jangid; Pramod Pareek; and Yussef and the Iqbal Express. In Jaipur, particular thanks to all at the *Sunder Palace Guest House* for making my first visit to the city so comfortable; and to the indefatigable Satinder Pal Singh of the *Pearl Palace Hotel* for providing an endless supply of entertainment, information and assistance. In London, special thanks to our editorial captain Karoline Densley for keeping the ship afloat and on course; to Harriet Mills (sorely missed) for all things photographic; to Kate and Martin for giving me the gig; and to Claire for putting in a good word. Thanks also to Sarah, who first took me to India and introduced me to the glories of the *charbagh*; to Laura and Jamie, even though neither is yet quite sure where India is or what it consists of; and of course to Allison, with whom I once travelled the length and breadth of the Subcontinent, and who I hope will one day see a tiger for herself.

Photo credits

Full page
Taj Mahal © Gavin Thomas

Introduction
Jaipur Elephant Festival © Glen Allison/Image
  Bank/Getty
Pink City, Jaipur © Gavin Thomas
Chandni Chowk, Old Delhi © Ian Cumming/Axiom
Bazaar, Bundi © Gavin Thomas

Things not to miss
02 Pushkar Camel Mela © Hans Petersen/
  Photolibrary.com
03 Main temple at Ranakpur © Gavin Thomas
04 Sammidheshwar Temple, Chittaurgarh Fort
  © age fotostock/SuperStock
07 Bengal tigress, Ranthambore NP © Anup
  Shah/naturepl.com
08 Deshnok rat temple © Daniel Jacobs
09 Biriyani and dhal dishes © Simon Reddy/
  Alamy
10 Jhunjhunu, Shekhawati haveli © Gavin
  Thomas
11 Baha'i Temple © Scott Stickland
12 Fatehpur Sikri © Gavin Thomas
13 Pelicans, Keoladeo NP © Jean-Pierre
  Zwaenepoel/naturepl.com
14 Pink City, Jaipur © Gavin Thomas
17 Lake Pichola, Udaipur © Gavin Thomas

Colour section: Forts and palaces of Rajasthan
Jaipur City Palace © Ananth Padmanabhan
Mural, Bundi City Palace © Gavin Thomas
Amber Fort © Kate Berens
Agra Fort, Diwan-i-Am © Superstock

Colour section: Rajasthani handicrafts
Sari factory, Rajasthan © Bruno Morandi/Robert
  Harding

Black and white pictures
p.80 Jama Masjid © Daniel Jacobs
p.104 India Gate © Scott Stickland
p.109 Cow in Paharganj © Daniel Jacobs
p.121 Khari Baoli spice market © Daniel Jacobs
p.133 Qtub Minar © Scott Stickland
p.158 Diwan-i-Am, Agra Fort © Alice Garrard/
  Superstock
p.178 Inlay work, Itimad ud Daulah © Gavin
  Thomas
p.192 Detail of Fatehpur Sikri Birpal © Gavin
  Thomas
p.198 Jaipur City Palace © Gavin Thomas
p.211 Jantar Mantar, Jaipur © Gavin Thomas
p.242 Ramgarh haveli detail © Gavin Thomas
p.246 Lake and City Palace, Alwar © Gavin
  Thomas
p.262 Jaisalmer Fort © age fotostock/Superstock
p.270 Baradaris, Ana Sagar, Ajmer © Daniel
  Jacobs
p.279 Camel fair, Pushkar © P. Narayan/
  Superstock
p.310 Jain temple carving, Lodruva © Daniel
  Jacobs
p.330 Lake Pichola, Udaipur © Gavin Thomas
p.350 Marble elephants, Mount Abu © eWILDz/
  Alamy
p.365 Vijay Stambh, Chittaurgarh © Gavin
  Thomas
p.368 Chogan Gate, Bundi © Gavin Thomas

SMALL PRINT

Index

Map entries are in colour.

INDEX

456

INDEX

INDEX

459

Map symbols

maps are listed in the full index using coloured text

– – –	Chapter boundary	@	Internet café
– – – ·	International boundary	(i)	Tourist office
– – · ·	State boundary	⊠	Post office
———	Main road	⊞	Hospital
———	Minor road	◉	Accommodation
–■–■–	Railway	♟	Fortress
– – – –	Track/trail	◨	Haveli
·············	Coastline/river	⌂	Palace
———	Wall	∴	Ruin/ Archeological site
⊠—⊠	Gate	—	Boat
⊐⊏	Bridge	⅃	Golf course
ᴖᴖᴖᴖ	Rocks	◪	Mosque/Muslim monument
⌄⌄	Mountains	▲	Hindu/Jain temple
▲	Peak	⊟	Ghat
/||\	Hill	⬭	Stadium
ᴛᴧᴧ	Swamp	▬	Building
⬇	Viewpoint	⊡	Church
Ⓜ	Metro station	⊤⊤	Cemetery
★	Bus stop	▦	Park
◆	Point of interest	▦	Mudflats
⛽	Fuel station